D1200345

The Columbia Literary History of Eastern Europe Since 1945

The COLUMBIA LITERARY HISTORY of EASTERN EUROPE

Since 1945

Harold B. Segel

COLUMBIA UNIVERSITY PRESS   New York

Columbia University Press
Publishers Since 1893
New York   Chichester, West Sussex
Copyright © 2008 Columbia University Press
All rights reserved.

Library of Congress Cataloging-in-Publication Data
Segel, Harold B., 1930–
    The Columbia literary history of Eastern Europe since 1945 / Harold B. Segel.
        p.   cm.
    Includes bibliographical references and index.
    ISBN 978-0-231-13306-7 (cloth : alk. paper) —
    ISBN 978-0-231-50804-9 (e-book)
        1. East European literature—20th century—History and criticism.   2. East European
    literature—21st century—History and criticism.   I. Title.
    PN849.E9S44 2008
    809'.933584709045—dc22

                                                                                    2007040577

♾

Columbia University Press books are printed on permanent and durable acid-free paper.
Printed in the United States of America
c 10 9 8 7 6 5 4 3 2 1

Contents

PREFACE *vii*
ACKNOWLEDGMENTS *xv*

1   World War II in the Literatures of Eastern Europe   *1*

2   Postwar Colonialism, Communist Style   *39*

3   In the Aftermath of the Great Dictator's Death   *66*

4   Fleeing the System: Literature and Emigration   *92*

5   Internal Exile and the Literature of Escape   *113*

6   Writers Behind Bars:
    Eastern European Prison Literature, 1945–1990   *143*

7   The Reform Imperative in Eastern Europe:
    From Solidarity to Postmodernism   *191*

8   Eastern European Women Poets of the 1980s and 1990s   *233*

9   The House of Cards Collapses:
    The Literary Fallout of the Yugoslav Crises of the 1990s   *264*

10 Glimpses of the Other World:
    America Through Eastern European Eyes   *290*

11 The Postcolonial Literary Scene in Eastern Europe Since 1991   *318*

NOTES   *371*
FURTHER READING   *379*
INDEX   *383*

The literature of Eastern Europe is a mirror of the calamities, and extraordinary changes, that have occurred throughout the region since it was plunged into the costliest war in human history on 1 September 1939. By the time Poland was invaded, the Czech lands had been appropriated by Nazi Germany under the guise of the Protectorate of Bohemia and Moravia, and Slovakia was well on its way to being shaped into a quasi-independent state under the leadership of a Nazi puppet. By the time World War II ended in May 1945, much of Eastern Europe lay in ruins, millions of innocents as well as combatants were dead, cultural treasures had been massively despoiled, and national borders and populations were soon to be shifted like so many pawns on a chessboard. Again, as after the first "world war"—that grand illusion of a war to end all wars—Eastern Europe was being remapped.

To enable us to better come to terms with the enormity of the transformation Eastern Europe underwent from 1945 to the collapse of communism, and from that momentous event to the present, a periodic reexamination of the forces shaping the region is necessary. We will be doing that in this book in the context of a broad consideration of the literary culture of Eastern Europe as a whole from the end of World War II to the early years of the twenty-first century. The legacy of the war itself is complicated by the realization that if in the wider sense all of Eastern Europe was a victim between 1939 and 1945, some of the presumed victims were also in fact victimizers. The capitulation of the Czechs, followed by the swift invasion and devastation of Poland, and the ruthless German and Italian campaigns in Yugoslavia, Albania, and Greece were offset by the compliance in the German scheme of conquest by Bulgaria, Hungary, Romania, and the puppet states of Croatia and Slovakia. When ultimate German victory seemed probable, the compliant Eastern European states made little determined effort to resist mounting pressure to enter the war on the German side.

As has often been the case in history, the primary incentive to this cooperation was territorial aggrandizement. This was certainly true for Romania, anxious to hold on to the rich region of Transylvania ceded to it by Hungary after World War I. For the Hungarians, reacquiring, with German backing, as much of Slovakia as it could after the disintegration of the Habsburg empire in 1918, and having the hope always of at least some return of Transylvanian lands, there could be no question as to where their allegiance would go. And for Bulgaria, certainly the least compliant of Nazi Germany's Eastern European allies, there were parts of Serbia, Macedonia, and Greece that beckoned. For the Croatians, the opportunity to become independent of the prewar Kingdom of Yugoslavia, with its Serb preponderance, was irresistible. Thus the Independent State of Croatia was established in 1941 under German and Italian sponsorship. It included, in addition to Croatia proper, Bosnia-Herzegovina and those parts of Dalmatia that had not already been ceded to Italy. The head of the new Croatian state was Ante Pavelić (1889–1959), who was backed up by the Ustaša terror organization that he headed.

If less animosity characterized Czech-Slovak relations through the centuries, the long-nurtured Slovak sense of inferior status in the Czechoslovak state—politically, economically, and culturally—won considerable backing for the Nazi-engineered independent Slovak Republic led by Monsignor Jozef Tiso (1887–1947). The Slovaks had little choice in the matter. Fascist Hungary had already begun gobbling up parts of Slovakia it had lost by the terms of the Versailles Treaty, and further delay by the Slovaks threatened even greater loss of territory. Collaboration with the Germans meant, in the case of the Croatians, willing participation in the campaign against the Serbs and Tito's partisans, and, in the case of the Slovaks, a supply of cannon fodder in battles against the Soviet Union.

In both instances, compliance also entailed deportation of Jews to concentration camps in Germany and Poland or, in the case of the Croatians, to the few that were established on Croatian soil, above all Jasenovac. The eagerness of the Croatians to persecute Jews (as well as Serbs and Gypsies) was at least mitigated among the Slovaks by a lesser degree of enthusiasm and on occasion even some resistance. The situation among the Bulgarians and the Romanians was more complex. Widely hailed for protecting their small indigenous Jewish population of less that fifty thousand, the Bulgarians nevertheless assisted in deportations of Jews to German concentration camps in countries where they were occupiers, such as Greece and Macedonia. The Romanian record is infinitely worse. Although claiming to protect the Jewish population of the historic Kingdom of Romania (the Regat), the Romanian authorities, especially under the regime of Marshal Ion Antonescu, subjected Jews to every conceivable kind of mistreatment. The Iaşi pogrom of July 1942 remains one of the worst atrocities of the entire war. What spared the lives of many Romanian Jews was the inconsistency and haphazardness with which the anti-Jewish measures were applied. The brunt of the Romanian Holocaust was borne, however, by the large Jewish populations of such regions as Bessarabia and Bukovina, which had been occupied by the Soviet army and then subsequently recaptured by Romanian troops. The most horrendous slaughter was carried out in Transnistria, which

Antonescu's forces seized from the USSR and temporarily incorporated into greater Romania. By the war's end, Romania's prewar Jewish population of eight hundred thousand had been reduced by more than half.

When the turning of the tide had become so obvious that denial was no longer possible, Hitler's Eastern European collaborators scrambled to realign themselves. Romania switched to the allied side on 23 August 1944, after the Soviets had begun their invasion of the country. The Bulgarian Otechestven Front (Fatherland Front), a coalition of resistance groups, staged a successful coup against the wartime regime on 9 September 1944 and threw its support to the Soviet forces that had already entered the country. The Croatian Ustaša state was defeated by Tito's partisans and was disbanded. Ante Pavelić had already fled the country; with the considerable assistance of the Vatican he was provided safe haven in Argentina, until his whereabouts were discovered and he was forced to flee again, this time to Spain. A failed attempt on his life in 1957 left him wounded, and he eventually died in Madrid on 28 December 1959.

As Soviet units began advancing into eastern Slovakia in the summer of 1944, a national resistance movement (known as the Slovak National Uprising) erupted on 29 August 1944. Although invested with the status of myth in Slovak culture, the weakly organized rebellion was handily crushed by the Germans. The Soviets captured Slovakia, and Tiso was hung on 18 April 1947. Only the Hungarians, led in the late stages of the war by the head of the fascist Nyilaskereszt (Arrow Cross), Ferenc Szálasi (1897–1946)—the ruler of Hungary since 15 October 1944—held out to the very end, continuing to round up Jews and slaughtering them even as the Russians and their Johnny-come-lately allies, the Romanians, were banging on the doors of Budapest. Like Tiso, Szálasi was captured and hanged in 1946.

The grim memories of the war throughout Eastern Europe, and the discord and enmity sown by it, have dogged the peoples of the region down to the present, as witnessed, for example, in the Balkan wars of the 1990s and the as-yet-unresolved issue of Kosovo's final status. The imposition of communist rule in the immediate postwar years, by sheer power or deception (and lasting until 1989–1991), was a direct outcome of the war and the Soviet occupation of most of the region. To the trauma of the war years was now added the trauma of communist neocolonialism. The nearly half-century of communist rule in Eastern Europe may be likened to a foreign body invading an organism that then periodically erupts in a desperate effort to expel it. The Berlin workers' strikes of June 1953 in the German Democratic Republic; the Poznań riots in Poland three years later; the outbreak of the Hungarian Revolution that same year; the promise of hope embodied in the Prague Spring of 1968, only to be dashed by the Soviet-led Warsaw Pact invasion; the rise, fall, and rebirth of the Solidarity movement in Poland in the 1980s; the dismantling of the Berlin Wall in 1989; the outbreak of revolution in Romania that same year and the summary execution of Nicolae and Elena Ceaușescu; and finally the unimaginable collapse of the Soviet Union itself in 1991 ended the long struggle to expel from Eastern Europe the foreign body that was communism.

But Eastern Europe was still not spared further tremors. The vicious and costly Balkan wars of the 1990s—the wars, that is, of the Yugoslav secession—were brought to an end definitively only in the late 1990s. By then, mass murder had been uncovered; new war criminals were being sought for justice (a dragnet some have still managed to elude); "ethnic cleansing" had entered the international vocabulary; and American and British NATO bombers had unleashed a seventy-eight day onslaught against a truculent Serbia led by Slobodan Milošević, who was subsequently put on trial for war crimes in the Hague but who died before a verdict was handed down. The Yugoslavia that had come together again after World War II under the leadership of Tito lay in ruins, replaced by the newly independent states of Slovenia, Croatia, Bosnia-Herzegovina, Serbia-Montenegro, and Macedonia, undoing the work of a generation of cartographers. National borders were further redefined following the peaceful separation of Montenegro from Serbia while the Serbian province of Kosovo and Metohija—which the Serbs have long regarded as the cradle of Serbian nationhood—was well on its way to becoming in all probability an independent nation under Albanian rule. Two new states in the heart of Europe came into existence in 1993 when the never wholly satisfying relationship between Czechs and Slovaks was acknowledged and the truncation of Czechoslovakia into the Czech Republic and the Republic of Slovakia was declared.

The fervently sought and much-celebrated collapse of communism throughout Eastern Europe has been accompanied by free enterprise and slow but steady economic progress. Most states in the region have finally been accorded the highly prized membership in the European Union and, in a few instances, in NATO. Yet political, economic, and social problems have persisted to the present day. New stirrings of nationalism have emerged that have discomforted minorities in the region, especially Gypsies. Albanian-Slav tensions have spilled over into Macedonia from the conflict in Kosovo. The expulsion of the Germans of Romania, begun under the dictatorship of Ceauşescu, has by now cleared Romania of this once thriving and distinct community. The position of Hungarians in Romania as well as in Ukraine and Slovakia has also been at times contentious in the postcommunist period. Problems with the Turkish citizens of Bulgaria flared in the 1980s and resulted in the expulsion of a large number of people, some of whom have eventually been allowed to resettle. Economic mismanagement led to riots in Albania in 1996–1997 and in Hungary more recently in 2006. Russian political meddling in the affairs of Belarus, Ukraine, and Estonia has proven an unsavory reminder of earlier Soviet expansionism. Although considerably smaller in size than in the period between the two world wars, the Jewish population of Eastern Europe has, despite many obstacles, shown signs of limited renewal. But reemergent nationalism in the region has also brought with it new manifestations of anti-Semitism, although fewer and less virulent than before, during, or immediately after World War II.

Although communism is no longer a political force in Eastern Europe, its legacy continues to be actively debated and its capacity for disrupting people's lives is manifestly evident. As secret police and other government archives open

up, the extent of collaboration with the communist regimes on the part of ordinary citizens, artists, intellectuals, and even members of the clergy (as, for example, in Poland, as revealed in early 2007) becomes better known—a source
of sometimes bitter acrimony and recrimination, with the end not yet in sight.

The new prosperity in Eastern Europe, unevenly distributed across the region, has produced its own share of social problems. Millionaires and multimillionaires are no longer a rarity, as indeed they are not in newly prosperous
yet still communist-ruled China. But the gulf separating the wealthy and the
many unable to keep up with rising costs of virtually every commodity grows
ever wider. Corruption has created fertile ground for the spread of indigenous
Mafia-like organizations, with a resultant increase in the crime rate. Political
assassinations (the murders of courageous journalists, for example, in Russia,
Lithuania, and elsewhere), prostitution, and drugs have become a new kind of
urban blight. Environmental issues, created by years of communist neglect and
mismanagement, have not yet been wholly and satisfactorily resolved.

Its problems notwithstanding, Eastern Europe—now more complex than
ever after the breakup of such multiethnic and multinational states as Yugoslavia
and the Soviet Union and the separation of the Czechs and Slovaks—continues
to exert a fascination of its own. But the proliferation of nation-states, with
their many different cultures and languages, makes the challenge of acquaintance daunting. However desirable it may seem to want to explore the cultures
of the region on an individual basis, a more reasonable approach may be—at
least initially—to expand our field of vision to take the region as a whole into
view. To move, in other words, from an understanding of the commonalities of
the region to a keener appreciation of individual national differences within the
framework of these commonalities.

With the goal in mind of facilitating a more comfortable grasp of the complexity of the entire region, as prelude to an accommodation of its discrete
cultures, I have organized this book primarily along chronological-topical lines.
This is to say that I address certain topics I regard as characteristic and important within a chronological structure beginning with the post–World War II
period and continuing to the present. The familiar "linear" literary history has
thus been set aside, because of the large number of literatures involved and the
inability to do real justice to each one by means of a traditional literary-historical
strategy. Instead, the primary focus will be on essentially common responses
to external, largely political, stimuli. Even in the postcolonial, postcommunist
period since 1991, literature throughout Eastern Europe—while free of the constraints of communist ideology—has responded much the same way to the social, economic, and political adjustments and readjustments taking place across
the length and breadth of the large region.

The book is divided into eleven chapters. The first explores the varieties of
literary responses to the calamities of World War II, taking due note of the
expectedly different perspectives of writers from occupied lands as opposed
to those from countries allied with the Axis for most of the war. The second
chapter addresses the cultural fallout of the postwar transformation of Eastern

Europe along Soviet-model political and economic lines and the accommodation of and resistance to socialist realism. In the third chapter the emphasis falls on strategies of literary subterfuge in the aftermath of Stalin's death in 1953, in order to expose the banalities and absurdities of communist rule. Chapters 4 and 5 consider the two faces of exile and emigration: (a) the physical departure of a number of writers out of Eastern Europe for the purpose of being able to create in freedom, and (b) the inner exile of writers who remained in place in their respective societies and probed different means of remaining productive as they tested the limits of censorship within the constraints of communist literary bureaucracy. The harassment, curtailment, and imprisonment of writers in Eastern Europe throughout the entire communist period—the Eastern European gulag, in other words—less known than its Soviet counterpart but scarcely less dehumanizing—is the subject of chapter 6.

The seventh chapter deals with the perhaps not immediately apparent nexus between the rise of the Solidarity movement in Poland in the 1980s and the emergence of Eastern European postmodernism as an expression of the growing demand for liberalization and democratization in the sociopolitical as well as cultural spheres. With the eighth chapter we take a movement sideways, if you will, to consider the appearance of a remarkable body of Eastern European women poets of the 1980s and 1990s, who collectively represent the demand for the freedom of women to address issues of gender in the same spirit as the imperative for liberalization embodied in the Solidarity and postmodernist movements. Chapter 9 returns again to the catastrophe of war as it takes up the literary legacy of the implosion of Yugoslavia amid the Balkan wars of the 1990s, the effects of which linger to the present day. Before proceeding to a consideration of the literature of the postcolonial and postcommunist period since 1991, we move laterally again, this time to look at texts by Eastern European writers who were able to achieve during the communist period that coveted goal of being able to visit the United States, many within the framework of the renowned International Writing Program sponsored by the University of Iowa. In the eleventh, and final, chapter—the longest in the book—we consider common trends in postcommunist Eastern European literary experience. The inclusion of major writers in Lithuanian and Ukrainian acknowledges the independence of Lithuania and Ukraine in the aftermath of the breakup of the Soviet Union and the significant achievements of their literatures.

This book represents one approach—I hope an interesting one—to the literary world of Eastern Europe in the sixty or so years since the end of World War II. It is obviously not, nor can it be, the whole story. Because of considerations of space, some names have been omitted and others have been skimmed over. I do indeed regret this, but I take some comfort from the expectation that this book will encourage further exploration.

Technical Notes

Authors' dates and the publication dates of literary and other texts are generally not repeated after the initial mention. The original titles of literary works are also provided only initially. They are subsequently referred to by their translated titles. Titles of published translations are italicized; others are not. Quotations are footnoted on first appearance. Subsequent references to the same text are indicated in the main body of the book by pages numbers in parentheses. Unless indicated otherwise, all translations in the book are my own.

Acknowledgments

I wish to express my sincere thanks to Jamie Warren, then of Columbia University Press, for initially proposing this book and for his help and kindness with my previous project, *The Columbia Guide to the Literatures of Eastern Europe Since 1945*. I much appreciate the assistance I received from Frank Sciacca of Hamilton College in retrieving some texts by Lilian Ursu that were unavailable elsewhere. Many thanks as well to two splendid contemporary Romanian poets—Mircea Cărtărescu, for the full text of his poem "Occidentul" and permission to translate from it, and Daniela Crăsnaru, for information concerning her American poems of 1993—and to that fine Macedonian poet and scholar Katica Kulavkova, for the original text of her poem "Mistikata na tvojot jazik" and permission to translate from it. I am also grateful to have had the opportunity to translate from poems by Mimoza Ahmeti, Bisera Alikadić, Ruxandra Cesereanu, Ferida Duraković, Luljeta Lleshanaku, Mariana Marin, Simona Popescu, and Oksana Zabuzhko. My association with Jamie Warren's successor, Juree Sondker, who inherited this project, has been friendly and helpful throughout. Kerri Sullivan, my manuscript editor, deserves special mention for her admirably diligent reading of the text, her many helpful suggestions, and especially for her patience and understanding.

The Columbia Literary History of Eastern Europe Since 1945

World War II in the Literatures of Eastern Europe

The Mad Dogs of War Unleashed: The Fall of Poland

World War II started when German forces attacked Poland on the first of September, 1939. Until then, many believed that after the Anschluss with Austria in 1938 and then the occupation of the Sudetenland in Czechoslovakia, Hitler's appetite for territorial expansion would be appeased and European fears of war would abate. But the assault on Poland put that pipe dream to rest.

For the Poles, the war was devastating. Not only did they become the first victims in the savage German onslaught that spared neither property nor humankind, but Polish culture too was brought under siege. Libraries, centers of learning, scholars themselves were targeted in the Nazi campaign to destroy whatever they could of Polish culture and reduce the population to slave status. But the war in Poland hit harder still at the huge Jewish population of the country, destroying millions of people and all but wiping out a way of life that had existed for hundreds of years. The execution of the Holocaust on Polish soil further traumatized the Poles, whose reputation for anti-Semitism was unenviable though often exaggerated. Polish literature dealing with the war and the consequences of the war thus has a double focus: on the valor of the Poles who resisted the German onslaught and on the complex relations between Poles and Jews during the occupation.

If the brevity of the woefully inadequate Polish armed resistance to the German invasion understandably provided little inspiration for works of fiction in the postwar period, the situation was quite different with respect to the participation of Polish units fighting with the Allies in campaigns in the western European theater of operations. Polish pilots stationed in England and Scotland served with distinction in the RAF; Polish seamen saw action in the North Atlantic; and Polish ground troops fought in the Italian and North African campaigns. Although their exploits eventually became well documented, the communists made a concerted effort for some time to deny them their due. The reasons for such neglect were simple. Many of the overseas Polish combatants were antagonists of the new postwar regime and loyal to the London-based Polish Government-in-Exile. As such, it was in the best interests of the communists to suppress knowledge of their role in the war. Attention was also systematically directed away from the Polish overseas units to the Polish First Army—organized under the command of General Zygmunt Berling and raised on Soviet soil—which took part in the reconquest of Poland together with the Soviet army. Since these troops were under communist leadership, it obviously behooved the postwar regime to highlight their part in the war at the expense of the deeds of the "free" Poles who fought in the west.

Of the literature generated by the Polish participation in campaigns of the western Allies, the most famous perhaps is Melchior Wańkowicz's (1892–1974) monumental three-volume novel, *Bitwa o Monte Cassino* (The Battle for Monte Cassino, published in Rome between 1945 and 1947). Because of censorship, the novel was not permitted to appear in its entirety in Poland until 1989. In essence a documentary work, it deals exhaustively with the heroic but costly efforts by troops of the Polish II Corps under the command of General Władysław Anders to dislodge the Germans from their strongly entrenched positions atop the mountain. This was by all standards one of the great battles of World War II. Wańkowicz himself took part in it as a reporter and tested his own observations of the events against the narrations of the soldiers who were the principal combatants. A great strength of the novel is the meticulous care with which Wańkowicz conducts his readers through the several phases of the battle, from its beginnings through the various Polish attacks and setbacks until German resistance was overcome and victory finally achieved. That victory opened up the road to Rome for the Allied armies. So detailed and all-encompassing is Wańkowicz's account that the book took three years to come to press. When it appeared, it was copiously illustrated, with nearly two thousand pictures, apart from maps, battle plans, and aerial photos.

Polish fiction about the war set in occupied Poland tended for the most part to concentrate on partisan fighting. Some of the best of such writing came from writers with a strong regional orientation, such as Leopold Buczkowski, Włodzimierz Odojewski, and Tadeusz Konwicki.

Attracted to prose experimentation in the late interwar period, Buczkowski (1905–1989) made his mark in the postwar period with his novel *Czarny potok* (*Black Torrents*, 1954). A native of the southeastern Podolian region of prewar Poland, Buczkowski used this offbeat setting of ethnic diversity (Poles, Jews, Ukrainians, Gypsies) for several works, beginning with his novel *Wertepy* (Byways) in 1937. *Black Torrents* takes place in and around the largely Jewish town of Szabasów between 1941 and 1943. The physical destruction and degradation of the world of the combatants is paralleled by the destruction of the traditional prose narrative. From the very first page, the reader is plunged into chaotic action with no clear idea of the affiliations of the combatants or their relation to one another or even of the precise geographical setting. Characters dart in and out of forests, and the Germans are a definite part of the landscape, as are bands of armed Ukrainians and Jews who seem to be both civilians and combatants. Mayhem is everywhere as people are shot at random, brutal interrogations occur, and bodies litter the streets and roads. Before much time elapses it becomes evident that the setting is Szabasów. Yet even that spatial delimitation still does not shed greater light on the nature of much of the action. Of particular interest in the novel is the intertwining of the fates of the Polish and Jewish inhabitants of the area as they try to withstand the German assault.

The Germans were not the sole invaders of Poland in 1939. The secret terms of the Molotov-Ribbentrop pact signed on 23 August 1939 in Moscow effectively divided Poland between the two powers. The pact permitted the Soviets to advance into Poland and occupy lands east of the Narew, Wisła (Vistula), and San rivers. Germany would then keep all Polish territory to the west of that area. The Soviets were not long in moving into Poland after the German invasion of 1 September. On 17 September Soviet armies began rolling westward. Shocked by Soviet cynicism and the Realpolitik behind the German-Soviet pact, Polish writers, particularly those who were native to the area being overrun by the Soviets, sought to depict the true nature of the Soviet occupation.

Włodzimierz Odojewski (b. 1930) deals with these same events in much of his fiction. His so-called Podolian cycle—consisting of *Zmierzch świata* (The Twilight of the World, 1963), *Wyspa ocalenia* (*Island of Salvation*, 1964; his only work available in English), and *Zasypie wszystko, zawieje . . .* (Snow Covers, Snow Buries Everything . . .), which he published in 1973 with the Polish émigré publishing house Biblioteka "Kultura" in Paris—recreates the annihilation by the Soviets of the Podolian region in 1943 and 1944. At its core the novel is a severe indictment of Polish-Ukrainian rivalries and ethnic conflicts, even within closely related families. In Snow Covers, Snow Buries Everything . . . , Odojewski made greater use of interior monologues in order to bring the psychological as well as mythographic components of the novel more to the fore. Polish censors originally demanded that Odojewski expunge from the novel any references to the Katyń murders of 15,000 Polish military officers later definitively attributed to the Soviets. The most lyrical of the novels in the Podolian cycle, *Island of Salvation,* traces the return of a young man to a family country retreat with which he has idyllic associations going back to his childhood. But the setting is the wartime fighting in the region, including the merciless hunting down of Jews and the bloody attacks on Poles by Ukrainians aligned with the Germans. Before the war the area had been a haven of multiethnic tranquility, and the young man wistfully recalls his boyhood friendships with Ukrainians his own age whose language he spoke. But those friendships are meaningless now as the Ukrainians team up with the Germans in an effort to defeat the Soviets and rid the area of as many Poles as they can in order to lay claim to the territory for an independent Ukraine. Military conflict is not Odojewski's prime concern in *Island of Salvation,* as it is in Buczkowski's *Black Torrents;* fighting is alluded to rather than portrayed. Instead, Odojewski emphasizes his belief that in times of crises there are no safe havens, that no "islands of salvation" conjured from the past exist. Only when the central character of

Island of Salvation achieves that realization, by the end of the novel, does it become possible for him to face the future with the will to endure.

Józef Czapski's (1896–1993) book *Na nieludzkiej ziemi* (In an Inhuman Land, 1949), which somewhat recalls the Albanian writer Ismail Kadare's *The General of a Dead Army,* encompasses a detailed description of a journey through Russia in search of slain Polish officers. It was written, it should be noted, before the discovery of the mass graves at Katyń. The book is at the same time an indictment of Russia, the "inhuman land" of the title, which to Czapski was a land of wretchedness and profound hostility toward Poland. Czapski had good reason to portray the Soviet Union as he does in his works. Like other writers of his generation, he was a survivor of Stalin's prison camps, in his case Starobielsk, which he recalls vividly in his memoirs, *Wspomnienia starobielskie* (Starobielsk Memories, 1944).

A different slant on the war comes in the writing of Józef Mackiewicz (1902–1985). In *Nie trzeba głośno mówić* (There's No Need to Raise Your Voice, 1969), the subject is the German invasion of the Soviet Union in 1941 and the tensions between the Poles, who regarded the Germans as their real foes, and the Ukrainians and Lithuanians, who first looked to the Germans as their saviors from a detested communism until German disinterest in them proved a shattering disillusionment. A relentless foe of communism and the Soviet Union, Mackiewicz excoriates both in the novel. The western Allies are also taken to task for their abandonment of Eastern Europe to the Soviets. The novel has a decidedly journalistic quality to it, above all in Mackiewicz's liberal use of historical information. In so blurring the boundaries between traditional epic narration and documentary writing, There's No Need to Raise Your Voice was a continuation of Mackiewicz's earlier novel *Droga donikąd* (*The Road to Nowhere,* 1955), which deals with the situation in Lithuania in the period of the first Soviet occupation of the country in 1940–1941. Mackiewicz is particularly adept at depicting the strength of opposition to Sovietization among the local bourgeoisie and more prosperous farmers, to whom collectivization in particular is anathema. Slowly but surely, however, the Soviets move to crush all opposition and toward the end of the novel begin mass deportations regardless of nationality or religion. The futility of efforts to evade the Soviet dragnet is epitomized by the flight by cart of one Polish couple. As they try to make their way through dense woods they seem to be directionless—on a road, in other words, to nowhere, hence the title of the novel.

As one may well imagine, conditions in occupied Poland, the tragic fate of the Jews, and resistance to the German occupiers commanded the attention of several prominent writers. Of the non-Jewish writers who addressed the plight of the Jews in Poland during the war, the most outstanding were Jerzy Andrzejewski, Leopold Buczkowski, Jarosław Marek Rymkiewicz, and Andrzej Szczypiorski. Whether rightly or wrongly, the Poles have had to contend with accusations that they did not do enough to help the Jews. The question of how much assistance they were indeed in a position to offer is highly problematic in view of their own situation: an occupied people whose losses in the war amounted to over three million and who faced death for aiding Jews. But given the burden of moral and ethical responsibility they have long had to bear, the preoccupation of many Poles with their behavior vis-à-vis Jews during the German occupation (and even after the war, when serious Polish anti-Jewish incidents, such as the Kielce massacre of 1946, did occur) gave rise to several important fictional texts in the postwar period.

The earliest chronologically was the novella *Wielki Tydzień* (*Holy Week*, 1955) by the prolific writer Jerzy Andrzejewski (1909–1983). Andrzejewski's previous novel, *Popiół i diament* (*Ashes and Diamonds*, 1948), is by far his best known, most popular, and most widely translated work. This effective, but somewhat melodramatic, novel is set in 1945 and depicts the political and military strife in immediate postwar Poland. *Holy Week* takes place during the occupation, in fact during the uprising in the Jewish ghetto of Warsaw that began on 19 April 1943 and continued, much to most people's surprise, until 16 May 1943. The uprising erupted at the beginning of the Jewish holiday of Passover and ended with the important Christian holidays of Good Friday and Easter. The irony of the underlying symbolism of the holy days, one Jewish, the other Christian, is inescapable. Passover is a week-long celebration of the deliverance of the Jews from Egyptian slavery and their return to freedom in the Holy Land. Good Friday and Easter, on the other hand, celebrate the crucifixion of Jesus and the Resurrection. The Ghetto Uprising, however heroic, ended in defeat and death, the opposite of the deliverance of Passover. The death of Jesus on the cross and his resurrection hold forth, in Christian teaching, the redemption of all men. It is the absence of this sense of redemption that Andrzejewski bemoans in *Holy Week*, in which the reader is made to see mostly Christian indifference and animosity toward the plight of the Jews, and even their betrayal.

Betrayal of Jews also runs through Andrzej Szczypiorski's well-regarded novel *Początek* (The Beginning, published in Paris in 1986 and in Poland in 1989; translated as *The Beautiful Mrs. Seidenman*). The story of a beautiful, "Aryan-looking" Jewish woman who is able to pass for a Christian and live beyond the walls of the ghetto, the novel tries to be evenhanded, as Szczypiorski indicts not only Polish Christians for their betrayal of Jews out of hatred or petty greed, but also Jews themselves who seek to stay alive by turning in fellow Jews to the Germans. This attempt at evenhandedness on Szczypiorski's part makes for some curious juxtapositions in his novel. Out of a desire to save the life of a Jewish girl, Joasia, an aristocratic Polish judge named Romnicki brings her for safekeeping for the duration of the war to a convent, where she is taken in by a nun, Sister Veronika. But aware of the nun's anti-Semitism, Romnicki cautions her against her obvious intention to raise Joasia, like her other Jewish wards, as a good Catholic. And when after the war Joasia migrates to Israel and assumes the name of Miriam, her pride in Jewishness and in the state of Israel is shaken when she witnesses mistreatment of Palestinian fedayeen by Israeli soldiers. Szczypiorski's point here is that when fortunes are reversed, the oppressed can just as easily become oppressors. Hence, the implied cautionary note about a rush to judgment against the Germans. However debatable Szczypiorski's reasoning may be here, there is little doubt that this dimension of *The Beautiful Mrs. Seidenman* became one of the reasons for his considerable popularity in the German-speaking world.

Andrzejewski's *Holy Week* is the most impressive Polish literary work dealing with the Jewish Ghetto Uprising written by a non-Jew. Even then, however, the focus is less on what transpired in the ghetto itself than on perceptions, attitudes, and behavior among Poles outside the ghetto walls. This is also the perspective of Czesław Miłosz in his two well-known poems "Campo di fiori" and "Biedny chrześcianin patrzy na ghetto" ("A Poor Christian Looks at the Ghetto").

The Ghetto Uprising broke out and was quashed in the spring of 1943. Over a year later, the Poles themselves rose up against their German occupiers in what is known as the Warsaw Uprising (1 August–9 October 1944). Because of the number of people involved, its duration, the destruction it brought to the city of Warsaw, and the fact that it appears to have been falsely encouraged by the Soviets who were camped across the Vistula River, the Warsaw Uprising is regarded as the centerpiece of Polish resistance to the Germans during the occupation. Understandably, it has also received its share of important literary attention, and two works stand out vividly because of the way their authors chose to deal with the uprising. Both were written by poets who themselves were participants in the event, Anna Świrszczyńska (1909–1984), who is also known under the pseudonym Anna Swir, and Miron Białoszewski (1922–1983). The success of both their works—Swir's *Budowałam barykadę* (*Building the Barricade*, 1974) and Białoszewski's *Pamiętnik z powstania warszawskiego* (*A Memoir of the Warsaw Uprising*, 1970)—lies in the immediacy of experience they convey. A poet of the older generation whose career seemed to take off suddenly in the early 1970s with the provocatively titled, intensely feminine volume of poems *Jestem baba* (I'm a Dame, 1972), Swir's *Building the Barricade* is an account in poetic prose of her own experiences setting up and manning barricades during the street fighting in Warsaw. Białoszewski's work is in some ways the more compelling. In a radical departure from the Polish Romantic tradition of nobility, heroism, and grand gestures, Białoszewski stresses the randomness and unpredictability of events. This deliberate eschewal of the heroic is striking. Somewhat in the manner of Tolstoy's *War and Peace,* the larger picture is sacrificed to the small steps taken by everyday people suddenly thrust into the midst of seemingly chaotic events that threaten to engulf them at any moment. The action is fragmentary, as if without logical sequence, and the more effective narratively.

Although he is also a respected poet, playwright, and essayist, Jarosław Marek Rymkiewicz's (b. 1935) international literary fame rests on his book *Umschlagplatz* (translated as *The Final Station: Umschlagplatz*). Published in 1988 by the Paris-based Polish Instytut Literacki (Institut Litteraire), the book is a provocative, intellectually stimulating narrative aimed at exposing the complex attitudes of the Poles toward the Holocaust. *Umschlagplatz* is the German word for the area of the Warsaw ghetto where Jews were assembled for deportation to the concentration camps. A non-Jew, Rymkiewicz became obsessed with the tragedy that had befallen the Polish Jews and set out to reconstruct the Umschlagplatz as it had existed during the war. This then became the launching pad, as it were, for his exploration of Polish-Jewish relations before, during, and after the war. Of particular interest is what his book reveals of Polish attitudes toward Jews in the postwar period. Rymkiewicz had previously addressed the matter of Polish-Jewish relations in his novel *Rozmowy polskie latem 1983* (Polish Conversations in the Summer of 1983, 1984). Written against the background of the rise of Solidarity and the attempted suppression of it, Rymkiewicz's novel acquires additional interest for its ruminations on Polish history and its evident pessimism concerning Poland's future.

Among Jewish writers who survived the war and wrote about it, Adolf Rudnicki (1912–1992) towers above others. Already an established writer in the interwar period, like Buczkowski, on the basis of such novels as *Szczury* (Rats, 1932), *Żołnierze* (Soldiers, 1933), based on his own military service, and *Niekochana* (Unloved, 1937), Rudnicki saw action in World War II and was captured by the Germans, but succeeded in escaping to Lwów (now Lviv, Ukraine) in the Soviet-occupied zone of the country. He returned to Warsaw in 1942, where he lived outside the walls of the Jewish ghetto on false papers and became active in the literary underground. He took part in the Warsaw Uprising of 1944 and became a member of the important Kuźnica literary group in the city of Łódź after the war. He returned to Warsaw in 1949 and pursued an active literary career as a novelist, short-story writer, and journalist.

Rudnicki's major contribution to the Polish literature on World War II was a multivolume chronicle of the Holocaust to which he devoted himself with passion and deep moral commitment. Collectively titled *Epoka pieców* (The Epoch of the Crematoria), the cycle includes the early short-story collections *Szekspir* (Shakespeare, 1948) and *Ucieczka z Jasnej Polany* (Flight from Yasnaya Polana, 1949), and especially the major collection *Żywe i martwe morze* (*The Dead and the Living Sea,* 1952). This latter volume (which was enlarged for new editions in 1955 and 1956 and was further revised in 1957) deals mostly with the fate of Polish Jews during the German occupation. Rudnicki's pictures of Jewish betrayal, self-denial, and suffering are poignant, moving, and bitterly true to life. They are among the best Holocaust-inspired fiction in any language. The last work in the Epoch of Crematoria cycle, *Kupiec Łódzki* (The Merchant of Łódź, 1963), is a fictionalized biography of Chaim Rumkowski (1877–1944), the chairman of the Jewish Council during the days of the Łódź ghetto.

The most resonant Polish literary work about life in the concentration camps was written by a non-Jew, Tadeusz Borowski (1922–1951). Borowski's is a tragic story of survival, hope, disillusionment, and suicide. He began his career as a poet in occupied Poland not long after beginning his studies in Polish language and literature at the underground Warsaw University. His first collection of poems, *Gdziekolwiek ziemia* (Wherever the Earth), was published clandestinely during this period. In 1943 Borowski was arrested, along with his fiancée, by the Germans and sent into the hell of the concentration camps. In Auschwitz and finally Dachau there seems to have been no form of brutality and suffering he did not personally witness. The memories were searing, and he later returned to them in his writing. After Poland's liberation by the Red Army in 1945, he moved to Munich briefly before returning to Poland on 31 May 1946. Once there he was able to reunite with his fiancée, from whom he had been long separated. Borowski's desire to commit to paper his concentration camp memories while they were still fresh in his mind resulted in the publication in 1947 and 1948, respectively, of two collections of short stories, *Pożegnania z Marią* (Farewell to Maria) and *Kamienny świat* (World of Stone). The title of one of the stories in Farewell to Maria, "Proszę państwa do gazu" ("This Way for the Gas, Ladies and Gentlemen"), was used for the title of the first English translation of the stories, published in 1967.

Borowski joined the communist Polish Workers' Party not long after the appearance of Farewell to Maria and World of Stone, in the belief that only communism could assure the future safety and independence of Poland. Despite his literary success (he was awarded the National Literary Prize, Second Degree, in 1950), based not only on his poems and short stories but also on his hack political works in the service of the party, he began to become deeply disillusioned with the Polish communist regime and his idealistic commitment to it. On 1 July 1951, at the age of twenty-nine, he took his own life by inhaling gas from a stove.

Borowski is remembered most for the stories in his two Polish collections, *Po żegnanie z Marią* and *Kamienny świat*. Obviously autobiographical, the stories are presented as fictional narratives and do not always square with the known facts of Borowski's life during and after the war. Nevertheless, they make an extraordinary impression on the reader not for any graphic depiction of the horrors of the camps, but for their largely matter-of-fact, dispassionate, unhysterical tone. As a *kapo,* or "privileged" concentration camp inmate-trustee, Borowski personally helped unload half-dead Jews from the boxcars that had transported them to the camps, helping himself along with other *kapos* to what food they had with them and at times assisting in their transfer to the gas chambers. Yet despite the range of degradation and barbarity that he witnessed, Borowski rarely ever sounds a note of pathos in his writings. Instead he highlights the ordinariness, even the banality, of what was going on all around as people connived to stay alive if only for another day. It is this unheroic treatment of the experiences of his narrator that brought Borowski much criticism from within the Polish literary community. And yet the great power of Borowski's stories lies in their very matter-of-factness, as if he deliberately sought, in this understated, unemotional way, to underline the monumentality of mere survival.

Recollection of another sort is also at the heart of a memorable work of Polish fiction dealing with the war and its aftermath, *Sennik współczesny* (*Dreambook for Our Time,* 1963), by one of the leading literary lights of postwar Poland, Tadeusz Konwicki (b. 1926). Mysterious, even enigmatic in some ways, *Dreambook for Our Time* recalls the partisan fighting that took place in the forests of what was then eastern Poland. Konwicki knew the area well both as a Pole from the former Lithuanian region of the country and as a combatant in a unit of the Home Army. The narrator is a former anticommunist partisan who has survived the war but has been deeply troubled ever since by conflicting memories of the past. On a journey of self-discovery, he has made his way to a remote village that he associates with his unsettling memories. After a failed suicide attempt, he regains consciousness surrounded by local people who seem as enigmatic as his recollections. Rumors circulate that a mysterious holdover from the anticommunist partisans named Hunjady still roams the forests, occasionally firing a rusty old pistol. The narrator's quest for information about the past becomes more urgent with the knowledge that the village is doomed to extinction because of a government dam-building project that necessitates its flooding. Of the motley group of people the narrator comes to know in the village, perhaps the most mysterious is Józef Car, who may be a Jew.

Nothing is ever certain in Konwicki's novel. It is Car who holds the key, or so it seems, to the resolution of the narrator's dilemma. The leader in the present of a strange redemptionist cult, Car seems bound up with the narrator's past. Through a series of flashbacks, this past begins to cohere. In the most important of these, the narrator is one of the remnants of a Home Army unit who hide out in snow-covered forests after the war and carry out partisan warfare against the communists. We learn that he has been ordered to kill a presumed traitor; unable to carry out the order, he only wounds the man and thereafter becomes burdened with the guilt of a failed mission. As he continues to grapple with his demons, the narrator becomes convinced that the man he was supposed to assassinate is none other than Car. Moreover, he conflates the elusive Hunjady with a former sergeant in the Home Army named Korwin who afterward became his commander in the anticommunist partisans and had ordered the assassination of Car. As the floodwaters close in on the strange, isolated village and its residents prepare to leave, Car preaches to his flock the wiping away of all the sins of the past. When the time comes for the narrator to leave the village, he does so with some questions still unanswered but with a greater sense that the past can at last be laid to rest.

A novel that succeeds to a great extent because of its strangeness and elusiveness, *Dreambook for Our Time* also insinuates Konwicki's belief that, so many years after the war, the time had come to give up the Polish obsession with the past, the Polish penchant for reliving the past and fighting the old battles of the past. The time had come, in other words, to accept the reality of a new day. There are many in Poland who still believe that of his many novels *Dreambook for Our Time* is Konwicki's finest.

Occupied Czechoslovakia

Certainly the most prolific author to address the matter of the German occupation of the Czech lands during World War II is the Prague native Arnošt

Lustig (b. 1926). A novelist and short story writer, Lustig was sixteen when, as a Jew, he was deported to the Theresienstadt concentration camp. In 1944 he was transferred to Auschwitz and then Buchenwald. During a death transport to Dachau in the spring of 1945 he managed to escape under the cover of an American air raid and hide out in Prague until the end of the war. The Soviet invasion of Czechoslovakia in 1968 occurred while Lustig was in Italy. He decided to remain abroad in protest. In 1970 he immigrated to the United States, following a year each in Israel and Yugoslavia. After a summer as a guest of the International Writing Program at the University of Iowa, he moved to Washington, D.C., where he had been offered a teaching position in literature and film at American University.

Lustig's literary career was shaped by his personal experiences of the wartime death camps; most of his writing deals in one way or another with the plight of the Jews during World War II. Often his leading characters are young women; the compassionate and understanding portrayal of these women is a hallmark of his style. His first books of stories, *Noc a naděje* (*Night and Hope,* 1957), *Démanty noci* (*Diamonds of the Night,* 1958), and *Ulice ztracených bratří* (*Street of Lost Brothers,* 1959), laid the foundation for such later works as his compelling short novel *Tma nemá stín* (*Darkness Casts No Shadow,* 1976), about two Jewish children who survive the Holocaust by hiding in the woods; *Nemilovaná: Z deníku sedmnáctileté Perly Sch.* (*The Unloved: From the Diary of [Seventeen-year-old] Perla S.,* 1979), a poignant tale in diary form of five months in the life of an adolescent prostitute in the Theresienstadt concentration camp; and *Modlitba pro Kateřinu Horovitzovou* (*A Prayer for Katerina Horovitzova,* 1964), about the gassing of a small group of Jews with American passports who were caught in Italy in 1943, among them the beautiful young dancer Kateřina Horovitzova, who moments before her death yanks a gun from the holster of one of her tormentors and shoots two German officers.

In *Neslušné sny* (*Indecent Dreams,* early 1960s), a collection of three novellas set in Prague during the German occupation, Lustig not only shifts the focus from the death camps to the squalor of occupied Prague not long before the liberation, but brings non-Jewish heroines to the fore. The three novellas comprising *Indecent Dreams* pivot in different ways on the motif of vengeance: in "Blue Day"—one of Lustig's best shorter works—a provincial German prostitute finds herself in the ironic position of being asked for shelter by a haughty Nazi military judge on the eve of the German surrender; in "The Girl with the Scar," his unlikely hero is an orphaned Czech schoolgirl who summons the courage to murder a German NCO who has taken a fancy to her; and in "Indecent Dreams" German deserters meet a swift death while Czech women prove as adept at men in exacting revenge on the remaining enemy.

Despite the grim context of most of his fiction, Lustig is not a depressing writer. Unsentimental and free of self-pity, his emphasis is on the triumph of the human spirit in the terrifying conditions of the camps. In *The Unloved: From the Diary of Perla S.,* for example, the young prostitute finds refuge from the horrors around her in dreams and fantasy and in recalling normal aspects of life in conversations with two other adolescent camp inmates. The problem of adjustment in postwar society of survivors of the war and the concentration camps is splendidly explored by Lustig in *Dita Saxová* (1962). This is a finely crafted and poignant novel about the emotional and erotic problems experienced by a lovely nineteen-year-old Jewish survivor of the camps as she tries to reconcile the horrors she has lived through with the need to create a semblance of normal existence in the postwar world. That Lustig's lasting literary fame will rest on his remarkable writings about the Holocaust is evident from the fact that they are now to be published under the collective title "Children of the Holocaust."

Jiří Weil's novels about the Czechs under German occupation—*Na střeše je Mendelssohn* (*Mendelssohn on the Roof*, 1960) and *Život s hvězdou* (*Life with a Star*, 1964)—are grim accounts of what it meant to be a Jew living in Nazi-occupied Prague. But they also highlight the ironies of German rule. Weil (1900–1959) came by his knowledge at first hand. Already an established writer in the 1930s, Weil had an intense dislike for totalitarianism in any form. He gave ample evidence of this in his book *Moskva–hranice* (From Moscow to the Border), which was based on his observations of the Soviet Union while he was working in the Czech section of the Comintern publishing house in Moscow before the war. After the German invasion of Czechoslovakia, Weil was slated to be hauled off to a concentration camp in 1942. However, he succeeded in faking his suicide and hiding out in occupied Prague for the rest of the war—no small feat. Despite difficulties with the communist authorities in the postwar period, he was made director of the State Jewish Museum in Prague, and subsequently was readmitted to the Writers' Union, from which he had been expelled in the early 1950s. In his first postwar novel about the occupation, *Life with a Star*, Weil drew heavily on his own experiences while hiding out in the Czech capital. Narrated in the first person, the novel is a compelling look into the everyday life-and-death struggle of Prague's Jewish community under the Nazis.

Mendelssohn on the Roof, which was published posthumously in 1960 after Weil's death from cancer in 1959, is similar in nature to *Life with a Star*, but with a twist. While still presenting a vivid picture of what Jews (and others) had to endure at German hands, it also isolates an incident that encapsulates the absurdity and banality of German rule. An ambitious SS officer named Julius Schlesinger is under orders to remove the statue of the German Jewish composer Felix Mendelssohn from atop the roof of the Prague concert hall. But there are several statues on the roof, and no indication which one is Mendelssohn. Falling back on his instruction in "racial science," by which he was taught how to distinguish Jews from other nationalities, Schlesinger determines that he will look for the statue with the biggest nose. The statue he finally orders his men to pull down turns out to be none other than that of Richard Wagner. The episode with the Mendelssohn statue provides an element of comic relief in an otherwise depressing novel of occupation, humiliation, and death.

One of the few Czech literary works dealing with the underground resistance during the war came, unexpectedly, from the pen of a former schoolteacher in her eighties named Věra Hoffmanová (who wrote under the pen name Květa

Legátová). Born in 1919, Legátová made her debut with the short-story collection *Želary,* the name of the fictional village in interwar eastern Moravia where the stories are set. Actually written in the 1960s, the book was published for the first time only in 2001 and proved an immediate success. Legátová's followup work, *Jozova Hanule* (Joza's Hanule), was published in 2002. A novella linked to the Želary stories, it deals with the resistance in the Moravian capital, Brno, during the German occupation. The work focuses on a young female medical student (Eliska) who becomes a nurse in a provincial hospital after the German invasion has made it impossible for her to complete her medical studies. She falls in love with a surgeon and before long the two of them become involved in the anti-German resistance movement. When the existence of her group is discovered by the Germans, the surgeon manages to flee the country, while Eliska is spirited away to a mountain hideaway in the remote village of Želary, the setting of Legátová's first cycle of stories. She is taken in by a uncultured mountain man named Joza, a blacksmith, to whom she had earlier given blood when he was brought in, wounded, to her hospital. Their common blood type becomes a powerful bond between them. Eliska is also given false documents and a new identity as Hana. Moreover, to safeguard her new identity she must also marry Joza. Against the background of wartime resistance, Legátová has crafted a compelling psychological tale in which her primary concern is the nature of the complex relationship between the urbane, educated Eliska and her unlikely husband, the good-hearted but primitive "child of nature," Joza. Legátgová's novella was made into an immensely popular film by Ondřej Trojan and in 2004 won an Academy Award as Best Foreign Language Film.

The Campaigns in the Balkans: Yugoslavia and Albania

Yugoslavs: Partisans and Chetniks

Yugoslavia proved to be a much more complex theater of operations than might ordinarily have been expected. After the fall of France in June 1940, Hitler began putting considerable pressure on the Balkan states to sign the so-called Tripartite Pact and align themselves with the Axis. Romania signed in November 1940 and Bulgaria in March 1941.

Hoping for support from the Soviet Union and the western Allies, the Yugoslavs held out as long as they could, until March 1941, when the situation appeared so hopeless that no course seemed to remain but to sign a protocol of adherence to the Tripartite Pact. In exchange, the Germans agreed to respect Yugoslav territorial integrity and sovereignty. But Yugoslav defiance, in the form of public demonstrations against Nazism and a military coup d'etat that elevated the sixteen-year-old presumptive heir, Petar, to the throne, sealed the country's fate. In April 1941 the Germans bombed Belgrade and other cities. Before long the country had been occupied and then truncated. The western parts of Yugoslavia as well as Bosnia-Herzegovina were assigned to the so-called Nezavisna Država Hrvatska (Independent State of Croatia), or NDH, which was nothing more than a Nazi puppet entity presided over by a military man, Ante Pavelić, and the Croatian fascist organization known as Ustasha (*Ustaša* in Croatian). The northern Serb territories were annexed by Hungary, with southern and eastern lands taken over by Bulgaria. The Germans occupied the rest of the country. Albania, under the domination of Mussolini's Italy at the time, took control of most of the predominantly Albanian province of Kosovo and Metohija as well as of parts of Montenegro, which then were occupied by Italian troops. The Slovene lands in the north of the Kingdom of Yugoslavia were divided between Germany and Italy.

Since any thought of serious military opposition to the German and Italian invaders had long been abandoned, resistance came mainly from Serb-organized partisan groups that coalesced around two prominent leaders, Jozef Broz Tito (1892–1980), who was partly of Croatian origin, and Draža Mihailović (1893–1946), a former royalist military officer. Tito's partisans, though predominantly Serbs, were recruited from the various Yugoslav ethnic communities. They were also generally of communist persuasion or inclination and opposed the restoration of the monarchy. The troops who grouped around Mihailović were largely Serb royalists who called themselves chetniks (*četnik* in Serbian; an old term for a militant Serb nationalist). Early in the war Mihailović was the man of the hour, internationally celebrated for his resistance to a ruthless German occupation and the horrific outrages of the Croatian Ustasha. But by the late summer of 1943 the tide had turned against Mihailović. The rivalry between Tito's partisans and Mihailović's chetniks led to bitter internecine strife so intense at times that it seemed to take precedence over the struggle against the Germans and Italians.

In vying for the considerable aid available from the western Allies, Mihailović fell victim to cleverly engineered rumors that he and his forces were collaborating with the Germans against Tito's partisans. Before long, the British and Americans cut off supplies to Mihailović and threw their support to Tito. With this Anglo-American backing, Tito and the partisans eventually came out on top. By the end of the war, and with Soviet assistance, they had reclaimed all the territories lost to the Germans and their allies. In order to strengthen the grip of the communists on the reigns of the postwar government, Tito and his loyalists made no secret of their desire to rid the country of Mihailović and the nationalists. The general himself was hanged in Belgrade on 17 July 1946 after an intense manhunt by Tito's forces. Ante Pavelić, who had presided over the wartime Croatian fascist state, managed to escape to Spain, where he lived until his death in Madrid in 1959.

Yugoslav fiction about World War II differs in certain major respects from that of other Eastern European countries. Bulgaria, Hungary, and Romania, as we have seen, became allies of Nazi Germany, both in response to considerable pressure and from the desire for territorial aggrandizement. Croatia and Slovakia were soon fashioned into puppet pro-Nazi fascist states. The Czech lands and Poland were quickly overrun and occupied, and even though some partisan fighting against the Germans occurred in Poland, it was insignificant compared to the Yugoslav resistance. The situation in tiny Albania most resembled that of Yugoslavia: stiff internal resistance to the Italian and German occupiers and internecine strife between partisans of the communist-organized Ushtria Çlirimtare Kombëtare (National Liberation Movement) and the nationalist anticommunist troops of the Balli Kombëtar (National Front). As the war progressed, a Tito-like authoritarian figure emerged in Albania in the form of Enver Hoxha (1908–1955) who, like Tito, led his country into the postwar period under communist banners.

The virtual capitulation of Yugoslavia to the Germans meant that the primary focus of war literature would be on the partisan struggle. But the communist grip on literary production in much of the postwar period guaranteed that the story of this struggle would be told almost wholly from the vantage point of Tito's partisans. Mihailović and the chetniks are either absent from the pages of this literature, as if indeed they never existed, or are presented only in a negative light, as the forces of reaction thwarting, or trying to thwart, the partisan campaign.

One of the most prominent literary figures of postwar Yugoslavia, Oskar Davičo (1909–1989), a poet and prose writer, drew on his own experiences as a member of Tito's partisans for his novels *Medju Markosovim partizanima* (Among Marko's Partisans, 1947) and *Pesma* (*The Poem,* 1952). The latter is by far the better known of the two. Set in German-occupied Belgrade during World War II, the large novel covers a time span of only thirty-six hours. It concerns the earnest attempt by a poet to join the partisans and the opposition to him by a morally overzealous young communist. This sets up a tragic situation in which the poet tries to vindicate himself by means of a public denunciation of the occupation, an act that leads to his arrest and imprisonment by the Germans. The action by partisans to free him proves successful but results in the death of the young communist. The cautionary note about communist overzealousness was sounded by Davičo at an appropriate time in the early postwar period—Tito had broken with the Soviet Union in 1948 and was engaged in a ruthless campaign to expunge the party of pro-Soviet and pro-Stalin elements.

The desire to avoid direct depiction of partisan-chetnik fighting on the part of writers dealing with the war is exemplified by Mihailo Lalić (1914–1992). A native of Montenegro, Lalić became a communist during his university years (in Belgrade), like so many other young Serbs and Montenegrans at the time, and fought with Tito's partisans during the war. His major work was the novel *Lelejska gora* (*The Wailing Mountain,* 1957), a first-person narrative by a partisan who is being hunted down by chetniks in the Montenegran mountains. A very atmospheric novel in terms of landscape, its main focus is not on military conflict, which is virtually absent, but on the relations between the partisan and the various people, mostly villagers, he encounters on his way and his ability to survive amid the strange but magnificent nature all around him.

The social and political crosscurrents in Yugoslavia before and during World War II are at the core of the major novel, *Ocevi i oci* (*Fathers and Forefathers,*

1985), by the prolific Serbian writer Slobodan Selenić (1933–1995). With its candid look at the tangled web of prewar Serbian and Yugoslav politics, and its unalloyed anticommunism, the novel would obviously have been difficult to bring to market before the death of Tito. It was written in 1981, by which time Selenić had been allowed to resume a public literary career after being ostracized for several years for political reasons, and was published in 1985. The story of the relationship between a member of the Serbian bourgeoisie, Stevan Medaković, and an Englishwoman whom he meets in the early 1920s while studying in England, marries, and brings back to Serbia spans the politically tumultuous years of the 1930s and World War II. Through a series of first-person narrations (the husband's memoirs; the wife's correspondence with a Serbian-Jewish woman married to an Englishman and living in England), Selenić skillfully intertwines the family and political dramas. As the wife attempts to integrate into middle-class Serbian society, the husband, a legal scholar, struggles to avoid becoming a pawn in the hands of various political factions vying for his support. In the late years of the war, the ever-deeper involvement of Medaković's son in the partisan movement and his obvious sympathies with the communists provide Selenić the opportunity to vent his distaste for the cynical maneuvering of the communists and his disdain for the nationalist politics of many of his fellow Serbs. Stoking the son, Mihailo's, partisan sympathies is his need to prove his Serbianness in the light of his mother's English background, which the son comes to spurn in his quest for self-identity. Eventually, Mihailo joins the partisans and is sent off to fight in the Battle of Srem near war's end. He is killed, and in the most moving part of the book, his father, Stevan, manages to get to the battlefield, where he joins many other Serbs in reclaiming the mangled bodies of their dead sons and loved ones.

Although the bitter campaigns in Yugoslavia would hardly have seemed conducive to levity, this was not the case with the novels of another Montenegran writer, the well-known Miodrag Bulatović (1930–1991). One of his best novels about the war, *Heroj na magarcu* (*Hero on a Donkey,* 1965), is a work of graphic realism about Montenegro under Italian occupation during World War II. At first meeting, it may seem a lighthearted treatment of a fairly benign Italian military presence in a Montenegran town. Interaction between the Italians and the Montenegran townspeople is casual, often amusing, and the Italians seem far more interested in sex than heroics. As in his earlier novel, *Crveni petao leti prema nebu* (*The Red Cock Flies to Heaven,* 1959), Bulatović's "hero" is again a simple man—a bar-cum-brothel keeper named Malić—whom nobody takes seriously. But as events develop, Malić turns into an ardent Marxist and supporter of the partisans, who gradually close in on the Italians. In the aftermath of Malić's comico-serious transformation, the novel acquires a previously negligible nationalism as the Italians are finally vanquished by the partisans.

Bulatović sought to repeat the success of *Hero on a Donkey* in a sequel entitled *Rat je bio bolji* (*The War Was Better,* 1977). But despite the reappearance of ribaldry, frolicsome Italian soldiers, and the newly Marxist Malić, this sprawling, almost phantasmagoric novel about a postwar, communized Slavic "invasion" of Europe spearheaded by Malić is ultimately less successful than *Hero on a Donkey*—doomed, to a large extent, by its own flamboyance.

One of the most compelling bodies of Yugoslav writing based on World War II experiences falls outside the realm of imaginative literature but should be considered in the present context. The very important Slovenian writer and religious thinker Edvard Kocbek (1904–1981) joined Tito's partisans in 1942 and saw action in various campaigns throughout the war. From November 1941 to June 1942 he also edited the political and cultural journal *Osvobodilna fronta*. Kocbek's major contribution to the Yugoslav literature on the war consists of diaries chronicling his experiences and observations as a World War II partisan. These include *Tovarišija: Dnevniški zapiski od 17 maja 1942 do 1 maja 1943* (Comradeship: Diary Notes from 17 May 1942 to 1 May 1943, 1949); *Slovensko poslanstvo: Dnevnik s poti v Jajce 1943* (The Slovenian Mission: Diary en Route in Jajka 1943, 1964); *Pred viharjem* (Before the Storm, 1980), which in fact includes fragments of diaries from the years 1938, 1940, 1941, and 1942; and *Listina: Dnevniški zapiski od 3 maja do 2 decembra 1943* (Document: Diary Notes from 3 May to 2 December 1943, 1967). Apart from their factual content, the diaries are especially interesting for Kocbek's reconciliation of Christianity and communism. Kocbek's most controversial literary work proved to be *Strah in pogum* (Fear and Courage, 1951), a collection of four novellas inspired by the wartime conflict. The controversy surrounding the book was provoked by the moral and ethical questions (above all, the Christian attitude toward killing) raised by Kocbek, which to many Yugoslavs seemed to be motivated by the desire to strip the partisan war of some of its mythic glory. So hostile in fact was the reaction to Fear and Courage that Kocbek was forced into virtual ostracism from Yugoslav literary and public life for nearly a decade.

Another major Slovenian novelist, Poris Pahor (b. 1913), a member of Trieste's large Slovene community, was pressed into Italian military service while a student at the University of Bologna. He served in North Africa, but after the Italian capitulation in 1943 was imprisoned in German concentration camps (Dachau, Belsen, and Natzweiler) for the last fourteen months of the war. He completed his university education in 1947 and lived for a time as a freelance writer before accepting an academic appointment in Trieste. A prolific novelist, short-story writer, diarist, and essayist, Pahor has had two principal concerns as a writer: his concentration camp experiences, and the tenuous situation of Slovenian culture in Trieste—the latter the subject of his novels *Mesto v zalivu* (City on the Gulf, 1955), *Parnik trobi nji* (The Steamship Signals Us, 1964), and *V labirintu* (In the Labyrinth, 1984), as well as his short-story collection *Kres v pristanu* (Bonfire in Port, 1959). Pahor's concentration camp experiences are recorded primarily in his splendidly written and aptly titled novel *Nekropola* (Necropolis, 1967; translated as *Pilgrim Among the Shadows*).

Although apparently able to conceal his Jewish origins behind his Italian military service, Pahor nevertheless bore witness as a camp medic to scenes of unspeakable human depravity in the camps. His unemotional, almost matter-of-fact first-person narration lends them an even greater sense of horror. *Pilgrim Among the Shadows* is constructed of a series of recollections of a former camp inmate (Pahor) triggered by a visit in 1966 to the restored Natzweiler-Struthof concentration camp, located about thirty-one miles southwest of Strasbourg in the Vosges Mountains in eastern France. The camp, which was intended to hold only about 1,500 inmates, was originally designed for German criminals, French Resistance fighters, and Gypsies. In the time that Pahor was imprisoned there, it was also used for the gassing of about 87 Jews (30 of them women). They were sent for that purpose from other camps so that Dr. Josef Hirt of the University of Strasbourg could have freshly gassed bodies free of wounds from beatings or other bodily "damage" in order to conduct experiments on their corpses aimed at demonstrating Jewish racial inferiority. This sordid episode in the history of Natzweiler-Struthof is alluded to by Pahor in the same dispassionate style in which the rest of *Pilgrim Among the Shadows* is narrated. Lending the narrative an almost surreal element is the fact that what Pahor describes was taking place even as the war was drawing to an end and punishing Allied air raids over the area were an almost daily event. Dispassionate though his narrative may be, Pahor examines his own behavior throughout his ordeal and raises profound questions about the limits of human endurance and human cruelty.

Albania: Communists and Nationalists

Albanian literature about World War II follows patterns similar to those of Yugoslavia—the Albanians' closest ally during the war—but with some distinctions. A number of writers had fought in partisan units and were able to draw on their experiences in their fiction and poetry. Among the more important of these were Shevqet Musaraj, Petro Marko, Fatmir Gjata, Ali Abdihoxha, and Dalan Shapllo. Later secretary-general of the Albanian Union of Writers and Artists, and a member of the People's Assembly, Musaraj (1914–1986) was a lifelong communist and a former partisan who had fought with the First [Albanian] Partisan Division. His major works about the war were in fact published in 1944, before the end of hostilities: *Epopeja e Ballit Kombëtar* (The Epic of the National Front), a condemnation of the nationalist anticommunist organization, and a basically factual account of wartime service under the title *Shtek më shtek me partizanët* (On Mountains and Hills with the Partisans). In 1959 Musaraj further enhanced his reputation with his prize-winning short-story collection *Isha unë Çobo Rrapushi* (It Was I, Çobo Rrapushi), which is set primarily against the background of the harshly enforced agricultural collectivization in Albania in the 1950s.

Petro Marko (1913–1991), a longtime communist who had fought on the side of the Republic in the Spanish Civil War of the late 1930s, served as well in World War II. He drew on these experiences in two novels, *Qyteti i fundit* (The Last City, 1960) and *Nata e Ustikës* (Ustica Night, 1989). Surrealist in style, The Last City focuses on the collapse of the Italian campaign in Albania by the summer of 1943 and the end of their occupation. Ustica Night was based on Marko's wartime internment together with many other Balkan prisoners on the isolated island of Ustica in the Tyrrhenian Sea north of Sicily.

Like Musaraj, the versatile writer Fatmir Gjata (1922–1989), a graduate of the Gorky Institute of World Literature in Moscow, also fought in the mountains during the war as a partisan and later became a political commissar. Although his acknowledged masterpiece remains *Këneta* (The Marsh, 1959), a novel dealing with the attempted sabotage of an important swamp-draining project and reflecting the widespread paranoia of the time about foreign (mostly Anglo-American) intrigue, Gjata also earned the respect of readers for such wartime novels as *Pika gjaku* (Drops of Blood, 1945), *Ujët fle, hasmi s'fle* (The Waters Slumber, but Not the Enemy, 1951), *Kënga e partizanit Benko* (The Song of Partisan Benko, 1951), and *Përmbysja* (The Overthrow, 1954). The best of these may well be The Overthrow, in which the emphasis shifts from war and combat to the growth of political consciousness in a peasant boy during the national liberation struggle.

Ali Abdihoxha (b. 1923), a novelist, short-story writer, and critic, rose to the rank of battalion commander in the Albanian partisan army during the war. He joined the Communist Party in 1944 and after the war eventually held positions in the Ministry of Education and Culture. Like other Albanian writers of his generation, he completed higher studies at the Gorky Institute of World Literature in Moscow. A prolific writer, Abdihoxha is best known for a series of well-crafted novels, inspired by his wartime experiences, in which he equates patriotism and communism. These include: *Një vjeshtë me stuhi* (A Stormy Autumn, 1959), his one work to be translated into a foreign language (French); the four-part *Tri ngjyra të kohës* (Three Colors of Time, 1965–1972), comprising *Në prag të luftës* (On the Threshold of War, 1965), *Lufta* (The Battle, 1969), *Përsëri lufta* (The Struggle Renewed, 1969), and *Lufta vazhdon* (The War Continues, 1972); and *Kronika e një nate* (Chronicle of a Night, 1984). Although wholly within the spirit of socialist realism, Abdihoxha still manages some taut war fiction. If the huge Three Colors of Time expectedly focuses on the impact of the conflict on the Albanian peasantry, his most widely acclaimed work, A Stormy Autumn, explores the moral and ideological crosscurrents within a group of young partisans who want to set up a clandestine press during the war. Chronicle of a Night, acknowledged as one of Abdihoxha's best novels, is set primarily in the last days of the war but also addresses the political background to Albania's entry into the communist camp in the postwar period.

Dalan Shapllo (b. 1928), a former partisan who had studied at the Lomonosov University in Moscow after the war, had a fruitful career as an editor (primarily at the journal *Nëntori),* critic, literary scholar (at Tirana University), and prose writer. Apart from a serious study of socialist realism under the title *Vepra dhe probleme të realizmit socialist* (Works and Problems of Socialist Realism, 1982), Shapllo's main entry in the field of imaginative literature was the World War II novel *Kohë lufte* (A Time of Battle, 1971).

Towering above other Albanian literary works about World War II are two novels by the celebrated Albanian writer Ismail Kadare (b. 1936). The first, which also happens to be Kadare's first published novel, *Gjenerali i ustrishë së vdekur* (*The General of the Dead Army*, 1963), is actually set in the postwar period. It is the story of an Italian general who returns to Albania twenty years after the war to reclaim the bodies of Italian soldiers who gave up their lives in the Albanian campaign. Accompanied by dental records, identification tags, maps, hired gravediggers, a dour priest, and near constant gloomy weather, the general sets about his grim mission in a spirit of noble purpose likened by the narrator to ancient Greek myths. But as exhumed bodies begin piling up, the general's mood shifts from exalted to depressed. The deeper he plunges into his task, the more aware he becomes of the animosity of his Albanian assistants and other observers and the ultimate futility of his massive undertaking. The parallel mission of a German general only heightens his sense of despair. In an emotionally intense scene near the end of the novel, at a peasant wedding to which he has come uninvited, the general is compelled to render account for the crimes of Italy and all other nations that have invaded Albania and ravaged its land. This outburst of Albanian nationalism and patriotism at the end of *The General of the Dead Army* is what apparently saved Kadare from damaging criticism for having written a work featuring the sympathetically drawn figure of a former enemy of the Albanian nation.

Eight years after the appearance of *The General of the Dead Enemy*, Kadare brought out another novel with a more direct World War II setting, *Kronikë në gur* (*Chronicle in Stone*, 1971). Richly evocative and imaginative, the novel is at once a tribute to the city that is Kadare's birthplace, Gjirokastër, and a touching journey into the mind of a young boy experiencing war for the first time. Gjirokastër, which is in southern Albania, not far from the Greek border, was also the birthplace of the now-deceased Albanian communist dictator, Enver Hoxha, who actually figures in the novel. A city renowned for its narrow cobblestoned streets, mountainside setting, and stone-roofed, fortress-like homes of Ottoman Turkish inspiration, Gjirokastër endured several occupations during the war—Greek, Italian, and German. These are all seen through the eyes and imagination of the novel's central character, a boy who constructs a fantasy world of things he observes and overhears. These rather than any accounts of chaos and destruction are what occupy center stage and infuse Kadare's novel with its atmosphere of magical realism. The work brings to mind a somewhat similar, albeit less exotic, novel, *Ljubezen* (Love, 1979), by the Slovenian writer Marjan Rožanc (1930–1990); in this instance, the patently autobiographical subject is a young boy's life in Ljubljana during World War II.

Four years after the publication of *Chronicle in Stone*, in 1975, Kadare produced another novel with a World War II setting, *Nëntori i një kryeqyteti* (November of a Capital City). But unlike *The General of a Dead Army* and *Chronicle in Stone*, it is a work of outright propaganda attributable to the downward turn in Albanian cultural life at the time. During the Fourth Plenary Session of the Central Committee of the Albanian Communist Party on 26–28

June 1973, the so-called Purge of Liberals was instituted, which caused grave consternation among writers and other intellectuals. Mindful of his prominence, and the precariousness of his situation, Kadare clearly sought to keep on the good side of the Hoxha regime by turning out a novel about Albanian partisan heroism in battle against the German occupiers of Tirana in 1944. In this respect, *November of a Capital City* is more easily reconciled with the war novels of Musaraj, Marko, Abdihoxha, and Shapllo.

Allies of the Axis

World War II has been a justifiably bitter memory for most Eastern Europeans. The occupied recall it only in terms of their suffering or heroism. The occupiers prefer to pass over it in silence when possible. The Bulgarians like to make much of the fact that they protected their small Jewish population, engaging in neither mass killings nor mass deportations. But the Bulgarians were occupiers in other lands—Greece, Macedonia, Serbia—and did indeed participate in deportations of Jews, if not in their actual murder. A somewhat similar claim is made by the Romanians with respect to the Jews of the historical kingdom of Romania. But the behavior of the Romanian army in lands seized from the Soviet Union and regarded as properly Romanian (Bessarabia, Bukovina, Transnistria) was horrific and resulted in the slaughter of large numbers of Jews. It is not something recalled with pride. The Romanian participation in the Battle of Stalingrad (on the German side, of course), which cost an extraordinary number of lives, is also usually relegated to the darker recesses of the mind. The Croatians and Hungarians have similarly grim memories. The killings of large numbers of Serbian Orthodox priests, Jews, and Gypsies by the Croatian Ustasha and the maintenance of concentration camps on Croatian soil during the war are seldom recalled by the Croatians themselves. The Jew-hunting and Jew-killing pursued so frenziedly by the Hungarians in the late years of the war, especially after Ferenc Szálasi and the Arrow Cross came to power, return to life almost exclusively in works of Hungarian Jews of the literary stature of Imre Kertész and Ernő Szép.

Before we consider the one Eastern European country—Slovakia—that has, at least in its own national consciousness, something it can look back on with a measure of dignity despite its wartime service to Nazi Germany as a puppet state, let us first review the Eastern European literature of collaboration, beginning with Hungary.

Hungary

As in postwar Czechoslovakia, the few Hungarian writers who have attempted to deal with Hungary's role in the war and the fate of the Hungarian Jewish population have been mostly Hungarian Jews. Certainly the best known, due to his receipt of the coveted Nobel Prize in Literature in 2002, is Imre Kertész

(b. 1929). Although a well-published author, Kertész is celebrated above all for two novels related to the Holocaust and obviously based on personal experiences, *Sorstalanság* (*Fatelessness*, 1975) and *Kaddis a meg nem szlületett gyermekért* (*Kaddish for a Child Not Born*, 1990). Narrated in the first person by a fifteen-year-old Hungarian Jewish boy, *Fatelessness* follows the young narrator from his roundup in Budapest in 1944 through his experiences in the Auschwitz and Buchenwald concentration camps, until his liberation by American troops and his return to Budapest after the war. The privations of the camps and the inhuman conditions on the freight trains that transport their human cargo there are recounted in a bland style appropriate to the age of the narrator, who only slowly perceives the true reality and larger dimensions of what is going on around him. Although the novel is well detailed, the emphasis is less on the horrors of the camps, few of which are described, than on the perceptions of the narrator, who is neither emotional nor self-pitying. In this respect the influence of the Pole Tadeusz Borowski, which Kertész has acknowledged, is clearly evident. The novelty of *Fatelessness,* given its grim subject, lies in the tendency of the narrator to see things in the best possible light, which carries over into the immediate postwar period, when he declares that "when anyone asks about the hardships, and the 'horrors,'" he will respond that "they will always remain for me the most memorable experience. Yes, if I'm ever asked, I'll say that the happiness from the concentration camps is the closest to my heart."[1] By happiness he means the contacts with other inmates of different nationalities, the beauties of nature he is able to savor every now and then, the ability to adapt to camp food, the occasional humane treatment shown him, and his preservation of a certain youthful innocence.

A shorter work, *Kaddish for a Child Not Born* is a touching, and disturbing, account of the impact of the narrator's concentration camp experiences on his marriage. Because of what he experienced as a Jew, and his deeply rooted fear that Jews might again become victims of persecution, he refuses to allow his wife to become pregnant, thereby destroying his marriage. His wife remarries a Christian and has two children whom the narrator eventually meets, pained by the knowledge that they could just as well have been his. Beautifully written in the form of a philosophically tinged personal narrative unbroken into chapters and only rarely into paragraphs in the original, *Kaddish for a Child Not Born* illuminates the deeper consequences of the Holocaust among those for whom even survival brought little peace.

Kertész's preoccupation with the Holocaust is also evident from such later works as *A kudarc* (Fiasco, 1988) and *Felszámolás* (Liquidation, 2003). Fiasco, which has been translated into several European languages but not English, is a novel about the writing of a novel. An "old" writer during the Brezhnev era in Hungary is laboriously working on a second novel. It will carry the title "Fiasco" and will be set in the Stalinist period. The central figure in the new work is also a writer, this time young, who ponders the subject of his first novel. In the end, he comes to realize that the only thing possible for him to write about is the war and the Holocaust. The story now comes full circle, with the "old" writer of the frame narrative understanding that he has already written such a novel. The real hero of Fiasco is thus Kertész himself, who recounts the circumstances—his own concentration camp experiences, the hardships he had to endure, his problems in trying to make a literary career, and so on—that led to the writing of *Fatelessness*.

Liquidation, which, like Fiasco, still awaits English translation but is available in other languages, deals with similar issues critical to Kertész: the impact of the Holocaust even years after the event, the corrosive influence of the tragedy on personal relationships, the difficulties of the writer in a communist society, and the hardships and frustrations of the creative process in general. The autobiographical element in Kertész's writings is never far from the surface. A curiously structured work in which the dialogue of a play alternates with the prose narrative and characters in the novel proper also appear in the dramatic fragments, Liquidation pivots on a mystery. A writer and translator identified only as B., a Jew, who was born in Auschwitz in 1944 of uncertain parentage, has committed suicide in the late 1990s by means of an overdose of morphine. The principal narrator of the novel is a publishing house editor named Keserű who was a friend of B. and who sets out to uncover the circumstances surrounding his death. As the informal caretaker of B.'s literary legacy, much of which he has removed from the death scene before the arrival of the police, Keserű had been entrusted with the manuscript of a three-act "comedy" by B. It is from this text, which seems to prophesy the behavior of people close to B., including Keserű, in the chaos of the postcommunist transformation in Hungary, that the dialogue with which Liquidation is interspersed has been taken. The title of the novel, Liquidation, has a twofold meaning. It refers obviously to the Holocaust, of which B. is a victim, and also to the impending liquidation of the publishing house with which Keserű himself is affiliated, yet another casualty of the social and economic changes besetting Hungary after the collapse of communism. Besides wanting to understand what caused his friend to commit suicide, Keserű is intent on coming across the "novel of life" he believes B. had completed before taking his own life. As other characters enter the novel (and the play within the novel), including B.'s former wife, with whom Keserű also had a brief affair, Liquidation takes on the intricacy of a crime novel.

In the end, it is B.'s wife who holds the key to the mystery. Profoundly troubled by his experience of the Holocaust, his own lack of identity, and his conviction that life is a concentration camp created by God for people on earth, B. entrusted his manuscript to his wife with the understanding that she would burn it in the eventuality of his death. When he finally learns the truth about the missing novel, and the part played by B.'s wife in its destruction and in the writer's suicide, Keserű's disappointment at not being able to read the novel is acute. At times seeming like a series of confessions, Liquidation is a novel of unrelieved gloom. Apart from the profound misery of B. and the psychological torment to which he subjected his wife until she could no longer stay with him, Keserű himself is a wretched figure, a man haunted by his arrest and brief imprisonment in the communist era on a false charge of distributing illegal journals, an event that destroyed his personal life and brought him to the brink of suicide.

Although almost all his literary work preceded World War II, Ernő Szép (1884–1953), one of Hungary's most popular and prolific writers, wrote a straightforward, unsentimental, but vivid memoir of what he himself experienced as a Jew in Budapest when, after the fall of the Horthy government on 15 October 1944, the extremist Arrow Cross party of Ferenc Szálasi took power and then joined forces with the Germans in a desperate three-month defense of the Hungarian capital against the approaching Soviet army. This bleak period is also the background of the well-known novel *Az ötödik pecsét* (*The Fifth Seal*, 1963), and the film based on it (1976), by the Hungarian writer Ferenc Sánta (b. 1927). Sixty years old at the time, Szép was forced to dig earthworks around the outskirts of Budapest along with thousands of other Hungarian Jews who had not been deported to death camps in the massive German roundup of 19 March 1944. Szep's memoir, *Emberszag* (*The Smell of Humans*), was first published in 1945 and was reprinted in 1984. It remains the only work by Szép available in English translation.

A different perspective on the plight of the Hungarian Jews in wartime Budapest came from the pen of Ferenc Karinthy (1921–1992), the son of the immensely respected writer Frigyes Karinthy (1887–1938). The author of many novels, short stories, and plays, a scholar in linguistics, and an accomplished sportsman, Ferenc Karinthy may be best known for his widely translated novel *Budapesti tavasz* (*Spring Comes to Budapest,* 1953), which was awarded the prestigious Kossuth Prize and was made into a very successful film by Félix Máriássy. Karinthy's first major novel after the coming to power of the Hungarian communist regime, *Spring Comes to Budapest* tells the story of Zoltán Pintér, an apolitical scholarly youth who deserts the army and joins the wartime resistance when he falls in love with a doomed Jewish girl taken captive by the Arrow Cross. The novel proved very popular and was published, with some slight revisions by Karinthy, more than twenty times between 1955 and 1980. A key to its success was Karinthy's skill at capturing the mood of Budapest in the last days of the war when the Russians entered the city and bitter street fighting ensued. With the enemy at last defeated, people venture into the streets to breathe the fresh air of liberation. A Hungarian band befriended by Soviet troops plays the Rákóczi March and Karinthy writes at the end: "It was so long now since music had been heard in the city that, as they listened, drinking it in, men and women wiped their eyes not knowing whether they were weeping or laughing."[2]

Aranyidő (The Age of Gold), which appeared in 1972, is arguably Karinthy's principal work of fiction dealing with World War II. Bizarre, entertaining, and ironic, it relates the escapades of a young Hungarian Jew named József Beregi during the Soviet siege of Budapest in December 1944. In advance of the Soviet penetration of the capital, the Germans desperately tried to round up as many Jews as they could for deportation to the death camps in Poland. Their Hungarian Arrow Cross collaborators simultaneously conducted their own reign of terror, hunting down Jews and dragging them to the banks of the Danube to be shot and their bodies dumped into the river. Beregi miraculously manages to escape this fate as well as the compulsory service at the Soviet front imposed on young Hungarian men. Partly concealed behind a huge moustache, he capitalizes on his Don Juan–esque success with women to hide out in their homes. The horror taking place all around him is the inescapable context of Beregi's story, but Karinthy succeeds in maintaining a balance between the madness engulfing the Hungarian Jews and Beregi's carefree romancing, which at one point carries him into a sexual encounter with a female officer of the Arrow Cross who has come to arrest him. On other occasions Beregi is provided shelter by a prostitute, a well-to-do woman, a street-smart adolescent, and, of course, the Arrow Cross officer. Karinthy—who lost his own mother, who was Jewish, in the Auschwitz death camp, and was a deserter from the Hungarian army—knew full well the terrible dangers and uncertainties of life in Budapest in 1944. This awareness is reflected in his novel, but Beregi's stubborn pursuit of pleasures, especially those of the flesh, provides a life-affirming counterpoint to the destruction surrounding him at the time.

Despite the success of *Spring Comes to Budapest,* and his previous enthusiasm for the postwar Hungarian communist regime, Karinthy eventually became disillusioned with the political climate in Hungary and began participating in the activities of the Petöfi Circle, which welcomed the reformist premiership of Imre Nágy (1896–1958). But a subsequent hardening of government policy caused Karinthy to desist from further political activity. When many of his literary friends fled Hungary in the wake of the Revolution of 1956, Karinthy chose to remain in the country on the grounds that his language was his life. His weaker novel about the revolution, *Budapesti ösz* (Autumn in Budapest), a sequel of sorts to *Spring Comes to Budapest,* appeared for the first time in Hungarian only in 1982.

After the suppression of the revolution, Karinthy busied himself primarily with translation and extensive collaboration with Hungarian theaters. Although he published a few collections of partly autobiographical sports stories and light theatrical pieces in the late 1950s and 1960s, his return to serious literary activity came in 1970, when more relaxed censorship in Hungary permitted publication of his dystopian novel *Epepe.* Immensely popular with readers, the novel reestablished Karinthy's celebrity.

A wholly non-Jewish Hungarian writer who wrote about the war was Tibor Cseres (1915–1993), who served in the army for some four and a half years before deserting, as an officer, in 1944. His first, and best-known, novel, *Hideg napok* (*Cold Days,* 1964), and the film based on it by András Kovács, won him instant fame. Cseres's focus in this work and in its much later sequel, *Vérbosszú Bácskában* (*Vendetta in Bácska,* 1991), is on the fighting in the Vojvodina (Hungarian Bácska, or Banat) region of the former Yugoslavia. Located along the southern border of Hungary in northeastern Serbia, the region, which had once been part of Hungary, had been ceded to the Kingdom of Serbs, Croats, and Slovenes (later Yugoslavia) by the Paris Peace Treaty of 1921. It was heavily

Serbian in population, but had a substantial Hungarian population as well as a small Jewish community. Its capital was Novi sad (Hungarian Új vidék). After the German occupation of Yugoslavia in 1941, Hungarian troops invaded Vojvodina on 11 April and reclaimed it for Hungary. A civilian administration was subsequently installed, with public safety entrusted to the Royal Hungarian Gendarmerie.

In response to Yugoslav partisan activity in the region after 22 June 1941, the Hungarians authorized a large-scale raid. Martial law was first declared and the raid was eventually mounted on 20 January 1942 under the command of Colonel József Grassy, one of the Hungarian Chiefs of Staff. Most of the action was concentrated in and around the city of Novi sad. With little hard evidence as to the location and identity of the Yugoslav partisans, the raid was carried out over a three-day period in the form mostly of random savagery that cost the lives of nearly four thousand people, primarily Serbs but also including 810 Jews, a small number of Russian refugees who had fled Russia after the Bolshevik Revolution, and even some local Hungarians. The "clean-up" action was ordered suspended on the night of 23 January. Although prominent members of the Hungarian military and government had had doubts about the rationale for the raid even before it was launched, the order to halt it came too late. Cognizant of the potential harm to Hungarian-Western relations posed by the raid, the Hungarians sought to limit the damage by bringing those held responsible to justice. Three generals and a dozen Gendarmerie officers were tried in December 1943 and convicted. Restitution to the families of innocent victims was ordered to be paid out as of 1 April 1944.

These are the bare bones of the incident dubbed the "cold days" by Cseres, referring to the three winter days on which the Novi sad massacre occurred. His novel, published over twenty years after the events, was rooted in Cseres's desire to find some historical justification for the massive Serbian retaliation against the Hungarians in late 1944. That reprisal, which extended over forty-five days, became the subject of Cseres's *Vérbosszú Bácskában*. In the introduction to this book, Cseres says that he had the idea for it as early as 1944 but then decided to shelve the project until the end of the Tito regime. It thus lay dormant for forty-six years. If Cseres sought to redeem the honor of the Hungarian nation by publishing *Cold Days*, there is little doubt that he was also motivated by the desire to show that the Novi sad events of 1942 set the stage for inevitable Serbian retaliation.

There is a considerable difference between *Cold Days* and *Vendetta in Bácska*. The first is a recreation of the infamous Hungarian massacre of January 1942, as described in the conversations and reminiscences of four Hungarian soldiers who took part in it—Pozdor, Szabó, Búky, and Tarpataki—and who now appear in a common prison cell awaiting punishment. The narratives of the four men, which Cseres uses to view the events from different perspectives, are interspersed with authorial comments on the separate narratives of the soldiers. To his credit, Cseres does not flinch from describing acts of individual and group brutality that, when taken together, paint a grim picture of the paranoia driving the Hungarian response to the perceived threat of Yugoslav partisan activity. In the end, of course, it was mostly innocent civilians who paid the price. If the soldiers in Cseres's novel are portrayed by and large as reluctant participants in the massacre, their reminiscences make it quite clear that many of their fellow soldiers and officers had no qualms about the random slaughter.

With *Vendetta in Bácska,* Cseres's aim was to settle scores with the Serbs in a big way. If the Hungarians bore responsibility for the massacre of 1942, the Serbs—in his view—carried a heavier burden for the massive retaliation of 1944. What seems to have troubled Cseres in particular—apart from all the bloodshed—was the absence of any Yugoslav apology for the later slaughter or any attempt whatsoever to hold the guilty accountable for their actions. Cseres indeed stresses Hungarian moral superiority in this regard. Avoiding fictional strategies in *Vendetta in Bácska,* Cseres has written what can only be described as an indictment. That he wanted the world to know the true nature of what he alleged to be the Serb crimes against the Hungarian civilian population of Bácska is evident from the English translation published by a small Hungarian-affiliated press in Buffalo, New York, in 1993 under the revealing title *Titoist Atrocities in Vojvodina, 1944–1945: Serbian Vendetta in Bácska,* and the fact that the entire work was subsequently made available on the Internet. *Vendetta in Bácska* is grim reading. Cseres pulls out all the stops in describing, in detail, horrible atrocities he claims the Serbs committed against the Hungarians, for which they went unpunished.

A native of Transylvania, Cseres also had strong views regarding the legitimacy of Hungarian claims to that area. These are much in evidence in *Őseink kertje: Erdély* (The Garden of Our Forefathers: Transylvania, 1990). Relatively more objective were his two previous novels dealing with the Hungarian-Romanian relationship, both, incidentally, with World War I settings: *Foksányi-szoros* (Focşani Pass, 1985), about a famous battle between Hungarian and Romanian forces during the war, and *Vízaknai csaták* (The Battles of Vízakna, 1988), dealing with Hungarian-Romanian relations in a small ethnically mixed Transylvanian salt-mining village.

János Pilinszky (1921–1981), one of the most highly regarded poets of post–World War II Hungary, was called up for military service in 1944 and served on the western front. What he saw of the remnants of the concentration camps and the terrible destruction of German cities inspired him to compose some of the most moving poems written by a Hungarian about the war. His first published collection, *Trapéz és korlát* (Trapeze and Parallel Bars), which appeared a year after the end of the war, in 1946, blended Christian religious imagery (Pilinszky was an ardent Catholic) and an abiding sense of isolation and desolation. The war itself and the mass extermination of the Jews are addressed more directly in the poems in his next collection, *Harmadnapon* (On the Third Day, 1959), and in the dramatic "oratorio" "KZ-oratórium" ("Concentration Camp Oratorio"), included in his major collection, *Nagyvárosi ikonok: Összegyűjtött versek, 1940–1970* (Metropolitan Icons: Collected Poems, 1940–1970, 1970, 1971; translated as *Metropolitan Icons: Selected Poems by János Pilinszky in*

Hungarian and in English, 1995). Later in his career, as his reputation grew and he began traveling extensively in the West, Pilinszky developed a friendship with the English poet Ted Hughes, who, in collaboration with János Csokits, became Pilinszky's first translator into English. In 1972 he lectured at the Sorbonne at invitation of the French Catholic existentialist philosopher Gabriel Marcel, and in 1975 at Columbia University.

Croatia

Even more so than the Hungarians, the Croats would seem to have little or nothing to contribute by way of war fiction. Absent writers of Jewish origin, and nothing positive to spin from their wartime collaboration with the Germans, Croatian writers have generally preferred to shy away from World War II in their fiction. But there is one exception, and a notable one at that. Ivan Aralica (b. 1930), one of the most respected contemporary Croatian literary figures, is a nationalist who served as vice president of the Croatian Parliament under independent Croatia's first president, the reactionary Franjo Tudjman. In 1997 Aralica published his only novel with a World War II setting, *Četverored* (By Rows of Four). Dealing with the explosive subject of the Serbian partisan massacre of thousands of Croats, Ustasha and civilians alike, at Bleiburg, Austria, in 1945 as they were attempting to flee across the border, Aralica's text assumes an undeniably revisionist perspective. The brutality of the Serbs, and the complicity as well of the British occupying army in Austria at the time, made Bleiburg almost a taboo topic for years after the war. Aralica may deserve some credit for even broaching the "Croatian Calvary" in his novel, but his nationalistic bias—which the film based on it by Jakov Sedlar emphasizes all the more— greatly weakens the work. For a devastating review of novel and film, the article by the liberal young Croatian writer Miljenko Jergović (b. 1966), published in the Croatian satirical magazine *Feral Tribunea* (Feral Tribune) on 27 December 1999, is required reading.

Romania

It was only as recently as the winter of 2004—fifty-nine years after the conclusion of World War II—that the Romanian president officially apologized for Romania's treatment of its Jews during the war. Previously, accusations of the Romanian slaughter of Jews in Bessarabia and Bukovina, territories liberated from Soviet rule in 1941, and in Transnistria, which the Romanians carved out for themselves from Soviet territory during the war, were either met with stony silence or flatly rejected. Similarly, the sometimes vicious and all-pervasive Romanian anti-Semitism of the 1930s has been rejected as anti-Romanian slander or grossly exaggerated. The diary of the Romanian Jewish playwright and novelist Mihail Sebastian (1907–1945), which was first published in Romania amid a storm of protest in 1996 (an English translation appeared in 2000 under the title *Journal, 1935–1944: The Fascist Years*), is a depressing account of the sprawling anti-Semitism that accompanied the rise to power of the extreme right wing in Romania in the late 1930s.

The Garda de fier (Iron Guard) legionnaires, formed by "Captain" Corneliu Zelea Codreanu (1899–1938), were savage in their treatment of Jews, especially after their attempted coup d'etat on 21 January 1941. Despite the crushing of the rebellion by the Romanian prime minister, General Ion Antonescu, who feared a takeover of the wartime Romanian state by the Iron Guard, the Jews had no cause for celebration. The provinces of Bessarabia and Bukovina in northern Romania, which had substantial Jewish populations, had been annexed by the Soviet Union in 1940. When combined German and Romanian forces retook the territories in the summer of 1941, Antonescu ordered the mass deportation of Jews during the period 15 September 1941 to fall 1942. The rationale for this was the alleged cooperation of the Bessarabian and Bukovinian Jews with the Soviets. The majority were transported to the territory of Transnistria. Of the nearly 150,000 Jews deported to Transnistria, some 90,000 perished. The zeal with which Romanian soldiers went about slaughtering Jews at times so astonished the Germans that, as difficult as it may be to believe, they ordered them to slow the pace of the killing.

Against the background of Romania's wartime record, the paucity of fiction dealing with the war should hardly come as a surprise. There were, however, a few exceptions. Perhaps the most interesting for its scope is the novel *Străinul* (*The Stranger*, 1957) by Titus Popovici (1930–1994; real name Titus Viorel). A former member of the Central Committee of the Romanian Communist Party, Popovici veered little from the official communist view of interwar Romanian society and politics, World War II, and the immediate postwar period of reconstruction. But given these ideological limitations, he still managed to turn out two respectable novels, *The Stranger* and *Setea* (Thirst, 1958). Our concern at this point is with *The Stranger*. A large novel, *The Stranger* takes place primarily in wartime Romania but does not address directly Romania's calamitous collaboration with Hitler, its staggering losses at Stalingrad, or the Allied raids on the country, especially the Ploeşti oil fields. Although these events all permeate the atmosphere of the novel, they are not its principal focus. Popovici's concern lies instead with an expansive depiction of the social and political scene, both during and after the war. His contempt for Codreanu's prewar Iron Guard movement, the wartime government of Ion Antonescu, and right-wing, nationalistic Romanian society in general, is conveyed through the central figure of the novel, Andrei, whom we first meet as a rebellious high school student opposed to injustice and war. Because of a school paper that he has written, which is considered suspiciously idealistic and inferentially hostile to the Antonescu regime, he is virtually ostracized by many teachers and schoolmates and is threatened with expulsion. By setting Andrei at odds with peers and adults alike, Popovici is able to paint a broad spectrum of Romanian society in the early 1940s, ranging from members of fashionable society who support Antonescu and cannot imagine a German defeat in the war to a variety of steadfast naysayers and recent converts who regret Romania's close embrace of Germany and predict a Russian victory, at no small cost to their own country.

The turning point is reached with the breakout of the Romanian antifascist movement and the country's exit from the Axis. Given, of course, Popovici's expected emphasis on the guiding communist role in the resistance, he does a credible job of capturing the mood of the time, euphoria mingled with anxiety. The panic in the countryside that follows raids by German planes and advancing German and Hungarian troops not long before the main Russian thrust into Romania is depicted in vivid detail. When Romanian nationalist fighters counterattack and at one point seize a town with a Hungarian minority, their frustration at not being able to immediately claim Transylvania for Romania— which they attribute to Soviet power politics—leads them to commit atrocities against the Hungarians. Andrei witnesses the beheading of some Hungarian civilians and intends to publicize the event for humanitarian reasons. Despite pressure from diehard Romanian nationalists who want the news about the massacre kept quiet, he stands by his commitment. By now Andrei has made common cause with the communists, who represent the future of Romania, in his view, and who support his stand.

The obvious ideological orientation of *The Stranger* notwithstanding, Popovici has succeeded by and large in bringing to life the social and political crosscurrents in Romania in the chaotic 1940s. The ultimate victory of the Red Army and of the Romanian communists as they stand poised to take over the country at war's end is rather much what one would expect. More interesting is the well-detailed portrait Popovici paints of the elements in Romanian society that supported first Codreanu's Iron Guard and then the Antonescu regime. A writer of communist persuasion like Popovici would not have been expected to depict the Romanian right wing any other way. But it is the social panorama and lifelike portraiture that make *The Stranger* the literary success that it has been.

The Slovak National Uprising

A powerful symbol of the Slovak resistance to fascism, the short-lived and ultimately unsuccessful Slovak National Uprising (SNP; in Slovak: Slovenské narodné povstanie) against the Germans during World War II has long been a dominant theme in postwar Slovak literature. "The uprising was an obvious proof and demonstration that the Slovaks had nothing in common with the fascism of which the uncrowned king was Hitler," declares the highly respected Slovak writer Ladislav Ťažký, as documented by the journalist Jozef Leikert in a book of interviews with Ťažký under the title *Testament svedomia* (Testament of Conscience, 1995).[3] Ťažký's words echo a familiar refrain of postwar Slovak writing about the event. To the Slovaks, the uprising was a vindication of their fundamental commitment to democracy despite wartime Slovakia's role as a

Nazi puppet state headed by the Roman Catholic cleric Monsignor Jozef Tiso. The need for such vindication would seem obvious in the light of the contrary status of the Czechs as an occupied people during the war and the Slovaks' participation in the Holocaust by reason of their deportation of Slovak Jews to the German death camps. The Czechs, in other words, behaved honorably and suffered the privations of an enemy occupation during the war. By contrast, the Slovaks were understood to be both anti-Semitic and anti-Czech and thus ripe for German bidding once an "independent" Slovak state, the first in history, was declared.

The threatened dismemberment of the Slovak part of Czechoslovakia considered by Hitler and the Hungarian leader, Admiral Horthy, whereby western Slovakia would become a part of Greater Germany, the territory up to the Hron River would be taken over by Hungary, and the northern part of the country would fall to the Poles, was another cudgel with which to beat the Slovaks into submission. The stand of the Poles, in particular, was a bitter blow to the Slovaks, who had long felt close to their neighbors to the north and believed in their support. But such support never materialized. And so, feeling abandoned and alone in the world—as they believe they often have been through the centuries—the Slovaks reasoned that they had no choice but to cooperate with the Germans. But the quasi-independence they achieved under German patronage came with a heavy price, as Ťažký points out in Testament of Conscience: "The loss of the southern territory, participation in the war against the Soviet Union, and the deportation of Jews to the concentration camps." And even though, as Ťažký mentions, Jews were deported from other countries in Eastern Europe—Hungary, Poland, Ukraine, Russia, and the Baltic states—such are the discreditors of Slovakia that they insist on using the deportations as evidence that "the Slovaks are fascists, despite the fact that the contrary is true" (54).

But even the "redemption" by blood in the form of the Slovak National Uprising was not enough to erase the shame that was felt by some over the maltreatment of the Jews. This is not so much the case with Ťažký, who seems more concerned with defending his fellow Slovaks against charges of fascism than with the fate of the Jews. Milo Urban (1904–1982), on the other hand, whose literary reputation in Slovakia yields nothing to Ťažký's, is more willing to confront the matter directly, as he does in his book of memoirs *Sloboda nie je špás* (Freedom Is No Joke, 1995): "In truth the Jews did not grow into our society; they isolated themselves from it on every level. But what we did to them under German pressure transgressed the limits of humanity and resisted the most fundamental claims of morality and social life. Should this be denied, even marginally? Should this tragedy be barred from one's consciousness, even today when it is sufficiently known to everyone? Only perhaps by a person without feeling, without a conscience."[4]

The significance of the Slovak National Uprising to the Slovaks, as well as its scope and almost legendary quality, seemed best accommodated by the larger dimensions of the novel. Among the many works in this genre, spanning the wide range of attitudes toward the uprising, were the partisan novel *Stretnutia v lasoch* (Encounters in the Forests, 1947) by Hela Volanská (1912–1996); *Hory mlčia* (The Mountains Are Silent, 1947), a lyricized depiction of the growth of Slovak resistance to the Germans, by Jozef Horák (1907–1974); *Víťazné stretnutie* (Victorious Encounter, 1949), a glorification of the role of the Soviet army in the uprising, by Samo Faľtan (b. 1920), a strongly pro-Soviet writer and the author of such nonfictional accounts of the uprising and the Soviet role in it as *Slovaci v partizánských bojoch v Sovietskom sväze* (Slovaks in Partisan Battles in the Soviet Union, 1957), *Partizánska vojna na Slovensku* (The Partisan War in Slovakia, 1959), *Partizani na Slovensku* (Partisans in Slovakia, 1960), and *O Slovanskom národnom povstaní* (On the Slovak National Uprising, 1964); *Smrť chodi po horách* (Death Walks the Mountains, 1948), dealing with the partisan fighting, by Vladimir Mináč (1922–1992), as well as Mináč's *Generácia* (Generation, consisting of the separate novels *Dlhý čas čakania* [The Long Wait, 1959], *Živi a mŕtvi* [The Living and the Dead, 1959], and *Zvony zvonia na deň* [The Bells Ring by Day, 1961]), a procommunist trilogy about the uprising but relatively free of deference to the role of the Soviet army, a stance that became possible after 1956; and Ladislav Mňačko's (1919–1994) *Smrť sa volá Engelchen* (*Death Is Called Engelchen*, 1959).

In his novel *Mŕtvi nespievajú* (The Dead Do Not Sing, 1961 or 1962)—the only other Slovak novel about the uprising besides Mňačko's *Death Is Called Engelchen* to be translated into English (under the title *Dead Soldiers Don't Sing*)—which deals primarily with elements of the German and Slovak armies fighting the Russians on the eastern front, Rudolf Jašík (1919–1960) touched on certain issues that would become more prominent as the literature of the Slovak National Uprising evolved. Shifting back and forth between the almost static battlefront and the rural home setting of many of the Slovak troops, Jašík shuns mythopoeia. Despite some exceptions, the German and Slovak soldiers are anything but comrades in arms. The Germans tend to distrust and look down on the Slovaks, and the Slovaks generally dislike the Germans, not least for their haughty attitudes. Striking a note that resounds through much of the Slovak fiction about the war, Jašík depicts the Slovaks as unenthusiastic about fighting the Russians, whom they regard as fellow Slavs. To the Slovaks, the kinship with the Russians overrides ideology. While he captures with some fidelity the social and political crosscurrents on the home front, Jašík's outlook becomes clearest in the battle scenes. The emphasis there is wholly on negatives: war as ubiquitous death, badly deteriorating German-Slovak relations, and the eventual desertion of a large number of Slovak troops, who decide either to make their way home as best they can or to go over to the Russian side.

Ladislav Ťažký also drew inspiration from the Slovak participation in the war as well as the Slovak National Uprising for his major novel *Ámenmária, samí dobrí vojaci* (Amenmaria, the Very Best Soldiers, 1964). The main protagonist, Matúš Zraz, is a sixteen-year-old student of mapmaking when the war breaks out; he is forced to serve on the eastern front fighting Russians with whom he and his fellow Slovaks feel close kinship ties. They decide, therefore, to join the advancing Soviet forces at the first opportunity. But they let the chance slip by and then have to merge with the rest of the Slovak forces on the eastern front on their long odyssey through Bessarabia and Romania to Hungary in flight from the Red Army. Only in the chaos of the retreat, disarmed by the Germans, do Zraz and his fellow Slovaks end up being taken prisoner by the Russians and then fighting the common enemy, the Germans, alongside them. Ťažký's other books dealing with the war include the novels *Dunajské hroby* (Danubian Graves, 1964), *Pochoval som ho nahého* (I Buried Him Naked, 1970), and *Evanjelium čatára Matúša* (The Gospel of Squad Leader Matúš, 1979), as well as the short-story collection *Vojenský zbeh* (The Army Deserter, 1979). Ťažký himself had been taken prisoner by the Romanians, interned in Romania, recaptured by the Hungarians, and pressed into a labor brigade in Austria.

In the first of two earlier novels dealing with World War II, *Farská republika* (The Parish Republic, 1948), the important Slovak writer Dominik Tatarka (1913–1989) excoriated the so-called Republic of Slovakia headed by the notorious Monsignor Jozef Tiso, who after the war was branded a traitor. With his second novel, *Prvý a druhý úder* (The First and Second Blow, 1950), he sought to explore the transition in Slovak society from the wartime uprising to the early postwar reconstruction of the Czechoslovak state. But the novel fell flat as a kind of communist hack work in which the protagonist, a partisan first in Ukraine and then in Slovakia, later becomes a heroic socialist builder of bridges.

As we can see, the literature of the Slovak National Uprising articulates a range of attitudes toward this defining moment in modern Slovak history. The overwhelming majority of works concentrate on the heroism of the Slovak resistance fighters and their opposition to Hitlerian fascism. The uprising easily lent itself to mythmaking as, for example, in Horák's The Mountains Are Silent. Some writers, and none more so than Samo Faľtan, placed their greatest emphasis on the leadership role of the Soviet Union. Others preferred to concentrate on the crimes against humanity of the Germans without allowing any light to fall on the deeds of their Slovak collaborators. Rudolf Jašík's position represents a more candid look at the deteriorating relations between the Germans and their Slovak allies and the Slovak reluctance to fight against the Russians. In *Death Is Called Engelchen,* Mňačko depicts German brutality, as in the burning of a peasant village and all its male inhabitants, but tends more to emphasize the close relationship of Russian and Slovak partisans in the guerilla fighting. In fact, the narrator of the novel is a badly wounded Russian partisan named Volodya who recalls the events that led up to the destruction of the village of Ploština and still agonizes over the possibility that somehow he and his fellow partisans may inadvertently have caused the tragedy.

There was hardly any Slovak writer who could bring himself to condemn the uprising, but one clearly did, and in no uncertain terms. That was none other than one of the grand old men of twentieth-century Slovak literature, Jozef Ciger Hronský (1896–1960). A well-respected writer on the basis of such pre–World War II novels as *Chlieb* (Bread, 1931) and *Jozef Mak* (1933), Hronský was one of a number of nationalistic and anticommunist Catholic Slovaks who fled the country after 1945. He first settled in Rome but later moved on to the safer haven of Argentina, fearful that the communists were pursuing him. Resentful of the tendency among some Slovak writers to deconstruct the myth of the Slovak National Uprising, above all by portraying the Slovak troops who fought alongside the Germans in a less than favorable light, he sought to oppose this trend with his novel *Svet na trasovisku* (A World in the Quagmire, 1960). By arguing that the antifascist resistance in wartime Slovakia was a Russian and Bolshevik import alien to the Slovak nature, however, all Hronský accomplished was to have his book regarded as taboo in Slovakia for nearly thirty years after its publication.

The treatment of Slovak Jews by the Slovaks during the war and the uprising attracted the attention of only a few Slovak writers. In one of his best novels, *Námestie svätej Alžbety* (St. Elizabeth Square, 1958), Rudolf Jašík addresses the ramifications for Jewish-Slovak relations, especially among young people, of the entry of the German army into a Slovak town under the control of the fascist Hlinka Guard. Pulling no punches, Jašík exposes the pettiness of some of the Slovaks, who never seemed to have anything against Jews, as they compete with one another in various schemes to earn money from Jewish suffering. In order to save his Jewish girlfriend, Eva, Igor proposes taking a large sum of money from her businessman father in order to get a local parish priest to issue a document declaring her to be a Christian. But her father refuses to deal with him. Along with other Jews, Eva is finally shot. Slovaks do the killing under German supervision. At the end of novel, the Germans quit the town as Slovak resistance fighters, with the Soviet troops not far behind them, draw nearer. A despondent Igor reluctantly flees under cover of night.

Fedor Cádra (b. 1926), although a less prominent writer than Jašík, wrote a gripping novel, *Jediný deň života* (A Single Day of Life, 1959), in which the saving of a Jew's life exposes the tension between a person's struggle for human dignity and the spiritual and moral corruption sown by totalitarianism. Of major Slovak writers—besides Jašík—who took up the matter of the plight of the Slovak Jews during the war, the most important has been Ján Johanides (b. 1934). His two best works dealing with the issue are *Súkromie* (Privacy, 1963) and *Slony v Mauthausene* (Elephants in Mathausen, 1985). A collection of five stories, Privacy is noteworthy above all for Johanides's indictment of the passive collaboration of the Slovaks in the deportation of Jews to the German death camps. One of these death camps, Mauthausen, becomes the springboard of the action in his later novel, Elephants in Mauthausen. Again exposing the moral relativism of the Slovaks in their treatment of Jews during the war, Johanides brings together in his novel several survivors of the camp in the postwar period. Apart from further recalling the horrors of the camps under the Germans, the novel fulfills another goal—exposing the ahistorical pursuit of bourgeois self-gratification in the postwar period, here exemplified by a Dutch survivor of Mauthausen and his children.

Similarly focused on the postwar period—while still considering the legacy of the wartime plight of the Slovak Jews—were the major writers Anton Baláž

(b. 1943) and Alfonz Bednár (1914–1989). Baláž took up a Jewish theme in his novel *Krajina zabudnutia* (Land of Oblivion, 2000), which follows the destinies of two Jewish female survivors of the Holocaust—the Slovak Miriam and the Hungarian Erna—who meet unexpectedly in Slovakia after surviving Auschwitz. The novel is set in the early 1950s, when the Iron Curtain was being drawn tighter around Eastern Europe and the communist antennae were out for "Zionist plots." Erna has escaped from Hungary just ahead of the secret police, and hopes eventually to make her way to the United States. Miriam, on the other hand, has been working for the Jewish Agency in a risky operation to help other Jewish survivors reach Israel, the "land of oblivion" of the title, where they can try to put the Holocaust behind them. The pair become a triangle when fate brings them together with the young photographer Jakub, a non-Jew, through whom Miriam expects to obtain photos for false passports and visas. Complicating matters further is the Israeli secret agent Neguš who had known Miriam previously and with whom he had a brief romantic fling. While sympathetic to the efforts to help smuggle Jews into Israel, his own mission in Czechoslovakia is to purchase weapons for the new Israeli army before the communist regime cracks down on such trade. Matters come to a head when the authorities in Prague become wise to the illegality of the Jewish emigrant operation, which they regard as the scheme of Jewish "wreckers" supported by American imperialism. At the end, with avenues of escape rapidly closing, Erna, posing as a Polish woman, and Neguš leave for Vienna while Miriam and Jakub, whose position now in Slovakia is precarious, take a train to Germany under assumed names. When Jakub tells her that it won't be easy for her in Germany because of the past, she says she will always carry the memories of Auschwitz with her but will make a new life, and that even Jakub himself will have to come to terms with it.

Anton Baláž's *Tábor padlých žien* (The Camp of Fallen Women, 1993) introduces the wartime Jewish theme in a more oblique way. Set in the late 1940s, not long after the communists have taken power in Czechoslovakia, the novel recounts the attempt on the part of government officials and young zealots to relocate a group of prostitutes from their habitual quarters in the capital, Bratislava, to a camp used for Jews during World War II. Although emphasis is on the way the prostitutes deal with the matter of their "reeducation," Baláž manages to expose a lingering Slovak resentment toward Jews and a certain banalization of anti-Semitism and the Holocaust. In speaking of the camp itself, an official acknowledges that the place is now "a pile of Jewish tatters, but that during the war it was a Jewish camp. . . . Here they suffered and from here the priestly regime [a reference to the wartime regime of Monsignor Jozef Tiso] allowed them to be transported to German concentration camps, where they were gassed. Therefore even these tatters will be spoken about with respect, understand? . . . No whores' words will be tolerated here anymore!"[5] He thus admonishes the women that "the spreading of anti-Semitism in the camp is a punishable offense." All this comes by way of a response to the consternation of a few of the women when they are given old clothes upon their arrival in the camp. When one is handed a blouse, she notices a patch on it and asks for a better garment without any patches. But another woman looks at the blouse and declares: "That's not a patch, but a Jewish star. You just have to rip it off!" "What?" screams the other one (Ernička) and then says to her friend Carmen: "You give us rags left behind by Jews? Phuy! I won't wear anything belonging to dirty Jews!"

With Alfonz Bednár, some of whose best works date from the 1950s and early 1960s, interest in the mythology of the Slovak National Uprising and the Slovak treatment of Jews during World War II is replaced by a concern with the consequences of these events on human behavior. *Sklený vrch* (The Glass Hill, 1954), one of his most resonant novels, is constructed in the form of an intimate diary, covering the period from winter 1951 to early spring 1952, by a young woman who tries to come to grips with her own past and ends tragically. The diary itself is preceded by a short prefatory section in italics in which Jožo Solan, the husband of the author of the diary, readies himself for a trip. As he picks up a sweater woven for him by his wife, a pile of letters tumble out. He becomes engrossed in reading them, and finally puts them down the following morning. The letters are, in fact, the diary of his wife, Ema. Not long after reading the penultimate entry, Solan receives a phone call informing him that his wife has just been killed in an industrial accident. Although interesting primarily for the novelty at the time of a female lead character drawn with greater individuality than had previously been the case in postwar Slovak literature, Ema's diary offers revealing glimpses into the lingering memories of the war and the Slovak National Uprising as well as into the slothfulness, backbiting, and intrigues typical of the immediate postwar socialist society. Ema and her husband, who are childless, are both employed in a state construction project with which most of the characters in the novel are associated.

In his development of the figure of Ema, Bednár broke with the familiar schematism of the socialist realism of the early 1950s; this is what attracted the most attention to the novel. Ema's individualism, as conceived by Bednár, lies in her candor, about her relationships with other men, her sometimes distant relationship with her husband—who resents her outgoing nature and her many friendships—and her inability to bear children, which she herself caused, a fact she has concealed from her husband. The past intrudes unpleasantly on the present when an envious and troublemaking fellow worker (Tretina) spreads accusations about Ema's role in the death of a mutual friend named Tkáčik, a fighter in the Slovak National Uprising. Tkáčik is rumored to have been led into a German ambush and subsequently killed because of a letter attributed to Ema. Ema's vigorous defense, and her denial of actual participation in the uprising alongside Tkáčik, may leave lingering questions about what actually happened in the nearby mountains during the dark days of the war, but serve to establish her forthrightness and resistance to intimidation. Ema's account of the war, her almost idyllic attachment to the region where the novel is set, and her relations with her husband and the other men who come in and out of her life give the novel its depth. Long regarded as a herald of the thaw in Slovak literature, as the beginning of a reaction to the schematic and demagogic descriptions of communist heroism during the Stalinist period, Bednár's The Glass Hill was an exceptional occurrence when it first appeared in 1954. Long on monologue and dialogue and short on narration, the novel also won admirers for its style, in particular Bednár's accurate reproduction of the spoken Slovak of the time.

The Glass Hill was followed by *Hodiny a minúty* (Hours and Minutes, 1956). A collection of half a dozen novellas spanning the Slovak National Uprising and the early decades of the postwar period—the same time frame, in fact, as *The Glass Hill*—it has been much admired by some Slovak literary critics for its unvarnished revelation of the "cursed face" of the uprising and the true social circumstances of World War II. The collection originally included the story "Rozostavaný dom" ("The Unfinished House"), but this text was subsequently condemned for, among other things, its "abstract humanism" and was deleted from the second edition of 1962. It was restored in a new edition in 1964.

The (East) German Perspective on the War

In the light of the German role in World War II, the literary response to it by writers of the German Democratic Republic is a matter of more than passing interest. However, a survey of the topic suggests a high degree of predictability, but still with a few surprises. In line with the official ideology, the operative assumption was that the war was the direct outcome of the triumph of the Nazis in prewar Germany and that the postwar state of the Federal Republic of Germany (Bundesrepublik) was the logical heir to prewar Nazism. The main source of opposition to the Nazis before the outbreak of war was the communists and their followers on the political left; after the war, the East German state (the German Democratic Republic [GDR]) was the sole voice of opposition to a right-wing West Germany. East German writers were thus obliged to depict West Germany as a safe harbor for many Nazis and former members of the SS, and the heroic Soviet Union as both the great victor over Nazi Germany and the bulwark against any resurgence of Nazism in the postwar era.

Although East German writers adhered by and large to these formulae, they did try on more than one occasion to work around the constraints for the sake of a more realistic depiction of events. Take, for example, the major novel *Nackt unter Wölfen* (*Naked Among Wolves,* 1957) by Bruno Apitz (1900–1979). Set in the Buchenwald concentration camp in the last year of the war, 1945, it tells the story of the resistance to the SS by a clandestine communist-led organization within the camp. No surprise here. After all, who but the communists, so the line went, were capable of organizing opposition to the SS within a concentration camp? But the more original dimension of the novel concerns the concealment by a band of conspirators of a Polish-Jewish child. The transfer of the child from one hiding place to another also becomes the means whereby Apitz familiarizes the reader with the landscape of the camp as well as with its daily routine. *Naked Among Wolves* was the first work by an East German writer to gain international recognition. The novel has been translated into over two dozen languages and in 1963 was made into a film by the German DEFA company.

Franz Fühmann (1922–1984), a major figure in the literary culture of the GDR, enlisted in the Wehrmacht in 1939 and saw action on several fronts in World War II. He was captured by Soviet troops and released only in 1949 after a long period of "reeducation" that left him a Marxist convert anxious to atone for the evils of the Nazi era. As a writer he is known in the West above all for his only work to be translated into English, *Das Judenauto: Vierzehn Tage aus zwei Jahrzehnten* (The Jew Car: Fourteen Days out of Two Decades, 1968; translated as *The Car with the Yellow Star: Fourteen Days out of Two Decades*). The pearl of this impressive collection is the title story, "The Jew Car," which vividly recalls the growth of prewar anti-Semitism in Germany. A similar look back at his own past, including his early youth in the Sudetenland and his assimilation of Nazi ideology before his political "rehabilitation," characterizes such heavily autobiographical later work as *Böhmen am Meer* (Bohemia on the Sea, 1962).

Fühmann also wrote directly about World War II. Published in 1953, his first two volumes of poetry—*Die Nelke Nikos Gedichte* (The Nelke Nikos Poem) and the autobiographical *Fahrt nach Stalingrad* (Journey to Stalingrad, 1953)—are almost sycophantic exercises in praise of the heroic defenders of Stalingrad and postwar socialist construction. However, with such subsequent works as the novellas *Kamaraden* (Comrades, 1955), based on his experiences in June 1941 just prior to the German invasion of the Soviet Union, *Kapitulation* (Capitulation, 1958), and *Das Gottesgericht* (The Judgment of the Lord, 1959), Fühmann demonstrated his ability to move beyond merely politically correct literary exercises. These texts also evidence the greater prominence of the autobiographical in his writing. In 1975 Fühmann was one of the contributors to the important anthology *Menschen im Krieg: Erzählungen über den 2. Weltkrieg von Autoren aus der Deutschen Demokratischen Republik und der Sowjetunion* (People in War: Stories About World War II by Authors in the German Democratic Republic and the Soviet Union).

Of Jewish origin, Stephan Hermlin (1915–1979; real name Rudolf Leder) had a close affiliation with the communists from the time he joined the German Communist Youth Organization at the age of sixteen. For this reason as well as his antifascist activities, he felt compelled to leave Germany in 1936. After several years in Egypt, Palestine, England, Spain (where he fought on the side of the Republic in the Civil War), France (where he was a member of the Resistance), and Switzerland, where he was interned in 1944 / 1945, he returned to Germany in 1945. In 1947 he resettled in East Germany, where he promptly joined the Socialist Unity Party. Over time Hermlin rose to positions of prominence in the East German Writers' Union, until he was accused of "decadence" and forced to give up his official posts in 1963. A firm Marxist who supported the poetic avant garde in the GDR and opposed the Communist Party's politics of cultural repression, Hermlin was widely respected and, in 1975, chosen vice president of the International Pen Club.

Like Franz Fühmann, Hermlin wrote about the war and also recalled his prewar years. His major work of fiction, *Die Zeit der Gemeinsamkeit* (The Time of Togetherness, 1949; translated as *City on a Hill*), is a collection of World War II stories. The best of these, the story from which the collection derives its title, deals with the Warsaw Ghetto Uprising of 1943 and underlines the need for Christian-Jewish solidarity. As in his other writings, Hermlin clings loyally to a belief in the rightness of communism and the leadership of the Soviet Union in the ongoing struggle against fascism. Hermlin's later novel, *Abendlicht* (*Evening Light,* 1983), is a small, elegantly written book of personal reminiscences on his youth in Berlin in the 1930s, his discovery of Marxism and membership in the Communist Party, the rise of National Socialism, and his participation in the fight against fascism.

A curious treatment indeed of the Warsaw Uprising of 1944 (not to be confused with the Jewish Ghetto Uprising of 1943) was written by one of the leading East German writers of mysteries and spy fiction, Wolfgang Schreyer (b. 1927). A native of Magdeburg who saw service in World War II, Schreyer returned from a prisoner-of-war camp in 1946 and worked as a pharmacist before turning to a literary career in 1952. Schreyer is associated with a theory of the novel of fact (*Tatsachenroman,* in German) in which fiction and journalism are combined. This is exemplified by the novel for which he is perhaps best known, *Unternehmen Thunderstorm* (Operation Thunderstorm, 1954). Based in part on Schreyer's own wartime experiences, this curious work purports to reveal the British plan to thwart the Soviet Union and the Polish People's Army during the Warsaw Uprising of 1944 in order to return Poland to capitalism. Schreyer was on firmer ground with the genre of the criminal novel, of which he wrote some half dozen into the early 1990s, as well as with other specimens of the Tatsachenroman that had Central American settings, such as, for example, *Dominikanische Tragödie* (Dominican Tragedy, 1982).

World War II rewrote the map of Eastern Europe for nearly the rest of the twentieth century. The imposition of a Soviet-style political and economic system drastically altered patterns of social and cultural life developed in the period between the first and second world wars. These far-reaching changes and the ways by which they were assimilated, contested, modified, or ultimately rejected in Eastern Europe over the nearly fifty years of communist domination will be explored in the following chapters.

2

Postwar Colonialism, Communist Style

Building the Postwar Order

The cessation of hostilities in 1945 found much of Eastern Europe in ruins. The calamitous toll in human lives was paralleled by the wholesale destruction of property and the loss of countless cultural artifacts. Adding to the misery that was the legacy of the war were the population shifts of the immediate postwar era necessitated by the new geopolitical realities—the incorporation of a large part of eastern Poland as well as the Baltic states of Lithuania, Latvia, and Estonia into the Soviet Union, the division of Germany, and the transfer to Poland of parts of Germany—sanctioned by the terms of the Yalta Treaty, which effectively split Europe into two competing spheres of influence.

Red Army control of Eastern Europe after the war, including the eastern part of the newly divided Germany, laid the groundwork for the imposition of Soviet-model regimes throughout the region. In some cases, the establishment of a communist regime did not go unchallenged—as, for example, in Poland, where military units loyal to the wartime government-in-exile in London undertook operations against the communists. In other cases, communist-engineered coups followed hard on the heels of liberation, as in Bulgaria. Elsewhere in the region the communists went through the motions of supporting multiparty elections while conspiring to undermine them at every turn until they achieved effective political control, as in Czechoslovakia, Yugoslavia, Hungary, and Romania.

By 1948 the communist stranglehold over all of Eastern Europe was incontrovertible. What followed, logically, was the implementation of the mechanisms for the new political, economic, and social order. The changes that were then instituted throughout the length and breadth of Eastern Europe were almost indescribably wrenching. The interwar period was consigned to oblivion and vilified as bourgeois, feudal, and protofascist. With few exceptions, the only cultural products of that period that continued to enjoy legitimacy were those of communist or left-wing origin. A new style of art in the form of Soviet socialist realism became the law of the land and endured beyond Stalin's death in 1953. By the early 1960s, however, the chinks in the armor of this totalitarian construct had become too evident to ignore, and before long only communist diehards were still paying it lip service. With industry, education, and land ownership now in the hands of the state, people found themselves working for a monstrous bureaucracy whose tentacles seemed to reach everywhere. The sheer unwieldiness of the system, magnified by endemic corruption and mismanagement—which contained the obvious seeds of its own eventual demise—had a damping effect on the creative impulse and gave rise to widespread malaise. In time it fueled a literature of its own derision.

Seizures of Power

Although not an easy subject to write about throughout much of the communist period, the process by which the new communist regimes gained control over the war-ravaged societies of Eastern Europe in the period 1945–1948 became the subject of several noteworthy literary works. Two of them were by well-known Polish writers, Jerzy Andrzejewski and Czesław Miłosz (1911–2004). Andrzejewski's second novel, and by far his most celebrated and most widely translated, *Ashes and Diamonds* (1948), was awarded the literary prize of the literary weekly *Odrodzenie* and was made into a highly successful film by the renowned Polish director Andrzej Wajda. The taut novel, set in 1945, deals with the internal turmoil in Poland in the immediate aftermath of the war when the communists were not yet firmly in control and were being challenged by fanatic right-wingers and members of the Armia Krajowa (Home Army) operating on behalf of the Polish Government-in-Exile.

After quitting his diplomatic position with the new Polish communist regime, Czesław Miłosz defected in 1951, during the darkest period of postwar Stalinism, and sought political asylum in France. Within the space of just a few years he published two works of prose—in a departure from his previous poetic writing—whose clear intent was to unmask the means by which the Soviets came to power in Eastern Europe—in this instance in his own Poland—and the steps taken to secure the support of artists and intellectuals. The first book, *Zniewolony umysł* (*The Captive Mind*, 1953), which was published by the Instytut Literacki in Paris, appeared in simultaneous English and French translations. After a theoretical discussion of how communist authorities seduce artists and intellectuals into cooperating with them, Miłosz introduces four portraits of Polish writers—referred to only as Alpha, Beta, Gamma, and Delta—as exemplars of those who succumbed to communist blandishments, in effect becoming Communist Party stooges. Despite the attempt at concealing the identities of the writers, most Poles in and out of Poland had no trouble determining who they were: the novelists Jerzy Andrzejewski, Tadeusz Borowski, and Jerzy Putrament, and the poet and satirist Konstanty Ildefons Gałczyński.

Miłosz's thinly veiled allusions to real personages, writers whom in fact he had known and whom he was now singling out as typical of those who were willing to compromise their integrity for the sake of communist favors, did not sit well with many Polish readers, at home and abroad. They regarded this as an act of betrayal on Miłosz's part. Nevertheless, *The Captive Mind* was celebrated in the West for its revelatory nature and has since become a classic of anticommunist literature in the same mold as Arthur Koestler's *Darkness at Noon* and George Orwell's *1984*. It may also be possible to view the writing of *The Captive Mind* as reflecting Miłosz's conscious desire to establish his anticommunist credentials among Western readers as well as among fiercely anticommunist Polish émigrés in Paris and elsewhere.

The likelihood of this is strengthened by consideration of Miłosz's next publication, the novel *Zdobycie władzy* (*The Seizure of Power*, 1955), a work of political intrigue, at times melodramatic, that focuses on the role of the Soviet Union in the communist assumption of political power in Poland. Like *The Captive Mind,* it is also a roman à clef. For Polish readers, discovering beneath their literary masks the true faces both of such writers as Jerzy Borejsza, Jerzy Putrament, Janusz Minkiewicz, and Adolf Rudnicki, and of General Karol Świerczewski was not particularly difficult. The central character of the novel, Piotr Kwinto, obviously modeled on the poet and essayist Paweł Hertz, also incorporates features of Miłosz himself.

The setting of *The Seizure of Power* is the summer of 1944, when the late July Red Army offensive against the Germans halted on the eastern side of the Vistula River, followed shortly afterward by the Warsaw Uprising, which lasted for more than two months, until the much-beleaguered insurgents surrendered. The Russian offensive resumed on 17 January 1945, and was to go all the way to Berlin. Behind the lines, in the city of Lublin to the east of Warsaw, the new procommunist Polish government that had been set up in Moscow and called the Committee on National Liberation was busy consolidating its power. Kwinto, a former political prisoner and now a political education officer in the First Polish Division (which was formed on Soviet soil and led the main thrust into Warsaw after the collapse of the uprising), initially accepts the historical necessity of replacing the prewar social order to which he himself belonged with a new communist government. But his acceptance is mixed with apprehension over the possibility that the Soviets and their Polish henchmen will impose a Soviet-style regime in Poland. When he is mustered out of the service, he continues nursing his doubts but is eventually persuaded, by arguments such as the following, to accept a position in the Polish Embassy in Paris (as Miłosz himself had done):

"You're with us. Whoever's with us will have everything. Money, which for people like us doesn't matter, books, travel. You see for yourself. You want to travel and you do. And there you'll see everything more clearly than here."[1]

But in the end Wolin, the commissar who has been handling Kwinto's "reeducation," develops serious doubts about the wisdom of letting him leave the country and tries—unsuccessfully—to stop his flight. Kwinto is thus off to breathe fresher air and, perhaps like Miłosz, to remain permanently in the West. The guile by which the pro-Soviet "reeducators" set about trying to win over hesitant and ideologically as yet unpersuaded Polish intellectuals is also exemplified in Wolin's words to Michał Kamieński, a former member of the Polish Home Army who loathes communism and the Russians:

> "Let's put our cards on the table," said the inquisitor. "You will let us use your name. In exchange, you will legally be able to practice spiritual resistance. At this moment we are quite sure of victory. We might test our strengths. Your Nietzsche understood, belatedly, that God was dead. Hegel's Trinity derived from your Catholic Trinity. And this was more important than the attacks of anti-Trinitarians. Our goal is to find people who, while not themselves Marxists, will support the economic reconstruction of the country. As for the rest, you'll play for time. And we too will play for time. It's in our interest to give you a *carte blanche*." (191)

Miłosz's *Seizure of Power* was written for a literary competition, the Prix Littéraire Européen, which it won; promptly thereafter it was translated into French. Apart from launching Miłosz's international reputation—at this early stage as an anticommunist Polish exile writer—it also reveals certain undeniable traits of Miłosz himself. In both *The Captive Mind* and *The Seizure of Power* he was willing to turn on former literary associates by exposing them as morally flabby and thus susceptible to communist blandishments. He was also clearly intent on attracting the literary attention of the West to himself as a freedom-loving Pole who had had enough of the communist system, had defected from it, and had launched his literary career in the West with such political "exposés" as *The Captive Mind* and *The Seizure of Power*.

The pattern of politically rooted internecine strife in Poland both toward the end of the war and in its immediate aftermath recalls the intense rivalry in wartime Yugoslavia between Tito's partisans and Mihailović's chetniks. The settling of scores after the war, and the relentless undermining of multiparty politics by the communists, wrote a bitter chapter in the long history of the effort to establish a viable state comprised of those south Slavs (Serbs, Croats, and Slovenes) who had entered the war under the banner of the Yugoslavia founded in 1929. The truly Byzantine tangle of politicians and parties in the period 1945 to 1949—until the establishment of the communist-dominated Federal Republic of Yugoslavia—might well have given rise to a sizeable body of fiction had it not been for the rigors of censorship. The ascension to power of Tito and the communists, the subversion of the postwar political parties, and the wartime role of Mihailović and his supporters (unless depicted in wholly negative terms) were virtually taboo topics, as taboo in fact as Tito's network of prison camps, above all the notorious Goli otok (Barren Island) in the Adriatic Sea, subsequently became.

One Yugoslav writer, the Serb Slobodan Selenić first demonstrated his willingness to discomfort the establishment with his early novel *Memoari Pere Bogalja* (The Memoirs of Pera the Cripple, 1968), a scornful treatment of the Yugoslav leadership written during the brief cultural "thaw" of the late 1960s. With the retrenchment of the 1970s, Selenić stopped publishing fiction until after Tito's death, when a limited easing of previous constraints made possible the appearance of literary works by writers anxious to probe the limits of the new environment. Narrated in the first person by the rather simple-minded eponymous character, The Memoirs of Pera the Cripple recall his coming of age in the Tito era and contain a number of passages mocking the communists and their world outlook. These become the more telling in view of the narrator's seriousness and his lack of intention to mock:

In any case, I raced like a centaur about the poor and empty streets of Belgrade at dawn, leaving after me a cloud of dust and the whistle of wind that beats in my pricked up ears like the victorious march of the National Liberation Army and partisan detachments of Yugoslavia. . . .[2]

The seventh-graders asserted that for a long time they had noticed how stupid Russian films were. The eighth-graders appealed to proletarian internationalism. The seventh-graders replied that we can't make doormats of our national pride and liberty. The eighth-graders feared that without the Russians the specter of capitalist imperialism would swallow us up. The seventh-graders wiggled out of that by pointing out that the USSR was in a pact with the Hitlerite Germans that completely took us by surprise and of course convinced us that even the Russians could be wrong. The eighth-graders shot back that it was in the interest of socialism. (183)

The internationally acclaimed Czech novelist Milan Kundera (b. 1929) is a witty, satirical, and intellectual writer with a particular interest in the foibles of romantic couples. Sex is never far from his mind and he is as attentive to its more ludicrous aspects as he is to its deeper ones. But there is another dimension to Kundera's writing besides the light and erotic. Undeniably evident in several of his novels and stories is the crushing weight of a political and social system that dehumanizes for the sake of the collective and brooks no questioning or deviation. The underlying disillusionment with communism is barely concealed beneath a mask of wry humor. Although his literary breakthrough came with the comico-serious novel *Žert* (*The Joke*, 1967), Kundera's career in a sense began with another work, *Život je jinde* (*Life Is Elsewhere*). He finished it in 1969, but the novel was prohibited from being published in Czechoslovakia. A French translation in 1973, followed by one in English in 1974, paved the way for Kundera's international acclaim. Kundera himself tells us that the idea for the book arose in the mid 1950s, hence in all probability before the genesis of *The Joke*.

Life Is Elsewhere is in essence the story of a grossly unappealing young Czech poet named Jaromil—whom Kundera delights in conflating at times with such great poets of the European Romantic and modernist traditions as Lermontov, Shelley, and Rimbaud—and his obsessive mother, to whom he swears undying love. Kundera's choice of subject at this early juncture in his career was motivated by his preoccupation with the historic role of the poet in Eastern European culture. In Kundera's view, the "last brief European period when the poet played his great public role was the period of post-1945 communist revolutions in Central Europe."[3] This is when many young artists and intellectuals were full of revolutionary ardor and believed heart and soul that the new order being imported from Soviet Russia after World War II would mark the beginning of a wonderful new stage in the development of human history.

The farcical aspects of Jaromil's behavior, both as a lover and as a poet who fervently embraces the Communist Party and its policies soon after its takeover in Czechoslovakia, are unmistakable. Conceived broadly as a lampoon of the poets who accepted revolutionary communism with an unquestioning zeal bordering on the fanatic, Jaromil trades morality for ideology. When his girlfriend shares with him the terrible secret that her brother intends to emigrate from Czechoslovakia, Jaromil is beside himself:

> What's that? Her brother wants to abandon our young socialist republic? He wants to betray the revolution? Her brother wants to become an emigrant? Doesn't he know what it means to be an emigrant? Doesn't he know that every emigrant automatically becomes an employee of foreign espionage services bent on destroying our country?[4]

And so he rushes off to the security police to betray her brother and, naively, the sister as well. She returns a few years later, but the brother never. Jaromil is so filled with himself as a defender of the state that he is beyond remorse.

In what was in fact his first novel, *The Joke,* Kundera takes us even closer to the heart of Kafkaesque darkness. Again outwardly frivolous and erotic, though less mocking than *Life Is Elsewhere,* the joke of the title proves to be anything but funny. In the early years of communism in Czechoslovakia a young man has a romantic relationship with a young woman who is a communist zealot and who takes everything literally. When she is away one summer at a party training course he sends her, as a jest, a provocative postcard declaring that optimism is the opiate of the people, not religion (as Marxism-Leninism taught), and seeming to espouse Trotsky. Before long the innocent jest snowballs into not one, but several interrogations, with the full cooperation of the young woman, who was politically offended by the card. The young man is now a virtual enemy of the state and is treated as such. He is stripped of party membership and functions, bounced from his university, and then called up for punitive military service and made to work in mines for a few years. When he returns to civilian life he is consumed with desire for revenge against those who wronged him.

Although this vengeance becomes the principal concern of the second half of the novel, Kundera devotes almost equal space to a consideration of the place of folklore, and especially folk music and song, in the new communist society (primarily in Moravia). Giving the communists their due, he argues that by destroying the old collective life of the countryside, capitalism had deprived folk art of its foundations. But the new postwar socialism created a new collectivity united by a common interest. The result was a rebirth of folk art, greatly nourished by the communists, who while lending it considerable support, at the same time skillfully began utilizing folklore for their own ideological purposes. Kundera's fine knowledge of music (comparable to Josef Škvorecký's interest in and knowledge of jazz), exhibited in much of his writing, informs the analysis of the communist support of traditional folk art with a definite sense of authority and adds an extra measure of interest to *The Joke*.

Kundera's fascination with the complexities of the male-female relationship, and his fondness for interlocking multiple perspectives through which the major characters are viewed, explains much of the appeal of his writing. But he is no less impressive in his portrayal of the mood of the late 1940s in Czechoslovakia, when the communists were consolidating their hold on the country. On one level, *The Jest, Life Is Elsewhere,* and *Kniha smíchu a zapomnění* (*The Book of Laughter and Forgetting,* 1978) are chilling pictures of the fanaticism and intolerance of so many communist "believers" in the first postwar years. The cruel suppression of individuality and freedom of opinion in a society newly emergent from war exacted a huge toll in shattered lives, and no Czech writer has taken the measure of this calamity as dramatically as Kundera. The opening scene of *The Book of Laughter and Forgetting* beautifully demonstrates the precariousness of existence at the time even on the highest stratum of party and government:

In February 1948 Communist leader Klement Gottwald stepped out on the balcony of a Baroque palace in Prague to address the hundreds of thousands of his fellow citizens crowded into Old Town Square. It was a historical moment in Czech history. A fateful moment of the kind that occurs once or twice in a millennium.

Gottwald was flanked by his comrades, with Clementis standing close to him. Snow flurries were in the air, it was cold, and Gottwald was bareheaded. The solicitous Clementis took off his own fur cap and set it on Gottwald's head.

The official propaganda section distributed hundreds of thousands of copies of a photograph of that balcony with Gottwald, a lambskin cap on his head and comrades at his side, speaking to the nation. The history of communist Czechoslovakia had its beginnings on that balcony. Every child knew the photograph from posters, schoolbooks, and museums.

Four years later Clementis was charged with treason and hanged. The propaganda section immediately erased him from history and, obviously, from all the photographs as well. Ever since, Gottwald has stood on that balcony alone. . . . All that remains of Clementis is the cap on Gottwald's head.[5]

The eventual disillusionment to which this period of ideological rigidity gave rise also forms part of the subject of *The Book of Laughter and Forgetting*. In relatively few lines, Kundera charts the course of the dynamic reversal that led to the "Prague Spring" of 1968 and its sad outcome:

> Historical events usually imitate one another without talent, but in Czechoslovakia, it seems to me, history staged an unprecedented experiment. Instead of the familiar pattern of one group of people (a class, a nation) rising up against another, people (an entire generation of people) revolted against their own youth. . . .
>
> This is the period commonly referred to as the Prague Spring: the guardians of the idyll had to remove microphones from private dwellings, the borders were opened, and notes began abandoning the score of Bach's grand fugue and singing their own lines. The atmosphere was unbelievably joyous, a real carnival!
>
> Russia, who composed the grand fugue for the globe, could not allow notes taking off on their own. On 21 August 1968 it sent an army of half a million men into the Czech lands. Not long afterward, about a hundred and twenty thousand Czechs left their country, and of those who remained about five hundred thousand had to leave their jobs for manual labor in the country, at the conveyor belt of a rural factory, behind the steering wheel of a truck—in other words, for the kinds of places from where no one would ever hear their voices. (19–20)

The reversal of young communist revolutionary zeal is also effectively dramatized by the Polish writer Kazimierz Brandys (1916–2000) in his novella *Obrona Grenady* (*The Defense of the Grenada,* 1956) and in his novel of the following year, *Matka Królów* (The Mother of Króls; translated as *Sons and Comrades*—ironically *król* in Polish means "king"). In *The Defense of the Grenada,* a group of young people sympathetic to the new order and filled with revolutionary zeal want to stage a production of Vladimir Mayakovsky's 1920s Soviet satire *Banya* (*The Bath*). But the party officials who oversee such matters are wary of a comedy, even by an artist of Mayakovsky's credentials, in which communist petty functionaries are held up to ridicule. The young enthusiasts are put through an ideological ringer aimed at so sanitizing the production that it threatens to become unrecognizable. Their spirits eventually broken, they agree to forego the Mayakovsky play in favor of some innocuous socialist realist work. In The Mother of Króls the mother of the title, a proletarian, loses all her sons, devoted communists who either die in the struggle against fascism or as scapegoats when party policies go wrong.

Before writing *The Defense of the Grenada* and The Mother of Króls, Brandys was known primarily as the author of a fictionalized account of the Warsaw Uprising of 1944, *Miasto niepokonane* (The Invincible City, 1946), and the huge tetralogy *Między wojnami* (Between the Wars). Comprising *Samson* (1948), *Antygona* (Antigone, 1948), *Troja miasto otwarte* (Troy, the Open City, 1949), and *Człowiek nie umiera* (Man Does Not Die, 1951), the tetralogy is a communist-inspired picture of the prewar intelligentsia—a favorite target of the communists—which Brandys portrays as politically naive and spineless. The responsibility for perceiving the real danger of fascism and the nexus between fascism and capitalism falls to the communists, who are the only effective lever of change in society. At this time in his career Brandys was a literary handmaiden of the party. But by the time he came to write *The Defense of the Grenada* and The Mother of Króls, however, his attitude had undergone a transformation, in reflection of the post-1956 "thaw" in Poland.

Socialist Realism: The New Straitjacket

The number of literary works generated by writers responding to the summons by the Communist Party that they adhere to the norms of socialist realism is staggering. Most rarely rise above the level of outright propaganda. The writers who produced these works were by no means among the less talented. In the days when that dreary Soviet import was the literary law of the land, few writers had the courage to resist it. Some went along out of conviction, like Kazimierz Brandys and Adam Ważyk (1905–1981). In his 1954 novel *Obywatele* (Citizens), which for a time was held up as a model of socialist realism, Brandys tells the story of high school students who act as self-appointed vigilantes striving to ferret out anything redolent of "bourgeois decadence" in their teachers. Their dogged efforts are crowned with success when they unmask a true class enemy, nothing less than a foreign agent.

Other writers attempted to resist the conformist pressures of socialist realism, and paid for their defiance by being ostracized from literature, if not worse. Drawing on their talents, some made a sincere effort to nudge the socialist realist work at least onto the threshold of art. The challenge was enormous—to remain faithful to the dicta of socialist realism while at the same time trying to preserve a fair measure of artistic integrity. In some cases they were successful; in others they failed dismally.

A prominent member of the prewar avant-garde, Adam Ważyk spent the years of World War II in the Soviet Union, from which he returned to Poland both as an officer in the Polish communist-backed army raised on Soviet soil and as a vigorous proponent of socialist realism. After the death of Stalin in 1953, yet before the easing of conditions in Poland in the aftermath of the Poznań riots of 1956, however, Ważyk startled the Polish literary world when in 1955 he published his sensational and controversial *Poemat dla dorosłych* (A Poem for Adults). Not merely a repudiation of socialist realism by one of its previously staunchest supporters, the work is perhaps even more impressive as an outright rejection of political and cultural totalitarianism. *A Poem for Adults* was a true herald of the post-Stalinist cultural "thaw" in Poland.

A somewhat related put-down of socialist realism came from the talented Hungarian writer Péter Esterházy (b. 1950). The scion of an illustrious Hungarian aristocratic family—which he made the subject of his huge novel

Harmonia caelestis (*Celestial Harmonies,* 2000)—first attracted serious attention in 1979 with his novel *Termelési-regény* (A Production Novel). Anticipating
postmodernist style with its playfulness, parodic impulses, and subversion of
conventional narrative, Esterházy's virtual parody of the communist-favored
"production novel" and socialist realism in general set the pattern for a subsequent series of novels collectively titled *Bevezetés szépirodalomba* (An
Introduction to Literature) and including *Függő* (Suspended, 1981), *Tizenkét
hattyúk* (Seventeen Swans, 1987), *Kis magyar pornográfia* (*A Little Hungarian
Pornography,* 1984), *A szív segédigéi* (*Helping Verbs of the Heart,* 1985), *Hahn-
Hahn grófnő pillantása* (*The Glance of Countess Hahn-Hahn,* 1994), *Hrabal
könyve* (*The Book of Hrabal,* 1990), and *Egy nő* (*She Loves Me,* 1996). These
individual "parts" of An Introduction to Literature can also be seen as representing a "supra-novel" comprising a broad range of historical and philosophical interests and concerned, like much of subsequent postmodernist fiction, with
the act of literary creation.

One of the most curious cases of a talented writer who struggled to satisfy
the demand for works of a genuinely socialist realist character is that of the
Albanian Ismail Kadare. In such books as *Ftesë në studio* (Invitation to a Writer's
Studio, 1990) and *Printemps Albanais* (Albanian Spring, 1991) Kadare portrays
himself as a vigorous champion of democratization in Albania. Although he has
had his conflicts with the communist regime, which he describes in detail, especially in Invitation to a Writer's Studio, Kadare is also the author of a few texts
clearly intended to meet the criteria of an authentic socialist realist literature.
This would hardly be considered unusual for a writer who had studied at the
Gorky Institute of Literature in Moscow.

Chief among Kadare's socialist realist works is the novel *Dasma* (*The Wedding,* 1967). The BBC produced a theatrical adaptation of it under the title
The Wedding and the Phantom.[6] The centerpiece of the novel is a wedding
celebration between a construction worker and a girl from the mountains. The
celebration takes place at an unnamed railroad station in an out-of-the-way
area where the foundations of a new town are being laid. The workers present
at the celebration are mainly involved in construction related to the new town.
Much is made of the town (and similar towns being constructed throughout
Albania) as the fulfillment of the promise of socialism. The workers, the collective "positive hero" of the novel, are uniformly enthusiastic about the challenge
of building socialism in backward Albania.

Since the socialist realist work must portray the coming together of the workers and right-minded intelligentsia, a writer identified only as S. K. is introduced
into the novel as the articulate expression of progressive ideas. In this sense he
is contrasted with a scholar-bureaucrat from the Institute of Folklore who interrupts a train trip in order to join the celebration for the purpose of chronicling
the mores of the celebrants. The celebration and its participants are no more
than laboratory animals to the folklore researcher, whose principal failing is
his inability to identify with the masses. For the sake of some semblance of a
plot, Kadare has introduced the melodramatic discovery of damaged rail lines,

hinting at sabotage against the state—a common theme in much communist-era Albanian literature and exemplified above all in Neshat Tozaj's novel *Thikat* (The Knives). But before long the "saboteurs" are revealed to be just some of the boisterous participants in the wedding celebration and the damage is quickly repaired.

More important as a potential source of intrigue in the novel is the mysterious figure of an old man, who turns out to be the father of the bride, a superstitious mountaineer who embodies the spirit of the medieval Canon of Lek Dukagjini, which sanctions blood feuds. The father is merely the instrument by which Kadare takes issue with the evils of the Canon, which the Albanian communist regime had sworn to eradicate as a vestige of medievalism. Although suspicions of sinister deeds related to the wedding as well as to the tradition of the Canon of Lek Dukagjini are voiced throughout the novel, they come only meekly to fruition, in the form of a minor offstage disturbance nearly at the very end of the work.

In his illuminating *Dialogue avec Alain Bosquet* (Dialogue with Alain Bosquet, 1995), which appeared in French a year before publication of the Albanian edition (itself a translation from the French), Kadare acknowledged that he had written *The Wedding* in a spirit of conformity and that it was his "most schematic" work (86). It came after the successes of *The General of the Dead Army* and *Përbindëshi* (The Monster, 1965, 1990) and at a time when, he says, he felt ready to explore new and original structures. But in response to the negative critical reception of *The Wedding*, Kadare determined henceforth to avoid further "dogmatic schematism" (86). This was in 1967, at the height of Enver Hoxha's campaign against cultural liberalism. It was also an echo of the Chinese "cultural revolution." Foreign plays were banned; churches and mosques were destroyed; school textbooks were revised accordingly; and writers and intellectuals were sent off to work as laborers or farmers. Literary conformity and pseudo-revolutionary exaltation were the order of the day. Unqualified praise for the policies of Enver Hoxha and revolutionary ardor were expected of all writers who hoped ever to see their works published.

Although it was well received in official circles, Kadare felt that *The Wedding* signaled his complete submission to dogmatism. Even with the support of friends who sought to convince him that it was not as bad a text as he believed, he grew discouraged and melancholic. Publication of the novel in Norway and Sweden, the appearance of an English translation published in Albania, and its adaptation to the stage by the BBC did little to assuage his mood. He understood that writing and publishing such a work was the "beginning of a writer's death" and he swore that henceforth he would make no such concessions in literature. On the other hand, he also understood that he could not abandon literature, that for him to do so would be a death of another sort, but still a death.

The Wedding, however, was hardly the black sheep in Kadare's otherwise lily-white oeuvre. To realize the extent to which he was willing to compromise himself during this period, one need but consider the typical kind of party-mandated anti-Americanism of his poems on the war in Vietnam, the shooting down over the USSR of an American U-2 spy plane, and his fulsome praise in verse of such Soviet technological advances as the Sputniks and the T-104 airplane.[7] Needless to say, when Kadare no longer needed to make such compromises, he deleted these texts from any newer anthologies of his poetry.

The talented Albanian poet Dritëro Agolli (b. 1931), one of the stars of contemporary Albanian literature, was also more than willing to assume the appropriate posture, as his long poems "Devoll, Devoll" (1964) and "Baballarët" ("The Fathers," 1969) reveal. In the first poem, about his native region, he delivered himself of a paean to communism that includes the line: "I remain a communist for all eternity."[8] In his equally celebratory poem about communism, "The Fathers," he wrote: "And we have taken into account your good dreams, / the most beautiful secular dreams / Of liberty and free lands, / Of humanity and peaceful hearths, / And we have joined them to our grand dream, / With the dream that is called communism. . . ."[9]

Other specimens of Albanian socialist realism from the early postwar period are also worth reviewing. Because of his own peasant background, Sterio Spasse (1914–1989)—one of the most durable of Albanian postwar literary figures, and a Marxist—was well qualified to appreciate the plight of the peasantry in the harsh years of the Zog regime in the 1930s, and he made it the subject of some of his best writing. He began his literary career in 1935 with the book publication of his novel *Pse?* (Why?); he remained active as a writer until the year of his death. Spasse's first real literary success was the popular novel *Afërdita* (1944). A typical socialist realist work, *Afërdita* took up the subject of a dedicated young teacher (Afërdita) who is intent on serving her country by teaching in a village school, thereby spreading literacy and culture among the peasantry in the spirit of the land reforms of 1944–1947. Despite the setbacks she encounters along the way, the positive heroine triumphs in the end and becomes a shining example of what was possible in backward, rural Albania. The ending of the novel is clearly utopian, but Spasse's belief in the eventual transformation of such a utopian vision into reality is beyond doubt. Taking advantage of the popularity of this novel, Spasse published a sequel to it in 1955 under the title *Afërdita përsëri në fshat* (Afërdita Again in a Village).

Between the first and second *Afërdita* novels, Spasse published his most acclaimed novel, *Ata nuk ishen vetëm* (They Were Not Alone, 1952). Like *Afërdita,* it deals with the Albanian peasantry in the years 1934 to 1936. But in contrast to the utopian earlier work, They Were Not Alone has a definite political dimension. Besides depicting the exploitation and degradation to which the majority of peasants were subjected before World War II, it also traces the development of political consciousness among this class. Under the tutelage, as may be expected, of the communists, this political consciousness culminates in acts of courageous defiance. Once they find their voice, and their ability to challenge authority, their attack on the manor of an abusive *bey* forces capitulation, and the peasants celebrate their victory at the end as the dawning of a new day. This same line continues into Afërdita Again in a Village, which carries the action into the troubled postwar years of 1944 to 1947. No longer an idealistic young woman of bourgeois background, the later Afërdita has become an active fighter for the rights of the peasants to own their own land. Strongly realistic and emotional, much of the interest of the novel centers on the old man, Nelo; attired in his Sunday finest, he sets out to work for the first time the land that is rightfully his, and is murdered by those who would still deny him that right.

Like other postwar Albanian writers, including Ismail Kadare, Spasse studied at the Gorky Institute of World Literature in Moscow. It was there in particular that he became well grounded in the principles of socialist realism. The great Russian writer for whom the institute was named became a literary hero to those Albanians who studied in the Soviet Union, and Spasse was no exception. With its revolutionary theme, Gorky's novel *Mat'* (Mother, 1905)—which had already been translated into Albanian—quite naturally proved to be one of the most influential works for Spasse. Inspirational reference to it in They Were Not Alone comes as no surprise.

Cast in much the same spirit is Shevqet Musaraj's (1914–1986) longish story "Isha unë Çobo Rrapushi" ("It Was I, Çobo Rrapushi"), from the volume of stories with the same title published in 1960 at a competition opened on the occasion of the fifteenth anniversary of Albania's liberation in World War II. The story is narrated by the eponymous hero, a villager who, on his return from the war, no longer wishes to live and work in his native village, expecting the routine to be much as it had been in the time of the prewar landowners. He goes off to Tirana to enjoy the big city and above all the hospitality of a town-dwelling nephew and his family. But as he moves about the capital and its outskirts as well as other Albanian towns, he is surprised by the amount of new construction he sees all around him. After a few years he decides to return to his native village and the family he had left behind there. He is amazed by the transformation of village life under the leadership of the communists and the enthusiasm of the villagers for the new agricultural collective. Overcoming his reputation as a laggard (which resulted from his refusal to remain in the village and work there after the war), he goes on to become a highly respected worker and a pride of the collective. The story is framed as a response by Çobo Rrapushi himself to a request for a newspaper interview.

Other Albanian writers in the late 1940s and 1950s also promoted the official line by combining war fiction with criticism directed against the prewar social order. In his major novel *Lumi i vdekur* (The Dead River, 1965), Jakov Xoxa (1923–1979) wrote about the revolts of the downtrodden Albanian peasants against the "feudal-bourgeois" regime of King Zog. He had dealt with similar material in two previous collections of short stories, one published in 1949 and the other in 1958. In one typical story a peasant from the Myzeqe region who has been badly exploited—first at the hands of a landowner in his own village and then by a greedy merchant in the port city of Durrës—eventually becomes a partisan fighter during the war and turns the tables on his former persecutors. The Dead River, another "masterpiece" of Albanian socialist realism, is set in the time of the monarchy and deals with a river that becomes the basis of a decision by a dishonest judge to rule against a peasant whose parcel of land has been lost to a *bey*. The ruling alleges that the river, which once separated the *bey*'s land from the peasant's, shifted course after a great inundation and now encompasses the lot in question. The peasant then moves to the city, where he experiences only hardship at the hands of merchants and *beys*. His daughter, who works as a servant in a *bey*'s mansion, is nearly raped by the master of the house. But she fights him off and though Christian herself eventually runs off with a Muslim from Kosovo.

Even more episodic and melodramatic, *Juga e bardhë* (The South Wind, 1971), Xoxa's other novel, deals with a peasant girl from the Myzeqe plain who, while still a teenager, falls in love with a shepherd, who goes on to become the party secretary of the village youth organization. But he is burned to death trying to save his tractor and the girl is never quite able to rid herself of the disturbing memory of him throughout the rest of the novel. She has an affair with the party instructor in charge of collectivization, an honest though inefficient young man, but eventually marries a pilot, who survives the crash of his airplane. The structure of the novel is episodic, often melodramatic, and trots out a series of barely developed characters who fill their lives with flirtations, affairs, gossip, and petty intrigue. As in other Albanian socialist realist novels of the period, natural disasters loom large and shape much of the action.

A better writer for the most part than Spasse and Xoxa, Fatmir Gjata (1922–1989) was the author of two major novels, *Tana* (1955) and *Këneta* (The Marsh, 1959), the latter considered his major contribution to postwar Albanian prose. Wholly in line with socialist realism, the main figure of The Marsh is a party secretary (Stavri Lara) who embodies all the virtues of the communist positive hero. A former mechanic who served as a partisan during the war and went on to become a communist, he is a fierce fighter for what he believes to be the interests of the people, disdains bureaucrats, is a fine administrator, and remains faithful and sincere in his private life. Two forces typical of early postwar Albanian socialist realism are at work in the novel. On the level of socialist construction, the title of the novel refers to the daunting land-reclamation project in the Maliq marsh. The other is the familiar plot to sabotage the undertaking orchestrated by those intent on destroying the new Albanian communist state. In this case Gjata pins the blame on the Americans—specifically, on two Albanian engineers who happen to be graduates of the American Vocational School founded by the American Harry Fultz, who later became head of the American Military Mission in Albania. The plot is discovered in time, however, and the Albanians are hanged.

According to the Albanian literary scholar and political émigré Arshi Pipa, Gjata has played loose with the actual facts of the case. Two such engineers involved in the project were indeed hanged, but not because of their involvement in any American-backed plot to sabotage the Maliq land-reclamation undertaking. They just happened to be convenient scapegoats to back up the government's claim that the Americans had indeed planned to overthrow the Albanian communist regime. Equipped with primitive tools and lacking basic necessities, the workers drafted into the marsh-draining project faced an impossible task.

When the project was finally completed, years later, it was thanks to the large number of political and other prisoners brought in to continue the work of the original "volunteers."

In some instances Soviet influence was even more direct. Dhimitër Xhuvani's *Përsëri në këmbë* (Back on One's Feet, 1970) is an outright imitation of the Soviet classic *Kak zakalyalas' stal'* (*How the Steel Was Tempered*, 1917) by Nikolai Ostrovskii. It tells the tale of yet another positive hero, this time a mechanic named Din Hyka who has lost his legs in a train accident. Anxious to play a role in the building of socialism despite his severe handicap, he constructs his own prostheses and walks to an employment office looking for a job. He finds work in a junkyard, which he turns into a shop for spare parts—not without significance at a time when Albania was in dire need of machinery as a result of foreign embargoes. He also becomes a successful inventor when he constructs a "jack with three interpenetrating cylinders" based on the idea of replacing the hydraulic system with a pneumatic one. Back on One's Feet sat very well with the communist authorities, who awarded the novel the prestigious Prize of the Republic and hailed the work as a shining example of socialist realist literature.

Ever the skeptic, Arshi Pipa, however, prefers to view the novel as a "bitter satire" written after Xhuvani's "more realistic novel, *Tuneli* (The Tunnel), featuring a disaster of socialist construction, was vilified as antisocialist."[10] When it first appeared in 1966, The Tunnel, which deals with the construction of the Bystrica hydroelectric power station, was dismissed as a prototype of negative writing and Xhuvani himself was angrily denounced for everything from political and ideological errors to his foreign bourgeois revisionist ideas and betrayal of socialism and the working class. Apart from the internal exile imposed on him, Xhuvani was sent to the Bystrica site to work as a manual laborer. What had so infuriated party officials was Xhuvani's depiction of the devoted young engineer who saves the tunnel from being flooded as a dull workaholic whose wife is driven to an adulterous affair with another young engineer—who is a "spoiled child" and, at bottom, a "petty bourgeois individualist" who considers it beneath his dignity to mix with workers. The workers themselves are portrayed most of the time in the novel as addicted to drink and idle chatter, whereas the local party secretary, far from being a model character, is depicted rather much as a robotlike bureaucrat. The party organization itself, which must in the representative socialist realist literary work be visible as a source of guidance and inspiration, is nowhere to be seen in The Tunnel. When all is said and done, the novel was perceived as denigrating the building of socialism and the socialist work ethic.

Xhuvani was made to pay a heavy price for The Tunnel and never fully recovered from the experience, even after publishing Back on One's Feet and resuming a productive literary career once he was permitted to return to Tirana. In an interesting symbolic interpretation of Back on One's Feet, Arshi Pipa sees the work as being motivated by Xhuvani's desire to "get even" with the party by writing a thinly disguised autobiographical novel in which Din Hyka's loss of his legs under the wheel of a train (symbolizing the party) operates as a metaphor for the party's destruction of his, Xhuvani's, own career. By creating a work so fundamentally scornful of socialist realism, Xhuvani has regained his own legs, metaphorically speaking, and reentered the literary mainstream.

The sycophantic party-mandated depiction of the West—so obvious in the case of Kadare, Agolli, and other writers in Albania—was paralleled elsewhere in Eastern Europe, such as, for example, Romania. A talented writer who had been allied with the left-wing press as a journalist in the interwar period, Eugen Jebeleanu (1911–1991) threw his wholehearted support to the new post–World War II communist leadership. So ardent was his embrace of the regime that he became an aggressive propagandist for socialist realism as well as for the official ideology. Much of his postwar writing deals with the struggle against fascism throughout the world; he also champions the Romanian revolutionary tradition going back to 1848. Nevertheless, in such postwar volumes of poetry as *Ceea ce nu se uită* (What Cannot Be Forgotten, 1945), *Scutul pacii* (The Shield of Peace, 1949), and *Poeme de pace şi de luptă* (Poems of Peace and War, 1950), Jebeleanu demonstrated a talent that raised him above the level of a mere verse pamphleteer. In the work that brought him international recognition—*Surîsul Hiroşimei* (The Smile of Hiroshima, 1958)—he took a politically correct antinuclear stand, with its clear indictment of the United States for the atomic bombing of Hiroshima and Nagasaki. However, in 1963, in his new collection of poems, *Lidice, Cîntece împotriva morţii* (Lidice, Songs Against Death), the universal humanism with which the volume is informed is the result of his visit to the site of the Czech town of Lidice, which together with all its inhabitants was totally destroyed by the Germans in World War II as an act of revenge for the Czech assassination of the "Hangman of Prague," Reinhard Heydrich. By the time he came to write the poems in his fine collection *Elegie pentru floarea secerată* (Elegies for the Cut Flower, 1966), Jebeleanu had for the most part left engaged poetry behind him and showed himself capable of writing exquisite lyrics.

Petru Dumitriu (b. 1924) represents a typical case of the Romanian writer compelled to accept the constraints of socialist realism but who demonstrated a certain willingness and ability to loosen these constraints when conditions were favorable. His works from the late 1940s and early 1950s were wholly in the idiom of socialist realism: *Duşmănie* (Enmity, 1948), *O sută de kilometri* (One Hundred Kilometers, 1949), *Nopţile de iunie* (June Nights, 1950), and above all the Soviet-style potboiler *Drum fără pulbere* (Road Without Dust, 1950), in which the building of the Danube–Black Sea Canal, a forced-labor project, is presented as a triumph of communism. But by the time Dumitriu came to write the novel regarded in Romania as his best, *Cronică de familie* (Family Chronicle, 1956), it had become evident that he was trying to reconcile a more personal vision of literature with the demands of communist ideology. After immigrating to West Berlin in 1960, Dumitriu became a prolific writer in French with a broad range of interests. His first two novels in French, *Rendez-vous au Jugement dernier* (Meeting at the Last Judgment, 1961) and *Incognito* (1962), were satires on Romanian themes. With such subsequent novels as *L'Extrème Occident* (*The Extreme Occident*) and *Les Initiés* (The Initiates), both published in 1966, *Le Sourire sarde* (*The Sardinian Smile,* 1967), and *L'Homme aux yeux gris* (The Man with the Gray Eyes, 1968), he directed his satire against the West. Dumitriu's reputation outside of Romania rests as well on several novels of a religious character, perhaps the best regarded of which is *Au Dieu inconnu* (*To the Unknown God,* 1979).

Forced Collectivization: Acquiescence and Resistance

Whatever the dislocations occasioned elsewhere in Eastern European societies by the ascendant postwar communist regimes, there is little doubt that in this largely agrarian region of Europe, agriculture and rural life were hit the hardest. Centuries-old patterns of village life were disrupted by the frenzied push toward collectivization and socialist construction. Peasants were uprooted and thrust into an ever-expanding network of industrial plants. Families were torn apart and set adrift. Traditional values were subverted. The result was that the lives of millions of people were invariably altered. So devastating was the impact of forced collectivization in Eastern Europe in the 1950s and 1960s that it brought forth an enormous response from writers throughout the region (with the exception notably of Poland, which was not collectivized), some of it—by party literary enthusiasts—certainly supportive of the changes, but much of it, however, negative in its attempt to come to grips with the scope of the calamity.

The transformation of the Romanian countryside by the advent of communism was perhaps the most traumatic in Eastern Europe as a whole. On the eve of World War II Romania was an overwhelmingly agricultural country. Its peasant class was large, conservative, and traditional. It was this traditional Romanian peasant culture that had become over time the backbone of Romanian literature. If much of the character of Polish literature down to the end of the nineteenth century was shaped by the history and outlook of the landowning nobility known as *szlachta* in Polish, then in the case of the Romanians a similar role was played by the peasantry. Indeed, when the two literatures are compared it may be fair to say that the thematic grip of the village on Romanian literature lasted even longer, in fact down to the outbreak of World War II. Some of the most revered names in the history of Romanian literature are all identified with the culture of the village—Ion Creangă (1837–1889); Ioan Slavici (1848–1925), whose peasant novel *Mara* (1906) is regarded as the first important Romanian effort in that genre; and Liviu Rebreanu (1885–1944), whose novels *Răfuiala* (Settling Accounts, 1919), *Ion* (1920), and *Răscoala* (The Uprising, 1932) represent a powerful collective portrait of the Romanian peasantry in the late nineteenth and early twentieth centuries, when the winds of change first began blowing through the countryside.

With the end of World War II and the communist ascendancy in Romania, fiction based on village life showed no immediate signs of losing its grip on the national literature. However, beginning with Zaharia Stancu's important novel *Descult* (Barefoot, 1948), it became obvious that new paths were being struck. Of a poor peasant background himself, Stancu (1902–1974) drew heavily on this experience as he sought to break with the idealized village literature of the past. The title of his novel gives it away: the emphasis of the work is on the wretched poverty of the Romanian peasant at the turn of the twentieth century and its psychic and even biological ramifications. These are seen through the eyes of the novel's central figure, the young peasant Darie, who is the narrator and clearly a reflection of Stancu himself. Stancu in fact built an entire series of novels around this character: *Rădăcinile sînt amare* (The Roots Are Bitter, 1958/1959), a five-volume cycle in which Darie appears as the chronicler of events ranging from the interwar period to the election campaign of 1946; *Jocul cu moartea* (The Game of Death, 1962), set against the German-Austrian occupation of a large part of Romanian territory in 1917; and *Pădurea nebună* (The Mad Forest, 1963), where he appears in the setting of a provincial town as a builder of the new (socialist) order. Stancu also wrote a trilogy of novels in 1960 devoted to the same thematics as Barefoot: *Clopote şi struguri* (Bells and Grapes), *Printre stele* (Among the Stars), and *Carul cu foc* (The Fire Wagon). But it was essentially only with his novel *Uruma* (1974) that Stancu achieved the success of Barefoot. Darie again figures in it. Returning to a provincial town to complete his previously interrupted secondary school education, he confronts the stifling atmosphere of contemporary small-town Romanian life, whose only redeeming feature is the Tartar girl Uruma, with whom he falls in love.

Before Marin Preda (1922–1981) scored his first great success as a writer in 1955, with the first volume of his monumental novel of peasant life, *Moromeţii* (*The Morometes*), he published three novellas dealing with the devastating impact of collectivization on the Romanian village: *Desfăşurarea* (The Unfolding, 1952; translated as *In a Village: A Story*), *Ferestre întunecate* (Windows in Darkness, 1956), and *Îndrăzneala* (Daring, 1959). These were followed by several political novels set against the background of Romania in the oppressive 1960s: *Risipitorii* (The Squanderers, 1962) and *Întrusul* (The Intruder, 1968). One of Preda's most highly regarded works, *Cel mai iubit dintre pămînteni* (The Most Beloved Man on Earth), is constructed along similar lines but appeared only in 1980. The much-delayed second part of *The Morometes*, now set in the postwar period and concerned more with the collective than with the central figure of Ilie Moromete—as had been the case in the first volume—appeared in 1967.

A kind of village epic, and intended by Preda as the first in a novelistic cycle that was to include at least *Marele singuratic* (The Great Loner, 1972) and *Delirul* (Frenzy, 1975), *The Morometes* paints an engrossing picture of peasant life in the Danubian plain area a few years before the outbreak of World War II. Although a fairly large number of characters figure in the novel, the focus is primarily on the reasonably well-off peasant Ilie Moromete and his family. Preda's intention is to present a realistic view of Romanian peasant life, eschewing the idealization and romanticization characteristic of much Romanian fiction. His characters are hardly charming in any folkloric way. They are unsentimental, coarse, shrewd, gossipy, overbearing, quarrelsome, and sometimes brutal. They are much concerned with money, loans, and taxes and quarrel among themselves over land acquisition. Their attachment to the soil is deep and abiding, and they are loath to give up rural life for the town. Political issues play no great role in their lives, but they are not politically naive. Preda is good at sketching the machinations (the "buying" of votes, for example) of local politicians. Moromete himself is an erstwhile alderman with a reputation for honesty and fairness, but he suffers because of a dubious relationship with the village mayor, Aristide. Money—the lack of it or the need for it—is the motor of much of the novel's action. Its corrupting power is obvious above all in the tortured relations between Moromete and his cheating sons, especially Paraschiv and Nilă. The other son, Nicolae, who remains loyal to his father and yearns for an education, will go on to become the lead character in the next novel in the Morometes cycle, The Great Loner.

At the end of *The Morometes*, the seemingly never-ending routine of struggle and compromise has taken its toll even of the resilient Ilie Moromete. His decline, Preda would have us understand, mirrors that of the peasant households in general as they fell deeper into ruin. World War II and its devastation, followed by the postwar turbulence, were just a few years away and with all this the end forever of the peasant way of life depicted in *The Morometes*. Although Preda did not flinch from dealing with the crippling blow dealt the peasant village by collectivization in the late 1940s and 1950s, it seems clear that with his great novel he sought to convey the belief that the traditional way of life of the Romanian village had already come to ruin.

Addressing the subject of the more ruthless means employed by the new communist regime in Romania to achieve the collectivization of agriculture in the "dark days" of the 1950s, the important Romanian writer Dumitru Radu Popescu (b. 1935) produced one of the most striking literary works of post–World War II Romanian fiction, the essentially allegorical *Vînătoarea regală* (*The Royal Hunt*, 1975). Part of a large novelistic cycle titled simply *F*, the novel —the best-known part of the cycle and the only work by Popescu available in English—is an account of the madness that grips an out-of-the-way Romanian town when word spreads that an outbreak of rabies has occurred. Whether real or imaginary, the townspeople set about killing as many dogs as they can, then other animals from geese to horses, until they finally set upon each other like mad dogs—in a sense merging into a single species with the animals they are destroying. The chilling nature of the narrative is enhanced by Popescu's shunning of paragraph divisions and dialogue demarcation in order to convey the torrent of a runaway epidemic. The story is recounted by an eyewitness to the events, a young boy named Nicanor, now a grown man and a doctor, who recalls the horrific things that took place during his youth. He is accompanied, and assisted, in the recollection process by his friend Tică Dunărințu, a criminal investigator looking into the circumstances of his father's death.

As the novel progresses, a nexus is established between the frenzy that over-
takes the village and political intrigue. Because of what appear to be trumped
up charges of foreign intrigue and espionage—a reflection of all-too-familiar
communist paranoia—a local party official named Calagheroviç is singled out
for assassination. False witnesses and people loyal to Calagheroviç are similarly targeted. At a time when small towns and villages such as the one in *The
Royal Hunt* were being radically, and painfully, transformed by the political,
economic, and social changes brought to the Romanian countryside by the communist regime, a distraction such as the rabies "epidemic" of the novel was welcomed by the authorities. As one character quotes Calagheroviç in *The Royal
Hunt*:

> He said it like this: we need a disease so that people can forget about the disaster
> of the war, and the misery that followed, and can forget that even now they don't
> have what they need, and can't have it as long as the old wounds aren't healed.
> You understand?[11]

The superstitious villagers interpret the epidemic as a punishment for their
breaking the interdiction against hunting on a particular day of the year, when
such activity was reserved for the king; hence the title of the novel, *The Royal
Hunt*. According to the local belief, whenever people go hunting on that day
and thus defy the law, someone is destined to die. At the beginning of the novel,
a fake death is staged as a way of trying to keep real death from occurring.
Shortly thereafter, however, news begins to spread about an outbreak of rabies.
The ensuing madness of villagers as they resort to ever more desperate measures
to avoid contracting the dread disease ineluctably assumes the contours of allegory. The vividly portrayed collective panic of the villagers in the novel can
be viewed as the panic sweeping similar villages throughout Romania as their
inhabitants attempted to come to grips with the changes then turning their lives
inside out.

The metamorphosis of the villagers from pursued to pursuers, from hunted
to hunters, is especially terrifying as the novel moves to its horrific finale. On a
wild rampage to destroy anything and anyone threatening disease, susceptible
to the slightest rumor of infection, they pursue Dănilă, the only man who was
not taken in by the mass hysteria, drive him into the Danube, and then allow
him to be torn to pieces by dogs whipped into indescribable frenzy by guns being fired all around them. Although the mosaic structure of the *F* cycle makes
for some inconsistencies and contradictions in chronology and narrative logic,
the work as a whole is a compelling, often chilling inquiry into the subversion
of a traditional way of life at the hands of Communist Party functionaries who
brook no opposition to the realization of their goals.

Popescu's earlier works suggest, however, an ideological orientation different from that of *The Royal Hunt*. His literary career began in earnest in 1958
with a volume of stories—published under the title *Fuga* (The Flight)—in which

village life in the present is contrasted with that in the past. Obviously because of the political situation in Romania at the time, Popescu felt constrained to show how much better off the peasants were in the contemporary village as a result of beneficent communist policies than they had been previously. Much the same perspective characterizes his first novel, *Zilele săptămânii* (Week Days, 1959), where he again develops the contrast between the new way of life and work during a single week in the routine of a village and the traditionalism and conservatism still lingering as obstacles to progress.

Of broader sweep, but similar ideologically, was Titus Popovici's next novel after *The Stranger, Setea* (Thirst, 1958). A sprawling family chronicle spanning the pre–World War I and early post–World War II years, the novel concentrates on the trials and tribulations of the rural Transylvanian family of Mihai and Ana Moţ, their children, and their grandchildren. Early-twentieth-century Romanian rural life is here depicted as an almost never-ending series of calamities. Unlike in *The Stranger,* Popovici exhibits little interest in politics, for his concern is primarily with the struggle for survival of the villagers as they live through the calamities of World War I, temporary resettlement in Hungary— where economic opportunities seem better until the revolution in 1919—and return to Romania, and the slow improvement of their lot until the arrival of new calamities brought by World War II, chief among them the loss of so many Romanian troops at the Battle of Stalingrad.

Popovici is adept at delineating the strengths and weaknesses of his characters, above all the stoic acceptance of fate and refusal to surrender to despair of Ana Moţ, a wife, mother, and grandmother who emerges as a pillar of strength guiding the fortunes of her family through thick and thin after the death of her husband. Again, as in *The Stranger,* Popovici has chosen to end his novel on the upbeat. The future looms bright because of the sweeping reforms being promised by the communists as they stand poised to assume power at war's end. The terrible disillusionment that lies just ahead with Soviet-style forced collectivization remains uncharted, except, obviously, in the minds of Popovici's readers in the late 1950s.

The powerful Romanian literary impulse to preserve the traditional image of village life, as if frozen in time, indeed even to idealize it, remained alive and well for some time after World War II. Typical in this respect is Fănuş Neagu (b. 1932), whose collection of stories *Ningea în Bărăgan* (It Was Snowing in the Bărăgan, 1959) exemplifies the romantic treatment of the peasant milieu. His folkish narrative technique also owes much to his eminent predecessor Mihai Sadoveanu (1880–1961). The landscape and atmospherics of the Danubian region were also heavily influenced by the works of Panait Istrati (1884–1935). Neagu's typical blending of the realistic and fantastic shows up as well in such subsequent collections of stories as *Somnul de la amiază* (The Afternoon Nap, 1960) and *Dincolo de nisipuri* (Beyond the Sands, 1962), and the award-winning *Cantonul părăsit* (The Abandoned Station Attendant's House, 1964).

A different approach to a traditional landscape was taken by the talented prose writer Nicolae Velea (1936–1987). Born into a family of rural schoolteachers, he graduated the Faculty of Philology of Bucharest University in 1958. That same year he made his literary debut with a short story in *Gazeta literară*. From 1958 to 1964 he was a member of the editorial board of *Gazeta literară* along with such other well-known writers as Nichita Stănescu, Ştefan Bănulescu, Matei Călinescu, and Cezar Baltag. Velea's first published book was the short-story collection *Poarta* (The Gate), which appeared in 1960. The book won the Ion Creangă Prize of the Romanian Academy. That same year his first novel, *Întâlnire târzie* (A Late Meeting), was awarded a prize of the *Viaţa Românească* review. Several other collections of short stories and novellas appeared between 1963 and 1975: *Opt povestiri* (Eight Stories, 1963), *Paznic la armonii* (Guardian of Harmony, 1965), *Zbor jos* (Flying Low, 1968), *Cutia cu greieri* (The Box of Crickets, 1970), *În razboi un pogon cu flori* (In War an Acre of Flowers, 1972), *Vorbă-n colţuri şi rotundă* (A Word in Curls and Round, 1973), which won a Writers' Union prize, *Dumitraş şi cele două zile* (Dumitraş and the Two Days, 1974), and *Călător printre înţelepciuni* (Traveler Amidst Wisdom, 1975).

Velea found his subjects primarily among rural people caught up in the great drama, or tragedy, of forced collectivization. Parting company as best he could with the usual socialist realist depiction of masses of happy peasants enthusiastically greeting the new order, he focused instead on individual psychological and emotional responses to the changes taking place. With a gift for language and a keen sense of humor, Velea succeeded in painting realistic and individualistic portraits of his people. If, however, he succeeded in stretching the stylistic and characterological limits of socialist realism, it should be noted that the overall picture he painted of collectivization is positive. The changes were difficult, but in the end brought worthwhile reforms to the village. Whether Velea truly believed this or not, there were some limits he clearly was unable to transcend at the time.

The means by which the communists wore down resistance to collectivization are described by the Czech novelist Alexandr Kliment (b. 1929) in his novel *Nuda v Čechách* (Boredom in Bohemia, 2001; translated as *Living Parallel*):

> In the fields they were plowing the balks. Some of the settlers still resisted, but then the cooperative made them all sign a document. Whoever didn't sign, whoever resisted socialization, would be forcibly moved to another region, would be discoursed to death, worn down, signed out, shut in, put in his place, condemned, and then released so that he could wear, sign, and shut *himself* down, out, and in, always pointlessly. Today everyone farms in concord, as if nothing had ever happened. And for the last decade, little has, not even a snowstorm.[12]

The heavy hand of communist-mandated conformity was felt not only in agriculture but also in city planning. This is demonstrated vividly in *Boredom in Bohemia*, where the focus is primarily on the attempts of an architect to preserve his integrity in the face of relentless pressure to conform. When the architect pleads his case for the residential housing he has designed for workers, he is rebuffed by his superior in the following dialogue:

> "The exigencies and tendencies are clear. Build quickly, build cheaply, near factories and according to a single model. I don't need to tell you which model. Build tactfully, inconspicuously."
>
> "Today we should build our workers' housing worse than a capitalist would have eighty years ago?" I objected. "On the road across from smokestacks that spit out ashes? And in the future the highway will head west."
>
> "First a highway will be built heading east, and that will last at least twenty years. Only then will Prague allow this area to have a highway to the west. Then we'll let everything fall into ruin. It's really a question of whether after twenty or thirty years the aging factories will be producing anything. But now there is one clear, relevant exigency: two thousand apartment units for each of four- to five-year plans. We must fulfill this exigency according to given, clearly defined notions."
>
> "Consider this a provisional situation and do not try to bring together aesthetic aspirations and sociological issues. Fulfill your tasks. This doesn't mean you can't preserve the continuity of your thought processes. Keep it up. The future will show that you were right." (104)

The noted Hungarian writer György Konrád (b. 1933) also dealt with the subject of the impact of changing politics on architecture and city planning in his bleak novel, *A városalapító* (*The City Planner*, 1977). Coming a few years after his first major success, the equally controversial *A látogató* (*The Case Worker*, 1969), *The City Planner* encountered a storm of official protest and led to the imposition of a total ban on Konrád's further publication. For the next twelve years, he published only with the underground press.

For a Bulgarian perspective on forced collectivization of the peasantry shortly after the communists took power in the country in 1944, consider such novels as *Nonkinata liubov* (Nonka's Love, 1956) and the much later *Haika za vultsi* (Wolf Hunt, 1982, 1986) by Ivailo Petrov (1923–2005; real name Prodan Petrov Kiuchukov), one of Bulgaria's most interesting post–World War II novelists. Closer chronologically to the events themselves, Nonka's Love deals with the grave impact on a young peasant woman of the transformation of Bulgarian rural society wrought by forced collectivization, industrialization, and the exodus of peasants from the village to the city in search of employment. At this early stage in his career, Petrov followed the path trod by so many Bulgarian writers before him—depicting village life in a lyrical, idealized way similar to traditional Romanian village literature. But Petrov was not to remain in this rut forever. In what is regarded as one of his finest works, the autobiographical *Predi da se rodia i sled tova* (Before I Was Born and Afterward, 1973)—which begins in fact before his actual birth—he abandoned the hackneyed approach to the Bulgarian village. Now drawing attention to the reality of its hardships and poverty, he also took aim at the nostalgic depiction of it in Bulgarian literature of the 1960s.

The subject proper of Before I Was Born and Afterward is the arranged marriage of his peasant parents in the 1920s in the Dobrudja region of Bulgaria along the Romanian border. Stretching from the Danube to the Black Sea, the Dobrudja had long been a bone of contention between the two Balkan countries. Petrov's text is divided into two parts. The first recounts his family life, including that of his grandparents, and culminates in his birth. Petrov faithfully portrays the life of the peasants, which he knew so well, without any embellishment but with good-natured humor. In the second part of the work, which ends when baby Ivailo begins taking his first steps, the routine of village life and the mores of the villagers come even more vividly to the fore. It was as if, in the postcommunist period, when so much Eastern European literary talent was being expended on recollections of the past, Petrov took stock of his own origins and sought, in his first major work—Before I Was Born and Afterward—to make up for the prettified portrayal of the village in his previous writing.

It was, however, in his novel Wolf Hunt, arguably his best work of fiction—the complete text of which was allowed to appear for the first time only in 1987—that Petrov was able to deal candidly with the brutality with which the collectivization of Bulgarian agriculture was carried out in the 1940s and 1950s. Wolf Hunt is set, once again, in a Dobrudja village. Polyphonic in structure, the novel develops out of the personal stories of six men gathered together in a cafe in the dead of winter to taste different locally produced wines. As they talk, and argue, tempers begin rising, until one of their number, Ivan Chibilev, announces that a shepherd has seen three wolves in the vicinity and that several sheep are missing. A hunt for the wolves is quickly organized. Within this narrative structure, each of the successive chapters of the novel pivots on a separate participant in the hunt. The device thus allows the reader entry into the world of the hunters, their backgrounds—reaching back in some instances to the 1920s—their private lives, and their personal and social conflicts. What emerges is a kind of collective portrait of the Bulgarian folk at a critical juncture in the nation's history.

Hungarian playwright and short-story writer Imre Sarkadi (1921–1961), who liked tempting fate and either committed suicide or died accidentally as the result of a fall from the windowsill of a Budapest apartment house one night in 1961, has two claims to literary fame. On the basis of his novella *A gyáva* (*The Coward*) he is well regarded for his cynical look at the contemporary Budapest intelligentsia. In Sarkadi's view, and as represented above all by the young woman Éva, the "heroine" of the tale, the intelligentsia are a self-indulgent, bored, amoral, heavy-drinking, and gossipy bunch who play at love and slip from one casual affair into another. Éva clings to her sculptor husband (whom she secretly despises) because of the material benefits she enjoys in the marriage. She has an affair with an old high school chum, an engineer who loves her and wants to marry her, but cannot bring herself to give up the life she has with her husband. Her disdain for the countryside and the simple pleasures of rural life become only too apparent when she briefly considers marrying the engineer and settling down with him in a small agricultural community where he has been offered a job.

Sarkadi's own enthusiasm in the 1950s for the "authenticity" of rural as opposed to urban life was bound up with his support for the transformation of the peasantry through agrarian reform and collectivization. Although not usually reckoned among his best works, such typical texts of the time as the plays *Út a tanyákról* (Road from the Farm, 1952) and *Szeptember* (September, 1953) and the short story "A kútban" ("In the Well")—the basis of the Hungarian film *Körhinta* (Merry-Go-Round), which won a prize at the Cannes film festival in 1954—make his views unmistakably clear and explain the negativity of *The Coward*.

The subject of village life in Germany both before and after the establishment of the German Democratic Republic is amply represented in East German literature. The self-educated and much honored writer Erwin Strittmater (1912–1994)—who in 1959 became First Secretary of the Writers' Association of the GDR—drew largely on his own experiences as a small farmer in several of his most important literary works. His first novel, *Ochsenkutscher* (Oxcart Drivers, 1950), presents a bleak picture of the village proletariat in the time of the Weimar Republic, thereby setting the stage for the more favorable depiction of rural life under the communists in his later fiction. Strittmater's play *Katzgraben: Szenen aus der Bauernleben* (The Village of Katzgraben: Scenes from Peasant Life, 1953), which deals with the modern class struggle in the village and is thematically related to Oxcart Drivers, was produced by an admiring Bertolt Brecht at the Berliner Ensemble theater in the 1952 / 1953 season.

Although he is the author of many subsequent works, mostly of an autobiographical character, Strittmater's acknowledged masterpiece remains the novel *Ole Bienkopp* (Ole Beehead, 1963), in which, surprisingly, he appears to be questioning the dominant role of the Communist Party in the German Democratic Republic. The eponymous hero of Ole Bienkopp is the forester's son Ole Hansen, nicknamed "Beehead" because of his cultivation of bees. After his return from the war, Ole (like Strittmater himself) receives a farm under the communist land-reform program. Ole eventually becomes an enthusiast of collectivization but runs into unexpected difficulty with party functionaries, who accuse him of anti-party activity. Angered, Ole quits the party but not long afterward is acclaimed a foresighted hero when in June 1952 collective farming is introduced as national policy. However, this is not the end of Ole's troubles. After a series of farm production mishaps for which he is unjustly blamed and then removed as director of the collective, Ole dies in a futile attempt to dig up marl to use as a low-cost fertilizer in the absence of an excavator. An able collective-farm manager, Ole, unlike the party, had foreseen the difficulties involved in trying to raise meat production by bringing in imported cattle without proper stalls and adequate supplies of fodder. An activist who sees problems before they arise, Ole becomes involved in a tug of war with party bureaucrats, who are more concerned with protecting their positions than helping him achieve his goals for the greater good of the collective. Further adding to the hostile reception in some quarters to Strittmater's novel was the obvious satire of party bureaucratese by which Strittmater intended to show the huge gap between socialist activists like Ole and communist functionaries who are out of touch with the people and whose directives are full of hackneyed words and phrases.

Another East German writer of modest background who also addressed the rural theme in his writing—though less prominently than Strittmater—is Martin Stade (b. 1931). A manual laborer until he devoted himself wholly to his writing in 1959, Stade attended the Johannes R. Becher Literary Institute but was expelled before completing his studies. He was also later expelled from the Writers' Union for his increasingly more antiestablishment attitude, as evidenced by his joining in the protests over the withdrawal of GDR citizenship from the popular writer Wolf Biermann in 1976. Stade's own writing, mostly short stories and novels, has two principal themes: the hardships rural people face in trying to come to terms with the new postwar agricultural realities under communism, primarily in his native Thuringia, and historical novels frequently viewed as allegories on the nexus of power and culture in the GDR.

What Stade sought to show in his village fiction—collected for the most part in such short-story volumes as *Der himmelblaue Zeppelin* (The Sky-Blue Zeppelin, 1974), *Der Präsentkorb* (The Gift Basket, 1983), and *Der Windsucher und andere Dorfgeschichten* (The Wind Searcher and Other Village Stories, 1984)—was the profoundly unsettling nature of the communist transformation of the countryside and the disorientation endured by villagers compelled to alter centuries-old patterns of rural life.

The mine field the rural theme could be for a writer willing to address the matter of collectivization is demonstrated by the case of the highly talented East German dramatist Heiner Müller (1929–1995), long regarded as the most important German dramatist after Brecht. In 1961 a student production of the play *Die Umsiedlerin; oder Das Leben auf dem Lande* (The Resettled Woman; or, Life in the Country), which Müller and his wife Inge had worked on intermittently from the mid-1950s, opened to a relentless barrage of criticism. The production was immediately withdrawn from the stage. Although Müller attempted a revision of the play in 1964 under the title *Die Bauern* (The Peasants), it fared no better with critics and was banned. Inge Müller's name was dropped as co-author and Müller himself was expelled from the Writers' Union for an indefinite period of time.

It is a moot point whether Müller realized the implications of his work and attempted to throw critics off the track by means of roguish characters, sex, and drunkenness, or whether he really did not anticipate the storm that would descend on him. The result was the same. An engrossing panorama of rural life in East Germany after 1945, set in a small Mecklenburg village, The Resettled Woman takes its title from the central figure, Niet, who is being lodged in a room in the home of the mayor of the village. Pregnant by a shiftless drunk, her main concern is for the future of her child. The time frame of the play is the sweeping land redistribution policy of the period 1945 to 1951, followed by the collectivization of 1952 to 1960. Although the breakup of large estates brought small parcels of land to peasants and was, at least initially, favorably received, the land was almost worthless without the necessities of farm life—from seed to machines, all of which were woefully lacking. Out to feather his own nest, the corrupt mayor picks the wrong moment to press for the immediate and total collectivization of the village. But since this is not yet party policy he is removed from his post and the local party secretary, a former concentration camp inmate, is named the new mayor. In his first official act, he assigns Niet the farm left behind by an old-time resident of the village who was driven to suicide by economic pressures.

Whatever the distractions of the plot, the characters, and Müller's fine handling of language in the play, there is no escaping the message The Resettled Woman sends concerning the contradictions in the party's agricultural policy at the time. The hope for a new and better life, embodied above all in the play's female characters, is at least temporarily thwarted by the often unforeseen dislocations caused by the ineptness of the rural land-reform program, a situation that was repeated across almost all of Eastern Europe during this turbulent period.

3

In the Aftermath of the Great Dictator's Death

The death in 1953 of the Soviet dictator Josef Stalin had a profound impact on Eastern Europe. It gave many millions of people the hope that the nightmare of Stalinism had at last come to an end and the belief that life was bound to improve. But it also filled them with anxiety and fear: anxiety rooted in uncertainty as to what lay ahead, and fear that things could get even worse, that conceivably new upheavals could again tear their countries apart. If fear was soon replaced by uncertainty about the future, hope about the inevitability of radical change was also doomed to disillusionment.

Tremors were felt within just a few years of the Great Dictator's passing. The outbreak of the workers' riots in Berlin on 16 and 17 June 1953 in protest over a 10 percent increase in "norms" for industrial workers was a grim reminder of the power of pent up emotions and the impossibility of forever keeping a lid on people's aspirations for a better life. The event became the subject of the talented and much-respected East German writer Stephan Heym's novel *Fünf Tage im Juni: Der Tag X* (Five Days in June: Day X, first published in West Germany in 1974 and in the GDR only in 1989). Three years after the Berlin strikes were suppressed by Soviet troops, riots in Poznań, Poland, broke out in the fall of 1956 over economic issues as well as over the continued presence of Soviet troops in the country after the end of World War II. But even worse events were just around the corner. In November of that same year, the bloody Hungarian Revolution erupted and could be quelled only after Soviet troops and tanks were poured into the country. The Soviet-led Warsaw Pact invasion of Czechoslovakia, which dealt a crushing blow to the hopes for democratic reform embodied in the Prague Spring, was not to occur until 1968, another twelve years away.

In order to appease restless populations ever more willing to stand up to oppression and even to take up arms in revolt, the Eastern European communist regimes began making limited concessions. The Soviet armed presence in Poland was decreased and made less obvious; certain economic ameliorations were introduced; and in the cultural sphere, censorship was relaxed. Previously banned literary works from the interwar period began to be republished, and Western cultural products became more accessible. Hungary, which suffered severe repression in the wake of the revolution of 1956, went on to become one of the more liberal regimes in subsequent years but in a way that did not attract undue attention to itself.

As if the mere news of Stalin's death were not enough, visual and tangible evidence of the end of the tyrant's reign came in the euphoric toppling of the gigantic statues erected in his honor in various Eastern European capitals. The Stalin monuments in Budapest were torn down in the course of the revolution in 1956. Parenthetically, those that were not razed, along with other specimens of Soviet monumentalist architecture in the Hungarian capital, were eventually gathered together and put on display in a separate park, primarily as a tourist attraction. The atmosphere surrounding such demolition in Prague was splendidly captured by Alexandr Kliment in his novel Boredom in Bohemia:

> One more anniversary of the Great Russian Socialist Revolution, celebrated in Prague with a parade of the masses and a demonstration in Old Town Square. Then, it seemed to me, that one of the sculptors had survived his own death, and even the sculpture's death, and had levitated up next to my shoulder to watch the show with me. . . .
>
> Along the embankment at the base of Letná Hill, stretching to the left and to the right, march processions of Praguers holding banners, slogans, and pictures of politicians. The dearest of generalissimos is already missing among the portraits. . . .
>
> During that brief moment, the music stops. All you can hear are footsteps. The collective vision of the mass of taciturn people marching past is fascinated by the statue, which just the day before had been a symbol of unshakability. Today it is a geyser of bursting fantasies flashing into the sky. Tattered rags, a ferrous fossil of the stormy cloud of a revolution that has blown over. Already given an autopsy with dynamite and jackhammers, the torso is scrawled all over with the black lines and curves of steel reinforcement rods.[1]

As we know from subsequent events, the euphoria felt in the immediate aftermath of Stalin's death soon evaporated. Communism did not fold up its tent and steal away under cover of darkness, nor did it release its grip on political power throughout the region. In some cases changes forced by events were largely cosmetic; in others, in response to local conditions, they went deeper. The relaxation of censorship in the 1950s and early 1960s permitted somewhat greater freedom of expression as the tenacious hold of socialist realism on literature slackened. One characteristic manifestation of this was the emergence of a bold literature of the absurd and grotesque. Although comparisons with related Western phenomena have often been drawn, the cultivation of the absurd and grotesque in the Eastern European post-Stalinist context is best thought of as essentially indigenous. Aesopian forms of literary expression and Kafkaesque nightmarishness had ample precursor traditions to draw on and did not have to be nourished from alien wellsprings. Whatever its harshness, the communist system was anything but an efficient and smoothly operating mechanism. It was monstrously corrupt, inefficient, bungling, and wasteful.

Writers were quick to pick up on the frailties of the system and to exploit them for artistic purposes, ever mindful (or perhaps better said, aware) that to do so without stratagems of literary evasion could invite repression even in the relatively milder post-Stalinist period. These stratagems generally involved the subterfuge of the absurd and the distortions of the grotesque. By transforming the everyday into the implausible and surreal, the elements of truth concealed beneath the cloak of absurdity could be made that much more difficult to discern. Distorting reality through the caricatures of the grotesque operated in a similar way.

There is hardly an Eastern European country in the postwar period unable to claim a literature of the absurd and grotesque, but some stand out more vividly than others. Fiction and drama of the absurd are represented in Poland by Tadeusz Różewicz and Sławomir Mrożek; in Czechoslovakia by Vacláv Havel, Bohumil Hrabal, Milan Kundera, Ludvík Vaculik, Martin Šimecká, and Zuzana Brabcová; and in Hungary by István Örkény, Istvan Csurka, Árpád Göncz, György Spiró, and György Konrád.

The lifting of the ban in Poland on new editions of the avant-garde writers of the 1920s and 1930s—Stanisław Ignacy Witkiewicz, Witold Gombrowicz, and Bruno Schulz—accompanied by the easing of restrictions on Western cultural products, had two very important consequences. It opened up the impressive Polish interwar avant-garde to readers who had little or no knowledge of this literature, and at the same time brought the then-fashionable Western theater of the absurd to the attention of Polish readers and theatergoers. The intersection of the two created fertile ground for the cultivation of an indigenous Polish postwar literature of the absurd and grotesque, represented above all by Tadeusz Różewicz and Sławomir Mrożek.

An accomplished poet and prose writer, Różewicz (b. 1921) began his career as a playwright with *Będą się bili* (They Will Fight) in 1948. However, it was not until 1960 that he scored his first important theatrical success, with *Kartoteka* (*The Card Index*). Notwithstanding the outward levity of the play, attributable to its absurdist style, its subject was anything but humorous—the numbing impact of World War II on Różewicz's own generation. It was a subject he could relate to personally as a former member of the Polish Home Army during the war. Written in 1959, the original censored version of the play appeared in 1960; the complete text appeared for the first time only in 1972. Perceiving that no conventional realistic drama could convey his dark vision of the world, Różewicz opted instead for a play of dreamlike discontinuities and shifting planes of reality. Everything is filtered through the consciousness of Hero, who lies on a bed throughout the play observing the movement of his limbs as if rediscovering his physical existence after emerging from a dream or surgery. Various characters enter, one after another, engage Hero in meaningless conversation, then leave. Only when a young German girl enters and Hero talks to her about the war and the mutual hunting of Poles and Germans does the subtext of *The Card File* become visible.

The final visitor is a journalist who asks basic questions of Hero, such as the meaning of his life, if he is glad to be alive, does he believe in God, does he have political views—questions that Hero seems unable to answer. When the journalist asks him if he realizes that humanity will perish in the event of nuclear warfare and, if so, what is he doing to prevent the explosion, Hero has little to say. As the journalist leaves, saying that he hasn't learned much from talking to him, Hero tells him that he came too late. The patent anti-heroism of Hero is further set in bold relief by the regular appearance of a Chorus of Elders borrowed from the Polish Romantic poet Adam Mickiewicz's drama *Dziady* (*Forefathers*, 1833). The lofty Romantic ideal of heroic sacrifice propagated by the play is turned upside down by Hero by virtue of his very posture and words.

Other plays followed *The Card File* in rapid succession in the 1960s and 1970s, among them *Grupa Laokoona* (The Laocoön Group), one of Różewicz's best works and a deflation of artistic and intellectual pretentiousness; *Świadkowie albo nasza mała stabilizacja* (*Witnesses; or, Our Small Stabilization*), a grotesque satire on the reemergence of petit-bourgeois values in postwar Polish society; *Śmieszny staruszek* (*The Funny Old Man*), one of Różewicz's not wholly successful minor works in which a seventy-year-old man stands before a beautiful young female judge (who appears initially as a puppet figure) to discourse, in a long, rambling monologue, on his obsession with dolls and his eventual transformation into a killer of mice. For all its brevity, the play manages to touch on some of Różewicz's own pet obsessions—the world as a garbage heap, the grotesque nature of life in the Stalinist period, and sex; *Akt przerywany* (The Interrupted Act), in which Różewicz makes a mockery of dramatic conventions and the entire notion of the illusion of theater as a reflection of reality; *Wyszedł z domu* (*He Left Home*), one of Różewicz's most effective texts for the stage, in which a wife desperately sets about "reconstructing" her husband after he mysteriously leaves home, is brought back, but has no memory; *Stara kobieta wysiaduje* (*The Old Woman Broods*), a reflection on the pathetic state of the modern world built around the metaphor of an ever-expanding garbage heap; *Na czworakach* (On All Fours), a takeoff on Goethe's *Faust* aimed at literary elitism in which the actors are required to move on all fours; *Białe małżeństwo* (White Marriage; translated as *Marriage Blanc*), a play on the theme of unbridled sexuality that became immensely successful worldwide notwithstanding its censure on grounds of licentiousness by Stefan Cardinal Wyszyński on 9 May 1976; and *Pułapka* (The Trap), based on the life of Franz Kafka and the first in which Różewicz deals with the Holocaust (which consumed Kafka's three sisters).

Political themes tend to be more obvious in the plays of Sławomir Mrożek (b. 1930) than in those of Różewicz, whose principal purpose in cultivating the absurd and grotesque was to effect nothing less than a transformation of theater. Mrożek's early one-act plays—*Policja* (*The Police*, 1958), *Męczeństwo Piotra Oheya* (*The Martyrdom of Peter Ohey*, 1950), *Na pełnym morzu* (*Out at Sea*, 1961), *Karol* (*Charlie*, 1961), and *Striptease* (1961)—clearly allude to the realities of the political situation of the time, without, however, attacking it directly. In *Striptease* Mrożek turns an erotic nightclub act into a political and philosophical metaphor for exploring human self-delusion and cowardice in the face of arbitrary power. Two characters—one an intellectual, the other an activist—find themselves in a room where a gigantic hand instructs them to remove their clothes until both perform an elaborate dance of rationalized submission. In *Charlie* Mrożek addresses the issue of irrational fear and paranoia. A grandson takes his grandfather to an optometrist for a pair of glasses that will enable him, hopefully, to see and shoot to death an unknown enemy known only as Charlie. Before long, grandson and grandfather are convinced that the optometrist must be Charlie because of his objections to the grandfather's desire to kill someone he doesn't even know. To save his own neck, the optometrist shifts gears, praises shooting, but tries to convince the grandson and grandfather that there may be more than one Charlie and that all of them should be shot. In the end, they wind up shooting an arriving patient because the optometrist has convinced them he is a Charlie. The dead body, now a dummy, is hauled into the room and concealed by the optometrist. The phone then rings, and it is a new patient calling to make an appointment. He gives his name as Charlie. The optometrist rushes to call the grandfather, who barely has any recollection of what has already transpired.

A somewhat similar motif is developed in Mrożek's longer play of 1970, *Vatzlav*. Mrożek had by now become an émigré (after protesting the Soviet-led Warsaw Pact invasion of Czechoslovakia in 1968) and wrote the play in France. Because of his status as a refugee, a ban was placed on further productions of his plays in Poland. It was only following the signing of accords between the Polish government and Solidarity in August 1980 that the first public performance of *Vatzlav* in Poland became possible. Consisting of sixty fast-moving scenes, cinematographic in structure, the play follows the travels of a former slave who, after a shipwreck, sets out to begin a new life in quest of riches and fame. But the longer he journeys through the land of the ostensibly free, the more discouraged he becomes by the similarities he finds to life in slavery. His decision to continue his flight is prompted at the end of the play by his encounter with General Barbar, who is on a rampage to punish the rich, the capitalists, and just about anyone else he runs across. When a character wearing a bear mask is brought before him (scene 51), Barbar asks him who he is. When the man behind the mask says that he is a bear, Barbar insists he is a camel even if he has no hump or a long neck. After all, according to Barbar,

> If you have [a hump], then you're hiding it, because I don't see it. Or you're cheating the authorities. And if you haven't got a hump you certainly would have hidden it if you had one. One way or the other, you're guilty because nowadays

everybody's either cheating or would like to be cheating. In any case, we'll say you're a camel.[2]

The good general then orders him castrated ("Take this camel aside and cut off his camelhood. His voice is way too deep"). To Barbar, Vatzlav too is just another "camel" and he orders him executed.

Vatzlav escapes by a ruse and makes his way to the sea. He is accompanied by baby Justyna, whom the "daughter" of the Genius has borne without knowing where babies come from (the head, she first believed, as the Genius told her). When he hears a police whistle blowing after him, Vatzlav decides to cross the sea with the infant despite his professed dislike for children. "See the other shore?," he says to the infant. "Neither do I. But if we could get there you might grow up into something decent. Here, though, in the best of cases you'll be raised by a hangman." Turning to the audience as he proceeds to enter the water, Vatzlav says—in words that would have required no explanation for Poles at the time—"You wait here. If I don't come back, that'll mean I made it. Then you can follow" (58–59).

Mrożek's most resonant play, his most famous and most widely translated and performed, remains the three-act *Tango* (1965). A wry commentary on the nature of power in a totalitarian society, the absurdist comedy exposes the cunning nature of brute power and the vacuum created for it by the failure of the intelligentsia to lead. Mrożek also makes the case for a balance between the need for tradition and the right of every new generation to rebel against it. In one of the most memorable moments in post–World War II Polish theater, the playing of a tango at the end—with the curtain still suspended—accompanies a ritualized dance of power and submission.

A comparison of Czech and Polish absurdist drama shows the preoccupation of the Poles with the nature and exercise of power, which seems less important to the Czechs than the grotesqueness of communist bureaucracy and the debasement of language under the communists. The differences may perhaps be explained in part by the way a communist regime was imposed on each country. In the case of the Poles, the ruination of Poland in World War II left it virtually helpless before the power of the victorious Red Army, which could work its will easily amid the devastation. A Soviet-backed communist alternative to the Polish Government-in-Exile in London was already established in Lublin as early as 1944. The opposition of units of the Home Army still loyal to the London exile government, and still operating in Poland after the war, could keep the pot boiling for a while but represented no real threat to the Soviets or their Polish puppets. Czechoslovakia, on the other hand, had capitulated to the Germans and suffered little physical damage during the war. The niceties of parliamentary democracy were observed in the immediate aftermath of the war as political parties set about trying to form a viable government, and the veteran political figure, Eduard Beneš, became president in 1946. But building on their

38 percent vote in the 1946 election, and beneath the facade of a National Front Government, the communists, led at the time by Klement Gottwald and with Soviet approval, carried on an intense campaign of manipulation and intimidation in advance of the election of June 1948. The victory of the communists in the election, followed somewhat later by the defenestration of the popular diplomat Jan Masaryk, the son of Thomas Masaryk, the first president of the new Czechoslovak state in 1918, paved the way for the assumption of full political power in Czechoslovakia by the Soviet lackey, Gottwald. The notorious anti-American and anti-Jewish show trials of Rudolf Slanský and others in 1952 left no doubt as to the ruthlessness of the new Czechoslovak regime.

The plays of Vacláv Havel are an appropriate point of departure for any consideration of absurdist drama in Czechoslovakia. Beginning with *Zahradní slavnost* (*The Garden Party*, 1963), Havel delighted in exposing the absurdity of communist bureaucratic culture and communist bureaucratic jargon. The central character of *The Garden Party* is Hugo Pludek, a half-wit who spouts an endless stream of absurdities, inanities, non sequiturs, and borrowed phrases, and impresses the officials of a government Inauguration Service, who think they can make use of him in their campaign against the Liquidation Office, another government bureau. The Inauguration Service, however, is duly liquidated, and before long Hugo becomes the head of a newly created Central Commission for Inauguration and Liquidation. His lengthy address as head of the new office near the end of the play makes Havel's satirical purpose abundantly clear:

> Today is no longer the time of static and unchangeable categories, when A was only A, and B always only B; today we all know very well that A may often be B and that B likewise A; that B may be B, but equally A and C; just as C may be not only C, but also A, B, and D; and in certain circumstances even F may become O, Q, and Y, and even Ř! You yourselves must feel that what you feel today you didn't feel yesterday, and what you felt yesterday you don't feel today, but might perhaps again feel tomorrow; while what you might feel the day after tomorrow you may never have felt before. Do you feel that?[3]

In his well-known *Vyrozumění* (*The Memorandum*, 1965), the nexus between bureaucratese and language debasement is at the heart of the play. A tissue of absurdity from start to finish, like *The Garden Party*, *The Memorandum* introduces a new artificial language known as Ptydepe that a government bureau is required to learn. Its purpose is to make office communications more accurate and introduce precision and order into their terminology. Ptydepe looks like this:

> Ra ko hutu d dekotu ely trebomu emusohe, vdegar yd, stro renu er gryk kendy, alyv zvyde dezu, kvyndal fer tekynu serly. Degto yl tre entvester kyleg gh: orka epyl y bodur deptydepe emete. (105)

At the beginning of the eighth scene we see the classroom where clerks are being taught the "language"; the lengthy explanation of the advantages of Ptydepe over natural languages by the instructor, J. V. Perina, is a highpoint of the play and parallels Pludek's triumphal speech at the end of *The Garden Party*. Much of Perina's efforts go into the teaching of Ptydepe interjections:

> Well now, our "ah!" becomes "zukybaj," our "ouch" becomes "bykur," our "oh!" becomes "hayf dy doretob," our "my oh my" becomes "bolypak juz," the interjection of surprise becomes "zyk," while our "well, well!" is not "zykzyk," as some students erroneously say to me, but "zykzym." (162)

Eventually, Ptydepe is jettisoned as being utterly nonsensical, and all hail the reestablishment of natural language—"Death to all artificial languages! Long live natural human speech! Long live man!" At the end, it is appropriately Perina who steps forward in another scholarly speech to point out the basic mistakes of Ptydepe but in the same breath to announce the creation of a new synthetic language, Chorukor. It is left to the sane and wise managing director, Josef Gross, in opposing this, too, to pronounce the meaning of everything that has transpired:

> In other words, our life has lost a sort of higher axis, and we are unrestrainedly falling apart, more and more profoundly alienated from the world, from other people, from ourselves. . . . Manipulated, fetishized, automatized, man loses the experience of his own totality; horrified, he stares like a stranger at himself, without the possibility of not being what he is not, nor to be what he is. (194–195)

So important was it to Havel to communicate these sentiments as unambiguously as possible that he elevated the character of Gross to the role of a raisonneur.

Other plays by Havel make similar use of scientific institutes and intellectuals. In *Ztížená možnost soustředění* (The Increased Difficulty of Concentration, 1968), one of Havel's best comedies, the lead figure is the social scientist Huml, who is given important lines concerning universal human rights and the individual's right to a private life. However, in view of the existing realities in Czechoslovakia at the time, Havel deflects attention from the play's true intent to Huml's nonstop philandering and a malfunctioning computerized robot (Puzuk) with a definite mind of its own. The lead figure in the later *Largo Desolato* (1984) is a paranoid, hypochondriacal professor of philosophy who is afraid even to leave his own quarters because of his assumption that "they" will come to get him at any moment and take him "there." The deliberate ambiguities of the play enhance its atmosphere of dread. Seizing on certain of his publications, people urge the professor to become their leader, and to do more, but about what remains unclear. When "they" finally do appear, they want the professor to renounce a pamphlet he has written simply by declaring that he is not the author of it. But the professor refuses on the grounds that he would be denying his own existence. Eventually, "they" set aside their case against the professor, but he still lives in dread of their return visit.

Pokoušení (Temptation, 1986), like *Largo Desolato,* also takes aim squarely at intimidation by the secret police and the widespread use of informers. The setting is a scientific institute whose purpose is to defeat the "hermetic" tendencies of the young, meaning their attraction to mysticism and other irrational notions. The institute is headed by a gay director who makes unambiguous advances toward other members of the institute, a few of whom are also busy pursuing their own romances, including the scientist Foustka's sadistic-erotic relationship with his girlfriend Vilma. The plot turns on the relationship between Foustka, who has many of the play's wisest lines on what becomes of a society that drives God from its heart, and a seedy character named Fistula, who presents himself as a representative of the very hermeticism Foustka is studying but who turns out to be an informer for the institute director. After Fistula's true role is revealed, the play ends with an increasingly frenzied dance at a party inspired by the same magic the institute has been organized to defeat. The director accuses Foustka of wanting to denounce modern science as the true source of all evil. Foustka responds that his sole wish is to "charge you with the pride of intolerant, self-loving power that is capable of anything and that uses science as a handy bow to shoot down anything that threatens it. That is to say, anything that does not owe its authority to that power, or relates to some authority outside itself."[4]

Ludvík Vaculik (b. 1926) caused a stir in the Czechoslovak literary world with the publication in 1960 of his novel *Sekyra (The Axe).* It is narrated in the first person by a Prague journalist who angers the authorities by his candid reporting of the suicide of a girl denied admission to high school. The journalist's return to his beloved native Moravia (Vaculík, himself of Moravian origin, was a trained journalist) becomes a journey of self-discovery as he warmly and nostalgically recalls the life of his deceased father, a sincere communist of great integrity whose faith was ultimately shattered by the sacrifices demanded of him in the name of socialism. By means of letters and monologues by his father interpolated into the text of the journalist's narrative, and recollections of conversations between father and son, the indictment of the corrupt Stalinist bureaucracy of his, the journalist's, own time acquires added depth. As the journalist exposes the workings of the bureaucracy in an urban newspaper office, the father paints an unsettling picture of the communists' mismanagement of agriculture. But apart from its undeniable political character, Vaculík's *The Axe* is a fond look back at his native Moravia, which comes alive in the novel in its landscape and seasonal changes as well as in the customs and speech of its rural population.

A champion of democratization—notwithstanding his earlier collaboration with the regime—Vaculík's boldness in stating his views at the Fourth Congress of the Czechoslovak Writers' Union in June 1967 resulted in his expulsion from the Communist Party. He was readmitted in 1968, but again ran afoul of the authorities by joining a number of other Czech and Slovak writers in active support of the reformist policy of Alexander Dubček. When it seemed that Dubček might cave in to Soviet demands that he curtail reform, Vaculík composed the *Dva tisíce slov* (Two Thousand Words) manifesto, which was published in the literary journal *Literární listy,* of which Vaculík was once editor, in June 1968. The manifesto had broad public appeal and further enhanced Vaculík's reputation. However, party conservatives and the Soviets regarded it as a dangerous provocation engineered by Dubček himself. That it became one of the factors prompting the Soviets to intervene in Czechoslovakia in 1968 seems understandable. In the aftermath of the invasion, Vaculík was again expelled from the party and prohibited from publishing any of his books in his own country. In the 1970s he founded Edice Petlice (Padlock Editions) as an outlet for writers unable or unwilling to cooperate with the official publishing houses in Czechoslovakia. Edice Petlice books were distributed only in the form of typewritten copies.

Vaculík's championship of democratic reforms in Czechoslovakia continued well into the late 1970s. Together with Vacláv Havel and the actor Pavel Landovský, he was one of the founding fathers of the Charter 77 human and civil rights movement. In January 1977, as Vaculík, Havel, and Landovský were on their way in Landovský's car to deliver the first copies of the charter to the authorities, they were arrested and taken into custody. After many interrogations, and harassment—which he writes about in his feuilletons[5]—Vaculík was released. Havel and Landovský fared less well; both were sentenced to prison terms. Given the subject of Vaculík's first novel, *The Axe,* and his troubled relationship with the Czechoslovak communist regime, it was virtually certain that his most intriguing novel, the Kafkaesque *Morčata* (*The Guinea Pigs*), would not make it past the censors. And so it was that in 1970 the novel was initially circulated in typewritten form by Edice Petlice.

The central character of *The Guinea Pigs,* who is also its narrator, becomes interested in guinea pigs (Peruvian variety) after hearing about them from a colleague at the bank where he is employed. Despite his wife's objections, he buys one as a Christmas gift for his sons. The guinea pig soon becomes a diversion from the narrator's principal concern—the regular pilfering of money from the bank by its employees. What astonishes him, however, is that even when confiscated by bank guards, the money does not seem to reenter the economy. This causes, he believes, a drop in the amount of currency in circulation, not just relatively, but absolutely. His fear is that when it falls below a certain limit, the bank will have to start laying off employees and before long the entire economy of the country will be adversely affected. As time goes on, however, the complexities of the bank's finances take a back seat to the bank clerk's now obsessive fascination with guinea pigs. To the one that he already has, others are added, and he and his children speak of their "menagerie."

The narrator becomes so morbidly fascinated with the guinea pigs that he studies virtually their every movement. As this point Vaculík shifts from first-person to third-person narration so as to put his former narrator's obsession in different perspective. This obsession has a macabre side to it. Not content merely to observe the guinea pigs, the bank clerk occasionally takes a perverse delight in putting one or another of them in potentially life-threatening situations as, for example, allowing one to nearly drown in a tub of water and then reviving it. This state of affairs continues to the end of the novel, when in a kind of nightmarish sequence reminiscent of Kafka, the bank clerk disappears forever. Although the work is often characterized as a commentary on the dehumanizing nature of communist repression, Vaculík is less obvious than that. The shenanigans of the bank employees, and allusions to the precarious state of the economy in communist Czechoslovakia, are clearly an important dimension of *The Guinea Pigs*. But Vaculík adroitly avoids obvious symbolism in the twisted relationship between the bank clerk and the guinea pigs by means of cultivated ambiguity. If anything, this makes the novel even more intriguing, open as it is to more than a single interpretation.

Two years after *The Guinea Pigs* appeared, Zdena Salivarová (b. 1933), the wife of the novelist Josef Škvorecký, published a patently autobiographical novel about the grim atmosphere of suspicion and betrayal in communist Czechoslovakia in the 1960s. Because of its subject, *Honzlová: Protestsong* (1972, 1976, 1991; translated as *Summer in Prague*) had to be published in emigration. Although long banned in Czechoslovakia, it was widely acclaimed elsewhere and appeared in print in Czechoslovakia only in 1991. Narrated in the first person in a casual manner by a young woman (Jana Honzlová) who belongs to a folklore chorus that is permitted to travel abroad, the novel paints a depressing picture of the breakdown of human relations in totalitarian Czechoslovakia, which is dominated by a Stalinist bureaucracy and the secret police. Questioning the arbitrariness of the decision-making process by which she is allowed to travel to some Western countries but not others (France, for example, but not Finland), she manages to gain access to secret files kept on her by her superiors. To her horror, she discovers that they are full of negative comments and assessments of everything from her professional work to her love life. It as if a campaign of intimidation had been stealthily organized against her, to be used as the authorities saw fit. And, moreover, this campaign was nourished by the willingness of a variety of people, including so-called friends, to spread gossip about her, denounce her privately, and try in various ways to advance their own careers at her expense. Obviously, those willing to act as such informers are well rewarded.

Using the negative documentation against her and also her possible involvement in the death of an elderly cleaning woman who befriended her, a member of the Interior Ministry and the police try to pressure her into becoming an informer herself. They also hold out the possibility of her being allowed to go on more trips abroad. But she staunchly refuses. In the end, after her very young brother dies in a tragic accident and her world seems to be collapsing around her, a secret police agent who has wanted to befriend her but whom she deeply mistrusts arranges for her to leave Czechoslovakia for France to begin a new life.

Also aimed at the mindless repression and bleak ordinariness of communist Czechoslovakia is the celebrated novel *Žabí rok* (*The Year of the Frog*, 1983) by the Slovak writer Martin Šimečká (b. 1957). Long active in the Czechoslovak literary underground, Šimečká originally circulated his novel in samizdat editions as a series of three novellas during the 1980s. Publication in book form had to wait until 1990, by which time the communist grip on Czechoslovakia had been definitively broken. In May 1992 the novel was honored with the Pegasus Prize for Literature established by the Mobil Corporation to introduce American readers to distinguished works of fiction in less familiar literatures.

Set in Slovakia in the early 1980s, the novel is constructed in the form of a first-person narration by a highly intelligent, introspective, cynical young man who seeks to come to grips with his own identity amid the repression and dreariness of a communist society that punishes the children for the sins, real or imagined, of their parents. Milan, a long-distance runner who has been prohibited by the communist authorities from attending university because of the imprisonment of his father on political grounds, takes on different menial jobs before becoming an orderly in the neurosurgery unit of a local hospital. Working alongside the surgeons during operations (which Šimečka describes in considerable graphic detail) awakens him to the fragility of life and helps him to see things from a different perspective. His experience of suffering, physical and emotional, is further enhanced when he transfers to a maternity ward, where he witnesses a number of abortions. Apart from the relief he derives from his running, the greatest joy of his life is his loving relationship with his girlfriend Tania, a less complex and introspective university student of Jewish background whom he eventually marries. Milan achieves an even deeper, more stoic acceptance of life when his wife becomes pregnant, gives birth prematurely, and loses the child soon after.

Not a political novel as such, *The Year of the Frog* succeeds admirably in capturing the police-state mentality of communist-era Czechoslovakia. Because of the imprisonment of his father, Milan not only is denied admission to a university but also lives with the constant fear of being picked up by the police on one charge or another. Uncertainty defines his life, and his long-distance running is not only a sport but a flight from the uncertainties and humiliations of his society. So, too, in another sense, is his love affair with Tania, who does not hold his lack of student status against him. But working first in the neurosurgery unit and then in the maternity ward of a hospital exposes Milan to the graver uncertainties of life beyond the merely political, thereby hastening his maturation and strengthening his resolve to move on.

A less cynical, but darker view of life under communism permeates the Czech writer Zuzana Brabcová's first published novel, *Daleko od stromu* (Far from the Tree, 1984). One of the most important Czech literary figures of the 1980s, Brabcová (b. 1959) had no recourse—given her subject of a disillusioned young woman's attempted suicide and confinement in a lunatic asylum—but to circulate Far from the Tree in samizdat editions before it was published by the Czech émigré house Index in Cologne, Germany, in 1987. The novel appeared in Czechoslovakia only in 1991 and was honored with the prestigious Jiří Orten Prize.

The motif of an alienated and joyless citizen for whom life in an asylum seems preferable to the society on the outside is hardly new in Eastern European fiction. But it acquires an undeniable poignancy in the intricately crafted design and poetic style of Brabcová's novel. Fragmentary and chronologically nonlinear, the work is narrated in the first person by the principal character, Vera, who seeks a haven from her "poor, autistic, and alcoholic" generation. Educated, highly literate, sensitive, and imaginative, she is familiar with the works of Chekhov, Dostoevsky, Edgar Allan Poe, James Joyce, and other literary luminaries. If it is too late for her to give birth to a son, as she declares soon after the novel begins, she wants at least to be able to write a book, which she says she is now attempting "with the blade of a knife at my throat." Much of Far from the Tree is taken up with Vera's random memories of the past, of members of her family and of family events. She also indulges in reflections on the remote past, and in philosophical observations.

She dreams of writing about the beauties of the Czech lands, about their past, and about water, with which she is obsessed. This obsession, and her sense that everything around her is being submerged in a flood, is obvious from the first page of the novel. Prague itself strikes her as a city made of glass, devoid of people, and threatened with submersion in a flood. The image of an imminent deluge is often encountered in Czech prose of the 1970s and 1980s, as, for example, in works by Bohumil Hrabal and Ivan Klíma. When the recollection of her first childish love, with which she starts her book, strikes her as banal, she stops short, dismissing the recollection and declaring:

> That murky water ahead of me is sure to have flooded the ground floor of this building by now.

In an obvious political allusion to the existing state of affairs in Czechoslovakia, she continues:

> I can still hear the crash of doors, the cracking motion of cupboards, the stamp of heavy studded boots, vague yellings, and damp confusion—that's the others trying to move their offices from the ground floor up to higher stories, attempting to save their card files and telephones and revolvers and their porter and their detainees from the water, from that undisciplined element that put a spoke in their wheel, that wasn't in their plan, and that cannot now be frightened off. . . .
>
> Of course, we shall perish with them, but so what? Out of the sea we came in the form of a little trilobite and into the sea we shall go again, in the guise of culture and with the mask of civilization. But, before this happens, I am here as part of their arsenal, I in a cell, in me a book.[6]

A central image of Brabcová's novel also relates to the "tree" of the title. This is the large plane tree on the tiny Prague island of Kampa in the Vltava River just off the Charles Bridge. Kampa was especially known as the home of two prominent figures of contemporary Czech culture, the poet Vladimír Holan and the cabaret comedian and conférencier Jan Werich.

A strikingly original novel, which weaves together reality and fantasy, Far from the Tree is nevertheless an unmistakable indictment of the bleakness and spiritual bankruptcy of the communist system in Czechoslovakia. Recalling the once-proud history of the Czech lands, Brabcová's heroine seems to be looking for an anchor in a swirling sea of malaise and malcontent. But that anchor exists only within her and her belief in the inevitability of a great inundation sinking everything beneath the water and then issuing life anew.

Absurdist theater in Hungary is associated, above all, with the names of Istvan Örkény, Istvan Csurka, Árpád Göncz, and György Spiró. A successful and highly regarded writer of prose fiction, known especially for his witty and ironic *Egyperces novellák* (*One Minute Stories*, 1968), Örkény (1912–1979) also made a name for himself as a playwright on the strength of over a dozen plays. In one of his most popular works for the stage, the two-part absurdist comedy *Pisti a vérzivatarban* (Pisti in the Bloodbath, written 1969, staged ten years later; translated as *Stevie in the Bloodbath*), the central figure, Pisti, represents a kind of Hungarian and Eastern European Everyman, indeed the Hungarian nation itself, whose three alter egos (all named Pisti) encapsulate the horrors of the twentieth century, with its wars, genocides, atomic bomb, and momentous social and political upheavals. Wholly absurdist in language and style, the play gives the impression of randomness and incoherence. But despite its lack of unity, surreal effects, and the multiple identities of the main character, there is no escaping the ultimate meaning of this descent in dramatic form into the terrifying abyss of the twentieth century.

On 2 May 1990, the writer Árpád Göncz (b. 1922) became Hungary's first democratically elected president in four decades. Besides his many short stories and voluminous translations from American literature, Göncz was the author of several plays, among them *Rácsok* (*Iron Bars*, 1968), *Sarusok* (Sandal Makers, 1975; translated as *Men of God*), and *Magyar Médeia* (Hungarian Medea) and *Persephone,* both published in 1979. *Men of God* is a political allegory set in the city of Sopron in 1401 and dealing with the persecution of Hungarian followers of the so-called Waldensian heresy. But the historical decor is mere window dressing for the true subject of the play, the post–Mátyás Rákocsi era in Hungary. *Iron Bars,* which alone among Göncz's plays has a contemporary setting—although unspecified—is based on a variation of the inversion motif as embodied, for example, in Sławomir Mrożek's *Police.* This time, however, the imprisoned is a popular poet named Emmanuel, who has been behind bars for ten years when the play begins. The charge against him? Emmanuel has the audacity to claim that he—and not his former friend, the president of the unnamed country where the action takes place—is the true author of the national anthem. Of course, Emmanuel is the author, but since the president now claims that he is the sole author of the anthem, Emmanuel cannot be released from prison unless he signs a document swearing that the only role he played in the anthem's composition was editorial. This he stubbornly refuses to do, and so must remain in prison.

But the situation has become an embarrassment to the authorities and they plead with him to change his mind, offering him various perks to get him to do so, not the least of which is the chance to leave prison and write his poems on bonded paper with a fountain pen instead of on scraps of toilet paper with the broken tip of a pencil. When this fails, they promise him recognition as the anthem's co-author. However, Emmanuel prefers to stay in prison, arguing that he is a very dangerous man on the outside, an enemy, and that even if he does sign their statement, he still wants to be kept where he is. But soon Emmanuel is released on the president's personal order and sent home to his wife and son. Delivery men begin showing up with new furniture, a phone, a beautifully bound set of the president's writings, and an immense gold-framed portrait of the president. Yet even though his wife and an old girlfriend plead with him to enjoy his freedom and be happy, he still yearns to return to prison. In the play's final act, doctors in an insane asylum are about to examine the straitjacketed Emmanuel, who is presumed to be mad because of his insistence on being returned to prison. He is later visited by the president, who tries to justify Emmanuel's fate in terms of historical necessity and then, in a gesture of reconciliation, offers Emmanuel the position of the nation's second poet, half of whose output will be officially credited to the president. After rejecting this obviously final offer, Emmanuel is returned to confinement and given a roll of toilet paper and enough pencil lead to last for two weeks. When he asks whom he will write for, the woman doctor handling his case tells him, why, for yourself, of course.

Playwright-in-residence at the Vígszínház (Comedy Theater) of Budapest, István Csurka (b. 1934) is the author of novels and short stories as well as plays that usually address contemporary social problems in a spirit of skepticism and disenchantment. This is evident, for example, in his sole play available in English translation, the one-act *Túrógombóc* (*Cheese Dumplings,* 1980). At once grotesque in its humor and absurd, the comedy is set in a radio studio where leading intellectuals have been invited to appear as guests on a popular talk show to discuss social issues of importance to lesser mortals. Kept in the dark as to the show's subject for the sake of spontaneity, the guests reduce the event to a shambles when they learn that they are to address the issue of stupidity and its role in society. The befuddlement of the intellectuals exposes them as inept, unimaginative, and, well, stupid. The play's title refers to a recipe for cheese dumplings shared with the audience by a cook who comes on after the intellectuals' discussion. When asked after she shares the recipe why cheese dumplings are called a spring dish, she says she has no idea and reinforces the absurdity of the play as a whole when she declares that it doesn't make much difference anyway.

Another widely known and versatile Hungarian writer, György Spiró (b. 1946), received his doctorate from Budapest's Eötvös Loránd University in

Slavic languages and literatures, primarily Polish. His enthusiasm for and knowledge of Polish culture is reflected in his best novel, *Az ikszék* (The X's, 1981), which is based on the life of the late-eighteenth- and early-nineteenth-century Polish actor and director Wojciech Bogusławski, and in his 1986 published dissertation on the early-twentieth-century Polish visual artist and dramatist Stanisław Wyspiański. Spiró's play *Az imposztor* (*The Impostor,* 1982), an allegory alluding to the struggle of Eastern European artists to achieve freedom of expression in the face of repressive, antidemocratic regimes, also draws on the life of Wojciech Bogusławski and was inspired by a specific episode in Spiró's novel The X's.

Without doubt, however, Spiró's most popular work for the theater remains the grotesque comedy *Csirkefej* (*Chicken Head*). Published in 1987, it presents a sordid yet in some ways poignant picture of lower-class urban Hungarian society in the 1980s. The poignancy is conveyed first by a lonely old woman's affection for her cat, whom a couple of local boys kill out of malice, and then by the boys themselves, who are on leave from a state institution where they were sent after the breakup of their families. The climax of the play comes when one of the boys murders the old woman in cold blood with a meat cleaver in the belief that she is responsible for his family's woes. The boys are immediately taken into custody by police who happen to be nearby. *Chicken Head* can be read in part as a commentary on a social system that has contributed to the disintegration of family life and traditional values.

That the appeal of the absurd and grotesque transcended the theatrical genre is exemplified by the important Hungarian novelist and essayist György Konrád (b. 1933). A Budapest native of Jewish origin, he barely missed being sent to Auschwitz. Although expelled from Eötvös Loránd University on several occasions, he was permitted to graduate in 1956, the year of the Hungarian Revolution. After its suppression by the Soviets, Konrád chose to remain in Hungary. After the political stillbirth of a new magazine of "critical thought" of which he had become a staff member, and now with a family to support, Konrád found employment as a social worker. He held this position for seven years. In 1965 he became an urban sociologist at the Budapest Institute of Urban Planning, but lost his job in 1973 as a result of pressure from the secret police. He was subsequently banned from all employment for the next sixteen years, until 1989 and the collapse of communism in Hungary.

Konrád catapulted to literary fame with his first novel, *A látogáto* (The Case Worker, 1969). Condemned in Hungary for its bleakness and preoccupation with the sordid, the novel did very well internationally. Clearly derived from Konrád's own experiences as a social worker, the case worker of the title is employed by a state institution charged with the responsibility of resetting orphans or children from homes where they are being abused or where parents are no longer capable of caring for them. The novel takes the form of a first-person narrative by the case worker, who identifies himself as living a comfortable middle-class life among people of similar status and income. However, his work brings him into some of the most squalid parts of Budapest, and his observations there form the bulk of his narrative. Well written, *The Case Worker* is, by and large, an exercise in the grotesque. The narrator's focus as he makes his rounds is almost wholly on the degradation and wretchedness he sees all around him. He encounters nothing but poverty, indifference, resignation, abuse, and an abiding sense of death and madness as the only means of escape. The people the case worker describes are often physically grotesque in one way or another.

The plot as such revolves around the case worker's decision to take under his own care a five-year-old idiot son of a couple who committed suicide. The boy himself is wholly a grotesque construct, whatever compassion his circumstances may arouse. Since the narrator deems it impossible out of consideration for his family to bring the boy into his own home, he decides to leave his family at least temporarily in order to move into the wretched flat where the boy lived with his parents. But at a certain point he is made to understand that unless he allows the boy to be removed to an appropriate facility, he will lose his job. The case worker yields reluctantly and resumes his previous way of life but in a spirit or resignation and with a sense of dreary predictability. He has demonstrated his ability to cross over to the other side and make a place for himself in a world of utter degradation. But when he picks up the threads of his previous life, he seems to perceive it as a another kind of hell.

After *The City Planner*, which was previously mentioned, Konrád wrote two predominantly autobiographical novels dealing with Jewish experience in Hungary during World War II and the Hungarian Revolution of 1956. The first, *A cinkos* (*The Loser*, 1982), is about a cynical and disillusioned Jewish intellectual for whom communism has lost all credibility and who is happy being confined to an insane asylum. The second, *Kerti mulatság* (*A Feast in the Garden*, 1989), in essence an experimental novel, is also a somber review of Hungarian Jewish history during and after the war and the bleak period of communist rule. Both novels were originally published in samizdat editions. Similarly incorporating autobiographical elements, Konrád's last published novel, the sprawling and long-winded *Kőóra* (*Stonedial*, 1995), again addresses the fate of the Hungarian Jews during the war and the Revolution of 1956.

Besides his fiction, Konrád was a prolific and gifted essayist who wrote about many of the most pressing issues of his time and place. His major collections of essays and articles include, among others: *Az értelmiség újta az osztály-hatalomhoz* (*The Intellectuals on the Road to Class Power*, 1979); *Antipolitika* (*Antipolitics*, originally a samizdat publication, which appeared in English in 1984); *Európa köldöken: Esszék, 1979–1989* (*In the Heart of Europe: Essays, 1979–1989*, 1990); *Ujjászületés melankóliája* (*The Melancholy of Rebirth*, 1991), a book of essays from the period 1989 to 1994; *Útrakészen: Egy berlini műteremben* (In a Berlin Studio, 1999); *Láthatatlan hang: Zsidó tárgyú elmélkedések* (*The Invisible Voice: Meditations on Jewish Themes*, 1997); and *A közép tágulása: Gondolkodás Európáról* (The Expansion of the Center: A Meditation About Europe) and *Az író és a város* (The Writer and the City), both of which appeared in 2004. Apart from his concern with Jewish issues, Konrád deals, extensively and insightfully, with Eastern European politics during and after communism and the dismal failure of the communist system.

As the most isolated and bizarre communist state, Albania succumbed to a pathological paranoia that saw, behind nearly every bush, foreign spies, saboteurs, and traitors hell-bent on bringing harm to the Hoxha regime. Three of Albania's leading post–World War II writers—Dritëro Agolli, Neshat Tozaj, and Ismail Kadare—have explored the full range of absurdity to which this paranoia gave rise.

One of the most respected postwar Albanian literary figures, Dritëro Agolli (b. 1931), a poet and prose writer, had impeccable credentials as a communist loyalist during the Hoxha regime. Long a member of the Central Committee of the Communist Party of Albania, he became president of the Union of Writers following the purge of the liberal faction headed by the dramatist Fadil Paçrami (b. 1922) and then head of Albanian Radio and TV, Todi Lubonja (b. 1923). In this capacity he wrote works supportive of the official ideology, such as *Baballarët* (The Fathers, 1969) and especially *Nënë Shqipëri* (*Mother Albania*, 1979). In his first book published after the fall of the Hoxha regime, *Pellegrini i vonuar* (The Belated Pilgrim, 1993), Agolli captured the mood of the country, the sense of bewilderment and drift, in the aftermath of the collapse of communism. At the same time he appealed to poets to look to the future while trying to make sense of the past.

Of the three novels of the 1970s on which Agolli's reputation as a prose writer rests—*Komisar Memo* (Commissar Memo, 1970), *Njeriu me top* (The Man with a Cannon, 1975), and *Shkëlqimi dhe rënia e shokut Zylo* (The Splendor and Fall of Comrade Zilo, 1973)—it is the last that has come to be acknowledged as his masterpiece. A surprising novel for a writer as ideologically committed as Agolli indeed was, The Splendor and Fall of Comrade Zilo traces the rise and downfall of an overbearing, ideologically zealous government official who heads a fairly minor department of cultural affairs that deals with, among other things, village folklore. Respected by some, mocked by others, Zilo sets himself up for his inevitable tumble when he criticizes a play as "immature" and "ideologically erroneous" and it is later praised by his superiors. Zilo's indictment is aimed not just at the play, then in dress rehearsal, but at the contemporary stage in general:

> Theatrical illnesses, such as displays of naturalism, melodramatism, schematism, pomposity, and so on, have joined with the low ideo-professional level of a large part of our theaters. . . . This often confuses the important with the unimportant, the general physiognomy of people with their unique features. As a result, the coherence of stylistic tonalities is undermined by incoherence and an abnormal intensity.[7]

But the novel may not be as transparent as it seems. If it comes across as a put-down of socialist realism and the workings of communist bureaucracy, a look beneath the surface discloses another probable dimension. Through the character of Zilo, Agolli appears to be discrediting a liberal journalist by the name of Jusuf Alibali (b. 1922), who was a friend of Fadil Paçrami and the notorious General Mehmet Shehu. Alibali, who has several literary works to his credit, eventually went into exile.

More obvious in intent than Agolli's The Splendor and Fall of Comrade Zilo, Neshat Tozaj's (b. 1943) novel *Thikat* (The Knives) was something of a literary sensation when it first appeared in 1989. So enthusiastic was Ismail Kadare about the work that he wrote a very favorable review of it for the journal *Drita*. Like Agolli, Tozaj was a dedicated communist who joined the party at an early age and remained loyal to it to the end. In his memoiristic *Pse flas: Retrospektivë* (Why I Speak: Retrospectives, 1993), he tells us, often in considerable detail, about the ups and downs of his career as a government employee in the Ministry of the Interior. Although the book begins with the year 1966, it is not at all a diarylike record of Tozaj's experiences. Instead Tozaj tends to focus on certain events in his life that enable him to cast himself in the light of a sometimes-ardent champion of a more liberal approach toward Albanian artists and intellectuals as well as toward human rights in general. Much of the volume is taken up with the arduous path Tozaj had to follow in order to bring The Knives to light and the problems he had with officialdom subsequent to the book's appearance.

As a longtime employee of the Ministry of the Interior with an intimate knowledge of the workings of the Sigurimi (the Albanian secret police), Tozaj's intention with The Knives was to demonstrate the almost mind-boggling paranoia prevalent in both government bodies. Tozaj had already built a reputation as a writer on the basis of such short-story collections and novels about spies and various plots, foreign and native, aimed at toppling the Hoxha regime as *Takimi i fundit* (The Last Meeting, 1976), *Në gjurmë të të tretit* (On the Trail of the Third, 1979), *Rrëmbimi i arkivit* (The Theft of the Archives, 1977), *Dora e ngrohtë* (The Warm Hand, 1983), *Në emër të popullit* (In the Name of the People, 1984), *Mes nesh* (In Our Midst, 1986), and *Bisede për një shok* (Conversations About a Friend, 1988). In The Knives, inspired possibly by the case involving the explosion of a bomb on the grounds of the Yugoslav Embassy in Tirana and written at a time of increased tensions between Albania and Yugoslavia, the isolated act of a deranged person who sets about cutting the tires of automobiles belonging to foreign embassies in Tirana turns into a monstrous power play by the Ministry of the Interior, which is intent on uncovering a nonexistent plot against the Albanian state. The candor with which Tozaj exposes the mindset of those in power in Albania at the time is the most striking feature of the novel. Most recently, Tozaj published in novel form, under the title *Shalom* (2004), an account of the shelter provided the Jewish community in Albania during the Italian and German occupations during World War II.

Conflating the nightmarish landscape of Kafka's fiction and the surreal vision of imperial St. Petersburg conjured up by the nineteenth-century master of the grotesque, Nikolai Gogol, Albania's best-known writer, Ismail Kadare, has carried the theme of Albanian paranoia beyond that of Tozaj's The Knives. Banned upon its appearance in Albania in 1981, *Nëpunësi i pallatit të ëndrrave* (The Official of the Palace of Dreams; a revised version appeared in 1996 under the title *Pallati i ëndrrave* [*The Palace of Dreams*]) is, in Kadare's own words, "The most courageous book I have written. In literary terms it is perhaps the best."[8] It is, in effect, a chilling vision of national paranoia and state mind control. Set in a vast empire clearly suggestive of nineteenth-century Ottoman Turkey that is ruled by a sultan, the novel follows the career of its main character, a young man named Mark-Alem, of the prominent and powerful Albanian Quprili family, after he accepts a position in the Palace of Dreams of the mysterious and ultrasecret Tabir Sarrail. Put simply, the Palace of Dreams is the agency through which all the dreams of the inhabitants of the empire are reported, sorted, and analyzed; it is staffed by an army of mostly low-level bureaucrats who could have been recruited from the pages of Gogol's *Petersburg Stories*. In the novel, dreams, for their strange insights and putative prophetic power, are regarded as more valuable than actions in determining state policies. Because of his family connections, Mark-Alem is rapidly moved up the bureaucratic leader, until he eventually becomes second in command.

Although an air of mystery and foreboding hangs heavy over Kadare's narrative, the emphasis is mainly on depicting the diabolical nature of the Palace of Dreams and the sterility and impersonality of the institution. Things heat up when an ominous dream brought in from the provinces foreshadows conflict between the illustrious Quprili family and the imperial authorities. The conflict is precipitated by the arrival at the home of Mark-Alem's uncle, the Vizier, of a group of ethnic Albanian rhapsodists who recite the ancient epic about the Quprili clan that has long been a bone of contention between the family and the Sovereign. Previously, the epic had been chanted by Serbian rhapsodists in an apparently less menacing version; but its performance on this occasion by Albanians is deemed threatening, and the rhapsodists are slain. Connecting the Albanian version of the epic to relations between Slav and non-Slav peoples, such as the Albanians, within the empire, and big-power politics involving Austria and Russia, the Sovereign feels constrained not only to have the Albanian rhapsodists killed but also to reach into Albania and root out the epic itself. Ultimately, a successful countercoup against the Sovereign is mounted by the Quprilis, and Mark-Alem winds up virtually in control of the Tabir Sarrail.

While the structural importance of the Serbian-Albanian epic to *The Palace of Dreams* may be open to question (it is, in other words, not truly essential to the plot), its inclusion is a reflection of Kadare's serious interest in the Albanian epic in relation to both the Serbian and the Homeric traditions. This interest also underlay two other works by Kadare from the same period—*Autobiografia e popullit në vargje* (*The Autobiography of the People in Verse*, 1980), a rather nationalistic essay on the Albanian popular song, and *Dosja H.* (*The File on H,*

1981), an entertaining novel in which Kadare uses the visit to Albania in the 1930s of two Irish-born American Homeric scholars to argue for the greater antiquity of the Albanian oral tradition in comparison to the Serbian.

As if the political embodiment of the absurd in the wake of Stalin's death, nothing commands the attention so much as the Albania-China love fest of the 1960s. The on-again, off-again romance between tiny Albania and the great Soviet Union, on one hand, and between tiny Albania and the great People's Republic of China, on the other, also illustrates the extreme, and sometimes ludicrous, paranoia of small states behind the Iron Curtain and the great power rivalry between the Soviet Union and China.

The death of Stalin only deepened the Albanian sense of insecurity. Proud of its staunch Marxist-Leninist and Stalinist character, the Albanian regime remained firm in its resolve to stay the course despite the thaw that had begun to creep across Eastern Europe in the wake of the Soviet dictator's passing. But by the late 1950s the steady erosion of Soviet support for Albania could no longer be denied. Albanian belief in the indestructibility of the Soviet-Albanian alliance, especially in the economic sphere, was now badly shattered. At least fifty percent of Albania's foreign commerce in the period 1946 to 1961 was with the Soviet Union. But when the Soviets announced in no uncertain terms an end to further support for Albania in early 1961, China stepped in to fill the vacuum. The new closer relationship between tiny Albania and colossal China had advantages for both. Situated strategically on the Adriatic, Albania was ideologically desirable to the Chinese as a forward base in the struggle against Soviet power and Yugoslav revisionism. From the Albanian point of view, Chinese economic support came at a critical point in time. Politically, the Sino-Albanian alliance buttressed the Albanian position with respect to Titoist Yugoslavia.

Beginning thus with the Albanian Third Five-Year Plan (1961–1965), the Chinese stepped in to fill the role vacated by the Soviet Union. The relationship between Albania and China, strengthened by Zhou Enlai's personal visit to Tirana in January 1964, as well as by the Soviet-led Warsaw Pact invasion of Czechoslovakia in 1968—which prompted Albania's withdrawal from the pact—endured until 1978. But the ominous handwriting on the wall was there to be read in 1971 with the new reality of Sino-American rapprochement heralded by President Richard Nixon's visit to China in the summer of that year. The angry protestations by the Albanians (as, for example, in the letter of the Central Committee of the Albanian Communist Party on 6 August 1971) only served to deepen the wedge between Albania and China. Insult was added to injury when, within a year after the death of Mao Zedong on 9 September 1976, Tito made a warmly received state visit to China from 30 August to 7 September 1977. Another round of denunciation from the Albanians made any possible repair of the frayed relationship all but impossible. Thus on 13 July 1978, China announced that it was officially cutting off all aid to Albania. Stunned, the Albanians retreated further into an ever deeper paranoia and xenophobia, marked in part by an exaggerated program of national self-reliance by which the country refused to incur any further foreign debt or become newly dependent to any extent on foreign aid.

The Sino-Albanian alliance and its eventual demise found resonance in Albanian literature, above all in the work of Ismail Kadare. Previously Kadare had taken up the matter of the Soviet-Albanian rift in his novel *Dimri i madh* (The Great Winter, 1977), which originally appeared in 1973 in a shorter version under the title *Dimri i vetmisë së madhe* (The Winter of Great Solitude). The title "The Great Winter" alludes to the severe winter of 1960 / 1961, when the definitive break between Albania and the Soviet Union abruptly cut off Soviet grain supplies to impoverished Albania precisely at a time when they were most urgently needed. Adding salt to the wound was Nikita Khrushchev's remark on the occasion of an earlier visit to Albania that mice in Soviet grain silos consumed more grain than Albania was able to produce. The Great Winter operates, as it were, on two levels, the political—where Kadare takes his readers into the Kremlin for the tense negotiations between the Soviets and Albanians— and the domestic and personal, whereby Kadare portrays the devastating impact on ordinary people of the grain cutoff. The political dimension of the novel is conveyed through the character of the Albanian journalist Besnik Struga, who accompanies the Albanian delegation to Moscow as an interpreter and is privy to the top-level negotiations. The feeling of authenticity surrounding the novel derives from the fact that Kadare based much of the dialogue on the minutes of actual negotiations and on the memoirs of Enver Hoxha. Hoxha himself is rather favorably portrayed in The Great Winter, a career- (and possibly life-) saving tactic on Kadare's part.

The traumatic Sino-Albanian rupture forms the subject of Kadare's novel *Koncert në fund të dimrit* (A Concert at the End of Winter; translated as *The Concert*, 1988). It was a large work (more than seven hundred pages) dealing with the breakup of the once-close relations between Albania and China in 1978, and Kadare had worked on it from 1978 to 1988. Neither austere nor allegorical in the manner of *The Palace of Dreams*, *The Concert* is rooted in its own time and elevates Albanian paranoia to the level of hyperbole. In capturing the mood of the Albanians in the period of the Sino-Albanian rupture, Kadare shows how all-pervasive the concern with political issues could be. From the average man in the street to high-placed government officials, the interpretation of Chinese intentions toward small Albania was the leading topic of the day, relegating virtually everything else to a secondary status. Since the Albanians had already been through something similar in previous years, first with Yugoslavia and then with the Soviet Union, the anxiety was certainly understandable. Kadare is especially good at extracting humor from the situation. The accidental injuring of the foot of a visiting Chinese by a local Albanian threatens to become an international incident, with people hanging on the results of an X-ray. An Albanian who has learned Chinese praises himself on his ability to fathom the depths of Chairman Mao's thoughts and is so consumed with everything Chinese that he cannot refrain from Chinese utterances during intimate moments with his Albanian wife.

Much of the action of *The Concert* takes place in China, which Kadare knew firsthand as a result of his visits there as a member of official Albanian writers' delegations. The tense movements of Albanians in and out of China serve as the means by which China and its leaders are introduced into the novel. Although a keen follower of the political drama unfolding at the time, Kadare may exaggerate his knowledge of China and the Chinese when he devotes considerable space to monologues intended to expose the thoughts of Chairman Mao and other high-placed dignitaries such as Zhou Enlai. The irony at the heart of the novel is that along with depicting the almost-pathological paranoia of the Albanians, Kadare also bares the paranoia of the Chinese, as exemplified by the attempt to listen in on or record as many conversations of their citizens as possible and by intense speculation over the cause of Mao's death.

Communism, to Kadare, was nightmarish, and novels such as *The Palace of Dreams*, The Great Winter, and *The Concert* make the point convincingly. Communist society, whether in Albania, the Soviet Union, or China, was dominated by an arrogant party leadership intent on self-preservation and by a subservient and mindless bureaucracy. The inanity—and absurdity—of party and other official meetings is delineated at great length, and Kadare's satirical purpose is beyond question. If Albania, cut off from the rest of Europe, the Soviet Union, and then China, is shown to be a country isolated in a world of its own imagining, China fares even worse. Monstrous plans for the destruction of Western civilization and the eradication of all culture and human individuality are ironically juxtaposed to the appalling backwardness of the Chinese, who for a time grotesquely remain Albania's sole link to the outside world.

The Sino-Albanian alliance has also served relatively more recently as the subject of a novel by the important Albanian writer Fatos Kongoli (b. 1944). Known primarily as the author of such literary exposés of the rot and corruption beneath the surface of the Hoxha regime as the novels *I humburi* (The Lost, 1992) and *Kufoma* (The Cadaver, 1994), Kongoli in 1999 published the novel *Dragoi i fildishtë* (The Ivory Dragon). Drawing on Kongoli's experiences in China earlier in his career, The Ivory Dragon is a first-person account of the everyday life of an Albanian student in China against the background of the Sino-Albanian relationship in the 1960s and '70s. Kongoli is candid in what he recounts, especially with respect to his friendships with other foreign students and his relations with women.

East German writers were among the most daring in their desire to expose the banality of life under the communists and the petty repressions of the everyday. A case in point is the novel *Es geht seinen Gang oder Mühen in unserer Ebene* (It Takes Its Course; or, Trouble on Our Level, 1978) by Erich Loest (b. 1926), one of the most highly regarded literary figures of the former GDR. A novelist, short-story writer, journalist, and playwright, Loest was called to military service while still in school. He served mostly in Slovakia. After the war he finally received his secondary-school diploma and immediately signed on as a correspondent with the *Leipziger Volkszeitung*. His membership in the Socialist Unity Party (communist) in 1947 proved of little use when his first novel, *Jungen, die übrig bleiben* (Young People Left Behind, 1950), was harshly reviewed in the *Tagliche Rundschau* (the organ of the Soviet military administration) and he was dismissed from his job. Nevertheless, in 1952 he was elected head of the Leipzig branch of the Writers' Union. He ran into further trouble because of his outspoken views on the Berlin workers' uprising on 17 June 1953, but the furor soon diminished and in 1955–1956 he was permitted to attend that East German literary finishing school, the Johannes R. Becher Literary Institute in Leipzig. Loest's opposition to the Stalinist "cult of personality" and dogmatism in GDR cultural life resulted in his arrest in 1957 on charges of having organized "counterrevolutionary groups." He was given a seven-and-a-half-year prison sentence. After his release, he was taken back into the Writers' Union, but he left it in 1979 after signing a letter condemning censorship. Loest quit the GDR for good in 1981 after receiving an exit visa.

Loest made his literary debut in 1950 with a collection of stories under the title *Nacht über dem See* (Night at Sea, 1950), which, like much of his fiction, deals with the trauma experienced by young people raised in the spirit of Nazi ideology in the aftermath of World War II. This concern is manifest as well in his autobiography *Durch die Erde ein Riss* (A Tear in the Earth, 1981) in which he addresses the matter of cultural repression in the GDR. Elsewhere in his fiction Loest writes about everyday life under socialism, as in It Takes Its Own Course; or, Trouble on Our Level (the title was drawn from a well-known poem by Bertolt Brecht). Once he left the GDR and especially after the fall of the Berlin Wall and the reunification of Germany, Loest published several books of a largely autobiographical nature focusing in particular on literary censorship in the GDR, his prison experiences, and his trials and tribulations at the hands of the East German secret police, the Stasi.

It Takes Its Own Course is a lively, often entertaining work that encompasses a wide swath of GDR society and paints an unflattering picture of it. The novel is narrated in the first person by the lead character, Wolfgang Wülff, a twenty-six-year-old native of Leipzig and an engineer. Wülff's disenchantment began when he was in his teens and, like so many other German youth, East and West, was wild about the Beatles. This enthusiasm culminated in the unfortunate event Wülff refers to as "die Schlacht auf dem Leuschnerplatz" ("the battle on Leuschnerplatz"). The Beatles brought long-haired hippies in their wake and before long imitators were springing up throughout the GDR. The best-known of these was the group calling itself the Old-Kings-Combo. That this would inevitably bring down the wrath of the authorities goes without saying, in view of the official condemnation of Western pop culture enunciated in no uncertain terms by the East German Communist Party head Erich Honecker at the eleventh meeting of the Central Committee of the Party in December 1965. This would, of course, have been the time frame of Wülff's recollection. The members of the Old-Kings-Combo were taken into police custody and a protest demonstration was scheduled for several days later, to be held in the

Leuschnerplatz. Needless to say, the public was warned not to take part in the demonstration. Like many other young people, Wülff was defiant in his eagerness to participate in it. When the police moved in en masse to break up the protest, Wülff was bitten by a police dog as he tried to flee the scene. The episode with the dog, to say nothing of the protest demonstration itself and the disproportionate might of the state arrayed against it, marked the beginning of Wülff's disenchantment.

Increasingly more cynical toward his self-serving colleagues at work and his superiors, he is no longer able to play the game of career advancement. His previous feelings of well-being in the material sense—a decent place to live with his wife and child and his Trabant automobile (in fact, the cheapest East German vehicle produced)—are no longer satisfying and he lapses into a state of negative passivity toward the society around him and the communist regime in general. When his antipathy gets the best of her, his wife divorces him and takes custody of their child as well as the Trabant. He consoles himself with a widow (Margrid) with a child from a previous marriage and some means at her disposal. Thinking primarily now in terms of his own needs, he decides to go ahead and marry Margrid, a senior postal employee. After all, she has a decent flat he can move into and so finally leave his mother's place, where he had settled after his own divorce. And when Margrid proposes that they pool their resources to buy a car, he confesses that he doesn't have enough even for that. But she reassures him that she can swing the purchase on her own but that for the time being it will have to be a used car, in fact a used Trabant (affectionately referred to as a Trabbi). At novel's end, Wülff sees himself setting forth on the same East German bourgeois path he had trod before, with the difference that he no longer has any illusions, these having begun to fade from the time of the episode on the Leuschnerplatz when he was ten years younger.

East German official dissatisfaction with the candor and obvious cynicism of Loest's novel should hardly raise eyebrows. His description of the defiant enthusiasm among East German youth for Western cultural phenomena, represented in the novel by the Beatles, and his obvious sarcasm and even mockery when writing about the mentality and behavior of the loyal communist functionary, embodied in the figure of Wülff's colleague, Huppel, were simply bound to get Loest into trouble. Writing about the appeal of the Beatles, at that time an icon of Western pop culture, Loest puts these words into Wülff's mouth:

> From one day to the next in our class the talk was only of the Beatles, the Beatles, yeah! . . .
>
> With the "yeah" came the hippies and with them the long hair, and here and there these types prowled the streets with defiant looks on their faces. Politically savvy waiters refused to serve the long-haired ones. In our school bashful dispositions rose to new heights. Whoever wore long hair was a beatnik. Whoever wore long hair, I heard at home, was a shirker and had lice. . . . We sat in our basement and imagined that we too had locks flowing to our shoulders, that we too could play terrific guitar and had a fantastic sound and knew English perfectly.

We banged on all kinds of covers and bellowed something that sounded like English, and since the basement was small, the racket was something awful, and the sound was enormous.[9]

And this sound grew in enormity until just eleven years after Loest's novel first saw the light of day, when it drowned out the hollow bellowing of totalitarianism for all time.

4

Fleeing the System

Literature and Emigration

When the loss of creative and personal freedoms became too painful for many writers to bear, in some instances in more than just the psychic sense, emigration seemed the only viable option. But emigration was not available as an option for many. The inability to part with one's native culture, with the sustenance of the native tongue, or with family and friends kept many from leaving even had this path been open to them. So they stayed, survived as best they could, but kept their dignity by means of an inner migration. Some simply retreated from further active participation in public literary life, with its censorship and repression. If they wrote, they did so for young people, or they kept body and soul together by translating for a living. In some instances they wrote for posterity and made no effort to have works published for which they knew no publication would be possible.

Whatever the hardships, many Eastern European writers chose to resettle in other lands. Some left their native country at an earlier point in time, such as Czesław Miłosz, who settled in the United States in 1961, and Milan Kundera, who was allowed to immigrate to France in 1975; others went later, like the distinguished Albanian Ismail Kadare, who parted company with his homeland in 1990. Whether emigration came earlier or later, most writers continued to cultivate their native language, even after acquiring proficiency in the language of their host country. Kundera, however, switched to French from Czech in the mid 1990s, publishing a series of novels written originally in that language. Some writers were destined to live their entire literary careers as émigrés in obscurity. Others, like Miłosz, Kundera, and Kadare, attained international celebrity. Miłosz was awarded the Nobel Prize in Literature in 1980, and Kadare and Kundera have been seriously considered for it at other times.

Miłosz and Kadare: Opposite Ends of the Spectrum

Miłosz's is a particular interesting case. To begin with, he was not an ordinary literary émigré, if one can say "ordinary" in this context. He was in fact a member of the Polish diplomatic corps when he went into exile after first defecting. After diplomatic service in New York City and Washington, D.C., from early 1947 to 1950, he returned to Europe to assume the post of first secretary of the Polish Embassy in Paris. His family remained in the United States. However, in December 1950 he was recalled to Poland, where he was stripped of his passport. In January 1951 he was able to return to his post in Paris but less than a month later requested political asylum of the French authorities. When he stepped out of the Polish Embassy, never to return, Miłosz was on the threshold of becoming a known writer. Before the war he had published two books, the poetry collection *Trzy zimy* (Three Winters, 1936) and the novella *Obrachunki* (Settling Scores, 1938). During World War II he eventually settled in Warsaw, where he published a small volume of poems (*Wiersze*) under the pen name Jan Syruć and became active in the literary underground. It was in this period (1942) that his best-known wartime work was published, the poetry anthology *Pieśń niepodległa* (Song of Independence).

Miłosz's first publications after his defection reveal both his state of mind at the time and the obvious laying of the foundation for a new life as an émigré. From a preoccupation primarily with poetic writing, Miłosz now shifted almost wholly to prose. His first book as an exile was the internationally celebrated *Zniewolony umysł* (*The Captive Mind*), which first appeared in 1953 in Polish under the imprint of the Instytut Literacki in Paris. The book is at once a rejection of the intellectual culture of the communist state from which he had just defected and at the same time a settling of scores, to an extent, with certain Polish fellow writers who were still part of the system. An attack on the blandishments by which the communists secured the loyalty of members of the literary community, *The Captive Mind* also underscores the ease with which writers and intellectuals were capable of compromising their integrity when offered the appropriate incentives. The book is constructed essentially along the lines of a case study, with thinly veiled allusions to specific personalities. *The Captive Mind* clearly established Miłosz's credentials as an anticommunist at a time when his past diplomatic service to the postwar Polish communist regime was being used to discredit the sincerity of his defection in some Polish émigré circles.

Miłosz's next book, *Zdobycie władzy* (*The Seizure of Power*, 1953), followed immediately on the heels of *The Captive Mind*. No less motivated by the desire to solidify his position as an anticommunist writer, Miłosz this time zeroed in on the military and political intrigue behind the Soviet takeover of Poland even before World War II had ended. A political novel, *The Seizure of Power* found a receptive audience among French readers when the major French publishing house Gallimard published it in translation as *La prise du pouvoir*. The timing was excellent for the appearance of both books. 1953 was the year of Stalin's death, Cold War tensions were high, and revelations about the nature of Soviet power and communist rule by insiders had a ready market in the West. The rapid publication of *The Seizure of Power* in French and the Prix Littéraire Européen that Miłosz was awarded for it catapulted him to international literary fame. In this same period *The Captive Mind* had begun appearing in foreign translations, further enhancing Miłosz's reputation.

In 1959 Miłosz received offers both from the University of California, Berkeley, and from Indiana University to join their faculties. The following year he accepted a visiting lectureship at Berkeley and in 1961 received a permanent professorship there. Miłosz remained at Berkeley until resettling in Kraków a few years before his death. Prior to leaving France for the United States he published two other prose works that much enhanced his already considerable reputation: *Dolina Issy* (*The Issa Valley*, Polish and French editions in 1955) and *Rodzinna Europa* (Native Europe; translated into English as *Native Realm*; first Polish edition, 1958). As if conceived in a spirit of reconciliation both with his homeland and with the Polish émigré community in Paris, these works are retrospective and nostalgic in nature. *The Issa Valley* is a thinly veiled, almost idyllic recollection of the author's Lithuanian childhood. It could not have helped but endear him to many of his fellow émigrés, themselves of similar background. *Native Realm* is as close as Miłosz ever came to writing an autobiography. Here he describes his school and university years in Wilno (now the Lithuanian capital Vilnius) and ruminates on the cultural and intellectual experiences of a young man growing up in that corner of Eastern Europe.

After becoming established in Berkeley in his new role as a university professor, Miłosz led an extraordinarily productive life as a writer of poetry and prose, capped by his winning of the Nobel Prize in Literature in 1980. His was a truly distinguished and remarkable literary career. Like the majority of émigré writers from Eastern Europe, Miłosz remained faithful to his native tongue. However, unlike the majority of émigré writers, he began soon after settling in Berkeley to actively promote his own career in English by working with American translators to get virtually all of his poetry into the American literary marketplace. His many volumes of prose, covering a wide range of topics, have had perhaps even greater resonance.

Immensely fortunate though Miłosz was as a writer in exile, his case has few parallels elsewhere in the Eastern European émigré literary experience. One parallel that suggests itself, albeit not perfect, is that of Ismail Kadare. A poet and prose writer like Miłosz, Kadare's reputation rests largely on his prose fiction. Like Miłosz, Kadare has never strayed from his fidelity to his native language. However, because of the paucity of translators from Albanian, his works have become known almost entirely in French translations and English translations based mostly on the French. Another far more important distinction to be made when comparing the careers of Miłosz and Kadare is the latter's considerably later self-exile from Albania. Long a controversial writer because of the boldness of some of his works, Kadare also managed to maintain a reasonably civilized relationship with communist officialdom as well as with the Albanian dictator Enver Hoxha when he was alive. Kadare's knowledge of and reverence for Albanian antiquity, his skillful use of allegory, his keen awareness of certain lines that were better left uncrossed, and an undeniable nationalism in some of his writings enabled him to avoid sharp conflicts with the regime until nearly its end. The fact that Kadare had studied at the Gorky Institute of Literature in Moscow when relations between Albania and the Soviet Union were still warm and that he never seemed to want to overtly defy the Albanian regime also cushioned his position.

Kadare published his first novel, *The General of the Dead Army,* in 1963. It reappeared in a revised edition in 1967. The novel was a considerable success despite official discontent with the fairly sympathetic treatment of the central figure of an Italian general. Kadare encountered even more trouble with censorship over his next novel *Përbindëshi* (The Monster), a curious reworking of the Trojan Horse legend with political implications. It was first published in 1965 in the official Tirana literary journal *Nëntori,* but was soon suppressed; it was republished in a revised version only in 1990 and 1991. Kadare's next two novels, *Dasma* (*The Wedding,* 1967), and *Kështjella* (*The Fortress,* 1970), also contained controversial elements. *The Wedding* is considered by some to be a mockery of socialist realism while others insist on reading the work as a good example of the official literary policy. On the surface a historical novel about the Turkish siege of an unnamed Albanian fortress defended by the Albanian national hero, Skenderberg (1405–1468), *The Fortress* also admits of more than a single reading. Skenderberg himself in fact never appears in the novel, which can be viewed as alluding to the tensions at the time between Albania and the Soviet Union. There are also those who interpret it as a debunking of the most pervasive of Albanian myths, that surrounding the figure of Skenderberg.

Apart from the patently autobiographical *Chronicle in Stone* (1971), which deals with a young boy's experiences in Kadare's hometown of Gjirokastër during World War II, Kadare's next few works were essentially political in nature. The somewhat weak novel November of a Capital City (1973; revised in 1989–1990 to expunge requisite procommunist propaganda in the original edition) has a World War II setting but was inspired by the Albanian purge of 1973–1975. *Dimri i madh* (The Great Winter), which Kadare wrote in the period 1971–1976 and which reflects Albania's rift with the Soviet Union in 1961, originally appeared in 1973 under the title *Dimri i vetmisë së madhe* (The Winter of the Great Solitude), but had to be rewritten because of the sensitive nature of its subject; it was finally reprinted in 1977. As these novels demonstrate, Kadare was willing on occasion to challenge official policy, but at the same time did not stand on principle when pressure was brought to bear on him to revise his works in conformity with that policy. When Miłosz was still part of the communist system, he wrote nothing to challenge it. That changed dramatically the moment he became a political exile. Kadare, on the other hand, showed little interest in becoming an exile for most of his career. Instead he was willing to test the limits of literary control while living under Hoxha and later staked a claim for himself as a vigorous defender of democratization and human rights in Albania.

Of Kadare's subsequent prose writings, the best were historical novels set in the Albanian Middle Ages, such as *Ura me tri harqe* (*The Three-Arched*

Bridge, 1978) and *Kush e solli Doruntinën?* (Who Brought Back Doruntine?, translated as *Doruntine,* 1980), an atmospheric and intriguing novel based on the Albanian folk legend of Constantine and his sister Doruntine. Although set in the 1930s, *Prilli i thyer* (*Broken April,* 1980) revolves around the ancient Albanian tradition of the blood feud (the Canon of Lek Dukagjini). *Nata me hënë* (A Moonlit Night), which followed Who Brought Back Doruntine? and *Broken April* in 1985, was banned a few months after publication for its frank depiction of the status of women in the patriarchal and intolerant Albanian society of Kadare's own time. This was the first instance of a work by Kadare being officially banned after its release.

Like Miłosz—who learned Hebrew to translate the Book of Psalms, the Book of Job, and the Books of the Five Megilot and classical Greek in order to translate the Gospel of Mark and the Apocalypse of John—Kadare had an excellent knowledge of classical and modern Greek and translated from both languages. He contributed translations of modern Greek poetry to an Albanian anthology of Greek poetry published in 1986, and in 1988 brought out a study of Aeschylus under the title *Eskili, ky humbës i madh* (Aeschylus; or, the Eternal Loser, 1988). He also published a translation of the *Orestia.* These classical interests were paralleled by an equally serious interest in Albanian oral epics as well as in the Homeric tradition in the Balkans. This is reflected in such works as *Autobiografia e popullit në vargje* (*The Autobiography of the People in Verse,* 1980) and his short novel *Dosja H.* (*The File on H.,* 1981).

Kadare's literary productivity continued unabated in the 1990s. *Ftesë në studio* (Invitation to the Studio, 1990) was Kadare's last publication in Albania before he left for France in 1990. It contains a selection of thirty-two poems, verse translations from several languages (including Chinese and Russian), and personal reflections on a broad variety of subjects, from literature to current events. Several of his pieces amount to a caustic settling of scores with other easily identified Albanian writers (to a certain extent thus resembling Miłosz's *The Captive Mind*). For some time Kadare's bête noire was the writer-scholar Arshi Pipa, who had long been a stern critic of Kadare, now portraying him as a lackey of communism, now hailing him for his anticommunist writings. It was especially the latter with which Kadare took issue, on the grounds that Pipa's characterization of him as anticommunist in the time frame in which this was done could have cost Kadare at the very least imprisonment. The implication on Kadare's part is that Pipa could not have been unaware of the possible consequences of his opinions.[1] Here is how Kadare portrays Pipa in his book *Nga një dhjetor në tjetrin: Kronikë, këmbim letrash, persiatje* (From One December to the Next: Chronicle, Correspondence, Reflections, 1991; translated into English as *Albanian Spring: The Anatomy of Tyranny):* "Though he described himself as a friend of democracy, whenever something happened in Albania that might quicken hope, A. Pipa promptly began discouraging people. When in December 1990, contrary to his prophecies, the first opposition party was actually established, he was one of the rare Albanians to make pronouncements against it.

The first democratic party and its founders were attacked equally by hostile forces like the Albanian Sigurimi and by the most confirmed reactionaries."[2] Kadare also asserts: "It was my novel *Chronicle in Stone* that A. Pipa referred to and about which he offered a monstrous interpretation that might very well have earned me a death sentence."

Kadare's next work, *Pesha e kryqit* (The Weight of the Cross, 1991), was originally designed as an appendix to Invitation to the Studio, which is why both works were published as a single volume in French translation under the title *Invitation à l'atelier de l'écrivain: suivi de, Le poids de la croix* (Invitation to the Writer's Studio, followed by The Weight of the Cross). *Albanian Spring* is a sequel to Invitation to the Studio and together with it and The Weight of the Cross forms a kind of trilogy of a distinctly autobiographical character that provides many insights into Kadare and his world. It is a personal chronicle of events covering the transitional period in Kadare's life from December 1989 to December 1990 and written in much the same tone and spirit as Invitation to the Studio.

Kadare's break with the Albanian regime of Hoxha's successor, Ramiz Alia—with whom he had had good relations since the days when Alia was Albanian director of propaganda and culture—was precipitated by the downfall of the Ceauşescus in Romania. Expectations of unrest in the last remaining communist country in Europe were running high, although Alia was still widely admired into the spring of 1990 as the leader who would finally bring democratic change to Albania. Believing that the time was right, Kadare went to see Alia personally to express his support for moves that had been taken in the name of democratization and to press the case against further violation of human rights. Of particular concern to Kadare were continued police violence, imprisonment, and the violation of laws. But while getting some agreement on certain points from Alia, Kadare opened a hornet's nest when he broached the matter of the widespread belief that the regime was deliberately keeping Albania poor in order to better control it. Kadare has left an eminently readable and quite detailed account of his rupture with the Albanian regime and his flight from Albania to France in *Albanian Spring*. The work also contains the complete texts of his exchange of correspondence with Alia, of 3 May 1990, 21 May 1990, and 23 October 1990. Kadare writes of his disillusionment and subsequent decision to leave Albania in these terms:

> I was thinking that I had done everything in my power to bring about a relaxation of the government. I had told myself that the day the totalitarian state agreed to live with a genuine literature would be the first real sign of reform, of the regime's attempt to humanize itself. Through my work, I've held this dream up to the Albanian people and to thousands of readers around the world. Now I understood that, although there is something authentic in the dream, the illusion was no more than an illusion. To make it a reality there had to be some new impulse. That impulse would be my *absence*.[3]

France, Nearly Everyone's Home Away from Home

The ranks of Eastern European exiles in Paris kept swelling from the early 1950s onward, and the French capital seemed to have a unique capacity for absorbing them all. If the Albanian exile literary community was necessarily small and overshadowed after 1990 by Ismail Kadare and his talented translator Jusup Vrioni, the Polish and Romanian contingents were another story entirely.

The Polish Story

To begin with, the Poles had a long history of seeking political asylum in France, going back to the defeat of the November Insurrection of 1830. It was then that nearly the entire Polish literary and intellectual elite clustered in Paris, in many cases never to return to Poland except in caskets. Before long, a library and cultural center—the Bibliotheque Polonaise—and a network of Polish schools were established as the so-called Great Emigration gradually cohered and became a new Poland in emigration. Printing in Polish also soon became possible and before long a thriving émigré publishing enterprise was underway. So in a sense it was natural for Polish malcontents and others to gravitate to Paris during the communist era. Although it still stands, the Bibliotheque Polonaise was replaced as the principal venue of Polish émigré literary activity by the Instytut Literacki (Institut Litteraire), which was founded in 1946. Its principal mission has been to publish the high-quality quarterly review *Kultura,* thus affording émigré writers a prominent place of publication within the Polish émigré community. Czesław Miłosz, of course, looms largest among the Polish émigré writers in Paris in the 1950s. But Polish émigré literary culture in the French capital came to be well represented by the likes of other talented writers, among them Sławomir Mrożek and Adam Zagajewski.

Zagajewski came to the fore of the "generation of 1968" as a poet who reveled in spoofing the totalitarian state and making a mockery of the official language. He became known for an extremely spare style, but one that he soon outgrew as his horizon expanded and he moved into realms of poetic imagination far distant from political opposition. A poet deeply embedded in European culture, Zagajewski was the author of several poems on such composers as Beethoven and Schubert and on the philosophers Schopenhauer, Kierkegaard, and Hegel. In 1974 he and his fellow poet Julian Kornhauser published a collection of sketches entitled *Świat nie przedstawiony* (Unrepresented World), a kind of programmatic manifesto attacking contemporary Polish poetry and prose for fleeing from contemporaneity and for a lack of ambition in taking up its problems. After he immigrated to Paris in 1983, Zagajewski became affiliated with the new Polish émigré quarterly *Zeszyty Literackie,* which was edited by Barbara Toruńczyk. In 1986 Zagajewski published in Paris a collection of essays on the Polish democratic opposition of the 1970s as well as on the political and cultural changes in Poland in the 1980s under the title *Solidarność i samotność* (*Solidarity, Solitude*). Of particular interest in the collection is his polemic on Central (or Eastern) Europe with the well-known essay on the subject by Milan Kundera.

A Romanian Exile Quartet

The careers of four prominent Romanian writers who became expatriates at various times in their careers shed considerable light on the range of exile experience among members of the same cultural space: Mircea Eliade, Norman Manea, Bujor Nedelcovici, and Dumitru Țepeneag. Paul Goma, the outstanding dissident of communist Romania, who also became an exile in Paris, will be discussed in the context of Eastern European prison literature in chapter 6.

A native of Bucharest, Mircea Eliade (1907–1986) was arguably the most prominent Romanian thinker of the twentieth century. After graduating from Bucharest University in 1928, having written a thesis on the philosophy of the Renaissance, Eliade spent the next three years at Calcutta University studying Indian philosophy. When he returned to Romania, he received his doctorate from Bucharest University in 1933 with a dissertation on yoga. Until 1939 he taught philosophy and the history of religions at the university. From 1940 to 1945 Eliade served as Romanian cultural attaché, first in London and then in Lisbon. When World War II ended, he did not return to Romania but took up residence in Paris. He remained in the French capital until 1956, lecturing on philosophy at the Sorbonne as well as other European universities. It was in this period that Eliade established himself as an international authority on religion and myth. In 1956 he accepted a professorship in the history of religions at the University of Chicago and remained there until his retirement in 1983. He was Sewell L. Avery Distinguished Service Professor in the Divinity School and professor in the Committee of Social Thought. A chair was named for him at the university after he retired. He died in Chicago in 1986.

Eliade's career falls into two main categories: scholarship and fiction. His scholarly works, dealing primarily with myth, magic, yoga, shamanism, and the history of religions, include, to mention only those available in English: *Le mythe de l'éternel retour* (1949; translated as *The Myth of the Eternal Return,* 1954); *Traité d'histoire des religions* (1949; translated as *Patterns in Comparative Religions,* 1958); *Le chamanisme et les techniques archaïques de l'extase* (1951; translated as *Shamanism,* 1964); and *Le yoga: Immortalité et liberté* (1952; translated as *Yoga: Immortality and Freedom,* 1964). His crowning scholarly achievement was the three-volume *Histoire des croyances et des idées religieuses* (The History of Beliefs and Religious Ideas, 1976–1983; translated as *A History of Religious Ideas*).

Eliade's creative writing began early, and before long he was recognized as an important figure in Romanian modernism on the basis especially of his novels and stories with Indian settings, reflecting his stay in India, and his works of an occult and supernatural character. The most important of Eliade's "Indian" tales is *Maitreyi* (1933; translated as *Bengal Nights*), about the love between a young European and an Indian teenage girl. Also set in India are

Şantier (Work in Progress, 1935) and the travel book *India* (1991). Eliade's literature of the fantastic includes: *Isabel şi apele diavolului* (Isabel and the Devil's Waters, 1930); *Domnişoara Christina* (Miss Christina, 1936); *Şarpele* (The Snake, 1937); the two tales of the occult included in *Secretul Doctorului Honigberger* (The Secret of Dr. Honigberger, 1940; translated as *Two Tales of the Occult*, 1972; reprinted as *Two Strange Tales,* 1986); and *Noaptea de Sanzieni* (St. John's Night, 1971; translated as *The Forbidden Forest*). His other fictional works include "Pelerina" ("The Cape," 1975; first published in German in 1976 and in Romanian, in the Paris-based émigré journal *Ethos,* in 1982); "Tinereţe fără de tinereţe" ("Youth Without Youth"; first published in Romanian in the Munich émigré journal *Revista Scriitorilor Români* in 1978 and 1979, and in French translation in 1981); and "Nouăsprezece trandafiri" ("Nineteen Roses"; the Romanian original appeared as a separate volume published by *Ethos* in Paris in 1980, and in French translation in 1982).

A novelist, short-story writer, and essayist, now living in New York, Norman Manea (b. 1936) was born in Bukovina, of Jewish origin. His first experience of imprisonment and privation came at the age of five when he spent five years in a Ukrainian internment camp in the aftermath of the Soviet takeover of Bessarabia in 1940. Manea was already an established writer before he emigrated to the United States in 1988 (from West Berlin, where he had resettled two years previously) on the basis of his novels *Captivi* (Captives, 1970), *Atrium* (1974), and *Cartea fiului* (The Boy's Book, 1976), and the title novella in the collection *Zilele şi jocul* (Happy Times, 1977; translated as *Compulsory Happiness*). The literary and political circumstances that prompted his emigration are recounted in a collection of essays written between 1988 and 1991, *Despre clovni: Dictatorul şi artistul* (On Clowns: The Dictator and the Artist, 1992).

Manea's literary reputation rests mainly on works published in English translation in the United States after his emigration from Romania. Apart from his essays, these include the novel *Plicul negru* (The Black Envelope, 1986), *Compulsory Happiness* (published in English in 1992), and a collection of fifteen haunting stories under the title *Octombrie oră opt* (October, Eight O'Clock, 1981). Set in Bucharest in the 1980s, and suffused with the mood of malaise and paranoia endemic to communist Romania, *The Black Envelope* is an almost surreal tale of a disgraced professor's attempt to solve the mystery of his father's death some forty years earlier. The novellas in the ironically titled *Compulsory Happiness* share the common theme of the nightmarishness of life in Ceauşescu's Romania. The first novella, "The Interrogation"—the best of the four—details the unspeakable mental and physical brutality with which agents of the Securitate pursue the interrogation of a woman prisoner. In "A Window on the Working Class" and "The Trenchcoat" trivial things assume huge significance in a deeply paranoid state obsessed with security and burdened with a mindless bureaucracy. The longest of the stories, "Composite Biography," was originally published in Romania in 1981 while the Ceauşescu regime was still in power. The careers of a loyal party member and a group of his coworkers in a bank are examined through the looking glass of an "Institute of Futurology." The essays in *On Clowns: The Dictator and the Artist* provide compelling insights especially into the workings of the cultural establishment under the Ceauşescu regime. *Ani de ucenicie ai lui August Prostul* (Auguste the Fool's Apprenticeship Years, 1979), on the other hand, is a humorous collection of fragmentary selections from one of the Romanian cultural periodicals from the period 1949–1965 intended to expose the banal policies of the literary establishment under the communists. Manea is now a professor of literature at Bard College in New York.

The immediate cause of Bujor Nedelcovici's (b. 1936) departure from Romania was bound up with the fate of his sixth novel, *Al doilea mesager* (The Second Messenger). He had begun his career as a writer of prose fiction in 1970 with his first novel, *Ultimii* (The Last). Three more novels followed between 1972 and 1977: *Fără vîsle* (Without Oars), *Noaptea* (The Night), and *Grădina Icoanei* (The Garden of the Icon). His first big success came with *Zile de nisip* (Days of Sand, 1979), which was awarded the Prize of the Romanian Writers' Union, was made into a film, and was subsequently translated into French. But in 1982 things took a turn for the worse for Nedelcovici. His new novel, The Second Messenger, was rejected for publication by the censors because of its Orwellian content. It was, however, published in French translation by the Albin Michel publishing house (Paris) and soon won the French Prix de la Liberté. A Romanian version appeared in 1991 and the following year was awarded the Prize of the Romanian-American Academy of Arts and Sciences. It was then adapted to film under the title *Somnul insulei* (The Dream of the Island); it premiered in 1995 at the French Festival of Arachon. The Romanian edition of the novel triggered some polemics. An article by the prominent critic Nicolae Manolescu in the review *România Literară* (number 27, 1991), which was apparently not to the liking of Nedelcovici's friend Norman Manea, brought a response by Manea in the 39th number (1991) of the journal. Nedelcovici himself replied in the 44th number (1991). But by now he was resident in Paris and thus far from the imbroglio.

Nedelcovici had in fact suffered few ill effects from the initial ban on The Second Messenger. In 1982, the year the censors rejected his novel, he became editor in chief of *Almanul literar* and head of the section of the Bucharest Writers' Association. But then he was informed that he was henceforth forbidden to publish anything under his own name; he also fell victim to political and police harassment. He decided to seek asylum in France and settled in Paris. As he notes in his book of essays *Aici şi acum* (Here and Now, 1996), this was in effect his second exile: "After a double interior exile (12 years at 'work down below' [a reference to his forced labor in a hydroelectric station and on various construction sites] and several years being prohibited from publishing anything), there then followed an exterior exile—both imposed by a demoniacal political system."[4]

Comfortable with French and quick to gain entry into Parisian as well as Romanian émigré circles, Nedelcovici adjusted easily. Indeed, he never looked back. In 1990 he was made a Knight of the Order of Arts and Letters in France and also became a member of the editorial staff of the review *Esprit.* By 1992 he was enjoying further literary recognition. He was made a titular member of the Society of Authors and Dramatic Composers and was inducted into the Society of Men of French Letters. Nedelcovici also began mending fences with the publishing community in Bucharest. In 1991 his novel *Îmblînzitorul de lupi* (The Tamer of Wolves) was published in Bucharest; a French version was brought out three years later. The following year his play *Noaptea de solstiţiu* (The Night of the Solstice) was performed in Baia Mare (Romania) and a volume of his short stories appeared in Bucharest. His first French novel, *Le matin d'un miracle* (The Morning of a Miracle), was also published in 1992; a Romanian edition came out in 1993 (as *Dimineaţa unui miracol*) and was honored with the Prize of the Writers' Union.

Unlike many other Eastern European literary exiles, Nedelcovici succeeded in making a secure niche for himself in the host culture as a respected writer in French. At the same time, while still officially in exile, he had returned to the literary scene in Romania and had again begun winning prestigious awards for his books. In 1994–1995, as if by way of confirmation of his international literary celebrity, Nedelcovici held a series of lectures at several universities in California. Prolific as ever, he also published another two books before the end of the century: *Aici şi acum* (Here and Now, 1996), a collection of essays, and the novel *Provocatorul* (The Provocateur, 1997). The novel shows how far Nedelcovici had come as a French writer. Moving from Paris to Montreal, San Francisco, and Mexico City, the work is cosmopolitan, romantic, erotic, and parodic, and combines a love story with critical analysis of contemporary French society. Its characters are entirely French.

A diligent diarist, Nedelcovici recorded his experiences in the journal he published in 1998 under the title *Jurnal infidel: Pagini din exil, 1987–1993* (Unreliable Journal: Pages from Exile, 1987–1993). Often quite fragmentary, the diary covers the years of Nedelcovici's exile in Paris beginning with an entry for 31 December 1996. It is preceded by a preface of sorts consisting of diary notations from 31 December 1996 and 1 January 1997, as well as from July and August 1997. Many of the entries are taken up with brief descriptions of Nedelcovici's meetings in Paris with other Romanian literary and intellectual exiles, among them Monica Lovinescu, Virgil Ierunca, Şerban Cristovici, Paul Goma, Mircea Eliade, Vintilă Horia, and others. One of the topics they discussed among themselves was the possible establishment of a Union of (Romanian) Exile Writers. But misunderstandings with Dumitru Ţepeneag and Paul Goma, in particular, as well as other problems, eventually left the plan unrealized. Although a political exile in France, Nedelcovici, and other émigrés, was still invited to the Romanian Embassy on the occasion of the anniversary of Romanian independence in 1872. Life in exile for Nedelcovici was anything but bleak. Apart from the many contacts he had and, for the most part, apparently enjoyed with fellow Romanian exiles, there were also the undoubtedly pleasant meetings with his publisher, Albin Michel, and with his translator, Alain Paruit. At one of the meetings at Albin Michel, Nedelcovici was introduced, for example, to Vladimir Nabokov, who was then the director of the literary and translation section of the publishing house. At a cocktail party on 23 June 1988, Nedelcovici recalls meeting the Russian writers Andrei Bitov and Andrei Sinyavsky. There were also several trips abroad, to Greece, Morocco, England, Canada, the United States, and elsewhere.

His status as an exile and the phenomenon of exile in general, however, were never far from Nedelcovici's mind, and his *Journal* is full of remarks on the subject. In an entry for 9 April 1987, for example, he declares: "Yoga: When I eat, I eat. When I drink, I drink. When I sleep, I sleep. And when you're in exile, you're in exile and nothing else."[5] In the entry for 7 June 1987, he declares: "I believe that exile was inscribed in my genetic code. In 1971, when my brother sought asylum in Geneva, Mama said to me: 'And you'll be going somewhere too.' 'No!' I replied. 'A writer cannot desert the language and country in which he was born.' I did everything possible to honor my faith and convictions. In 1985 I returned from Paris, even when I knew that the Albin Michel publishing house was going to publish my novel The Second Messenger. In 1987 it became necessary . . . to leave Romania. Mama had been entirely right! I was predestined to exile" (57). Keenly aware of a deep sense of loss, Nedelcovici wrote on 28 May 1987: "I have lost my country, my home, my family, my friends, my library, the past, my parents, memories, my youth. . . . Now I have to reconstruct everything on other grounds! . . . Transformed, transfigured, another identity (even though I will be bearing the same name), another country, another world. *I am another person*" (47–48).

After the Romanian revolution of December 1989—which he writes about, though not at great length, in his *Jurnal*—Nedelcovici, like other Romanian exiles in France and elsewhere, began giving thought to returning home. He finally made up his mind to go back in March 1990. Once there, he first thought that he would remain. But problems arose as soon as he started attending meetings of the Writers' Union (to which he had belonged before his exile). Admission was open only to writers who had already published two books. But Nedelcovici thought the rule ought to be relaxed in view of the difficulties many writers had experienced under the old regime and in exile and that in considering them for admission to the union their activity over many years should be taken into account. However, the president of the union, Mircea Dinescu, dismissed Nedelcovici's argument in an insolent tone. Nedelcovici was also upset over the fact that no provisions were being made to discipline writers who had collaborated with the regime, such as Eugen Barbu, Adrian Păunescu, and Corneliu Vadim Tudor, and he contrasted the situation in France, where stern justice was meted out to writers who had collaborated with the Nazis, mentioning specifically the cases of Louis-Ferdinand Céline and Pierre Drieu la Rochelle. Nedelcovici's attitude toward the post-Ceauşescu literary scene in Romania became increasingly more skeptical and critical. The sense of estrangement was now undeniable. Having rooted himself so much in the Parisian literary milieu, he decided to remain in exile rather than return permanently to his native country, which henceforth he would visit only on relatively short trips.

Dumitru Ţepeneag (b. 1937) was in the forefront of the younger generation of writers at the end of the 1960s who were opposed to the rigid social and cultural controls of the Communist Party. The flash point was the publication in 1971 of his collection of short stories *Aşteptare* (Waiting), which had to be withdrawn from bookstores in official censure of Ţepeneag's increasing radicalism of the early 1970s. Nonetheless, he was permitted by the authorities to travel to Paris, where he subsequently learned of the loss of his Romanian citizenship. During his stay in the French capital, Ţepeneag remained an active writer, publishing several works in French, including a book on chess, *La défense Alékhine* (The Alekhin Defense, 1983). After the fall of the Ceauşescu regime, Ţepeneag, now again able to publish in Romania, issued two new books in the 1990s recounting his exile from Romania and his early experiences in France: *Zadarnică e arta fugii* (The Futile Art of Running, 1991) and *Român la Paris: Pagini de journal, 1970–1972* (A Romanian in Paris: Pages of a Journal, 1970–1972, 1993).

In late 1995 he finally made a return visit to Romania, when he and the French writer Alain Robbe-Grillet, some of whose works Ţepeneag had translated into Romanian, were invited to the French Cultural Institute in the western Romanian city of Timişoara. But the trip did not unfold as Ţepeneag might have desired. Acrimonious interviews in the press and elsewhere during Ţepeneag's stay in Cluj and Bucharest, mostly dealing with the place of the émigré writer in Romanian literature, made his return to his native land distasteful. Three years later he published a description of the entire episode under the title *Călătorie neizbutită* (An Unsuccessful Trip). This is small book about the linguistic, psychological, and literary ramifications of a writer's decision to abandon his native language in order to write in a foreign one.

Czechs Who Stay and Czechs Who Go

Alexandr Kliment is less well known than his contemporaries Josef Škvorecký, Pavel Kohout, Milan Kundera, and Václav Havel—despite publication in 2001 of an English translation of his novel *Nuda v Čechách* (Boredom in Bohemia; translated as *Living Parallel*). But Boredom in Bohemia splendidly captures the dilemma of the Czech intellectual who is torn between love of his native land and hatred for the political system that has so turned him against it that he yearns to escape it. This finely wrought novel of love and politics in pre-1968 Czechoslovakia is narrated in the first person by a youngish architect named Mikuláš Svoboda, whose frustrations in his career are paralleled by his frustrations in love. His idealistic visions of attractive and environmentally sensitive housing projects are shelved by a compassionate superior, who tries to make him understand that deviations from the socialist realist norm simply would not be tolerated in the prevailing circumstances.

Moving back and forth in time, Mikuláš recalls his relationship with his first wife, Jarmila, which subsequently ended in divorce, and his current relationship with the divorced Olga, an artist who holds dual citizenship and encourages him to resettle with her in France. But as Mikuláš considers the idea of exile, he finds it hard, if not impossible, to imagine distancing himself permanently from the Czech, and Prague, landscape that has become so much a part of him. He travels about Prague, mostly on foot, and his mind is consumed by the landmarks he sees wherever he goes. He sets these in the appropriate historical context and understands finally that he is psychically incapable of leaving behind his native land, despite everything he has lived through. In the end, Olga will go away alone, after an erotic triple coupling with Jarmila and Mikuláš. Reunion with the former wife, with whom he is friendly and still intimate on occasion, is also out of the question. And even the hope of a new relationship with the railroad station baggage claim attendant Míladka also evaporates when she marries another man. Mikuláš is left a solitary figure comforted only by childhood memories. Even when changes in the political climate encourage hope that his old architectural plans may yet be revived, he is wrenched from these illusions by his former superior, who tells him that younger people, with different ideas, have now taken over and that both of them are superfluous.

Lyrical and polyphonic, poignant and erotic, Boredom in Bohemia was not intended primarily as a political novel. But as Mikuláš reviews events in Czech history since the communist takeover in 1948—the flickering out of the last vestiges of Czech democracy, the coming to power of the communists, the harsh implementation of collectivized architecture, the cult of Stalin and the impact on the Czechs of his death, the intractability, insensitivity, and banality of communist thought as, for example, in architecture—a depressing picture emerges of the profound disillusionment to which a younger person of vision could succumb under the communist regime.

Boredom in Bohemia obviously could not have been published in Czechoslovakia in 1977, when it was written. Kliment had already angered the official critics in 1960 when his first novel, *Marie*, appeared. Deliberately eschewing the political, Kliment made personal relationships the main focus of the work. A poet, playwright, and author of children's books, as well as a novelist, Kliment felt the full weight of communist censorship after the suppression of the Prague Spring of 1968. From 1970 to 1989 he was banned from publishing anything in Czechoslovakia and was not permitted any public literary career. It was only thanks to Czech émigré presses, including the famous Sixty-Eight Publishers in Toronto, Canada, that *Nuda v Čechách* saw the light of day. Appropriately, it was one of the first novels to be published in Czechoslovakia after the downfall of the communist regime.

Sixty-Eight Publishers was the brainchild of the prominent Czech writer Josef Škvorecký (b. 1924) and his wife, the writer, singer, and actress Zdena Salivarová (b. 1933). One of the most prolific contemporary Czech writers, Škvorecký had made a name for himself with the appearance of his first novel, *Zbabělci* (*The Cowards*), which he wrote in 1948/1949; publication, however, was delayed for a decade. In the form of a first-person chronicle covering a single week in the year 1945, the novel was banned not long after publication because of official displeasure with its central character, the irreverent young Daniel Smiřický, and its apparent mockery of the Red Army, something obviously not calculated to win favor with the communists so soon after World War II. Subsequent works by Škvorecký, such as *Konec nylonového věku* (The End of the Nylon Age) and *Tankový prapor* (The Tank Brigade), were similarly rejected for publication. When *The Cowards* was finally permitted to appear in print in 1958, the controversy that swirled about the novel cost Škvorecký his position as editor in chief of a literary bimonthly and his ability to participate freely in his country's literary life.

Fluent in English, which he had begun studying seriously before World War II, he earned what living he could by translating American fiction and writing a series of popular crime novels either alone or in tandem with Jan Zábrana. By the time the first of his famous Lieutenant Borůvka detective novels, *Smutek poručíka Borůvky* (*The Mournful Manner of Lieutenant Borůvka*), appeared in 1966, the winds of change had begun sweeping across Czechoslovakia and ushered in an all-too-brief period of greater tolerance. The Czech Writers' Union presented Škvorecký with its award for the year's best fiction on the basis of The End of the Nylon Age in 1967. Other works by Škvorecký also began appearing. But the Soviet-led Warsaw Pact invasion of Czechoslovakia in 1968 put an end to the "thaw" and to Škvorecký's literary career in his country. After considering all the pros and cons of emigration, much like Mikuláš Svoboda in Kliment's Boredom in Bohemia, Škvorecký and Salivarová left Czechoslovakia permanently for Canada on 31 January 1969. They settled in Toronto, where Škvorecký himself went on to an immensely successful career as a writer and professor in the Department of English at the University of Toronto.

Apart from the further development of their literary careers, both Škvorecký and Salivarová undertook one of the most important developments in communist-era Czech literary history. In 1972 they founded Sixty-Eight Publishers, which was devoted to publishing works by Czech émigré, exile, and underground writers. What began as a modest but immensely valuable undertaking grew to become the principal publishing house of the Czech emigration. By the time the communist regime had been toppled from power and the new Czech president, Václav Havel, was in a position to invite the Škvoreckys back to Prague in order to decorate them, Sixty-Eight Publishers had published several hundred Czech literary works.

One of the most prominent, and controversial, Czech dissidents both before and after the suppression of the Prague Spring and the Charter 77 episode was the playwright and novelist Pavel Kohout (b. 1928). Although he had served as second cultural attaché of the Czechoslovak Embassy in Moscow from 1949 to 1950, and until 1955 edited the cultural section of the army publication *Československý voják,* Kohout was not destined to remain for too long a loyal servant of the state. His theatrical career began in the 1960s, when from 1963 to 1966 he served as dramatic adviser to the famous Divadlo na Vinohradech (Theater in the Vineyards). But this appointment ended when he resigned his membership on the governing board of the Czechoslovak Writers' Union in protest over its cultural and political orientation. His speech at the Fourth Congress of the Union in 1967 earned him the same kind of disciplinary measures meted out to other literary liberals. His active role in the Prague Spring of 1968 and his collaboration in the drafting of Charter 77 resulted in his dismissal from the party and the writers' union.

He was permitted to accept an invitation to visit Austria in 1979 as a guest director and playwright, but neither he nor his wife was subsequently allowed to return to Czechoslovakia; they were also stripped of their citizenship. Kohout remained in Vienna for a decade, returning to his native country only after the downfall of communism. During this period most of his works were written in German and published in Austria or Germany. Apart from his dramatic writing, Kohout began turning out mostly political texts, beginning in the late 1960s. *Z deníku kontrarevolucionáře* (From the Diary of a Counterrevolutionary, 1969), the first of these, is a kind of collage of diary notes and supplemental material covering the period from the 1940s to the Soviet invasion in 1968. *Kde je zakopán pes* (Where the Dog Lies Buried), which was eventually published in 1987, is in essence a "memoir novel" wherein Kohout obviously draws on his own experiences in order to trace the evolution of a dissident and his conflicts with the authorities.

This novel was followed by *Bílá kniha: O kauze Adam Juráček* (The White Book: About the Adam Juráček Case), which was published in 1970 in an expanded German edition as *Das Weissbuch in Sachen Adam Juraček*; in English in 1977 as *White Book. Adam Juráček, Professor of Drawing and Physical Education at the Pedagogical Institute in K., vs. Sir Isaac Newton, Professor of Physics at the University of Cambridge, Reconstructed from Contemporary Records and Supplemented by Most Interesting Documents by Pavel Kohout*; and in 1978 in the Czech original by Sixty-Eight Publishers.

Taking aim at the "normalization" introduced in Czechoslovakia after the suppression of the Prague Spring, *White Book* is a political allegory in the form of an absurdist text about the case of Adam Juráček, who through sheer force of will disproves Newton's law of gravity by standing on a ceiling. What follows is a hilarious escalating investigation by local officials that mimics typical communist-era investigations, interrogations, and arbitrary assignments of dissidents to mental hospitals. Initially Adam Juráček is praised for his "unsparing scientific and human endeavors, leading to a crowning discovery that promises to liberate our fellow citizens, as well as progressive mankind, from our very last shackles—the shackles of gravity."[6] But matters soon take a different turn. Juráček is ordered removed to a psychiatric clinic for observation. The Board of the Academy of Sciences then convenes to deliberate the matter and reaches the conclusion that "the law of gravity is today an indispensable component of an unshakable construct from which humanity sets out for the stars" (76). Under pressure from the higher bodies of the state, local officials then reverse their earlier decision. Juráček is disciplined, but public demonstrations break out in his support. Juráček is taken into custody in handcuffs and imprisoned. A professor of physics at Charles University is asked to conduct his own investigation and determines that Juráček is indeed capable of defying the laws of gravity; however, a confrontation breaks out between this professor and another one, also from Charles University, who rejects his findings. The Criminal Court of Prague hears the case and acquits Juráček of the charge of committing punishable acts by virtue of the fact that his defiance of gravity took place only in the imagination of the world around him, as a "result of a so-called mass-hypnosis called forth by the suggestive powers of the Accused" (172). Juráček is declared unfit and is committed to a psychiatric sanatorium and subjected to a variety of experiments.

The much-celebrated Milan Kundera—another Czech exile since 1975— seemed to be off to a politically secure course when he joined the Communist Party shortly after World War II. But he was expelled from it after the communists took power in Czechoslovakia in February 1948. Before settling on a career in literature and film, Kundera earned his way as a laborer and jazz musician. He eventually became a professor at the Prague Institute for Advanced Cinematographic Studies, which produced several of the most compelling Czech films of the postwar period.

Kundera's literary career was launched with his first novel, *The Joke*, which was published in Czechoslovakia in 1967, a year before the Soviet invasion. It immediately established him as one of the most gifted Czech writers of the postwar period; at the same time, however, it adumbrated his future difficulties with the authorities. Like most of his fiction, *The Joke* is a deft combination of wry humor, irony, sex, and political candor. Essentially a tale about a love affair turned sour, it was taken primarily as a negative picture of communist rule in Czechoslovakia. *The Joke* was followed by one of Kundera's most popular works, *Směšné lásky* (*Laughable Loves*, 1965; enlarged ed., 1981), a collection of highly entertaining stories pivoting on sex. It was the last work by Kundera that the Czech communists allowed to be published in Czechoslovakia. One of the first literary victims of the repression that followed the quashing of the Prague Spring, he was dismissed from his position at the Institute for Advanced Cinematographic Studies in 1970, and all his books were thereafter removed from public libraries in Czechoslovakia.

Kundera was allowed to go into exile in 1975. He eventually settled in Paris and continued to write prolifically. But since his books could no longer be published in Czechoslovakia, they first appeared in French; the Czech originals were subsequently published by Sixty-Eight Publishers in Toronto. After *Laughable Loves*, Kundera published, in French, *Life Is Elsewhere* (1973). It won the Prix Médicis for the best foreign novel published in France that year. *Valčík na rozloučenou* (*The Farewell Party*) appeared next, in 1976, followed by *The Book of Laughter and Forgetting*) in 1979 and *Nesnesitelná lehkost bytí* (*The Unbearable Lightness of Being*) in 1984. Kundera is imaginative, humorous, and skilled at injecting glancing blows at the political system he left behind without overpowering his readers with tendentiousness.

Kundera's loosely constructed *The Book of Laughter and Forgetting* comprises seven almost autonomous sections built around his familiar themes of male–female relations, primarily sexual, both successful and unsuccessful. He injects himself as a character on occasion and takes time off from his story to talk about his narrative as well as literature, music, sex (of course), and the state of the world. Throughout the game-playing of Kundera's different couples, the reader is kept aware of the calamities of Czech history, from the ruinous defeat at the hands of the Habsburgs in the seventeenth century to the Soviet invasion of 1968. In the wake of the events of 1968, many Czechs were incarcerated and executed and well over a hundred thousand went into exile. While the "laughter" of the title alludes to the resilience of the Czechs as a nation in the face of devastating assaults on their national identity, and to the absurdity of the human situation in general, the "forgetting" has a very special referent—the disastrous assault on Czech culture in the time of Gustáv Husák (1913–1991), the Soviet stooge who became the country's boss right after the Soviet invasion of 1968. To Kundera, and indeed to a great many Czechs, it seemed that Husák's rule could be interpreted as a diabolical plot sponsored by the Russians to erase Czech history. In a telling passage later in the book he writes: "Or is it true that a nation will not go live across a desert of organized forgetfulness? None of us knows what will be. However, one thing is certain. In moments of clairvoyance the Czech nation can glimpse the image of its own death up close. Not as an accomplished fact, nor as the inevitable future, but as a perfectly concrete possibility. Its death is by its side."[7]

Arguably Kundera's masterpiece, *The Unbearable Lightness of Being* further exemplifies his unquenchable interest in human sexuality and the dialectics of the male–female relationship. It explores the emotional and erotic intricacies in the relations of two couples, a compulsively womanizing and politically humiliated surgeon who falls in love with and marries a sensitive woman but is unable to change his sexual ways, and his lively artist mistress and her other married lover. Humorous and wise in the ways of the world, thoughtful and compassionate, *The Unbearable Lightness of Being* is also the most politically engaged of Kundera's novels, set as it is during the Soviet invasion in 1968 and the dreary aftermath of dehumanizing repression. Death is no stranger to Kundera's fiction, but instead of approaching it with a sense of dread he seems to suggest that it can be a beneficent release from the trap the world has become. If any novel by Kundera can lay claim to the title of masterpiece, it is surely this work.

The Unbearable Lightness of Being was the last work Kundera wrote originally in Czech. His subsequent novels—*Immortality* (1990), *Slowness* (1996), *Identity* (1997), and *Ignorance* (2002)—were all written in French, as if he intended to reinvent himself as a French writer at home on the European stage of letters. Of these novels, *Immortality* and *Ignorance* have done the best critically. The others are so different from what Kundera had written previously that critics and public alike were unsure how to receive them. Another important facet of Kundera's fiction in French is his abandonment of Czech settings and characters. The one exception is *Ignorance*, in which he explores the realities and implications of emigration at greater depth than in any previous work. The issue of emigration had appeared, to be sure, in *The Incredible Lightness of Being*:

Tomáš, the surgeon, had emigrated to Zurich, but was persuaded by his new wife, Tereza, to return to Prague. Sabina, the mistress, eventually immigrates to the United States after the death of her lover Franz. But emigration in this novel is marginal, something that happens but is not explored psychologically or philosophically, as it is in *Ignorance.*

By the time he came to write *Ignorance,* Kundera had lived in emigration for over twenty years. The novel is the fruit of an obviously long consideration of the matter of exile and possible return. It focuses on two Czech émigrés, Irena and Josef, who, like Kundera himself, have been living in emigration for twenty years, she in France and he in Denmark. Both are middle-aged and have lost their spouses. Irena and her husband left Czechoslovakia primarily because of her desire to flee a domineering mother. With her husband now dead and her children grown, she has reluctantly returned to Prague with her lover, a Swedish businessman whose company has set up shop in the Czech capital and who has persuaded Irena to return there with him. Josef, who had left everything behind in order to emigrate to Denmark, has also returned to Czechoslovakia after the death of his wife. Their parallel stories briefly converge when they meet by chance in a Paris airport. Irena remembers Josef from a single fleeting encounter years before when she felt a certain liking for him. But he has no memory of her whatsoever. They agree, however, to get together in Prague.

Ignorance is interesting, above all, as a meditation in fictional form on emigration and return. Neither Irena nor Josef is overly enthusiastic about returning to Prague, or of seriously considering a permanent return to Czechoslovakia. What they discover, in a sense, is that they can't go back and pick up the threads of lives dropped a long time ago. The people they meet in their own country show little or no interest in their lives in emigration and, to a certain degree, seem to fault them for having left Czechoslovakia in the first place. Irena and Josef's promise to meet again in Prague culminates in an afternoon of torrid sex in his hotel room. Still strongly attached to the memory of his wife and their home in Denmark, Josef gives no thought to remaining in Prague and maintaining some relationship with Irena. He leaves her, asleep on his bed in the hotel, and then flies back to Denmark. In a grotesque parallel scene to the coupling of Irena and Josef, Irena's mother seduces Irena's by-now unloved lover, Gustaf, who pleasantly contemplates an unentangling relationship with her mother when in a Prague to which Irena no longer feels any compelling ties. There is often an element of erudition in Kundera's writing, usually involving language, history, or literature. In *Ignorance,* the *Odyssey* is frequently brought up as a frame of reference, reminiscent of Kundera's use of allusions to Sophocles' *Oedipus* in *The Unbearable Lightness of Being.* The long separation of Ulysses from home and the circumstances of his return are echoed in the mixed feelings toward return after two decades in emigration of Irena and Josef.

Of the relatively younger Czech writers who sooner or later sought refuge in the West, and subsequently turned their experiences into fiction, by far the most colorful is Iva Pekárková (b. 1963). Her literary fame rests entirely on three thinly veiled autobiographical novels she wrote about her life before and after she came to America. The first is *Péra a perutě* (Plumes and Pinions, 1989; translated as *Truck Stop Rainbows*), which Pekárková published with Sixty-Eight Publishers three years after emigrating from Czechoslovakia in 1986. It was followed by *Kulatý svět* (*The World Is Round*, 1993). In 1996, the year of her return to her native Prague, she published the last of what may be regarded as her expatriate trilogy, *Dej mi ty prachy* (*Gimme the Money*).

A tough, sexually graphic first-person narration by a happy-go-lucky twenty-something university student of psychology (named Fialka), *Truck Stop Rainbows* is essentially a road novel in which the lead character sleeps her way through Czechoslovakia and neighboring countries with truck drivers she picks up whenever and wherever possible. A passionate street photographer who strives to record on film the horrendous environmental pollution, wretched housing, neglect, and decay attributable to years of communist indifference, she spares nothing in her pursuit of truth, in both her picture-taking and her comments on the life she sees around her. A brutally honest picture of the conditions of the time, *Truck Stop Rainbows* obviously could not have been published in Czechoslovakia. It thus became the first literary fruit of Pekárková's personal exodus, chronicling her arduous journey from a grimly depressing Czechoslovakia through a nightmarish ten months in a refugee camp in Austria, and thence to the perhaps-unexpected hardships of life in the New World.

The World Is Round follows the flight to the West of (presumably) the heroine of the first novel. Although she receives permission to emigrate to the United States, nothing of her life in America forms a part of the novel. Instead the entire focus is on the degrading life of refugees from throughout the former Eastern bloc who are thrown together in a detention camp in Austria (and based on Pekárková's own stay in the Traiskirchen refugee camp, to be precise the Flüchtlingslager Traiskirchen bei Wien). Narrated again in the first person, often interspersed with lengthy conversations among various refugees, the novel captures the dreams for freedom and a new life as well as the disillusionment of the inmates. In a kind of short epilogue, the narrator speaks of her new existence in America, with a husband and with a baby on the way.

This epilogue becomes, as it were, the point of departure for Pekárková's next novel, *Gimme the Money*. However, in a switch from first- to third-person narration, the heroine is now Jindřiška, a Czech repatriate who has settled in Manhattan and, in order to earn a living, has become a cab driver. She is also married to a difficult-to-get-along-with, French-speaking African Muslim immigrant named Talibe. *Gimme the Money* captures much of the hardship, and flavor, of the immigrant's money-grubbing existence in New York, as indeed it does that of the world of the big-city immigrant cab driver.

The Tragedy of Emigration: A Yugoslav Case

That some Eastern European writers were constitutionally incapable of surviving in exile is exemplified by the tragic case of the Croatian poet Viktor Vida

(1913–1960). Born on the island of Kotor off the Dalmatian coast, Vida was educated in secondary schools in Kotor and Podgorica; after this his parents resettled in Zagreb. He studied South Slavic and other languages and literatures at Zagreb University and graduated the Faculty of Philosophy in 1937. He then left for Rome on a scholarship from the Italian Institute in Zagreb. When he returned to Croatia two years later, he began work as a librarian at the institute. In 1941 he taught at a Zagreb high school, and then quit in 1942, when he resettled in Rome and joined the Italian-Croatian News Agency. When this closed in 1943 after the fall of Italy in World War II, Vida remained largely unemployed, until in 1946 he found a job as a clerk at the Commissione Pontificia d'Assistenza. Obviously restless, Vida packed himself and his family off to Argentina, arriving in Buenos Aires at the beginning of 1948. Although he lived a threadbare existence in Argentina, Vida began publishing poems, essays, and reviews in a variety of Croatian émigré journals, becoming in time a frequent contributor to the *Hrvatska revija* edited by Vinko Nikolić. His first books of poetry, *Svemir osobe* (The Universe of a Person, 1951) and *Sužanj vremena* (Slave of Time, 1956), were published with the help of friends. In response to the growing, largely political divisions within the Croatian émigré community in Argentina, Vida, an able essayist, wrote, with Ivo Bogdan, *Obrana hrvatske cjelokupnosti i javnih radnika* (A Defense of Croatian Integrity and Public Workers, 1954).

In 1960, for reasons never successfully clarified, Vida committed suicide by throwing himself under the wheels of a train. Despite his deep feelings of emptiness and isolation as an émigré, Vida apparently never seriously considered returning to postwar Yugoslavia. He chose instead to deal from the distance of emigration with many of the questions then being addressed by writers in Croatia itself as well as those elsewhere in emigration. The long neglect of Vida's poetry in Croatia ended in 1962 with the publication of his collected poems (*Sabrane pjesme*); the collection is preceded by a sensitive analysis by the critic Ivo Lendić in which he demonstrates Vida's modernity and contemporaneity.

The compromises demanded of writers by emigration are never easy. But as the case of Vida demonstrates, there were occasions when they could prove unbearable. The successful transitions to a new life and literary career in emigration of Miłosz, Kundera, Kohout, Pekárková, Škvorecký, Kadare, Manea, Nedelcovici, Vida's fellow Yugoslav writer Danilo Kiš, and others—however impressive—were certainly not normative.

5

Internal Exile and the Literature of Escape

As a way around their inability to deal honestly with issues of contemporary relevance, and in the face at times of severe cultural repression, Eastern European writers often pursued a variety of stratagems. Those with the inclination, and talent, cultivated the absurd and grotesque, as we have seen, hoping in this way to establish a dialogue with readers under the noses of the censors. Many other writers simply stopped participating in public literary life and wrote instead "for the drawer," thereby waiting for a better tomorrow when these private works might see the light of day and they themselves could return to literary normalcy.

When this practice proved unsatisfactory, and necessarily gave way to the normal desire of the writer to have contact with readers and fellow authors alike, the great era of Eastern European samizdat began. In his introduction to the English edition of *A Cup of Coffee with My Interrogator: The Prague Chronicles of Ludvík Vaculík* (1987), Václav Havel describes the genesis of the phenomenon:

It was in this gloomy period that the idea of trying to escape from the closed world of writing "for the drawer" was born. Starting with a small circle of mostly strictly "forbidden" authors (Kohout, Klíma, Kliment, Vaculík, myself, and a few others), these writers began to exchange their manuscripts with a view to copying them and circulating them to a wider readership. They started writing regular *feuilletons,* short literary essays which they sent to one another with the same intention. Others joined in and our pieces got around. . . . Today there are a great many *samizdat* series circulating in Czechoslovakia, consisting of periodicals, individual articles and entire books, polemics, and various other texts, all this via a widespread network that has come about quite spontaneously, without any central organization. Many of these articles and books find their way abroad and then return to our readers by courtesy of émigré publishers and Czech and Slovak broadcasting stations.[1]

There were, of course, other stratagems for remaining in public literary life and at the same time circumventing censorship; one of the most widely cultivated of these was historical fiction. Although practiced in a variety of forms, there was a definite preference for the novel. This was in a sense a type of escapist literature, but at the same time it could also make claim to relevance by insinuating parallels between events in the past and contemporary reality. This historical fiction had certain definite chronological foci.

World War I and the Interwar Period

The considerable interest in World War I is wholly understandable in the light of the remapping of Eastern Europe after the breakup of the colonial empires of Austria-Hungary, Germany, and Ottoman Turkey. Most of the modern states of Eastern Europe owe their existence to the defeat of the Central Powers, as they were known. In the aftermath of the war, Austria and Hungary became new republics of considerably shrunken dimensions. Transfers of territory also made one state larger at the expense of another, as, for example, in the case of Romania, with its newly acquired postwar Transylvanian region.

The "war to end all wars" became the subject of several outstanding novels, among them the Romanian Zaharia Stancu's epic-picaresque *Jocul cu moartea* (*A Gamble with Death*, 1962) and especially the Serbian writer Dobrica Ćosić's (b. 1921) four-volume *Vreme smrti* (*A Time of Death*, originally published between 1972 and 1979). *A Gamble with Death* is essentially a picaresque novel about the escape from German imprisonment and subsequent travels through the war-torn Balkans of the central character of much of Stancu's prose fiction—his alter ego, Darie. Far broader in scope, Ćosić's *A Time of Death* chronicles the hardships of the Serbian nation during World War I. A Serbian patriot and nationalist, Ćosić, who held the office of president of the truncated Yugoslavia (consisting just of Serbia and Montenegro) from 1992 to 1993, delivers a stern indictment of high-placed political and military figures on both sides of the conflict whose policies brought untold suffering to millions of people. His is also a strong brief against the Western allies (England, France, and Italy), who seemed quite willing to abandon the Balkans. Only Russia, the longtime ally of Serbia, is depicted in a favorable light. The tetralogy ends with the defeat of the ill-equipped Serbian army and the grim retreat of the survivors through a perilous Albania. For Ćosić, World War I was the crucible in which the new state of the Serbs, Croats, and Slovenes, later to be known as Yugoslavia, was formed. The underlying message of *A Time of Death* was the natural right of the Serbs to hegemony among the southern Slavs, a right achieved through monumental suffering and sacrifice. Ćosić's championship of the Serb cause continued right down to the Balkan wars of the 1990s and his relatively brief tenure in the office of president of Serbia-Montenegro.

Notwithstanding the euphoria of postwar sovereignty, most of Eastern Europe experienced conditions of serious instability, politically and economically, in the interwar period. In most cases this instability led to a rise in nationalism and the ascendancy of right-wing and/or fascist regimes. For the Bulgarian writer in the communist era who had any interest in the interwar period, the singular political event of that time had to be the abortive communist uprising of September 1923 that followed the successful right-wing coup against the agrarian regime of Aleksandur Stambolinski on 9 June 1923. The events leading up to the September Uprising, as it came to be known, and its suppression by the new government of Aleksandur Tsankov—which dealt a crippling blow to the political left in interwar Bulgaria—served as the officially encouraged inspiration for many literary works. Typical was the much respected writer Emiliian Stanev's (1907–1979) historical romance, *Ivan Kondarev* (1958), about one of the leading figures of the uprising and for which Stanev was awarded the Dimitrov Prize.

The Distant and Far Distant Past

For many South Slavic writers, recollection of the past meant above all the national struggle against the centuries of Turkish oppression. Among Macedonians this is the principal thrust of historical fiction and poetry, as exemplified by the extraordinarily prolific and talented Slavko Janevski (1920–2000). One of Macedonia's most celebrated writers, Janesvki is credited with the authorship of the first novel in modern Macedonian, *Selo zad sedumte jaseni* (A Village Beyond the Seven Ash Trees, 1952). The author of a large body of poetry published between 1945 and 1992, Janevski also wrote a substantial number of novels. His outstanding achievement in this genre is the so-called Kukulino octology, which traces life in the archetypical Macedonian village of Kukulino from the year 700 to the future date of 2096. Two of the novels have been translated into English, *Čudotvorci* (*The Miracle Workers*, 1988) and *Devet Kerubinovi vekovi* (*The Nine Centuries of Kerubin*, 1986). Arguably the best novel in the octology, *The Miracle Workers* tells the story of Turkish assaults on the village of Kukulino in 1719 and the subsequent fate of the village. The events of 1719 comprise the bulk of the novel, which is divided into three major sections: "characters before events," wherein the main characters are introduced in the context of the rituals and legends by which the town lives; "events before the end," in which various legends and portentous events are narrated prior to the Turkish assault on Kukulino for the purpose of forcing its inhabitants to accept Islam; and "the end before oblivion," written in the style of an authentic old chronicle by a chronicler named Milentij Kletnik, and covering, year by year, everything that transpired in Kukulino from 1719 to 1756. Absent some interest in Macedonia, ancient or modern, Janevski's novel may not be to everyone's taste. But it is rich in color and handsomely narrated by a writer well able to bring the far distant past to life.

When we approach more modern times, nothing loomed larger to Macedonian writers of historical fiction than the Ilinden Uprising of 15 August 1903, the pivotal event in their national awakening. It was then that the Macedonians at last rose up against the Turks, succeeded in capturing the mountain town of Kruševo, and immediately thereafter declared Macedonia a republic. The air was full of idealistic rhetoric about revolutionary social goals, but the euphoria of Macedonian independence was short-lived. The new "republic" lasted just ten days. Although this episode is the subject of a number of works of fiction, none surpassed *Solunski atentatori* (The Assassins of Salonika, 1961) by Jovan Boškovski (1920–1968), whose collection of short stories, *Rastrel* (The Shot, 1947), has the distinction of being the first book of narrative prose to appear in the Macedonian language. The Assassins of Salonika is based on actual events and conceived in the style of a fast-paced conspiratorial novel, and Boškovski's main goal is to portray as faithfully as possible the mindset of the young Macedonian revolutionaries—who were in fact terrorists—as they knowingly set about undertaking actions that could result only in their deaths.

In the case of the Bulgarians, an even greater attraction for writers of historical fiction was the compelling and brilliant history of the first and second Bulgarian kingdoms (852–1018, 1185–1393), possibly the greatest gems of Slavic antiquity. This was clearly the case with Emiliian Stanev's later novel, *Legenda za Sibin, preslavskiia kniaz* (The Legend of Sibin, Prince of Preslav, 1974). Set in the time of the second Bulgarian kingdom, it deals with the dilemma of a ruler who was attracted neither to Orthodox Christianity nor to the rapidly spreading and influential Bogomil heresy, which essentially rejected Orthodox doctrine. The daughter of the prominent historian Petur Mutafchiev, Vera Mutafchieva (b. 1929), herself a well-known historian, also breathed new life into the genre of the historical novel. Her particular fields of interest were ancient Byzantium and nineteenth-century Bulgaria and Ottoman Turkey. *Letopis na smutnoto vreme* (Chronicle of the Time of Trouble), which deals with Rumelia in the time of the Turkish sultan Selim III (1789–1807), was published in 1965–1966. It was followed in rapid succession by such other historical novels with similar settings as *Sluchaiat Cem* (The Case of Cem, 1967), about Prince Cem, the son of the Turkish sultan Mehmed II (1459–1495), *Poslednite Shishmanovtsi* (The Last of the Shishmans, 1969), and *Ritsariat* (The Knight, 1970). In these historical novels as well as in her scholarly writing, Mutafchieva was one of the few Bulgarian intellectuals who demonstrated positive aspects of Ottoman rule in Bulgaria. Later Bulgarian history also drew her attention, as evidenced by the novel *Suedinenieto pravi silata* (Strength Through Union, 1985), which was based on the Serb-Bulgarian war of 1885.

Dimitur Mantov (b. 1930) has been by far the most prolific of the Bulgarian historical novelists. His best-known text in the genre of historical fiction, *Ludite glavi* (The Wild Ones, 1976), has as its subject the Bulgarian uprising of April 1876, a pivotal moment in the struggle for liberation from the Ottoman Turks and the development of a Bulgarian national consciousness. The Wild Ones forms a part of Mantov's huge family chronicle *Pradedi i pravnutsi* (Grandfathers and Grandsons, 1990), which also includes *Haidushka kruv* (A Brigand's Blood, 1969), *Zla zemia* (Bad Land, 1970), *Zubato sluntse*

(The Jagged Sun, 1975), and *Cherven kalendar* (Red Calendar, 1976). Mantov's other historical novels include *Ivan Asen II* (1960; Asen ruled from 1218 to 1241) and its sequel, *Ivan Asen II: Tsar i samodurets* (Ivan Asen II: Czar and Autocrat, 1970); *Kaloian, tsar na bulgarite* (Kaloian, Czar of the Bulgarians, 1969; Kaloian was the ruler of the second Bulgarian kingdom from 1197 to 1207); *Han Krum* (Khan Krum, 1973), based on the life of the early Bulgarian ruler who conquered Byzantium; *Albigoiska legenda* (The Albigensian Legend, 1974); *Kniaz Boris I* (Prince Boris I, 1978; ruled from 852 to 888); *Tsar Simeon* (Czar Simeon, 1979; ruled from 893 to 927); and *Tsar Petrovo vreme* (In the Time of Czar Petur, 1981; ruled from 927 to 970). Although Mantov later evolved into a more sophisticated writer with a greater interest in the psychology of his characters, much of his historical fiction is largely descriptive and shallow, though often immensely colorful.

The rich tapestry of Bosnian history and the country's predominantly Muslim population—so integral a part of the Ottoman Turkish world for so long—have provided fertile ground for modern Bosnian writers of historical fiction. The best known of these was Ivo Andrić (1892–1975), who was catapulted to international fame by his receipt of the Nobel Prize in Literature in 1961. Although raised and educated in Bosnia, Andrić was in fact born a Croat and baptized a Roman Catholic. Notwithstanding these facts, as well as his long identification with the Bosnian landscape and culture, he was appropriated by Serbia after his death and hailed as one of that country's greatest writers. But Andrić's credentials as a Bosnian writer are impeccable. In his youth he was imprisoned for his involvement in the nationalistic, anti-Habsburg Young Bosnia organization, which was implicated in the assassination of the Archduke Franz-Ferdinand and his wife in Sarajevo in 1914. In 1924 he earned a doctorate in history from the University of Graz (Austria) for his dissertation on the development of intellectual life in Bosnia under Turkish domination. During the German occupation of Belgrade in World War II, Andrić, who was living in the city at the time as an official of the Yugoslav Ministry of Foreign Affairs, was forced into virtual isolation in his apartment. He made superb use of the situation by undertaking his most important, and impressive, literary work, a huge trilogy of novels based on Bosnian history. The first novel remains his most acclaimed, *Na Drini ćuprija* (*The Bridge on the Drina*). It was followed by *Travnička hronika* (translated alternately as *Bosnian Chronicle, Bosnian Story*, or *The Days of the Consuls*), and, finally, *Gospodjica* (Miss; translated as *The Woman from Sarajevo*). All three volumes were published for the first time in 1945, the year World War II ended.

Andrić went on to write many more works, but the most memorable, above all from the viewpoint of his obvious affection for the Bosnian past, remains the so-called Bosnian trilogy. The best known novel of the trilogy, *The Bridge on the Drina,* handsomely exemplifies Andrić's ability to recreate the Bosnian past with color and remarkable narrative skill. The focus of the novel is the bridge over the Drina River in Travnik (Bosnia) that was built in the sixteenth century on order of a Turkish grand vizier. Andrić follows the intertwining of destinies of the bridge and the people whose lives it touches from its initial construction to the merciless pounding it received in World War I. *The Days of the Consuls*, the second part of the Balkan Trilogy, spans the seven-year period 1807–1814, when the Dalmatian littoral fell under French rule in the wake of Napoleon's conquests. The arrival in Travnik of a French consul was soon followed by the appearance of other consuls from such rival countries as Germany, Russia, and Austria. The interaction of the Europeans with one another, their relations individually and collectively with the Turkish viziers already in the town, and the reactions of the ethnically diverse townspeople to the foreign diplomats in their midst form the basis of the novel. In the third novel of the trilogy, *The Woman from Sarajevo*, history recedes in importance as Andrić's attention is drawn now to the moral tale of a woman whose desire to live frugally after her father's financial decline and premature death turns into a pathological love of money that condemns her to a life of solitude and ultimately destroys her.

Another renowned representative of Bosnian literature, Meša Selimović (1910–1982), also found literary glory in dredging the Bosnian past. Born in Tuzla, Bosnia, into a Muslim family, Selimović is justifiably regarded as one of the finest writers in Serbo-Croatian of the twentieth century. He attended Belgrade University in the 1930s, where he concentrated on the Serbo-Croatian language and Yugoslav literatures. During World War II he was captured by the Croatian Ustasha and imprisoned from September 1942 to January 1943. He then managed to escape and join Tito's partisan Yugoslav Army of National Liberation.

Selimović's fame, both nationally and internationally, rests principally on his novel *Derviš i smrt* (*Death and the Dervish*, 1966). Inspired in part by the court-martial and execution of his brother Šefkija Selimović, a partisan officer like himself, toward the end of 1944, the novel is set in the late period of Ottoman rule over Bosnia but alludes to the Yugoslavia of Selimović's own time. Using a stream-of-consciousness technique, Selimović weaves an intriguing tale of murky power politics as Ahmed Nuruddin, the head of an order of dervishes in Sarajevo, tries to free his brother, who has been arrested and is later killed by the local authorities for no valid reason. In the misguided belief that he can change the repressive system from within, Nuruddin eventually becomes a part of it, even reaching high office, but in the end is devoured by the system to which his brother fell victim.

Selimović won instant fame for this novel, which has been widely translated. He was made a member of the Serbian Academy of Arts and Sciences and of the Academy of Arts and Sciences of Bosnia and Herzegovina, and was awarded honorary doctorate degrees by the universities of Belgrade and Sarajevo. He also won a Njegoš Prize for his literary work in general and for *Death and the Dervish* in particular on 10 October 1969. Moreover, he was a candidate for a Nobel Prize in Literature.

In *Tišine* (Silences, 1961), which antedates *Death and the Dervish* by five years, Selimović recreates the historical atmosphere of the period immediately following World War II. The story pivots on the troubles experienced by a former soldier as he tries to adapt to the sweeping social changes in postwar Yugoslavia. A war veteran (Ahmet Šabo) also figures in *Trvava* (*The Fortress,* 1970), but the setting this time is the aftermath of the Battle of Khotin in the late seventeenth century and the veteran is a Bosnian Muslim who fought in the Ottoman Turkish army against the Russians. Narrated in the first person, the long novel chronicles the hardships of Šabo's life in Sarajevo after the war, various intrigues in the town, and conflicts with the religious hierarchy, which brooks no questioning of its authority (symbolized by the fortress that stands menacingly on a hill overlooking the town).

The Bosnian Dževad Karahasan (b. 1953), known best for his poignant account of the siege of Sarajevo during the Bosnian war of 1991–1995, *Dnevnik selidbe* (Diary of an Exodus, 1984; translated as *Sarajevo: Exodus of a City* (1994), reached farther back in time for his richly imaginative novel *Istočni divan* (The Oriental Divan). When it first appeared in 1989 it scored an immediate success and was honored as the best Yugoslav novel of the year. Set in Baghdad (the "new center of the world") in the eighth century, The Oriental Divan is a colorful mosaic of history, literature, and fable united in a historical novel that has as its leading figures such towering representatives of medieval Islamic culture as the writer al-Muqaffa, the mystic al-Hallag, and the philosopher at-Tauhidi. Although detached from anything specifically Bosnian, the work reflects the appeal of the ancient Middle East and its culture to a Bosnian Muslim writer like Karahasan.

That Bosnian poets would also have the same enthusiasm for the culture of the past as writers of prose fiction is amply demonstrated by perhaps the finest Bosnian poet of the century, Mak Dizdar (1917–1971; real name Mehmed Alija Dizdar). As a poet, Dizdar is esteemed above all for his book *Kameni spavač* (*Stone Sleeper*), which was originally published in 1966. A posthumous 1973 edition contains extensive revisions made by the author not long before his death. The lavish bilingual Serbo-Croatian–English edition of the book published in Sarajevo in 1999 is based on this revised text. The title *Stone Sleeper* alludes to the white limestone tombs of *krstjani* (Christians), followers of the schismatic medieval Bosnian church denounced and persecuted by the Orthodox and Roman Catholic religious establishments as a dualist heresy influenced by the ancient South Slavic Bogomil faith. Bosnian Muslims regard themselves as the direct spiritual and historical descendants of the medieval *krstjani,* whose separatist church survived until it was outlawed by the Bosnian king Stefan Tomaš in an effort to appease the Vatican and win its support in the campaign against the Turks. The tombs, or *stećci,* that dot the Bosnian landscape are inscribed with various enigmatic signs interpreted by Dizdar as the spirit of Bosnia expressed by means of an esoteric symbolism of mixed Christian and Islamic origin. Composed in elegantly simple verses of great metric and stanzaic variety, Dizdar's *Stone Sleeper* is an admirable work of poetic beauty and spiritual depth. It was preceded in 1960 by a collection of old Bosnian grave inscriptions, *Stari bosanski epitafi* (Old Bosnian Epitaphs), and followed in 1969 by a collection of old Bosnian texts, *Stari bosanski tekstovi* (Old Bosnian Texts).

The Croatian novelist Ivan Aralica, a native of Dalmatia—whom we met in chapter 1 as the author of the controversial World War II novel By Rows of Four (1997)—had acquitted himself far more impressively with a series of much-honored historical novels published between 1979 and 1986. Arguably the best of them, *Psi u trgovištu* (Dogs in a Marketplace, 1979) draws on old chronicles of Franciscan friars and travelers' diaries to paint a vivid picture of a Dalmatia caught in the crossfire of Ottoman Turkish and Venetian conflict during the sixteenth to eighteenth centuries. Similarly colorful and intriguing in their narrative design are such subsequent novels as *Put bez sna* (Dreamless Journey, 1982), *Duše robova* (The Souls of Slaves, 1984), *Graditelj svratišta* (The Inn Builder, 1986), and *Asmodejev šal* (Asmodey's Shawl, 1988), in which Aralica follows the fortunes of a Croatian family from seventeenth-century Ottoman-Venetian warfare through the early nineteenth century, when Dalmatia fell under Napoleon's control. In 1994 Aralica returned to an earlier period of Croatian history with his novel *Knjiga gorkog prijekora* (A Book of Bitter Reproach), about Zadar under Venetian rule in the fourteenth century. Although Aralica has many admirers in his native Croatia, there are those who have expressed reservations concerning the conservative Christian and Catholic sensibility permeating much of his writing.

Like the South Slavs, the Albanians also endured Turkish rule for many centuries, and made it the principal focus of their own historical fiction. This fiction rarely reaches back to the early periods of Turkish domination but instead concentrates on events related to the Rilindja, or Renaissance, of the late nineteenth century. Novels by Sterjo Spasse (1914–1989), written well after the end of World War II, are typical in this respect. In *Pishtarë* (Torches, 1975), the first of his Rilindja cycle *Rilindasit* (literally, Representatives of the [Albanian] Renaissance), Spasse's concern is primarily with the ethnic, political, and religious dimensions of the struggle that culminated in the declaration of Albanian independence in 1912. His subsequent novel, *Kryengritësit* (The Insurgents, 1983), focuses instead on the military aspect of the anti-Turkish insurgency that began with the formation of the Albanian League of Prizren (Kosovo) of 1878–1881. The avowed purpose of the league was the unification of all Albanians in a single autonomous state within the Ottoman Empire. A leading representative of socialist realism, Spasse began his career as a writer in the 1930s.

Although interesting for their historical details, his Rilindja cycle falls much below the literary level of his first novel, *Nga jeta në jetë: Pse?* (From One Year to the Next: Why?), which first appeared in 1935 and in some ways still remains Spasse's major contribution to Albanian literature. But in the light of the harsh criticism of the novel by communist critics because of its alleged nihilism and despair, Spasse must have felt that it behooved him in the Enver Hoxha era to create positive heroes in the style of socialist realism, hence his historical cycle and his later novels about a socialist heroine, the schoolteacher Afërdita, who brings enlightenment to a backward Albanian village. *Ata nuk ishin vetëm* (They Weren't Alone, 1952), which won the Prize of the Republic, is arguably Spasse's best postwar work. It is set in the interwar era and deals specifically with the peasant disturbances of 1934–1936, in which the communists played an active role.

Among Polish writers of historical fiction, the names Andrzej Kuśniewicz (1904–1993), Antoni Gołubiew (1907–1974), and Teodor Parnicki (1908–1988) stand out prominently. With an ancient history less resplendent than that of the Bulgarians, the Poles tended to focus on the tenth and eleventh centuries, which was the early, formative period of the Polish state under the Piast kings. This Polish historical fiction began first appearing immediately after World War II, when the uncertain political climate tended to favor literary works with innocuous, remote settings. But there was more to the cultivation of this genre than just a strategy of censorship evasion. In the immediate aftermath of the war, the Poles were moved to recall past episodes of German aggression and successful Polish resistance. The shifting of the Polish borders from east to west in fulfillment of the Yalta agreements also validated historical fiction depicting the territorial expansion of the early Piast state.

In his multivolume *Bolesław Chrobry* (Bolesław the Brave, 1947), one of the first major historical novels to appear in the postwar period, Gołubiew tapped into these various currents. He tended for the most part to stick close to the documented history but still managed to generate controversy through his bold linguistic stylization. Although dealing with the same historical period, Teodor Parnicki's novel *Srebrne orły* (Silver Eagles, first published in Jerusalem in 1944 and in Poland in 1949) was set in the much broader context of medieval Europe as a whole. The great breadth of Parnicki's historical fiction was in fact its most distinguishing feature. This is true not only for his novels with Polish settings but even more so for such historical novels of non-Polish content as his esteemed *Słowo i ciało* (The Word and the Flesh, 1959), a fanciful work about a man of Persian-Greek origin detained by the Romans in early-third-century Alexandria, and *Twarz księżyca* (The Face of the Moon, 1961), set at the turn of the third and fourth centuries A.D. in Choresm, near the Caspian Sea, Illyria, and Rome.

Parnicki seemed to reach his zenith in the 1960s, when perhaps his greatest historical novel, the multivolume *Nowa baśń* (A New Fairy Tale), began appearing. Consisting of six volumes published between 1962 and 1970, the immense novel projects Polish eleventh- and twelfth-century history onto a vast canvas extending from Novgorod to Ireland. Apart from Parnicki's use of medieval literature and chronicles as well as Celtic and Scandinavian tales, the novel also reflects the time Parnicki spent in Mexico, first as a refugee from the German occupation of Poland and then, in 1944/1945, as the cultural attaché of the Polish Embassy. Keenly interested in ancient Mexican culture and mythology, Parnicki used this background in the composition of A New Fairy Tale. While working on A New Fairy Tale, Parnicki still found time to publish two other works in the historical vein, *I u możnych dziwny* (The Powerful Too Are Strange, 1965), with a seventeenth-century setting, and *Koła na piasku* (Wheels in the Sand, 1966), dealing with the rise and fall of Hellenistic culture in Asia and set in the year 160 B.C.

Although he began his literary career at the age of fifty-two, Andrzej Kuśnie-wicz more than made up for his late start. Apart from four volumes of po-etry, he published eleven novels between 1963 and 1987, most notably *Eroica* (1963); *W drodze do Koryntu* (On the Way to Corinth, 1964); *Król obojga Sycylii* (*The King of the Two Sicilies*, 1970), which won the Seguyr Prize for the most outstanding foreign novel published in France that year; *Stan nieważkości* (State of Weightlessness, 1973); *Trzecie królestwo* (The Third Kingdom, 1975); *Lekcja martwego języka* (Lesson of a Dead Language, 1977); and *Nawrócenie* (Conversion, 1987). The elegantly written *King of the Two Sicilies* is Kuśnie-wicz's acknowledged masterpiece and his only work translated into English. In it Kuśniewicz trained his sights on a period he knew well, the twilight years of the Habsburg Empire and World War I. Sweeping with light, deft strokes across the panorama of events leading up to the war, Kuśniewicz lavishes much attention on the colorful, multiethnic Habsburg military on the eve of its last hurrah. At the same time, he delicately balances the novel's inner psychologi-cal drama—the incestuous relationship between a young, well-born, and effete Viennese officer in the elite Twelfth Regiment of the King of the Two Sicilies and his headstrong, domineering sister—and the mystery surrounding the mur-der of a young Gypsy girl. The officer's suicidal jump from a moving train on the way to the front at the end of the novel seems to epitomize the passing of an imperial culture as irrelevant as the Kingdom of the Two Sicilies itself.

The historical genre was reasonably well represented also in Slovak litera-ture, especially by the prolific and highly respected Milan Ferko (b. 1929). His first historical novel, *Krádež svätoštefanskiej koruny* (The Theft of the Crown of St. Stefan), appeared in 1970. It deals, perhaps unexpectedly, with the relation-ship between Queen Elizabeth I of England and her chambermaid. Although it enjoyed a good reception, it was in fact the only historical novel by Ferko set outside of his native Slovakia. In 1975 Ferko published *Svätopluk*, the first volume of a trilogy based on the life of Svätopluk, duke of Moravia (d. 894). The remaining two volumes of the trilogy are *Svätopluk a Metod: Oheň života, oheň skazy* (Svätopluk and Methodius: Fire of Life, Fire of Devastation, 1985), dealing with the relations between the ruler of the Great Moravian state and Saint Methodius, Apostle to the Slavs (ca. 824–884/885), and *Svätoplukovo dedičstvo* (The Legacy of Svätopluk, 1989). By subordinating the Christianizing mission of Saints Cyril and Methodius in the Great Moravian Kingdom to the political crosscurrents of the time, Ferko played up the acceptance of the Slavic liturgical language devised by Cyril and Methodius as a necessary strategy against the further encroachment of German religious and political interests in the region. Ferko's other historical writing includes the intriguing novel *Medzi ženou a Rímom* (Between Woman and Rome, 1980), about the sojourn of the Roman emperor Marcus Aurelius in the land that became Slovakia.

In general the bulk of Ferko's historical fiction should be seen in the context of his deep commitment to the promotion of what may be called, for want of a better term, Slovakdom. He was a vigorous promoter, for example, of the richness of the Slovak language, as in *Prvá láska nastorako* (First Love Askew, 1989). His 1994 book, *Stary narod, mladý štát* (Old Nation, Young State), remains his sole work available in English (as *Slovak Republic: Old Nation, Young State*). In *Otváranie studničiek* (The Opening of the Wells, 1988) he celebrated the self-sacrificing devotion of Slovak womanhood against the background of historical events in the early twentieth century. Further books by Ferko on Slovak themes include *Sto slávnych Slovákov* (One Hundred Famous Slovaks, 1995); *Šestdesiat jeden krokov k slovenskej identite: Zvrchované Slovensko* (Sixty-One Steps to Slovak Identity: A Sovereign Slovakia, 1996), a collection of documents of which he was one of three contributors; and *Slováci a mad'ari: Subor študii* (Slovaks and Hungarians: A Collection of Studies, 1996). Apart from his historical fiction, Ferko was also a historian and in 1990 published *Velkomoravské záhady* (Great Moravian Puzzles), an account of Moravia from earliest times to the year 906.

Another Slovak writer, L'udo Zúbek (1907–1969), also commanded attention for his cultivation of the biography as a type of historical writing. His first work in this genre was the novella *Oltar majstera Pavla* (The Altar of Master Paul, 1956), based on the life of the creator of the splendid altar in the church of Saint Jacob in the culturally important Slovak town of Levoča. Master Paul also happened to have been a student of the renowned Wit Stwosz, the artist responsible for the celebrated triptych in the Church of Mary in Kraków, Poland. Zúbek's yet more impressive biography of Doctor Jesenius (*Doktor Jesenius*, 1973), the rector of Prague University in the early days of the Thirty-Year War, presented a broad canvas of contemporary Prague life interspersed with the complexities of confessional, political, and national concerns. Zúbek's pseudo-memoir based on the life of L'udovít Štúr, the codifier of the Slovak literary language and the man esteemed as the father of his nation, appeared in 1957 under the title *Jar Adely Ostrolúckej* (The Spring of Adela Ostrolúcka).

Zúbek's other major contribution to the historical-biographical genre is *Farebný sen* (The Colored Dream, 1965), actually a new version of his biographical novel of 1938 originally published as *Ján Kupecký*. Kupecký (1667–1740) was a prolific and highly regarded Czech portraitist born into a family of (Protestant) Czech Brethren who were persecuted in the Czech lands for their religious beliefs. The noteworthy feature of The Colored Dream is that, in a deviation from most biographical novels, Zúbek drew primarily on his imagination to compensate for the relative paucity of factual data about his subject. In Zúbek's version, Kupecký's life—for which he had only the meager sketch written by Kupecký's much younger assistant, Caspar Füssli, to rely on for basic facts—was one of many trials and ultimate success. Separated from his family at an early age, married to a much younger woman of another religion who bears him two children (who eventually die) and who proves unfaithful to him, Kupecký was forced to flee the religious intolerance of Vienna at the time and to struggle to make his own way as an artist. Zúbek's choice of narrative strategy enhances, as it were, the authenticity of his novel. Kupecky's world is portrayed through the eyes of the artist himself in a highly subjective, fragmentary, at times chronologically disjointed style as he reviews his life near the moment of his passing from it.

Another period of interest to Slovak historical writers, such as Rudo Moric (1921–1985), was the Spring of Nations of 1848, when Slovaks placed themselves on the side of the Habsburgs, ultimately to no avail. The interest in this event was shared as well by Romanian writers, such as, for example, Camil Petrescu (1894–1957), whose three-volume novel *Un om între oameni* (A Man Amongst Men, 1955–1957) pivots on the central figure of the scholar and political figure Nicolae Bălcescu (1819–1852) against the background of the revolution of 1848 in Wallachia. Petrescu had previously also made Bălcescu the subject of his play *Bălcescu* (1949).

A multifaceted writer who at one time practiced journalism in Bucharest while pursuing a sports career as a soccer player and coach, Eugen Barbu (1924–1993) also held impeccable Communist Party credentials. He was a member of the Central Committee of the Party and, for several years, editor in chief of the important cultural and political weekly *Săptămînă*. The well-known Romanian émigré writer Norman Manea refers to him as the "socialist boss" of *Săptămînă* in his book *On Clowns: The Dictator and the Artist* (1992). Barbu's reputation as a writer was established by his first major literary success, the social novel *Groapa* (The Hollow, 1957), and was reaffirmed by arguably his best work of prose, *Princepele* (The Prince, 1968). Set in the time of the Phanariot rulers of Romania (1711–1821), this richly evocative historical novel—which combines much authentic data with fictional elements—assumes the character of a parable on political power with contemporary relevance. Barbu's interest in the subject of The Prince did not end with publication of the novel. In 1972 he began publishing a series of source materials for the novel under the title *Caietele princepelui* (The Prince Notebooks) and in 1975 also brought out a collection of stories, *Miresele* (The Bride and Groom), related to The Prince. Considering his novel primarily a "historical compilation," Barbu stressed that his aim was to write a symbolic tale in which all of Romanian history would be encapsulated in an epoch of servitude, referring to the impoverishment of Romania by the Phanariotes. The prince himself is meant to typify all the negative qualities of the Phanariote rulers of Moldavia and Wallachia in the period 1711–1821. Barbu again took up Romanian history, this time in the twentieth century, in 1976 in the first volume of a massive tetralogy to which he gave the title *Încognito: Cine-roman* (Incognito: A Cinema Novel). The tetralogy represents a nationalistically colored overview of Romanian history between 1914 and 1944. The last volume appeared in 1980. The novel has proven somewhat controversial in the light of suspicions of plagiarism on Barbu's part.

An even more massive undertaking, but one happily free of Romanian nationalism à la Barbu, is the ongoing cycle of historical novels, projected to range in time from ancient Babylonia to the twentieth century, by Gheorghe Schwartz (b. 1945). A former cultural attaché of the Romanian Embassy in Bonn, Germany, in 1992 and 1993, and currently dean of the Faculty of Humanities and Social

Sciences in the University of Aurel Vlaicu in Arad (his native city), Schwartz has had a productive career as a writer since the appearance of his first novel *Martorul* (The Witness) in 1972. The volumes published so far in the historical cycle include *Cei o suta: Anabasis* (The Hundred: Anabasis, 1988); *Cei o suta: Ecce homo* (The Hundred: Ecce homo, 1993); *Oul de aur* (The Golden Egg, 1998), for which Schwartz won the Writers' Union prize for prose; and *Mâna albă* (The White Hand, 2000). Noteworthy above all for its colorful characters, plot complexities, and Schwartz's grasp of history, the series still has a long way to go before completion. The most recent volume, The White Hand, covers the period A.D. 471–768, that is, from the fall of Rome to Charlemagne.

Among former East German writers who cultivated the genre of historical fiction, perhaps the most interesting is Martin Stade. His literary debut in 1971 was the appearance of the historical novel *Meister von Sanssouci* (Master of Sanssouci). Stade was keenly interested in the nature of relations between artists and intellectuals, on the one hand, and political authority on the other. In his competently written, and interesting, Master of Sanssouci he draws a contrast between the imperious and obstinate Prussian ruler Friedrich II (the Great) and the young and talented architect G. W. von Knobelsdorf, who embellished the design of the splendid Sanssouci Palace in Potsdam. Stade explored a similar theme in his highly praised *Der König und sein Narr* (The King and His Jester, 1975), in which he develops the portrait of the academician Jacob Paul von Grundling, who, as he is about to die, reviews his life from its peak—when he was president of the Academy of Sciences—to his fall to the status of court jester. A professor of history, law, and literature, Grundling encounters an antagonist at court who is none other than the new king, Friedrich Wilhelm I. The tug of war between the two men is rooted in Grundling's unwillingness to compromise his ideas and ideals and the king's desire to transform him into an intellectual lackey. Although easily read as a commentary on the state of culture in the German Democratic Republic in Stade's time there, the novel is compelling reading even without any contemporary political interpretation. In 1981 The King and His Jester was made into a successful film in West Germany under the direction of Frank Beyer. Stade's other historical novels include *Der närrische Krieg* (The Foolish War, 1981) and two works based on the life of Bach, *Junge Bach* (Young Bach, 1985) and *Zwischen Schlehdorn und Paradies: Der junge Bach* (Between Schlehdorn and Paradise: The Young Bach, 1990).

Allegory

The domestic fame of the Czech dramatist Milan Uhde (b. 1949) rests mostly on his 1964 cabaret-like farce *Král Vávra* (King Vávra), subtitled *Nonstop Nonsense*. It was inspired by the epic poem *Král Lávra* (King Lávra, 1854) by the Czech writer Karel Havlíček Borovský (1821–1856). Borovský's poem is in turn an adaptation of an Irish folktale called *The King with the Horse's Ears*. Neither Borovský nor Uhde altered the original Irish setting of their works.

Czech features are absent in both texts, although the allegorical subtext is obvious in each. Borovský was a major figure in the Czech national revival movement of the nineteenth century, which sought to resuscitate the nearly moribund Czech language and restore dignity once again to a Czech culture that had suffered gravely under centuries of Habsburg rule. To Borovský, and indeed to other contemporary Czech revivalists, obvious parallels existed between the Czechs and the Irish. Both peoples were proud of their ancient heritages, but had been struggling for a very long period of time—politically, culturally, and linguistically—under foreign imperial rule. British imperialism had imposed colonial rule over the Irish; Habsburg imperialism had reduced the Czechs to a distinctly inferior status within the realm and had pursued a policy of eradicating Czech identity by means of an aggressive policy of Germanization.

Although Uhde was uncomfortable with any allegorical interpretation of King Vávra as a political satire aimed at Soviet imperialism, especially in the Stalinist period, and Soviet-style totalitarianism in Czechoslovakia, such a reading is impossible to avoid. Now instead of Habsburg imperialism being the target, it is Soviet imperialism, which, Uhde infers, is another colonial power. Uhde has tailored his play to the times. King Vávra, who in fact is not of royal lineage at all, but a former peasant who was chosen for the position because his first name just happened to be "král" ("king"), is a close relative of Alfred Jarry's justifiably famous Ubu Roi. He is ruler of half the world, with the other half ruled by the English. In one of the more resonant absurdist elements in the play, the operations of King Vávra's realm are directed not from some super-high-tech center, but from a drab little office where ordinary household items take the place of sophisticated machinery. The implied commentary by Uhde on the national mood of submissiveness and complacency in Czechoslovakia in the 1960s easily accords with other texts from the same period aimed at exposing the inability of the individual to influence history. Cynicism, materialism, opportunism, and the standardization, and indeed mechanization, of human existence have taken complete hold of society. Life truly has become "nonstop nonsense," as the play's subtitle informs.

When King Vávra opened at the satirical theater Večerní Divadlo in the Moravian capital of Brno within three months of Václav Havel's *The Garden Party*, it was an immense success. No matter how much Uhde cautioned against interpreting the absurdist play as political allegory, it was widely so understood by audiences. Further enhancing its appeal was Uhde's use of cabaret and music hall techniques in the tradition of the famous Prague theater of the 1930s of Jiří Voskovec and Jan Werich ("V+W").

Uhde also drew inspiration from antiquity for his second allegorical play, *Děvka z města Théby* (The Wench from the Town of Thebes, 1967). A free adaptation of Sophocles's tragedy *Antigone,* in Uhde's hands it became a parable on power and the failure of idealism. When Antigone defies Creon and has her brother Polyneices buried—in defiance of Creon's order and as a direct challenge to his authority—Antigone fully expects to be punished. She is thus willing to sacrifice herself to achieve her goal of toppling Creon, whom she holds responsible for the decline of morality in Thebes. But not only does Creon not have her punished, he praises her courage and in a surprise twist begs her to kill him as punishment for his misdeeds. He confesses his wrongdoing and the weakness that has brought about the ruination of his own once-lofty ambitions. In another reversal, Antigone refuses to murder him, as she had planned, seeing Creon's death as now futile and a betrayal of her own earlier idealism. She becomes instead a disillusioned skeptic, abandoning any hope of achieving change in the fortunes of the state. Seeking happiness in sensual pleasures, she becomes a whore.

When Pavel Kohout was asked in 1962 to write a play for the beleaguered Vinohrady theater in Prague, he said he preferred doing an adaptation, as that was less likely to create problems with the censors. Indeed, several of Kohout's greatest successes as a playwright were adaptations of works by Chekhov, Jules Verne, Karel Čapek, Jaroslav Hašek, and Leonid Andreev. When Kohout's new play was ready it was titled *August August, August*. It opened at the Vinohrady on 12 May 1967. Often interpreted as a political allegory, the play is set in a circus reminiscent of Andreev's most famous play internationally, *He Who Gets Slapped*. In the Russian play the central figure of the tragi-comic clown becomes a laughingstock by virtue of the slaps he receives in abundance. Beholding the humiliation of the clown, who must grin through it all, the audience delights in feelings of superiority. Kohout has preserved this element of the Russian play. His clown, August, hardly steps into the ring before he is slapped by the Circus Manager. Other circus personnel also slap him. But through it all, August never caves in, his joy of life nurtured by his dream of training eight white Lipizzaner horses for a special dressage act. This is the climax of each show, and as a rule is reserved for the Manager. Because of declining attendance, however, the Manager decides to let August take over on this one occasion. The fact that he knows nothing about horses has no place in August's thinking—or, better said, daydreaming.

The allegorical dimension of the play relates to the way August's supreme ambition is treated by his superiors. They never discourage him, and neither do they ridicule him. Instead they feed his ambition incrementally, having him perform a series of tasks to amuse the public before letting him handle the dressage. At last August is given his great chance. With his wife and son looking on, he is outfitted with a top hat, tails, and a whip. While the preparations for the dressage are being made, a huge cage is set up and the roar of beasts is heard from offstage. As the performance is about to begin, the Circus Manager warns August that a dream should remain just that; otherwise it will be killed. August indicates that he does understand, although his literalmindedness and naiveté negate that possibility. All he has on his mind is the fulfillment of his dream—the performance with the eight white Lipizzaners. But instead of horses, wild beasts rush toward August as the lights go out and a horrendously loud drum roll reverberates through the big tent. A few seconds later, the lights come on again, but August is no longer among the performers, who take their bows from an empty ring. The performance, and play, end with the parting words of the

Circus Manager, who wishes the audience well on its way home. The allegorical implications of Kohout's play, one of his most successful, are unmistakable. The Circus Manager embodies the cynical exploitativeness of the powerful, who manipulate the idealism of others as it suits them. But when this idealism threatens to get out of hand, it is as mercilessly snuffed out as Kohout's clown. Apart from its underlying premise, August August, August is an appealing circus play full of verbal gags and clownish routines.

In the case of the Albanian writer Ismail Kadare, a classical legend, this time that of the Trojan horse, was referenced directly and then decked out in modern dress. *Përbindëshi* (The Monster)—originally written in 1965 (and thus one of Kadare's earliest prose works), almost immediately banned, and republished only in 1991—is set in Tirana, the Albanian capital, in the 1960s. In an approach unlike Uhde's, Kadare calls attention to his referent, the *Iliad*, throughout his book. The modern-day Helen of Troy is the fiancée of the inspector of museums who runs off with a young man named Gent Ruvina, a student of philosophy who has just returned from Moscow as a result of the worsening relations between Albania and the USSR. The heroine (Lena) is from a small town where all blondes named Lena began to be called Helen of Troy after the showing of a movie based on the story of the Trojan horse. While Lena and Gent carry on, an old police wagon concealing a group of men, including the jilted museum inspector, sits a few kilometers from the center of Tirana, awaiting the moment when they can enter the city and turn it to rubble.

Kadare has thus intertwined the classical story of the *Iliad* with one about the rising paranoia in official circles and beyond after the break with the Soviet Union. The mere suspicion that this modernized version of the *Iliad*, which at times moves back and forth from classical antiquity to Albania in the 1960s, had more to do with Stalinist Albania than with Homer's time was enough to warrant its suppression. That a text like this could even emerge at the height of socialist realism in Albania must have seemed strange. A scholar of classical antiquity with a commendable knowledge of Greek, ancient and modern, Kadare might well have assumed that The Monster would arouse little suspicion in the light of his classical interests. But its distance from the norms of socialist realism and the allusions to contemporary Albanian political events in the novel rang enough alarms to cause problems with the censors almost from the moment of its publication in the official Tirana literary journal *Nëntori*.

Kadare was also the author of a much later political allegory, *Piramida* (The Pyramid, 1993). In its original form it was a short story serialized in the initial issues of the first Tirana opposition newspaper, *Rilindja Demokratike*, in January 1991; once in exile in Paris, Kadare expanded it to novel length. One of Kadare's most effective, and impressive, works of fiction, *The Pyramid* is set in ancient Egypt, in the time of the pharaoh Cheops. The short novel recounts the original intention of Cheops to break with previous pharaonic tradition by not ordering the construction of a pyramid in his own honor. But he eventually yields to the influence of the high priest Hemiunu, who convinces him that the pyramid will be

Your Secret Police. Your army, Your navy, Your sweet-smelling harem. The higher it rises, the weaker the citizen will seem beneath its shadow. And the smaller your citizen, the higher you, and your power, become. . . . The pyramid is the pillar that holds power high. If it wavers, everything collapses.[2]

And so with the pharaoh's blessings, work on the pyramid was begun. Hundreds of thousands of workers were pressed into the construction of the stupendous project, and word of it spread far and wide. Very soon, however, delays and other problems beset the undertaking and were attributed to conspiracies. There were many investigations and arrests, and even Hemiunu was replaced. But as work continued and the pyramid rose ever taller, the mood of the people turned more fearful, as they were overwhelmed by the unnatural immensity of the structure and believed that it was destined to consume all Egypt. Moreover, the pharaoh himself had fallen into a state of mental derangement over it. His death came exactly three years after the great pyramid that was to be his tomb was completed. The last pages of the novel describe the ravages visited on the pyramid by time.

Were Kadare a Romanian writer, one could easily imagine that the target of his allegorical novel was the great white elephant, the "Palace of the People," raised in Bucharest on the ruins of an enormous swath of the city by command of the (later-executed) dictator Nicolae Ceaușescu. But Kadare is Albanian, not Romanian, and the allegory in *The Pyramid* aims squarely at the Enver Hoxha Museum, which was erected on the main square of Tirana to the memory of the communist dictator before the collapse of the regime. The huge white marble edifice, very much resembling a modernistic pyramid (and often referred to as "Pyramid"), still stands, of course; but the huge red star of plastic that once crowned it was removed in the aftermath of the regime's downfall. The "Pyramid" is now Tirana's International Center of Culture.

A less obvious type of allegory is pursued in a few works by the internationally respected Polish journalist Ryszard Kapuściński (1932–2007). Imbued with a passion for faraway places and revolutionary strife, above all in the Third World, Kapuściński has become undoubtedly the most acclaimed and most widely translated writer of reportage in Poland (and indeed Eastern Europe as a whole) since 1945. A lover of adventure, he threw himself into the heart of the action from one end of the globe to the other. His success as a writer of reportage rests on his keen eye for the ironic and grotesque and his ability to get people from all walks of life to open up to him. Much of his story-writing is woven out of such interviews. Kapuściński first achieved fame with *Cesarz* (Emperor, 1978; translated as *The Emperor: Downfall of an Autocrat*), about the downfall in 1974 of the last emperor of Ethiopia, Haile Selassie I (1892–1975). It was followed by such equally successful books of reportage as *Szachinszach* (*Shah of Shahs*, 1982), covering the collapse of the Iranian regime of the last shah, Mohammed Reza Pahlavi (1919–1980); *Jeszcze dzień życia* (*Another Day of Life*, 1986), on the revolution in Angola in the late 1960s and '70s;

Wojna futbolowa (*The Soccer War,* 1987), about a war between Honduras and San Salvador (the title piece of the collection) as well as upheavals in Ghana, Nigeria, Mozambique, the Congo, and Algeria; and *Imperium* (1993), which chronicles the final years of the Soviet Union.

The two books by Kapuściński that lend themselves most to interpretation as political allegory are *The Emperor* and *Shah of Shahs.* Both seem directed at Edward Gierek (1913–2001), a longtime communist who in 1970 replaced Władysław Gomułka as head of the party and the government following the workers' riots of that year. His scheme to solve the country's dire economic problems by undertaking an overly ambitious program of industrialization only served to worsen matters. Poland became heavily debt-ridden and in 1980 also began experiencing food shortages. In August of that same year, Lech Wałęsa, now the head of the Solidarity union with a huge membership, led the famous Gdańsk shipyard strike, which sparked a series of strikes throughout the country. The agreement signed by the regime and Solidarity on 31 August 1980 recognized the right of Polish workers to strike and to organize their own independent union. Fearing possible Soviet intervention over the turn of developments in Poland, General Wojciech Jaruzelski replaced Gierek as head of the party in Poland and imposed martial law in December 1981, at the same time declaring Solidarity an illegal organization. Both of Kapuściński's works, *The Emperor* and *Shah of Shahs,* are built around the central figure of a vain, imperious ruler who tolerates no opposition and has become gravely out of touch with his people.

Utopian fiction, which was reasonably well cultivated by Eastern European writers in the communist period and which may be regarded as a genre closely related to allegory, had a major representative in the Hungarian writer Tibor Déry (1894–1977). One of the outstanding Hungarian writers of the twentieth century, Déry began writing as early as 1917 and scored his first major success with the novel *A befejezetlen mondat* (The Unfinished Sentence) in 1949. In this work as well as in his next novel, *Felelet* (The Answer, 1951), Déry dealt, respectively, with the interwar Hungarian bourgeoisie and with the working class. Communist Party dissatisfaction with Déry's perspective on the Hungarian workers' movement—it was denounced as harmful by the then Hungarian Minister of Culture, József Révai—as well as his increasingly activist role in events leading up to the Hungarian Revolution of October 1956—set the stage for Déry's imprisonment from 1957 to 1960. While serving his prison term, which lasted longer than many had expected and which brought forth appeals for his release from writers' groups around the world, Déry had ample time to continue literary activity, so long as writing implements were supplied him. Two of the most important works he managed to complete during his incarceration were the autobiographical *Börtönnapok hordáleká: Önéletrajzi jegyzetek* (Prison Days Deposits: Autobiographical Notes) and a huge dystopian novel, *G.A. úr X.-ben* (Mr. G.A. in X., 1964).

Despite his fine reputation in Hungary, Déry has not been widely translated. Apart from a couple of collections of short stories, he is known in English principally as the author of the novel *Niki, egy kutya története* (*Niki: The Story of a Dog,* 1956). It was based on Déry's relationship with his own pet. He has fared somewhat better in other languages (French, German, Italian, Russian), in which, perhaps curiously, his best-known work is Mr. G. A. in X.

Mr. G. A. in X. employs the familiar strategy of the publication of someone else's manuscript, in this case an old school friend (Mr. G. A.) of Déry's who abandoned Paris at a certain point, leaving in Déry's care a manuscript, entitled "Mr. G. A. in X.," about his subsequent adventures. Déry was supposed to destroy the manuscript after reading it, but instead hung onto it for some twenty years before finally deciding to release it for publication. Composed in the 1920s, "Mr. G. A. in X." is a long, densely detailed account of Mr. G. A.'s journey from Europe to a place called X., to which he was able to take a train up to a certain point but then had to proceed on foot for fifteen days. The city of X. and surrounding landscape are drab and depressing, to say the least. When he inquires after a hotel, he is told that with the possible exception of the Excelsior, which has twenty pleasant rooms, all the others are closed. On the way there, he stops at a huge restaurant, where a few tables are occupied by solitary diners who seem to eat rapidly and leave immediately after the last bite. Service is unbelievably slow and a menu is nonexistent. Instead G. A. is given the only meal apparently available—soup served in a white iron bowl, a piece of sour-smelling meat covered with a grayish sauce on a cracked porcelain plate, and a paper-thin slice of bread. When G. A. asks if anything else is available he is told that this is all they have been serving for some years. When G. A. continues his search for a hotel, he eventually comes across the gigantic and grand Hotel Astoria, but is struck by the virtual absence of people. This and other oddities (elevators, for example, that do not indicate the floor) establish the absurd nature of life in X., where people actually dislike the sun and have no idea of spring, and where it rains much of the time.

Déry's own prison experiences are reflected in Mr. G. A. in X. in the rather long episode in chapter 16 involving the narrator's visit to a certain Mr. Bowen, who was incarcerated on the charge of having committed the most serious crime in a civilized society—the limitation of another person's individual freedom. Mr. Bowen's crime is in keeping with the absurdity of Déry's novel as a whole. After perceiving what he interpreted as a decline in his young wife's romantic interest in him, Mr. Bowen stopped eating and sleeping, lost weight, and infected those around him with his own sadness. The specific criminal act for which he was imprisoned was that on the pretext of being unable to live without his wife, he ever so tenderly persuaded her not to die, thus curtailing her individual liberty! The absurdity is compounded by the description of the circumstances of Mr. Bowen's imprisonment. He is treated deferentially, lives and eats well, and, like the other prisoners, is free to leave and return at will. But he has no desire to leave since he has no craving for freedom. As he declares to a prison official present at the time: "It is in your establishment that I have come to understand what it is to live in a manner worthy of a man. I would never have believed that a prison sentence could have a beneficial and educative effect on the wayward soul of a criminal." When the narrator asks him if he never desires to return to a free life, he replies: "Man was not created to be free, my dear sir." "But what will happen when you are old?," inquires the narrator. Mr. Bowen's answer is: "We will never die! And if we never die, why should we grow old? Isn't that so? Death is nothing but a superstition, sir, the same as unhappy love. The intelligent man can readily do without both of them."[3]

A less ponderous, less confusing, and in some ways more successful Hungarian allegorical novel was the hugely popular *Epepe* (1970) by the popular writer Ferenc Karinthy. A linguist by training, Karinthy used his novel to bring his discipline into the realm of fiction. The protagonist of the novel is none other than a linguist named Budai, who is on his way to a conference in Helsinki, Finland. But he mysteriously lands in another city, where people speak a strange language that he cannot identity. Nevertheless, things go well enough for him in the beginning, as he relies on gestures to communicate. When he begins exploring the city, it seems normal enough, except for the fact that there is a steady stream of pedestrians moving through the streets. At one point he is carried along by the crowd into a sports arena (in a further reflection of Karinthy's own interest in sports), where a strange ball game is being played that involves several teams and at least eight balls and where Budai has trouble differentiating one opponent from another.

Other strange occurrences follow: a nightclub where each customer is limited to a ten-minute stay; a cathedral where believers are led up to the steeple as part of the service; his hotel bill has no date; a newspaper without a title page; an elevator girl whom he enlists in his effort to learn something about the exotic language but who never pronounces words the same way twice; the discovery of a Hungarian theater journal that has been out of print for thirty years on the stairs of a metro station he enters; the mysterious man he tries to stop in the metro but who disappears, quickly having spoken just the words, "You too?" During a blackout at his hotel, Budai has sex with the elevator girl, who has come to his room and with whom he finds he is able to communicate. By now, however, Budai has run out of money, is evicted from his hotel, becomes homeless, takes to drinking, but consoles himself that he can at least understand the people he meets in taverns. One day Budai finds himself in the middle of a revolution, with people marching in the streets, tanks rolling through, summary executions, more tanks appearing with men in different uniform. When he emerges from hiding in the underground metro, the city has begun returning to normal, except for scaffolding on some buildings. He sits down to eat in a park, and when he throws the paper the food was wrapped in into a small pond, the pond turns out to be a brook that Budai hopes to follow and thereby find his way home again.

Apart from the multiplicity of strange episodes common to much dystopian allegorical fiction, *Epepe* is interesting for its concern with communication, or the lack of it. Budai's efforts to decipher the mysterious language of the unknown city he has come to are certainly the high points of the novel. It is also in this way that Karinthy has found common ground with other Eastern European writers who sought to address the debasement of language under communism and the use, or misuse, of language as a means of widening the gap between the ruled and the ruling.

Outer Space, Fantasy, and the James Bond/007 Syndrome, Eastern European–Style

At the mention of science fiction from Eastern Europe, the one name that leaps to mind is that of the Pole Stanisław Lem. Not only is Lem undoubtedly the most prolific science-fiction writer in all of Eastern Europe, he is also certainly the most widely translated and the best known. His following in the United States alone has been so great that Lem clubs and Web sites have proliferated to the point that it is no exaggeration to speak of a Lem cult. If *Solaris* still remains Lem's most popular work, *Tales of Pirx the Pilot*—about the adventures, or misadventures, of the genial bumbler Pirx—*More Tales of Pirx the Pilot, The Cyberiad, The Futurological Congress,* and *The Star Diaries* do not lag far behind.

The key to Lem's phenomenal success is the irresistible combination of extraordinary knowledge of apparently everything related to space travel and the ability to write about it with wit, whimsy, and humor. The ability also to produce book after book through some of the most troubled years of post–World War II Poland is attributable, obviously, to the largely apolitical nature of Lem's writing. But it would be a mistake to assume that Lem never introduced anything political into his novels and stories. If we consider just a single example, *Pokój na ziemi (Peace on Earth),* which was published in 1987, we can see how Lem was able to bring together the realities of the Cold War and science fiction in a fairly innocuous way. Narrated in the first person by one of Lem's favorite characters, the astronaut Ijon Tichy, the novel pits the Soviets and the West against each other in a frantic race to discover the secret intentions of self-programming robots on the moon (are they planning to invade Earth?). Tichy is sent on a highly secret mission to investigate. But when his corpus callosum is severed by a ray, his brain no longer allows him to recall what he discovered. A tug of war between East and West, and within Tichy himself, then ensues. Although lighthearted and amusing, the grim reality of East-West Cold War competition for supremacy in space as well as on our planet is inescapable.

Of the other Eastern European nations with an impressive literature of the fantastic, Romania stands head and shoulders above the rest. Because of his formidable intellectual stature, and his importance as a forerunner of post–World War II Romanian fantastic literature, Mircea Eliade leads the list. Eliade made his considerable reputation primarily as an authority on myth, folklore, and religion, as we have seen. But there was another facet to his creativity: he was also a writer of fiction with a penchant for the fantastic. This is evident in such works as *Miss Christina* (1936), The Snake (1937), and *The Secret of Doctor Honigsberger* (1940). After the war, and his resettlement in the United States, Eliade published another major novel, St. John's Night (1970; translated as *The Forbidden Forest*). His continued commitment to the genre of the fantastic was demonstrated by the postwar collection published in Madrid in 1963 under the title *Nuvele* (Novellas), which includes "La țigănci" (translated into English as "With the Gypsy Girls'), and in the novellas *Pe strada Mântuleasa* (On Mântuleasa Street, 1968; translated as *The Old Man and the Bureaucrats*), *Youth Without Youth* (translated as *Rejuvenation by Lightning*, 1968), and Nineteen Roses (1980).

As early as the prewar tales of terror, *Miss Christina* and *The Secret of Dr. Honigsberger,* certain emphases stand out clearly in Eliade's approach to the genre of the fantastic. One is his preference generally for Romanian settings and for characters often drawn from the world of academia, science, and the arts. This latter facet of his writing explains its intellectual dimension. There are learned discussions (seldom overdrawn) about archaeological digs, exotic travel, literature, Indian philosophy, books of the occult and magic, alchemy, and so on. The occult dimension of *The Secret of Dr. Honigsberger* builds up gradually, as a professor—invited to inspect the impressive library of a widow's late husband—is gradually drawn into the world of a Saxon specialist on India named Dr. Johann Honigsberger of Brașov and the mysterious disappearance of the widow's husband, a man fascinated by Indian thought and obsessed with attaining a mastery of Sanskrit. As the professor plunges deeper into the mysteries of the diaries of the deceased, he begins to appreciate the depth of his subject's fascination with even arcane aspects of Indian philosophy and yoga. But when he attempts to return to the library after a hiatus of several weeks, everyone in the widow's house, including the widow herself, denies knowing the professor; they claim, moreover, that the library the professor has been investigating was dispersed many years previously, after the death of the widow's husband. Eliade has woven an intriguing yarn that provided him the pretext for displaying his vast erudition on the subject of Indian thought and culture; the sudden lapse of memory of the widow and what follows thereafter may well have been his way of extricating himself from an intricate plot with no place to go.

Another facet of Eliade's literature of the fantastic is the folkloric, in which he remained deeply interested throughout his career. In *Miss Christina* the plot becomes increasingly more terrifying as Eliade plunges the reader into the dark tale of young gentry woman (Christina) whose appetite for cruelty at the expense of peasants resulted in her murder and whose body disappeared, giving rise to local legends. A young artist visiting the estate where Christina had lived suffers nightmares that seem so real they are virtually indistinguishable from reality; in them, Christina comes to his room demanding love and sex. The erotic dimension of the story is by no means uncommon in Eliade's fiction, as noted especially in his earlier works as, for example, the "Indian" novel *Maitreyi.*

One of Eliade's best-known novellas of the occult, *Youth Without Youth* (also translated under the title *Rejuvenation by Lightning*), examines the rejuvenating potential of electricity. Instead of being killed by a powerful bolt of lightning, a man experiences a remarkable transformation. His skin and teeth grow back, scars vanish from his body, his limbs recover their strength, and, additionally, he finds himself possessed of a phenomenal memory and an uncanny knowledge of languages he never studied. Although his doctors try to keep the case as secret as possible, the news still leaks out, and before long the German Gestapo begins plotting to abduct him to Germany, where he can be studied further by a mysterious doctor involved in research into similar phenomena. The Germans are eventually thrown off the track; the man, facially made over, survives the war and lives well into the 1960s, at one point celebrating his one hundredth birthday. The longer the novella continues, however, the more convoluted it gets, as Eliade succumbs to the temptation to explore the philosophical, metaphysical, and even political implications of rejuvenation. At the end, when the rejuvenated man returns to his hometown in Romania in the dead of winter, he meets old friends in a popular cafe who have no idea what he is talking about when he refers to events after 1938, when he was first struck by lightning. In the kind of occult ending familiar from other stories along similar lines, as the man makes his way home in the snow, he begins discarding his teeth in a reversion to his immediate post-lightning state and rapidly declines into old age. When his body is found the next day, he is much smaller than the clothes he has on and is identified by a passport in his pocket as someone completely different.

Another quite talented Romanian writer of the fantastic, Vasile Voiculescu (1884–1963), was also a poet and much admired especially for his "translations" of Shakespeare's "lost" sonnets. Besides his poetry and plays, all of which enjoyed a considerable revival in Romania after his death, Voiculescu was attracted to the genre of the fantastic. His collection of tales of fantasy and magic, *Povestiri* (Tales), was published posthumously in 1966. It contains two of his best stories, "Capul de zimbru" ("The Auroch's Head") and "Ultimul Berevoi" ("The Last of the Berevois"). Lively and entertaining, Voiculescu's tales generally have traditional Romanian village settings, but seem to transform the village into a realm of myth and legend, in a way reminiscent of Chagall's paintings of the Russian Jewish *shtetl,* or village. Some Romanian critics have viewed this as an antireality juxtaposed to the grim reality of Stalinist Romania in the 1950s.

Among South Slavs, several writers stand out for their contribution to the literature of the fantastic. Two are Croatian: Stjepan Čuić (b. 1945), a Zagreb University graduate in South Slavic and Russian studies and a fairly prominent nationalist writer and journalist; and Goran Tribuson (b. 1948), an exceptionally versatile and popular writer of occult and fantastic fiction who also teaches screen-writing at the Academy of Dramatic Arts in Zagreb. In the area of fiction, Čuić is best known for his tales of the occult, a vein he has mined with impressive results in his two collections of short stories, *Stalinjova slika i drugi priče* (Stalin's Picture and Other Tales, 1975) and *Tridesetogodišnje priče* (Thirty-Year-Old Stories, 1979). Besides such imaginative short fiction as, for example, his collection *Praška smrt* (Death in Prague, 1975), Tribuson is also the author of the fantastic novel *Snijeg u Heidelbergu* (Snow in Heidelberg, 1980). In relatively more recent years he has earned perhaps even greater prominence as the author of a series of popularly oriented "hard-boiled" crime novels, including *Zavirivanje* (Peeping, 1985), *Siva zona* (The Gray Zone, 1989), *Dublja strana zaljeva* (The Deeper End of the Bay, 1991), *Noćna smjena* (Night Shift, 1996), *Bijesne lisice* (Rabid Foxes, 2000), and *Gorka čokolada* (Bitter Chocolate, 2004). Linking most of these novels is the figure of private investigator Nikola Banić, who is clearly modeled on the famous American sleuth Philip Marlowe and also recalls Josef Škvorecký's famous Lieutenant Borůvka. Among Serbian writers of the fantastic, the most celebrated is a Belgrade native, Zoran Živković (b. 1948). Well represented in English translation, and winner of several awards, Živković is much admired for his imaginative plots, considerable narrative skill, and use of postmodernist techniques. The work with which he is most identified is his five-part "mosaic novel" collection *Nemogući priče* (Impossible Stories, 2004), which includes the World Fantasy Award–winning story cycle "Biblioteka" ("The Library").

The Bulgarian writer Andrei Guliashki (b. 1914) is beyond doubt the Eastern European master of the spy thriller. A prolific and varied writer, with interests ranging from urban and environmental problems to socialist realist–inspired novels lauding the achievements of the postwar regime in undoing the wrongs to Bulgarian village life inflicted by the prewar fascist government, Guliashki really came into his own with his spy novels. Although politically predictable— Cold War anti-Bulgarian and anti-Soviet intrigues on the part of the unscrupulous West, aided and abetted by the seemingly never-ending machinations of die-hard Bulgarian anticommunists—Guliashki's novels are fairly well crafted and entertaining. Guliashki even managed to create a Bulgarian counterpart to Ian Fleming's James Bond ("007")—the counterespionage officer Avakum Zahov. The novels in the Zahov series include *Prikliucheniiata na Avakum Zahov* (The Adventures of Avakum Zahov, 1962; translated as *The Zahov Mission*), *Sreshtu 007* (Faceoff with 007, 1966), *Poslednoto prikliuchenie na Avakum Zahov* (The Last Adventure of Avakum Zahov, 1976), and the two-volume *Zhivotut i prikliucheniiata na Avakum Zahov* (The Life and Adventures of Avakum Zahov, 1977). Guliashki also wrote several murder mysteries, perhaps the best of which was his later *Ubiistvoto na ulitsa "Chekhova"* (The Murder on Chekhov Street, 1985). In 1979 he brought out a collection of three novellas under the title *Otdelenie za reanimatsiia* (The Reanimation Section).

Pavel Vezhinov (1914–1983), another popular Bulgarian writer of Guliashki's generation, published his first novel, *Siniiat zalez* (Blue Sunset), in 1947. This was a time, just a few years after the end of the war, when socialist realism was being rammed down writers' throats and deviations were viewed harshly. Vezhinov's preoccupation with criminality in Blue Sunset and the novel's erotic elements brought down the wrath of critics and made things difficult for him for a while. But his subsequent humorous and parodic stories, a war novel, *Vtora rata* (The Second Brigade, 1959), and a couple of party-line antifascist novels, especially *Daleche ot bregovite* (*Far from the Shore*, 1967), nudged him back into the literary mainstream. *Far from the Shore* is an improbable adventure yarn, set in the 1930s, about a small band of Slav communists who commandeer a boat from Bulgaria with the intention of making their way to the Soviet Union and the "free life." Vezhinov also became known in the 1960s, '70s, and '80s as the author of several popular mystery and science-fiction novels, including *Chovekut u siankata* (The Man in the Shadows, 1965), actually a collection of mystery tales; such science-fiction works as *Nauchnofantastichni noveli* (Science-Fiction Novellas) and *Sinite peperudi* (The Blue Butterflies), both published in 1988; *Gibelta na Aiaks* (The Death of Ajax) and *Nad vsichko* (Above All), both published in 1973; and *Az sum atomna* (I Am Atomic, 1981).

Crime and Punishment

Although never encouraged as a literary genre by the communists on ideological grounds (crime being regarded as endemic to bourgeois society), the crime novel ("Krimi," in German) nevertheless remained popular with Eastern European readers throughout the period. Like historical literature, science fiction, fantasies, and spy stories, the crime novel was a form of escapist literature. But since such writing tended to be held in light esteem, authors of crime fiction often favored pen names for their works. This was, however, not the case with one of the earliest practitioners of the genre in post–World War II Eastern Europe, the Pole Leopold Tyrmand (1920–1985).

A brash and popular writer, Tyrmand left Poland for the United States in 1966 and thereafter devoted himself to publishing books, in English as well as Polish, exposing the nature of communist rule in Poland and throughout Eastern Europe. Of his four novels, by far the most successful was *Zły* (The Evil One, 1957; translated as *The Man with the White Eyes*). What made the work a sensation was the fact that nothing like it had yet appeared in postwar Poland—a large, tough novel set by and large in the teeming Warsaw underworld of the 1950s. As a well-connected journalist and sports writer, Tyrmand had an impressive knowledge of the gangs of young hoodlums that preyed on the innocent, the wheeling and dealing of black marketeers, and the big business of sports-events ticket scalping, and he poured this knowledge into his novel. The character for whom the novel is named is a shadowy but powerful individual (himself a former gangster now reformed) who sets out on a kind of personal crusade to rid Warsaw of its hoodlums, racketeers, and gangsters. With its inside look into the seamiest corners of Warsaw a little over a decade after the end of the war, and its robust action and earthy language, the novel has long held a special place in the history of postwar Polish fiction.

A decade after Tyrmand published *Zły* (1957), the Czech writer Josef Škvorecký brought out the first of a series of his own crime novels built around the figure of police lieutenant Borůvka: *The Mournful Demeanor of Lieutenant*

Borůvka (1966). A collection of twelve case studies from Borůvka's long career, each pivots on a murder, with two of them set in Italy, where the lieutenant has gone on vacation with his daughter. Not exactly the model of a suave professional detective, Borůvka is a plumpish, short, middle-aged man, somewhat on the melancholic side (hence the title of the novel). The next novel in the series, *Konec poručíka Borůvky* (*The End of Lieutenant Borůvka*, 1975), was written after Škvorecký and his wife, the Czech writer Zdena Salivarová, had already emigrated from Czechoslovakia and were living in Canada. Like *The Mournful Manner of Lieutenant Borůvka*, it is also a collection of stories, in this case five. They are all set in Czechoslovakia after the Soviet invasion of 1968 and highlight the conflict between the regular criminal police of which Borůvka is a member and the secret police.

Although more political in nature than the first Borůvka novel, *The End of Lieutenant Borůvka* does not transform the lieutenant into any kind of patriotic-heroic figure. On the contrary: bowing to pressure, he denounces Dubček and his regime for revisionism and even goes so far as to support the Soviet invasion of his country. The last story of the collection is highly melodramatic and partially rehabilitates Borůvka politically. When he and his squad are ordered to block the planned kidnapping of a young girl by men hired by her parents, who managed to flee Czechoslovakia after the 1968 invasion, Borůvka turns his gun on his own men, thereby allowing the plane to take off. He is soon taken into custody and sentenced to fifteen years in prison.

Návrat poručíka Borůvky (*The Return of Lieutenant Borůvka*, 1980) is different in a few important respects from the preceding novels. A full-scale crime novel rather than a collection of closely related short stories, it employs first-person narration and the figure of a Canadian narrator (Neil Danby), who can observe and comment on the Czech émigré community without being a part of it. Borůvka himself is now also an émigré, having escaped from prison in Czechoslovakia and fled to Canada, where he works as a security guard at a Toronto parking lot. If not exactly a marginal character in the novel, he still has been reduced to the level of a minor figure, despite his contribution to the solution of the murder of the narrator's sister, Heather.

Škvorecký's fondness for the crime genre did not end with the Borůvka cycle. In 1973 he published the clever and entertaining novel *Hříchy pro pátera Knoxe* (*Sins for Father Knox*, 1973). This refers to the career of Ronald Arbuthnot Knox (1888–1957), an Eton and Oxford–trained theologian who in 1917 converted to Roman Catholicism, became a priest, and in time came to be an important figure in English Catholicism. Knox is important to the history of crime fiction both as a result of his satirical essay on Sherlock Holmes, in which the famed sleuth is treated as a historical figure, and because of his ten postulates for the successful detective novel, which were adopted as the basis of the famous Detection Club headed by G. K. Chesterton, a friend of Knox's; these inform Knox's own crime novels, among them *The Viaduct Murder* (1926), *Footsteps at the Lock* (1928), and *The Body in the Silo* (1933). Škvorecký has taken the ten postulates of Knox and made them the bases of separate crime stories alternately subtitled, in English, "Whodunit," "Howdunit," and "Whydunit." However, in a surprise twist of his own, Škvorecký abandons one or more of Knox's principles in each story and leaves it up to the reader to figure out which (the correct answer for each story is provided at the end of the collection).

When the Czech writer Karel Pecka (1927–1997) completed his early novel, *Pasáž* (Passage), in 1974, he may have had little idea that its publication would bring him together with Škvorecký's and Salivarová's Sixty-Eight Publishers. A talented and at times strikingly original writer, Pecka has unfortunately become better known as the author of an extraordinarily detailed account of his eleven years (1949–1960) as a Czech political prisoner for distributing pamphlets regarded as inimical to the communist regime. Passage is an arresting novel for its Kafkaesque, surreal character and its twists of plot. During a traffic jam, in heavy rain, the main figure of the novel, a man named Antonín Tvrz (the name means "citadel" in Czech), abandons his broken-down car and heads for an underground passage. A young girl he notices smiles at him alluringly and he follows her inside. When he enters a restroom, he encounters a beautiful blonde prostitute with wicked red heels, who literally screws her clients to death. Continuing to follow the little girl, he soon finds himself trapped in a labyrinth of shops. It is now past midnight, and Tvrz chooses to exchange his identity papers for a key that gives him access to all areas of the underground. After running into a dead school friend, Tvrz witnesses himself hours before on a movie screen and then goes on to have sex with the prostitute, who is now a simple flower-seller. At this point the novel ends, with Tvrz no longer the possible madman he may have seemed to the reader, but rather an actor in a film about his own recent experiences.

The mysteriousness of Pecka's novel, to say nothing of its erotic and criminal elements, made it impossible to publish in Czechoslovakia. By then, Sixty-Eight Publishers was firmly established in Canada and was turning out a number of works of Czech fiction by émigré or banned writers. Pecka turned to Škvorecký for help, the novel was accepted by Sixty-Eight Publishers, and it appeared in print for the first time in 1976. It was also adapted for the cinema in 1998 and directed by the Czech director Juraj Herz.

The last major work by the multifaceted Pavel Kohout was the novel *Hvězdná hodina vrahů* (The Stellar Hour of Murderers, 1995; translated as *The Widow Killer*). A suspenseful thriller set in the final months of the German occupation of Prague during World War II, it chronicles a series of gruesome ritual slayings of German and Czech widows by a mad killer. Of particular interest in the novel is the sympathetic relationship that develops between a young Czech detective (Jan Morava) and a German police official (Erwin Buback), himself of partly Czech origin, who works in the Prague Gestapo. The cat-and-mouse game between the detectives and the psychotic killer continues until the end of the novel. By this time the German occupation of Czechoslovakia is coming to a chaotic finale, and the fate of the detectives and the madman they are pursuing becomes intertwined with the conflict that erupts between the long-suppressed Czechs and their former masters desperately trying to quit the country. A long novel in which the gore may be carried too far, *The Widow Killer* neverthe-less makes a vivid impression, especially in its depiction of the last days of the German occupation of Prague.

Lest the Slovaks appear underrepresented in the area of crime fiction, we have but to consider the work of the often-intriguing Dušan Krist Mitana (b. 1946). The author of several novels and collections of short stories, Mitana is known for a propensity for the mysterious and irrational, as in his first published col-lection of short stories, *Nočné správy* (Nightly News, 1976). His fascination with crime and punishment, with detection and the seemingly inexplicable, is reflected in one of his better works, *Koniec hry* (The End of the Game, 1984), a novel about the murder of his pregnant journalist wife in a jealous rage by a television director named Peter Slávik. The growing hostility of Slávik toward his wife had already been aggravated by Slávik's mother, who disliked the wife and never lost an occasion to complain about her to her son. The "game" of the title refers both to the wife's lighthearted attitude to life and to the game of deception Slávik plays with police captain Števurka in order to conceal his crime. In the end, his mother's "confession"—which the police accept but do not believe—saves his neck but leaves him to ponder his mother's altruism and his own reluctance to accept responsibility for his actions. True to his profes-sion, he imagines the *real* film he will sometime be able to make of the events and use to find the sense in them.

Disappearance, search, and mystery, combined at times with the absurd and philosophical, are at the core of Mitana's short-story collection *Na prahu* (On the Threshold, 1987) and his most intriguing text, the self-mocking and paro-distic postmodern experimental novel *Hl'adanie stráténého autora* (The Search for a Missing Author, 1991), in which an author named Tomáš Eliáš, who published under the pseudonym Dušan Mitana, has disappeared.

Another prominent Slav writer of crime fiction is the Slovene Peter Božič (b. 1932). In 1972 he published a rather slight contemporary crime novel with the title *Jaz sem ubil Anito* (I Killed Anita, 1972). Consisting mainly of dialogue, its primary appeal was the novelty of its squalid setting and characters, some-thing new for Slovenian literature at the time. The Anita of the title is a ciga-rette butt–collecting down-and-out prostitute in trouble with the police, who is strangled at the end. After his World War II novel *Očeta Vincenca smrt* (Father Vincenc's Death, 1979) and a few plays, Božič returned to the kind of "hard-boiled" fiction with which he became identified with I Killed Anita. In 1987 he brought out his highly popular *Chubby Was Here* (original title in English), which deals with the unlikely subject of the Ljubljana subculture of homeless youths, bohemians, and eccentrics of the 1960s and '70s. The novel in some ways recalls the Pole Leopold Tyrmand's *The Man with the White Eyes*. Božič's more recent novels—*Človek in senca* (Man and Shadow, 1990) and *Zdaj, ko je nova oblast* (Behold the New Authority, 1993)—deal similarly with the dark undercurrents of contemporary urban life.

Crime fiction also had an enthusiastic popular following in the German Democratic Republic, despite the fact that this type of writing was officially discouraged. Notwithstanding the regime's attempts to crack down on the circulation of Western crime fiction throughout the communist period, a complete ban on it as well as on the cultivation of the genre by domestic writers was an impossibility. To the authorities, crime fiction was incompatible with the high moral purposes of state-sponsored socialist realism and deserved to be outlawed. Crime was regarded as a product of a decadent bourgeois capitalist system; absent the roots of such a system in communism it follows that crime would simply not exist. Reality taught otherwise, however, and no curbs imposed on crime fiction, imported or domestic, could be truly effective. The authorities then tried a communist-style appropriation of the genre by supporting the writing of works designed to illustrate that crime in a socialist society resulted from the assimilation of Western ways and ideas. Instead of the lone-wolf type of detective common to much Western crime fiction, the practitioners of the new communist alternative sought to replace such a crimebuster with the collective figure of the security police or good solid everyday socialist citizens, who were often portrayed as working in tandem with the police in the solving of a crime or crimes.

A classic of this new type of Eastern European crime fiction is the GDR writer Hans Pfeiffer's (b. 1925) *Mord ohne Motiv* (Murder Without a Motive, 1965), about the police investigation of an apparently motiveless murder by a young thug. The novel was designed to expose the harmful influences on the young of improper upbringing by parents (in terms, that is, of the implanting in the young of false values) and of Western literature and television programs. Besides his authorship in the 1960s and '70s of a few crime novels besides Murder Without Motive—*Sieben Tote brauchen einen Mörder* (Seven Deaths Need a Murderer, 1964) and *Tote Strohmbahnen* (Dead Currents, 1974)—Pfeiffer was also an authority on crime fiction in East Germany and on various aspects of criminality. As early as 1960 he published *Die Mumie im Glassarg: Bemerkungen zur Kriminalliteratur* (The Mummy in the Glass Coffin: Observations on Crime Fiction) and in the 1980s followed it up with two further books, *Phantasiemorde: Ein Streifzug durch den DDR-Kriminalroman* (Fictional Murders: An Expedition Through the GDR Crime Novel, 1985) and the short *Kochrezepte für Kriminalgerechte, oder, Wie man einen Kriminalroman schreibt* (Recipes for Criminal Rights; or, How to Write a Crime Novel, 1987).

Among the foremost East German writers of crime fiction were Erich Loest—whom we have met previously as the author of the controversial novel It Takes Its Course; or, Trouble on Our Level (1978)—and Wolfgang Hilbig (1941–2007). Loest wrote a few popular "Krimis" in the 1980s under the pseudonyms Hans Walldorf and Waldemar Nass. These include *Pistole mit sechzehn* (The 16-Round Pistol, 1984), *Ein Sachse in Osnabrück* (A Saxon in Osnabrück, 1986), and *Froschkonzert* (String Concert, 1987). A different kind of writer than Loest, but one no less attracted to the crime genre, Wolfgang Hilbig was a poet, a critic, and the author of such intriguing and intellectually provocative novels as *Der Brief* (The Letter, 1985), *Die Weiber* (The Women, 1987), *Eine Übertragung* (A Transfer, 1989), and *Ich* (I, 1993). A hallmark of

Hilbig's postmodern style is the complex layering of narratives, which textually represent identity crises rooted in the disparity between official representations of society and the sober reality of the protagonists' everyday lives.

With the exception of The Women, which explores the nature of sexual repression in a closed society like the GDR, Hilbig's other three works operate in unfamiliar ways with the familiar motifs of crime fiction. Perhaps the best of these novels, *I* is truly Hilbig at his best. A substantial novel of nearly four hundred pages, it is a first-person account by a "Stasi-Spitzel" ("Stasi informer") named Cambert, a writer who is ordered to shadow a mysterious author suspected of a hostile agenda toward the state. Sinister and grotesque at the same time, the novel has an almost Gogolian character. Cambert is a ludicrous figure who inhabits a dark subterranean world of cellars and whose spying is complicated by the fact that the author being shadowed has no intention of publishing his works. Plagued by doubt about the necessity of his undertaking, Cambert also wonders how seriously he himself is being taken by the GDR Ministry for State Security. An "underground man," Cambert rents a depressing room from Frau Falbe, who barely acknowledges his existence, and where growing insecurity about his role as an informer begins blurring the lines between creativity and the reports he is obliged to provide the Stasi. Masterfully written, with an abundance of comic touches and allusions to the genre of the "Krimi" itself as well as intertextual references to such modern authors as Foucault, Pynchon, Beckett, and Mailer, Hilbig's *I* is as much about literature and the generation of the text as it is a caricature of the Stasi's by now well-known practice of employing East German writers as informers.

In A Transfer, a novel about the murder of a female postal worker named Kora Lippold, the narrator is a young boy who, like his friends, bemoans his inability to freely get his hands on Western crime fiction and other forms of bourgeois literary trash. They live in the provinces, far from a major urban center like Berlin, and so in the end are driven to invent their own kind of crime fiction. The criminal is seen here as an individual who flouts the authority of the state in order to find the "escape" of prison.

As we shall see later on, the popularity of crime fiction has outlived the communist era and has become one of the staples of the literary marketplace in Eastern Europe since 1990. The emergence of large-scale crime and corruption in new postsocialist societies assimilating free market economics has created a remarkably fertile field for a new wave of crime fiction, one that often makes its communist predecessor seem tame by comparison.

6

Writers Behind Bars

Eastern European Prison Literature, 1945–1990

Since the collapse of the former Soviet Union, the world has come to better understand the enormity of the network of prison camps, known as the *gulag,* that existed throughout that vast state. The opening of a window onto the wretchedness and brutality of the camps came initially with the publication of Aleksandr Solzhenitsyn's novel *Odin den´ v zhizni Ivana Denisovicha* (*A Day in the Life of Ivan Denisovich,* 1962). Later Solzhenitsyn determined to go beyond his novel by compiling a more comprehensive record of the entire Soviet gulag, drawing on not only what he himself had endured but also the accounts of other prisoners. This work, *Arkhipelag Gulag* (The Gulag Archipelago), was first published in Paris in three volumes between 1973 and 1975. The blockbuster book left a lasting impact on readers throughout the world and dispelled any lingering doubts concerning the Soviet Union's capacity for inhumanity. Solzhenitsyn was roundly denounced for the book after the publication of the first volume and the following year was exiled from his homeland.

In large measure due to Solzhenitsyn's extraordinary books, and the research encouraged by them, the gulag phenomenon in the former Soviet Union has been well studied and has become widely known. But the same cannot be said for Eastern Europe as well as the former German Democratic Republic, which must be situated within the context of communist Eastern Europe for the nearly half-century of its existence. The possible explanation for this relative neglect may be found in the complexity of the region when compared to the Soviet monolith. The multiplicity of cultures (and languages) obviously presents a formidable challenge to broad research beyond the area. In Eastern Europe itself any effort to deal directly with the prison camp issue had to wait until obvious political impediments had disappeared with the downfall of the communist system. A great deal has become known since the early 1990s, but there is much yet to be uncovered. Even given the understandable temptation to bring to light the grimmer aspects of life under communism, and the natural tendency to want to settle scores with the past, not a great deal has been written about the world—perhaps better said, the culture—of the Eastern European prison camps. To be sure, the system was less extensive than that of the Soviet Union. Across the region as a whole there was no "archipelago" of the nature described by Solzhenitsyn. Nor were forced labor and/or prison camps everywhere the same from one country to another. But whatever their variance in number and repressiveness, the sad fact remains that the number of people sentenced to them for whatever length of time was huge. That intellectuals and artists suffered perhaps disproportionately when compared to the rest of the populace can be accepted as a given even just on the basis of Solzhenitsyn's accounts.

My intention at this point is not to attempt any systematic study of the communist-era Eastern European prison camps—that would truly exceed my own range of interest and the scope of this book—but rather to develop a sense of the nature of the prison camps through a focus primarily on Eastern European writers who served time in them. The approach will be twofold: to review the circumstances that led the individual writer to be incarcerated for any period of time, and then to consider the impact of prison experience on literary output, both expository and fictional. When all is said and done, it was the Eastern European literary community that has so far left the most vivid and moving writing about the prison camps. It is that simple fact that is being acknowledged here.

In view of the large number of writers involved, and the quantity of literary works generated by camp experience, it is not really feasible to discuss every case on an individual basis. Some writers, and texts, will be mentioned only in passing. The emphasis will be on the most significant, and the most interesting. It would also be nice if the material lent itself to some more disciplined organization, but it does not, and so a certain arbitrariness in the order of presentation is inevitable. Writers will be discussed on a country-by-country basis, beginning with those states with the most notorious camp systems. And although the concern here is, of course, with the post–World War II period, certain earlier authors and works may be introduced for the sake of background.

Romania

The intense paranoia of the little-educated, uncultured, and megalomaniacal dictator Nicolae Ceauşescu—until his execution in the bloody revolution in 1989—created a fertile climate for the extreme intrusiveness into daily life of the Romanian security police known as Securitate. This was abetted by the development of a fairly extensive network of notorious prison camps between 1949 and 1960 under the leadership of the then–Communist Party boss, Gheorghe Gheorghiu-Dej. It is has been estimated that during those years alone more than a million people were interned in camps.[1] Since writers were deemed among the least trustworthy members of the intellectual class and the most obviously at odds with the regime over censorship, it stands to reason that they would be targeted for police surveillance and incarceration. The most outstanding cases of such repression and incarceration involved two quite dissimilar writers, Paul Goma and Nicolae Steinhardt.

Paul Goma (b. 1935) remains the most famous dissident of Ceauşescu's Romania and the first Romanian writer to shed a bright light on the extent to which the country had been transformed into a vast prison camp between the years 1948 and 1964. He has often been compared to Solzhenitsyn, but the comparison is only superficially apt. Goma was born in the Bessarabian village of Mana. After the Soviet takeover of Bessarabia in 1940, his family found refuge in Romania. However, his father was arrested by the NKVD and deported to Siberia in 1943. Eventually reunited, the Goma family established residence in the village of Buia in the Tîrnava Mare district. Most of the future dissident's early education was in schools in the Sibiu (Transylvania) area. In 1952 he was expelled for political reasons. He finally graduated a school in the town of Făgăraş, between Sibiu and Braşov, after vain attempts to enter schools in Sighişoara and Braşov. Upon graduation, he was admitted to both the Faculty of Philosophy of Bucharest University and the M. Eminescu School of Literature, and he choose to attend the latter.

Because he was a natural-born rebel and nonconformist, it was only a matter of time before Goma clashed with the authorities. After the Hungarian uprising of 1956, which he greeted enthusiastically, he was imprisoned for two years in the maximum security penitentiary at Gherla. An old Transylvanian town in the Cluj area, known at least since the Middle Ages, Gherla in time became famous for its penitentiary, which had been in fact a fortress with a rich history and the largest structure in the town. On 20 October 1785 a decree of the Habsburg emperor Joseph II officially transformed the fortress into an imperial prison, known as Carcer Magni Principatus Transilvaniae.

After his release from Gherla, Goma was sentenced to an additional three years of house arrest (1960–1963) in the village of Lăteşti. As a free man, relatively speaking, he worked at a variety of odd jobs in Transylvania until resuming his studies in Bucharest in 1965. But his past continued to dog him and in 1967, weary in part because of the physical harassment he had to endure, he quit the university. It was then that Goma decided to try to make his way as a freelance writer. He made his debut in 1966 with a short story published in the prominent Romanian literary review *Luceafărul*. He also began collaborating with such well-known papers as *Gazetă literară, Viaţa Românească,* and *Ateneu.* In 1968 he published his first volume of stories, *Camera de alături* (The Room Next Door). His novel *Ostinato* (the title refers to a term in musical composition, from Italian *ostinato,* "obstinate") appeared in Germany in 1971 after being rejected by Romanian publishers. This set the pattern for most of Goma's subsequent publications until the overthrow of the communist regime. *Uşa* (The Door), his next novel, was also published in Germany in 1972. A French translation, with the title *Elles étaient quatre* (They Were Four), followed two years later.

Not long after the publication of that volume, Goma was again arrested but freed after a well-organized international campaign of protest on his behalf.

He claims, however, that he continued to be harassed by the Securitate, beaten in the streets, and threatened by death. Matters came to a head in 1977, when Goma was forced to emigrate. He and his family received political asylum in France, and they settled in Paris. Until it again became possible for him to publish in Romania after the revolution of 1989, all his books in the late 1970s and '80s appeared in France and in the French language. His novel *Gherla* was first published, in 1976, in French by Gallimard before Goma emigrated. *Gherla* was followed by such novels as *Dans le cercle* (Inside the Circle, 1977), *Garde inverse* (Reverse Guard, 1979), *Le tremblement des hommes: Peut-on vivre en Roumanie aujourd'hui* (The Trembling of People: Can One Live in Romania Today?, 1979), *Chassée-croisé* (Crossroads, 1983), *Les chiens de la mort, ou, La passion selon Pitesti* (The Dogs of Death; or, The Passion According to Piteşti, 1981; reissued in Romanian in 1990 as *Patimile după Piteşti*), which details his prison experiences in the Piteşti prison in the 1950s, and *Bonifacia* (1986). The autobiographical *Din Calidor: o copilărie basarabeană* (In Calidor: A Bessarabian Childhood, 1990; translated into English as *My Childhood at the Gate of Unrest*), which was originally published in the Romanian émigré journal *Dialog* (edited by Ion Solacolu), had appeared in French in 1987.

Apart from his fictional and autobiographical writings, Goma was an ardent diarist and published five volumes of diaries, all brought out in Romania in 1997 and 1998, and of particular interest for the light they shed on his later life and career. These include *Alte jurnale* (Other Journals), which covers his stay in the United States in the fall of 1978 but concentrates primarily on the period 1994–1996; *Jurnal I: Jurnal pe sărite* (Journal I: By Leaps and Bounds, 1997); *Jurnal II: Jurnal de căldura mare* (Journal II: Journal of the Great Heat, 1997), devoted to the period June–July 1989; *Jurnal III: Jurnal de noapte lungă* (Journal III: Journal of the Long Night, 1997), covering the period September to December 1993; and *Jurnal unui jurnal 1997* (Journal of a Journal, 1997), which deals just with the year 1997.

Goma was a productive writer and, in a sense, a man with a mission. That mission was to expose, against the background of his own experiences, the totalitarianism of the Ceauşescu regime in all its grotesque paranoia and inhumanity. Taken together, his work is a grimly persuasive record of repression, which, in Goma's own case, followed him even into exile. Perhaps the two most revealing of Goma's novels with respect to the world of the Romanian prison camp in the Ceauşescu era are his first, *Ostinato* (translated into French as *La cellule des libérables*, The Cell of Those Soon to Be Freed), and, of course, *Gherla*, arguably the most compelling book by him based on his prison camp years.

Written between 1965 and 1969, *Ostinato* features a large cast of characters but tells the story principally of a Bucharest University student named Ilarie Langa who is arrested and sentenced to seven years in prison on a charge of having committed euthanasia. In order to put an end to his mother's terrible suffering from cancer, he gave her a strong dose of morphine. After he makes two failed attempts at escape, his sentence is lengthened to eleven years in full. At the beginning of the novel Ilarie is in a cell with other prisoners who are scheduled to be released soon. But after eight months there he still has no clear idea of when he himself is going to be a free man again and becomes dispirited. The review of his life in which he then engages becomes Goma's way of addressing some of the most serious problems of Romanian life and culture in the decade of the 1950s. As Ilarie speculates on what society holds for him and his fellow detainees on the outside, he becomes haunted by the idea of the Ideal Female. This then becomes a thread running through the entire novel. Drawing obviously on his own experiences, Goma uses the first part of the novel to paint a grim but stunningly accurate picture of the inner workings of a contemporary Romanian prison. In the case of Ilarie, the eleven years that he has spent in camps and prisons—including several months at hard labor, to which political inmates were often condemned—have taken their toll on his health and above all his nerves. The question naturally arises as to how well he will be able to adapt to life beyond prison after so many years behind bars and after everything he has endured. The last two parts of *Ostinato* are devoted primarily to these questions and their ramifications; at the end of the novel, when Ilarie is about to open the gate that will readmit him to society, these issues still remain unresolved.

Half the size of *Ostinato, Gherla,* which was first published in France in 1976, aims, more so than *Ostinato,* at opening the eyes of Western readers to the full range of horrors of the prison camp system in Ceauşescu's Romania. Goma's premise is that while the West has learned much about the Soviet gulag, it knows next to nothing about the extent of repression and human degradation in Eastern Europe, above all in Romania. Starting out as a conversation between a former Gherla inmate and a French friend about the former's prison years, the dialogue produces an ever-broader canvas of revelations; these in turn are buttressed by the tales of other inmates that are integrated into the narrative. The early discussion between the former inmate and his friend takes on another dimension of interest in the exchange between the two concerning narrative strategy. It is clear from the inmate's arguments that he is strongly motivated to speak as he does because of the silence of his contemporaries. He wants not only to raise the consciousness of the West about what has taken place in Romania, but especially to rouse fellow former inmates to speak boldly of their own experiences.

Nicolae Steinhardt's death in 1989 ended the career of one of the most unusual figures in twentieth-century Romanian literature and culture. He is still little known outside his own country, notwithstanding his pre–World War II publications in French and the appearance in 1995 of a UNESCO-sponsored French translation of his most important literary text, *Jurnalul fericirii* (Journal of Happiness), followed a year later by an Italian translation of the work. A highly idiosyncratic account of his years of imprisonment under the Ceauşescu regime, the title of the book would initially strike the reader as ironic, and was probably meant to create that impression, at least in part. But as improbable as it may seem, Steinhardt found spiritual joy, indeed an epiphany of sorts, in prison that changed the course of the rest of his life.

Nicolae, or Nicu-Aurelian, Steinhardt was born on 12 July 1912 in the Bucharest district of Pentelimon, the son of Jewish parents distantly related on his father's side to the Freuds of Vienna. In Steinhardt's case it is important to take note of his ethnic origins, since his attitude, or attitudes, toward Judaism became one of his central moral, intellectual, and literary concerns. After attending secondary school in Bucharest, Steinhardt went on to Bucharest University, from which he received a degree in law in 1934. That same year he launched his literary career with a small book that in its irreverence and liveliness was to foreshadow much of his subsequent writing. Published under the pseudonym Antisthius—the name of a figure in the French satirist de La Bruyère's *Les Charactères* (1688)—*În genul lui Cioran, Noica, Eliade . . .* (In the Style of Cioran, Noica, Eliade . . .) is a brash parody of the styles of the leading representatives of the 1930s generation of Romanian writers and thinkers.

Within a year of the appearance of his book of parodies, Steinhardt demonstrated his precociousness and broad range of interests when he and his friend Emmanuel Neuman published a short study, in French, of Catholic concepts of Judaism under the title *Essai sur une conception catholique du judaisme* (An Essay on a Catholic Conception of Judaism). Two years later, in 1937, the year after Steinhardt received his doctorate in constitutional law, he published, also with Neuman and also in French, a study devoted wholly to Jewish matters, *Illusions et réalités juives* (Jewish Illusions and Realities).

After an extended two-year trip through Western Europe, Steinhardt, now back in Romania, accepted Camil Petrescu's invitation to collaborate with the prestigious monthly *Revista Fundaţiilor Regale* (The Review of the Royal Foundations). He held the position until 1940, when he fell victim to the policy of vicious anti-Semitism introduced at the time by Horia Sima, the leader of the Romanian fascist Iron Guard in 1938 after the assassination of its founder, Corneliu Zelia Codreanu, and in 1940 Romanian deputy prime minister.

Steinhardt's position deteriorated still further when the communists took over Romania after World War II. Inalterably opposed to totalitarianism in any form, he was unable to make the moral and intellectual compromises necessary to reach an accommodation with the new regime. The advancement of his literary career was severely hampered by the obstacles put in the way of his publishing, and he was barely able to scrape together a living by means of small editorial jobs. Fearless in his personal integrity, he staunchly refused to sever or even cut back on his relations with intellectual companions whose ideological views had already set them at a distance from the regime. What eventually cost him his freedom was his unwavering support for the philosopher Constantin Noica—notwithstanding his earlier parody of him—who had become a particular target of the Securitate. Steinhardt, along with other close supporters of the much-beleaguered philosopher, was taken into custody in 1959, tried in court, and sentenced to thirteen years of hard labor. Thus began Steinhardt's journey through the nightmare world of Romania's gulag.

At the beginning of January 1960, Steinhardt was incarcerated in the notorious prison at Jilava. It was there, on 15 March that same year, that he was baptized into the Romanian Orthodox faith by one of his fellow prisoners, a monk named Mina. Here is how he writes of this pivotal event in his life in the entry dated "15 March 1960" of his *Journal of Happiness*:

> The catechization is over. The baptism, set for the day of the fifteenth, takes place as agreed upon. Father Mina chooses the moment that seems to him the most opportune: the return "from the air" [the outdoor exercise period for prisoners], when the screws are busiest, and when activity is at a peak. We have to work fast, and clandestinely, in sight of everybody. . . .
>
> When the torrent of men returns with a lot of racket, carrying, by twos, the tank, the bucket, and a reservoir of water, Father Mina, without removing his cloak, pounces on the only pitcher in the room—a red pitcher, with cracked enamel, greasy and disgusting—and fills it with stagnant water brought in in the "reservoir" carried by him and another detainee. The two Greco-Catholic priests and my sponsor come over to my bed. . . .
>
> Two detainees, our accomplices, take up position right in front of the peep-hole, thereby blocking it. At any moment a guard might come in order to have a look, but now when the prisoners have been discharged for the exercise period, or have already been bought back, it is less probable. Hastily—but with that clergyman's skill whereby speed does not impede clear speech—Father Mina pronounces the required words, makes the sign of the cross over me, spreads over my head and shoulders the full contents of the jug (the tankard is a kind of stumpy kettle), and baptizes me in the name of the Father and of the Son and of the Holy Spirit. As to my confession, I did it summarily: the baptism erases all my sins. I am reborn, in fetid water and in a spirit of haste.[2]

Until an amnesty for political prisoners made Steinhardt a free man in August 1964, he had spent time elsewhere in the Romanian prison system, including and especially Gherla. Once returned to civilian life, Steinhardt was as intractable as ever, showing not the slightest inclination to collaborate with the communist regime despite the relative political liberalization of the period. Assisted by his friends Constantin Noica and Alexandru Paleologu (1919–2005), who was also released from prison in 1964, Steinhardt was able to devote himself entirely to literary pursuits.

It was probably in the late 1960s that Steinhardt began working on *Journal of Happiness*; he regarded this book as his literary testament. The first version of the text, running about 570 typed pages, was confiscated by the Securitate. Steinhardt considered it lost and during the next several years attempted to re-constitute it, this time producing a text of 760 pages. But it was to be some time before it saw the light of day. Thanks to a concerted effort by the Romanian Writers' Union, Steinhardt eventually obtained his original manuscript and set about recasting it as a text of 480 pages. It was then smuggled to the West, where large excerpts from it were broadcast in 1988–1989 by Radio Free Europe. Fearing that the authorities would move to confiscate his works and papers as a form of revenge, Steinhardt entrusted them to a friend, the writer Virgil Ciomoş. It was Ciomoş who edited Journal of Happiness for the Dacia publishing house of Cluj in 1991. The edition was based on Steinhardt's original version but incorporated changes he had made to both the first and second versions of the work. In 1992 Journal of Happiness was honored as the Best Book of the Year in Romania.

A large, sometimes ponderous book, Steinhardt's Journal of Happiness is in some ways a remarkable text. Apart from the often minutely detailed descriptions of everyday life in prison, it splendidly reflects Steinhardt's extraordinary erudition—and, at the same, a certain inability to keep his journal from overflowing with almost countless literary, political, historical, and biblical references. It is a text that demands annotation, which the original Romanian edition sadly lacks. The journal is also structured idiosyncratically, jumping back and forth in time, with no apparent reason, in the chronological ordering. An entry for November 1960, for example, is followed by one for November 1970, another for January 1964, then one for February 1934, and one from 1953. Also adding to the curiosity of the text is Steinhardt's practice of inserting every so often italicized sections, generally of no more than a paragraph or two, in which events, or conversations, are recalled. These serve the purpose, for the most part, of introducing a different perspective on an issue he may be discussing at the time. They are all similarly titled—"Bughi Mambo Rag" ("Boogie, Mambo, Rag")—as if to suggest a change of rhythm in the text. Whatever the complexities of Journal of Happiness, it remains by far one of the most unusual books of recollection to come out of an Eastern European's experience of prison. It is also the story of the discovery of faith by a remarkable Romanian intellectual.

After finishing Journal of Happiness and then seeing its chances for publication destroyed when the Securitate confiscated his typescript, Steinhardt returned to essay writing and by the mid-1970s had completed a book of essays under the title *Între viaţă şi cărţi* (Between Life and Books). With some half of its pages expurgated by the censors, the collection was published in 1976. His next publication, a book of literary studies, *Incertitudini literare* (Literary Uncertainties), came out in 1980 and won the Grand Prize for Literary Criticism. That same year, Steinhardt took the vows of a monk and entered the monastery at Rohia in the northern Murameş region. It was a move he had considered for some time.

The popular image of a monk as a man renouncing worldly interests in order to devote himself wholly to the spiritual hardly applied to Steinhardt. As a new member of the Rohia community he lost little time in taking charge of the badly needed task of putting the monastery's huge library in order. He also undertook the editing of sermons and other religious publications. And far from avoiding the sphere of worldly concerns, he vigorously renewed his active participation in Bucharest's literary life. There was hardly a cultural event of note at which he was not present, and his essays on literature and the arts again appeared in a variety of journals.

Albania

Despite its much smaller size, Albania weighs in a close second to Romania in terms of its prison camps in the era of the communist dictator Enver Hoxha. No less paranoid an authoritarian figure than Ceauşescu, albeit better educated and with a wartime partisan mystique that his Romanian counterpart lacked, Hoxha was as nationalistic and independent-minded as Ceauşescu. Relations with Yugoslavia, a staunch Albanian ally during World War II, were sundered after Tito's break with Stalin in 1948. This act of disloyalty was harshly condemned in ultra-Stalinist Albania and set the tiny country off in pursuit of another large protector, this time China. The Albanian-Chinese alliance lasted through most of the 1960s, and when that too ended, it left in its wake an isolated, economically backward, xenophobic, deeply distrustful state able and willing to imprison anyone on the slightest suspicion of plotting against its interests. Again, as in Romania, one of the prime targets of the Segurimi, the Albanian secret police, was the small intellectual elite. So many people, however, passed through the gates of the Albanian prison camp system in Hoxha's time that it may indeed have seemed that at one time or another most of the country was behind bars.

The Albanian writers who got caught in the Sigurimi dragnet included, among many others, such prominent figures as the scholar and poet Arshi Pipa, the poet Visar Zhiti, Bashkim Shehu, the son of the much-feared general and later prime minister Mehmet Shehu (1913–1981), and Besnik Mustafaj, a novelist, short-story writer, and essayist, and, in the post-Hoxha period, Albanian ambassador to France. If the Albanians did not produce a dissident and prison camp alumnus of the outspokenness and literary productivity of Paul Goma, the backwardness of Albanian society under Hoxha and its tight muzzling of writers for so long does not mean for a moment that Albania produced little of merit in this regard. In fact, quite the contrary.

Arshi Pipa (1920–2002) is the first to be discussed both for chronological reasons and because deep hostility to the Hoxha regime, and to communism in general, led him to publish in exile a series of books of a more-or-less scholarly nature that sought to expose the Albanian dictatorship in the way that Goma sought to expose Romanian tyranny under Ceauşescu through his fiction. Talented and courageous, Arshi Pipa was a poet, novelist, literary scholar, and political writer. Attracted to Italy and Italian culture at an early age, he later studied in Florence and upon completion of his studies taught Italian in various schools in Albania. His knowledge of Italian, combined with an enthusiasm for poetry, resulted eventually in a study of the influence of Dante on the Italian poet Eugenio Montale (1896–1981), published in 1944 under the title *Montale and Dante*. Pipa was twenty-four years old at the time and the Italians had already invaded Albania. That same year Pipa also published his first volume of poetry, *Lundërtarë* (Seamen). During the war he edited the review *Kritika letrare* (Literary Criticism), and after the liberation of Albania his credentials earned him a place on the editorial board of *Bota e re,* the organ of the League of Albanian Writers.

By now the communists had taken over Albania, and it was not long afterward that Pipa found himself out of favor with the new regime. Because of his views concerning freedom of expression, he became a political prisoner from 1946 to 1956. The First Congress of Albanian Writers, which took place in Tirana in October 1945, was made up at this time mostly of noncommunists. The organization soon began publishing its own journal, *Bota e re* (New World). Pipa was one of two noncommunists on the editorial board. He had previously written an article on the major interwar Albanian writer Migjeni, and was asked to commemorate him on the eighth anniversary of his death (26 August 1938). But, Pipa claims, the party ideologists did not like his speech, and as a measure of their disapproval he was demoted to the then-unfinished Durrës lyceum. Not long afterward, at a poetry reading at the Tirana House of Culture, he further antagonized the authorities with his recitation of lyrics from a translation of Goethe's *Faust* that also included these lines from Goethe's "Song of the Flea": "Und war sogleich Minister, / Und hatt' einen grossen Stern" ("And right away he became a minister, / and wore a huge star"). Pipa conjectures that this could have been misconstrued as an oblique reference to the general secretary of the Ministry of Education, Shemshi Totozani.

Pipa was taken into custody, tried, and sentenced to two years of conditional "reclusion." But when it was reported, four months after his incarceration, that he had not recanted, he was abruptly taken from the prison section of the Durrës hospital, made to undergo a second trial *in camera,* and was found guilty of "counterrevolutionary" activities. The whole process lasted, he recalls, some fifteen minutes, after which he was sentenced to twenty years imprisonment. An amnesty later cut his time to ten years, which he served in various prisons and in a forced labor camp. The most notorious of these was the Burrel prison, where the Hoxha regime incarcerated the political prisoners it regarded as the most dangerous. It was built in the 1930s during the reign of King Zog in his birthplace, Mat.

Pipa was freed in 1957, following which he fled to Yugoslavia, living for a time in Sarajevo. In 1959 he published a verse account of his years in prison under the title *Libri i burgut* (The Prison Book). Consisting for the most part of separate poems on the theme of freedom and tyranny, the book also includes praise, for example, of the Hungarians for their courage and heroism in revolting against communist despotism. While in prison in 1955 he also wrote the epic-like *Rusha* (1968), a Romeo and Juliet tale of love and vendetta between Albanians and Serbs in the second half of the fourteenth century.

The year in which The Prison Book was published, Pipa immigrated to the United States, where he was able to pursue a productive academic career as a scholar and university teacher. With little call for Albanian, Pipa had to be content to make his way up the academic ladder as a teacher of Italian and French, primarily the former. But there was still ample opportunity for him to become involved in Albanian studies on different levels, working with established scholars in those institutions where scholarship in Albanian was being conducted and publishing in journals with some interest in Albanian. He first obtained a professorial rank at Adelphi College, where he became an assistant professor in Italian but also conducted an occasional course in philosophy. The University of Minnesota eventually became his home. He was a member of the faculty from 1966 to 1989 and held the rank first of associate professor (1966–1969) then full professor and head of the Department of French and Italian (after 1968, the Department of Romance Languages).

The two main thrusts of Pipa's writing in the United States were scholarly and political. As a scholar in Albanian, Pipa's major contribution was the "Trilogia Albanica," consisting of *Albanian Folk Verse: Structure and Genre* (1978), *Hieronymus De Rada* (1978), a monograph on the Italo-Albanian writer Girolamo De Rada (1814–1903), and *Albanian Literature: Social Perspectives* (1989). In the political area, Pipa devoted himself to writing books exposing the true nature of the Hoxha regime, as he perceived it, and particularly its repression of culture. The first of these was *The Politics of Language in Socialist Albania* (1989), in which he argues that the disappearance of literary Gheg—with reference to the Gheg dialect of northern Albania—left Albanian literature deprived of "half of its creative potential." Tosk, the other main Albanian dialect, spoken in the southern part of the country, happened to be the idiom of the majority of those Albanians who dominated the Communist Party and state apparatus for many years after World War II. In 1972, when so-called unified literary Albanian was officially adopted as the only written form of the Albanian language, Gheg—which Pipa himself spoke and favored—virtually disappeared from the cultural landscape.

The Politics of Language in Socialist Albania was followed by a no-holds-barred attack on the Hoxha regime under the title *Albanian Stalinism* (1990) and, the following year, by *Contemporary Albanian Literature* (1991), a personal and obviously ideologically slanted interpretation of the course of Albanian literature from the immediate postwar period to his own day. Pipa's subsequent polemics with Ismail Kadare can be traced to this book, in which Pipa paints Kadare as a staunch foe of the Hoxha regime whose writings in the main constitute a negation of official ideology. Kadare had not yet exiled himself from Albania and regarded Pipa's assessment of his writings as slanderous and an attempt to cause him trouble with the regime. Kadare, as we saw earlier, settled scores with Pipa (and others) in writings from his post-1993 Parisian exile.

In his *Autobiography: 1988,* published in English in Albania in 2000, Pipa wrote poignantly of his prison experiences, recalling in one poem ("Neli") his close relationship with a fellow prisoner named Neli:

> A peasant he was from Central Albania,
> plagued by malaria, rheumatism, an unhealed
> knee wounded while a guerrilla fighter,
> when his brothers were killed.

Suffering also from hunger
for having left at home
three motherless children
in care of his old folks.
Yet in such need and misery
I never saw or heard him
complain, get angry, envy
the guy receiving
a parcel, speak badly of others,
let alone quarrel with them
for an inch of room on the floor,
and generous to the point
of undergoing torture
not to denounce a fellow
who was not even a friend.
In prison much I learned
not found in books. Humanity
plucked bare of feathers
I saw, and was disgusted.
Yet something else I saw,
the like of Neli, no scores,
the good seed of perhaps
a better future.
So I accepted life,
And could live out my fate.[3]

In the very revealing poem titled simply "Autobiography," Pipa gives us an idea of his intellectual defiance, when he recalls his experiences as a student in Florence, Italy:

Those were the days when I was reading Lenin.
Unfortunately for him, I read last
his empiro-criticism book.
The result was brain constipation.
Idealism I regurgitated
by coping with Bergson. I was to appear
in black shirt and then to praise
his recent conversion to Christian mysticism.
I did neither one, thus igniting the wrath
of my Catholic pro-fascist adviser.
. . . .
My brother was then in jail
in Ventotene. Later he went through
the Nazi camp of Priština,

then joined the partisans, and ended up
tortured to death. I learned his fate
during my second, *in camera*, trial.
And I have sworn upon my brother's blood
to fight Stalinism no less than fascism
to the last drop of my blood. . . . (53–54)

In keeping with his role as an ardent champion of Albanian democracy, Pipa
also took up the cause of the rights of the Albanian population of Kosovo, publishing two major political studies on the subject: in Albanian, *Zhvillimi politik
i shtetit shqiptar, 1912–1962* (Albanian Political and National Development,
1912–1962, 1962), and in English, *Studies on Kosova* (1984).

The case of Visar Zhiti (b. 1952) epitomizes the precarious situation of the
writer in Enver Hoxha's Albania. He was born in the port city of Durrës, but
grew up in Lushnjë, where he finished high school in 1970. He then began
teaching in Kukës, in northern Albania near the Kosovo border. In 1973, just as
he was preparing to publish his first book of poems *Rapsodia e jetës së trënda-
filave* (Rhapsody of the Life of Roses), he fell victim to the purge of Albanian
artists and intellectuals triggered by the Fourth Plenary Session of the Albanian
Communist Party. His manuscript was rejected by the Naim Frashëri publishing house, to which he had submitted it, as ideologically unacceptable. Unable
to publish anything, Zhiti continued to live and teach in Kukës until his arrest
there in 1979. After several months in solitary confinement he was sentenced in
April 1980 to ten years imprisonment. He was released in 1987 and allowed to
work in a brick factory in Lushnjë.

While in solitary confinement—especially in the Qafë-Bari prison camp in
the mountainous north of Albania, with its harsh winters—and denied writing implements, Zhiti composed and committed to memory nearly a hundred
poems reflecting his harrowing experiences. He was finally able to publish these
in book form in 1993, two years after the downfall of the Albanian communist
regime, under the title *Kujtesa e ajrit* (The Memory of the Air). A second volume
of prison poems, *Hedh një kafkë te këmbit tuaja: Poezitë e burgut* (I Toss a Skull
at Your Feet: Prison Poems), appeared in 1994.

Zhiti's prison poems are a grim record of ideological persecution under the
Enver Hoxha regime and at the same time a testimony to the poet's strength of
will and resolve to create a powerful poetic account of what he lived through.
The frightful loneliness of prison, the sense of extreme isolation and hopelessness, is the subject of the short poem "Çastet ikin" ("Moments Pass"), from
The Memory of the Air collection: "Moments pass / like lice / over my body /
In this prison ditch / full of the mud of suffering / I sit and wait / How sad /
to be a warrior / without a war."[4] In another poem from the same volume,
"Epilogu (që koha e bën parathënie)" ("The Epilogue: Of Which Time Makes
a Preface"), which he composed while in prison in Lushnjë, also considers what
poetry has cost him and yet its immense meaning to his life:

> Life is less than hope
> yet, despite that, I write poems
> although no one reads them.
> Perhaps the wind does not read the stars at night,
> and perhaps the cliff at the shore of the sea
> feels nothing of the rage of the waves.
> Yet, despite that, I write poems,
> that have destroyed my life. For seven years
> they wound barbed wire around my body.
> They rent my skin and torrents of life flowed
> like torrents of blood
> down to the bottom of my feet.
> But if it was impossible for me to save my soul,
> all of my soul,
> I was able to pull out a particle
> from the crevices of my body
> and I sent it
> to love
> to poetry.
> I now live
> with particles of soul, little ones
> like lost bees
> . . . .
> And if you consider
> that even inscriptions on gravestones
> have readers . . . ,
> then poetry is greater than hope! (83–84)

The Memory of the Air also contains a cycle of poems written after his release and dealing in part with his visits, for the first time, to Austria and Italy. When he entered the Colosseum, as he writes in "Koloseu" ("The Colosseum"), the marks of his own imprisonment were still fresh and he could identify with those who had been slain there: "At last I came to the Colosseum, / the last slave. With still unhealed wounds. / With the tiger teeth of dictatorship still in my body. / . . . / Over there, the place where my rulers sat. / I see their fat, evil thumbs / pointing down, demanding my death" (181).

The later collection, I Toss a Skull a Your Feet, contains several of the bleakest of Zhiti's prison poems. In "Vdekja vazhdon" ("Death Continues"), composed in Spaç on 16 January 1983, he describes this all too common scene:

> He fell down the stairs
> and did not get up again
> (afterward death continued the journey).

. . . they'll bury him in the ground . . . no one knows where . . .
without a coffin! . . .
The planks were used for the bed.
(Building 2, Room 7, Row 3, No. 51)

. . . without a funeral . . .
 (the crowds had accompanied him once
when he went to trial—in handcuffs)

. . . nor a stone on his grave . . .
though for all those years he had extracted stone, stone, stone. . . .[5]

Death again is the subject of "Vdekja këtu nuk trondit kërkënd" (Death Unsettles No One Here"), dated 9 March 1983: "The tunnel caved in / and a prisoner was killed / (the chains he wore have not yet been killed). / And the work gang returned to camp / with one man less, / with one corpse more / that will not be sent home for burial. . . ." (116).

Zhiti wrote several other works after the two volumes of prison poems: *Mbjellja e vetëtimave* (Sowing Lightning, 1994); *Valixhja e shqyer e përrallave* (The Tattered Traveling Bag of Tales, 1996), a collection of light stories for "girls of every age"; *Këmba e Davidit* (The Feet of David, 1996); *Si shkohet në Kosovë* (Going to Kosovo, 2000); *Rruget e ferrit* (The Paths of Hell, 2001); and *Ferri i çarë* (Hell Divided, 2002). The last two books are based wholly on his prison experiences. The Paths of Hell, which he wrote between 1998 and 2001 in Rome and Tirana, is divided into ten chapters, three of which are subdivided into several smaller sections. Besides discussing the prison camps of Burrel, Spaç, and Qafë-Bari, Zhiti brings up the cases of Arshi Pipa and Kadare's controversial novel *The Palace of Dreams*. Hell Divided, which Zhiti subtitled *Roman i vërtetë* (A Real Novel), was written from 1999 to 2002, also in Rome and Tirana. Although called a novel, it is not one in any strict, fictional sense. Zhiti has won several literary prizes, among them the Italian Leopardi Gold Prize for Poetry (1991) and the Ada Negri Prize (1997), and the Albanian National Prize for The Memory of the Air (1998). In 1996 he was elected a delegate to the Albanian Parliament and subsequently held the position of cultural adviser to the Albanian Embassy in Rome.

Bashkim Shehu (b. 1955) was by all means one of the most interesting if improbable long-term inmates of the Albanian prison camp system. The son of one of the most powerful men in twentieth-century Albanian history, general of the army and later prime minister Mehmet Shehu (1913–1981), Bashkim Shehu was born and educated in Tirana. He began his career as a screenwriter with Albanian Film Studios and in 1966 published his first literary work, *Një kohë tjetër: Novelë e tregime* (Another Age: Novellas and Short Stories). Although born into privilege, he suffered a serious reversal of fortune after his father's probable murder. He was forced to spend the next eight years in a prison camp and then a year and a half in political internment. Once a free man, Shehu moved to Budapest in 1992 and the following year published an autobiography of sorts, the principal thrust of which was not to chronicle his years in prison but rather to meticulously recreate the circumstances surrounding his father's death. The purpose was to make as strong a case as possible for the murder of Mehmet Shehu on Enver Hoxha's orders and to explore the reasons Hoxha had felt that this was necessary. First published in France, in French, as *L'automne de la peur* (Autumn of Fear), it appeared in Albanian in 1994 under the title *Vjeshta e ankthit*. The probable murder of Mehmet Shehu is also the subject of Ismail Kadare's 2003 novel *Pasardhësi* (*The Successor*).

But it has not been only Bashkim Shehu who became obsessed with the official version of the suicide of Mehmet Shehu during the night of 18 December 1981. The alleged suicide itself, as well as the mysterious internment of his remains, has long been the subject of rumor and speculation in Albania and beyond. Autumn of Fear is Bashkim Shehu's attempt to come to grips with the sordid events of that night and to discover his father's final resting place. Writing as a scholar of politics, Arshi Pipa, whom Bashkim Shehu mentions by name in Autumn of Fear, addressed the Mehmet Shehu case in his book *Albanian Stalinism* (1990), quoting extensively from Enver Hoxha's own account of Mehmet Shehu in his book *The Titoites: Historical Notes* (1992).

Bashkim Shehu subsequently left Budapest and returned to Tirana to resume his career as a writer. In 1995 the first of two major novels by him appeared, *Rrugëtimi i mbramë i Ago Ymerit* (*The Last Journey of Ago Ymeri*), followed in 1996 by *Gostia* (The Dinner Party). *The Last Journey of Ago Ymeri* is the more interesting of the two. Ago Ymeri is the hero of an Albanian folk ballad who is allowed to return from the underworld for a single day. This forms a dimension of Shehu's novel in which the leader of a totalitarian state, now prince of the underworld, sets out to destroy an intellectual and popular balladeer named Viktor Dragoti, who appears one day in a remote Albanian seaside village and is rumored to be a man killed several years earlier while trying to swim to freedom. The novel is clearly intended as a glimpse into the machinery of totalitarian persecution implicitly likened to a half-century of Stalinist rule in Albania. When Dragoti appears out of nowhere in the village, he is recruited to serve as a witness to the marriage of the sister of a local inhabitant named Mira. Both she and her friend, Rita, have taken to the streets in search of two such "external" witnesses. Viktor agrees, but leaves as soon as possible for Tirana. In the meantime, the local official who has taken notice of him, Qemal, decides to track him down on the way to Tirana. He succeeds after overtaking the bus carrying Dragoti. When the two men meet, Qemal can hardly believe his eyes. Dragoti is an old school chum of his whom he knows for certain had been killed when trying to escape from Albania by sea some nine years earlier. Dragoti, however, claims that he has no recollection of the event and insists that he has come back from the other world. But the file cannot be located and the hapless Qemal is taken into custody and placed in an asylum.

Another writer made to bear the heavy burden of the "sins" of a father is Fatos T. Lubonja (b. 1951). A well-known journalist who has been a leading activist for democratic reform in postcommunist Albania, Fatos is the son of Todi Lubonja (b. 1923), the general director of Albanian Radio and Television, whose purge in 1974 enabled the prominent writer and orthodox communist Dritëro Agolli to assume the leadership of the Union of Writers and Artists (a position he held until 1992). The same year as his father's purge, Fatos, a recent graduate in physics from Tirana University, was himself taken into custody and sentenced to seven years' imprisonment on the basis of diaries critical of Enver Hoxha found in an uncle's attic. He was assigned to the notorious Spaç copper mine. Another sixteen years in prison were added to his initial sentence in 1979, when he was accused, together with other inmates, of "counterrevolutionary" agitation while in prison. He made his second trial and imprisonment the subject of his documentary novel *Ridënimi* (The New Sentence, 1996). Lubonja was released only in 1991. Once out of prison, he became active in human rights and in 1994 founded the influential cultural and political quarterly *Përpjekja* (The Endeavor). An English-language anthology of pieces from *Përpjekja*, with writings also by prominent Albanian and Kosovar intellectuals, was published in Tirana in 2003 under the title *Endeavor*.

Lubonja has written extensively of his prison experiences in his book of memoirs, *Në vitin e shtatëmbëdhjetë: Ditar burgu, 1990–1991* (In the Seventeenth Year: Prison Diary, 1990–1991, 1994) as well as in The New Sentence. His drama, *Ploja e mbramë* (The Last Slaughter, 1994), was composed during Lubonja's incarceration in Burrel prison in 1988 and 1989. Since his return to cultural and political life, he has won international recognition. In 2002 and 2004, respectively, he was awarded two highly prestigious European literary prizes—the Italian Alberto Moravia Prize and the German Herder Prize.

Besnik Mustafaj (b. 1958), a few years younger than Fatos Lubonja, has been one of the most prominent literary figures in postcommunist Albania. A native of Bajram Curri and educated at Tirana University, he began his career as a poet, publishing two volumes of verse in 1978 and 1987. Since then he has concentrated entirely on prose. His first novel was the short *Vera pa kthim* (Summer of No Return, 1989). It was followed by *Vapa* (Locusts, 1993), *Një saga e vogël* (A Small Prison Saga, 1994), *Daullja prej letre* (The Paper Drum, 1996), and *Boshi* (The Abyss, 1998). He has also published two books of nonfiction: *Midis krimeve dhe mirazheve: Ese* (Between Crime and Illusion: Essays, 1991), on the precarious situation of the Albanians in Kosovo and the historic animosity between Albanians and Serbs, and *Fletorja rezervat: Shënime jashtë valixhes diplomatikë* (Reserved Pages: Notes Outside the Diplomatic Pouch, 1995), an account of his experiences in the French capital as his country's ambassador to France from 1992 to 1997.

Most of Mustafaj's work reflects his long and ardent opposition to the Hoxha regime in Albania. The terror of repression is strikingly vivid in such novels as A Small Prison Saga and The Abyss. A novelistic triptych, A Small Prison Saga develops the image of Albania as a political prison from Ottoman times through the Hoxha era. The three parts of the novel recount the grim prison experiences of various members of a single family who for one reason or another have been victimized by the oppressive machinery of the state, above all in the time of King Zog in the interwar period and then by post–World War II communists. In the most poignant, second, part of the work, the eagerly anticipated first conjugal visit permitted a prisoner and his wife becomes a nightmare of physical and psychic impotence. The absurd and grotesque come to the fore in the third part, when the old jailer of the prison, faced with an absence of prisoners after the fall of the dictatorship, loses his mind and fills cells with rocks to overcome the void he feels. He is, in fact, the father of the prisoner's wife in part 2. She believes she became pregnant after the conjugal visit with her husband but gives birth instead to a rock.

The Abyss, like A Small Prison Saga, has the quality of fable and allegory combined. While on an assignment about chrome miners, a young woman photojournalist uncovers the grim evidence of a cave-in. She thereafter becomes a "nonperson." Her parents, employer, and ex-fiancé refuse to acknowledge her existence when she attempts to resume her previous routine in Tirana. She returns to the small town near the mine, hoping to be helped by an agricultural engineer she met there and with whom she had an affair. But when he retraces her steps in Tirana, he runs into the same wall of denial. Upon his return to the town and the hotel where he left Ana B., she is nowhere to be found and everyone denies ever having had a guest by that name. While he himself did not personally undergo the trauma of imprisonment, Mustafaj obviously knew of the horrors of the camps and made them the subject of some of his most important fictional writing.

Yugoslavia

Western opinion was long seduced by the benign image of a liberal Yugoslavia. Tito had split with the Soviet Union, after all, and had pursued an independent path of socialism. For some time in the post–World War II period the Yugoslavs were economically better off than the rest of Eastern Europe and they seemed to enjoy a freer political climate. Workers' management, never very well understood in the West, offered proof of a kind of grassroots democracy—so it was believed—and this in turn was bolstered by the official Yugoslav foreign policy of nonalignment—not capitalist, not communist in the sense of being part of the Soviet bloc, but "nonaligned." Eventual Anglo-American backing for Tito and his partisans during the war also predisposed the West toward a generally favorable view of Yugoslav socialism.

This attitude persisted for a long time, until the country fell apart within a relatively short period after Tito's death. Nationalist enmity then burst into the open, and before long the federal Yugoslav state began coming apart at the seams in bloody ethnic conflict. By the early years of the twenty-first century, Yugoslavia had been replaced by the newly independent former republics of Bosnia-Herzegovina, Croatia, Serbia-Montenegro, Slovenia, and Macedonia, and the former leader of Serbia and the shrunken state of Yugoslavia-Montenegro—Slobodan Milošević—was sitting before the World Court in the Hague on charges of fomenting a campaign of ethnic cleansing in Bosnia-Herzegovina and Kosovo amid the worst fighting in Europe since World War II. Now, Milošević is dead, Montenegro has split from Serbia, and Kosovo seems headed for independence despite strong Serbian objections.

Until the great unraveling of Yugoslavia in the late 1990s, few in the West had any real idea of the existence and nature of a Yugoslav prison camp system. Croatia's wartime fascist alliance with Nazi Germany, its enthusiastic participation in the rounding up and deportation of Yugoslav Jews to the German death camps, and the existence of one major concentration camp on Croatian soil— Jasenovac, where terrible crimes were committed—eventually did become fairly well known. But Titoist Yugoslavia was long spared a similar blackening of its national reputation. Yugoslav literature has had few readers in the West and so revelations concerning a Yugoslav gulag network centered on the Adriatic island of Goli otok (Barren Island) were slow in coming to foreign attention.

One of the earliest books about Goli otok appeared in 1984, in English, by a former prisoner named Venko Markovski. The book, *Goli Otok: The Island of Death. A Diary in Letters,* was published in Boulder, Colorado, in the Social Science Monograph series. Markovski was a Macedonian Stalinist at odds with Tito over the break with the Soviet Union in 1948. Following his release from Goli otok, he lived in Bulgaria and eventually served in the Bulgarian Parliament. He was born in Macedonia in 1915 and went to Bulgaria for the first time in 1937. In 1956 he was arrested for clandestinely circulating a scathing poem about Tito and his circle under the title "Suvremenni paradoksi" ("Contemporary Paradoxes"). He was sentenced to five years imprisonment on Goli otok, the "Devil's Island" of Titoist Yugoslavia. After serving his full term, he was released in 1961 and allowed to return to Skopje, the Macedonian capital, where he lived under virtual house arrest. Finally, in 1966, he was allowed to leave Yugoslavia.

Markovski's book, *Goli Otok: The Island of Death,* is written in the form of forty-four letters and an epilogue composed after the fact, since no writing implements were available to him on the island. A passionate anti-Titoist, he fills much of his account of life on the island with denunciations of Tito and his close associates for their betrayal of Yugoslavia and the ideals by which the wartime partisans had been motivated. Also, he excoriates Tito for turning against his fellow partisans and transforming patriots and heroes into political criminals. When not recounting the issues involved in the Yugoslav-Soviet split, from the viewpoint of course of a staunch supporter of the Soviet Union and Stalin, Markovski's diary is straightforward, with a heavy emphasis on the inhuman tortures inflicted on the prisoners, beginning with the forced marching they were made to endure when they first arrived on the island and above all the extent to which prisoners were turned on other prisoners. Markovski also describes in detail his periods of isolation.

The dramatic and emotional style of much of the book is apparent from the following passage:

> Shadows—not real human beings—dwell on Goli Otok, shadows of our former freedom fighters. On Goli Otok human beings are reduced to things, to numbers; they are treated as mere quantities; they live in rags and tatters. From dawn to dusk a sorrowful train of people moves back and forth across the desert that is Goli Otok. Their eyes are sunken; their hands have been broken in inhuman toiling. Their legs drag as if bound by heavy chains, their heads are bent low. They don't talk, they don't even look around. Each of these shadows is a loose page from a shattered life.[6]

As an introduction, so to speak, to Goli otok intended for a foreign audience, Markovski's book may be forgiven for its emotionalism and strong Soviet bias. More compelling reading by far are texts that appeared in Yugoslavia itself and so far have not been translated. One of the earliest, which came in the wake of Tito's death in 1980 when the country enjoyed a temporarily more open state-run press, was the 1982 novel *Tren 2* (Train 2) by Antonije Isaković (1923–2002). The short work describes the notorious Goli otok prison camp and portrays the partisans as crude Stalinists. Of much greater scope was the huge documentary *Goli otok,* which appeared in Belgrade in 1990, by the Serbian writer Dragoslav Mihailović (b. 1930).

A native of Ćuprija, Mihailović belongs to the generation of Yugoslav writers who came to the fore in the 1960s. After secondary school he enrolled in 1949 in the Faculty of Philosophy of Belgrade University, where he studied Yugoslav literature and the Serbo-Croatian language. His studies, however, were interrupted by a serious bout of tuberculosis early in 1950, arrest and imprisonment on Goli otok until the spring of 1952, and obligatory military service in 1952 and 1953. His first book of short stories, *Frede, laku noć* (Good Night, Fred), appeared in 1967 and drew on the author's own experiences on Goli otok. Like so many other Yugoslavs, as we have seen from Markovski's book, Mihailović was sent to Goli otok following Yugoslavia's break with the Soviet Union, when many people suspected of Soviet sympathies became political detainees. These events, as well as teen violence—which Mihailović also deals with—could be written about openly only in the 1960s.

Until his much later blockbuster, *Goli otok,* Mihailović was best known for his novel *Kad su cvetale tikve* (When the Pumpkins Blossomed, 1968). Drawing on Mihailović's own background as a boxer, the novel deals with the life of a Yugoslav expatriate former boxer married to a Swede and living in Sweden. It was adapted for the stage but was withdrawn after fewer than a dozen performances, presumably because of objections on the part of Tito himself. Of Mihailović's other works, the short-story collection *Lov na stenice* (Hunt for Bedbugs), which was published in 1993, hence after *Goli otok,* also has prison life as its principal theme. Mihailović received the October Prize of the City of

Belgrade in 1967 for Good Night, Fred, and the Andrić Prize in 1976 for his second novel, *Petrijin venac* (Petrija's Wreath, 1975). In May 1981 he was made a corresponding member of the Serbian Academy of Sciences.

Mihailović's massive *Goli otok* consists in the main of lengthy interviews with former inmates of the notorious island prison camp. Each interview is preceded by prefatory, italicized, personal reminiscences of the interviewee by Mihailović himself. The interviews are quite substantial. The first, for example, with Jovan Dimitrievič and titled "Kad čovek prestaje da bude čovek" ("When a Man Ceases to Be a Man"), is 192 pages long. The second interview, with Nikola Nikić, "Bosanski lonac" ("The Bosnian Vase"), is considerably shorter, at 84 pages, but still relatively long. The third interview, with Nikola Mićanović, "Mali vodar dugo pamti" ("The Little Water Carrier with a Long Memory"), runs 120 pages in length. *Goli otok* itself is a book of 682 pages. Over half the text is thus taken up with these three interviews. The rest of the narrative part of the book, extending from pages 409 to 663, is made up of appendices in the form of factual pieces—mostly by Mihailović himself, but some by separate investigators—about the various forms of punishment inflicted on the Goli otok inmates. Detailed descriptions and analyses of certain ailments and diseases to which prisoners succumbed on the island are also included. The last fifteen pages of the book consist of the names of 452 inmates.

A few parts of *Goli otok* had appeared separately before the book itself came on the market. This was the case, for example, with the piece "Od jedan put su ubili dvadesetak ljudi" ("Twenty People Were Killed at One Time"), which was published in Belgrade in February 1989. It was written or dictated by "N. N." and handed over to Mihailović. It is one of the most chilling accounts of conditions on the island in the entire book. The author notes that the killing of inmates on Goli otok began in the second half of July 1949, after the arrival of the Bosnians, mostly Muslims, who were in charge of the punishments. The killings took the form mostly of severe beatings and also included stomping on an inmate's chest. Bodies were then piled on top of one another, like so much wood, and at night taken beyond the camp and buried.

No less compelling an account of life in Tito' s prisons was written by the prominent novelist Boris Pekić (1930–1993). One of Yugoslavia's most acclaimed men of letters, Pekić left Yugoslavia in 1971 and lived in England until his death twenty-two years later. His experience with the Yugoslav gulag came at an early age. In 1948 he was accused of organizing a student conspiracy against the state and was sentenced to fifteen years at hard labor. He was pardoned in 1954. Ten years later he won a major Yugoslav literary prize for his biblical novel *Vreme cuda* (The Time of Miracles, 1964). Prior to his resettlement in England, Pekić had published a second major novel, *Hodočašće Arsenija Njegovana* (translated under the title *The Houses of Belgrade*, 1970).

The change in politics and culture required by the shift from Yugoslavia to England had no apparent impact on Pekić's literary output. Between 1975 and the year of his death he published over a dozen new books. Apart from novels, including one called *Sentimentalna povest Britanskog carstva* (A Sentimental

Novel of the British Monarchy, 1993), there was a book comparing Yugoslav and English politics, *Poslednja pisma iz tudine* (Last Writings from Abroad, 1991), and two more of a political nature: *Kako upokojiti vampira* (How to Pacify a Vampire, 1977),[7] an intriguing if dense philosophically oriented work about the attempt by a professor of medieval history at Heidelberg University and a former Gestapo officer to come to grips with his past in the form of a series of letters to his brother-in-law, and *Odmor od istorije* (A Vacation from History, 1992), a collection of essays on Yugoslav and Serbian politics in 1945 and 1991, edited by Radoslav Bratić. The most important of Pekić's nonfiction in the London period remains, however, his massive three-volume work based on his prison and postprison experiences. The first two volumes are grouped under the title *Godine koje su pojeli skakavci: Uspomene iz zatvora ili antropopeja, 1948–1954* (The Years the Locusts Consumed: A Prison Memoir; or, Anthropopeia, 1948–1954, 1987). The third volume bears the title *Skinuto sa trake: Dnevničke zabaleške i razmišljanja, 1954–1983* (Stripped of My Stripes: Daily Notes and Thoughts, 1954–1983, 1991).

Pekić is a tougher read than Mihailović. The latter's *Goli otok* involves by and large first-person narration and the speech is colloquial in nature much of the time. The reader becomes rather quickly engaged in the personality and experiences of the narrator. Pekić, on the other hand, was an erudite and, truth be told, prolix writer, with impressive knowledge and a fondness for a great many, often long footnotes. The footnotes are certainly not without interest, but they are time-consuming in the reading. Nevertheless, the impact The Years the Locusts Consumed makes is in its very detail. Pekić describes, seemingly from the moment he is carted off to prison, everything that happens to him, and everything he thinks about what is happening to him, in considerable detail. His interest in the psychological, on the part of prisoners and officials alike, is impressive and adds depth to the narration. Interrogations and conversations are reconstructed in minute detail, as if they were being recorded on the spot, and are used by Pekić to analyze the mindset of the police in a totalitarian state.

A leading poet of the 1960s and a prominent dissident in communist Yugoslavia as well as a champion of democracy under the authoritarian rule of President Franjo Tudjman (died 1999) of Croatia, Vlado Gotovac (1930–2000) also came to know the prison camps at first hand. A respected journalist as well as radio and television editor, he turned to the writing of poetry in 1956 and by 1995 had published seventeen volumes. Essentially an urban poet despite a rural upbringing, Gotovac became identified with a highly philosophical poetry deeply committed to the integrity of the individual and the need to preserve democratic freedoms. His prose writings are addressed to social issues, including totalitarianism and, later, the Balkan wars of the 1990s. He was, in the words of one of his editors, "an engaged writer who was not directly engaged in politics."[8] Gotovac had already written about political rights in Yugoslavia in his book *U svakodnevnom* (The Daily Routine), which first appeared in 1970.

Gotovac's willingness to confront sensitive issues reflected the liberalization in Yugoslavia in the period 1965 to 1971. Some Croatian leaders, seeking to extend the accommodations, began pressing more openly for an easing of what they regarded as unfair taxes and federal controls imposed on the wealthier republics of Croatia and Slovenia for the sake of the less well off sister republics. This growing Croatian nationalism gave rise to the Croatian Mass Movement (*Masovni pokret* in Croatian, or Maspok, for short), with communists and noncommunists alike vying for control of the organization and agitating for still greater liberties for Croatia, including, among others, a separate army and banking system and a separate seat at the United Nations.

Tito's move to suppress Maspok in 1971 and the resultant purges and arrests of Croatian political figures, artists, and intellectuals did not spare Gotovac. The immediate source of his difficulties was his five-month stint (22 August–3 December, 1971) as editor in chief of the weekly *Hrvatksi tjednik*, which was put out by the important Croatian cultural and publishing institution Matica Hrvatska. After a meeting of the Central Committee of the Communist League of Yugoslavia on 1 December 1971 and changes in the Croatian political leadership, *Hrvatski tjednik* was shut down. On 11 January 1972 Gotovac was taken into custody, and on 27 November of that same year he was sentenced to four years in a maximum security prison. An additional three years were slapped on him for "criminal activity against the nation and state by means of counter-revolutionary attacks against the state and social system." Gotovac was also prohibited from all forms of public activity for a period of three years. Despite appeals on his behalf by international organizations of writers and other foreign institutions, he was again hauled into court, because of conversations he had had with two foreign journalists about the possibility of employment with their news organizations, conversations that were reported back to the authorities. On 5 June 1981 Gotovac was again sentenced to prison (this time an ordinary one as opposed to a maximum security facility) for two years with an additional four-year prohibition on public activity.

Although certainly an advocate for greater autonomy for Croatia within the Yugoslav federal system, Gotovac was hardly a rabid nationalist and never advocated Croatia's secession from Yugoslavia. He had also never written anything that could be misconstrued as anti-Serbian. Like his poetry, his prose writings are imbued with a sense of the philosophical and moral, even when he is discussing such issues as nationalism, tyranny, and the reform movement. Indeed, Gotovac did not run afoul of the authorities for his writings but rather, at least in the case of the first indictment brought against him, because of his association with *Hrvatski tjednik*, which was accused of supporting the program of counterrevolutionary groups.

By the late 1980s, thus several years after Tito's death, Gotovac was willing to take a more active role in the political life of his country. In 1989 he founded the Croatian Social-Liberal Party, which lost Croatia's first multiparty elections, in spring 1990, to Franjo Tudjman's Croatian Democratic Union. His preoccupation with the conflict resulting from the breakup of Yugoslavia led to his participation with other writers in a discourse on Yugoslavia published as *Okovana Bosna: Razgovor* (Bosnia in Chains: A Conversation, 1995) and his editing of the Bosnian Croatian writer Juraj Njavro's book *Glava dolje ruke na ledja* (Head Down, Hands Behind You, 1992), which deals mainly with the siege of the Croatian city of Vukovar in some of the worst fighting of the Balkan wars of the 1990s. His first book about his earlier time in prison, *Pisma protiv tiranije* (Letters Against Tyranny), appeared in 1981. It was followed by *Moj slučaj* (My Case, 1989), which consists of separately published essays. Another book, a collection of "notes" covering the years 1972–1973, appeared in 1995 under the title *Zvjezdana kuga: Zatvorski zapisi, 1972–1973* (Star-Studded Plague: Prison Notes, 1972–1973).

Marjan Rožanc (1930–1990), a prominent Slovenian writer, earned three and a half years in prison on a charge of disseminating hostile propaganda against the Yugoslav regime. Known for his versatility and intellectual strengths, Rožanc turned out several well-received novels, short-story collections, and plays. He is also widely admired as a brilliant essayist and for such autobiographical novels as *Slepo oko gospoda Janka* (The Blind Eye of Mister Janko, 1972); *Ljubezen* (Love, 1979), perhaps his best work of fiction, a first-person account of a boy's life in Italian-occupied Ljubljana during World War II; *Roman o knjigah* (A Novel About Books, 1983); *Sentimentalni časi* (Sentimental Times, 1985); *Hudodelci* (Criminals, 1981), which follows the career of a post–World War II rebel and criminal; and *Metulj* (The Butterfly, 1981), a sequel to *Criminals*. Unlike Boris Pekić, Vlado Gotovac, and others, Rožanc did not write a specific work recalling his prison years. Instead, his experiences are reflected in much of his writing, particularly the autobiographical novels.

Two other well-known Slovenian writers, Vitomil Zupan (1914–1987) and Ivan Potrč (1913–1993), also figure in any discussion of post–World War II Yugoslav prison literature. In the case of Zupan, experience of prison was direct and is so reflected in his book *Levitan* (1982). Potrč, on the other hand, had been imprisoned for his communist activism as a young man before the outbreak of World War II and, in a sense, drew on this much earlier experience in his major novel *Na kmetih* (translated into English as *The Land and the Flesh*, 1959). He was also imprisoned by the Germans during the war but escaped in 1943 and joined Tito's partisans. Thus two different experiences, at very different intervals in his life, helped shape the prison dimension of *The Land and the Flesh*.

A versatile writer, Zupan was in Italian internment for a while during World War II and, like Potrč, managed eventually to join the Slovenian partisans. After the war, he worked for Radio Ljubljana until 1947, when he became a freelance writer. In 1948 he was ordered taken into custody as a "suspicious intellectual" and in 1949 was sentenced to eighteen years in prison. He was released, however, in 1954, whereupon he resumed his education, receiving a degree in civil engineering from Ljubljana University in 1958. Soon after, he returned to freelance writing. His first major work was *Andante patetico* (1945), a psychologically interesting novella with a wartime partisan setting. It was critically dismissed as "decadent." Zupan eventually published another dozen novels, three of the best being *Menuet za kitaro* (Minuet for a Guitar, 1975), about a chance meeting at a Spanish resort decades after the war of a former Slovene partisan and a former German officer; the autobiographical *Igra s hudičevim repom* (Playing with the Devil's Tail, 1978); and *Levitan* (1982).

Written at least a decade before it was published, *Levitan* could not be published earlier because of its subject. And when it appeared, it caused a sensation. Its title derived from the name of its principal character, the former partisan Jakob Levitan, the "novel" certainly deserves to be ranked among the most unusual in the annals of Eastern European prison literature. As Levitan-Zupan calmly, unemotionally, recalls his years in prison, it soon becomes obvious that this is no conventional account of imprisonment. Although he minces no words throughout about his disdain for the communist system, he prefers setting aside political issues and the circumstances of his arrest and imprisonment. Instead, he focuses on the sexual dimension of life behind bars. He, and his fellow prisoners, think—and talk—a great deal about sex, potency and impotency, the charms of women and their own reactions to them, both before and while in prison, homosexuality, sadism, masochism, the sexual exploitation of younger men by older ones, and so on.

Levitan deals primarily with the psychology of his fellow prisoners, above all in terms of their attitudes toward sex. Zupan had already established a precedent for such willingness to deal openly with sexual matters—although previously denied admittance into mainstream Slovenian literature—with his 1978 novel, Playing with the Devil's Tail. The candor, and extent, to which he addresses sexual issues in *Levitan,* and his casualness of style, are what make the work so unusual among Eastern European prison narratives. A compelling literary work in its own way, *Levitan*'s absence of chapter divisions seems if anything to enhance the reader's desire to stay with it from beginning to end.

Potrč's best-known work, *The Land and the Flesh,* is a naturalistic tale of lust and unbridled passion. It takes the form of a lengthy confession by a young peasant whom the narrator meets in prison. As the two inmates draw closer, the young man tells him about the events that led up to his sordid affair first with the older wife of a dying neighbor and then with one of her two daughters. In both cases the women become pregnant and bear children. When the affair with the older woman eventually palls and the peasant feels himself caught in a trap from which there is no escape, he strangles her, for which he is arrested and sent to prison. The confessional narration by the young inmate takes place within the context of prison and allows Potrč to draw on his personal understanding of prison life and patterns of interaction among prisoners.

Two of the most distinguished figures in twentieth-century, not just post—World War II, Yugoslav literature—Ivo Andrić and Milovan Djilas—also endured their share of prison life and made it the focus of some of their more important writings. Almost all of Andrić's fictional works appeared after World War II. Before the war his career was primarily that of a diplomat. After a cosmopolitan education that included study at the universities of Zagreb, Vienna, Kraków, and Graz, he entered diplomatic service and was posted to such European cities as Rome, Geneva, Madrid, Bucharest, Trieste, Graz, and

Belgrade. On the eve of World War II he held the position of minister in Berlin. An ardent Bosnian patriot, Andrić was imprisoned for three years during World War I because of his involvement in the Young Bosnia movement, which was suspected of having a hand in the assassination of Archduke Franz Ferdinand and his wife in Sarajevo in 1914. Although Andrić's prison experiences antedate the scope of this book, and were never repeated in the period of communist Yugoslavia, they are reflected in his fiction, most notably the novella *Prokleta avlija* (*The Devil's Yard,* 1954). Set in the period before World War I, *The Devil's Yard* comprises a series of loosely structured stories-within-the-story about various prisoners in the notorious Turkish prison known unofficially as "Devil's Yard" in Istanbul.

One of the legendary figures of modern Yugoslav history, the Montenegran Milovan Djilas (1911–1995), joined the Communist Party while a student at Belgrade University in 1932. His political persuasion and antiroyalist passion landed him three years in jail during the prewar Kingdom of the Serbs, Croats, and Slovenes. Thus began his intimate familiarity with prison life. A close friend and ally of Tito through the years of World War II, Djilas met the future ruler of communist Yugoslavia in 1937, when, as Josif Broz (Tito), he was the secretary-general of the Yugoslav Communist Party. Djilas joined the party's Central Committee in 1938 and, two years later, its Politburo. An ardent Marxist and Leninist, he believed firmly in the rightness of the communist cause and, later, the Yugoslav nationalism espoused by Tito. During the war he was a major player in the partisan resistance movement and Tito's right-hand man. After the war he rose steadily in rank and power, becoming in 1953 one of Yugoslavia's four vice presidents and, in December of that year, president of the Federal People's Assembly. He staunchly supported Tito's break with the Soviet Union in 1948.

Things began going downhill for Djilas not long after his appointment as president of the Federal People's Assembly. His growing criticism of the Communist Party for what he saw as its betrayal of the ideals of communism for the sake of privilege and power, and his increasingly more stubborn insistence on greater liberalization, prompted his dismissal from office and, in April 1954, his resignation from the party. By now his relations with Tito himself had soured beyond repair. After first receiving an eighteen-month suspended sentence, Djilas was imprisoned in 1956 for writing an article for an American magazine supporting the Hungarian Revolution of 1956. As if this were not provocative enough, he brought a nine-year prison sentence down on himself by smuggling out to New York the manuscript of his most famous book, *The New Class* (*Nova klasa*). The publication of the book in 1957 resulted in the serious charge against him of seeking to undermine socialism as an idea. Ironically, the prison to which he was sentenced was the same one in which he had done time in the prewar royalist period.

While still in prison, Djilas went even further in his defiance of the regime by smuggling out for publication in the West yet another book of revelation and denunciation, *Conversations with Stalin* (*Razgovori sa Staljinom* in Serbo-

Croatian), based on his wartime missions to Moscow and his personal meetings with Stalin. The book appeared originally in English, like *The New Class,* in 1962. Once out of prison, and after Tito's death in 1980, Djilas elaborated on the ideas in *The New Class* and published a sequel of sorts under the title *Fall of the New Class (Pad nove klase* in Serbo-Croatian), tellingly subtitled in the English edition *A History of Communism's Self-Destruction.* Before his death in 1997, Djilas had managed to complete four volumes of his political autobiography—*Land Without Justice* (1958), *Memoir of a Revolutionary* (1973), *Wartime* (1977), and *Rise and Fall* (1985), all of which appeared in English before publication of the originals.

Apart from his often-impressive autobiographical writings, his less compelling fictional works, and his rather weak biography of Tito, *Tito: The Story from Inside* (1980), Djilas wrote a collection of essays based on his years in prison entitled *Tamnica i idea (Of Prisons and Ideas;* English translation 1986). Loosely structured, the essays in the collection fall short on concrete ideas, generally covering familiar ground, albeit at times too abstractly. However, in view of the fact that Djilas spent much time in solitary confinement, perhaps it could not have been otherwise. The book succeeds most in the specifics of his recollections of everyday prison life. The pictures Djilas paints are vivid if unsettling—for example, his account of the use of a chamber pot by inmates to smuggle pamphlets from cell to cell or his sketches of peasant convicts who had been jailed for settling old grudges by murder.

Czechoslovakia

Except for the fairly short interval of the Prague Spring of 1968, which, as we know, was ended by the Soviet invasion, the Czechoslovak state was one of the most repressive in all of communist Eastern Europe. Its often antiquated, inadequate, and at times downright primitive prison system (politely referred to by the regime as "corrective educational facilities") was on more than one occasion the target of negative foreign reporting. The number of writers who endured imprisonment and chose to write about it—which in itself could be regarded as a punishable offense—lent further support to the poor press the system has had. Among such writers, the most prominent that come to mind are—chronologically in terms of their imprisonment—Jiří Mucha, the son of the famous Art Nouveau painter Alfons Mucha; the poets Jan Zahradníček and František Daniel Merth; the prose writers Karel Pecka, Jiří Hejda, and Vladimír Škutina; two prominent women writers, Lenka Reinerová and Eva Kantůrková; and the celebrated dramatist Václav Havel, who became president of Czechoslovakia after the downfall of the communist regime.

The biographer of his father and a World War II associate of the Czechoslovak Government-in-Exile and the BBC, Jiří Mucha (1915–1991) returned to Prague at war's end, where in 1947 he published his first book, a set of war memoirs entitled *Oheň proti ohni* (Fire Against Fire). When the communists took effective control of Czechoslovakia in 1948, Mucha, like so many other Czechs who had joined or tried to join the RAF or the British army, was considered suspect and was taken into custody. On unsubstantiated charges of being a spy for the West, he was sentenced in 1951 to six years in prison. However, after the death in 1953 of Klement Gottwald, the first communist president of Czechoslovakia, he was released as part of an amnesty for political prisoners.

When Mucha returned to civilian life in 1954 he began working for the Barandov film studios, where he produced several films under an alias. His background as a political prisoner all but guaranteed that anything he wrote was unlikely to be published. Things changed for the better, however, only in 1962, when he helped arrange an exhibition of works by his then largely forgotten father. This led to the publication in 1966 in English of two books on Alfons Mucha that did much to awaken new interest in the artist. Although he spent much of his later life outside of Czechoslovakia, Mucha was in Prague to witness the success of the Velvet Revolution in 1989, which brought Václav Havel to the presidency of the Czechoslovak state. By now his health had begun to decline rapidly and he died two years later, shortly after his seventy-sixth birthday.

The book by Mucha that interests us most here is *Living and Partly Living*, which was first published in 1967 by Hogarth of London in a translation by that prolific English translator of Czech literature, Ewald Osers. Its title borrowed from a line in T. S. Eliot's *Murder in the Cathedral*, *Living and Partly Living* is written in the form of a diary composed eighteen hundred feet below ground in a labor camp coal mine and in total darkness save for the illumination provided by a miner's lamp. Before then Mucha had spent the better part of a year in solitary confinement. The time was 1952, and the notorious purge trials of Rudolf Slanský, the former deputy premier of Czechoslovakia and Communist Party secretary, and other communist functionaries accused of alleged Anglo-American espionage was in full swing. Mucha's arrest and sentencing to six years of hard labor is best seen in the context of the extreme paranoia of the Czechoslovak communist government in the early 1950s and the anti-Semitism that was also a part of that paranoia. Under "November" in *Living and Partly Living,* Mucha indeed recalls the Slanský trials and the open expressions of anti-Semitism they gave rise to (Slanský himself was Jewish), including those in his camp, where there were a few Jewish inmates.

Living and Partly Living is composed in the form of a year-long month-by-month diary beginning in July and ending in June. The year itself is unspecified. Apart from this one structural aspect, the book is loosely organized and random in nature. The often very detailed descriptions of Mucha's confinement in coal and uranium mines obviously take center stage, but Mucha's interests range broadly and incorporate reminiscences of his childhood, the prewar and war years, his extensive travels, his broad literary interests, from Fleuron to Tagore, reflections on art and culture in general, and the awakening of his desire to become a writer. It was as if his incarceration provided him the welcome opportunity to reflect on, and order, the experiences and impressions of his life. Mucha's memoirs were written by and large during the time that he was in various labor camps. This was anything but an easy task, as paper and writing implements were officially forbidden (as in the case of the Albanian writer Visar Zhiti) though not impossible to obtain by stealth, as Mucha relates early in his book:

> One of the miners works in my section and provides my link with the outside world. He gets me my pencils and small notebooks, which I keep hidden in a hollow behind the wooden shuttering, and he takes my written pages out with him.[9]

Whatever the privations of the camp, they were partially offset at least by Mucha's ability to read. The camp actually had a library from which he was able to take books, especially those by Russian authors. Books were not the only form of culture permitted at the camp. There was a musical organization that performed on occasion and theatricals were also offered. But it was in reading as well as in his own writing that Mucha made the hell of the mines at least minimally bearable. Working in the mines was always hazardous, and the pages of *Living and Partly Living* are full of terrifying descriptions of the many accidents that occurred and the injuries and deaths they caused.

Throughout his incarceration, with its horrific working conditions and occasional sudden changes of prison camp, Mucha retained an admirable optimism. He depicts himself in his book as a man whose spirit simply cannot be broken and who can find cause for happiness even in the grimmest of circumstances. This is not wholly unusual for people who have spent long periods of time behind prison walls. Indeed, Mucha regarded his experiences at Prague-Pankrác, Ostrava, and other places of internment as collectively representing some of the most pleasant moments of his life!

The impact of the news of Stalin's death in 1953, which occurred while Mucha was still in prison camp, had an electrifying effect on the camp routine. The inmates themselves seem to have taken the news in stride. But among the camp officials fear, perhaps of the unknown, became the order of the day:

> Fear. Doubled sentries every night. Orders to fire at the slightest sign of the men forming groups. . . . During the morning the radio played the funeral march from Moscow. Heavy tragic music. The end of an epoch. Everybody can feel it, on both sides, and that is what engenders fear. Fear of the unknown, of the new, of the future. (102–103)

Beyond these few remarks, Mucha has nothing more to say about the passing of the Soviet dictator.

Mucha's voice is not the only one heard in *Living and Partly Living*. Dialogues involving several other inmates are also woven into the narration, providing glimpses into the camp from different perspectives as well as different patterns of speech. Often featured in the dialogues are criminal, as opposed to political, prisoners, with the result that their usually colloquial and earthy idiom stands in contrast to the educated and sometimes poetic style of Mucha himself. But notwithstanding the eloquence, for example, of the closing passage of the book, it is, in the final analysis, the incredible grimness and inhumanity of prison life that stands out starkly and vividly in *Living and Partly Living* and gives the memoir its true power.

No less interesting, although lesser known in the West, are the prison writings of the poets Jan Zahradníček and František Daniel Merth, the prose writer and poet Jiří Hejda, and the prose writers Lenka Reinerová, Karel Pecka, and Vladimír Skutina.

Jan Zahradníček (1905–1960) is widely esteemed as one of the great Czech poets of Catholic mysticism. If, in his earlier poetry, he seemed haunted by visions of suffering and death, in his later writing he found sustenance in the spiritual traditions of his native land and the saints who watched over her destiny. In 1951, after suppression of his book, *Znamení moci* (Sign of Power, 1948), on the communist acquisition of power in Czechoslovakia, he was arrested on charges of illegal association and treason, and was sentenced to thirteen years in prison. He was granted a temporary reprieve in 1956 in order to sit by the deathbed of his two daughters, who died after eating poisonous mushrooms, but was returned to prison immediately after their funeral. He was finally released in 1960, but died that same year. Although he was subsequently cleared of all charges, he became a nonperson in official Czech literary histories; for the next forty years only one of his books was reprinted. His posthumously published books of poems, *Čtyři léta* (Four Years, 1969) and *Dům strach* (Fear House, first published in Toronto in 1981), deal primarily with the latter four years of his imprisonment. Zahradníček's account of his struggle to preserve his sanity through long hours of solitary isolation and to compose poems in his own head, in the absence of writing materials, constitutes some of the most poignant writing in the annals of Czech prison literature.

František Daniel Merth (b. 1915) was a Catholic priest who made his debut as a writer in 1937 with the verse collection *Refrigerium*. During World War II he published nothing. In 1948 he was arrested and sentenced to five years' incarceration. Following his release, he was permitted to resume his career as a priest only in 1971. His first literary work published after his prison years was a collection of poems in prose under the title *Nokturny* (Nocturnes, 1966). The following year he brought out another book of poems, *Den Madian* (Madian's Day, 1968). With an introduction by Zdeněk Kalist, who had shared Merth's imprisonment, it is beautifully illustrated by a photographic assemblage of symbolic objects. It was privately printed outside Prague and distributed to a select circle of readers. Characterized by lonely introspection, strange dreams, and hallucinations, the poems are clearly those of a poet who had left the society of men for an inner exile of the spirit. Before a prohibition against further publication was imposed on him in 1971, Merth succeeded in issuing another three volumes of poetry: *Kahany* (1969), *Na jihu království* (In His Kingdom, 1969), and *Orančína píseň* (Orange Song, 1970). A subsequent small collection of poems, originally composed in 1976, circulated unprinted under the title *Sedm básnů* (Seven Poems) until 1994, a few years after the fall of communism in Czechoslovakia, when it made its first appearance in print—with a slight change of title, *Sedm písní* (Seven Songs). The "seven" of the title refers to the seven cycles of poems of which the book consists.

The bulk of Jiří Hejda's (1895–1985) published work deals with his prison experiences, beginning with the novel *Útěk* (Flight), which appeared in 1969 and offers a chilling account of life in the notorious Leopoldov prison in Slovakia. Hejda's subsequent publications all came out in the 1990s and include *Žil jsem zbytečně: Román mého života* (I Lived Superfluously: The Story of My Life, 1991), a large two-part autobiography that covers his life from World War I to 1973, and *Sonety zpívané šeptem ve stínu šibenice: Ruzyně–Pankrác–Mirov–Leopoldov–Valdice, 1950–1962* (Sonnets Chanted in a Whisper in the Shadow of the Gallows: Ruzyně–Pankrác–Mirov–Leopoldov–Valdice, 1950–1962, 1993), the very title of which tells the whole story.

Hejda recounts in much detail the circumstances of his arrest, trial, and sentencing in I Lived Superfluously: The Story of My Life.[10] The salient facts are these: Hejda was one of the thirteen-member group of alleged antistate terrorists led by the well-known political activist Dr. Milada Horáková (1901–1950) that was tried and convicted in 1950. In the most notorious communist-era show trial preceding the Rudolf Slanský case of 1952, Horáková, a former member of the Czech Parliament who had been active in the resistance during World War II, was sentenced to death despite pleas from around the world for an amelioration of the court's judgment. But the Czech president Klement Gottwald refused to budge, and so on 27 June 1950 Horáková and three codefendants were hanged. The rest of what was called at the time "Horáková & Co." were given long prison terms.

Hejda, who was taken into custody on 21 December 1949, was kept out of touch with his family for the next six months. His trial, which was billed as "public" and began on 31 May, was also barred to them. Spared the death penalty, which relieved his wife and children of their greatest fear, he was, however, sentenced to over a dozen years in prison. His long ordeal then began. Before his arrest and incarceration, Hejda had been engaged primarily in industry and finance and was also an attorney. In prison he became a poet. In order to keep from succumbing to utter despair and hopelessness, he took refuge in verse. Poetry truly became his salvation. Without paper and pencil, he had to compose his poems in his head and commit them to memory—an astonishing, seemingly impossible feat, but one nevertheless brought off successfully by more than one Eastern European writer in prison under the communists, as we have seen.

The fruit of Hejda's creativity was the sonnet collection Sonnets Chanted in a Whisper in the Shadow of the Gallows: Ruzyně –Pankrác–Mirov–Leopoldov–

Valdice, 1950–1962. That Hejda in fact conceived of the 153 poems in the ten-part collection as a cycle is evident from their linked nature. Throughout the entire text, the last line of each sonnet is repeated as the first line of the following. The prefatory poem "Louisa," which Hejda dedicated to his wife, sets the tone of the sonnet cycle as a whole:

> For half a century I didn't have a free moment
> to write verse, not even in a diary.
> . . . Now it is surely strange
> for someone so old to turn up
> in the guild of poets.
> It's not my fault. Prison garb put me there.
> This is by way of an apology.
> If these verses, rhymed casually
> and in solitude, without paper, in the dark
> and from memory, bring You only
> a measure of the happiness they gave me,
> then I shall be at peace in the depths of my soul.[11]

Addressing himself in the sonnets, Hejda conveys a deep sense of disillusionment in humankind. If the act of composing the sonnets, in all their intricacy, helped sustain him during the many days and nights of his imprisonment, they themselves are still full of the despair he sought to avoid as much as possible. "You gained everything," he writes in one sonnet, "power, wealth, and love, / independence and self-confidence, / and you lost everything" (24). Elsewhere, he speaks of the finality of death: "Death, that is the end, afterward there's nothing. / A voice, captured on a tape-recorder, / a face, smiling from picture postcards, / that's all that will remain after your demise" (104). Running throughout the sonnets like a leitmotif is Hejda's desire to build a new and better world. Acknowledging the fact that the world pays little attention to events in a small, easily conquered country in the middle of Europe, he laments its becoming a "plaything in the hands of new Tamerlanes," an obvious allusion to the Soviets. At the end, yoking the death camps of World War II and the Czech prison system, he laments: "Terezín, Dachau, Pankrác, Auschwitz. / That is our destiny! Perhaps we are cursed" (139).

As if the deprivation of his liberty and the long separation from his family were not enough to crush his spirit, Hejda also suffered the loss of his wife, Louisa, while in prison. In early August 1955 he received a note from his eldest daughter, Jitka, informing him that his wife had passed away on the morning of 2 August. He was sixty at the time. He composed a sonnet on her death ("Na smrt Luisy," "On Louisa's Death"), recalling their happiness together and lamenting the fact that now they would not be able to discuss his sonnets, to which he had been so looking forward.

I was happy that one day I would come home,
that we would discuss these verses.
. . . We lived together like two birds in the shadow of thunder,
and we had our own world in our nest
for fair weather and in the roaring of thunder,
here on the outside it resembled the wings of a stage
behind which the actors were performing a strange farce,
and then you were dead to me.—I remained alone,
I no longer have a home; this was taken away from me.
And the sonnets dedicated to you
others may read, but not you. (109)

The extraordinary feat of memory and creativity represented by Hejda's sonnets, and the poignancy and emotional range of the poems themselves, establishes the collection as one of the memorable achievements of Eastern European
prison camp literature.

A remnant of the once-thriving German-speaking Jewish community of
Prague, and billed as the last female writer of that city to write in German,
Lenka Reinerová (b. 1916) was long affiliated with left-wing and communist
causes. While working as a journalist, she fled Czechoslovakia in 1939 after
the German takeover and sought refuge in France. But after the German invasion of that country she was taken into custody and interned for a time in
the women's camp in Rieucros. Once she managed to make her way to the
so-called unoccupied zone of France, she—like other German-language writers from Czechoslovakia who were either Jews or communists, or both (Anna
Seghers, Egon Erwin Kisch, and Bodo Uhse, among others)—was assisted by
the American League of Writers in securing a visa to Mexico.

With war's end, she and her husband, the writer and medical doctor Theodor
Balk, returned to Prague in 1948 after a few years residence in Belgrade,
Yugoslavia, where she worked for Radio Belgrade. But in spring 1952 she was
arrested in conjunction with the Slanský affair and was placed in investigative
detention for fifteen months, after which she and her family were required to
live in the provinces, away from Prague. The charges against her were high
treason, espionage for the class enemy, and Zionism, especially the latter. She
was "rehabilitated" in 1964, but in 1968—after the suppression of the Prague
Spring—she was dismissed from the Czechoslovak Communist Party, banned
from further publication, and made to give up her job as editor in chief of the
German-language monthly *Im Herzen Europas*.

Her book *Alle Farben der Sonne und der Nacht* (All the Colors of Sun and
Night, 2003) is an account of her arrest and imprisonment in a windowless
cell, where, in the company of another female prisoner named Dana, she reviews events in her life both big and small. When not reminiscing about her student days, her work with a group helping refugees from Nazi Germany resettle

in Prague before the invasion of Czechoslovakia, her wartime internment in France, her flight to Mexico, her postwar stay in Yugoslavia, and her eventual return to Czechoslovakia, Reinerová undergoes interrogation after interrogation. Indeed, imprisonment becomes a seemingly never-ending series of interrogations to which, and from which, she is conducted blindfolded. The suddenness of her initial arrest and incarceration are recalled in these words:

> For an entire month I was detained in an improvised cell in the basement of a splendid villa belonging to State Security. Then one morning they bound my eyes, bundled me into some vehicle, and drove off. Everything without a single word of explanation. After the auto had stopped for a certain length of time, I was taken out—with my eyes still bound—and led into some building. Stale cold air surrounded me. A gate creaked, I was pushed in somewhere, and then came the command: "Remove the blind from your eyes!" I was standing in a prison cell, at the beginning of my solitary confinement. Nobody bothered to tell me that the institution I was in was the notorious Ruzyně. The interrogations that were now initiated were irregular, but frequent. Mostly during the day, but sometimes I was also fetched at night.[12]

As to what her interrogations were aimed at discovering, Reinerová recalls that there was hardly a facet of her life that had not become suspect. The conditions of her imprisonment were degrading but typical:

> Mornings, we had to get up at 5:30 and only at 9:30 at night were we allowed to lie down. Our days consisted of sixteen long hours. The burdensome idleness resulted only in burdensome fatigue. The cell was insufficiently aired out, and was outfitted with just two small flap seats covered in metal and a barely larger slab that served as an eating table. During the day our two straw mattresses were folded against the wall; at night, the seats and the so-called table. The cell was so small this entire setup could not be let down from the wall all at once.
>
> A Turkish privy was located in a corner, above which we also washed ourselves. For drinking, we were given a paper cup into which you could collect water if you stood with one foot on the privy and with the other on a bar directly above it. That was nearly an acrobatic feat. Apart from the cup and the daily ration of bread nothing else was to be kept in the cell. The most basic hygienic items also had to be requested each time from the guard, who gave you—three sheets of toilet paper per day or none at all, depending on his mood. (85)

And then one day, as abruptly as she was first taken into custody, she was again blindfolded and, after a series of maneuvers worthy of any spy novel, then set free. It seems that Comrade Stalin and Comrade Klement Gottwald, the Czech head of state, had both recently died, the Slanský trials had ended with everyone being hanged, and Lenka Reinerová was no longer a person of interest to State Security.

Karel Pecka has been often referred as the Czech Solzhenitsyn, on the basis of his 1970s book *Motáky nezvěstnému* (Uncensored Letters to the Missing), a two-part novel based on his prison camp experiences and written between February 1975 and May 1978. The book first circulated in samizdat in Prague and was subsequently published by Sixty-Eight Publishers in Toronto in 1980. Pecka was arrested as early as 1949 for contributing to an illegal newspaper (the charge was "high treason") and was sentenced to eleven years' imprisonment in the labor camp at Bytíz u Příbrami. This was the first of several camps to which he was assigned. On his release in 1959 he found employment as a scenery technician for the National Theater. During the political thaw of the mid-1960s, leading up to the invasion of Czechoslovakia in 1968, he resumed his literary career as the author of several novels, among them *Úniky* (Evasions, 1966), *Veliký slunovrat* (The Great Solstice, 1968), and, perhaps the most important of them, *Na co umírají muži* (What Men Die Of, 1968), which he had written in prison.

In the 1970s and '80s Pecka was very active in the dissident movement, and was a signatory of Charter 77. His literary career continued unabated, and by the time of his death in 1997 he had produced another eleven works of fiction. On the occasion of Pecka's fiftieth birthday, Ludvík Vaculík wrote a feuilleton entitled "On Heroism" in which he lauds Pecka's ability to bounce back from the privations of prison life:

> It is one thing if they imprison someone who knows exactly what he is doing and why, and quite another when a young, immature person lands in jail, more or less by accident. I was amazed, for instance, by the fate of Karel Pecka (a leading dissident who made his literary debut in the sixties), who frittered his youth away in the uranium mines. For someone to be able to pick up the pieces of such a wrecked life and to give it meaning and value I believe requires a kind of courage he surely did not possess before his prison experience.[13]

This resilience, if you will, is present in Pecka's prison writings. Uncensored Letters to the Missing is one of the best, and most readable, prison-camp books written by an Eastern European. A talented storyteller, as evidenced by the success of his fiction, Pecka recounts his experiences in an unpretentious, colloquial style free of sentiment or moralizing. Although the book is narrated in the first person, Pecka appears in the work as the inmate named Vilém Svoboda. "Svoboda" means freedom in Czech, and the name was chosen to point out the grim irony in the position of Pecka and his fellow political inmates. The largely first-person narrative extends over two parts, for a total length of 517 pages in the Sixty-Eight Publishers edition of 1980. It covers the transfers from one camp to another (among them Pankrác and Fierlinger) of Pecka and his fellow prisoners; their work in uranium mines somewhat similar to the ones Mucha writes about; their relations with one another, and with the camp authorities, including the ease with which they could, and did, report on one another when the pressure was great enough; the visits to the camps of family members and other loved ones; the musical programs arranged by the authorities utilizing inmates' talents; the publication of a camp newspaper; and the severe beatings an inmate might receive if he withheld information.

Fellow inmates (not all of whom were Czechs) and prison authorities are vividly recalled by Pecka, who weaves a considerable amount of dialogue into his narrative adding to its readability.

> "Talk, or it'll be still worse," the interrogator's voice rang out.
>
> I remained silent. I had to endure two more rounds, I reckoned in my mind. God, let me hold out; afterward it'll be credible. Ten more blows rained down, the heaviest and more frenzied from the right side, the weaker ones from the left. This idiot on the right's going to break my ribs; he's got to be a true believer. I bellowed like an ox, when someone hit me hard in the belly with his fist. I groaned and fell forward. My hands, shackled behind the back of a chair, tightened to the very bone, held me back.[14]

Vladimir Škutina (b. 1931) was arrested and imprisoned in 1962 but was released after serving ten months, on the grounds that he had not committed any legal offense. During the reform period he was a popular television personality, and in April 1969 received an award from the Ministry of Culture for his work in the field of television drama. The account he wrote about his imprisonment, *Presidentův vězeň* (Prisoner of the President; reissued in 1980 under the title *Presidentův vězeň na hradě plném bláznů* [Prisoner of the President in a Castle Full of Madmen]), was published by a local press in northern Bohemia in July 1969.

That same month, while vacationing in Yugoslavia with his family, he was prosecuted in absentia and arrested upon his return to Czechoslovakia. Together with the journalist J. Lederer, he became one of the first victims of renewed repression in the literary field after the suppression of the Prague Spring. Charged with defaming President Novotný by saying publicly that he was an ass, Škutina was held under arrest for three months and released in December 1969, rearrested in 1970, and sentenced to four years' imprisonment. He was finally set free again in 1974. Four years later, he and his family immigrated to Switzerland, where he has lived ever since.

Besides Prisoner of the President, most of Škutina's work has been in the lighter revue vein. These include such texts as *Lenin v Curychu* (Lenin in Zurich, 1985); *Josef Švejk a Josef K.: Dva osaměli chodci na Karlově most* (Josef Švejk and Josef K.: Two Solitary Pedestrians on the Charles Bridge, 1988); *Humor als Waffe: Leider die einzige* (Humor as Weapon: Unfortunately, the Only One,

1988); *Masarykové v Ženevě* (The Masaryks in Geneva, 1989); *Was ist Komik? Vladimir Škutina über Humor und Charles Chaplin* (What Is the Comic? Vladimir Škutina on Humor and Charles Chaplin, 1990); and others.

Two of the most unusual and gripping literary works to come out of the Czech prison milieu were Eva Kantůrková's *Dvanáct rozhovorů* (Twelve Conversations, 1980) and *Přítelkyně z domu smutku* (*My Companions in the Bleak House*, 1984). A well-known Czech novelist, short-story writer, and essayist, Kantůrková studied history and philosophy at Charles University and, after taking her degree in 1956, worked for roughly the next ten years as an editor before devoting herself full-time to writing in 1967. Although the daughter of the communist journalist Jiří Síla (1911–1960), she soon became an opponent of the Czechoslovak communist regime and a highly vocal spokesperson for liberal and democratic reform. Needless to say, it was next to impossible for her to publish anything in Czechoslovakia, with the result that until the collapse of the regime most of her works appeared in underground or overseas publications.

A very talented essayist who wrote mostly on literature and politics, and an able novelist with at least a half-dozen novels to her credit, Kantůrková secured her reputation as a dissident writer with Twelve Conversations and *My Companions in the Bleak House*. Originally an underground publication, Twelve Conversations consists of a series of conversations with twelve women whose husbands were imprisoned for political reasons. A similar publication, devoted to such well-known women dissidents as Olga Havlová, Mariá Rut Křížková, Elzbieta Ledererová, and others was published in Cologne, Germany, in the Czech Index series in 1980 under the title *Sešly jsme se v této knize* (We Met in This Book).

My Companions in the Bleak House is a book of vivid portraits of female prisoners that is based on Kantůrková's own one-year incarceration in the dreary Ruzyně prison on the outskirts of Prague after a charge of sedition. She touches on such subjects as the awful stench within the prison; the restrictions on contacts between the inmates; the dehumanization and humiliation the prison system works on those unlucky to be confined within its walls; the conduct of the guards and other officials toward the prisoners; the periodic body searches; the behavior of the inmates toward one another; and the sometimes long-lasting bonds that developed between them. In one of the memorable paragraphs in her introduction, Kantůrková imagines how the inside of her cell must have looked to someone viewing it through a peephole:

Six of us were lying crowded together, although the cell was intended for four; iron bedsteads painted gray, gray blankets, for the most part filthy, poorly washed and torn sheets, sagging beds; as for our pajamas, the less said the better—they were of coarse orange-colored cloth, the same cut for men and for women, one pair missing part of a sleeve, another with only one trouser leg, some with no elastic in the waist to hold them up. Our underwear was shabby and terribly laundered. Lying there hunched together under our gray blankets, we looked like plucked parrots nobody wanted. We were as miserable as only a human being can be miserable.[15]

Of the many aspects of women's prison life that she touches on in her book, perhaps the most bizarre in a sense is what she characterizes as the "toilet telephone." This became the most frequent means by which the women maintained contact with male prisoners on other floors. When she first heard of it, from a friend jailed ten years earlier for unorthodox political views, her reaction was one of horror:

"What? Talking into a toilet drain?" Oh! If that's all there was to it! You have to kneel down to the toilet when all the water had spilled out of the siphon so that you could hear through the drain pipe. Majka's fingernails were worn down to the skin from splashing water out the pipe. Every now and then we'd hear from a window: "Majka, flush it out! Libuška, flush it out!" Which meant: get all the water out of the siphon so we can talk. Majka's eyes were irritated and she had a rash on her forehead from the gaseous odors coming from the drainage. She also enticed me into making the acquaintance of someone the same way. . . . However much the idea nauseated me, I had to admit that for these dear girls this telephoning had to be their daily bread, and literally, for what other way does a woman have to get a man, in jail? . . . But some of the girlies babbled such filth into the toilet that the men couldn't flush the pipes and fill them with water again fast enough in order to drown their voices. (25–26)

Like other works by her, Kantůrková's *My Companions in the Bleak House* is a no-holds-barred look at life around her, raw and compelling. In this case, it is the life of women in prison. It was a life Kantůrková herself came to know well, from the inside. Relating her cellmates' stories with compassion and objectivity, she gives her reader not only a glimpse of the dark world of prison in the days of the Czechoslovak communist regime, but a cross section of contemporary society as well. It is not just Ruzyně prison that emerges as the "bleak house" of Kantůrková's book, but Czechoslovakia itself.

Václav Havel, whose formidable international reputation is based both on his work as a dramatist and on his highly visible involvement in politics, was imprisoned on four different occasions—in 1977, 1978–1979, 1979–1983, and 1989—for a total of nearly five years. After his trial on 22 and 23 October 1979, he was found guilty of the crime of subversion against the state. Havel himself was sentenced to four and a half years in prison. The first seven and a half months of his imprisonment were spent in Ruzyně prison, where he had been kept from the time of his initial arrest. On 7 January 1980 he was transferred to the prison at Heřmanice, outside Ostrava in northern Moravia. In July 1981 he was taken to the hospital at Pankrác prison, where it was discovered that he was suffering from a bowel tumor. After the removal of the tumor, he was transferred in August to yet another prison, Plzeň-Bory. Eventually, he was removed to a municipal hospital and, on medical grounds, soon released.

Unlike most of the writers we have looked at, Havel never wrote about his prison experiences as such. They affected him deeply, and it was to take him a long time to recover from them. His letters to his wife, Olga, which now rank highly among his writings, contain no information on the circumstances of his confinement. Prison rules and regulations forbade the incorporation into letters to family members of any references to life inside prison. The letters to Olga are instead filled with questions about her management of their household in his absence, about the myriad of mundane details that make up a person's day-to-day existence. They also include requests for items to be brought him when she and their son, Ivan, next visit (the family was allowed four visits per year). What her letters to him were about we can only guess, since they were all confiscated by the authorities. But the importance of his letters to her were of immense psychological value and cannot be overestimated. They provided his only link to the outside world for over four years and, in a sense, were an outlet, and an important one, for his creative impulses.

Once out of prison, Havel did write one small play with a prison setting. This was *Chyba* (Mistake), which he dedicated to Samuel Beckett as an expression of gratitude for Beckett's play *Catastrophe*, written by the Irish playwright in 1982 for the Avignon Festival and dedicated to Havel while he was still in prison. A five-page one-acter, like the Beckett play, *Mistake* dramatizes the indoctrination a new prisoner receives from his fellow inmates. Although they intend merely to give him an innocuous explanation of prison procedure, the other inmates mistake a lack of response from the newcomer as insolence and begin assaulting him. The truth of the matter is that he is a foreigner, possibly a Hungarian, who does not understand Czech. The point of *Mistake* is the potential for violence that lies just beneath the surface of prison life, where misunderstandings happen all too often, especially when inmates are transferred from cell to cell and from prison to prison, with sometimes dire consequences. Havel has spoken on more than one occasion of his personal knowledge of this more sinister aspect of prison experience.

Rudolf Dobiáš (b. 1934), a writer known primarily for works about and for children, was barely out of secondary school when he was arrested in 1953 on a baseless charge of antistate activity and sentenced to hard labor in the uranium mines in Jáchymov. He was given amnesty in 1960. After completing studies at the Technical Secondary Chemical School in Bratislava, he went on to become a freelance writer, specializing in children's literature, and for two years was also employed as a warden at a home for destitute children. From 1990 to 1993 he served as a journalist on the staff of the newspaper *Slovenský denník*.

Dobiáš eventually became active in the (Slovak) Confederation of Political Prisoners, and for several years was editor in chief of the magazine *Svedectvo*, which was published by the confederation. In conjunction with these responsibilities, Dobiáš wrote four works of a revelatory nature based on his own experiences as a political prisoner, as well as on those of others. The first was the documentary-like *Svedectvo troch krížov* (The Testimony of Three Crosses), the first work for adults Dobiáš wrote after the fall of the communist regime in 1989. It describes a contrived communist trial and the death of three of his fellow students from Trenčin gymnasium. *Temná zeleň* (Dark Green, 1996), which came next, is an award-winning collection of stories for adults. The book is essentially a caustic overview of the half-century of communist totalitarianism in Slovakia. *Tajni ľudia* (Secret People, 1999) is another collection of stories and novellas along similar lines, its title derived from the longest story in the book. In the majority of the texts, which are distinguished by a sharply etched period background, Dobiáš's protagonists attempt to free themselves from the past and to forget it, though not at the price of forgiveness.

Zvony a hroby (Bells and Graves, 2000), subtitled *Príbehy z prítmia* (Tales from the Shadows), originated during what Dobiáš has referred to as the longest winter of his life—late 1953 and early 1954—when he had to endure solitary confinement in the interrogation room of the state security police. It is a somber book that pays homage to fellow prisoners who died in incarceration. The first section, "Koniec šialeného storočia" ("The End of a Crazy Century"), leaves no doubt as to Dobiáš's attitude toward the hideous century of world war, mass murder, and political extremism through which he lived. This is followed by a series of somber "testimonies" of crosses, referring to dead prisoners and others. Clearly not a work of fiction, Bells and Graves is rather a collection of essays interspersed with prayers of a religious character offering thanks to God for freedom.

Hungary

Of the Hungarian writers who chose to write about prison camp experience or to transform it into fiction, the most interesting are Tibor Déry, Árpád Göncz, Ádám Bodor, and József Lengyel.

We have previously encountered Déry as the author of the dystopian novel Mr. A. G. in X. (1964). Prior to the post–World War II advent of communism in Hungary, Déry had already experienced brief stays in prison because of the conservative interwar regime's dissatisfaction with what they deemed the questionable morality of a few of his earlier literary works as well as his obviously pro-left sympathies. However, these earlier prison experiences pale by comparison with the much longer incarceration he was made to endure from the time he was taken into custody on 20 April 1957 until 1960. Again, the charges brought against him related to his writings and his politics. Denounced for his unacceptable treatment of the working class in *Felelet* (The Answer, 1951), Déry had already come under suspicion by the party. But his fate was sealed by his growing activism on behalf of democratic socialism in the days preceding the Hungarian Revolution of 1956 and during its aftermath.

Chronologically, Déry begin writing about his imprisonment almost from the time he was put in a cell in Budapest and had use of writing tools. Although not dealing for the most part with prison life, the autobiographical notes he began compiling in prison eventually appeared under the title *Börtönnapok hordaléka: Önélejtrazi egyzetek, 1958* (Prison Days Deposits: Autobiographical Notes, 1958, 1989; the original title had been simply *Önélejtrazi egyzetek*). Curiously, his very candid autobiography *Itélet nincs* (No Verdict), which appeared in 1969, is actually less valuable as a source for his period in prison than Prison Days Deposits.

Déry's deepest responses engendered by his incarceration appear in the series of letters he wrote principally to his mother, Ernestin Rosenberg, who was ninety-four years old at the time and bedridden, and to his third wife, the actress Erzsébet Kunsági (referred to as Böbe). The differences between the two sets of letters are striking. A devoted and loving son, who had visited his mother often and used her as the inspiration for a few of his literary characters, Déry simply did not have the heart to tell her of his arrest and subsequent imprisonment. Instead, and with his wife's complicity, he created a myth of domestic and foreign film and literary assignments that kept him away from her and often from Hungary. Fully aware of her feelings for him, he counted on her reluctance to do or say anything that might interfere with his career, no matter where it took him or for how long. The hoax was elaborate, but certainly well intentioned. Through the complicity of friends who happened to be in Italy, for example, Déry was able to generate letters to his mother with Italian addresses and Italian stamps.

Déry's letters to his wife were more straightforward. Circumspection was obviously necessary since the letters were read by more than just the intended recipient. There is little talk about the actual conditions of Déry's imprisonment but a great deal about friends and relatives, mutual concerns about health and medical care, and long lists of books that Déry wanted his wife to send him. But circumspection did not mean that the correspondents felt constrained to limit themselves just to the exchange of factual information. The correspondence is in fact often deeply emotional, and for this reason the letters of Tibor Déry and Böbe have been reckoned among the loveliest in Hungarian literature.

Déry's books, manuscripts, and even furniture were finally brought together in a single place in 1970, three years after his death—this was the Petőfi Literary Museum in Budapest. When the Déry materials began to be assembled there, a plan was developed to publish a series of volumes consisting in the main of previously unpublished and long-forgotten works, including the author's correspondence. The series was to be called the Déry Archive. Five volumes have appeared to date, including: *Három asszony* (Three Wives, 1995), the correspondence with his three wives, and *Liebe Mamuskam* (My Dear Mommy, 1998), his correspondence with his mother, a born Viennese whom he usually spoke with and wrote to in German.

On 2 May 1990 Árpád Göncz became Hungary's first democratically elected president in four decades. Before then he had been known as a playwright, short-story writer, essayist, and translator. After receiving his degree in law from Budapest University in 1944 he became a private in the army but also served in the Hungarian antifascist underground. When World War II ended, he was hired as an attorney by an agricultural bank in Budapest and continued his earlier collaboration with the Independent Smallholders Party, a left-of-center opposition group. The communist takeover of Hungary in 1948 cost him his job and forced him to find employment as an unskilled factory worker. He subsequently became involved in soil reclamation and studied agricultural engineering at Gödöllö University.

For his role in the revolution of 1956 he was sentenced to life imprisonment but served only six and a half years. He speaks of this imprisonment in the forward to the English translation of his collection of stories *Hazaérkezes* (*Homecoming*, 1990; translation published 1991):

> The revolution put an end to my studies. But I was lucky this time too: again I had witnessed too much inhumanity not to seek—together with friends—some political solution, a reasonable compromise involving a modus vivendi with the Soviet Union, so that we would not have to live through eight more such dreadful years. Our experiment failed. It was at that point I served my six years, the years—which I then believed—I owed the devil. After a closed, secret trial whose procedures were rushed through with no chance of appeal, I was sentenced to life imprisonment for conspiracy and treason, together with István Bibó, who, with the martyred communist prime minister Imre Nagy, was the major political hero of 1956. It was in prison that I learned the English language, and I still feel that for this, if nothing else, my confinement was worthwhile.[16]

Göncz began his study of English while in prison, as he tells us in the foreword to *Homecoming*. Once he was released from prison, Göncz was denied permission to work either as a lawyer or as an agricultural engineer. He turned instead to translation, first technical, then literary, and went on to achieve distinction in this area, as a translator of American, Canadian, and British literatures. He has translated, among others, works by James Baldwin, Truman Capote, Willa Cather, William Faulkner, Ernest Hemingway, John Updike, and Thomas Wolfe.

As a creative writer, Göncz is the author of a few plays and several short stories. Göncz's first play, *Rácsok* (Iron Bars, 1979), about a poet imprisoned because the president of an unnamed republic wants him to admit that he, the president, not the poet, was the author of the country's national anthem, was based on the experience of a fellow inmate in the Budapest prison (see discussion above in chapter 3). A collection of his plays was published in 1990 under the title *Mérleg: Hét drámaja* (Balance: Seven Plays). His short stories appear in two collections, *Találkozások* (Encounters, 1980) and *Hazaérkezes* (Homecoming, 1990). From terse vignettes about the horrors of World War II to an encounter several hundred years after her burning at the stake between Joan of Arc and Bishop Couchon, they are written in a spare, even laconic style.

But his prose works, like his plays, convey a deep respect for human dignity and a love of life.

The prison experiences of Ádám Bodor (b. 1936) and József Lengyel (1896–1975) were quite different from those of Déry and Göncz. Both were in fact incarcerated in foreign prisons. In the case of Bodor, a Transylvanian Hungarian who lived in Romania until 1982, when he was able to resettle in Hungary, he was taken into custody on political grounds and jailed from 1952 to 1954. Known primarily as the author of such strange yet compelling novels as *Sinistra körzet* (The Sinistra District, 1992) and *Az érsek látogatása* (The Archbishop's Visit, 1999), Bodor has more recently addressed the matter of his Romanian imprisonment in *A börtön szaga* (The Prison Saga, 2001). This is in fact a lengthy series of answers to questions posed in a radio interview by the Transylvanian Hungarian writer and journalist Zsófia Balla (b. 1949)—hence the subtitle of The Prison Saga, *Válasok Balla Zsófia kérdéseire: Egy korábbi rádióinterjú változata* (Answers to Zsófia Balla's Inquiry: Based on a Previous Radio Interview).

Bodor's descent into the nightmare of the Romanian gulag began when he was arrested at the age of seventeen by the Securitate for his establishment of IKESZ (Illegális Kommunistaellenes Szervezet [Illegal Anticommunist Organization]). He was an avowed anticommunist, as was his father, a well-known economist who had previously been brought up on charges of treason against the state for his involvement in the case of Áron Márton (1896–1980), the Roman Catholic Bishop of Transylvania who was sentenced to fifteen years in prison by a Bucharest court in 1951 for his support of the inclusion of Transylvania within the borders of the Hungarian state. He was released by the amnesty of 1955 but was placed under house arrest from 1956 to 1968. Like his father and Bishop Márton, Bodor believed passionately in the cause of Transylvanian independence from Romanian rule and actively subscribed to the violent overthrow of the Romanian communist state. As he himself declares in The Prison Saga, he dreamt of becoming a conspirator and political assassin and fashioned himself on characters in the crime fiction of Edgar Wallace. The Romanian secret police thwarted Bodor's dreams in no uncertain terms and hastened the transformation of the impetuous youth into the sober adult.

Since the secret police already knew virtually everything they needed to know about the IKESZ organization and Bodor's role in it, thanks to a loose-tongued IKESZ member who had cracked under pressure, they had no need to resort to physical violence to wring a confession from him. Bodor admits that he was treated well and never subjected to any beatings, or worse—this despite the fact that after an initial, fairly short term of incarceration in Cluj, he was transferred to the prison in Gherla, one of the most notorious in Romania, where he remained until his surprise release (which he attributes to outside influence). It was while at Gherla that Bodor came across former members of the Romanian fascist Iron Guard who were undergoing "reeducation." For much of the time that he was behind bars he shared a cell with other political prisoners, at first fellow members of IKESZ who had been caught in the same police dragnet as

Bodor himself. Conditions could hardly be described as ideal, but Bodor's main complaint had to do with food:

> Political prisoners were not entitled to visits, nor were they able to receive letters or any packages. So we had to make do with what the prison kitchen dished out. No denying, day and night we were hungry. But I have to admit that after the Securitate's food, despite the fact that the menu never changed for weeks on end—every day we got the same thing—we couldn't praise the prison chefs enough. By way of breakfast we were given a runny, sugary corn mush; at noon, like a kind of high tea, rations of bread were passed around. Later, a still unforgettable one-course meal was served: its base was beetroot soup, into which were tossed appropriately proportioned pieces of potato, celery and turnip, some crushed barley, or pearl barley, as it's called, and from this substantial enough mixture real little pieces of ox tongue and brains peered out. Ugh, my saliva immediately starts flowing. To be sure, a little lemon or sour cream wouldn't upset the balance of it. We swore that once we were free the same dish would steam on our tables at least once a week. This certainly doesn't mean that tongue and brains are indispensable in Romanian culinary culture; rather, I believe that they just habitually fell into our plates because some more finicky army quartermaster, an officers' mess head chef, had exiled them from the menu, so that thanks to his caprice every week a load of cattle heads from the neighboring army post was dispatched to the prison kitchen. Of course, there were less fortunate days when, for example, instead of brains, bits of hairy, gristly calves' ears were floating on the surface of the soup. But it also happened that from the mess kit spoon a mournful calf's eye every now and then stared accusingly at a convict.[17]

Bodor's recollections of his imprisonment in Romania offer a splendid look inside one of the most abusive prison systems in all of Eastern Europe in the communist era. If he himself suffered relatively little, many Romanian writers and intellectuals who passed through the same system have a different story to tell, as we have seen. But there are moments in Bodor's Prison Saga when he shares glimpses of the harsh treatment meted out at the hands of former Iron Guardists who worked as "kapos," or trustees, at Gherla.

The experiences of József Lengyel, a former prisoner in the Soviet gulag, make Bodor's three-year incarceration in Romania seem tolerable. An old-time communist, indeed one of the founding fathers of the Hungarian Communist Party, Lengyel was compelled to flee Hungary after the downfall of Béla Kun's Hungarian Republic of Soviets in 1919. After sojourns in Austria and Germany, he settled in the Soviet Union, where in 1938 he shared the fate of a number of other foreign communists then resident in the U.S.S.R. He was arrested, held in prison for several years on false charges, and finally deported to Siberia. He was released in 1953, after Stalin's death, and returned to Hungary two years later.

Several of his works deal with the victims of the Stalinist trials and draw heavily on his own experiences. In this regard, the novella *Elejétöl végig* (From

Beginning to End, 1984) remains his most compelling text. Its descriptions of horrific privation and inhumanity rival any in Solzhenitsyn's *A Day in the Life of Ivan Denisovich* or in Gustaw Herling-Grudziński's *Inny świat* (A World Apart, 1951) (see below).

Poland

The extension of the Soviet gulag into Poland began even before the communists came to power in the aftermath of World War II. After the German defeat of Poland early in the war, the country was effectively partitioned between Germany and the Soviet Union in accordance with secret agreements signed by the two governments. The Soviet Union got primarily eastern Poland, where it wasted no time in rooting out opposition, actual or potential. Two of the many Poles caught up in the Soviet dragnet were the writers Gustaw Herling-Grudziński and Leo Lipski (real name Lep Lipschuetz), both of whom wrote harrowing accounts of what it meant to be subjected to Soviet imprisonment.

One of the most admired contemporary Polish writers, Herling-Grudziński (1919–2000) is known most for his short stories and essays. His stories have appeared in such collections as *Skrzydła ołtarza* (Wings of the Altar, 1988), *Wieża i inne opowiadania* (The Tower, and Other Stories, 1988), *Portret wenecki: Trzy opowiadania* (Portrait of Venice: Three Stories, 1995), *Don Ildebrando: Opowiadania* (Don Ildebrando: Stories, 1997), *Opowiadania zebrane* (Collected Stories, 1999), and another collection of previously published stories from the period 1991–1995, *Gorący oddech pustyni* (The Hot Breath of the Desert, 2000). Several of Herling-Grudziński's best stories have Italian settings, past and present, a reflection of his long residence in Italy. Following his release from Soviet prison in 1942, he joined the Polish army raised by the London Government-in-Exile and took part in the Allied invasion of Italy. When the war ended, he decided to remain in Italy, making his home primarily in Naples.

A student of Polish literature in Warsaw when war erupted, Herling-Grudziński sought to flee the German occupation by seeking refuge farther to the east. But the rapid Soviet advance into eastern Poland in late 1939 made any hope of escape virtually impossible, and in 1940 he was taken captive and subsequently imprisoned in a Soviet labor camp on the White Sea. His narrative about his experiences there from 1940 to 1942 was published in Poland in 1951 under the title *Inny świat* (translated as *A World Apart*). When the English translation appeared in Britain in 1986 it carried an introduction by the philosopher Bertrand Russell.

A World Apart is an excruciatingly grim, minutely detailed account of life in a Soviet prison. It deserves to be ranked along with Solzhenitsyn's *A Day in the Life of Ivan Denisovich* as one of the masterpieces of Eastern European and Soviet prison literature. Although Herling-Grudziński's diaries—published between 1973 and 1998 in six volumes under the general title *Dziennik pisany nocą* (The Journal Written at Night)—by and large do not deal with his Soviet prison days, they nevertheless are engrossing reading for the light they shed on their author's life and travels in Italy, current events as seen through Herling-Grudziński's eyes, Polish and world literature (he had a special affinity for Russian literature despite everything he had been through and wrote about it with admirable insight), art, philosophy, and intellectual life. An immensely thoughtful man of letters who tasted life to the fullest, Herling-Grudziński wrote and published a number of works of fiction and essays after *A World Apart* and The Journal Written at Night, but it is these two works above all that remain the foundation of his literary reputation.[18]

Born in Zurich in 1918, Leo Lipski (as he is best known) was raised and educated in Kraków. After completing secondary school, he studied psychology and philosophy at the Jagiellonian University in Kraków. He began his literary career as a poet and prose writer before World War II. Like Herling-Grudziński he fled east in advance of the German army, which had begun overrunning Poland after the invasion on 1 September 1939. He first took refuge in the eastern Polish city of Lwów, but was arrested in 1940 and sent off to a Soviet labor camp. But he eventually managed to escape and made his way to the Middle East, where he joined the re-formed Polish army of General Władysław Anders. However, severe illness during the army's stay in Iran rendered him unfit for military service. In 1943 he settled permanently in Palestine.

Lipski, whose severe health problems (he later suffered a paralyzing stroke in Israel) curtailed his literary activity, is known above all for two works, the short-story collection *Dzień i noc* (Day and Night, 1957), a very short book of just 56 pages about the time of his Soviet imprisonment, and the 79-page novella *Piotruś: Apokryf* (Pete: An Apocryphal, 1960), a depressing Israel-based story of a lonely, disabled man who has nothing to look forward to except physical decay and death. Although they deal with similar material, the great brevity of Lipski's Day and Night makes it an entirely different work from Herling-Grudziński's *A World Apart* and its astonishing detail.

Postcommunist Polish prison literature may begin with the recollections of Herling-Grudziński and Lipski, but it hardly ends there. Far different in tone and spirit is the much younger writer Andrzej Stasiuk's (b. 1960) small volume of prison stories published in 1999 under the title *Mury Hebronu* (The Walls of Hebron). A natural-born rebel who was booted out of high school as a trouble-maker, Stasiuk joined the peace movement in the early 1980s, and then was put in prison for a year and a half after deserting from the Polish army. He has since made an admirable career as a writer. Stasiuk eventually parted company with the Warsaw literary community, which held little appeal for him, and in 1987 took up residence in an isolated village in the Carpathian Mountains near the Ukrainian border. Here, apart from breeding llamas, among other things, he and his wife founded the independent publishing house Czarne in 1996.

After attracting much favorable attention with his first novel, *Biały kruk* (*White Raven*), about an ill-fated winter vacation trip through the Carpathians, he further enhanced his reputation with *Opowieści galicyjskie* (*Tales of Galicia*, 2001), a book of stories dealing with the Carpathian village life Stasiuk has come to know so well; three small novels of contemporary Polish life, *Dukla* (1997), *Dziewięc* (Nine, 1999), and *Przez rzekę* (Across the River, 2001); and a book based on travel through Eastern Europe and the Balkans of the title *Jadąc do Babadag* (Riding to Babadag, 2004).

The Walls of Hebron, despite its brevity, is strong reading, not so much for its pictures of prison life—Herling-Grudziński's *A World Apart* is far richer in this respect—but because of the rawness of its prose and its acceptance of brutality as a way of life. As the narrator says early in the longest part of the book, "Opowieść jedney nocy" ("The Tale of One Night"):

> You're not on the other side of the wall, you're not in the future, you're not in freedom. You're here, so live here. I'm telling you that. You can believe me.[19]

Stasiuk's brushes with the law began in fact before his arrest for desertion. Cursing his mother in the belief that it was she who sold him out to the authorities on the occasion of his first offense, he recalls that his prison education began with this initial encounter with the police:

> After my first meeting with the police I had a banged up nose and sore kidneys. At night I was gushing blood and had to listen to a beating going on the other side of the wall. That's more than enough for a fifteen-year-old squirt.
>
> In the morning they tried to interrogate me. Nothing, not a word, not even a single word of the ones they wanted to hear. I don't know, I don't remember, I don't know, I don't remember, I don't know, I don't remember. I thought I was going to vomit up my own stomach. They banged me around only in the belly. I was sitting in a chair, one asked a question, waited for the answer, and then winked at the second one standing against the wall. This other guy approached and slammed his fist into my stomach, just once, then he had to pull me up together with the chair I was in since I went sailing a good half-meter. When he got tired of boxing, he grabbed me by the whiskers with two fingers, by the hair on the temples, yanked me up, then sat me down, yanked me up, then sat me down. If I ever run into him, I'll cut his throat. In cold blood.
>
> For two days I couldn't eat, my stomach shriveled so badly that it couldn't hold anything, absolutely nothing. They let me go. I don't know why I went home. (36)

The German Democratic Republic

One of the most vexing writers of the GDR—from the point of view of the communist authorities—was Erich Loest (b. 1926; pseudonyms Hans Walldorf, Waldemar Nass). His outspoken opposition to Stalinism and GDR cultural policies resulted in his arrest in 1957 on the charge of organizing "counter-revolutionary groups." He was sentenced to seven and a half years in prison, and strictly forbidden to write during this period. After his release in 1964 he rejoined the Writers' Union and resumed an active literary career, especially as the author of a series of criminal novels written under the pseudonym Hans Walldorf. But his continued opposition to censorship and other GDR cultural policies again brought him into collision with the regime, a situation further exacerbated by the book It Takes Its Course; or, Trouble on Our Level (1978).

Loest quit the Writers' Union in 1979, and two years later left for West Germany on a three-year exit visa. He returned to East Germany only after the fall of the Berlin Wall. Once in the West, he published several compelling books of a largely autobiographical nature, focusing in particular on literary censorship in the East German state, his prison experiences, and his run-ins with the Stasi, the East German secret police. These include *Der vierte Censor: Vom Entstehen und Sterben eines Romans in der DDR* (The Fourth Censor: The Emergence and Death of a Novel in the GDR, 1984), about his problems with the censors over It Takes Its Course; *Der Zorn des Schaffes: Aus meinen Tagewerk* (A Ninny's Rage: From My Day's Work, 1990); *Die Stasi war mein Eckermann, oder: Mein Leben mit der Wanze* (The Stasi Was My Eckermann; or, My Life with the Bedbug, 1991), consisting mostly of state and secret police files about his case; *Heute kommt Westbesuch* (Today We Have a Visitor from the West, 1992), a short work made up of monologues by two former citizens of the GDR who look back on their lives under the communist regime, which now seem senseless to them; and *Als wir in den Westen kamen: Gedanken eines literarischen Grenzgangers* (When We Came West: Thoughts of a Literary Border Crosser, 1997), a collection of fifty pieces on a wide variety of subjects, many of interest to historians of the GDR.

The case of the Silesian-born Hans Bienek (1930–1990), the son of a German father and Polish mother, recalls that of Polish and Hungarian writers who were unlucky enough to land in Soviet prison camps. Bienek and his family resettled in the Soviet zone of Berlin in 1946. In 1951, the year in which he joined Bertolt Brecht's Berliner Ensemble, he was taken into custody by the Stasi on grounds of anti-Soviet agitation. He was sentenced to twenty-five years of forced labor in the notorious Vorkuta camp in Siberia by a Soviet military tribunal. However, he was granted amnesty in 1955 and shortly thereafter moved to West Germany. Bienek settled in Munich, where he made his way primarily as a freelance writer. He is remembered most for his highly successful novel tetralogy (1975–1982)—*Die erste Polka* (The First Polka), *Septemberlicht* (September Light), *Zeit ohne Glocken* (Time Without Bells), and *Erde und Feuer* (Earth and Fire)—all dealing with his childhood and youth in Upper Silesia, and for his novel *Die Zelle* (*The Cell*, 1968), a sober, highly detailed account of the myriad of torments and humiliations he was made to endure at Vorkuta, including the confiscation of his eyeglasses.

The Reform Imperative in Eastern Europe

From Solidarity to Postmodernism

The Solidarity Movement in Poland and Its Literature

> The formation of Solidarity was no accident, no coincidence, but the crowning
> result of a process or breakthrough that had been years in the making and had
> already delineated itself in the early seventies. On the other hand, the shattering
> of Solidarity, or at least of its legal framework, although also not accidental, was
> the handiwork of a completely different force and logic, external in relation to
> the organic processes and changes in Polish political life.
>
> —Adam Zagajewski, *Solidarność i samotność,* page 9

The formation of the Solidarity movement in Poland was the most resonant
event in the history of post–World War II Eastern Europe prior to the dismantling of the Berlin Wall. The attempt to crush it, and everything it represented,
by means of martial law imposed by order of General Wojciech Jaruzelski on 13
December 1981 (lifted only in July 1983) gave rise to an impressive and socially
relevant body of nonfictional and fictional texts by writers closely related to or
affiliated with Solidarity: Janusz Anderman, Stanisław Barańczak, Kazimierz
Brandys, Tomasz Jastrun, Sławomir Mrożek, Marek Nowakowski, Andrzej
Szczypiorski, and Adam Zagajewski.

In his two sets of diaries, *Miesiące, 1978–1979* (Months, 1978–1979)
and *Miesiące, 1980–1981* (Months, 1980–1981), both issued by the Instytut
Literacki in Paris in 1981 and 1982, respectively, Brandys vividly recalls the
events leading up to the formation of Solidarity. A selection of passages from
both volumes, translated by Richard Lourie, was published by Random House
in 1983 under the title *A Warsaw Diary, 1978–1981.* Despite his achievements
as a novelist and short-story writer, The Dairies may well come to be regarded
as Brandy's most important literary legacy for the light they shed on a critical
juncture in Poland's post–World War II history.

Renowned primarily for his novels about the German occupation of Poland during World War II, especially *Początek* (The Beginning, 1986; translated as *The Beautiful Mrs. Seidenman*), Andrzej Szczypiorski (1924–2000), who began his career as a journalist, associated himself with the democratic opposition in the 1970s, took an active role in the Solidarity movement of the 1980s, and subsequently became a participant in the political life of postcommunist Poland. He was interned during Martial Law (1981–1982) and in 1989 was elected a senator to the Polish Diet, a position he held until 1991. His views on these events are contained above all in a collection of essays published in 1997 under the title *Grzechy, cnoty, pragnienia* (Sins, Virtues, Desires). The essays are grouped into two sections: "Z notatnika stanu przemian" ("From a Notebook of a State of Changes"; sometimes also appearing with the title "Z notatnika stanu wojennego" ["From the Martial Law Notebook"]), which was originally published in 1983 and addresses the plight of political prisoners during Solidarity and Martial Law, and "Grzechy bliźnich, cnoty własne" ("The Sins of Others, My Own Virtues").

Known primarily as a dramatist in the tradition of the theater of the absurd, Sławomir Mrożek was a staunch advocate of democratic rights in Poland. In protest over the Soviet invasion of Czechoslovakia in 1968, he went into exile in France in 1969. His subsequent support of the Solidarity movement and his denunciation of Martial Law in 1981 further alienated him from communist Poland. A small underground collection of his "Donosy" ("Denunciations") appeared in 1983; a more complete collection of his stories and "denunciations," from the emergence of Solidarity to the collapse of communist power in Poland in 1989, was published in 1994 under the title *Opowiadania i donosy: 1980–1989* (Stories and Denunciations: 1980–1989).

Until the declaration of Martial Law on 13 December 1981, Marek Nowakowski (b. 1935), a Warsaw native and graduate in law of Warsaw University, was admired as a prolific writer of short stories that collectively represent a kind of chronicle of everyday Polish life under communism. Nowakowski was an active supporter of Solidarity and, once Martial Law became the order of the day, the author of one of the most compelling accounts of its impact on Polish society and the Polish psyche. It was called *Raport o stanie wojennym* (Report on Martial Law; translated as *The Canary, and Other Tales of Martial Law*). Since the book obviously could not be printed in Poland, it appeared originally in Paris in two volumes in 1982 and 1983. In a manner somewhat reminiscent of Janusz Anderman's later "freeze frame" vignettes in his collection *Fotografie* (Photographs, 2002), Report on Martial Law consists of a series of "snapshots" depicting everyday life in Poland in the first weeks of Martial Law.

Also reminiscent of Anderman, Nowakowski's style is true-to-life and gritty. It was a style he had already honed in his stories about the tough fringe element in Warsaw in such collections as *Ten stary złodziej* (This Old Thief, 1958); *Benek kwiaciarz* (Benek the Flower Peddler, 1961); *Silna gorączka* (High Fever, 1963); *Trampolina* (The Trampoline, 1964); *Zapas* (Legacy, 1965); *Marynarska ballada* (A Sailor's Ballad, 1966); *Gonitwa* (The Chase, 1967); *Przystań* (The

Harbor, 1969); *Mizerikordia* (Misericordia, 1971); *Układ zamknięty* (A Settled Deal, 1972); *Zdarzenie w miasteczku* (Happening in a Small Town, 1972); *Śmierć żółwia* (The Death of a Turtle, 1973); *Gdzie jest droga na Walnę* (Where's the Road to Walna?, 1974); *Książe nocy* (The Prince of Night, 1978); *Chłopak z gołębiem na głowie* (The Boy with a Pigeon on His Head, 1979); and *Tutaj całować nie wolno* (No Kissing Here, 1979).

Like Report on Martial Law, Nowakowski's subsequent books about the period of Solidarity and Martial Law appeared first in Paris or, on one occasion, Chicago. These include *Notatki z codzienności: Grudień 1982–Lipiec 1983* (Everyday Notes: December 1982–July 1983, 1983); *Życiorys Tadeusza Nawalanego, czyli Solidarność ma głos* (The Biography of Tadeusz Nawalany; or, Solidarity Has the Floor, 1983); *Dwa dni z aniołem* (Two Days with an Angel, 1984); *Osiem dni w ojczyźnie* (Eight Days in the Fatherland, 1985); *"Grisza, ja tiebie skażu"* ("Listen Here, Grisha," 1986); *Kto to zrobił?* (Who Did It?, 1987); and *Karnawał i post* (Carnival and Fast, 1998).

Once Solidarity had achieved its goals, and the communist regime in Poland had been overthrown, Nowakowski turned his attention to the dynamics of social change in postcommunist Poland and wrote a series of stories on the subject, contained in the collections *Portret artysty z okresu dojrzałości* (Portrait of the Artist as an Adult, 1989); *Homo Polonicus* (Polish Man, 1992); *Grecki bożek* (The Little Greek God, 1993); *Rachunek* (The Reckoning, 1984); *Powidoki: Chłopcy z tamtych lat* (Snapshots: The Boys of Yesteryear, 1995); *Powidoki 2: Wspomnij ten domek na Gąsiówce?* (Snapshots 2: Remember the House in Gąsiówka?, 1996); *Reda* (Roads, 1998); *Tapeta i inne opowiadania* (Wallpaper, and Other Stories, 1996): *Strzały w motelu George* (Shots in Motel George, 1997): and *Powidoki 3: Warszawiak pilnie poszukiwany* (Snapshots 3: A Varsovian Eagerly Searched For, 1998). As tedious as it may perhaps seem to review a long list of Nowakowski's writings, it is important to appreciate his extraordinary literary output, much of which, taken together, constitutes an illuminating account of the most tumultuous period in Poland's post–World War II history.

One of the most important poets of his generation, Adam Zagajewski (b. 1945) plunged into dissident literary activity while still a student at the Jagiellonian University in Kraków. It was then that he began editing the dissident journal *Zapis*. In 1979 he was invited to Berlin by the Berliner Kunstlerprogramm, and did not return to Poland until September 1981. Martial Law was levied in December of that year, but by then Zagajewski had already become actively involved in Solidarity in Kraków, where he had been living since 1963. This involvement, in conjunction with his earlier editorship of *Zapis*, all but necessitated his emigration from Poland. In 1982, before the lifting of Martial Law, he settled in Paris, where he became editor of the quarterly Polish-language literary magazine *Zeszyty literackie/Cahiers littéraires*. The publication was relocated to Poland in the early 1990s after the collapse of the communist regime.

Zagajewski's clarity, intellectual sophistication, cosmopolitanism, and sense of moral responsibility—much like that of his illustrious predecessor Zbigniew

Herbert (1924–1998)—pervade all his poetry, from his first volume, *Komunikat* (Communique, 1972), through *Ziemia ognista* (Fiery Land, 1994). Although he was born after World War II, Zagajewski was appalled by the horrors of the war and alludes to them often in his writing. Similarly, the political upheaval represented by the emergence, suppression, and then rebirth of the Solidarity movement instilled in him a fear and loathing of dictatorial repression and deep feelings of anxiety, sorrow, and loneliness. These same sentiments are reflected not only in his poetry but also in *Świat nie przedstawiony* (Unrepresented World, 1972), an important collection of essays from 1971 to 1973 by both Zagajewski and the poet Julian Kornhauser. Perhaps the most resonant of these addresses the issue of "new poetry," understood by Kornhauser and Zagajewski as one

> that wishes to be contemporary through and through, and that means that it tries to deal seriously with Poland. It wants to be a political poetry, not the prettified kind to which we have been accustomed, not the kind that operated with phrases and generalities and got lost in a thicket of subtle mythological allusions that stirred up beautiful rebellious tenants and suburban villas, but the kind that would permit the citizen to see the world as it truly is, the naked, defenseless world, with its hypocrisy and ugliness, its absurd and stupid television, its morning newspaper, the marketplace and the university waking up early, the First of May and the Spartakiad.[1]

Zagajewski's principal other works include *Drugi oddech* (Second Wind, 1978), a collection of articles and reviews; *Solidarność i samotność* (Solidarity and Solitude, 1986; translated as *Solidarity, Solitude,* 1986); *Dwa miasta* (Two Cities, 1991); and *W cudzym pięknie* (*Another Beauty,* 1998).

A highly regarded poet, literary critic, and translator (especially of English and American authors), Stanisław Barańczak (b. 1946) has been a professor of Polish literature at Harvard University since 1981. By the time he left Poland his position had become all but untenable politically. After the workers' riots of June 1976, he became a cofounder of KOR (Committee for the Defense of Workers) and the clandestine quarterly *Zapis.* In 1983 he was one of the founders of the Paris *Zeszyty literackie,* with which Adam Zagajewski was also associated, and a regular contributor to the periodical *Teksty drugie* (Other Texts). Apart from his personal political activism, Barańczak has also used his poetry as a vehicle for his political and ethical ideas, without compromising their aesthetic appeal as poetry. A strong and consistent voice of conscience and morality in public affairs, he was a sharp critic of the Polish communist regime's abuse of the rights of workers and intellectuals.

Because of increasing censorship and security police surveillance, several of his books, beginning with his collection of essays *Ironia i harmonia: Szkice o najnowszej literaturze polskiej* (Irony and Harmony: Sketches on the Newest Polish Literature, 1973), had to be published illegally or outside of Poland in the Polish émigré presses in London and Paris. His works dealing directly with Solidarity and Martial Law include *Przed i po: Szkice o poezji krajowej przełomu lat siedemdziesiątych i osiemdziesiątych* (Before and After: Sketches on Poetry Inside Poland of the Late 1970s and 1980s, 1988), a study in essence of the impact of Martial Law on Polish poetry; *Przywracanie porządku* (The Return of Order, 1983), on immediate post–Martial Law Poland; and *Pomyślane przepaście: Osiem interpretacji* (Imagined Abysses: Eight Interpretations, 1995).

Janusz Anderman's (b. 1949) principal works from the Solidarity period, and dealing directly with it, were of necessity originally published outside of Poland. The immediacy of much Solidarity literature, like Anderman's, its caustic criticism and belittlement of the regime, made publication of such writing in Poland out of the question. Anderman's two small collections of short prose pieces from the 1980s—*Brak tchu* (Breathless; translated as *Poland Under Black Light*) and *Kraj świata* (*The Edge of the World*)—were originally brought out by Polish émigré publishers, *Poland Under Black Light* in 1983 by the London-based Polish PULS Publications and *The Edge of the World* by the Instytut Literacki in Paris in 1988 (English translation, 1985; in this instance the English translation appeared before the Polish edition).

Anderman is known above all for his sarcasm and mockery, which are addressed to such issues as an obsessive state paranoia that imagines plots against the regime under every rock and behind every tree, literary and other forms of censorship, official sloganeering, and the ubiquitousness of the security police. His fondness for the absurd and grotesque, inspired in part by the nineteenth-century Russian writer Nikolai Gogol, to whom there are occasional allusions in his works, is buttressed by Anderman's ability to capture the accents and rhythms of Polish vernacular speech of the period. This "acoustical" quality of his prose has been noted by several critics; while enriching the texture of his prose it also makes it all but impossible to translate into another language.

Anderman's snapshots of everyday Polish life from the 1970s and 1980s are grimly realistic, concerned as they are with the gritty abrasions of arrests, interrogations, and incarceration. As Anderman asks in one place: "When did it happen in this country? The well- nourished paddy wagon conducts people in an unknown direction; the tear gas bites into the deserted street. . . ."[2] In this same collection of stories, Poland itself comes to resemble a desolate armed camp, as he writes in "Ten kraj" ("This Land"): "The country is fading on the maps, more and more withering away . . . The streets end unexpectedly in army barracks . . . life according to the rules goes on, behind high prison walls; only there does hope continue. Barbed air wounds the lungs, people forget about the future, their world has the short life of film clips, notes lost on scattered cards" (5). The impact on the writer's ability to work in such conditions is devastating:

In this country at this time I haven't the courage to write. They wondered. I don't know if I'll ever be able to write about it. I couldn't hack it after October.

Couldn't hack it after December. Or after March. Those months are all screwed up in my mind . . . March was earlier . . . I couldn't get it together after June. They said those months didn't change people even the slightest compared to now. (50–51)

In the same story, "Temat współczesny" ("Contemporary Topic"), two writers wander through a bleak urban landscape wondering if they can ever write again—until they see a pigeon run over by a passing car after it swept down on a cigarette butt flung down by one of the writers. When another pigeon descends on it ("Look. The other one's fucking it"), the writers decide that they will jointly write about the incident ("We'll write it together. It's a topic, after all. Pity not to") (56). Anderman recounts the grim ironies of contemporary life, the tensions between the images propagated by the state media and the living reality, the bugging of conversations, the opening of mail, and the feeling that one is never alone to be able to freely speak one's mind or express an opinion.

One of Anderman's most effective books, *Fotografie* (2002), is a collection of short essays, more in the nature of feuilletons, that originally appeared on the pages of *Gazeta Wyborcza* between 1998 and 2002. The point of departure for many of the pieces, and hence the title of the collection, is a photograph (real or otherwise) taken by Anderman. A number of the pieces also deal with political and cultural events of the 1970s and 1980s and are quite topical. There are allusions to such prominent artists of the period as Adam Zagajewski, Marek Nowakowski, Andrzej Wajda, Tadeusz Nowakowski, Ryszard Krynicki, and Hanna Krall; his travels; the situation of the Jews (including the Kielce district killings of 1945 and 1946); his decision in 1984 to emigrate to London—where he coedited (from Poland) the émigré quarterly *Puls*—but his fear of having to ask for a passport at a time when the influential dissident Adam Michnik was strongly against people leaving Poland. However, after noting changes in the country after the Martial Law amnesty, Anderman decided against emigrating, reasoning that there was too much to do there.

A short eyewitness account of events leading up to the foundation of Solidarity and the subsequent internment of a number of its supporters during Martial Law was written by the poet Tomasz Jastrun (b. 1950). The editor of a Solidarity cultural journal in 1980 / 1981, he went into hiding after Martial Law was declared and was arrested in October 1982. He was imprisoned in Białołęka prison but was released by the terms of the general amnesty of 23 December 1982. Well known for such volumes of poems as *Bez usprawied-liwienia* (Without Justification, 1980), for which he won a Robert Graves Foundation Prize, *Kropla, kropla* (Drop by Drop, 1985), *Obok siebie* (At My Side, 1989), and *Tylko czułość idzie do nieba* (Only Tenderness Goes to Heaven, 2003), Jastrun is also represented in English through Daniel Bourne's translations, published under the title *On the Crossroads of Asia and Europe* (1999). His diary of moments in the rise of Solidarity covers the period 26 August 1980 to 1 September 1981 and was originally published in Germany in 1983 as

Zapiski z Błędnego Koła (Notes from a Vicious Circle). This edition also includes the prison notes *Białołęka 9 listopada–23 grudnia 1982* (Białołęka 9 November–23 December 1982), which had first appeared as a separate publication. Named for the prison where the Martial Law internees were kept, Białołęka 9 November–23 December 1982 comprises a small collection of thumbnail sketches of prison life.

Notes from a Vicious Circle was not Jastrun's only work on Solidarity and Martial Law. In 1985 he also published a small book on Anna Walentynowicz (b. 1929)—*Życie Anny Walentynowicz* (The Life of Anna Walentynowicz)—a Polish trade union activist who worked in the Lenin Shipyard in Gdańsk and became intimately bound up with Solidarity. Her firing on 7 August 1980, five months before she was due to retire, aroused fellow workers, who took up her cause and went on strike on 14 August. After the strike was settled, both Walentynowicz and Lech Wałęsa regained their positions and soon afterward the Solidarity union was established. Although later disagreements with the Solidarity leadership resulted in her break with the union, in January 2005 she received the Presidential Medal of Freedom in Washington on behalf of Solidarity. From 1990 to 1994, Jastrun himself served as cultural attaché in the Polish Embassy in Stockholm, Sweden.

Democratic Opposition, Postmodernism, and the Path to Revolution in Romania

Younger Romanian writers and intellectuals emerged as both the organizers and the leaders of democratic opposition to the continued rule of Nicolae Ceaușescu and his failed communist regime. This was true not only for Bucharest, the capital, but also in such provincial centers as Sibiu and Brașov in Transylvania and in the western city of Timișoara, where indeed the revolution that finally succeeded in toppling Ceaușescu first erupted. Many of these younger intellectuals banded together in the organization known as Alianța Civică (Civil Alliance).

The crystalizing movement for reform in Romanian civic and political life also had its literary corollaries. Tentative efforts to open Romanian literature to freer, more creative, and independent forms of expression drew inspiration, as previously noted, from interwar and immediate postwar surrealism. But this tradition, as important as it was, was unable to play any nurturing role in the harsher climate of the 1950s and early 1960s, when the imposition of socialist realism was an incontrovertible reality. The tentative efforts to loosen the restraints of this Soviet import by older writers like Vasile Voiculescu, who departed from realism by introducing elements of the surreal and fantastic, paved the way for bolder experiments by writers of the 1970s and early 1980s.

Although critics and scholars tend to characterize some of the more prominent literary works of the late 1980s and 1990s as postmodernist, impressive evidence of the emergence of a postmodernist current in Romanian literature can be traced back to the end of the decade of the 1960s. That was when, in 1969, the first volume of Mircea Horia Simionescu's (b. 1928) extraordinary (and massive) tetralogy, *Ingeniosul bine temperat* (The Well-Tempered Genius), first appeared. Bearing the scholarly title *Dicţionar onomastic* (An Onomastic Dictionary), it consisted of a pseudo-scholarly dictionary of names down to the letter "L"; names are followed by amusing and imaginative brief "definitions" or by much longer illustrative examples. The next volume, which carried the dictionary through the letter "Z," came out in 1976 under the title *Jumatate plus unu* (A Half Plus One), the change of title being a ploy to distract censors, who had already begun expressing dissatisfaction with Simionescu's work. But so innovative was the Dictionary that, reservations aside, it was awarded the Ion Creanga Prize of the Romanian Academy. The third volume, now titled *Breviarul (Historia calamitatum)* (The Breviary: A History of Calamities), appeared in 1980. The third and final volume was published three years later as *Toxicologia sau Dincolo de bine şi dincoace de rau* (Toxicology; or, On the Far Side of Good and on This Side of Bad).

Simionescu has had a long and noteworthy career in Romanian literature since his debut in the literary review *Luceafărul* in 1968. On the occasion of his seventieth birthday the Romanian Writers' Union awarded him its Opera omnia (All Works) Prize. Although best known for the volumes that comprise his highly idiosyncratic Well-Tempered Genius, he was also the author of a number of novels, among them *Dupa 1900, pe la amiază* (After 1900, About Noon, 1974), which won the prose prize of the Romanian Writers' Union; *Rapirea lui Ganymede* (The Abduction of Ganymede, 1975), characterized by Simionescu as a "false travel journal"; *Nesfârşitele primejdii* (Infinite Dangers, 1978); *Învăţaturi pentru Delfin* (Lessons for a Dauphin, 1979); *Redingota* (The Riding Coat, 1984); *Licitaţia* (Litigation, 1985); *Asediul locului comun* (The Siege of the Commonplace, 1988); and *Paltonul de vară* (The Summer Coat, 1996), which won the Writers' Union Prize. He has also published several volumes of short stories as well as travel books and a journal of the years 1963–1971 (*Febră*, Fever).

Long interested in onomastics, Simionescu mentions in the preface to the edition of *Dicţionar onomastic* published in 2000 that the idea of an independent onomastic dictionary—"a novel with a thousand characters"—crystalized in the spring of 1958 when his friend Radu Petrescu, who was then expecting the birth of his first child and concerned about what to name it, proposed to Simionescu that he draw up a list of a few dozen names, with brief descriptions, demonstrating "academically" how a "Mitica or Mache evolves differently from an August, Demosthenes, or Hidroxin." Simionescu at first collected some thirty names, but when these failed to satisfy his friend, he expanded the list to twelve hundred. The project obviously dragged on a while, during which period Petrescu's child was born. By the time Simionescu was through with it, it had assumed the proportions of a gigantic metanovel; indeed, in the judgment of the renowned Romanian critic Nicolae Manolescu, "The most original metanovel I know."[3] Imaginative, irreverent, playful, satirical, parodic, and, in the final analysis, an explosive act of creative liberation, Simionescu's "novel" paved the way for the impressive emergence of Romanian postmodernism in the late 1980s and '90s.

Another pioneer of Romanian literary postmodernism is a talented writer of Armenian heritage, Ştefan Agopian (b. 1947). His literary career began in earnest in 1971, when the editor of the large Cartea Românească publishing house, Alexandru Paleologu, impressed by some previous short stories by Agopian, suggested that he write a novel. Agopian did just that, in a year's time, and titled his work *Ziua mâniei* (The Day of Rage). It was to be a reconstruction through fragments of a single day in the turbulent lives of two families in the year 1915. However, for a variety of reasons, including at one point in 1978 a "lack of paper," the novel did not see the light of day until 1979; in the meantime, Agopian had begun other projects. Although he wrote two chapters of what was to become one of his best works, *Tache de catifea* (Velvet Tache), he abandoned this project in 1972 and instead began writing a work of historical fiction that he called *Manualul întâmplărilor* (The Manual of Happenings). After finishing it finally in 1978, he turned next to his partially written Velvet Tache and completed that book as well in 1980. It was published in 1981. Although the novel met with a certain indifference, it had powerful supporters within the literary community and was proposed for the Writers' Union Prize. This, however, was denied Agopian because a member of the jury ruled against it on the grounds that Agopian was not a member of the organization. Agopian then undertook the writing of pair of linked high-adventure historical novels with a biblical theme, *Tobit* (begun in 1980 and published in 1983) and *Sara* (begun in 1981–1982 and published, after several years of delays, in part because of difficulties with the censors, in 1987). Both novels were very well received and, together with the hugely successful publication in 1984 of The Manual of Happenings, established Agopian's reputation as one of the outstanding younger prose writers of the day. In April 1984 *Tobit* was awarded the prize of the Bucharest Writers' Association. The following year, The Manual of Happenings won the Writers' Union Prize.

Although he was nominated for a scholarship to the International Writing Program of the University of Iowa in 1986, he was denied a visa. And even after the novel *Sara* was honored with the prize of the review *Amfiteatru* for best literary work of the year, Agopian was also refused a visa to travel to the United States in 1988. Finally, in 1989, he was allowed to attend Iowa's International Writing Program. Once back in Romania, Agopian caused a minor scandal in 1993 with an erotic prose work under the title "Noapte de februarie" ("A February Night"), which appeared in the review *România Literară*. His international literary stature was enhanced when he was invited to participate in the Leipzig and Frankfurt book fairs in 1998, and the following year gave a literary reading in Berlin. In 2000 his first book of plays, *Republica pe eşafod* (Republic on the Scaffold), appeared, and in 2004 he brought out a new book of prose stories, *Fric* (Burnt), which was awarded the review *Cuvîntul*'s Best Book of Prose of the Year. State honors also came Agopian's way. In 2000 he was decorated by the President of Romania, Emil Constaninescu, with the National Order of Merit, Commander's Rank.

Agopian is justifiably regarded as one of the most important modernizers of Romanian prose writing; within his canon, the novel Velvet Tache of 1981 occupies a pivotal place. It is credited with hastening the emancipation of Romanian prose not only from the straitjacketing socialist realism of the 1950s, but from the constraints of realism in general. Set in the early Napoleonic period against the background of the Russo-Turkish war of 1769–1791, it tells the story of a Romanian boyar named Tache Vlădescu who sets out with friends to join an uprising against the Turks led by Tudor Vlădimirescu. Tache, however, takes a leisurely approach to the journey, stopping along the way at inns and estates; his meetings and conversations in these places collectively represent an important dimension of the book. By the time he reaches Vlădimirescu's camp, Vlădimirescu has been slain and Tache's travels have been in vain. Identified in an introduction as the author of the book, Tache mentions that he was born in 1800 and died fifty-eight years later, killed immediately after the revolution of Mamona the Young. Agopian creates a plausible world within a definite time frame, but one of total imagination. A novel of adventure in form, it seems to make merry with the genre itself in the spirit of postmodernist antitraditionalism.

Collaborative works of fiction involving more than two authors are fairly rare. But since postmodernism seems capable of accommodating almost anything, contemporary Romanian literature can boast of one such effort, of particular interest to Americans (who unfortunately have no translation to help them in this case). The work in question is the novel Femeia în roşu (The Lady in Red), a curious mixture of docudrama, historical novel, and self-reflective fiction, written by two men and a woman: Mircea Mihăieş, a graduate in English of Timişoara University, the author previously of a book on William Faulkner and the editor of the Timişoara opposition weekly Orizont; Mircea Nedelciu, the "uncontested prose leader of the 1980s" (to borrow Mircea Cărtărescu's characterization); and the sole woman participant in the joint composition of the novel, Adriana Babeţi, a writer, critic, and outspoken adversary of the post-Ceauşescu "neocommunist" government policies.

The story's main character is a Romanian woman named Ana Cumpanas (later Anne Sage, an Immigration Service "anglicization" of Suciu, the family name of her second husband, an attorney). A real person, she was born and grew up in the Banat province of southwestern Romania, which was once known for its multilingual mix of peoples (primarily Romanians, Serbs, and Germans). Ana was a beautiful, enterprising, immoral woman who ran speakeasies and bordellos and knew the gangster John Dillinger. She was, in fact, the famous (or infamous) "Lady in Red," who betrayed him to the police and federal agents hunting for him. But once Dillinger was killed, the verbal promises given her by the authorities that she might keep her immigration status were not honored and she was forced to return to her native land. Back in Romania, she led a quiet life, shunned publicity, and remained in the Banat region until her death in 1947.

The novel based on this unlikely character is an impressive mix of the fictional and the documentary. Appropriately, it includes a bibliography of books and periodicals used in its composition. The Lady in Red is also a book about the writing of a book. The authors are shown on the trail of clues, talking with peasant women in remote Romanian villages who speak perfectly idiomatic American English, and interacting with imaginary American reviewers of imaginary American literary journals. In a parallel, minute-by-minute account, the last hours of Dillinger's life are presented side-by-side with the goings-on in an ordinary sleepy town of the Banat. Just a few chapters earlier, carousing young Romanians in Vienna (this is the 1920s) try to get a peek into Dr. Freud's legendary cabinet and chat in a coffeehouse with the unidentified and still anonymous Elias Canetti.

Notwithstanding the importance for the development of Romanian postmodernism of such writers as Agopian and Simionescu, or of a work such as The Lady in Red, the undeniable leader of the postmodernist movement has been Mircea Cărtărescu (b. 1956). A prolific writer and a professor at Bucharest University, Cărtărescu's truly dominant role in Romanian postmodernism in the late 1980s and 1990s was established not only by several collections of poetry and by the novels *Visul* (The Dream, 1989; reissued in 1993 and 1997 with the new title *Nostalgia*), *Travesti* (In Disguise, 1994), and *Orbitor* (Dazzling, 1996), but by the publication in 1999 of his 1998 doctoral dissertation *Postmodernismul românesc* (Romanian Postmodernism). In its delineation of the emergence of postmodernism in Romania in the 1980s, this nearly 500-page book casts a very wide net. In developing a typology of Romanian postmodernism, Cărtărescu considers not only its antecedents in the Romanian surrealist tradition of the pre- and postwar years, but also those divergences from the postmodernism of the West that are largely attributable to the oppositional character of the Romanian movement in the context of the prevailing domestic political and social situation.

Cătărescu's is indeed an impressive performance. Conversant with Western theorists from Robert Scholes to Ihab Hassan, he cuts easily through the often-dense thicket of contradictory theorizations to a lucid exposition of the history and properties of postmodernism. At his best certainly when discussing postmodernism as it developed in Romania, he reconsiders the entire Romanian literary culture of the twentieth century before addressing the postwar period, with particular emphasis on modernism of the 1960s and '70s and its links with the interwar surrealist movement. Impartial, yet to a certain extent revisionist at the same time, Cărtărescu devotes perhaps his most important pages to his own generation of the 1980s, the last before the collapse of communism in Romania. It was the younger writers of this period who, faced with greater impediments to publication, were the most receptive to the subversive potential of postmodernist technique. Their range in poetry and prose, both structurally and stylistically, is dazzling.

The most stunning of Cărtărescu's works are by far *Nostalgia* and his epic poem in verse *Levantul* (The Levant, 1990). Although usually spoken of as a novel, *Nostalgia* is really a collection of five separate stories grouped under three headings: "Prolog," consisting of the story "Ruletistul" ("The Roulette Player"); "Nostalgia," containing "Mendebilul" ("Mentardy"), "Gemenii" ("The Twins"), and "REM"; and "Epilog," with the single story "Arhitectul" ("The Architect"). The Prologue and Epilogue, with one story each, serve as the frame for the main body of the novel, "Nostalgia," with its three stories. Underlying the stories, as separate as they may appear, is a single unifying vision and what Cărtărescu himself has called "the same stylistic calligraphy." In a sense, the stories mirror each other. It is in this way that *Nostalgia* lends itself to consideration as a novel.

Taken as a whole, *Nostalgia* brings together dreams, magical experiences, childhood recollections, literary allusions, and much self-referentiality. In this regard the novel is a compendium of postmodernist literary techniques. Notwithstanding shifting narrative voices, one constant remains throughout: the frequent intrusion of the author, who interrupts his storytelling to raise questions about storytelling in general, to wonder about the sense of what he is doing, to openly question the wisdom of continuing, to express his dissatisfaction with what he is writing, to discuss his literary compulsions, his moments of satisfaction and even greater moments of frustration, and the despair that he believes makes it impossible for him to write another word. Mystery, strangeness, humor, irony, and parody, especially self-parody, all contribute to the stylistic alchemy of the novel.

Regarded as arguably a greater tour de force is Cărtărescu's quasi-epic poem in verse The Levant. A comic masterpiece, it consists of twelve cantos (actually thirteen since the eleventh canto appears in two different variants). Its subject, broadly speaking, is the Oriental dimension of Romanian culture, to which Cărtărescu attributes a continuing relevance. The epic begins in the Greek archipelago, in the early nineteenth century, where a motley band of pirates, adventurers, and idealistic young men and women come together and proceed north to the Wallachian principalities, their native land. Their goal is to institute liberty and democracy and overthrow a hated oppressor. They achieve only a limited success, and when their grand adventure has run its course, they all get together in the author's present-day apartment and comment upon their past experiences.

For the Romanian reader the poem's most attractive feature is its language and style. Cărtărescu is a master of language who can bend it to just about any purpose he wishes. This may not make his texts easy for the foreign reader, as in the case, for example, of *Nostalgia,* but they are regarded as a sheer delight among Romanians. In The Levant, Cărtărescu takes his reader on a merry romp of rediscovery through different stages in the evolution of Romanian poetry while at the same time illuminating the progress of Romanian cultural history. Ironic, parodic, and postmodern, Cărtărescu thoroughly revels in jolting his reader out of the illusion of his epic narration by references to a heterogeneous assemblage of writers, thinkers, artists, and political figures, such as Borges, George Steiner, Leonardo da Vinci, Tasso, Shakespeare, Edgar Allan Poe, the

Romanian writers Ana Blandiana, Alexandru Muşina, Traian Coşovei, and Panait Istrati, the Russian literary scholar Bakhtin, Julio Cortázar, Gramsci, Che Guevara, Patrice Lumumba, the Romanian historian Bălcescu, John Lennon, the Red Rock Crossing, Arizona, music festival, and, of course, himself. One gravestone-like interpolation reads: "I, Mircea Cărtărescu, have written The Levant in a sad moment of my life at the age of thirty-one years, when, no longer believing in poetry (my whole life until now) and in the reality of the world and my destiny in this world, I have decided to spend my time hatching an illusion."[4] Rather than a rejection of the past, which its parodic character might lead one to assume, Cărtărescu's The Levant is instead a celebration of it.

Cărtărescu was also the author in 2001 of a nearly 500-page *Jurnal* (Journal) covering the years 1990 through 1996. This is in the tradition of modern Romanian diary writing practiced by such writers as Paul Goma, Mihai Sebastian, Nicolae Steinhardt, and Bujor Nedelcovici. Cărtărescu's journal, or diary, is less fragmentary than those of his predecessors but written essentially along similar lines. He tells us a great deal about himself, his mood swings (at one point declaring that books no longer interest him and that he's becoming neurasthenic), his dreams, his inspirations, his literary and other priorities, his present projects, his own writings, his trip to America in October, November, and December 1990, his later stays in France, Germany, and Holland, and so on. He shares with his readers his liking for and prodigious knowledge of contemporary American culture as well as his astonishingly cosmopolitan reading habits. Cărtărescu's sequel to his journal, covering the years 1997 to 2003, appeared in 2005 under the title *Jurnal II: 1997–2003*.

A further indication of the continuing importance of interwar Romanian surrealism in the post–World War II era—after the renewed interest of the later 1940s—is a book such as Simona Popescu's *Salvarea speciei: Despre suprarealism şi Gellu Naum* (The Salvation of the Species: On Surrealism and Gellu Naum, 2000). Popescu herself (b. 1965) is one of the more impressive younger poets to break into print in the 1990s, that is in the post-Ceauşescu years. Her first volume of poems *Xilofonul şi alte poeme* (The Xylophone, and Other Poems) appeared in 1990. It was followed in 1991 by the collection *Pauză de respiraţie* (Breathing Pause), which she and her fellow poets Andrei Bodiu, Caius Dobrescu, and Marius Oprea jointly composed. Two other volumes of poetry by Popescu herself appeared in 1994 and 1998, respectively: *Juventus* and *Noapte sau zi* (Night or Day), a seventy-eight-page text consisting of a single poem or, more precisely, poetic dialogue. Popescu has also published two works of prose, the novel *Exuvii* (Exuviae, 1997) and a collection of essays under the title *Volubilis* (1998). Her stern hairdo, parted in the middle and pulled back behind the ears, and her oversize granny glasses notwithstanding, Popescu is an entertaining and self-mocking poet. Fond of irony and sardonic wit, she is also bold, innovative, and full of surprises. These qualities may be what led her to the surrealism of Gellu Naum (1915–2001), on whom, at age twenty-two, she did a diploma study and subsequently published her book The Salvation of the Species.

In her novel Exuviae (1997), an exercise in postmodernist narcissism, Popescu alternates between first-person narrative and a second speaker who addresses her directly. This is a familiar postmodernist technique and opens another perspective on the main character, who is, of course, Popescu herself. The "exuviae" are the skin sheddings (or "skinswaps," to borrow from the title of a major collection of poems by the Slovenian poet Andrej Blatnik) experienced by the author-narrator as she passes from one phase of life to the next, taking on a new identity, as it were, with each shedding.

Postmodernism Elsewhere in Eastern Europe

The South Slavs

By the early 1990s literary postmodernism was well entrenched throughout Eastern Europe. It made its appearance in Yugoslavia before sectarian conflict tore the state apart. The father (in a sense) of Yugoslav postmodernism is the Serbian writer Milorad Pavić (b. 1929). His renown is both scholarly and literary. A professor at Belgrade University, Pavić is an acknowledged authority on older Serbian literature and is the author of books on the Baroque, classicism, and preromanticism. As a writer of fiction, he became an instant celebrity with the publication of his intricate, puzzle-like novel *Hazarski rečnik: Roman-leksikon u 100,000 reči* (*Dictionary of the Khazars: A Lexicon-Novel in 100,000 Words*, 1984). Besides winning the prestigious NIN Prize as the best novel in Serbo-Croatian in 1984, it has been translated into twenty-four languages.

Presented as a 1980s reconstruction and updating of a book by the same name from 1691—itself, in turn, a reconstruction of the lost "dictionary" of the ancient Khazar people—the entire novel is composed in the form of a great puzzle. Alphabetized entries out of chronological order and cross-referencing symbols invite readers to use the book as they would a dictionary. It can be taken in hand and read at any arbitrary point, from left to right, right to left, or even "diagonally." There is one major structural division—into three separately alphabetized books divided along religious lines (Christian, Hebrew, and Islamic), prefaced by preliminary notes and followed by appendixes that contain the lion's share of the narrative. The story itself is divided into three periods in time, each with its set of three characters. It was also published in male and female editions, different only by seventeen lines—according to Pavić, masculine and feminine stories cannot have the same ending.

Pavić pursued a similar game-playing technique in his subsequent novels *Predeo slikan čajem* (*Landscape Painted with Tea*, 1990) and *Unutrašnaja strana vetra ili roman o Kheri i Leandru* (*The Inner Side of the World; or, The Novel of Hero and Leander*, 1991). *Landscape Painted with Tea* is another large novel, this time in the form of a crossword puzzle woven out of the life and papers of a successful Serbian architect named Atanas Razin (alias Atanas Slivar), who settles in Los Angeles but eventually sells his engineering and pharmaceuticals company and moves to North Carolina. Along the way, Pavić provides instructions on how to solve the puzzle and discusses the novel with his readers.

The Inner Side of the Wind, a new reading of the ancient tale of Hero and Leander, includes both a male and female version within the same volume, differing in this respect from *Dictionary of the Khazars*. The book can also be opened from one side or the other; the two versions have identical title pages, and one is printed upside down from the other. The reader thus can start with whichever version he or she chooses. Hero's story is some twenty pages shorter than Leander's. The combined stories transpose the ancient tale onto seventeenth-century and contemporary Serbia. The story of Heroena Bukur (the Hero of the female book) is set in twentieth-century Yugoslavia and culminates in the violent death of the heroine. The narrative is anything but linear. It incorporates a direct intervention by Pavić at one point as well as a story-within-a-story by Heroena, covertly inserted into translations she makes of such French authors as Anatole France and Pierre Loti (copies of which she sends to her brother, with the interpolated passages indicated in lipstick). In Leander's story, Leander is the nickname given a young Serb by a Russian teacher of Latin in Belgrade's Serbian-Latin school when his class is assigned the reading of a Latin translation of the original Greek *Love and Death of Hero and Leander*. The story itself takes place during the seventeenth-century wars between the Serbs and Turks and ends with the violent death of the male protagonist.

After *The Inner Side of the Wind*, Pavić published *Poslednja ljubav u Carigradu* (*Last Love in Constantinople*, 1998), subtitled *A Tarot Novel for Divination*. Divided into a "special key" and twenty-one additional "keys" corresponding to Tarot cards, the book comes equipped with illustrations of the various cards, instructions on how to lay out the cards, an explanation of the use of the book for divination, and a section called "The Keys of the Great Secret for Ladies of Both Sexes." Pavić is also the author of several collections of short stories, among them *Stakleni puž: Priče sa interneta* (The Glass Snail: Stories from the Internet, 1998). Departing from his previous fascination with quasi-kabalistic numerology and Tarot, Pavić again demonstrates the indebtedness of postmodernism to computer culture. Adopting the persona of an Internet author, he presents the three stories that make up the collection as printouts from a Web site. After an epilogue in which he writes about himself as a third party, he offers his own URL: "khazaro.com".

After Pavić, arguably the most prominent name in Serbian postmodernism is Svetislav Basara (b. 1953). One of the most provocative of those Serbian writers who made their debut in the early 1980s, Basara launched his career with the short novel *Kinesko pismo* (*The Chinese Letter*, 1984). It was followed a year later by *Peking By Night* (original title in English, as befitting a work much indebted to American pop culture). Basara's later flamboyance, irreverence, iconoclastic humor, and existential concerns are already foreshadowed in *The Chinese Letter*. The narrator, who is unsure of his own name but nevertheless calls himself Fric (Fritz), is ordered by a couple of mysterious men "to write a statement of about one hundred pages."[5] He obliges by duly recording the bizarre occurrences of his daily life: his absurd conversations with his mother, who is abducted by slave traders; his visits to his friend, who is employed in the autopsy room of a hospital; and his sister's tumultuous marriage to the butcher's son, to mention just a few. Fragmentary and digressive, the novel has a serious underside despite its madcap narration. It is the means by which Basara tackles the issue of the emptiness of the contemporary world and the place in it of human individuality. Basara has said that he began writing the novel in the 1970s. Contrary to the widespread impression that this was a good period in Yugoslavia's post–World War II history, it was, in Basara's opinion, a wretched time of stagnation.

After *The Chinese Letter,* Basara wrote an impressive number of new novels: *Napuklo ogledalo* (The Cracked Mirror, 1986); *Fama o bickilistima* (The Fuss About Cyclists, 1988) and its sequel, *Na Gralovom tragu* (In Quest of the Grail, 1990); *Mongolski bedeker* (Mongolian Guidebook, 1992); *Tamna strana meseca* (The Dark Side of the Moon, 1992); *De bello civili* (On Civil War, 1995; original title in Latin), a work brimming with jibes at postmodernism, structuralism, and such prominent literary figures as Roland Barthes; *Ukleta zemlja* (The Accursed Land, 1995); *Looney Tunes: Manično-paranoična istorija srpske književnosti u periodu 1979–1990* (Looney Tunes: A Manic-Paranoic History of Serbian Literature in the Period 1979–1990, 1997) and its sequel, *Sveta mast: Manično-paranoična istorija srpske književnosti* (Holy Water: A Manic-Paranoic History of Serbian Literature, 1998). These last two texts will be looked at more closely in chapter 9, in the context of Basara's views on the collapse of Yugoslavia and on Serbian nationalism.

Ukleta zemlja (The Accursed Land) illustrates Basara's postmodernism at its most imaginative. The title actually refers to the interior novel (of sorts) within the novel. It is ascribed to one Robert T. Cincaid, who is said to have written it originally in English and first published it in the fictitious village of Krštrmrk in 1978. The preface to the novel was written by Basara, who tells us that, after abandoning the novel he was working on in the spring of 1992, he threw himself into the translation of Cincaid's book, which he found in a bookshop shortly after arriving in Krštrmrk.

The "action" of the novel is set in a country known as Etrastsia, the location of which is so difficult to find that Basara reaches the conclusion that the place simply does not exist—which, however, does not mean that it never will exist! In fact, as Basara states, he would not be at all surprised one day "to see fluttering before a skyscraper on the East River the red-blue-yellow-black-orange-green-violet flag of the Kingdom and Republic of Etrastsia."[6] The preface is followed by several pages of double-columned text that we are to presume has been taken from the first volume of an encyclopedia published by the Belgrade publisher Prosveta and containing an entry on Etrastsia; we learn that it was a kingdom from 1148 to 1945, a republic from 1945 to 1987, and both a kingdom and republic after 1987. It is said, "according to certain authorities," to be situated geographically between Hungary, Bulgaria, Romania, Albania, Yugoslavia, Turkey, Austria, and Greece. One of the authorities frequently cited by Basara about Etrastsia is the "liberal economist and Etrastsian poet, Salman Basri" [read, of course, Salman Rushdie].

What follows after the preface is a mind-boggling narrative of the absolute wretchedness, poverty, and paranoia of Etrastsia. The country is so poor that it cannot afford medications, which leads its despotic ruler to resolve the problem by declaring that the nation's citizens are healthy and so do not need pharmaceuticals. What scant resources Etrastsia has have to be reserved to keep the Americans from taking over the country. When the narrator, Cincaid, first came to Etrastsia he was married to his nineteen-year-old bride, Clio, in the Orthodox cathedral in Dunum, the capital of Etrastsia. As bride and groom were making their way down the steps of the cathedral after the ceremony, the bride was killed on the spot by a sniper's bullet. The case is solved only toward the end of the novel, by which time Cincaid, a cocaine user, has discovered that he is not a homosexual—which he believed he had been even at the time of his very brief marriage to Clio. The alleged murderer, who was arrested and put to death by the president himself, was a member of one of the rare opposition parties. The man, notes Cincaid, looked like a criminal, but then so does everyone in Etrastsia. In fact, Cincaid says that his own physiognomy has changed much for the worse since he arrived in the accursed country.

When the time came for the criminal's execution, reporters and cameramen from CNN, notes Cincaid, were already in place. The criminal was dispatched with a single bullet to the neck in full view of all those assembled. In a final letter to a colleague at the British Embassy in Istanbul (who had previously advised him to commit suicide), Cincaid announces his resignation from the diplomatic service and his intention to enter a secret monastery in Etrastsia together with Salman Basri. He then recommends that his colleague read Salman Basri's *Sveto opijanje* (Holy Intoxication), a work in praise of alcohol and drunkenness printed in Krštrmrk in 1977 and a copy of which he encloses. Then he goes on to explain the compatibility between Christianity and alcoholism and even substance abuse.

Two other South Slavic writers, one a Croatian and the other a Bulgarian, also evidence the strength of postmodernism in the Balkans. The Croatian, Vedrana Rudan (b. 1949), a native of Opatija, was a columnist for a Croatian daily until she was relieved of her position because of her opposition to Croatia's role in the Balkan wars. Since then she has resumed her career as a journalist for the prominent Croatian daily *Nacional*. Her first novel, *Ucho, grlo, nož* (Ear, Throat, Knife, 1999; translated as *Night*), is a caustic look at the reality of contemporary Croatia through the eyes of a writer who has no illusions and approaches her subject with a keen sense of irony and satire. To read what Rudan has to say about her own novel, the circumstances in which it came to be written, and its distinctly antifeminist character is to understand its essential autobiographical nature.[7]

The Bulgarian writer Georgi Gospodinov (b. 1968), now considered the *enfant terrible* of contemporary Bulgarian literature, won that reputation on the basis of his immensely popular first novel, *Estestven roman* (*Natural Novel*, 1999). Before the appearance of this work, Gospodinov had published two collections of poems, *Lapidarium* (1992) and *Cheresata na edin narod* (The Cherry Tree of One Nation, 1996). Narrated in the first person, *Natural Novel* takes the form of a series of extremely short chapters (most no more than a page or so), primarily but not exclusively about the author himself at a point of crisis in his life. His marriage has fallen apart and his wife, with whom he has not slept in six months, is pregnant by another man. At one point before they split up, the wife blurts out that she saw the baby on ultrasound and "it was tiny, just a centimeter and a half."[8] Although preoccupied with his family predicament, Gospodinov operates with a loose enough structure to allow for other narratives that have little or nothing to do with his own situation. It is, in a way, his attempt to write a "natural novel" in the sense of conveying life's chaotic rhythms. But what Gospodinov conveys much of the time is a taste for what would seem to be gratuitous violence and bathroom humor. Tripping the light fantastic as he spins his grotesque narrative, Gospodinov hops from one episode to another. Allusions to popular American culture—de rigueur in such Eastern European postmodernist writing—abound, as Gospodinov is happy to display his familiarity with such American cult films as *Pulp Fiction* and *Reservoir Dogs*. Needless to say, contemporary drug culture also receives its share of emphasis.

In fine postmodernist fashion, Gospodinov also discusses his ideas on novel-writing in more than one place. He muses, for example, about a novel only of beginnings, an "atomic novel of openings floating in the wilderness" (16). He then gives examples of what he has in mind:

> If read quickly one after the other they merge and move like frames on a film reel and become transfigured in a single general kinetics that works characters and events into some sort of new story. (19)

He also imagines endless possibilities:

> Yet nothing will be described in this Novel of Beginnings. It will only give the initial stimulus and will be sufficiently subtle to move into the shadow of the next opening and leave the characters to connect as they may. That's what I would call a Natural novel. (20)

He also toys with the idea of writing a novel using only verbs ("Only the verb is honest, indifferent, and precise" [38]). Quirky and self-conscious though it may be, Gospodinov's *Natural Novel* is a fitfully entertaining postmodernist romp with a serious issue at its core, the dissolution of a marriage.

Another noteworthy representative of South Slavic postmodernism, Berta Bojetu (1946–1997), was that rare phenomenon, a Jewish woman writer in Slovenia. Trained as an actress, she was the author of a few plays, including one for the puppet theater, in which she has also performed; two collections of poems of an assertive eroticism, *Žabon* (The Frog, 1979) and *Besede iz hiše* (Words from Home, 1988); and two novels, *Filio ni doma* (Filio Is Not at Home, 1990) and *Pticja hiša* (The Birdhouse, 1995).

Filio Is Not at Home, arguably her best prose work, is a feminine dystopian novel enveloped in an atmosphere of dread and danger. The setting is an unnamed island in an unnamed location, neatly divided between an Upper Town reserved for women and a Lower Town for men. Men are the absolute rulers of the island, their power embodied above all in the person of the Commander of the Guard (Poveljnik straža). Assisting the Commander in his control of the Upper Town are three brutal and malicious women who do the Commander's bidding in exchange for minor privileges.

The novel consists of three separate narratives. The first is related by Filio, who has come back to the island at the request of her dying grandmother, Helena Brass. After the older woman's death, Filio returns to the mainland, carrying with her Helena's diary. The diary is the heart of the novel, and its longest section. In it, Helena Brass, a forty-two-year-old widow, recalls how a shipwreck brought her to the infamous island, accompanied by her daughter (who remains unnamed in the novel) and a four-year-old boy who lost his mother in the shipwreck and whom she later names Uri. Uri's own account of events on the island forms the third part of the novel.

It is from Helena Brass's diary that the full extent of the monstrous nature of the island is revealed. Raped by the Commander soon after her arrival on the island, Helena becomes his mistress. This still does not spare her the wrath of his three female cohorts, who resent her relationship with him and try to make her life miserable. Her daughter in the meantime gives birth to a girl, whom Uri names Filio. Uri himself is soon taken away for special education with other boys and is reunited with Helena only several years later. While in the special school, he is exposed to the bizarre behavior among the boys and their superiors, including rape, homosexuality, and even bestiality. When Helena opens a school for Filio and other children, assisted by the Commander, so great is the anger against her that she is beaten badly and raped by an unknown man. Subsequently, her daughter is killed by a rock wielded by a man who had often slept with her. Filio, who has grown into a lovely young girl, feels that she is now in similar danger. Her mother's death, which she witnessed, has had a profound effect on her and she becomes obsessed with the image of her mother as a bird flying heavenward.

In the meantime, Uri has become an aide to the Commander, but he grows more ill at ease over conditions on the island. When he sees Filio's name on a list of women to receive visits by men (but only in the dark so as to minimize emotional ties), he changes places with the man designated to visit her and then tries to arrange to become her sole visitor. Even though the young couple are not allowed to see one another, Filio has a premonition as to Uri's identity. Filio eventually becomes pregnant, but the female underbosses of the island force her to undergo a brutal abortion. Later, with her grandmother's financial help, she manages to flee the island. She receives an education and in time becomes a well-known painter. The image of her mother as a bird that she still carries with her appears prominently in her art.

Not long after Filio's flight, Uri becomes the new commander of the island but soon leaves it to pursue Filio on the mainland. However, a life together seems impossible because of the scars they both bear from life on the island. After sixteen years on the mainland, Filio returns to the island for a final visit with her dying grandmother. When she returns to the mainland, she takes several things belonging to her grandmother, including her diary. She also finally realizes that she has loved Uri for all the time she has been on the mainland and still loves him.

Notwithstanding its fantasy-island character, overburdened plot, and sensationalism, Filio Is Not at Home is a grim indictment of a society that brutally forces women into subservience to men and the complicity of some women in such repression. Yet it is also a novel of feminine strength and survival, illustrating the ability of women to overcome adversity through a willingness to rebel and thereby force change. Highly imaginative, and well written—despite the twists and turns of its plot—Filio Is Not at Home became one of the sensations of contemporary Slovenian literature.

Czech and Slovak Postmodernism

Any consideration of Czech postmodernism must first acknowledge the preeminence of four writers: Jiří Kratochvil, Daniela Hodrová, Michal Ajvaz, and Jáchym Topol. They are, to be sure, not the only representatives of postmodernism in contemporary Czech literature, but they are certainly the most important and the most influential.

A self-proclaimed apostle of postmodernism, Jiří Kratochvil (b. 1940) is also one of its leading proponents. His allegorical short story (not quite two and a half pages) "Ma lásko, Postmoderno" ("Postmoderna, My Love") suggests itself as a statement of his attitude toward the uncoupling of literature from the social and political obligations forced on it under the Czechoslovak communist regime. The narrator of the story describes how he freed Postmoderna, his old childhood sweetheart, from a prison where she has been kept for forty years, hoisted her on his shoulders, and then carried her out into the world. The story was published in 1993, four years after the end of communism in Czechoslovakia. Kratochvil was to state the case yet more eloquently in the epilogue to his first novel, *Medvědi román*.

Before the fateful year of 1968, Kratochvil, a native of Brno, Moravia, had published in well-known literary journals as well as in the Czech literary underground. Nevertheless, he remained largely unknown until 1989. It was in 1990, just a year after the collapse of communism in Czechoslovakia, that Kratochvil's most important work of fiction to that time, the novel *Medvědí román* (Bear Novel), was published in its entirety. Kratochvil completed the novel in 1985, but it had to wait until the postcommunist era to see the light of day. The original version of the novel, free of the compromises Kratochvil felt constrained to introduce into the edition of 1990, reached the public under the title *Urmedvěd* (Ur-Bear, or Original Bear) in 1999. By then, on the basis of the text as it appeared in 1990, Kratochvil had become a literary celebrity. He was honored with the Tom Stoppard Prize in 1991; the prize of the review *Literární noviný* in 1993; the Egon Hostovský Prize in 1996; and the Karel Čapek Prize in 1998.

Kratochvil speaks of Bear Novel as "an open system, a novel as a living organism, living and moving before the reader's eyes, and its modes of expression are, for example, story variants and some kind of—how to put it?—finely chiseled improvisations."[9] In defending the experimentation of the work against his critics, Kratochvil contrasted the open system of the novel with the "closed" conditions prevailing in Czechoslovakia under communism. This coupling of postmodernism and implied political protest has already been observed in the case of the Romanians. Kratochvil had experienced the repression of the regime at first hand. He was ostracized after his father, Josef, a teacher and ornithologist who also wrote books for children, left Czechoslovakia for the United States in 1952 (later resettling in West Germany). Although he began gaining acceptance as a writer in the 1960s, Kratochvil was thrown out of work after the Soviet invasion of Czechoslovakia in 1968 and was forced to spend the 1970s as an unskilled laborer.

In familiar postmodernist fashion, much of Bear Novel concerns the creation of a novel. The writer-narrator describes the work as a "novel about how I am writing a novel about someone who is writing a novel" (168). Bear Novel begins as a kind of dystopian allegory of Czechoslovakia in the period of so-called normalization (1969–1989), when the reform movement led by Alexander Dubček was replaced after the Soviet invasion of 1968 by the hard-line regime of Gustav Husák. The novel is set in the fictional totalitarian state of Island and is marked by cruelty and absurdity. The ruler of the state is named Klitoris and Island is divided into six major cities, which all resemble each other. If a natural disaster damages part of one city, special squads are sent to all the other cities to inflict the same kind of damage. Echoes heard in one city are also heard in the other cities thanks to a complex monitoring system.

The first narrator to appear in Bear Novel is a petty thief named Ur (from Latin *ursus*, bear) who lives in an elevator and is trained by a mysterious figure named Savo to emulate the movements of a bear by walking on all fours. The plan is to penetrate circles of power by this novel means. The second part of Bear Novel returns the reader to the real Czechoslovakia and the period of "normalization" of the 1970s. The narrator is now Ondřej Béranek (the name means "young lamb" in Czech) who happens to be writing a work called Bear Novel. In the third part of the novel, another change of narrator occurs. The new narrator is Kratochvil himself, who relates the history of the heretical béranki ("young lambs") sect that arose in the second half of the seventeenth century and eventually became the Béranek clan of Moravia. Kratochvil then narrates the fate of František Béranek, the father of Ondřej Béranek, a village teacher who was accused of collaborating with the Germans during World War II. But František escaped execution disguised as a bear. However, the bearskin he throws over himself affects his character, turning him into an aggressive predator. It is at this point that Kratochvil draws the reader's attention away from the story to the time of the appearance of Bear Novel, of which he, Kratochvil, is the author, and to a consideration of the narrative process itself. In this way Kratochvil creates the illusion of the novel arising in a sense before the very eyes of the reader. In an epilogue, Kratochvil reintroduces Savo as the new president of Island who no longer needs to turn Ur into a pseudo-bear. Instead, he wants to marry him off so that the novel can conclude with a happy ending, which it does. However, Kratochvil himself, as narrator, does not end there. He introduces several new motifs, in fact never concluding his novel. Everything in the work can then be revised and modified; it is never a finished text but rather a game with ever-changing rules. And so, in the end, Kratochvil asserts, the novel Bear Novel is not at all the work he wanted to write, but something entirely different.

Bear Novel is, in fact, the first part of a trilogy that includes Kratochvil's subsequent novels *Uprostřed nocí zpěv* (Song in the Middle of the Night), published in samizdat in 1989 (an official edition appeared in 1992), and *Avion* (1995). Two intertwining plots are similarly at the heart of Song in the Middle of the Night. It is a work about the search for one's father and thus one's own identity. The theme of the loss of one's father, who is still alive somewhere on earth and therefore capable of being found, became understandably important in Kratochvil's writing and appears in several works. The quest for the missing father also becomes conflated with the reader's quest for a more accessible narrative, one that is unencumbered by the complexities of Bear Novel. Kratochvil himself addresses this issue in Song in the Middle of the Night:

> This time I decided to write a novel about the miserable fate of the children of post-February [1948] émigrés, and thus provide a testimony about them. In the thrall of this noble mission, I tried to write the novel in a way that would find it the greatest number of readers, and subordinated the means of literary expression to this communicative consideration, too.[10]

Song in the Middle of the Night has an obviously autobiographical character from the outset. It begins with an unnamed narrator recounting his life from the time Kratochvil's native Moravia was liberated by the Red Army, when his mother was presumably raped (and impregnated) by a man of uncertain nationality together with sixteen Soviet soldiers. It continues up to the narrator's marriage to the daughter of a party apparatchik. He believes that his father is a Brazilian priest named M. S. Prudencio and he begins sending him letters. In other chapters, a character named Petr Simonides narrates his own life story. He is the son of a schoolteacher and ornithologist (as was Kratochvil senior himself) who emigrated from Czechoslovakia in 1950. Toward the end of the book both protagonists merge into one. The unnamed narrator is now called Petr, while the story of Simonides is further narrated in the style of the unnamed hero.

In the last chapter Petr also addresses a letter to his presumed father, Father Prudencio. However, the reader is suddenly jarred by the appearance of the following metatextual declaration: "Whenever I come to a chapter I think could hold the key to the novel as a whole, I fall into a panic" (73). This may suggest that here indeed is the key to the novel in that the story of the unnamed figure is the creation of Petr. Furthermore, a reference to Simonides's schizophrenia also suggests that the story of the unnamed figure in this context may merely be a figment of a sick mind. In Bear Novel Kratochvil had offered the thesis, through the character of a university docent named Drop, that "schizophrenia and totalitarianism are isomorphic phenomena—that is, they have an identical structure—and a totalitarian society arises from the same causes as schizophrenic psychosis. In other words, it has the same roots, the same beginning, the same course, and the same end."[11] In the light of Kratochvil's ideas about literature as an open system, it seems entirely plausible that in his view literature might thus become a defense against, indeed an antidote to, the closed systems of schizophrenia and totalitarianism.

The third novel in Kratochvil's Bear trilogy, *Avion* (1995), derives its title from the name of a Brno hotel that was erected in 1927–1928; it is dedicated to the memory of the prominent Czech avant-garde architect Bohuslav Fuchs (1895–1972), the style of whose buildings influenced the composition of Kratochvil's novel. Indeed at the end of *Avion* Kratochvil notes that the work was completed in the Hotel Avion on 14 August 1994. He describes the attraction the hotel held for him in these words:

> The Hotel Avion for some time now has seemed to me the captivating model of a novel. I've always wanted to write such a novel: by no means expansive, rather narrow like the Avion (but just as deep!), the entire world of the novel compressed into a small space, a wonder of conciseness in which all the characters walked in full freedom (ten stories like the Avion—that is, ten chapters and an epilogue) and the whole thing would be (from the first chapter to the epilogue) mutually connected with striking views, unexpectedly connecting and mirroring various motifs and details from all the chapters of the novel . . . Its composition would evidently be influenced by the architecture of the Hotel Avion—a functionalistic novel, with pronounced functional novelistic structure.[12]

Hynek Kočka, the main personage of the novel and its narrator, and the figure created by him, František, meet in a hotel room, where they discover that they are both creative writers and that both of them are writing a novel, each about the other. We are again back to the motif, so frequent in Kratochvil's works, of the creation of a novel.

To Kratochvil, the text is a game, and he dismisses as misguided any attempt to treat literature as a mirror of reality. In relatively more recent fiction, Kratochvil has turned in other directions. With *Noční tango* (Night Tango, 1999) he initiates the search for a new style, whereas his *Lehni, bestie!* (Down, Beast!, 2002) represents the first Czech literary response to the attacks of 11 September 2001 in New York. The novel also reflects Kratochvil's desire to reestablish serious contact with the external world.

The outstanding contemporary Czech novelist Daniela Hodrová (b. 1946), a Prague native, has made a dual career. She is an academic, a literary theorist whose principal focus has been the genre of the novel, and in particular the initiation novel; she is also the author of several complex and intricate novels in a postmodernist style similar to that of her contemporary Jiří Kratochvil yet alluding to the Czech political situation in her own time. These include primarily the trilogy *Trýznivé město* (The Suffering City, 1991), consisting of the novels *Podobojí* (In Both Kinds, completed in 1977–1978 but first published in 1991), the title derived from the Czech Hussite demand that all should receive communion in both kinds; *Kukly* (Masks, written in 1981–1983 and first published in 1991); and *Théta* (Theta, published in 1992 but also written several years earlier). She is also the author of two later novels, *Perunův den* (Perun's Day, 1994) and *Komedie* (Comedy, 2003).

With Hodrová, it becomes difficult at times to know when the literary scholar ends and the novelist begins. In the manner of much postmodernist fiction, she favors loose structure, shifting perspectives whereby an event is seen and commented on by different characters, many references to her own literary endeavors as well to her own ideas concerning the design and structure of a novel, historical revisionism, an iconoclastic attitude toward tradition, a taste for the exotic and mysterious, passages in foreign languages, game-playing, and the blurring of the boundaries between fiction and reality and between art and non-art. Events often occur without meaning or explanation, such as the dog who sometimes can speak and other times not (in Perun's Day). Relying on rapid shifts of perspective—switching, in other words, from one character to the next—the omniscient narrator of Perun's Day relates often bizarre or mysterious events experienced by the four female protagonists who dominate the novel, each of whom is named for one of the Apostles: Miss John, Miss Matthew, Miss Luke, and Miss Mark. In most sections of the novel, an episode is limited to a single one of the main characters; on some occasions, however, the main characters are allowed to interact within a single episode.

In Théta, her best-known work to date, Hodrová appears both as the author of the novel and as a character in it. She recounts the dying of her father, a former actor, from lung cancer. At the same time as she describes events surrounding his care and ultimate death, she reveals that she is writing a novel about a certain Eliška Beránková, who is searching for her father. She herself is Eliška Beránková, and she is searching for the identity of her own father and, of course, of herself. She likens her search to that of Telemachus for Ulysses. "Who am I as I write this novel? Who do I want to be?," she asks.[13]

At another point, yielding to reality, she declares: "I am stripping off my skin. It is causing me unspeakable agony. My cuticle has already cracked in two places anyway—there where, some time ago, Truth nicked my throat, and on the forehead, where Reality dug its claw into me. I am not Eliška Beránková—I am Daniela Hodrová." But then she is disturbed by the thought that "having shed Eliška Beránková's cuticle (in several places on me it's still hanging in shreds), a strange feeling overcomes me. What if Eliška Beránková goes on living, independently of my will? What if all contrived characters from novels continue dwelling somewhere, just like the dead, enveloping our world in an increasingly airtight casing created even of all our feelings and memories?" (86). Interrupting the narrative to share questions, and doubts, with readers about the literary process itself is part and parcel of postmodernism.

Characters wander from one Hodrová novel to another. Masks consists of 126 "images" (*obrazy*), all built around the character of a young woman named Sofie Syslová (in a typical play on words, the name combines *Sofia,* the goddess of wisdom, and *sysel,* a ground squirrel). Sofie reappears in the later *Komedie* (Comedy), as does the character Diviš Paskal (the name suggests a union of Dionysus and the paschal lamb), also from Masks. Comedy exemplifies as well another common attribute of postmodernist fiction: its fondness for detail, especially of big-city locales. In the case of Comedy, the big city is Prague and the novel is so laden with landmarks and locations that readers unfamiliar with the city would have a difficult time navigating the text. Much of the novel in fact takes place between the walls of the Olšaný cemetery and its surroundings. These become the principal focus of the autobiographical dimension of the work and had appeared earlier in Théta. Olšaný is in fact the setting of Hodrová's trilogy as a whole.

Michal Ajvaz (b. 1949), a Prague native and graduate of Charles University with degrees in Czech literature and aesthetics, made his literary debut in 1989 with *Vražda v hotelu Intercontinental* (Murder in the Intercontinental Hotel). This is a small book consisting of rather long colloquial poems on Prague themes or reflecting his strong philosophical interests. His next book, *Návrat starého varana* (The Return of the Old Komodo Dragon, 1991), is a collection of twenty-one short stories almost all narrated in the first person and characterized by the combination of high intellect and rich imagination that inclines toward the strange.

Ajvaz's first novel, *Druhé město* (The Other City, 1993), like much of his earlier writing, demonstrates an all but obsessive interest in the city; but unlike Kratochvil's and Hodrová's works, this interest is unrelated to the past or to the quest for a long-absent father. The point of departure for the novel is the poem "Město" ("City"), from Murder in the Intercontinental Hotel, in which the narrator searches for the remnants of an ancient city on which Prague is believed to have been built. In the novel, the narrator first becomes aware of the "other city" that lies just beyond Prague when he comes across a book written in a strange alphabet in a secondhand bookshop. His discovery has the effect of shocking the narrator's perceptions about his world by suggesting the existence of possible realities of which heretofore he had no idea. This includes even speech, about which Ajvaz now declares: "Those few phonemes that we use are surrounded by an unknown jungle of sounds."[14] Thus awakened by the strange book, the narrator in The Other City overcomes his trepidation about crossing the boundaries of his own world into the uncertainties of the "other city." By entering into this new and strange space, the narrator signals his intention to reject all previous methods of cognition in order to embrace new possibilities as well as even possibly dangerous limitations. But like Kratochvil, who casts doubt on the purposefulness of his own undertaking in Bear Novel, Ajvaz cautions in The Other City that there is no certainty that even there will he discover any new truths.

After The Other City, Ajvaz published another two novels in rapid succession, *Tiché labyrinty* (Quiet Labyrinths, 1996) and *Tyrkysový orel* (The Turquoise Eagle, 1997). The more interesting of the two, The Turquoise Eagle is divided into two parts: "Bílí mravenci" ("White Ants") and "Zénónovy paradoxy" ("Zeno's Paradoxes"). Both of these, like The Other City, aim at casting doubt on the reality of our existence and of our world, at least with respect to its uniqueness vis-à-vis other possible worlds, including that of dreams. The more fanciful of the two stories, "White Ants," is a relation by an ethnographer about a species of white ants that secrete a green fluid capable of curing sleeping sickness and that have a remarkable way of defending themselves: when in danger the entire colony merges and forms a living sculpture, usually a white tiger lying with its jaws wide open. In "Zeno's Paradoxes," the narrator (Ajvaz) recalls what happened to him one snowy night on his way home from the Philosophical Faculty of Charles University when he dropped into a pub and overheard students discussing ancient philosophy.

The son of the dramatist Josef Topol, Jáchym Topol (b. 1962) caused a sensation with his first novel, *Sestra* (Sister, 1994; translated as *City Sister Silver*). A huge explosive work of the imagination, free-form in structure and at times almost hallucinogenic, it is a compelling picture of postcommunist Czech urban youth—amoral, cynical, hustling, and hedonistic. Since much of the interest of the book for native Czechs lies in its linguistic virtuosity, its play with and creation of words, its admixture of Czech and other languages, the work is extremely difficult to translate and the existing English translation offers at best only an approximation of the original (which the translator acknowledges). *City Sister Silver* won the prestigious Egon Hostovský Prize for best novel of the year.

Although a plot in any conventional sense would seem to be a minor ingredient of *City Sister Silver,* there is one. It pivots on the character of an actor and artist named Potok who has spent time in prison and psychiatric hospitals under the communists. Potok and his friends—who are "people of the Secret" ("lidi Tajemství") and members of the "Organization"—are engaged in almost every conceivable kind of shady get-rich-quick scheme, with the curious exception of weapons, drugs, and prostitution. They also become engaged in Mafia-like gang conflicts and are even used by a government agency to trace the whereabouts of a Vietnamese general who is conducting a campaign of terror against other Vietnamese and embassy staff in the Czech capital. Potok's main concern, however, is finding his great love, Little White She-Dog (Malá Bílá Psice), a nightclub singer and occasional prostitute whose real name is Barbara Zavorová but who is also often referred to as "Černá" ("Blackie").

As in Kratochvil, Hodrová, and Ajvaz, a sense of knowable reality is subverted by the blurred boundaries between dream and waking. Potok, at one point, gives an account of a dreamed tour of Auschwitz conducted by a talking skeleton. At another point, regular male menstrual cycles and even pregnancy are ascribed to Potok. Wild flights of the imagination, computer game-playing, and dizzying action, combined with the linguistic eccentricities of the text, make for slow reading. But the overall picture that emerges of the tumult of postcommunist society, echoed throughout Eastern Europe, is as compelling as it is intriguing.

City Sister Silver was followed in 1995 by two novellas by Topol, *Výlet k nadražní hale* (*A Trip to the Train Station*) and *Anděl* (*Angel*). Both again demonstrate Topol's knowledge of and skill at depicting the seamy underside of postcommunist Prague, with its native criminal element as well as foreign hustlers. If anything, given their shorter length, they offer even more disturbing and sensationalized pictures of Czech society in the 1990s, the immediate postcommunist years. Drug abuse is rampant and goes hand in hand with criminal behavior that does not stop short of murder.

A slightly younger contemporary of Jáchym Topol, and not quite in the same league as a writer, Ewald Murrer (b. 1964) exhibits a similar taste for the magical and surreal, but his writing lacks the social dimension of Topol's work. A native of Prague who began his literary career in the 1980s, primarily as a poet, Murrer's first major publication was the dreamlike *Zápisnik pana Pinkého* (Mr. Pinke's Notebook, 1986; translated as *The Diary of Mr. Pinke*). Murrer was working at the time as a gardener at the President's Office in Prague Castle, a job he held from 1985 to 1990. In 1992, after receiving a year's stipend from the Czech Literary Fund, he began a literary journal named *Iniciály*. He remained its editor in chief until 1994. After publishing the poetry collections *Mlha za zdí* (Fog Behind the Walls, 1992) and *Vyznamenání za prohranou válku* (Decoration for a Lost War, 1992), Murrer bought out his full-length prose work *Sny na konci noci* (*Dreams at the End of the Night*, 1996). Like *The Diary of Mr. Pinke*, it has been translated into English and published by Twisted Spoon Press of Prague.

Because he is a writer of such vivid imagination, Murrer's *Dreams at the End of the Night* would seem to be a natural extension of *The Diary of Mr. Pinke*. The earlier book assumes the form of a diary for an unspecified year ranging from March (6) to December (10). A small haiku-like verse utterance of anywhere from two to five lines begins each entry, followed by a short prose passage written in the first person, presumably Mr. Pinke himself. In a generally vague sort of way, the entries conjure up the atmosphere of an Eastern European village populated mainly by Jews, distantly recalling a painting by

Chagall. Everything, however, is enveloped in an aura of the mysterious, magical, and surreal. Animals talk, a goat scratches Talmudic symbols in the earth, a cat attends a funeral, a businessman named Fuks sells the horns of unicorns he captures in the region, a local rabbi secretly plays Tarot with a dog, the death of a resident named Issac Antan occasions a visit by none other than that famous Odessa Talmudist, Kuttenbrunz, and so on. In the style of postmodernist self-referentiality, Ewald Murrer appears as a visitor to the village under his own name. In the last entry, by Murrer, he mentions receiving a letter in the scratchy writing of a cat's paw inviting him to the village. When he arrives, he is greeted by the cat, of course, as well as all the village personalities, who then escort him to Mr. Pinke's house, where they present him the key. What this all means, or is supposed to mean, is, of course, anybody's guess.

Dreams at the End of the Night is akin in spirit to *The Diary of Mr. Pinke*. The work is divided into seventeen prose units, for a total of well over a hundred pages. Each narrative is marked off by a short quotation from some literary source (Celan, Heimito von Doderer, Kobo Abe, and so on). The heart of the short text is a journey initiated by a stranger who is particular about his appearance; silent and enigmatic, he prefers to converse with white sheets of paper and recalls visits to a number of other towns, everything enveloped again in Murrer's familiar surrealism. After the narrator recalls dreams, those he dreamt and those others dreamt, the reader is told that there were no towns and no dreams. Subsequent narratives offer the same recipe of enigma set in a surrealistic landscape tinged with elements of the grotesque and macabre.

Although a less familiar literary landscape than the Czech, its achievements also more easily overlooked after the uncontested divorce of the Czech and Slovak parts of the former Czechoslovakia in 1993, Slovakia nonetheless has made noteworthy contributions to European postmodernism. These are bound up with the names of such prominent writers as Pavel Vilikovský, Dušan Mitana, Jana Bodnárová, and Michal Hvorecký.

Respected as a writer of fiction as well as a translator of English and American literatures, Pavel Vilikovský (b. 1941) has made his reputation primarily on the basis of two small books published in 1989: the two-part *Kôň na poschodí, slepec vo Vrabl'och* (A Horse on the Staircase, a Blind Man in Vráble) and *Večne je zelený . . .* (Ever Green Is . . .). The lesser of the two works, *A Horse on the Staircase, a Blind Man in Vráble* is essentially a first-person narration of random thoughts about family, childhood, his mother's illness, and so on during a bus trip for no important reason to the historical town of Vráble. The horse of the title belongs, in fact, to a Russian soldier billeted in the same house in Bratislava as the narrator and his family at the end of World War II. Again, for no particular reason, the Russian decides at a certain point to ride his horse up a couple of flights of steps. Each section of the narrative is marked off by quotations from some equestrian manual, although the episode of the Russian and his horse comes up fairly near the end of the work. Vilikovský's musings on the bus trip to Vráble—introspective, humorous, mildly philosophical—suggest a belief in the absurdity of reality and the reality of absurdity. The horse on the staircase of an apartment house is no more or less absurd than the envy the narrator experiences when he notices standing on a corner of Vráble across from a bus stop a blind man attired in a light summer suit and a Panama hat with a black ribbon. As the bus pulls away, and the blind man also disappears from view, the narrator considers the different chronologies each represents. The bus will travel on from one stop to another, whereas the blind man will remain, and die, in Vráble. After he kills his ailing, bedridden mother by suffocating her with a pillow, the narrator remarks at the end of the novel that "everything is truly in its place. The horse on the staircase, the blind man in Vráble."

The much acclaimed *Ever Green Is . . .* , its title a parody of a line in Goethe's *Faust,* is narrated by a former Czech spy who claims to have been the lover of the infamous Austro-Hungarian World War I espionage agent Colonel Alfred Redl. At times humorous and witty, the now elderly narrator writes of his homosexual relationship with Redl, his experiences with Romanian chambermaids, his ruminations on interrogation and torture as an enemy agent, and his (anything but flattering) assessment of Slovakia and Slovaks. Sex, primarily heterosexual, occupies a prominent place in *Ever Green Is . . . ,* as indeed it does in most of Vilikovský's writings—as, for example, his romantic-erotic *Slovenský Casanova* (A Slovak Casanova, 1991).

Although a zealous pursuer of wit, who also enjoys playing games with his readers while at the same time mocking them, Vilikovský may perhaps carry his deconstruction of Slovak national myths in *Ever Green Is . . .* a bit too far. One can only imagine how his countrymen might have reacted to remarks like these, even though they come from the mouth of the Czech narrator:

> All nations want to plow a deep furrow in the history of humanity. . . . Only Slovaks, the children of God, see the meaning and fulfillment of their existence in the fact that they exist. Who else knows how to enjoy such childlike pleasure: "A hundred years have gone by already, and we're still here! We're not useless after all! We're still here, and that for sure means something!" And then, full of enthusiasm, they determine a clear goal: "Let's keep existing!"[15]

On the Slovak attitude toward Jews, a sensitive issue in post–World War II Slovakia, Vilikovský's narrator has this to say:

> Nowhere, I guess, was there such a deep-rooted hatred of Jews as there was right among the broad masses of the Slovak people, who used the pejorative term "židák" (Yid) for them. You really didn't know that? You're just getting to know Slovaks and I can see you've already developed a fondness for them. (58)

The prominence of rural themes in Slovak literature also comes in for its share of mockery in Vilikovský's book:

> Without the Slovak countryside there wouldn't be any Slovaks, and without Slovak writers there wouldn't be a Slovak countryside . . . at least definitely not today. Nowadays if a Slovak wants to come to in the lap of virginal nature, he simply opens some outstanding work of Slovak literature. Don't worry; in Slovak literature all works are outstanding, and so succeed with everyone. (65)

Even more exuberant an exponent of postmodernism than Vilikovský is Dušan Mitana (b. 1946), a leading contemporary Slovak writer well known for his nonconformity and eccentricity. Mitana's fascination with the irrational, mystical, and occult is amply evidenced in his collection of short stories *Nočné správy* (Nightly News, 1976). His penchant for narrative experimentation also informs his intriguing novel *Hľadanie stratèného autora* (The Search for a Missing Author, 1991). Mitana pulled out all the stops in his later *Návrat Krista* (The Return of Christ, 1999), subtitled "Fantasticko-faktografický pararoman s vesmírnou zápletkou, alebo Dejiny spasy v 10 častiach s prologom a epilogom" ("A Fantastic-Factographic Paranovel with a Cosmic Plot; or, The History of Salvation in Ten Parts with Prologue and Epilogue"). The book was published by L.C.A. (Literature & Culture Agency) of Levice, Slovakia. The "novel," using the term loosely, is another bold and curious work, less a piece of fiction than a long (nearly 400-page), highly idiosyncratic inquiry into the matter of Jesus Christ's inevitable return to earth.

Mitana draws on a vast range of sources for this work, among them astrology, Rudolf Steiner's anthroposophy, numerology, the Old and New Testaments, the Torah and other Jewish teaching and lore, mythology, the occult sciences, space exploration, the Nazi obsession with the occult, the literature on outer space (Carl Sagan, Paul Davies, Fred Hoyle, Erich von Däniken), New Age philosophy, and history and politics (Nazi Germany, Admiral Richard Byrd, Saddam Hussein, and the extreme Russian nationalist Vladimir Zhirinovsky). He is also conversant with most of if not all the speculative writings about UFOs, human contact with residents of other planets (expressing the belief that the gods of mythology were in fact otherworldly astronauts), highly secret underground tunnels in America and elsewhere, the mysterious American "Area 51," and so on. Since his book was published in the last year of the twentieth century, one can assume that the symbolism of the turn of the century as marking the beginning of a new historical epoch was an important element in the genesis of The Return of Christ.

One of Mitana's recurrent themes in the book is his belief that the Jews will eventually recognize Jesus as their true messiah, and that when this occurs conditions will be propitious for the Second Coming. Mitana's visionary reasoning is free of anti-Jewish prejudice or compulsion to convert. He is above that. As to the chronology of the Second Coming, he lays a particular emphasis on the year 2033:

> Two thousand years will have elapsed since the death and resurrection of Jesus Christ, according to the Gregorian calendar, in the year 2033. According to the reckoning of a solved biblical code, this date is also prophesied in the Torah as the end of the old era. And according to several astrologers it is also in the year 2033 that the age of the Fish ends and the epoch of the "fourth century"—of Cala Yuga—begins. Sectarians await the end of the world, confessors of the New Age religion and of the "new" world religion, the Bahai faith, hope that it will be the end of the Century of the Fish and the advent of the New Century, the Century of the Water-Snake, when the Great Guru destroys the boundaries between religions and the Golden Century arises. They are convinced that the Century of the Water-Snake will signify the end of the Judeo-Christian era. In effect, it will be the contrary![16]

As we can see from the above, Mitana does not shrink from tackling, and deflating, views that part company with his own, especially those of New Age philosophy. Mitana ends his work with these words:

> Speculation about the date of Christ's birth, death, and return are useless because they deflect attention from the fundamental question: Why did the Son of God have to come to this Earth two thousand years ago; why did he have to be born in a cave near a Bethlehem inn; why did he have to die on Golgotha; and why must he come again? In order to save us from self-destruction! (345)

In 2001 Mitana published *Krst ohnom* (Baptism of Fire), which might at first glance seem to be a sequel to The Return of Christ. It is instead an attempt on Mitana's part to explain his transformation from a nonconformist rebel to a messianist whose worldview pivots on the figure of Christ. Of particular interest in this collection of nine stories is the author's revisiting characters from his previous writing in order to recast them in conformity with his new spirituality. The "baptism of fire" of the title is the fire of hell through which the literary figures pass on their way to Christian rebirth.

A poet, novelist, and playwright, Jana Bodnárová (1950) began her career with the award-winning short-story collection *Aféra rozumu* (An Affair of the Mind) in 1990. It was followed by the verse collection *Terra nova* (New Land) and *Neviditel'ná sfinga* (The Invisible Sphynx), both in 1991; the novel *Z denníkov Ida V.* (From the Diaries of Ida V.) in 1993; two more verse collections, *Še-po-ty* (Whi-s-pers, 1995) and *bleskosvetlo/bleskotma* (flash-bright/flash-dark, 1996); the short-story collections *Závojovaná žena* (The Veiled Wife, 1996) and *2 cesty* (Two Roads, 1999); and the short novel *Tiene papradia*

(Shades of Bracken, 2002). Bodnárová is very much a woman's writer who views the world around her through the prism of feminine sensibility. Female characters are almost always at the center of her works, and their male counterparts come off as weaker or generally less interesting. But Bodnárová does not advance any feminist agenda. Her "heroines," often university students—a milieu she knows well—are placed in what at first appear to be everyday situations. But the richness of Bodnárová's imagination soon transforms the ordinary into the strange and even fantastic.

Her first collection of stories, An Affair of the Mind, set the pattern of much of her subsequent prose. Comfortable mostly in short forms, she usually prefers first-person narration, often by a literary persona, a focus primarily on feminine experience, a taste for the mysterious, an attachment to childhood recollections, and a strong affinity for photography (about which the very first story in An Affair of the Mind, "Prelud" ["Illusion"], is built). Other stories in this collection ("Vernisáž" ["Vernissage"]; "Smutný valčík" ["The Sad Waltz"]) as well as in The Veiled Lady ("Čas do popoludňajšieho kina" ["Time for the Afternoon Cinema"]) similarly make use of photographic motifs.

Reading Bodnárová, it is difficult to escape the feeling that her writing is essentially autobiographical. In From the Diaries of Ida V., the "nonheroine" is an academic in the field of English, a convert to Eastern Orthodoxy who quotes Robert Browning, T. S. Eliot, and William Burroughs, and who fills her diary entries with incidents from her daily routine (the comings and goings of family members) as well as her observations and thoughts on life, death (prompted by the early death of her father), illness, literature, and society. Dreams play an important role in her diary, especially toward the end of the work, where they engulf the text. All in all, Bodnárová's book is an intriguing look into the mind of an educated, thoughtful, and complex woman of her own time and place. Two Roads is a loosely structured, experimental short novel in two parts, "Chôdza v čase" ("A Walk in Time"), with five temporal levels—the '50s, the '60s, the '70s, the '80s, and the '90s—and the longer "Chôdza po úlomkach skla" ("A Walk Along Shards of Glass"). "A Walk in Time" suggests almost a personal reminiscence as the author follows the development of an unnamed sickly girl through the '50s, to the teenage Antónia of the '60s who experiences menstruation for the first time, to the tour guide Sabina in the '70s who has never been abroad and flirts with the idea of leaving Czechoslovakia but is discouraged from doing so by officials at the Czech-German border, to the romantic interest in an unnamed woman on the part of a stranger in the '80s who tries to convince her that her children and husband will leave her and that she will then be his, and finally into the '90s and the newly independent Republic of Slovakia with its new social problems.

Bodnárová's strong attraction to photography, both still and cinematic, also shows up in a series of so-called videopoviedky ("video tales") that read like miniature film scenarios. They are mostly descriptive "mood" scenes, often with elements of mystery and strangeness, again with women at the center, but also occasionally with exotic foreigners (a Buddhist monk, a Japanese performer).

With Shades of Bracken, possibly her best work to date despite its relative brevity, Bodnárová combines recollection and myth in an interesting example of contemporary Slovak postmodernism The "nonheroine" of the tale is a journalist named Oča (a shortened form of Očarovaná, "Enchanted"), who leaves on a trip to photograph a dying forest together with her unemployed and disaffected husband, a civil engineer who longs to build bridges but wonders if anyone still has any use for them. As they drive to their destination, which happens to be in Oča's native region, memories of her childhood are reawakened. She is of village origin, unlike her husband, and her recollections evoke vivid images of such figures as her grandmother, who was known as the village witch and who used to regale her with superstitions, dreams, and tales of magic; her mother, who hated rural life and sought only to flee it, eventually throwing herself from a mountain cliff; a certain Doctor Schulz, who never married and lived with his old mother; and a local amateur painter who was rumored to be a former professor and who aroused her enthusiasm for art and knowledge in general. The retrospective passages in the novel, identified by their own titles and the common subtitle *Exil pamäti* (Exile of Memory), mesh neatly with the events of the present and create an intriguing parallel world of myth and magic.

At the end of the novel, after Oča and her husband revisit the site where her mother leaped from a cliff, Oča seems to relive her childhood and to become as if magically transformed by it. Shedding her clothes, she asks her husband to photograph her as she whirls about, plucking the blades of a fern and ecstatically declaring: "Have a look at the strata of anthropocentric self-adoration!"[17] Unable to grasp her meaning or her ecstatic transport, Adam, the husband, feels increasingly more alienated from her, calling himself "an outsider" and preferring to be in a coffeehouse or a movie theater. He regards his wife as "insane," but still proclaims his love for her. She is off in another world, however, a "small part of the enchanted soul of the forest, a sister of nymphs, a plant woman. The eye of the sun intimately follows her from the deep." When Adam approaches the spot from which she has disappeared, at the bottom of the plants the camera catches a naked woman, motionless, dead. But the woman suddenly flings up one shoulder, then another, and with a laugh tosses from side to side. She resembles "a person who has left everything behind her and is now unburdened, free. Like a swimmer in green waters or like a musician who liberates himself through music." Disdaining his wife's concern for nature, for the mountain forests of her native region, Adam had previously dubbed her an "ecofeminist." Oča's love of nature and feeling of intimacy with nature, which the city-bred Adam does not share, reflects the environmentalism Bodnárová shares with other contemporary Slovak writers.

Another facet to the novel that propels Bodnárová into the mainstream of contemporary Slovak social concerns is its anxiety over the rise of neofascist racism. At one point in the work Adam is severely beaten by a gang of youths when he tries to defend a young Gypsy. The gang leaves a piece of paper on his chest with the message "LIQUIDATE JEWS, GYPSIES, FOREIGNERS," and is signed "The Exterminators."

The young and popular contemporary Slovak writer Michal Hvorecký (b. 1976)—who has also performed in a Bratislava rock band—published his first book, the critically well-received collection of macabre sci-fi stories *Silný pocit čistoty* (A Strong Sense of Purity) in 1998. In one of his best stories, "Mrakodrap" ("Skyscraper"), which typifies Hvorecký's fresh imagination, a skyscraper runs out of control and imprisons its inhabitants. Another story is intriguingly titled "Slizký mäsožravý mutant zo zmorenej planéty B2.44M, ktorý sa rýchlosťou svetla rúti na citadelu Vládcu hviezd a chce ju zničiť laserkinetickým delom" ("The Slimy Carnivorous Mutant from the Exhausted Planet B2.44M That Plummets with the Speed of Light Down on the Citadel Ruler of the Stars and Seeks to Destroy It with a Laser-Kinetic Weapon"). Hvorecký followed up A Strong Sense of Purity with a second collection of stories, *Lovci & zberači* (Hunters and Gatherers, 2002).

More aggressively postmodernist in his partly parodic embrace of the world of pop culture, Hvorecký makes free use of such everyday phenomena as the television sitcom, cyberpunk, the horror genre, street parties, and the supermarket. Everything is passed through the prism of cybernetics and information science. To Hvorecký, these new technologies are both transforming the world and at the same time reaching deep into human consciousness. The brand names of the contemporary computer world are everywhere, as characters stroll along Apple Macintosh Boulevard and down iBook, AppleWorks, Mac OS, and Power Mac streets. The competitive world of Microsoft is equally well represented.

Hvorecký's imagination is fueled as much by media coverage of demonstrations against globalization as by his vision of the supermarket of the future, in which it is not the consumers who select the products but the products that choose the buyers. This is the subject of perhaps his best story in Hunters and Gatherers, "Prvé víťazstvo supermarketov" ("The First Victory of the Supermarkets"). It is narrated in the first person by a supermarket designer who hits on the idea of having a team of MIT psychoanalysts, known previously for their work on a cranial opera, create music to enhance the shopper's sense of need by appealing to images in the subconscious. Accompanied by TV crews and a horde of shoppers, the narrator then rushes to try out his discovery in a newly opened gigantic store. But as he walks around with a shopping cart in hand, he finds that after putting one item in the cart he can't resist adding more and more. He suddenly notices that, like other shoppers, he begins crying from happiness, happiness based on the realization that they can get whatever they need in this store. This then leads to a mad frenzy of shopping as customers try to outdo each other in accumulating goods. The narrator describes the scene this way:

> But then I heard a penetrating, gnashing sound. I got my head together. I jumped over the saleswoman's body, blocked her with the cart, and ran further. All the other shoppers seemed to be hurrying as well. Perhaps many of them were trying to outdo me in purchases! I took stock of the situation. I heckled them. It was bedlam. I joined them. Around me, shelves with goods of dubious and cheap quality were winking. I suddenly had no idea what to do first. To move

forward or quickly buy here and continue later? I was at a loss. . . . Joining in the mad flight, I reached the closest shelf and pulled it. Dozens of different kinds of European mayonnaise came crashing to the floor. Someone fell and began swearing. I coughed in reply, then ran further. The rhythm of the music adapted to my steps. I reached hangers with teenage styles and felt a desire for colorful windbreakers and T-shirts I didn't really like very much. At such a price, though, it would be a shame not to buy them. I already had a full cart.[18]

Eventually the supermarket is reduced to a shambles, and the designer falls victim to his own invention. In one of the many interviews he has given since becoming a literary star, Hvorecký claims that the inspiration for the story came from the opening of a Swedish supermarket in Bratislava, where, several hours before the doors were to be opened, fighting broke out among the throng of shoppers anxious to enter.

As may well be imagined from the subjects he writes about, the American influence on Hvorecký is strong. The signposts of contemporary American culture are scattered throughout the pages of his works, and he has been mentioned in the context of such writers as Thomas Pynchon, William Gibson, and Jack Womack. In fact, Hvorecký was the Slovak translator of Womack's novel *Ambient,* which enjoys considerable cult status. Hvorecký's first novel, *Posledný hit* (The Last Hit, 2003), is in much the same spirit and style as his short-story collections. Up-to-date in the quasi-terrorist aspect of its plot, and replete with motifs related to almost every icon of contemporary culture, it has as its "hero" the unlikely figure of a highly popular Icelandic disc jockey named Alfred Raff. A denizen of big cities whose home is everywhere and nowhere, Raff becomes the front man in a newly formed boy-band named Icon. As he says, "My Icelandic origin, naturally, helped. Reykjavik nowadays is a mystical place for the music scene like Seattle was for the grunge scene, Rio de Janeiro for Brazil-electro, Cologne for minimal house, and New York for electroclash."[19]

Raff's cynical manner begins to dissolve after he falls in love with a singer he meets in London named Letizia. The romance, however, is short-lived. Letizia dies in an automobile accident and Alfred is emotionally crushed. His career nosedives, he loses interest in everything, and in a manifestation of his disinterest in the world he moves to the hinterlands, in this case Bratislava, the Slovak capital. He is sought out here by a journalist named Karisma Gas, who turns out to be an anti-globalization conspirator intent on bringing about, by nonlethal means, a new world order that would end the hegemony of American-generated high-tech instruments of deception and delusion and the CIA's insidious distribution of mind-controlling drugs and antidepressants. Aided by her accomplices, she whisks Raff away on a globe-trotting journey of indoctrination that includes, among other places, Iraq, Vietnam, and the United States, where he visits American "concentration camps," such as Fort Drum in New Jersey, Fort Huachua (sic) in Arizona, and Indiantown Gap and Allenwood in Pennsylvania.

Once installed in a luxury hotel in Dubai, in the United Arab Emirates, Raff has to undergo a program of extensive reading in all the genres of pop culture—thrillers, spy stories, science fiction, comics, "gore horror," Westerns, songs, commercials, pornographic literature and films. According to Karisma: "Pornography means the same for the present generation as oral sex did a decade ago" (108). Through pop culture the young in particular can be dominated and manipulated, and hence are the means Karisma and her followers chose to effect their revolution. As Raff muses at one point: "I understood that my road to superficiality was at an end. I don't know how I could have forgotten that today's teenagers are like Africa once was. You have to colonize them. By any and all means. I became one of the conquerors" (182). Toward this goal, Karisma asks Raff to compose a love ballad for a new campaign she and her cohorts are planning. In conditions of virtual imprisonment, he devotes considerable care to his composition, which he titles "The Last Hit." When the time comes to perform it before an enormous crowd, Karisma informs him that the program will contain subtle changes inserted by Karisma and her followers that Raff is not in any way to alter. Performed together with his old band, Icon, the concert proves to be a great media event, worthy of a famous rock star. The high point of the event is "The Last Hit," into which Raff has introduced his own subtle changes and a hidden message. His long journey through ideological combat at last at an end, Raff can now look forward to effecting the only revolt of which he is capable. Echoing the sentiments of "The First Supermarket Victory" and alluding to his earlier attempts at flight from Karisma and her gang, he declares:

> Oh, what kind of ludicrous protest did I attempt with escape? After all, I already knew that the last possible form of true revolt remaining to me was buying. Nowhere else on earth did I have such a possibility of free movement and decision-making as in shopping centers. That's the main reason why I liked rooting around in huge baskets filled with merchandise. I loved moving goods freely through salesrooms, pulling them from hangers, putting them in other departments, or in the end just tossing them on the floor. (213)

Polish Postmodernism: The Vision of Magdalena Tulli

Although not the only Polish writer whose texts may be regarded as postmodernist, Magdalena Tulli (b. 1955) may in some ways be the most compelling. She attracted national and international interest with the publication of her provocative and beautifully written first novel, the short *Sny i kamienie* (*Dreams and Stones*, 1995), which won the prestigious Koscielski Foundation Prize the year of its appearance. Tulli's second novel, *W czerwieni* (*In Red*, 1998), was soon translated into several European languages; and her next book of fiction, *Tryby* (Currents, 2003; translated into English as *Moving Parts*), has added to the luster of her reputation as one of Poland's most outstanding contemporary writers. In 2006 her newest novel, *Skaza* (Blemish), appeared.

Although much praised for the elegance of her prose, Tulli is a less accessible writer than her contemporary, Olga Tokarczuk. Her short novels are intellectually challenging, and demanding, as they indeed address everyday assumptions about both the world around us and the literary process itself. A work of a fertile imagination, *Dreams and Stones* reads less like fiction and more like a poetic parable-treatise on the city and modern urban culture, relating Tulli in this respect to other "urbanists" of contemporary Eastern European postmodernism, such as the Czechs Ajvaz, Topol, and Vopěnka. Her book also recalls in some ways Italo Calvino's *Le città invisibili* (*Invisible Cities*, 1972); Tulli, incidentally, has translated Calvino. Plot, events, and even characters, in any traditional sense, are conspicuous by their absence. Apart from faceless masses of urban dwellers and workers, the city is the novel's sole true character. It is anything but static, its growth compared at length to that of a tree. Tulli's universal city is in a state of constant flux, like memory itself, which plays an integral role in her imaginative cityscape.

At times undeniably humorous, In Red is in essence a deeply depressing tale about a small provincial Polish city named Ściegi and its inhabitants, who are doomed to suffering and ultimate self-destruction. The novel begins in the first thirty years of the twentieth century, although the chronology is as vague here as elsewhere in Tulli's fiction. That it alludes to the situation in postcommunist Eastern Europe seems obvious. Neither materialism in terms of the feverish acquisition of money and goods nor faith provide any lasting relief from overwhelming feelings of emptiness and frustration. These in turn give way to eventual violence and madness. The history of the city is conveyed impressionistically by the color red, the color of dawn but also the color connoting death and birth. Other associations touch all the town's inhabitants.

Tulli's lack of faith in contemporary civilization extends as well to her third novel, *Moving Parts*. Set amid the perplexing layout of a nameless hotel in a nameless city in an unspecified time, the novel comes across as yet another postmodernist experiment in multiple narration similar in some respects to the novels of the Czechs Jiří Kratochvil and Daniela Hodrová. A nameless, and hapless, narrator who has no wish to be one has been hired to tell the trite story of a romantic triangle that culminates in a violent crime. But he keeps on getting sidetracked, and ultimately derailed, by other narrators (and characters), who also want to have their say as they are all swept along on a fantastic journey resembling a romp through a fun-house maze. Any sense of permanence in life is undermined as Tulli paints a disturbing picture of fragility, vulnerability, and helplessness. Although she is frequently compared to Gogol and Kafka, the resemblances are superficial and Tulli has indeed created an unsettling world of her own design.

Hungarian Postmodernism

After Péter Esterházy made Hungarian postmodernism a part of the international literary landscape with such novels as A Production Novel, *A Little*

Hungarian Pornography, and *Helping Verbs of the Heart* (see chapter 2 above), its visibility was further elevated by the writings of László Krasznahorkai, the Romanian-born Adám Bodor, and Péter Nádas.

Ranked among the most intriguing, and challenging, of contemporary Hungarian postmodernists, László Krasznahorkai (b. 1954) combines flamboyance and reclusiveness with an extraordinarily convoluted yet spellbinding style. Beginning with his first novel *Sátántangó* (Satan Tango, 1986), which became the basis for a successful seven-and-a-half-hour black-and-white film directed by Béla Tarr in 1994, Krasznahorkai has attracted attention for his dark, pessimistic, indeed hopeless vision of the world. In a dense narrative in which dreams, fantasies, and a profoundly depressing image of the human condition commingle, his startlingly bleak residents of a failed collective farm wait around for an apocalypse that never appears. The setting is one frequently encountered in Krasznahorkai's fiction—a bleak, stagnant, out-of-the-way Hungarian town, in Satan Tango rendered all the gloomier by the poverty of its inhabitants, their fondness for drink, and incessant rain. Like Beckett's characters waiting for Godot, Krasznahorkai's townspeople wait for some savior of their own who will show them a way out of the desperation of their existence. When the "savior," Irimias, a former resident with the charisma of a prophet, finally appears, he is an ordinary con artist who merely takes advantage of their ignorance and naiveté. As in the Polish writer Olga Tokarczuk's works, or in those of the Colombian Gabriel García Márquez, the real and the surreal merge. Elements of the fantastic and hallucinatory become all-pervasive. The ceaseless rain that falls throughout sets the mood for and seems the appropriate accompaniment to Krasznahorkai's languid, at times even monotonous, style.

His next book, also published in 1986, the short-story collection *Kegyelmi viszonyok: Halálnovellák* (Relations of Grace: Tales of Death, 1986), has a similar character. The eight stories in the collection are built around wretched human creatures who appear at some point to achieve grace, only to suffer a reversal of fortune that ends in their death or suicide. In one of the best stories, "Herman, a vadőr" ("Herman, the Gamekeeper"), a former gamekeeper and renowned hunter develops a sudden compassion for an animal in a trap, thereafter changing his outlook and values. But this then leads him to the opposite extreme, of setting traps for humans, until he himself is hunted down and killed.

Az ellenállás melankóliája (*The Melancholy of Resistance,* 1989), Krasznahorkai's next, and most famous, novel (which was also made into a film in 2000) deals with the strange events that occur in a neglected, remote Hungarian town after the arrival of a circus featuring what it advertises as the largest whale in the world. Conceived as a parable alluding to the political climate in Eastern Europe in the late 1980s before and after the downfall of communism, the novel is anything but easy reading. The ponderousness of Krasznahorkai's style, as befitting the tenor of the work, is augmented by its division into chapters but not paragraphs.

Krasznahorkai's fondness for the offbeat and strange also informs the two novels after *The Melancholy of Resistance*—*Az urgai fogoly* (The Prisoner of Urga, 1992) and *Háború és háború* (*War and War*, 1999). The Prisoner of Urga—Urga, or the more common name, Ulan Bator, refers to the capital of Mongolia—was inspired by the Urga–Beijing leg of Krasznahorkai's journey to Siberia via China in the 1980s. The first-person narrator of the novel travels the route as a godless pilgrim in search of paradise, only to come up empty-handed. Upon his return to an Eastern Europe profoundly unsettled by the wars in the Balkans, he finds his questions have no answers and he is condemned to asking them all over again. The two central episodes of The Prisoner of Urga recount the performance of a traditional Chinese opera, in which a young actress makes a great impression on him, and the narrator's long illness during his trip. Krasznahorkai returned to his experiences in China in a second book, published in 2004, *Rombolás és bánat az Ég alatt* (Destruction and Distress Under Heaven). It comprises a series of ten essays dealing with different facets of Chinese life. Three of the essays, "A nagy utazás" ("The Big Trip"), "Beszéd a romokon" ("Conversation Amid the Ruins"), and "Suzhouban és mégsem Suzhouban" ("In Suzhou and Yet Not in Suzhou"), have further subdivisions. Several of the essays are in the form of conversations between the narrator and various Chinese intellectuals he encounters. The book also includes a number of explanatory notes and a guide to the pronunciation of Chinese names.

Háború és háború (*War and War*) is certainly among Krasznahorkai's strangest works. It is also one of his least successful. The fairly complex story involves a small-town archivist named Dr. György Korim whose life changes when he comes across the typescript of a book by an unknown writer that he believes deserves immortality. After leaving behind his family and job, he travels to New York, the world's epicenter, where he plans to type the manuscript into a computer and then launch it on the Worldwide Web, where he believes it properly belongs. Much of *War and War* is taken up with the hapless adventures of a now utterly disreputable-looking Korim as he makes his way around New York. Krasznahorkai's style matches Korim's compulsive manner. The novel is divided into eighty chapters, which are further subdivided into numbered subchapters, each comprising a single sentence, usually one or two pages in length; these are presented as the reported speech of Korim in conversations with people he meets or as details about or from the mysterious manuscript he has begun typing into a laptop acquired in New York. Although much about the manuscript remains elusive, it does seem, in the main, to be about five men (Kasser, Falke, Bengazza, Toot, and Mastemann) who appear in different locales and at different times in history, extending from ancient Crete to Cologne, Germany, just before the Franco-Prussian war. The common thread is the eternity of war that is history, with never any hope of true peace.

Toward the end of the novel, once the manuscript has been sent into the "heaven" of the Worldwide Web, Korim becomes entranced with the photo of a work of art representing an Eskimo igloo that was designed by the Italian

Arte Povera artist Mario Merz and housed in the Museum of Modern Art in Schaffhausen, Switzerland. The novel ends essentially with the disappearance of Korim after he visits the Schaffhausen museum. But as if to continue the story of Korim and his manuscript beyond the pages of his novel, Krasznahorkai had a commemorative plaque put up on a wall of the Swiss museum a few weeks after the publication of *War and War* that contained a message from Korim expressing the hope that the public who reads the plaque may find the peace that he had failed to find.

Another master of the exotic and strange is the older Transylvanian Hungarian novelist and short-story writer Ádám Bodor. After a two-year stint in prison, from 1952 to 1954, followed by a period of employment as a factory worker, Bodor in 1965 began publishing short stories in Hungary (where he settled permanently in 1984) (see further discussion in chapter 6 above). He became a full-time writer in 1968. Although arguably more successful in shorter genres, he scored a major triumph with his first novel, *Sinistra körzet: Egy regény fejezetei* (The Sinistra District: A Novel in Chapters, 1992). Bodor's proclivity for the bizarre, so evident in the stories and novellas in his collection *Az Eufratesz Babilonnál* (*The Euphrates at Babylon,* 1969), animates the whole of The Sinistra District. The novel is set in a mysterious military zone located in a high valley in the northern Carpathian Mountains, within the borders of Transylvania and Ukraine. It is a region, peopled with exotic and even monstrous people, where puzzling maladies and diseases occur. Narrated by a character who is identified by the alias Andrei Bodor, the novel has some superbly evoked landscapes and an overwhelming atmosphere of dread.

Bodor's newer novel, *Az érsek látogatása* (The Archbishop's Visit, 1999), is much shorter than The Sinistra District, but more attractive stylistically. The setting is essentially the same as in the earlier work, the border area between Romania and Ukraine, which Bodor obviously knew quite well. It is a region of despair and desperation where anything can happen and where the boundaries between the real and the imaginary dissolve. The novel is narrated in the first person by Colentina Dunka, who is the proprietress of a hairdressing salon; she is a part of the small world of the town of Bogdanska Dolina and indeed seems to take a certain pleasure in recounting her nightmarish story. Just beyond the town are huge heaps of rubbish whose unbearable stench shrouds the town in fog. Whereas the area had once been run by mountain infantry, as in The Sinistra District, it has since been taken over by Orthodox priests. The head of the religious community, Vicar Periprava, has been in a coma-like slumber for years, and so to end the malaise this has produced in the town, he is butchered and chopped up into small pieces on the order of his two deputies, who are known as archimandrites. For several years the town has also been anticipating the arrival of the archbishop, a visit that in theory should occur every weekend. Elaborate plans are made for the visit on a regular basis, but the archbishop in fact never shows up, and never will. At one point the narrator lets slip the news that the archbishop has really been blown up in an explosion at the railway station of a nearby town.

Bodor's fondness for the grotesque is amply displayed in the novel. In one instance, a woman who also works in Colina Dunka's salon finds a curious way of keeping in touch with her husband, a geography teacher, who has been shipped off to an internment camp. Both wife and husband maintain contact by means of small pieces of cloth soaked in saliva. These are ferried back and forth by another character who has access to the camp and who smuggles the items in a medical vial he conceals in his underpants. No matter what events occur in the town and to the principals of the story as time goes by, everything seems to stay exactly the same and Bogdanska Dolina remains mired in a cesspool of madness and degeneration.

Péter Nádas (b. 1942), a novelist, essayist, and playwright, is better known internationally than either the older Bodor or the younger Krasznahorkai. Because he is a more accessible writer, more of his works have become available in translation. His literary fame dates from the publication of his huge novel, *Emlékiratok könyve* (*The Book of Memoirs*), in 1986. Strongly objecting to the book's heavy eroticism as well as its political implications, the Hungarian censors kept it from reaching the market for several years. Complicated structurally in a way compatible with postmodernist trends, the novel comprises three interrelated sets of memoirs narrated in the first person. The main story concerns an unnamed Hungarian writer who, during a stay in East Germany in the 1970s (the atmosphere of which Nádas convincingly evokes), enters into a psychologically intricate relationship with an aging actress (Thea) and a young man (Melchior Thoenissen), with whom she is also in love. Interwoven into the writer's personal chronicle are sections of a novel he is composing about a fin-de-siècle German novelist named Thomas Thoenissen, who appears to be modeled on Thomas Mann. The repetition of the name Thoenissen serves to underscore the narrator's self-referentiality. Both writers, the author of one of the memoirs and his fictional construct, Thomas Thoenissen, are prone to incestuous longings, and both become involved in bisexual triangles. *A Book of Memoirs* is steeped in sexuality, sensuality, and an intense preoccupation with the body that takes up much space in the text and slows the reading. Nádas, however, moves effortlessly from the present into successive strata of the past and in so doing—in the context of a dense, provocative, and at times exasperating novel—splendidly captures the mood of Central and Eastern Europe in the post–World War II era as well as the impact of political events on the human psyche. At the end of *A Book of Memoirs* the principal narrator's childhood friend and homosexual lover (Krisztian), who is now living in the West, inherits his friend's manuscripts after his death and completes them by describing his last years and offering his, Krisztian's, own perspective on their relationship. This then becomes the third memoir of the novel.

After *A Book of Memoirs*, Nádas published a few other noteworthy novels. *A fotografia szép története* (*A Lovely Tale of Photography*, 1999), in part a reflection of Nádas's own experiences as a photojournalist and an intriguing blend of the visual and the literary, is a story about a female photographer who is put in a sanatorium and must now view life from a different perspective than through the lens of her camera. The postmodernist preoccupation with the self and with the genre of the memoir shows up clearly in a book by Nádas from the late 1980s, *Év könyv: Ezerkilencszáznyolcvanhét–ezerkilencszáznyolcvannyolc* (Yearbook: Nineteen Hundred Eighty-Seven–Nineteen Hundred Eighty-Eight, 1989), a month-by-month account of a year in the life of a writer living in the countryside with recollections of events back in Budapest. Nádas was also the author of several volumes of theatrical stories, a volume of plays, two film novellas, three volumes of essays and critical pieces, and a quirky but witty philosophy of love under the title *Az égi és a földi szerelemről* (On Celestial and Earthy Love, 1991).

The variety, vivacity, and originality of Eastern European literary postmodernism and its considerable role in the subversion of totalitarianism clearly deserve greater recognition in the West. Although never as abundant as one might like, there are already sufficient translations available to permit a better appreciation of this stunning body of writing.

8

Eastern European Women Poets of the 1980s and 1990s

Women writers in general, and among them, of course, women poets, have been a part of the literary culture of Eastern Europe for more than two centuries. To be sure, they never constituted more than a tiny minority until the late nineteenth century and the arrival of the emancipation movement. During the period between the first and second world wars, Eastern Europe could boast of a number of talented women poets, among them the Pole Maria Pawlikowska-Jasnorzewska (1891–1945), whose poetry volumes *Pocalunki* (Kisses, 1926) and *Surowy jedwab* (Raw Silk, 1932) were considered scandalous because of their frank eroticism and bold articulation of feminine sexuality; the Bulgarian Elisaveta Bagryana (1893–1981); and the Romanians Maria Banuş (1914–1999) and Magda Isanos (1916–1944).

The advent of post–World War II communism and its emphasis on the new equality of women in the workplace brought women into every facet of life, from the literary to the scientific. As the case of Maria Banuş demonstrates, however, this could just as well be a mixed blessing. Banuş's first volume of poems, *Ţara fetelor* (Land of Girls, 1937), was full of vitality and a sensuality rare for Romanian literature at the time. The volume catapulted Banuş to instant fame. But once communism overtook Romania, her poetry assumed an embarrassingly sycophantic character. Banuş embraced the communist regime and its ideology with a passion, extolling Stalin in one poem, for example, while in her collection *Ţie-ţi vorbesc, Americă* (I'm Speaking to You, America, 1955), she took on that favorite Cold War communist target, American "imperialism." Once communism had been swept away in Romania, Banuş made a wholly successful return to the kind of exquisite poetry for which she is justifiably admired.

Beginning in the postwar period, and especially after the thaw that followed the death of Stalin in 1953, women poets began publishing with ever greater frequency and winning larger circles of readers. By the 1970s it had become politically incorrect to speak of women writers as a breed apart. By the 1980s and 1990s they were in the front ranks of those clamoring for greater democracy and more individual freedoms, including the freedom to express themselves as women. Although there is no single Eastern European country in which women poets have stood out with any greater brilliance or prominence, Poland's status as the only one thus far to be able to boast of a Nobel Prize in Literature won by a woman poet—Wisława Szymborska—makes it an appropriate point of departure for our discussion.

Poland

Wisława Szymborska (b. 1923) is now in her eighties. She has published nine volumes of poetry, from *Dlatego żyjemy* (That's Why We're Alive) in 1952 to *Widok z garnkiem piasku* (View with a Grain of Sand) in 1996, in addition to numerous collections of selected poems. Unpretentious, down-to-earth, a poet of the everyday who also celebrates the miraculous in the ordinary, Szymborska often juxtaposes the small and seemingly trivial with the grand and monumental. This cavalier attitude toward the grandiose is perhaps nowhere better expressed than in the titular poem of her collection *Wielka liczba* (The Great Number, 1976) in which she writes: "Four billion people are on this earth, / but my imagination is the same as ever. / It doesn't handle big numbers well. / It is still constantly being moved by individuality. . . . / to a thunderous call-up I reply with a whisper. / I won't say how much I let go by in silence. . . . / My dreams, even they aren't as populous as they ought to be, / There is more solitude in them than crowds and tumult."[1] Much the same attitude defines Szymborska's attitude toward poetic language. In "Pod jedną gwiadzką" ("Beneath One Little Star"), from *Wszelki wypadek* (Every Case, 1972), she assumes this mock apologetic stance: "I apologize to great questions for small answers. . . . I apologize to everything for not being able to be everywhere. / I apologize to everyone that I am unable to be this man or that woman. / I know that so long as I live nothing justifies me, / because I alone stand in my way. / Don't think badly of me, speech, for borrowing big words / and then laboring to make them light" (195). In the poem "Jawa" ("Reality"), from *Koniec i początek* (The End and the Beginning, 1993), she posits the subservience of dream to reality: "Reality doesn't flee / the way dreams flee. / No rustle, no ring / scatters it, no shout nor crash / rises from it. / Images in dreams are / turbid and ambiguous, / which allows them to be interpreted / in many different ways. / Reality signifies reality, / and that's a greater riddle. . . . The volatility of dreams allows / memory to shake them off easily. / Reality needn't fear being forgotten" (296–297).

Although born in 1909, thus fourteen years older than Szymborska, the vigorously feminist poet Anna Swir (real name, Anna Świrszczyńska) has a twofold reputation. She first began attracting attention for poems of a highly personal nature. Many of these poems, in the three collections *Wiatr* (Wind, 1970), *Jestem baba* (I Am a Dame, 1972), and *Szczęśliwa jak psi ogon* (Happy as a Dog's Tail, 1978), are remarkable for their sensuality and eroticism, the more so when one realizes that they were composed when Swir was in her sixties.

The other major facet of Swir's creativity was the no less remarkable body of poems based on her experiences as a military nurse during the Warsaw Uprising of 1944. Swir, however, did not compose these poems at the time nor publish them soon after the events, as one might have expected. Thirty years had to elapse before she felt confident that she had found the right voice to describe the terrible events she had lived through. In 1974 her Warsaw Uprising book of poems, *Budowałam barykadę* (*Building the Barricade*), appeared in print. To this day, the book conveys an extraordinary sense of immediacy and remains one of the most impressive literary works spawned by the uprising.

Turning now to Swir's poems on love and the body, we find an unapologetic candor about the physical. Swir revels in a woman's physicality, in a woman's ability to create life. Acknowledging the transitory nature of the human and the bodily, she occasionally admits death into her verse as a reminder of what ultimately must be. But usually, however, Swir's poems on the body are celebratory in nature, ecstatic, as in this example from "Kobieta rozmawia ze swoim udem" ("A Woman Talks to Her Thigh") from the collection I Am a Woman:

It is only thanks to your charm
that I can take part
in the rites of love.
. . . The souls of my lovers
open to me in a moment of love
and I have them in my power.
I look as does a sculptor
on his work
at their faces slammed shut with eyelids,
martyred by ecstasy,
made dense
by happiness.
. . . O, many riches,
many precious truths
growing immense in a metaphysical echo,
many initiations
delicate and startling
I owe to you, my thigh.
The most exquisite beauty of my soul
would not give me any of those treasures
if not for the clear, smooth charm
of an amoral little animal.[2]

Like Szymborska, her contemporary Julia Hartwig (b. 1921) remains one of Poland's most respected women poets of the post–World War II period; in the opinion of many, she is the most important poet after Szymborska herself. After publishing her first poetry in the Lublin journal *Odrodzenie* in 1944, she spent the years 1947 to 1950 in Paris, first on a fellowship, then as an employee of the Polish embassy. Her exquisite knowledge of the French language and literature, evident in her translations from Guillaume Apollinaire, Blaise Cendrars, Max Jacob, Henri Michaux, and Pierre Reverdy, characterizes as well her books on the poets Apollinaire (1961) and Gérard de Neval (1972). Hartwig's first published volume of poetry appeared in 1956 under the title *Pożegnania* (Farewells). It was followed by *Wolne ręce* (Free Hands, 1969), *Dwoistość* (Duality, 1971), *Czuwanie* (Vigilance, 1978), *Chwila postoju* (A Moment's Rest, 1980), *Obcowanie* (Relations, 1987), *Czułość* (Tenderness, 1992), and three more volumes of original poetry, all published in 1999: *Zawsze od nowa: 100 wierszy* (Always Anew: 100 Poems), *Zobaczone* (Glimpsed), and *Przemija postać świata* (The Shape of the World Is Changing). Additionally, three volumes of Hartwig's collected poems have been published, the most comprehensive of which, *nim opatrzy się zieleń* (Before the Verdure Changes Color), appeared in 1995.

Although not a political poet as such, Hartwig often voices her disillusionment with the thwarting of freedoms in communist Poland after the calamities of World War II. She speaks directly to her readers—in usually short poems, many of them in prose—in a conversational style free of punctuation that belies the seriousness of the issues she writes about. In her prose poem "Mówiąc nie tylko do siebie" ("Speaking Not Just to Myself") from Tenderness, she admonishes people to take freedom for themselves rather than to wait for it to fall into their laps: "Make a little more room for yourself, human beast. / Even a dog pushes his way around on his master's knees in order to make / himself comfortable, and when he needs space, he dashes ahead, / paying no heed to any summons. / If you didn't manage to get freedom as a gift, / demand it just as boldly as you do meat and bread. / Make a little more room for yourself, pride and human dignity. / The Czech writer Hrabal said: I have as much freedom as I take for myself."[3] But Hartwig also conveys a deep sense of resignation, for which only writing grants her solace. She acknowledges the beauties of nature; but these are not enough to offset feelings of disappointment and resentment. She often expresses, as do so many other women poets, a strong need for intimacy while at the same time recognizing the inevitability of parting. This comes through clearly, if bitterly, in the poem "Westchnienie" ("A Sigh"), from Tenderness: "Oh, how I loved you, superfluous things, / friendship, boundless love, dedication, virtues, / met so rarely, dearly paid for, / and how I lamented every deceit, every / embezzlement, every abuse. / Oh, how I loved you, unnecessary things, / images, words, flowers, faces, / every blossoming meadow, sunsets and sunrises, / oh, how I loved you, almost beyond my strength, / and how it upset me that you are all so superfluous" (187).

Worthy successors of Szymborska and Hartwig include Halina Poświatowska, a talented poet of post–World War II Poland who died prematurely at the age of thirty-two; Ewa Lipska, a perennial favorite who was outspoken on political conditions in Poland in the communist period; Urszula Benka, a prize-winning poet who left Poland for Paris in the early 1980s and subsequently immigrated to the United States; and Marzena Broda.

After making her debut as a poet in the literary press in 1956, Poświatowska (1935–1967) received a degree in history from the Jagiellonian University in Kraków. She had also studied at Smith College in Northampton, Massachusetts, during a time when she had come to the United States for treatment for a heart condition. Several of her poems as well as her *Opowieść dla przyjaciela* (A Tale for a Friend, 1966), a prose account partly in diary form, were inspired by her stay in America. Poświatowska's first book of poems, *Hymn bałwochwalczy* (Idolatrous Hymn), appeared in 1958 and was followed by two more in her lifetime: *Dzień dzisiejszy* (This Very Day, 1963) and *Oda do rąk* (An Ode to Hands, 1966). A fourth book of poems, *Jeszcze jedne wspomnienie* (One More Remembrance), appeared posthumously in 1968. Sensitive and sensuous, Poświatowska's poetry is frequently erotic and at times hints at lesbian attraction. She wrote poems on the death of Marilyn Monroe, on black women, and on women living on the margins of society whom she encountered in the United States. Her eroticism is often autoerotic as she expresses pleasure with her own body, which she enjoyed viewing through the eyes of a lover. As she wrote in the poem "Lustro" ("Mirror") from the Idolatrous Hymn collection: "I am asphyxiated with the beauty of my own body."[4]

Ewa Lipska (b. 1945) made her debut as a poet in 1967 with the simply titled collection *Wiersze* (Poems). Four more numerically titled volumes appeared between 1970 and 1979. She subsequently published such collections as *Dom spokojnej młodości* (The House of Quiet Youth, 1978), *Żywa śmierć* (Living Death, 1979), and *Nie o śmierć tutaj chodzi, lecz o biały kordonek* (It's Not About Death Here but a White Chenille, 1982). In 1985 the underground Warsaw Independent Poets and Artists Publishing House brought out her collection *Przechowalnia ciemności* (Storeroom of Darkness), and in 1990 she published *Strefa ograniczonego postoju* (Short-Term Parking Lot, 1990). Other volumes of her poetry include *Ludzie dla początkujących* (People for Beginners, 1997); *Godziny poza godzinami* (Hours After Hours, 1998); *Sklepy zoologiczne* (*Pet Shops*, 2001); and *Gdzie indziej* (Somewhere Else, 2005). Several anthologies of her poetry have also appeared, including two bilingual (Polish-English) editions: *Białe truskawki / White Strawberries* (2000) and *Pet Shops, and Other Poems* (2002). In 1991 Lipska served as second secretary of the Polish Embassy in Vienna, in 1992 as first secretary, and in 1995 as councilor of the Embassy. Simultaneously in 1991 she held the position of vice director and in 1995 director of the Polish Institute in Vienna. She has received many honors for her poetry since receiving her first literary prize, named for Andrzej Bursa, in 1971.

Lipska's poetry embraces the political and the personal. She was acutely aware of the privations and uncertainties of life under communism, as she writes in "Tu pracuję" ("I Work Here"), from Short-Term Parking Lot: "I work here. In the East of Europe. / Surrounded by dogs. Small and awkward. / By people sad or drunk. / Or tragic like those of August Strindberg."[5] In

"Z sennika" ("From a Dreambook"), in her fifth collection of poems (1978), she had cautioned: "If you dream about power / don't leave your mouth / for a week" (233). The cynicism and disillusionment pervading much of her poetry stand out sharply in one of her most often quoted poems, "Instrukcja obsługi" ("Instruction Manual") from Short-Term Parking Lot: "I'm trying to get the country going. / I read the instruction manual carefully. / I turn the nation to the left. / I turn the nation to the right. / But the country doesn't work. / The nation is dead" (308). Her disillusionment is such that she even questions the wisdom of bringing a child into the world. She could cherish the child and love it, and though she conjures mental pictures of it, she counters the positive visions with the horrid ones.

An undeniable sense of loneliness, of a certain futility, yet a reaffirmation of physical existence characterizes much of Lipska's poetry. She also often adopts the persona of a poet of no particular importance, even of mediocrity. If Szymborska belittled lofty and grandiloquent means of expression, Lipska voices skepticism even about the communicative possibilities of language, as in "Ucz się śmierci" ("Learn Death"), from her fifth volume of poems, and is even cynical regarding her poetry recitations in other countries, as in "Sprawozdanie dla Alana Turnera" ("A Report for Alan Turner," 1991) where she writes: "Out of revenge I write a commissioned poem / for one hundred and fifty pounds. / I lease out my past for twenty minutes / to the assembled audience. / The breaking glass of applause. / I try to poison myself with truth / calls out one fanatic poet. / An interview with Menna Elfyn. / A feminist lunch. Exchange of addresses" (331). Close in some respects to the "linguistic poetry" of Miron Białoszewski and Tymoteusz Karpowicz, she shared their opposition to official language. Lipska is also a poet of impermanence, as underscored in her writings by the venues of hotels, boarding houses, waiting rooms, trains, airplanes, other countries, and constant traveling.

Urszula Benka (b. 1955), a relatively younger poet than Ewa Lipska, published her first book of poems, *Chronomea,* in 1977. It won the Stanisław Grochowiak Prize for Poetry. Four volumes followed between 1978 and 1991: *Dziwna rozkosz* (Strange Ecstasy, 1978), *Nic* (Nothing, 1984), *Perwersyjne dziewczynki* (Perverse Little Girls, 1984), and *Ta mała tabu* (This Little Taboo, 1991). An intensely personal poet of nocturnal moods much taken with the scrutiny of the emotions, Benka left Poland for France in the early 1980s and subsequently immigrated to the United States. Although she has lived in New York for some time, she continues to publish in Poland. The poems in This Little Taboo deal primarily with issues of love and parting and were written between 1985 and 1987, during her stay in Paris. The "Taboo" of the title refers to Benka's pet cat.

A member of the "Barbarian" group of poets who published mostly in the Kraków quarterly *bruLion,* Marzena Broda (b. 1960) issued her first book of poetry, *Światło przestrzeni* (The Light of Space), in 1990. It won the Kazimiera Iłłakowiczówna Prize. Her next book, *Cudzoziemszczyzna* (Foreignness), appeared in 1995 and contains poems from 1985 to 1995, many written in and reflecting her stay in the United States. Indeed the poem of the title was written in New York in March 1993 and questions whether the poet's real love is "foreignness." Other poems are addressed to women writers with whom Broda feels strong affinities, among them the French novelist Marguerite Yourcenar (1903–1987) and the Russian poets Marina Tsvetaeva (1892–1941) and Sofia Parnok (1885–1933). The epigraph to the collection is taken, in fact, from the elegy to Tsvetaeva written by the German poet Rainer Maria Rilke. In one long poem dated New Jersey, 27 February 1993, "Elegia dla miast" ("Elegy for Cities"), Broda speaks of cities named "Tsvetaevburg" and "Parnokgrad."

A formally disciplined poet given to long prosaic lines of verse, Broda invests her world with the qualities of loneliness, of a desire for isolation, and of nocturnal moods. As she writes in one of her best poems, "Anioły" ("Angels"), on the subject of loneliness: "Loneliness is better than the belief / that someone will be found who will not miss this loneliness."[6] In the tellingly titled poem "Miasto mojej samotności" ("City of My Loneliness"), written in Kraków in 1989, she speaks of the spatial limitations of a city in which "Bridges do not unite people, but distance the right / and the left shores of a city, shrinking the world to just a few streets. / And only the quiet contemplation of falling leaves awaits me" (25). As in her poem "Petersburg," cities enhance feelings of isolation and loneliness, which to Broda are not at all inimitable.

Czechs and Slovaks

Among the Czechs and Slovaks, the best-known women poets of the postwar era have been Sylva Fischerová, a Czech, and Jana Bodnárová and, more recently, Tat'jana Lehenová, both Slovaks.

Sylva Fischerová (b. 1963) published her first book of poetry, *Chvění závodních koní* (*The Tremor of Racehorses*), in 1986, five years before she received her doctorate in classical philology from Prague's Charles University, where she now holds an academic appointment. It was followed by the collections *Velká zrcadla* (Large Mirrors, 1990), *V podsvětním městě* (In an Underground Place, 1994), and *Šance* (Chances, 1999). Fischerová's poetry often combines the philosophical and the everyday. She is very much a feminine poet without being demonstratively feminist. Didacticism and moralizing are alien to her writing. Her style is compact but forceful; her well-crafted imagery striking, if often elusive, in some instances reminiscent of surrealism. She writes both short and long poems, but even in the longer poems the lines themselves are short, often no more than a few words. A suggestive poem such as the untitled "Hluboko do těl . . ." ("Deep Into the Body . . ."), from Large Mirrors, easily brings haiku to mind: "Deep into the body / our gestures withdraw, / deep into the sun / our glances are lowered / and smooth bare brows / rest on our palms. Silence, / the silence of a leafless tree by a railroad bridge. / Such pure / brush strokes, luminous colors / on the background of heaven."[7] But there is much more to Fischerová's poetic vision than a single poem can convey. She has written with irony and wit on the Soviet invasion of Czechoslovakia, on Czech strength and weakness, on the death of her father, and on the mythic and fantastic. Her imagination throughout is extraordinarily fertile.

Ranked among the foremost contemporary Slovak women writers, Jana Bodnárová, whom we have previously met as the author of such prose works as An Affair of the Mind and From the Diaries of Ida V.: The Confession of a Nonheroine, is also highly regarded for her poetry, much of which is in prose form. After her first two verse collections, *Terra nova* (New Land) and *Neviditel'ná sfinga* (The Invisible Sphinx), both published in 1991, Bodnárová came out with a small book of "psychogram-texts" from the period 1987–1994 under the title *Še-po-ty* (Whi-s-pers, 1995). The "psychogram-texts" are in essence short prose pieces, really prose poems, on such subjects as the tawdry aspects of life, indifference to suffering, and loneliness. The narrative voice is almost always female, as in the following example: "L'ahký dych stúpa k nebu" ("A Light Spirit Ascends to Heaven")—"I saw on the screen the death of a horse / He fell and just for a moment trembled / His rider faintly shouted / A defender of the rights of animals waved his fist— / Beneath it an old trace of a slashed wrist / And I had to go / eat a light lunch."[8]

The year after Whi-s-pers, Bodnárová published another collection of short prose texts, these more in the nature of ministories rather than prose poems. She titled the collection *bleskosvetlo/bleskotma,* which roughly translates as "flash-light/flash-dark." The stories in this small-format book of a little over a hundred pages run anywhere from a page and a half to eleven pages long. A few are in dialogue form. The majority are whimsical or fanciful, with exotic motifs, and featuring primarily female leads (the stories often begin with the word *žena,* "woman," or *dievča,* "girl"). Some of them were inspired by specific paintings by Caravaggio, Wolf Vostell, Daniel Spoerri, Jean Fautrier, Jan Vermeer, Wen Chen-ming, and Francisco de Zurbarán. Other books by Bodnárová, along similar lines, include *Závojovaná žena* (The Veiled Woman, 1996), *2 cesty* (Two Journeys, 1999), and *Tiene papradia* (Shades of Bracken, 2002).

A native of Bratislava who now resides in Prague, Tat'jana Lehenová (b. 1961) aroused considerable controversy when her first poem, "Malá nočná mora" ("A Little Nightmare Music"), appeared in the magazine *Romboid* in 1988. Some critics regarded the poem as scandalous, dismissing Lehenová's frank eroticism as little more than pornography. What they failed (or refused) to appreciate was the nature of Lehenová's rebellion against the strict regimentation of virtually every facet of a person's life under the previous Czechoslovak communist regime. When such regimentation finally ended, writers like Lehenová lost little time in stripping away the barriers and taboos that had kept Slovak culture so long straitjacketed, especially with respect to an individual's private life. This explains to a great extent the new preoccupation with the erotic and sexual in the late 1980s and early 1990s. Undeterred by her critics, Lehenová brought out her first volume of poetry, *Pre vybranú spoločnost'* (For the Chosen Few), the year after the appearance of "A Little Nightmare Music"; the collection also includes that controversial poem. The poet's bold assertion of the right of a woman writer to address the matter of her own eroticism and her physical pleasure in the sexual relationship was clearly made in the name of all women. Lehenová's next collection of verse, *Cigánský tábor* (The Gypsy Camp, 1991), conveys much the same embrace of a woman's otherness, although at times inclined toward greater reflection and greater experimentation, especially typographically.

The Balkans

Slovenia

Contemporary Slovenian poetry by women has been dominated by four figures: Saša Vegri (b. 1934; real name Albina Dobršek), Svetlana Makarovič (b. 1939), Maja Kne (b. 1951), and Maja Vidmar (b. 1961). Although now senior citizens, Vegri and Makarovič have remained productive into the twenty-first century. They are also deserving of attention for their role in the development of a recognizably feminine type of poetry in Slovenia.

Vegri's first book of poetry, *Mesečni konj* (The Moonstruck Horse), dates back to 1958. Writing at an unhurried pace, she published two more volumes in the 1960s, *Naplavljeni plen* (Abandoned Booty, 1961) and *Zajtrkujem v urejenem naročju* (We Breakfast in Proper Style, 1967); a fourth volume only a decade later, *Ofelija in trojni aksel* (Ophelia and the Triple Axel, 1977); her fifth book of poems, *Konstelacje* (Constellations), in 1980; and her most recent, *Tebi v tišino* (To You in Silence), after another long hiatus, in 2001. With the exception of the more experimental Constellations, Vegri has concentrated for the most part on short poems often of no more than a word or two, a style with which her much younger contemporary Maja Vidmar also seems most comfortable. A poet who makes women's experiences from adolescence to maturity her major area of concern, Vegri offers an immediate accessibility that contrasts with the somewhat more enigmatic imagery of, say, Vidmar. Perhaps a good introduction to Vegri's style might be found in these poems, the first from her 1961 collection, Abandoned Booty, and the second from her 2001 collection To You, in Silence: (1) "Women"—"Women are like lutes, / tranquil and devoted, / as they wait / for their bodies / to begin singing. / And when / someone / plays harmoniously / on them / they sing / of the sorrow of silver nights / when their men / leave them alone, / of birth / which they weave / in themselves, / and of love / stretched / like strings / from their mouths to their hips"[9]; (2) "These Are the Offspring"—"These are the offspring / of your young body, / but will you abandon them, / will you disown them / and the love of your young body? / A young body is beautiful. / A young body / lives from love / and for it / amazing, / amazing, / how long the body lives, / but when / will it cease being / when will we cease / calling / love blind?"[10]

Sometimes referred to as the "first lady of Slovenian poetry," Svetlana Makarović, a graduate of the Academy of Performing Arts in Ljubljana, has also published prose fiction, children's literature, and picture books. Moreover, she has made a name for herself, both nationally and internationally, as an actress, a cabaret performer, and a singer of popular songs. Although she rejects the idea of a female poetry as opposed to a male one, she is very much a woman's poet, intent on illuminating all aspects of femininity. A hallmark of her style is her sometimes novel use of elements of Slovenian folk culture, as well as her deceptively simple verse. In many instances, Makarović uses these sources in unexpected ways, for the purpose of subverting traditional, derived ideas about women and their place in society. After her first volume *Somrak* (Twilight, 1964), Makarović published an additional nine collections of poems, among them *Pelin žena* (Pele's Wife, 1973), *Pesmi o Sloveniji: Za tuje in domače goste* (Poems About Slovenia: For Foreign and Domestic Guests, 1985), *Križantema na klavirju: Šansonska besedila S.M.* (Chrysanthemums on the Piano: The Chanson Texts of S.M., 1990), *Tisti čas* (That Time, 1993), and *Kaj lepega povej* (Say Something Nice, 1993).

Two younger contemporary Slovenian women poets, Maja Kne and especially Maja Vidmar, have come to the fore of their generation. Although she has not published anything since 1980, Kne is well regarded on the basis of the collections *Popisovanje in rondo* (Cataloging and Rondeau, 1978) and *Ko bo s čudovito gladkim gibom ukazala finale* (When with a Wonderfully Smooth Movement She'll Order Finale, 1980). But her highly elusive imagery and the indefinable sense of her verse leave her a poet of limited accessibility. This is much less the case with Maja Vidmar, the publication of whose 1984 debut volume, *Razdalje telesa* (Distances of the Body), marked a more important literary event than the publication of Kne's two books of poems. Rejecting intellectuality and reflection, Vidmar's very spare but highly sensual lyrics fixate on the body and have an intensely female quality to them. They struck new, bolder notes in Slovenian poetry written by women and won an immediate following. Four years after Distances of the Body, in 1988, her second volume of verse, *Način vezave* (Method of Binding), appeared. After a hiatus of a decade, during which Vidmar married and bore two children, she returned to the literary limelight with her third book, *Ob vznožju* (At the Base, 1998), which contains poems striking for their eroticized images of death. Her most recent collection of poems *Prisotnost* (Presence)—judged by some critics her best yet—was honored with the 2005 Jenko Award by the Slovenian Writers' Association. As a measure of her growing international stature, a selection of her poetry was published in Austria under the title *Liebhaftige Gedichte*. It was awarded the Huberty-Burda-Stiftung Prize in 1998.

Croatia

An able writer in Croatian and German, which she studied along with archaeology at Zagreb University, Irena Vrkljan (b. 1929) rests her reputation primarily on two volumes of prose dealing with both autobiography and biography: *Svila, škare* (Silk and Shears, 1984; translated as *The Silk, the Shears and Marina; or,*

About Biography) and *Marina, ili, o biografii* (Marina; or, About Biography, 1986). These closely related books are at once an autobiography and a biography of another woman writer, the Russian poet Marina Tsvetaeva, in which biographical writing is explored as literature and as memory. Enthusiastically received, Silk and Shears consists of a three-part collection of autobiographical fragments covering Vrkljan's childhood in Belgrade before World War II, her prosperous family's move to Zagreb in 1941, the war itself, her postwar life in socialist Yugoslavia, and her subsequent career as a writer in Zagreb and Berlin. In *Marina; or, On Biography*, Vrkljan turns her attention to the life and career of Marina Tsvetaeva, to whom she was strongly attracted by her poetry and her suicide.

As a poet herself, Vrkljan was the author of the poetry collections *Paralele* (Parallels, 1957), *Soba, taj strašen vrt* (Room, This Frightful Garden, 1966), and *U koži moje sestre: Berlinske pjesme* (In My Sister's Skin: Berlin Poems, 1982). She was also the author of the novels *Stvari već daleka* (Matters Now Distant, 1962), *Doba prijatelstva* (Time of Friendship, 1963), *Dora ovaj jeseni* (Dora of That Spring, 1991), *Pred crvenim zidom, 1991–1993* (Before the Red Wall, 1991–1993, 1994), and *Posljednje putovanje u Beć* (The Last Trip to Vienna, 2000), a short mystery novel.

The daughter of the painter Ordan Petlevski, Sibila Petlevski (b. 1964) is now considered the leading woman poet of contemporary Croatia. Talented and sophisticated, with a keen interest in the visual arts, she published her first major book of poetry, *Skok s mjesta* (Standing Jump), in 1990. This includes the earlier collection "Kristal" ("Crystal"), which originally appeared in a portfolio with prints by the artist Nevenka Arbanas. In 1993 Petlevski published *Sto aleksandrijskih epigrama* (One Hundred Alexandrine Epigrams), a persuasive modern rendering of the elegiac distich, reflective of the poet's classical erudition. Petlevski's most impressive volume of poetry to date, *Francuska suita* (French Suite), appeared in 1996. Besides her active career as a poet, which has brought her international attention—she was a featured poet, for example, in the Munich literary journal *Literatur* in 1999—she has taken an active role in ongoing discussions of the future of an independent postcommunist Croatia in the context of the European family of nations.

Petlevski has also demonstrated her convincing knowledge of the English language and of English and American literatures on more than one occasion. In 1991 she published *Spin-Off: Antologija novijeg američkog pjesništva* (Spin-Off: An Anthology of Newer American Poetry), for which she wrote the introduction as well as the translations. And in 2002 she published the curious but in its own way impressive book *Koreografija patnje* (Choreography of Suffering). It consists of three main sections: "Gospodja ponoć" ("Queen Midnight"), containing fifty-eight very short prose pieces, essentially anecdotal in nature, from the lives of such English writers as Robert Herrick, John Milton, John Dryden, Samuel Johnson, Alexander Pope, William Cowper, John Masefield, Francis Thompson, W. E. Henley, and others; "Choreography of Suffering," a bilingual (English and Croatian) mini-anthology mostly of sonnets composed in

English by Petlevski and translated by her into Croatian that she began writing after the outbreak of the Croat-Serb war in 1991; and "Hrvatska koreografija" ("Croatian Choreography"), a collection of several prose pieces on literary and historical themes.

Bulgaria

Contemporary Bulgarian women poets owe their greatest debt to their gifted fore-runners Elisaveta Bagryana (1893–1981), Blaga Dimitrova (b. 1922), Nevena Stefanova (b. 1924), Lyudmila Isaeva (1926–1991), and Lilyana Stefanova (b. 1929). Successor poets such as Rada Alexandrova (b. 1943), Kalina Kovacheva (b. 1943), Vanya Petkova (b. 1951), Valentina Radinska (b. 1951), Nadya Popova (b. 1952), and Mirela Ivanova (b. 1964) have indeed had a very solid foundation on which to build. As products of a strongly traditional and masculine-oriented Balkan society, Bulgarian women poets faced an uphill struggle in order to assert their independence and their pride in femininity. In consequence, they became fiercely independent and outspoken, pushing aside taboos and expressing their innermost thoughts and feelings without regard for public scrutiny. In this respect, they have been among the most daring in all of Eastern Europe.

The way was opened up by Elisaveta Bagryana, who in her acknowledged masterpiece, *Vechnata i svyatata* (The Eternal and Holy Woman, 1927), introduced into modern Bulgarian poetry the themes of woman's sensuality and desire to taste life to the fullest. As she writes in her poem "Stihii" ("The Elements," 1925): "How can you hold me back—free, irreverent, unhumbled—disobedient wanderer, lover of freedom, / born sister to the wind, the water, and the wine, / for whom the unattainable, the infinite is seduction, / who always dreams of roads—unreached, uncrossed— / How can you hold me back?"[11]

Similar sentiments resound in the poetry of Blaga Dimitrova. In the 1977 poem "Dokosvaniya" ("Touch"), for example, she addresses the irony of boundaries:

> Everything is separated by a boundary line
> which is a contact to something else.
> The trunk is imprisoned in bark—
> Through it, it feels the wind and the rain.
> The fish is armored with scales—
> through them it senses the sound of waves.
> The sea is tensed by shores—
> through them it touches the thirsty land.
> I am nailed in a woman's skin—
> through it I know caress and wound.
> We make contact with the world
> only through our boundaries.
> And by becoming more boundless,
> we will become more lonely.[12]

Although now in her early eighties, Nevena Stefanova has been one of the most enduring talents in modern Bulgarian poetry. She has published many books of poetry, covering the years from 1938 to that of her most recent retrospective collection, *Pomruknali siyaniya* (The Radiances Have Grown Dark, 1997). A very personal yet emotionally uncluttered poet, resistant to some of the more extreme trends in contemporary poetic style, Stefanova has been deeply absorbed in the nature of femininity, and with the pleasures and burdens of being a woman. Confessing her ambivalent feelings about femininity in her poem "Osvobozhdenie" ("Liberation") from the collection *Otkroveniya* (Avowals, 1973), she writes: "O, femininity, die off! / You are pernicious, / your syncopes are so threatening / to an honorable and upright heart! / . . . Our mutual confessions / were self-condemnations, / frightened by outbursts of tenderness, / by the flow of feelings and longing / . . . But our wishes met / like the clouds charged with electricity. / We felt / liberated from that spell. / I threw away my armor— / that I may reveal / my heart is indefensible. / Femininity, forgive me, I almost / did away with you!"[13] Although not excessively preoccupied with the issue, Stefanova also writes with much sensitivity of the hardships of separation and loss, and of her fear of opening herself to others.

Another strong voice in twentieth-century Bulgarian poetry belongs to the no less durable and prolific Lilyana Stefanova. One of the South Slavic participants in the University of Iowa's International Writing Program (in 1980), Stefanova was also one of the most widely traveled Bulgarian poets of the century. Her impressive poetic output was initiated in 1956 with the publication of her first book of poems, *Kogato sme na dvadeset godini* (When We Are Twenty). More than two dozen books of original poems and selected verse followed before the turn of the century. Her most recent collection, *Byah—za da buda* (I Was—That I May Be), appeared in 2003. Stefanova is a consummate poet of love. In simply structured, often terse poems, usually written in the first person, she explores the many varieties of the love experience within the broader context of life in general. She is particularly sensitive to the ironies and mysteries of the male-female relationship and voices the need for magic in life to make it worth living.

Vanya Petkova's prolific career as a poet was launched with the publication in 1965 of her first volume, *Soleni vetrovi* (Winds of Salt). This was followed by another two books of poems before her breakthrough collection, *Greshnitsa* (A Sinner, 1968). A poet of assertive femininity virtually from the beginning of her career, Petkova became progressively more open and unapologetic about her right to an independent erotic life. The poem from which A Sinner takes its title unequivocally establishes the direction of her writing. "There you have it—I am a sinner," Petkova declares in the first line, and then proceeds to flaunt her spirit of independence in short lines of simple diction: "I say what I want, / I kiss lips that I seek, / and eyes the color of a lake, / and eyes the color of hazelnuts / I shall spill over to the very bottom. / As you see, I am a sinner. / There are contrived laws / that would destroy me. . . . But I shall remain a sinner / and amid all the hostile outcries / and after every sin / I write poems."[14] Welcoming love, she makes it clear in "Takava sum" ("This Is How I Am") that it is love itself that she loves and not any man: "I tried and understood. / I cannot love a man. / I love only love" (62).

Petkova's two later major collections of verse, *Tsiganski romans* (A Gypsy Romance, 1984) and *Zemetresenie* (Earthquake, 1988)—which followed another eight books of poems—contain previously published texts as well as new ones. Although the emotional intensity of her earlier poetry is still there in the new poems, there is now a greater sense of remembrance and recollection, of the price of ardor, and of the intrusion of the political into her life. As she writes in one of the poems in the "Gypsy Romance" cycle, "And I love, suffer, and burn, from politics, people, and the fates. / That I may not live to old age, I do not fear, / since my bark has already broken apart! / In this world a bullet loves me / and sentences me to death for love."[15] But love she must, as she recalls in "Lyubovna nosht" ("A Night of Love"): "I sought to bear you on my lips, / on my knees, on my fingers, in my eyes, / with the same rhythm with which we kissed, / and the chaos in which we loved each other" (61).

Petkova's accommodation of the political in her life and art may have been initiated by a trip to Cuba that yielded the decidedly pro-Cuban volume *Venceremos— Venseremos: Lirichni eseta za Kuba, sreshti s izvestni latinoamerikanski pisateli i revolutsioneri* (Venceremos—We Shall Triumph: A Lyrical Essay About Cuba, Meetings with Renowned Latin-American Writers and Revolutionaries, 1980). The fervent embrace of Cuba and Castro, as well as other Latin-American revolutionaries, was accompanied by the fashionable Eastern European America-bashing of the time. This is clearly in evidence in A Gypsy Romance, where one poem, "Biografiya" ("Biography"), recalls the assassinations of John F. Kennedy, Robert Kennedy, and Martin Luther King Jr. and another poem, "Edna negurka plache za men" ("A Black Woman Cries for Me"), is dedicated to the Marxist activist Angela Davis, the famed South African singer Miriam Makeba, and the black American pop singer Nancy Holloway, who became immensely popular in Paris, where she settled in the late 1950s after an abusive marriage. In her epigraph to the poem, Petkova mentions that these women "love me." Latin-American, black, and Cuban motifs also characterize several other poems in the same collection.

Macedonia

The position of women in Macedonian literature has been more modest than in that of neighboring Bulgaria, not only because of its tiny size and its larger Muslim population, but also because of the fact that a Macedonian literature in the Macedonian Slavic literary language arose only after World War II. Nevertheless, Macedonian literature has made great strides since then and can boast of a number of fine writers, including several women.

Undoubtedly, the most stellar woman poet of contemporary Macedonian literature is Katica Kulavkova (b. 1951), as she prefers her last name be transliterated and pronounced. A poet as well as a prominent literary scholar on the faculty of the Saints Cyril and Methodius University in Skopje, Kulavkova has a well-deserved international reputation. Apart from studies on Macedonian poetic language and tradition, she is the author of several books of original poetry, among them: *Našiot soglasnik* (Our Agreement, 1981), *Nova pot* (New Path, 1984), *Žedbi* (Thirsts, 1989), *Domino* (1998), and *Medjusvet* (Interworld, 2000). In July 1997 she was a guest of the Maison des écrivains étrangères et des traducteurs de Saint-Nazaire in France, which led to the publication a year later of a bilingual French-Macedonian edition of some of her poems under the title *Via lasciva.*

Forgoing the folkloric and patriarchal elements in the Macedonian literary tradition, Kulavkova writes a sophisticated, intellectual poetry reflective of her considerable literary culture and her interest in verse experimentation and wordplay. It looks back to the ancient Macedonian past, and antiquity in general, but is at once contemporaneous and universal in scope. The opening stanza of "Dolgovečnost" ("Longevity") in the Interworld collection clearly conveys the poet's obsession with the far-distant past: "Pretext for looking / into the unimaginable past—an unfathomable text. / Millions of years—a passage that someone / traversed on foot / astrally and imperceptibly—with the lightness of a vegetable / world, with the elegance of clear coloring and / unconcealed indifference / toward the ephemeral and intimate. . . ."[16] But at a certain point antiquity yields to this striking absurdist stanza: "Monkeys mutate, people evolve / sheep are cloned, fruits are grafted / gingo biloba always remains true to itself / even though they change its name, / transcription, or style: *yin-kuo, gimekio, gjingjir, gjumbur, mamelle,* / *tchitchi, bonsai, beobab,* phoenix, living fossil . . ." (16–17). At the end, Kulavkova asks the reader, "Are you really not interested in knowing who is composing this mosaic / and who is playing the card of understatement?"

Kulavkova's poetry can also be richly sensuous and even erotic, as, for example, in the poem "Mistikata na tvojot jazik" ("The Mysteriousness of Your Tongue") from the collection New Path: "The hymens of words are bursting / spurting blood—an unlyrical saliva / penetration lubricated in meaningfulness / fragrant lances sink inside / but right inside / the tongue's anagram is / an insatiable game / from your gullet to mine / the more archaic / the more festive / the dialect of love / the hymn of the lips / the red forecourt of the throat / give it to me / spirally / spiritually / ritually / coal-baked / peasant bread, tongue-bread / tongue on the spit, earth clay-red / take-it-from-me / give-it-to-me! . . ."[17]

Romania

Without doubt, Romanian literature has produced some of the most impressive Eastern European women poets of the 1980s and '90s. They include Nina Cassian, Ileana Mălăncioiu, Ana Blandiana, Ioana Ieronim, Liliana Ursu, Daniela Crăsnaru, Doina Uricariu, Denisa Comănescu, Elena Ștefoi, Marta Petreu, Magda Cârneci, Mariana Marin, Carmen Firan, and, the youngest of the group, Ruxandra Cesereanu and Simona Popescu.

One of the greatest and most widely known Romanian women poets of the twentieth century, Nina Cassian (b. 1924; real name Renée Annie Cassian) published her first book of poems, *La scara 1/1* (On the Scale of 1:1), in 1948. Its indebtedness to pre–World War II European and Romanian surrealism incurred the hostility of the new communist authorities and compelled her to seek other means of expression, at least through the 1950s. Her first few books after On the Scale of 1:1—*Sufletul nostru* (Our Soul, 1949), *An viu, nouă sute şi şaptesprezece* (Vital Year, 1917, 1949), *Horea nu mai este singur* (Horea Isn't Alone Anymore, 1952), and *Tinereţe* (Youth, 1953)—were obvious attempts to reach an accommodation with socialism realism. Cassian later rejected much of her own writing of this period. After Stalin's death in 1953, and during the Romanian cultural "thaw" of 1965 to 1970, Cassian published another nine volumes—which contain some of her best poems—among them *Cronofagie* (Time Devouring, 1969), a collection of poems composed between 1944 and 1969.

Between 1971 and 1983, despite the return of more repressive conditions, Cassian's output remained undiminished. In this period she brought out another nine books of poetry: *Recviem* (Requiem, 1971), *Marea conjugare* (The Big Conjugation, 1971), *Loto-poeme* (Lotto Poems, 1972), *Suave* (Suave, 1974), *Spectacol în aer liber* (Spectacle in Open Air, 1974), *O sută de poeme* (One Hundred Poems, 1974), *Viraje* (Orbits, 1978), *De îndurare* (For Mercy, 1981), and *Numărătoarea inversă* (Count Down, 1983), her last book to be published in Romania. In 1985 Cassian received a Fulbright Fellowship to teach creative writing at New York University as a visiting professor for the academic year 1985–1986. While she was in the United States, word reached her that verses by her satirizing the regime of Nicolae Ceauşescu had been found among papers belonging to her friend, the writer Gheorghe Ursu, who had been arrested. She resolved to seek political asylum in America. As her poetry became better known in English, she was invited to give a number of readings and in 1987 became a participant in the International Writing Program of the University of Iowa. In her native Romania she was awarded the State Prize in 1952, the Writers' Union Prize in 1964 and 1983, and the Writers' Association of Bucharest Prize in 1982.

As a poet, Cassian commands an extraordinary range, wit, sensuality, and vivacity as well as an appealing casualness. Intensely personal, she celebrates love but has no illusions about its potential to cause pain and disillusionment. She is also a compassionate poet whose writing demonstrates great concern for the human condition. Although most of her poems are short and simple in expression, some of her longer ones are among her best. By way of an introduction to Cassian's poetic universe, here is one of her short poems from the 1980s: "Gimnastica de dimineaţa" ("Morning Exercises")—"I wake up and say: I'm done for. / It's my first thought at dawn. / A nice way to start the day / with such a murderous thought. / God, take pity on me / —is the second thought, and then / I get out of bed / and live as if / nothing had happened."[18]

Ileana Mălăncioiu (b. 1940) has been a prolific, gifted, and prize-winning poet, with eleven books of poems to her credit between 1967 and 1996 as well as a book of short essays, *Calătorie spre mine însămi* (A Journey Toward Myself, 1987), most dealing with literary topics. She was also long affiliated as an editor with the journals *Argeş* and *Viaţa Românească;* for the latter she wrote a regular column under the heading "Cronica melancoliei" ("Chronicle of Melancholy"). The title could be applied to much of her poetry. Outwardly plain in style, eschewing the experimental and flamboyant, but with often startling transitions from the everyday to the ethereal, she writes of fear, loneliness, melancholy, resignation, the wintry (snow is a commonplace in her poetry), and the funereal.

Images of death and dying (of humans and animals), and of cemeteries, are frequent in her writing, occasioned it would seem by the death of her sister (which inspired the volume *Sora mea de dincolo* [My Sister Beyond, 1980]). In "Acord final" ("Finale"), from *Linia vieţii* (Lifeline, 1982), she declares: "I shall die and I shall know absolutely nothing about my death, / Just as I know absolutely nothing about my birth / I opened my eyes I cried and I laughed and I cried / I shall close them and I shall have nothing to say. / And yet my death is a real thing / More real than my birth, perhaps . . ."[19] In the title poem from her first published volume of poetry, *Pasărea tăiată* (The Slaughtered Fowl, 1967), Mălăncioiu draws the extraordinary image of her own body becoming the conduit of death from the severed head, which dies sooner, to the body of the fowl: "I take the head in one hand, the rest in the other / And I change hands when under the weight I sway / Before they die let them be tied together / Through my body, at least in this way, / The head however dies sooner / As if the killing hasn't been done properly maybe / And so that the body should not throb alone / I let the death flow into it through me."[20] Her poem "Boul jupuit" ("The Flayed Ox") in the same collection is similar in spirit if yet more disturbingly graphic.

Among the foremost Romanian women poets of the postwar period, and one of the most honored and widely translated, Ana Blandiana (b. 1942) has had an extraordinarily productive career. She first began publishing poems at the age of seventeen, in the review *Tribuna*. A few years later she won critical acclaim with her first collection of poetry, *Persoana întîi plural* (First Person Plural) in 1964. Other volumes followed in rapid succession, including *Octombrie, noiembre, decembrie* (October, November, December, 1972); *Somnul din somn* (The Dream Within a Dream, 1977); *Întimplări din gradina mea* (Goings-on in My Garden, 1980); *Ora de nisip* (The Hour of Sand, 1983); *Arhitectura valurilor* (The Architecture of Waves, 1990); *Imitaţie de coşmar* (Imitations of Nightmare, 1995); and *Balanţă cu un singur talger* (A Scale with One Tray, 1998). Besides her poetry, Blandiana has also published several books of essays, a travel book, two volumes of stories in the vein of the fantastic, and a novel.

Largely apolitical, Blandiana is a delicate and vulnerable poet who sees herself in everything created, who yearns for purity (often conveyed by images of snow), for stillness, and for the refuge of dream, and even of death. Sleep and dream are among the most recurrent images in her poetry, as is the eye that tends to look away from the world rather than at it and to see into the poet's dream world of animated plants and unpeopled landscapes, as she writes in "Cândva arborii aveau ochi" ("Once Upon a Time Trees Had Eyes)," from *October, November, December*: "Once upon a time, / Trees had eyes, / I can swear, / I know for sure / That when I was a tree I could see . . . Now I search in vain for the eyes of trees. / Perhaps I don't see them / Because I'm a tree no more."[21] A small poem from the collection *Ochiul de greier* (The Cricket's Eye, 1981), "Veşmînt" ("Clothes"), exemplifies Blandiana's need to be sheltered from the hurts of the day and her longing for solitude: "Sometimes in the morning I wake up frozen / And, still half asleep, / I pull, drowsy and shivering, / My young body, / warm, silky, / over myself / And wrap myself in it / Teeth chattering childishly, / Happy that for one more day, / One entire day / I will be / In a shelter from eternity."[22] After the downfall of the Ceauşescu regime, Blandiana became president of the newly reconstituted Romanian PEN and in 1994 the founder and president of the Academica Civica Foundation.

Ioana Ieronim (b. 1947; real name Ioana Brânduş), another of the impressive Romanian woman poets to emerge in the late 1970s and early '80s, published her first book of poems, *Vară timpurie* (Early Summer), in 1979. In this and in such subsequent volumes as *Proiecte de mitologie* (Plans for a Mythology, 1981), *Cortina* (The Curtain, 1983), *Eglogă* (Eclogue, 1984), *Poeme electronice* (Electronic Poems, 1986), and *Luni dimineaţa* (Monday Morning, 1987), she reveals herself as a poet of the seemingly small and insignificant, a poet of delicacy and subtle nuances. But it was in 1992 that Ieronim published the book for which she is now best known, a poignant collection of prose poems representing an autobiographical recollection of a childhood in a Transylvanian Saxon (German) community and the destruction of that community following the communist takeover of Romania. More on this in chapter 11.

Another accomplished poet of Transylvanian German ancestry is Grete Tartler (b. 1948). A musician by training, she also studied Arabic and English at Bucharest University, from which she graduated in 1976. By 1986 Tartler had also published several volumes of verse: *Apa vie* (The Water of Life, 1970), *Hore* (Dancing the Hora, 1977), *Astronomia ierbii* (The Astronomy of Herbs, 1981), *Scrisori de acreditare* (Credentials, 1982), and *Achene zburătoare* (Winged Achenes, 1986). Further volumes came out in the 1990s: *Materia signata* (Designated Matter, 1992), *Roşiile portocalii când sunt verzi sunt galbene* (Blood Oranges When They Are Unripe Are Yellow, 1997), and *Cuneiforme* (Cuneiforms, 1997), a collection of poems from 1970 to 1995. A small volume of her poems in English translation appeared in 1989. In addition to her poetry, Tartler has also published two books of essays, several books of nursery rhymes for children, and a number of translations from German and Arabic poetry. In 1978 and 1985 she was awarded the Poetry Prize of the Writers' Union, and in 1982 was also honored by the Romanian Academy. Tartler has served as Romanian cultural attaché in Vienna.

Of particular interest in Tartler's poetry are the motifs reflecting both her musical interests and her knowledge of Arabic and Islamic literature and culture, as in "Teatru de umbre" ("Shadow Theater")—"Silhouettes of freshly skinned hide / a hazel twig / sets them dancing / on the other side of the scorching air / like a curtain of transparent cambric— / and behind the source of light: / burning structures, torches— / and the artist, called *karagöz* in Turkish, / and the manipulator of the shadows, *pehlevan* . . ."[23] In recent years Tartler has taken an interest in issues related to nationalism in Europe; in 2001 she published the book *Europa națiunilor, Europa rațiunilor* (Europe of Nations, Europe of Motives).

A poet of wide range, Liliana Ursu (b. 1949) is the author of more than seven volumes of poetry, among them *Viața deasupra orașului* (Life Above the City, 1977), *Ordinea clipilor* (Time Sequences, 1978), *Piața aurarilor* (*Goldsmith Market*, 1980), *Zona de protecție* (Safety Zone, 1983), *Corali* (Coral, 1987), and *Înger călare pe fiară* (*Angel Riding a Beast*, 1996). Apart from her poems with American motifs, which we will meet in chapter 10, Ursu writes of poets and poetry, women, her native Romanian homeland, especially Sibiu (the Transylvanian town where she was born), foreign places she has visited, above all Italy and the Levant, the Romanian philosopher Constantin Noica, nature, the erotic life, and so on. Her imagery is often unexpected, unsuspected, clever. Wit is no stranger to her verse. Although not an autumnal or funereal poet as such, Ursu does not avoid images of death as, for example, in the small poem "Cea mai frumoasă sirenă" ("The Most Beautiful Siren") in the *Goldsmith Market* collection of 1980: "The fishermen could barely pull in their nets / and the sea was now a wild mare, / forever pulling away from them. / In the morning, they put their rations in salted sacks / and crossed themselves. They then set sail again for the open sea. / The sun began to burn dolphins' backs / before they understood that death is the most beautiful siren."[24] Although her canon includes texts in a variety of verse and stanzaic lengths, Ursu often favors relatively shorter poems, some of them reminiscent of Japanese haiku but with a touch of the surreal, as in the poems "Plouă la Siena" ("Rain in Siena") and "Cântec" ("Song") from the *Goldsmith Market*: "A fish swims inside each drop of rain. / The city breathes through their gills, / clean and white" (49); "With a chrysanthemum the poet strokes the smoky flanks of autumn / while his horse grazes on the belly of a violin" (92).

Keenly sensitive to the repressive atmosphere of the Ceaușescu era, Daniela Crăsnaru (b. 1950) vented her sense of confinement and entrapment in several books of poems published between 1973 and 1988: *Lumină cît umbră* (Light As Shadow, 1973); *Spațiul de grație* (The Space of Grace, 1976); *Arcașii orbi* (The Blind Archers, 1978); *Crîngul hipnotic* (The Hypnotic Grove, 1979); *Vînzătorul de indulgențe* (Saleswoman of Indulgences, 1981); *Șaizeci și nouă de poezii de dragoste* (Sixty-Nine Poems of Love, 1982); *Niagara de plumb* (Niagara of Lead, 1984); *Emisferele de Magdeburg* (The Hemispheres of Magdeburg, 1987); and *Fereastra în zid* (The Window in the Wall, 1988).

Facing inevitable censorship if she expressed her feelings directly, she devised a poetic idiom of indirection, ambiguity, and metaphor to keep the censors off balance. However, it was in a collection of poems she did not publish while Ceaușescu was still in power that she voiced her sense of the all but hopeless

reality of oppression. The poems were kept hidden in an aunt's cellar out of fear
of the consequences of their discovery in case Crăsnaru's own apartment was
searched. They appeared first in English translation, by Fleur Adcock, under the
title *Letters from Darkness,* in an edition published by Oxford University Press
in 1999. The Oxford edition also contains poems selected from Crăsnaru's
collections Niagara of Lead and The Hemispheres of Magdeburg. Prior to her
"political" poems, Crăsnaru had written often, in a tone of somber desperation,
of disappointments in love, and of loneliness in the aftermath of separation.
Arguably the best of her poems about love are collected in the volume Sixty-
Nine Poems of Love.

Born, like Crăsnaru, in 1950, Doina Uricariu also enjoys a fine reputation as
a poet and has been the recipient of a number of awards. After studying French
and Romanian literatures at Bucharest University, she became an editor at the
Eminescu Publishing House. A literary scholar as well as a poet, Uricariu has
published studies of the Romanian poet Emil Botta (1912–1977) and, in 1998,
her doctoral thesis on the poet Nichita Stănescu (1933–1985). That same year,
an eight-hundred-page edition of poems culled from all of her previous volumes
was published under the title *Vindecările* (Cures), the title of her first book of
poems in 1976. Uricariu's poetry often combines elusive but compelling images
turning often on the uncertain, even fearful experience of motherhood, as "Din
obrazul meu aşchii mici" ("Small Splinters from My Cheek") and "Duminica"
("On Sunday"): "Happiness blood from my blood. / Sometimes truth remains
silent / for the sake of seeming something else: / I talk about the claws of a bird, /
they scratch into my shoulder, / but this strange tale describes / the precise time
after nursing, / tender, ferocious, domestic, / hair in braids. / The small body has
turned its back toward you / and the serene joy submerges in me"; "On Sunday
night with great patience / I returned to myself a little, / thought puts a haughty
distance / between its light and the tiny flame flickering in the glass, / detached
from the body, / it struck me all at once like an ugly flower. / The child learns
how to run, how strangely, / how strangely he rejoices in knowing how to run, /
only our blood still crawls on all fours, / the helpless, the simple-minded, / and
the little flame, flickering in the glass, worships the same way."[25]

Denisa Comănescu (b. 1954), who has also translated from American and
English poetry, is the author of such verse collections as *Izgonierea din par-
adis* (Banishment from Paradise, 1979), *Cuţitul de argint* (The Silver Knife,
1983), *Barca pe valuri* (The Boat on the Waves, 1987), and *Urma de foc*
(The Trace of the Fire, 1999). In a casual, colloquial style, enlivened by unexpected, striking, and sometimes humorous images, she writes about the
misunderstandings and disappointments of everyday relationships—between
family members and between lovers—and about loneliness. In "Robinsonadă"
("Robinsonade"), from The Boat on the Waves, she imagines this nautical
dream: "I remain trapped in a room / and murder sentiments / with an iron /
like flies. / But this condition constrains me / like a corset. / I have confused
myself with a boiler / with a coffee grinder / with a can of diesel oil / with a bull-
dozer / with a very delicate night shirt. / Oh, were I a steamship / my love would

assure it / the loveliest sea / the lightest pitching / the miraculous island / with people."[26]

Elena Ştefoi (b. 1954) is the author of five books of poetry: *Linea de plutire* (Water Line, 1983), *Repetiţie zilnică* (Daily Rehearsal, 1985), *Schiţe şi povestiri* (Sketches and Stories, 1989), *Cîteva amănunte* (A Few Details, 1990), and *Alinierea la start* (Alignment for a Start, 1996). In general her writing conveys a certain sense of fear concerning forces in the world around her. Although she promises to indulge her sense of reality "as I would a baby," and to spoil it, she has at times felt that she is struggling in a mass grave where there is no room for even one word more. Yet defiance tinged with optimism characterizes other poems by her. Ştefoi shares the strong interest in political matters of other women writers in contemporary Eastern Europe. She has taken a special interest in minority affairs in Romania and in 1997 published a series of interviews with György Frunda, the head of the Hungarian community in Romania. That same year she was awarded a prize by the Association of Hungarian Journalists in Romania.

The author of five volumes of poems and two volumes of essays, Marta Petreu (b. 1955; real name Rodică Marta Crişan) is a respected writer in Romania who has also won admiration for the award-winning monthly journal *Apostrof* that she founded in Cluj-Napoca soon after the fall of the Ceauşescu regime in 1989. Her books of poetry include *Aduceţi verbele* (Bring Verbs, 1981), for which she won a Writers' Union prize; *Dimineaţa tinerelor doamne* (The Morning of Young Women, 1983); *Loc psichic* (A Psychic Place, 1991); and *Poeme neruşinate* (Impudent Verses, 1998). Petreu writes in a casual, contemporary idiom. In lines of various length of a generally rather prosaic character, she voices her thoughts on loneliness, the hardship and pleasure of writing poetry, and the private anguish of being a woman. Neither morose nor self-pitying, Petreu is clever, witty, and ironical. In recent years she has also branched out from poetry into the area of politics and philosophy, as, for example, in her only book published in English, *An Infamous Past: E. M. Cioran and the Rise of Fascism in Romania* (*Trecut deocheat sau "Schimbarea la faţă României,"* in Romanian, 2005).

Magda Cârneci (b. 1954; until 1990 wrote under the pseudonym Magdalena Ghica) began her career as a poet in the 1980s, eventually publishing such well-received volumes as *Hipermateria* (Hypermatter, 1980), *O tăcere asurzitoare* (A Deafening Silence, 1985), *Haosmos: Poeme, 1985–1989* (*Chaosmos: Poems, 1985–1989,* 1992), and *Psaume* (Psalms, published only in French translation in Marseille in 1997). A bilingual collection of her poems, *Poeme/Poems,* translated by Adam Sorkin and Cârneci herself, appeared in 2005. Cârneci is a poet of soaring, indeed cosmic, vision, as in the collections Hypermatter and *Chaosmos,* in which—in generally long prosaic lines of verse—she weaves sensuous, dazzling images of the universe as woman, of female awakening, of the birth cycle of woman and fetus, of male–female union projected onto the vast expanses of the galaxy.

Cârneci has also gained an admirable reputation as an art scholar. She received a doctorate in art history from the École des hautes études en sciences sociales in Paris and later became professor at the Institut national des langues and civilisations orientales, also in Paris. Her publications in the field of art include, among others, *Art of the 1980s in Eastern Europe: Texts on Postmodernism* (1999), *Artele plastice în România, 1945–1989* (The Plastic Arts in Romania, 1945–1989, 2000), and monographs on the Romanian artists Lucian Grigorescu (1895–1965) and Ion Ţuculescu (1910–1962). In 2002 she also published a collection of essays under the title *Poetrix: Texte despre poezie şi alte eseuri* (Poetrix: Texts on Poetry and Other Essays).

Mariana Marin (1956–2003) made her literary debut with her volume *Un război de o sută de ani* (The Hundred Years' War, 1981), for which she won the Writers' Union Prize for a first book of poetry. She subsequently published *Cinci* (Five, 1982), together with fellow poets Romulus Bucur, Ion Bogdan Lefter, Bogdan Ghiu, and Alexandru Muşina; *Aripa secretă* (The Secret Wing, 1986), in which the figure of Anne Frank is used to insinuate a parallel between Nazi oppression and that of Ceauşescu's Romania; *Atelierele, 1980–1984* (The Workshops, 1980–1984, 1990); and the prize-winning *Mutilaria artistului la tinereţe* (The Mutilation of the Artist as a Young Woman, 1999). Marin set the tone for much of her poetry in the poem "Casa morţii" ("The House of Death") in which she renounces childbearing: "Nothing more remains between us / than these paper children / whom we help every morning / to cross the street. / Refusal to continue the species. / My refusal to be another house of death / in such times."[27] A somber, sometimes difficult poet, Marin is frequently drawn to death, yoking love and death, *eros* and *thanatos,* as in her "Elegie, XII" ("Elegy XII):

> Death spent the night between my breasts.
> But between you and me (so to speak)
> will forever exist a Europe or a Red Sea.
> The language in which I imagine the word *death*
> is not the language in which you imagine the word *love*.
> What keeps us apart today (so to speak)
> will keep us even farther apart tomorrow.
> That is why, for all the darkness of our past,
> which we are unfolding now like
> a papyrus from ancient Egypt,
> I entreat you to run away with me into the abyss *that was given to us.*
> There, your freckles and your red hair
> will surely understand and will love
> the language of my breasts
> between which, even then, death will pass the night. (61)

Carmen Firan (b. 1958), a native of Craiova, is a talented and multifaceted writer who has been living in the United States since 2002, when she assumed directorship of the Romanian Cultural Center in New York City. Her several volumes of poetry include *Iluzii pe cont propriu* (Illusions on My Own Account, 1981), *Trepte sub mare* (Steps Beneath the Sea, 1990), *Negru pur* (Pure Black, 1995), and *Locuri de trăit singur* (Places of Lonely Living, 1997). While in the United States, she has published two bilingual collections of her poems: *In the Most Beautiful Life / În cea mai frumoasă viață* (2002) and, together with Adrian Sângeorzan, *Voci pe muchie de cuțit / Voices on the Razor's Edge* (2003). A writer also of prose fiction, Firan published a collection of novellas and short stories, *Farsa (Farce)*, in 2002; an English translation of the work appeared the following year. In 2004 a small volume of her poems, translated by Julian Semilian, was published under the title *Desperate Conquests,* and in 2005 her *Second Life* also appeared in English.

A poet who favors short poems and short lines, free of punctuation, Firan writes in a deceptively simple but highly imaginative and surreal style, often in the first person. Her poems are about poetry, women—who stand at the center of her poetic world—impermanence, insignificance, loneliness, and death. But no trace of sadness, melancholy, or self-pity clouds the horizon of her verse. In a typical poem, "Natură moartă cu scaune libere" ("Still Life with Empty Chairs"), from Places of Lonely Living, she writes: "There are nights when / a woman in a black / hat comes and writes / constantly on a piece of paper / a name / a surname / a street / she hides herself / behind the corner of a house / and comes / and sits / on all the empty / chairs / and tells me / that she is working on an encyclopedia / that will include / even me."[28]

Among women poets born in the 1960s, two in particular stand out for their ingenuity and provocativeness, despite considerable differences between them: Ruxandra Cesereanu (b. 1963), a native of Cluj-Napoca, and Simona Popescu (b. 1965), from Bucharest. A graduate of the Faculty of Letters of the "Babeş-Bolyai" University (in Cluj-Napoca) in 1985—where she is now a senior lecturer in the Faculty of Political Science and Journalism—Cesereanu was a member of the Equinox literary group while at the university. Her first book was the "mini-novel" *Călătorie prin oglinzi* (A Journey Through Looking Glasses, 1989). It was followed by five small collections of poetry—*Zona vie* (The Living Zone, 1993); *Gradină deliciilor* (Garden of Pleasures, 1993); *Căderea deasupra orașului* (The Fall Above the City, 1994); *Oceanul Schizoidian (The Schizoid Ocean,* 1997); and *Veneția cu vene violete: Scrisorile unei curtezane (Venice with Violet Veins: The Letters of a Courtesan,* 2000)—a collection of short stories, *Purgatoriile* (The Purgatories, 1997); the novel *Tricephalos* (2002); and two studies of the gulag and political torture in communist Romania (1998). In 1994 she was awarded the Poetry Prize of the Writers' Association of Cluj-Napoca.

Cesereanu's reputation, which has become international since the appearance of two books of poems in English, has much to do as well with her role in the founding in 2002 of Phantasma, the Center for Imagination Studies, at her university in Cluj-Napoca. As a poet, Cesereanu is known for rather lengthy poems of irregular, mostly long, prosaic lines of verse. Her subject matter, however, is anything but prosaic. Intent on extending the rich tradition of Romanian oneiric (dreamlike) poetry into the twenty-first century, she brings an exceptionally fertile imagination to an often macabre but fascinating surreal and psychedelic poetry, as in the poem "Maria Magdalina" ("Mary Magdalene"), from *Schizoid Ocean*. The opening lines suffice to demonstrate her style:

> For such a long time Mary Magdalene has dug into me with a shovel of glass
> and searches me like an empty tomb,
> inside the body a king of rats makes his home,
> only he will be bridegroom and chosen.
> No Christ have I, nor will I wash the holy feet of saints,
> nor have I womanly tears.
> Waiting for the spring rains I lay and lay.
> The skin is a cold lizard, the body is full of plagues,
> Industrious little angels are busy cleansing them,
> killing Satan's black flies.
> Mary Magdalene, how you stagger, tipsy,
> but your body is not any more slippery than my repulsive soul.
> Be a preacher of secrecy and deliver me.
> For such a long time I have sold myself to follies and perfidious beauties,
> rummage in the carcasses, vultures of prey,
> everything beneath the clouds is baobab of flesh. . . .[29]

Death, blood, suicide, madness, putrefaction, decapitation, grinding, ripping, twisted religious symbolism, an occasional Baroque-style figure poem, and much more make up the frightening world of Cesereanu's poetic vision.

Cesereanu's commitment to oneiric poetry is also evident in her anthology of Romanian oneiric poetry published in 2000, *Deliruri şi delire* (Deliriums and Deliria, translated into English as *Lunacies*). Covering a large number of poets, beginning with the classic Mihai Eminescu, she closes the anthology with a poem of her own, which she prefaces with this "confession," which encapsulates her outlook and style: "For me, the Schizoid Ocean has the value of Cambrian, Silurian, Devonian, because it is an 'archeo-unconscious' [*arheoin-conştient*] of mine. I have said 'Ocean' because I have the reverie of the aquatic, of submergence, of the uterine. But, of course, Schizoidian also has a connection with the world *schizo*. The poet as beast, as I see him, has to be a beast especially with regard to himself: that is to say, so that he may experience a fever of fourteen degrees Celsius. From this, what he perpetrates approaches delirium."[30]

No less talented than Cesereanu, and much more playful, Simona Popescu published her first book of poems, *Xilofonul şi altre poeme* (The Xylophone, and Other Poems), three years after graduating Bucharest University. Three other volumes of poems followed in the next few years: *Pauză de respiraţie* (Breathing Pause, 1991); *Juventus* (1994), a mixture of verse and prose; and the long poetic dialogue *Nopte sau zi* (Night or Day, 1998). Popescu writes in a wholly postmodernist manner. Disarmingly casual, often preferring the first person, antipoetic when it suits her, she can be narcissistic and self-mocking at the same time. Often ambivalent toward the world around her, she muses openly about the senselessness of existence, expresses loneliness yet self-reliance, and the comfort she derives from literary and intellectual pursuits. Her poem "Elice" ("Propeller") from The Xylophone collection, typifies Popescu's gift for irony and wry humor when addressing the dilemmas of existence:

> I came into the world
> in order to understand nothing
> and to make trouble for others
> for example, my mother
> I came into the world in order to wear glasses
> and I don't wear glasses
> and that is why I mistake men for women
> and that is why I like girls with short hair
> all around me colors moving light
> horizons dusty foggy
> indistinct flares
> I have a young face and an old one
> some people know the first
> and others the second but nobody knows both
> I came into the world
> to know it and to forget it
> and I can't grasp it
> and I can't forget it
> a motley fair enveloped in smoke smoke smoke
> I move every which way like a wound-up toy
> I overcome distance I return I pause
> I begin again senselessly I diffuse warmth
> I came into the world in order to bear
> hunger thirst somnolence heat and cold
> in order to feel
> and speak in many different ways
> in order to seek solutions to be indolent
> in order to wait so as not to have patience
> I sit in an upholstered chair
> like a bird on a branch
> (a mute bird)
> the azure of the sky
> the taste of ash in the mouth
> cruel silence
> and a propeller in my skull.[31]

Written in unrhymed poetic prose, in lines of varying length and with some pages entirely in prose, Popescu's lengthy dialogue *Noapte sau zi* (Night or Day) resembles in part an extended dream. Indeed, the central theme of the poem is the reality and unreality of dream. In the style of much postmodernist writing, the text of the poem is peppered with an eclectic array of literary and other allusions. Susan Sontag, Greenaway, Artaud, Keats, Coleridge, Marlowe, Wordsworth, Edward Lear, and Poe share space with the Surrealist painter Magritte as well as with Art Garfunkel, *Star Wars,* and figures from classical antiquity. Popescu is also fond of flavoring the Romanian text with passages in French and English.

Albania

The strongly traditionalist and predominantly Muslim Albanian society was not hospitable to women writers for much of its history. It was, in fact, only in 1970 that Elena Kadare (b. 1943), the wife of Ismail Kadare, became the first woman to publish a novel in Albanian. The situation is quite different today, and women writers are no longer a novelty. Among women poets, two in particular dominate the contemporary Albanian literary scene: Mimoza Ahmeti and the slightly younger Luljeta Lleshanaku.

A visual artist as well as a writer, Mimoza Ahmeti (b. 1963) in recent years has added to her already formidable reputation by acting as a singer of her own compositions. To date, she has published four major collections of poems: *Bëhu i bukur* (Become Beautiful), which appeared in 1986, the year she graduated from Tirana University; *Sidomos nesër* (Especially Tomorrow, 1989); *Delirium* (1994); and *Pjalmimi i luleve* (The Pollination of Flowers, 2002). Sardonic, playful, at times humorous, Ahmeti writes about the difficulties of her age, about flight, the inconstancy of men, the mysteries of love and life, Albanian delusions, and so on. In one of her more playful poems, from Delirium, "Jam i çmendur për kampari" ("I'm Mad About Campari"), Ahmeti writes (in the persona of a male) of a fondness for the Italian liqueur:

> I like Campari, ohhh, I like it very much.
> My wife, no, she doesn't drink Campari.
> I and my wife speak to each other five minutes a week
> and I am not number one for her.
> Oh, I'm mad about Campari.
> But I don't propose to die off
> in this manner.
> No, I'm not going to die this way.
> I'm going back to confront America
> and afterwards come back here.
> But do you know how one drinks Campari,
> diluted with water, with soda and lemon?
> Ohhh, it tastes good, very good.

Campari . . . I'm just wild about it.
America is a big supermarket . . .
I lost my way there / and you know how I found my way out?
With Campari.
Hemingway loved Campari,
not women . . .
Hemingway . . . wasn't the first
who loved Campari.
Will you come with me to America?
How? "In order to lose your way"?
I like that. That's what's called "irony."
I'm mad about Campari . . .
Campari is a girl
I like a lot.[32]

In a typical poem from The Pollination of Flowers, "Lufta për t´u bërë i za-konshem" ("The Struggle to Be Ordinary"), Ahmeti waxes ironic on the theme of commonness:

You are a genius, said my father
while I just wanted him to say: child.
I looked all around: raw nature,
people not fully formed and an ambiance
completely coarse.
And so, I was no older than three years
when I felt that I was alienated
and since then I continue to suffer
the peculiarity of my gaze.
I swear to you: No water, no heaven,
no sea is clearer
than the look of a three-year old . . .
I bore into them with my big eyes
read their tears, weight, flesh
and perceived their odors without even smelling them
and I had a magnificent nausea without needing a system of knowledge. . . .[33]

The gifted, if somewhat less sparkling, Luljeta Lleshanaku (b. 1968) has known the political repression of the Enver Hoxha regime at first hand. Because they were members of the political opposition, Lleshanaku's parents were kept under close scrutiny and she herself was forbidden either to enter a university—until 1990, after the end of the Albanian communist state—or to publish her poems. When she finally pursued a university education, she studied Albanian language and literature at Tirana University.

Lleshanaku's first book of poems, *Sytë e somnambulës* (The Eyes of a Somnambulist), came out in 1993. It was followed a year later by *Këmbanat e së dielës* (The Bells of Sunday), which in 1996 was awarded an "international lyric poetry prize" by the American periodical *Vision*. Her next volume, *Gjysmëkubizëm* (Demi-Cubism, 1996), won the best book of the year award from the Albanian Eurorilindja publishing house. *Antipastorale* (Antipastorals) followed in 1999, the year in which Lleshanaku became a participant in the University of Iowa's International Writing Program. *Palca e verdhë* (The Yellow Marrow), her most recent volume, appeared in 2000.

As a member of the first postcommunist Albanian literary generation, Lleshanaku has enjoyed the luxury of writing free of the familiar restraints of socialist realism. This has not, however, made for a poetry of lyric joy, for she still carries the baggage of the past. A sense of loneliness, of wintry desolation, are frequent in her poetry, notwithstanding the frequent quirkiness of her imagery. She writes often of erotic relationships and love, but the experiences seem destined to oblivion, as in the poem "Elektroliza" ("Electrolytes") from The Yellow Marrow: "For a long time now / your kisses have burned me / and your clean body frightened me / like sheets in a surgery ward / and your breath disappearing in my lungs / is like lilies dropped into a cesspool / in the dead of winter. / For a long time now / I have felt ashamed of my freedom. / Every day I pull a stake off your fence / and burn it for warmth. / My freedom . . . your freedom . . . / An atmosphere alive with electricity / my soul pawned for a nickel / yours slowly deserted by its ions and growing smaller every day."[34] Similarly bleak, and typical, is the poem "Pak më shumë se retrospektivë" ("Somewhat More Than a Retrospective") from Demi-Cubism: "I was born of a dead hope / like a blade of grass / between poorly joined slabs of sidewalk. / I learned my first words / behind poorly fitted doors. / I became acquainted with daylight / through the cracks in my body / through half-baked clay. / I learned to sing / like the cold current of air / between two misshapen bodies. / (But I can't get used to anxiety / like casinos / with new clients) / From one dead hope / straight to another that slows down rapidly / while approaching the first."[35]

The German Democratic Republic

Two women poets in particular stand out on the literary landscape of the German Democratic Republic between the time of its founding and its collapse in 1989: Elke Erb and Sarah Kirsch.

Dubbed "our flip-out Elke" by her fellow East German writer Volker Braun, Elke Erb (b. 1938) is the daughter of Marxist historian of literature Ewald Erb, who resettled with his family in the newly established GDR in 1949. A native of Scherbad/Eifel, she studied German and Slavic literatures at Halle University and later moved to what was then East Berlin. Strongly supported by members of the so-called Saxon school of poetry, notably Sarah Kirsch, Erb was quickly recognized as a leading representative of the young generation of East German poets born between 1934 and 1940. Characteristic of this group was their opposition to the exploitation of poetry for political and didactic aims and a rejection of then-prevailing social norms. In her earliest books of poetry, *Gutachten* (Expert Opinion, 1976), *Einer schreit: Nein!* (One Cries, No!, 1976), and *Der Faden der Geduld* (The Web of Guilt, 1978), collections primarily of very short prose pieces and a few dreamlike poems of no demonstrable social content, Erb exhibited both great concern for stylistic precision and a talent for irony. Typical of her short pieces, for example, is "Armut" ("Poverty") from The Web of Guilt: "I have too few things, and they're only the kind that would do in a real pinch. If they were any better, there could be fewer of them. I also don't have enough room for my things. Among them, I'm one of the things tossed out by someone who has too few of them."[36] The Web of Guilt contains an epigraph from the works of the Alsatian Dada poet Hans (Jean) Arp, whose influence is felt strongly in the small volume, along with a substantial interview with Christa Wolf that was based on a four-hour tape recording.

Erb published three more books of poems in the 1980s: *Trost: Gedichte und Prosa* (Consolation: Poetry and Prose, 1982), a selection of texts made by Sarah Kirsch; *Vexierbild* (Puzzle Picture, 1983), a similar collection of small prose and verse pieces; and *Kastanienallee* (Chestnut Alley), Erb's most mature volume of poetry to that time and especially interesting for the poet's comments on each poem set in smaller type at the bottom of the page or on the opposing page.

In 1985 Erb and the East German writer Sascha Anderson jointly edited an anti-establishment literary anthology under the title *Berührung ist nur eine Randerscheinung: Neue Literatur aus der DDR* (Contact Is Just a Peripheral Phenomenon: New Writing from the GDR). Erb's works published since the reunification of the two Germanys include, among others, *Der wilde Forst, der tiefe Wald: Auskünfte in Prosa* (The Primitive Forest, the Dense Woods: Information in Prose, 1995), an exceptionally interesting selection of essays, dialogues, and poems published originally between 1989 and 1995, a few of which deal specifically with East German themes (including the well-known "DDR und aus: Bemerkungen zu den Angriffen auf Christa Wolf" ["GDR and Beyond: Observations on the Attacks on Christa Wolf," 1990]). Erb has also translated such major Russian writers as Gogol, Blok, and Akhmatova, and has rendered into German the thirteenth-century Georgian romance *Vis and Ramin*.

One of the most highly regarded poets to come out of East Germany, Sarah Kirsch (real name Ingrid Bernstein; b. 1935) was born in Limlingerode, in the South Harz region. She adopted the first name "Sarah" as a protest against German anti-Semitism before, during, and after World War II. Kirsch studied biology, and from 1963 to 1965 also took writing courses at the J. R. Becher Institute of Literature in Leipzig. The impetus to her literary career owed much to her marriage (1958–1968) to the poet and essayist Rainer Kirsch, with whom she wrote her first book of poetry, *Gespräch mit dem Saurier* (Conversation with the Sauropod, 1965). In this collection, as well as in her next two volumes of poetry published under her own name—*Landaufenthalt* (A Stay in the Country,

1967) and *Zaubersprüche* (Magic Spells, 1973; translated as *Conjurations*)—
her interest is heavily in the realm of nature described in a strikingly simple
style, free of metaphor. Through her observations of nature, Kirsch leads her
reader to a contemplation of other issues both universal and contemporary,
such as the Holocaust, the division of Germany, and the war in Vietnam. Kirsch
never abandoned her attachment to nature and landscape, despite the prominence of other concerns in her subsequent poetry. Her volumes *Erdreich* (Soil,
1982), *Katzenleben* (*Catlives*, 1984), and *Schneewarme* (Snow Warmth, 1989),
which were published after she had resettled in West Germany, were inspired by
the North German countryside, especially in the winter season.

Notwithstanding Kirsch's previous inclination toward the introspective and
subjective, the breakup of her marriage to Rainer Kirsch intensified these tendencies in her writing. The profound impact of her divorce led to a new concentration on the crises of her own life. Kirsch's poetry henceforth became intensely
private and autobiographical as she sought ways of expressing and resolving
her own inner conflicts. A sense of anguish, hurt, and desolation coupled with
rage at a hostile fate and a passionate desire to reclaim what had been lost, inform, to various degrees, the poems in *Conjurations* and in such later volumes
as *Rückenwind* (Tail Wind, 1976), *Erlkönigs Tochter* (The Erl King's Daughter,
1992), and *Bodenlos* (Bottomless, 1996).

Although not an outspoken critic of the GDR regime on the order of the popular poet and singer Wolf Biermann, Kirsch had strong feelings about the artist's right to creative autonomy and made her position known mainly through
her spiritually independent and introspective poetry. Although much admired
as a poet, she was nevertheless chastised for her passivity and resignation at
the Sixth Writers' Congress of the GDR in 1969. It was, however, only after
Biermann was stripped of his GDR citizenship while on tour in West Germany
that Kirsch resolved to quit the GDR, which she did in 1977. Since resettling
there, Kirsch has been able to satisfy a fondness for travel, as manifest in such
volumes as *Catlives; Drachensteigen* (Dragon Paths, 1979), which grew out of
a year's stay in Italy; *La Pagerie* (1980), a small book of travel impressions inspired by the landscapes of Provence, in the form of very short prose fragments;
and *Soil*, which came in the wake of a visit to the United States. Rediscovering
the world of nature and foreign landscapes has had a calming effect on the
intense passion and tangled emotions of Kirsch's previous private and poetic
world.

Apart from her poetry, Kirsch has also written several books of prose. These
include the journalistic *Die Pantherfrau: Fünf unfrisierte Erzählungen aus dem
Kassetten-Recorder* (Panther Woman: Five Ungroomed Stories from the Cassette
Recorder, 1973; translated under the title *Panther Woman: Five Tales from the
Cassette Recorder*), a collection of minimally edited interviews with five women
from different walks of life in the GDR; *Die ungeheuren berghohen Wellen auf
See* (The Enormous Mountain-High Waves at Sea, 1973), a collection of seven
stories written between 1968 and 1972 and also dealing primarily with the
status of women in East Germany; *Irrstern* (Comet, 1986); *Allerlei-Rauh: Eine*

Chronik (Allerlei-Rauh: A Chronicle, 1988); *Schwingrasen* (Grassland, 1991); *Spreu* (Chaff, 1991); and *Das Simple Leben* (The Simple Life, 1994). These last five volumes consist in the main of often complex personal reflections and reminiscences from Kirsch's West German period; except for *Allerlei-Rauh* (its title derives from a well-known fairy tale by the Brothers Grimm), which is one continuous narrative, they are mostly in the form of small prose pieces of a random, disparate nature. Chaff is a verbally and visually playful diary of reading tours undertaken by Kirsch on the urging of her publisher between May 1988 and December 1990. Kirsch also contributed to the commemorative volume in honor of the German-Jewish poet Else Lasker-Schuler (1869–1945), *Meine Träume fallen in die Welt: Ein Else Lasker-Schuler Almanach* (My Tears Fall on the World: An Else Lasker-Schuler Almanac, 1995).

Much honored for her literary work, Kirsch was the recipient of the Kunstpreis der Stadt Halle in 1965; the Heinrich Heine Prize of the GDR in 1973; the Petrarca Prize in 1976; the Austrian State Prize and Kritikerpreis in 1981; the Roswitha-Gedenkenmedaille of the town of Bad Gandersheim in 1983; the Friedrich Hölderlin Prize in Bad Homburg in 1984; the Weinpreis der Literatur in 1986; the Kunstpreis des Landes Schleswig-Holstein and the Stadtschreiber-Literaturpreis of the city of Mainz in 1988; the Kulturpreis der Konrad-Adenauer-Stiftung in 1993; the Georg-Büchner Prize in 1996; and the Annette-von-Droste-Hülshoff Prize in 1997. In 1996 Kirsch was appointed to the Brothers Grimm Professorship at Kassel University.

In their vitality and versatility, the Eastern European women poets who came to the fore in the 1980s and 1990s have greatly enriched their respective literary cultures and the world of Eastern European poetry as a whole both in those last two decades of the twentieth century and in the first decade of the twenty-first. They have done so as gifted poets no less capable of embracing universal concerns than their often better-known male counterparts while at the same time informing their poetic vision with an undeniable feminine sensitivity.

9

The House of Cards Collapses

The Literary Fallout of the Yugoslav Crises of the 1990s

The collapse of communism in Eastern Europe was heralded by the dismantling of the Berlin Wall in 1989. When that ignominious barrier between East and West began to be torn down, it was as if the signal had been given to dismantle the entire communist apparatus throughout Eastern Europe. The process needed little encouragement. The weaknesses of the communist system had already begun manifesting themselves as early as the workers' strikes in East Berlin in 1953. By the late 1980s, after the upheavals in Poland and Hungary in 1956, the Soviet-led invasion of Czechoslovakia in 1968, the death of Tito in 1980 with its implications for the future integrity of the Yugoslav state, and the birth of the Solidarity movement in Poland in the early 1980s, Eastern Europe seemed ripe for sweeping change, if not imminent collapse.

Notwithstanding the violence in Bucharest and other Romanian cities accompanying the downfall of the Ceauşescus, the disintegration of Yugoslavia far surpassed in brutality anything seen elsewhere in Eastern Europe. To make matters worse, its legacy of ethnic strife has continued to the present day. The status of Albanian-dominated Kosovo still remains unsettled, Montenegro has elected to part company with Serbia—thus ending the fiction of a Yugoslav state comprising Serbia and Montenegro—and Albanian-Slav tensions in tiny Macedonia have yet to be resolved to the satisfaction of both parties. As clichéd as it may sound, the Balkans have truly been Balkanized.

In its heyday, the idea of Yugoslav supranationality had its logic. Tito's goal in the post–World War II period had been to implant the idea of Yugoslavism, of a sense of a Yugoslav identity taking precedence over the ethnic tribalism that has long been the curse of the South Slavic peoples. But the strength of the Yugoslav federated state depended on the will and charisma of a single individual, Tito himself. Once that individual passed from the scene, the pull of nationalistic factionalism proved irresistible. The career of the distinguished writer Danilo Kiš (1935–1989) demonstrates all too clearly the price to be paid by any strong advocate of the Yugoslav supranational ideal.

In 1976 Kiš published one of his best-known books, *Grobnica za Borisa Davidoviča* (*A Tomb for Boris Davidović*), a collection of linked stories about the fate of several characters (mostly Eastern European and Russian Jews) who in various ways become victims of Stalinist terror. The patent anti-Stalinism of the work did not sit well with the Yugoslav Writers' Union, which lost no time in launching a campaign of defamation against Kiš, accusing him above all of plagiarism. Not one to take anything like this lying down, Kiš struck back in 1978 with a book of essays entitled *Čas anatomije* (*The Anatomy Lesson*). Besides taking the dissecting scalpel to the arguments of his defamers, Kiš also took aim at both totalitarianism and nationalism. That the two were linked in his mind, and behind the hostile reception of *A Tomb for Boris Davidović,* is obvious from this statement from *The Anatomy Lesson:* "Nationalism is the ideology of banality. Nationalism is, moreover, a totalitarian ideology."[1]

By now, however, the climate had become so hostile that Kiš took off for his beloved France, where he had studied as a younger man. His French was fluent, and he was able to earn a living teaching the Serbo-Croatian language and lecturing on Yugoslav literature at the universities of Bordeaux, Lille, and Strasbourg. Although he was loath to regard his stay in Paris as an exile, Kiš in fact lived virtually the last ten years of his life in France, where he died in Paris on 15 October 1989. In addition to his demolition of totalitarianism and nationalism, Kiš also addresses the charge—in a small section of *The Anatomy Lesson* under the heading "Judaizam" ("Judaism")—that the prominence of Jewish characters in a *Tomb for Boris Davidović* was an indication of Kiš's Jewish ethnocentricity. Indeed, it may have been Kiš's sense of his own (partial) Jewishness that buttressed his support for the supranationality of Yugoslavism.

In his essay "Spomini na Jugoslavijo" ("Memories of Yugoslavia"), included in the collections *Razbiti vrč* (The Broken Jug, 1992) and *Konec tisočletja, račun stoletja* (End of a Millennium, Account of a Century, 1999), the celebrated Slovenian writer Drago Jančar expresses a view of Yugoslavia diametrically opposed to Kiš's. It was also a view that had wide support throughout the country before its breakup:

> I probably do not speak solely for myself when I say that I love Yugoslavia. But Yugoslavism, that is the Yugoslav idea, I despise with all my heart. Even more, I would suggest that it is precisely the so-called Yugoslovenians, indeed the zealots of this idea, who have definitively destroyed Yugoslavia. . . . Yugoslav nationalism and integralism, which forcibly and artificially concealed the actual, organic state of affairs, automatically produced the opposite effect—the collapse of Yugoslavia.[2]

Apart from such novels as *35* (1974), *Galjot* (The Galley, 1978), *Severni sij* (Northern Light, 1993), *Posmehljivo poželenje* (Mocking Desire, 1993), *Katarina, pav in jezuit* (Katarina, the Peacock, and the Jesuit, 2000), and his short-story collections *Smrt pri Mariji Snežni* (Death at Mary of the Snows, 1985) and *Augsburg in druge resnične pripovedi* (Augsburg, and Other True Stories, 1994), Jančar has also dealt seriously with Slovenian, Yugoslavian, and Eastern European intellectual and political life in the twentieth century— particularly in the period of communism and in the years since the collapse of Yugoslavia—in several other books of essays. These include *Sproti* (One Day at a Time, 1984); the bilingual *Ura evropske resnice za Slovenijo/The Hour of European Truth for Slovenia* (1997); *Temna stran meseca: Kratka zgodovina totalitarizma v Sloveniji 1945–1990* (The Dark Side of the Moon: A Short Journal of Totalitarianism in Slovenia, 1945–1990, 1998), essays and documents edited by Jančar; *Brioni* (2002); and *Duša Evrope* (The Soul of Europe, 2006).

When the wars of the Yugoslav secession broke out in 1991 after the declarations of independence of the Slovenian and Croatian republics were met with Serbian military intervention, the end of the unified Yugoslav state was in sight. Until the horrific campaign of ethnic cleansing in Kosovo, the bloodiest fighting was waged in Croatia and Bosnia-Herzegovina. Negotiations to end the conflict were long and difficult, but in November 1995 the Bosnian War at last came to an end when the various parties to it accepted the terms of the Dayton Agreement, whereby separate Muslim-Croat and Serb republics were to be created on the territory of the former Bosnia-Herzegovina. By then, Sarajevo, once one of the most attractive cities in Yugoslavia, was a ravaged wreck and Serb-Croat enmity was at an all-time high, with revelations of wartime massacres echoing the internal Yugoslav strife of World War II.

But the end of Balkan conflict was still not at hand. Within two years of Slobodan Milošević's ascension to the presidency of a new truncated Yugoslavia, composed of Serbia and Montenegro, Serb soldiers and irregulars were overrunning Kosovo and waging a new campaign of aggression against the Albanian population. It took NATO intervention and seventy-eight days of relentless American and British bombardment of Serbia in the spring of 1999 before Milošević agreed to remove Serbian troops from Kosovo. In 2000 he was voted out of power and replaced by a democratic government under Vojislav Kostunica. In late June the following year, Milošević was finally extradited to the Hague to stand trial for war crimes before an international tribunal. But before any decision could be reached, he died, presumably of heart problems, in 2006. In the meantime, random killings in Kosovo of both Albanians and Serbs and sporadic outbursts of fighting between the Albanian and Slav populations in Macedonia have been a clear indication that definitive peace in the region still remains elusive.

The War in Words: Bosnian Muslims and Bosnian Serbs

The siege of Sarajevo, as the focal point of the war in Bosnia, has generated a literature of its own. One of the most compelling texts, *Dnevnik selidbe* (Diary of an Exodus, 1994), was written by Dževad Karahasan, a Bosnian Muslim novelist and theater critic who held the position of dean of the Academy of Theatrical Arts at Sarajevo University during the Bosnian War. His reputation as a writer of fiction had been well established by his "Oriental" novel, *Istočni divan* (The Oriental Divan, 1989). Because of its content, *Dnevnik selidbe* obviously could not be published in Sarajevo or in Yugoslavia, and so Karahasan and his wife fled to Austria at no small risk to themselves. The book was translated into English and published as *Sarajevo: Exodus of a City*. Rather than a chronicle of the destruction of Sarajevo in 1992 and 1993, the book is more a lament for the unraveling of the intricately patterned fabric of the city's multiethnic culture, in which Bosnian Muslims and Christians (Croats and Serbs), Turks, and Jews had all managed to live both together and apart in peace and harmony for centuries. Not only a lament, Karahasan's work is a deeply thoughtful, often incisive, consideration of the role or roles of literature in a free society and the abuses to which it could be subjected and which it might itself perpetrate.

The experience of another Bosnian Muslim writer, Semezdin Mehmedinović (b. 1960), was similar. One of the most prominent members of the Bosnian Muslim literary community, Mehmedinović also studied in Sarajevo and remained in the Bosnian capital as an active contributor to the city's cultural life. His major literary work was the English-titled *Sarajevo Blues*. It was first published at the end of 1992 as the first book in the Ljubljana (Slovenia)–based series Biblioteka "egzil-abc," which provided a forum for Bosnian writers and translators under siege. *Sarajevo Blues,* which was reprinted in an expanded edition in 1995, consists of small essays, prose vignettes, and poems all written in the first person and reflecting the terrible ordeal of Sarajevo during the Bosnian War. The pieces are poignant and grim, and in some cases convey a sense of disbelief that such a fate could befall the city and shatter the peace and good will among its inhabitants. The disillusionment began in fact with the image of the Bosnian Serb leader Radovan Karadžić as a rabid nationalist now spewing hatred and encouraging violence, in stark contrast to the man who used to be known as good-natured and peace-loving. Yet in recalling the behavior of Karadžić (and others) during the student riots of 1968, Memedinović could see that he had the makings of what he calls "the perfect errand-boy for Milošević's nationalist-Stalinist project"[3] and recounts unspeakable acts of savagery perpetrated under the banner of Serbian nationalism.

In an interview with his translator at the end of *Sarajevo Blues,* Mehmedinović dwells at some length on the war as a tragic catalyst that came to make the world more conscious of Bosnian literature and culture as separate from the Serbian and the Croatian. This is borne out by the new attention to Bosnian literature in the English-speaking world, as evident—apart from the translations of Karahasan's and Mehmedinović's siege-inspired books—in the publication in 1998 of the anthology *Scar on the Stone: Contemporary Poetry from Bosnia,* edited by Chris Agee, and the appearance in English of the fine

Bosnian poet Ferida Duraković's collection *Heart of Darkness*. Like Karahasan, Mehmedinović and his family also fled Bosnia, in their case settling in the United States as political refugees in 1996.

Another Bosnian Muslim writer, Abdulah Sidran (b. 1944), who has won several awards for his writing, was working as chief dramatic adviser for Bosnia-Herzegovina Radio when the Bosnian War erupted in April 1992. Known for his volumes of poetry with Sarajevan themes, such as *Sarajevska zbirka* (The Sarajevo Collection, 1979), *Sarajevska zbirka i nove pjesme* (The Sarajevo Collection and New Poems, 1987), and *Slijepac pjeva svome gradu* (*The Blindman Sings to His City,* 1997), a collection of poems from 1975 to 1985, Sidran poured his anguish over the fate of his besieged city into his collection *Sarajevski tabut* (The Sarajevo Bier, 1993) and into the first group of poems in *The Blindman Sings to His City,* "Seven Poems Under the Siege (1992–1996)." Sidran also wrote the text for an illustrated book on the Bosnian War, with photographs by Zoran Filipović, published in France in 1994 by the Ministry of Culture, Department of International Affairs, under the title *Sarajevo.*

Two Bosnian women poets, Bisera Alikadić (b. 1939), a Muslim, and Ferida Duraković (b. 1957), a Serb, vented their own thoughts about the war in their poetry. An urban poet, who gained a reputation especially for sensitive poems about the emotional plight of women in the big city, Alikadić lived through the siege of Sarajevo and made it the subject of a volume of poetry entitled *Grad hrabrost* (*City of Courage*) and published in a bilingual Bosnian and English edition in 1995 by the Sarajevo-based International Center for Peace (Medjunarodni centar za mir).

The depth of Alikadić's outrage over the calamity that befell Sarajevo is felt painfully in every poem of *City of Courage*. A single example, such as "Plamteći neboder" ("Burning Skyscraper"), suffices:

> You'd like me to aestheticize
> this horror,
> to sing obliquely,
> wisely.
> No, I am screaming, screaming
> like a burning skyscraper
> in the middle of the city
> and the flame licks at the sky.
> If you like,
> if you still need
> symbols and metaphors
> then the skyscraper is beating
> with hundreds of hearts.
> The skyscraper is a beehive
> full of burning bees,
> horrified eyes,

objects, memories,
and conscience, Conscience.
Gentlemen and killers,
at the end of the twentieth century
in the heart of Europe
hell is served à la Dante.
After fire there is no illusion
a pile of ashes
emptiness staring.
If I am a poet even after
all this evil,
my poetry is a cry.[4]

By keeping her style plain, Alikadić makes her outrage, especially at the sense-less death of children, all the more sincere and intense.

Ferida Duraković began her career with the publication in 1977 of her first book of poetry, *Bal pod maskama* (Masked Ball). That was a year before she graduated Sarajevo University. She subsequently published another four collections of poems: *Oči koje me gledaju* (Eyes That Keep Watching Me, 1982); *Mala noćna svjetiljka* (A Little Night Lamp, 1989); *Selidba iz lijepog kraja gdje umiru ruže* (A Move from a Lovely Neighborhood Where Roses Die, 1993), which contains prose as well as poetry; and *Serce tame: Sarajevo, 1973–1993* (*Heart of Darkness: Sarajevo, 1973–1993*, 1994)—its title taken from the Joseph Conrad novel—her most famous volume.

Duraković decided to remain in Sarajevo during the war and to try to give voice in her poetry to the devastation of which she herself became a witness. As secretary of the Bosnian PEN Center in Sarajevo, she also earned wide respect for her courage and dedication in keeping the center open amid the strife. In the autumn of 1999, after the English-language publication of *Heart of Darkness*, she visited the United States on a speaking and poetry-reading tour. She traveled primarily in New England, visiting such college campuses as Harvard, Brandeis, and Holy Cross. She was awarded the PEN New England's 1999 Vasyl Stus Freedom-to-Write Award, which honored her decision to keep the Sarajevo PEN Center open during the war, and the Hellman-Hammer Grant for Free Expression.

Some of her poems from the Bosnian War are in the form of Japanese haiku; the stark simplicity and highly compressed style of the genre make her fleeting impressions of the war all the more striking. Her sense of perceived affinities with poets who also lived through cataclysmic times animates her poems on the Russian Anna Akhmatova, the Austrian Georg Trakl, who committed suicide during World War I, and the martyred Spanish poet Federico García Lorca. The inability of Westerners to comprehend the fighting in her native Bosnia inspired Duraković to compose the poem "Pisac sagledava domovinu dok učeni postmodernist ulazi u njegov grad" ("A Writer Observes His Homeland

While a Learned Postmodernist Enters His Town"), which alludes to the French philosopher B. H. Levy's visit to Bosnia during the siege:

> Cruelly and for a long time everything
> has been repeating and yet everything
> happens for the first time:
> the face of a young man whose life was flowing away
> all night through your fingers, through the hole
> in his back. . . .
> And a pool of blood: in the middle a loaf of bread
> soaked with blood as if with morning *milk from the hills* . . . No, you
> should not be trusted,
> you are coming from the heart
> of darkness that burst and gushed into the daylight.
> You are an unreliable witness,
> a prejudiced one besides.
> That is why
> the Professor came, utterly Parisian: *Mes enfants,*
> he started,
> and his fingers kept repeating: *Mes*
> *enfants, mes enfants, mes enfants.*
> In the Academy of Sciences
> wise gray heads could think
> only about his dazzlingly white shirt.
> *Mes enfants,*
> *Europe is dying here.*
> Then he arranged
> everything into a film, into images, into great words like
> *histoire, Europe,*
> *responsabilité,* and naturally,
> *les Bosniacs.* So this is how to look into the face of History,
> not like you: in crude irresponsible fragments,
> in a sniper shot that smashes into the skull,
> into graves already covered with tireless grass . . .[5]

A unexpectedly humorous perspective on the siege of Sarajevo characterizes the Bosnian Serb writer Nenad Veličković's best piece of prose fiction to date, the novel *Konačari* (*Lodgers*, 1995). Born in 1962, Veličković, a Sarajevo native, has had a productive career as the author of a number of TV and film scripts, radio plays, and works of fiction. He is also the author of a two-part dictionary of sex, one part—a straightforward dictionary—is printed one way; the other part, an illustrated, historical mini-survey of sex in art—is printed the opposite way, so that the book has to be turned upside down to go from one section to the other. Since January 1998 Veličković has held the position of teaching assistant in the Department of South Slavic Literatures at Sarajevo University.

Lodgers is narrated in the first person by a character named Maja, who combines naiveté and literary pretensions and who occasionally addresses the reader directly on such literary matters as the role of the narrator. Maja can't decide if she wants to write a diary of the siege, or a novel, or a diary in the form of a novel. Full of funny lines and episodes, the novel concentrates on the doings of Maja's eccentric family as it takes up lodgings in a Sarajevo museum directed by her father after the destruction of their own apartment. But the ever-present reality of the siege is inescapable. Although deflecting attention from the horrors taking place all around her by humor, wit, and irony, Maja on occasion admits them directly into her narrative as, for example, when the family dog (itself a source of humor in the novel) brings into the museum a human foot it has retrieved from a garbage heap. None of the terrible privations, anxieties, and fears of people during the siege pass unnoticed, but they are presented in the context of black humor characteristic of the narrator's style throughout. After a cow is slaughtered for food—its killing graphically described—its head is brought before a man identified as the commander. This description follows:

> Shiny with melted butter, the glassy eyes gazed at him. And he turned the head, together with the plate, first to one side and then the other, stood up theatrically, took aim and delivered a rabbit punch to the back of the cooked neck. Both glassy balls flew out of the buttered hollows and started rolling over the table. In my homeland, this blow is valued like a degree from Yale in America or a goal in the final of the World Cup in Brazil.[6]

Serbian responsibility for initiating the Bosnian War is never in question in Veličković's novel, but by means of his easygoing narrator, guilt is spread around evenly:

> The Serbs destroy, burn, loot, rape. They say they're defending their own land, but they're plundering other people's. Protect your own people, but persecute others. This is all being done by individuals. And there are individuals like that among the Muslims as well. Everyone rapes and loots and destroys and burns. Wherever they can and as it suites them! (102)

It would of course be simplistic to imagine that all Serbs rallied solidly behind the policy and tactics of the Bosnian Serbs under Radovan Karadžić during the Bosnian War. There were indeed Serbian writers who could see the larger picture and were appalled at the excesses of Serbian nationalism and the brutalities to which Bosnia and Sarajevo in particular were subjected. They were in some cases outspoken in their depiction of the brutality of the campaigns, first in Bosnia and later in Kosovo.

In his novel *Tunel: Lepa sela, lepo gore* (The Tunnel: Pretty Village, Pretty Flame, 1995), which originated as a journalistic report about an episode during the Bosnian War in the magazine *Duga,* Vanja Bulić (b. 1947) describes the Muslim siege of six Serbian soldiers trapped in a tunnel. Three of them manage to escape. Attention is thereafter concentrated mainly on the Serb Milan and his prewar Muslim friend Halil, from the same town, whom he now regards as a mortal enemy. Full of hatred for Muslims, Milan seeks to kill a wounded Muslim soldier in the same hospital where he has been taken but exhausts himself trying to reach him and bleeds to death. The novel, and even more graphically, the highly successful 1996 film based on it directed by Srdjan Dragojević, overlooks none of the atrocities committed by both sides as it targets the senselessness of the ethnic and religious hatreds from which the Bosnian conflict arose. Bulić followed *The Tunnel* with *RS: Ratna sreća* (Remembrance of War, 2002), which deals with Serbia in the aftermath of the Dayton Accords and focuses on war profiteers in Belgrade and the new morality of exploitation and profit.

Zlatko Dizdarević (b. 1949), a Muslim writer from Serbia, born in Belgrade, and the publisher of the much-respected newspaper *Oslobodjenje,* wrote two books about the Bosnian War, both about the fighting in Sarajevo: *Sarajevo: A War Journal* (a translation from the French by Anselm Hollo, 1993) and *Portraits of Sarajevo* (which has also never been published in the original language, 1994). *Sarajevo: A War Journal* is a diary with entries covering events in Sarajevo from 25 April 1992 to 18 August 1993. It is preceded by an entry dated 25 June 1993 addressed to the American reader and offering an explanation of why the war in Bosnia should not be regarded as either a civil war or a war of nationalities. The regular entries about the siege itself create a considerable sense of immediacy about the fighting, besides providing commentary on many peripheral issues, from the human interest to the political. With respect to the latter, Dizdarević is consistently critical of the peace-keeping role of the United Nations and other international bodies ("Someone must have felt bad about showing [François] Mitterand a devastated city. What will he think of us! No, we can't let that happen with the British dignitary when *he* comes to pay us a visit. We're known the world over for our hospitality, aren't we?"[7]). *Sarajevo: A War Journal* became a highly acclaimed book and in 1993 won the International Prize from Reporters Without Borders.

Conceived in a different vein, *Portraits of Sarajevo* is a more intimate text composed of generally quite short vignettes built around ordinary people trapped in the city during the siege who try as best they can to preserve some semblance of normal life despite the dangers and destruction all around them. Dizdarević's technique here is to introduce a character or characters, briefly sketch their background, and then let the people speak for themselves.

The Serbian writer David Albahari, one of Danilo Kiš's most talented followers has, like Kiš, rejected Serbian nationalism, socialist realism, and the postwar celebration of the legendary heroism of Tito's partisans. His formidable literary reputation rests primarily on such novels as *Sudija Dimitrijević* (Judge

Dimitrijević, 1978), *Cink* (*Tsing*, 1988), *Snežni čovek* (Snow Man, 1995), and *Mamac* (*Bait*, 1996) as well as on several highly regarded collections of short stories. Much concerned with language, the nature of literature, and the creative process, Albahari has studiously avoided the conventional in favor of the odd and the whimsical. Much of his inspiration derives from his recollections of family life, which he portrays in a series of vignettes, as in the short-story collection *Opis smrti* (A Description of Death, 1982). Of partly Jewish origin, like Kiš, Albahari has made the now-extinct world of small-town Jewish life in the former Yugoslavia the subject of a number of his stories without ranging far beyond the ambiguous Jewishness of his own family. He has also drawn on his extensive travels in the United States, Israel, Kenya, and his own native Yugoslavia.

In 1994, in the wake of the Balkan wars, Albahari and his family resettled in Canada. His experiences as a refugee in that country for two years form the subject, in part, of one of his most rewarding books, *Bait*. Undivided into chapters or paragraphs, the work is also to a large extent a family memoir. In the baggage the narrator has brought with him from Yugoslavia are three cassette tapes of his remarkably impressive mother, a convert to Judaism, recorded by him sixteen years earlier. As he replays the tapes, the narrator listens to his mother's voice recounting her life—as a Serb and as a Jew—the tragedy of which encapsulates that of Yugoslavia itself. The novel operates on two temporal planes. The tapes in a sense resurrect the mother and her experiences, whereas the narrator's comments on and recollections of his mother and his Yugoslav past occur in the present. So, too, do the discussions between the narrator and his alter ego, otherwise known as his friend Donald, himself a writer, which are interspersed throughout the novel. Despite the narrator's claims that he is not a writer, his conversations with Donald—about language and silence, literature and language, native language and adopted language, narration and time, and the legitimacy of the taped memoirs as a novelistic form—evince a keen interest in the literary art.

Of the many works of fiction inspired by the Balkan wars, *Bait* remains one of the most outstanding. As thought-provoking as any postmodernist inquiry into language and narration, the work deals sensitively with the interrelationship of past and present and the unique problems of an exile attempting to bridge the gap between a native language and an adopted language. Albahari's text is also extremely valuable for its insights into the Jewish presence in Serbia, from the prewar to the postwar periods, and the appalling impact of the wars of the 1990s on the cohesiveness of the Yugoslav ethnic mosaic.

The Literary Fallout of the Kosovo Campaign

The Serb onslaught against the Kosovo Albanians during and after the fighting in Bosnia was also viewed with disgust throughout the civilized world and similarly occasioned its share of literary engagement.

The fierce nationalism underlying the hostility between Serb and Croat and Serb and Muslim (Bosnian or Albanian) obviously had been nurtured over a very long period of time. What was needed to set it off was the collapse of Yugoslavia. The death of Tito in 1980 set the stage for the breakdown of the flimsy apparatus that tried to hold the state together after his demise. Slovenia's declaration of independence from Yugoslavia in 1991, followed shortly thereafter by a similar declaration on the part of Croatia, began the downward spiral that culminated in the Bosnian War of 1992–1996 and the Serbian campaign of "ethnic cleansing" in Kosovo in the late 1990s. Before reviewing the literature generated specifically by the campaign of ethnic cleansing in Kosovo, it may be instructive now to get a sense of the background to it by considering the writings of a few prominent Yugoslavs, both Serb and Croat.

The major Serbian writer in this regard is Dobrica Ćosić, the author of the massive tetralogy about the Serbs in World War I, *A Time of Death* (see chapter 5 above), a former member of the Central Committee of the Serbian Communist Party, and a member of the Yugoslav National Assembly. A long-time apologist for Serbian political aspirations as well as communist ideology (which he later repudiated), Ćosić not only supported the Serbian nationalism that gathered steam in the wake of Tito's death but is credited by many as one of the leading cultural figures most responsible for stoking it. Although he wrote one of the best novels dealing with the partisan resistance against the Germans in World War II, *Daleko je sunce* (*Far Away Is the Sun*, 1951), Ćosić's literary fame is still linked primarily with *A Time of Death*. That Ćosić has been consistent over time in his outlook is evident from two previous works of fiction, *Koreni* (Roots, 1954) and *Deobe* (Divisions, 1961), as well as two books on political themes both published in 1992, *Promene* (Changes), a collection of essays, and *Srpsko pitanje — demokratsko pitanje* (The Serbian Question—A Democratic Question). The latter consists mainly of lectures and speeches, some dealing with the Kosovo situation and collected under the title "Kosovska drama" ("The Kosovo Drama"), and others addressed to the fall of Yugoslavia ("Raspad Jugoslavije" ["The Fall of Yugoslavia"]).

During the Balkan crises of the 1990s, when Ćosić held the office of president of the Federal Republic of Yugoslavia, he was accused on several occasions of fomenting nationalist passions and for being ultimately responsible for the suffering of thousands of people. An article by a Czech translator and member of the Czech PEN Center in the Yugoslav daily newspaper *Danas* accused Ćosić of actually having ordered the shelling of the Croatian city of Vukovar during the Serb-Croat conflict. Ćosić took *Danas* to court, seeking damages in the amount of 100,000 euros because of the "mental pain" caused by the report, but the court eventually ruled against him. In order to present a different image to the world of both Ćosić and the Serb position in general, a collection of excerpts culled above all from Ćosić's The Serbian Question—A Democratic Question was published in French translation in 1994 under the title *L'Effondrement de la Yougoslavie: Positions d'un résistant* (translated by Slobodan Despot and published by L'Age d'Homme of Lausanne,

Switzerland). The book is prefaced by Miodrag Perišić, Minister of Information and Presidential Adviser of the First Federal Republic of Yugoslavia, of which Ćosić himself became president on 15 June 1992. The rationale for the book, according to Perišić, is to set the record straight concerning public utterances by Ćosić in his term as president that, according to Perišić, had been either misrepresented or misunderstood. On the surface, Ćosić's public utterances and writings about Serb-Albanian relations are all sweetness and light. His disavows any desire to curtail the Albanians' cultivation of their culture and the Muslim faith. But he makes the point repeatedly that Yugoslavia for centuries had been the battleground of Christianity and Islam and that the Yugoslav Muslims in fact should be regarded as an "artificial nation." What he will not countenance, however, is any actions by the Albanians in Kosovo that would advance the Kosovar separatist cause or lead to a union of Kosovo and Albania.

Still more a defense of the familiar Serbian position on Kosovo is the well-known writer Danko Popović's book *Božuri i trnje: Monografija o Dželetovićima* (Peonys and Brambles: A Monograph About the Dželetovići; translated into English as *The Bloodblossoms of Kosovo: A Chronicle About the Serbian Holy Land*). Popović, who was born in Arandjelovac, Serbia, in 1928, is known most as the author of the immensely popular novel *Knjiga o Milutinu* (The Book of Milutin, 1984). *The Bloodblossoms of Kosovo* is a purely ideological text lamenting the fate of the Serbs in Kosovo over time, the rightfulness of their claims to Kosovo as an integral part of Serbia, the gradual Albanianization of the province, and the pernicious role of the Yugoslav communists in further reducing the Serbian hold on Kosovo in favor of autonomous-region status for the province. The work begins with the resettlement of Serbs from Montenegro to Kosovo, the "cradle of the Serbian nation," beginning in 1921. Its focus is primarily on the Dželetović family, whose trials and tribulations trying to create a home for themselves in Kosovo and the indignities they suffer at the hands of Albanians and in consequence of the Yugoslav Communist Party's policies during Tito's reign are meant to be paradigmatic of the plight of the Serbs in Kosovo in general. *The Bloodblossoms of Kosovo* is a bitter work encapsulating the full dimension of Serbian disillusionment over their de facto loss of Kosovo.

A similarly jaundiced perspective on the Kosovo Albanians has come from the Serbian writer Radosav Stojanović (b. 1950). A native of Crna Trava in Kosovo and a graduate of Priština University, Stojanović had manifested an interest in Serb-Albanian relations in his short-story collection *Mrtva straža* (Death Watch, 1988). But the continuing deterioration of these relations prompted him to publish a chronicle of the anti-Serb campaign in Kosovo of the 1980s under the inflammatory title *Živeti s genocidom: Hronika kosovskog baš-čašća 1981–1989* (Living with Genocide: A Chronicle of the Kosovo Outrage, 1981–1989, 1990).

Understandably, Albanian (and Kosovar) writers have viewed the events in Kosovo from an entirely different perspective. This is nowhere more evident than in works by Ismail Kadare. His spare, deceptively simple novel *Ura me tri harqe* (*The Three-Arched Bridge,* 1978) looks far back in history at the roots of the Serb-Albanian crisis. Set in the fourteenth century, a dark age of warring, intrigues, and the steady encroachments of the Ottoman Turks, events are seen through the eyes of an Albanian monk-translator who keeps a journal of the times. With deft strokes, Kadare sketches the historical and political background before focusing in on the strange circumstances surrounding the building of a bridge over the mighty Ujana e Keqe (Evil Waters) River. Local reaction to the project is generally one of awe mixed with superstitious hostility. The bridge finally gets built and appears strong until late in the winter, when strange depressions appear in the masonry. This apparently sinister development also coincides with the monk's apprehensions concerning the growing presence of the Ottoman Turks in the Balkans. The idea then takes hold in this climate of fear, superstition, and irrationality that in order to survive the new bridge has to be somehow placated by a human sacrifice in the form of immurement. Someone, in other words, has to be immured within a wall of the bridge. This seems to have come to pass when one day the chalk-colored head, neck, and part of the chest of a man are discovered protruding from the bridge. People come from all over to view the phenomenon and the monk speculates that the corpse in the wall is probably that of a vandal who was discovered by the bridge builders, killed, and made a part of the bridge for the purpose of instilling dread. In the meantime, nothing is able to halt the Turkish advance after the downfall of Byzantium. Foretelling his own doom, like the man sacrificed to the bridge, the monk brings his chronicle to an end as Turkish forces appear on the horizon. Twelve years after the novel begins, in 1389, the battle of Kosovo Field was fought. The Serbian loss became miraculously transformed thereafter into the most powerful myth in Serbian culture and the cornerstone of Serbian nationalism.

In his subsequent book on Kosovo, *Tri këngë zie për Kosovën* (*Three Elegies for Kosovo,* 1998), Kadare has concentrated just on the events of the battle of 28 June 1389, which was fought by a combined army of Serbs, Bosnians, Albanians, and Romanians against an Ottoman Turkish army led by Sultan Murad I. The Turks were victorious, although at the cost of the life of Sultan Murad, who was buried in Kosovo. The first part of Kadare's work (the first "elegy") paints a vivid picture of the night before the momentous battle and the day of the battle itself. The focus is on the multinational forces arrayed against the Turks. Minstrels (who double as the narrators of the first two elegies) entertain the troops, but the songs they sing reveal the lingering animosity between Serbs and Albanians. The second part of *Three Elegies for Kosovo* begins at the end of the battle as the minstrels and others head west after the calamitous defeat. In the last part, "The Royal Prayer," the narrator is now the voice of the deceased Sultan Murad himself, coming from the tomb. Through Murad's narration, Kadare traces the subsequent dark history of Serb-Albanian relations down to the policy of ethnic cleansing of the Kosovo Albanians instituted under the leadership of the Serbian president Slobodan Milošević. Elegantly written, and moving, *Three Elegies for Kosovo* amply compensates for its brevity—the novel is less than a hundred pages long.

On the other side of the Serbian ledger from such rabid nationalists and apologists as Dobrica Ćosić and Danko Popović are the Serbian writers Mirko Kovač, Svetislav Basara, Vidosav Stevanović, and Vladimir Arsenijević. Kovač, a Serb, so irked the literary establishment, and others, in Serbia by his unconcealed loathing for Serbian nationalism that he voluntarily exiled himself to Croatia, where he lives on the island of Rovinj. If his repudiation of Serbianism in part shaped the novel for which he is best known, *Životopis Malvine Trifkovića* (The Life of Malvina Trifković, 1971), his only work thus far to be translated (into French), of equal importance in its genesis was Kovač's belief that both groups, Serbs and Croats alike, have been equally guilty of extreme nationalism and ethnic hatred.

A short, sordid work composed in the form of fifteen small manuscripts by the principals and others close to them, the novel would seem to belong primarily to the genre of the murder mystery. A young Serbian girl, Malvina Trifković, is sent to a Serbian Orthodox school for girls in Budapest. The time is the early twentieth century. Her model behavior quickly falls to pieces. She develops a lesbian affair with another girl, who commits suicide, after which she runs away from the school to marry a Croatian Roman Catholic (virtually an unpardonable sin). His large family is inhospitable to her, primarily because she is a Serb; the exception is her sister-in-law Katarina, who befriends her and with whom she also plunges into an intense lesbian relationship. This ends when Katarina becomes pregnant by a man she refuses to identify. After Katarina's premature death, the child, a daughter who is given the same name of Malvina, is brought up by stepmother Malvina, and in the Orthodox faith. When the girl is in her teens, the elder Malvina encourages her relationship with a Croat in his early thirties. The couple are wed. Not long afterward, their murdered bodies are discovered. Crosses have been cut into their bellies, their sexual parts have been mutilated, and the medical report on the young Malvina reveals that she was raped after the mutilation and murder. No one is brought to justice for the crime, and the elder Malvina retires into a Serbian convent.

The sensationalism of the novel, its clinical detail, and unanswered questions concerning various relationships make The Life of Malvina Trifković certainly a strange work. But what seems perfectly clear is Kovač's intention to show as graphically as possible the intense hatred between Serb and Croat. From the day she arrives in Tomislav Parčić's home as his new wife, Malvina is targeted for alienation. The sole friendship she establishes is with Tomislav's lesbian sister Katarina. Her marriage is undone through the machinations of Tomislav's brother Ivan, whose main goal in life is the preservation of Croatian honor and glory, which has been defiled, to his way of thinking, by his brother's marriage to a Serb. And when the elder Malvina's stepdaughter and husband are murdered at the end, the crime is perceived as clearly ethnically motivated. Thus, long before the outbreak of the Balkan wars of the 1990s, Kovač pinpointed the root cause of the conflict in his novel. Kovač is also the author of a book of short prose pieces under the title *Evropska trulež i drugi eseji* (European Rot, and Other Essays, 1994). Apart from a touching obituary for Danilo Kiš, the pieces deal for the most part with literary issues (South Slavic and Western), nationalism, totalitarianism, democracy, the future of Serbia, and, among the most interesting, the ties binding writers and dictators.

A case apart for the arsenal of literary weapons that he brings to his demolition of Serbian nationalism is Svetislav Basara, who appeared in chapter 7 as a leading representative of Serbian postmodernism. Brash, irreverent in the extreme, wildly imaginative, with a great flare for the absurd, Basara is at his liveliest when subverting Yugoslav and Serbian pseudo-mythologies, especially Serbian delusions of national grandeur. One of his favorite targets is Tito, whom he dehumanizes in his 1995 novel *De bello civile* (*On Civil War*; original title in Latin) within the context of a subversion of structuralism:

> If I am not mistaken, structuralism appeared here at the end of the seventies. At first it was just an outdated intellectual trend, but it would later cause a series of ultimately strange and dangerous events. . . . Many famous and not-so-famous structuralists visited Belgrade, held lectures, went bar-hopping, and took young female students of world literature to their rooms in luxurious hotels and made little structuralists. Up until then Yugoslavia was a rather pleasant cozy little nook. The Ruler [Tito] was still alive and firm in his decision never to die; time was marching on in a straight line; the sale of smoked meat products was on the rise; the birth rate was satisfactory; and the mutiny on the Bounty had long since been squelched in blood. . . . And not even dreaming of it, the Ruler was a structuralist. The later research of Dr. R. Hamsun of Uppsala University leaves no doubt about that. According to Dr. Hamsun, the Ruler had been so decoded already by 1950 that he had ceased to be a human being and had become a symbol. The same author claims that the Ruler would never have died if the deconstructionists had not interfered.[8]

The contradictions and absurdities of communism Yugoslav-style, and what Basara refers to as the "Yugonostalgia" of the period after the breakup of Yugoslavia, also come in for their share of mockery, above all in his two-part Manic-Paranoic History of Serbian Literature. Anything but a literary history, and with the flimsiest of plots, the book gives us Basara expressing himself on anything of interest to him, from Titoist Yugoslavia to political correctness in the terminology for homosexual men and women to postmodernism. Declaring himself an "inveterate anticommunist," he mockingly wonders aloud how he might yet save communism and still be an anticommunist since there will be nothing after communism. Communism, he declares, is the last stage of decomposition of the "huge idiot succinctly called the *nation*," and its collapse will be followed only by absolute chaos. Mixing real and fictitious characters, Basara drags a host of post–World War II Yugoslav and Serbian literary and political figures into his work, among them Danilo Kiš (of whom he speaks reverently) and Miodrag Bulatović (who appears in some of the funniest sequences in the novel). At the end of Holy Water (the second volume), by which time fighting has broken out in Kosovo, the American peacekeeper Richard Holbrook and the spokesman for the Kosovo Liberation Army, the "academic painter" Agim Kastrati, a recurrent figure in the Manic-Paranoic History of Serbian Literature, also put in appearances.

Virtualna kabala (Virtual Kabala), which immediately preceded Looney Tunes and Holy Water in 1996, is essentially a consideration of the collapse of Yugoslavia in somewhat less frivolous terms. As a dramatic writer, Basara is also the author of several black comedies in the vein of the absurd and fantastic: *Dolce-Vita, Hamlet-Remake, Budibogsnama* (God-Be-With-Us), in which Samuel Beckett and Albert Einstein appear as characters, and *Oximoron* (Oxymoron), which were published in a single collection in 1997 under the title *Sabrane pozorišne drame* (Collected Plays). Although clever and laugh-provoking, most of Basara's works, with the exception especially of his comedies, are so full of Yugoslav and Serbian topical allusions that they can best be appreciated only by a very knowledgeable reader.

Vidosav Stevanović (b. 1942) was also among the foremost Serbian writers to oppose the Serbian nationalism that led to the wars of the 1990s. In 1988, three years before he and his family fled Yugoslavia, Stevanović's protests against Slobodan Milošević resulted in his expulsion from the League of Communists and exclusion from all public functions. He also lost his position at the Prosveta publishing house, where he had managed to promote the publication of dissident works from elsewhere in Eastern Europe. Stevanović further alienated himself from the Milošević government when he founded the elitist oppositional Belgrade Circle. Stevanović and his family left Serbia at the outset of the Serb-Croat war of 1991 and sought refuge first in Macedonia and then in Greece. A few years later he was able to settle in France as a political exile, but even there—as subsequent events revealed—he was still unsafe from assaults on his person by Serbian nationalists deeply resentful of what they regarded as his denigration of their motherland. At the beginning of the new year, 1995, he was brutally attacked on a Parisian street, an incident that prompted a Croatian friend, the writer Predrag Matvejević, to address a letter to Pen Club International appealing for Stevanović's protection.

Stevanović's first major work dealing, however obliquely, with the Yugoslav situation was the highly imaginative novel *Testament: Roman u 52 bdenja* (Testament: A Novel in 52 Vigils, 1986). Narrated in the first person by a woman who later in the novel also addresses letters to family and friends about her experiences, it describes an apocalyptic journey through the hell of an imaginary Balkan country called Kao and no doubt meant to represent Serbia. A participant in the country's wars and insurrections, the narrator raises the question at the end of the novel whether she and the others on the journey are alive or dead or simply in fact the material from which a grand dream was constructed. Grotesque, bizarre, and fantastic images are commonplace in Stevanović's works and Testament is no exception.

Stevanović was awarded the prestigious NIN Prize for Testament in 1986. His most celebrated subsequent work was the novelistic trilogy *Sneg u Atini* (Snow in Athens, 1992), *Ostrvo Balkan* (The Balkan Island, 1993), and *Hristos i psi* (Christos and the Dogs, 1994). Allegorical, autobiographical, at times hallucinatory, the trilogy as a whole is a highly personal, in some ways idiosyncratic view of the disintegration of Yugoslavia in the wars of the 1990s. In the first novel the calamities that beset Yugoslavia (never identified as such) are traced through the first-person accounts of four members of a family who, like Stevanović and his own family, manage to escape the fighting for the safety of Greece. The Balkan Island has a less coherent structure than either Snow in Athens or Christos and the Dogs. It consists of twenty-one loosely related "chapters" generally narrated in the first person and divided into numbered paragraphs resembling a diary. Broadly speaking, the subject of the novel is the siege of the Bosnian capital Sarajevo, although the city remains unnamed. War has erupted, the city is being shelled mercilessly, and the devastation and human toll mount daily. The inhabitants take refuge in caves, while in the streets "defenders" and "liberators," who recognize each other only by the "stench of their hatred," confront one other. Everything is viewed through the eyes of the narrator, who enters the caves people are hiding in in order to be able to describe conditions in detail; he subsequently travels to the front to take notes on the action there. Wherever he goes he is a witness to horror.

The last novel of the trilogy, Christos and the Dogs, paints a dark and disturbing picture of Yugoslavia after the Balkan wars. As in Snow in Athens, each character introduces himself or herself in a simple way and then tells his or her story, about their arrival in Greece, the hardships they experience, their plans for the future, possible departure for America if the money for the trip can be found, and so on. These episodes alternate with "apocrypha" narrated by other characters, living and dead, who appear in hallucinatory sequences and are meant to represent the political figures responsible in one way or another for the debacle in the Balkans.

Stevanović's trilogy portrays the conflicts in Croatia and Bosnia in vivid, even nightmarish terms; like Testament, it aims squarely, if at times obliquely, at the anachronism and cost of Serbian nationalism. Combining biblical, fantastic, and macabre elements (trafficking, for example, in human organs retrieved from fresh corpses on the battlefield), the trilogy attracted considerable attention when first published in France in 1993 in two volumes: *La neige et les chiens* (The Snow and the Dogs) and *Christos et les chiens* (Christos and the Dogs).

In a somewhat later novel, *Ista stvar* (The Same Thing, 1995), Stevanović again confronts the madness of war, this time by means of a series of eleven hallucinatory monologues (or "circles") spoken by eleven people, male and female—among them a couple of young boys, a writer, a professor, and a sniper—who are exiles in France or survivors in the rubble of a phantom city in Eastern Europe. What they have in common is the desire to hide their origins and to suppress the history of a country that to all intents and purposes no longer lives. The sniper (known as "The Sixth"), for example, observes his victims through his sniperscope and at one point contemplates the economy of killing two people at the same time when he trains his sights on a pregnant woman walking on a street below him. She is, in fact, another character in the book identified as Sela. The boy Simon, just one of many children deprived of mothers and fathers by the war, has to step over the corpses of his slain parents in order to leave his hiding place and rejoin the outside world, where snipers' bullets rain down like hail and horrors abound on all sides. Another young refugee, Pavel, now calling himself Paul, lives in Paris, where he begs for money in the Paris Métro with his rubber snake and studies the faces of passengers in an effort to determine who will give him something and who will not. Following the same narrative pattern of his Balkan trilogy, Stevanović crisscrosses back and forth between his characters, ultimately creating a composite picture of mindless devastation in a relentless spiral of hatred and vengeance. His is a world without hope, a world of shattered lives and shattered dreams. In a broad sense what Stevanović is saying is that it has always been so when the mad dogs of war have been unleashed and so long as nations exist so, too, will war. And who will reap the profits? None other, of course, than the merchants and traffickers of arms.

When Stevanović's near-native city of Kragujevac voted out the socialists in local elections in early 1997 and the opposition coalition Zajedno took over the municipal administration, Stevanović was invited to accept the position of director of the "liberated" TV Kragujevac. But attempts by the authorities in Belgrade to take over the TV station led to a nasty fracas involving local residents and police from Belgrade and mass protests, with Stevanović again in the thick of things. The entire episode is recounted in the form of a month-by-month narrative from December 1996 to mid-July 1997—a period of two hundred days which, according to Stevanović, may not have changed the world but nearly changed Serbia. It was published in French translation in 2003 under the title *Voleurs de leur propre liberté* (Thieves of Their Own Liberty). In 2001 Stevanović gave full vent to his feelings about Slobodan Milošević in his book *Milošević: Jedan epitaf* (Milošević: An Epitaph). It was translated into English and published in 2004 with the less ambiguous subtitle *The People's Tyrant*.

A native of Pula, in northern Croatia, the Serbian novelist Vladimir Arsenijević (b. 1965) was the youngest Serbian writer to win the prestigious NIN Prize in 1994 for his first novel *U potpalublju* (In the Hold, 1994; translated as *Cloaca Maxima: In the Hold*). This was the first part of an intended tetralogy under the title *Cloaca Maxima*. Narrated in the first person by a young man whose wife is expecting the birth of their first child, the novel explores the psychological and emotional impact of the beginning Serb-Croat war of late 1991 on Belgrade youth, for whom drug use, rock music, and sexual license underscore their alienation from the rest of society. As the novel draws to an end, the calling up of reservists, early casualties at the front, and deaths among those who chose to flee the country in order to escape the war become an inescapable reality to the young couple. The second part of *Cloaca Maxima, Andjela* (Angela), subtitled *Sapunska opera* (A Soap Opera), appeared in 1997. Against the events of 1992, including the siege of Sarajevo, the narrator tells the story of his life and the role played in it by the young woman named Andjela who became his wife and with whom he flees Serbia to Greece at the end. Arsenijević's next book, *Mexico: Ratni dnevnik* (Mexico: A Diary of the War, 2000), encompasses a diary of the period 26 March 1999 to 26 May 1999. The diary is framed by a prefatory narrative consisting of a dialogue about the Balkan wars and the events in Kosovo between Arsenijević and the Albanian writer Bashkim Shehu, whom Arsenijević met for the first time in 1998, and a much longer concluding discussion about the NATO bombing of Serbia during the Kosovo conflict between the author and Serbian and Albanian friends in Mexico City, where he arrived on 26 May 1999 with a grant from the International Writers' Parliament.

Among the most vigorous proponents of the Croatian point of view in the ongoing clash of ideologies in the former Yugoslavia is Stjepan Čuić, who, as we have seen, is best known for his predilection for the grotesque and occult. In the 1990s Čuić also published two books of nonfiction dealing with contemporary Croatian politics and the Balkan wars: *Abeceda licemjerja* (The Alphabet of Hypocrisy, 1992), on Croatian self-determination, and *Lule mira* (Peace Pipes, 1994), a journalistic work dealing with the Croats in Bosnia during the conflicts of the 1990s. The Alphabet of Hypocrisy is arguably the more interesting of the two. Stressing throughout that Croatia is a European nation and not some extension of a greater Serbia, Čuić argues against an autonomous status for Croatia on the grounds that before long the Croats would be subject to Serbian hegemony, as they have been in the past. The Serbs, he argues, cannot accept the idea of a Croatian "national expression" and continue to advance the argument that Croatia is virtually by definition an Ustasha state, with reference to the Croatian fascist organization allied with Hitler during World War II. With an obvious paranoia-tinged resentment toward Europe for the mercenary considerations that have shaped its attitude toward Croatian aspirations for independence, he writes at one point:

> The Croats, a European nation, implore Europe to acknowledge them as such. They base their demand, to one and all, on their geography and political philosophy, on the right to independence and the ideal of freedom and democracy that smolders in their history as well as in their collective consciousness from the "bulwark of Christianity" to their sacrifices in the brutal war imposed on them.[9]

Elsewhere in his book Čuić also takes issues with those (Croatian) intellectuals who, like Slavenka Drakulić—whom he discusses at some length—appeared before the Helsinki Watch Commission and gave testimony that he considers detrimental to the cause of the Croatian nation, and almost solely because of what these intellectuals regarded as the revival of nationalism with its recollections of the wartime Ustasha. While disclaiming any sentiment for the Ustasha, Čuić argues the point that the problem with intellectuals like Drakulić is that they seize on the slightest evidence of a rebirth of Croatian nationalism to exaggerate the facts and thus—doubtless unintentionally—contribute to anti-Croatian sentiment. So obsessed are they with signs of renewed nationalism, and so ready are they to heap blame on the Croatians themselves, Čuić contends, that they ignore the crimes of the Serbs and the rabid nationalism behind them.

Slavenka Drakulić (b. 1949) herself is an internationally respected Croatian journalist and novelist who has spent much time in the West (including the United States) and whose ideas need no "spinning" by Čuić. Her celebrity owes much to such lively and intelligent books of political reportage as *How We Survived Communism and Even Laughed* (1992), *Balkan Express: Fragments from the Other Side of the War* (1993), and *Kao da me nema* (As If I Didn't Exist, 1999; translated into English as *S.: A Novel About the Balkans*). *How We Survived Communism and Even Laughed* originated as a series of short pieces on Eastern Europe after 1989 written originally in January and February 1990 on assignment for *Ms.* magazine in New York. Drakulić's intention was to focus on a less well covered aspect of the immediate aftermath of the collapse of communism, namely women—the impact on them of the changes taking place and their reactions to them.

Her next book of reportage, *Balkan Express: Fragments from the Other Side of the War* (1993), contains stories about the "less visible side" of the Yugoslav conflicts of the early 1990s. Drakulić wrote the pieces between April 1991 and May 1992, during which time she viewed the disintegration of the former Yugoslavia from her home in Zagreb, Croatia. Her third book of reportage, *Café Europa: Life After Communism* (1996), includes two dozen pieces written between 1992 and 1996. As in *How We Survived Communism and Even Laughed*, Drakulić's field of vision again expands to take in the whole of Eastern Europe after the fall of communism. Her essays deal with such subjects as the appalling condition of public toilets in Bucharest; the surprise return to Yugoslavia of Crown Prince Alexander; the graves of Nicolae and Elena Ceauşescu in Bucharest; reactions to her visit as a Croat to Israel in the light of the treatment of the Jews under the fascist puppet regime of Ante Pavelić; and her father's role in World War II. In her most recent book on the Balkan wars, *S.: A Novel About the Balkans,* Drakulić again focuses on the impact of the conflict on women, in this instance the plight of a Bosnian woman who is repeatedly raped by Serbian soldiers during the Bosnian War in 1992 and bears an unwanted child in exile.

Notwithstanding her acclaim as a journalist, Drakulić has also had some success with her novels. Curiously, perhaps, these have little to do with the issues to which her books of political reportage are devoted. Instead, they are fairly short texts, narrated in the first person by a young woman, doubtless autobiographical in part, and dealing by and large with serious illness, bizarre relationships, the body, and eroticism. *Hologrami strahu* (*Holograms of Fear*, 1992), for example, recounts a presumably successful kidney transplant undergone by the narrator. *The Taste of a Man*, published originally in English, is a macabre tale of a brief but extremely passionate love affair between a Polish female graduate student in New York and the young married Brazilian researcher on cannibalism she meets there. Unable to face the inevitability of her lover's return to Brazil, and out of a desire in a way to keep him wholly hers for the rest of her life, the Polish woman murders him, deposits his dismembered remains in different parts of New York, including Kennedy Airport, but not before partaking of some of his flesh. *Mramorna koža* (*Marble Skin*, 1989) is about a tortuous mother-daughter relationship in which the daughter, a sculptor, is unwholesomely obsessed with her mother's body, as if wanting to possess it completely and finding a release of sorts in sculpting it in marble. The illness and approaching death of the mother in *Marble Skin* echo the medical ambiance of *Holograms of Fear*, while the preoccupation with the body, intense sexuality, and blood link *Marble Skin* and *The Taste of a Man*.

Denounced for her independent views as well as her refusal to identify with the new nationalism of the post-Yugoslav Croatian state, Dubravka Ugrešić (b. 1949) went into exile in 1993 and has been living in Amsterdam ever since. Her literary career embraces both essayistic writing and fiction and includes such widely translated major books as *Forsiranje romana-reke* (*Fording the Stream of Consciousness*, 1991); *Na raljama života* (*In the Jaws of Life*, 1992); *Americki fictionar* (American Fictionary, 1993; translated as *Have a Nice Day: From the Balkan War to the American Dream*), which also deals with her travels in the United States, where she has frequently lectured; *Kultura laži: Antipolitički eseji* (*The Culture of Lies: Antipolitical Essays*, 1966), a collection of mostly breezy short pieces covering a wide range of Croatian and Yugoslav cultural and political topics; and two relatively recent works of fiction, *Muzej bezuslovne predaje* (*The Museum of Unconditional Surrender*, 1998) and *Ministarstvo boli* (*The Ministry of Pain*, 2005), both based heavily on Ugrešić's own experiences as an exile.

Ugrešić's first published piece of fiction since the collapse of Yugoslavia, *The Museum of Unconditional Surrender* is a novel in the form of fragments of various sorts (including self-contained short stories) that splendidly convey the emotional and intellectual dilemmas of an exile's homelessness. Less fragmentary in structure, *The Ministry of Pain* is a first-person narrative by a Croatian émigré academic living and teaching in Amsterdam. Much of the novel is taken up with her often unflattering analysis—often by means of language and speech—of the outlook and behavior of her fellow émigrés from the former Yugoslavia and the phenomenon of what she calls "Yugonostalgia." This "Yugonostalgia" shows up poignantly above all in the little essays the narrator asks her students from the former Yugoslavia to write about what they remember of their previous life. In the end, Ugrešić's *The Ministry of Pain* is, if nothing else, a testimony to her own very real "Yugonostalgia."

Miljenko Jergović (b. 1966), a native of Sarajevo, is another Croatian journalist (as well as poet, prose writer, and novelist), who, like Drakulić and Ugrešić, has espoused a liberal point of view of the Balkan wars. He is also representative of the Bosnian intellectuals who came of age in the 1980s. Jergović's work began appearing in the late 1980s in newspapers, magazines, and literary journals. His first book, a collection of poems under the title *Opservatorija Varšava* (Warsaw Observatory), won two prestigious prizes in 1988. His second book of poems, *Is Someone Studying Japanese in This City Tonight?* (original title in English), came out in 1990. From 1989 to the beginning of the Bosnian War in 1992 Jergović was a columnist for the Sarajevo daily *Oslobodjenje*. In the first months of the war he also wrote for the weekly magazine *DANI*. His third book of poems, *Himmel Commando*, was published in 1992. Jergović went to Zagreb in 1993, where he began publishing the texts that eventually went into the making of his book *Sarajevski Marlboro* (*Sarajevo Marlboro*, 1994). Jergović has since brought out several other books, among them a collection of poems by young Bosnians from 1992 to 1996, *Ovdje živi Conan* (Conan Lives Here, 1997); a collection of his own stories entitled *Mama Leone* (1999); and the popular novel *Buick Rivera* (2002).

Although he is an astute observer also of Croatian culture and politics, it was Jergović's vignettes in *Sarajevo Marlboro* of his native city before the outbreak of war, and during the conflict, that brought him his greatest fame. Narrated unpretentiously in the first person, with wry humor and a healthy dose of cynicism, the stories—in their totality—comprise one of the most readable and in some ways disturbing accounts of life in Sarajevo at the time. Even when writing directly about the war, Jergović manages never to lose sight of the small things of everyday life that can sustain people through the worst of times. In one story, "Kaktus" ("Cactus"), he recalls how he looked after the small cactus in a pot given him by his girlfriend during the siege of Sarajevo until it was unable to further stand the cold. In "Buba" ("Beetle"), his momentary relief that his house and car had survived the first bombardment of Sarajevo soon yields to a sense of the hopelessness of the whole situation. In some instances, as in the story "Hanumica" ("Muslim Doll"), tragedy and humor come together in a mix typical of Jergović's style. The oddball loner Ćipo allows a homeless Muslim girl, Mujesira, to share the huge apartment his aunt lets him use in her absence. But he avoids her like the plague, treating her only as a domestic servant. When a mortar explodes outside his front door, blowing off Mujesira's legs, and she lies dying in a hospital for the next two days, only then does he begin to perceive what she means to him.

When it suited him, Jergović could also shock the reader with graphic detail of war, as in the opening description of "Brada" ("Beard") when Dinka, the wife of a Croatian poet, Juraj, is led to what is left of his body:

Juraj's head lay in the mud like an empty dish into which the first raindrops fall. The soldiers marched past him indifferently. A few steps away his neighbor

Šimun, who was digging a two-meter trench, stared at the clay that was over-flowing with all the colors of the rainbow, with a peculiar feeling of emptiness in the back of his neck and with a premonition, free of fear, that his own head would be turned into a prison bucket for cleaning out latrines. Every now and then he glanced out of the corner of his eye at the place where an hour earlier Juraj had been digging; in his mind's eye he measured the hole from which Juraj's brain had burst out, and admired its regular contours as if a skillful potter had shaped it, sculpting with his fingers that which had been given by God as if it were dust and water. [10]

When all is said and done, perhaps the most lamentable victim of the Bosnian War was the harmony that had existed for a very long time between Serbs, Croats, Muslims, and Jews. Jergović was keenly aware of the loss and conveys in "Kondor" ("The Condor") the rapidity and ease with which neighbor would turn against neighbor in conditions of ethnic warfare. The light tone of the narration indeed sets in bolder relief the breakdown in relations then taking place, with the story of Izet, the Muslim, and Spasoje, the Serb, serving as a paradigm for what was happening throughout Bosnia:

The war happened upon Izet in Vraca. Before he could even bat an eyelash, let alone run away, Chetniks showed up on the threshold of his house and his neighbor Spasoje immediately made a grab for his neck. Just the day before, Spasoje had offered him a shot of *rakija*. He was on good terms with Izet and as harmless as a water-pistol. But on this day there he was all dressed up in a black uniform, a dagger shining at his waist, his beard grown out overnight as though he'd fertilized it with manure from the stable, and bellowing outside Izet's door that he'd slit his throat if he didn't open it. . . . Izet could smell the *rakija* on Spasoje's breath through the wooden door, and when he finally opened it, he was hit smack in the face by a rifle butt. Izet toppled over like a candle. (75–76)

In more recent years, the young Croatian writer and journalist Boris Dežulović (b. 1964), a native of Split, has weighed in on the Yugoslav tragedy of the 1990s. As a journalist he in fact covered the fighting in Kmin, Krajina, Mostar, and Dubrovnik, and was the first journalist in Serb-occupied Vukovar. Restless and rebellious by nature, Dežulović has worked at a variety of different jobs, several in connection with the alternative theater Epicenter, of which he was one of the founders. He was also a founder of the well-known satirical weekly *Feral Tribunea*—a supplement of the newspaper *Slobodna Dalmacija*—which he left in 1999 to become a columnist for the independent-minded Zagreb weekly *Globus*. That same year, 1999, Dežulović edited an anthology of "contemporary Croatian stupidity" ("antologia suvremene hrvatske gluposti") under the title (in English) *Greatest Shits*. His willingness to deflate national myths and shibboleths shows up as well in his second novel, *Jebo sad hiljadu dinara* (Who

Gives a Damn About a Thousand Dinars Now, 2005). Intent on exposing the insane folly of the Bosnian-Croatian War, Dežulović brings together a Croatian and a Bosnian unit, each on a secret mission and dressed in the uniform of the opposing side. The point of this satirical and tragicomic antiwar novel is to demonstrate the unnaturalness of the conflict between the two groups of men (twelve in toto) who essentially represent two sides of the same coin. This idea is reenforced through flashbacks pointing up the intertwined fates of the men, even before going into combat.

Released the same year, Dežulović's first collection of poetry, *Pjesme iz Lore* (Poems from Lora), conveys the same sentiments as his novel. Bold and brash, Dežulović aims squarely at the senselessness of war and the folly of nationalism. *Christkind* (Christchild, 2003), Dežulović's first novel and winner of a best fiction award in Croatia the year of its publication, is a work of a different sort. Here science-fiction time travel is combined with a moral dilemma regarding the killing of the baby Hitler. A young man returns to the past and finds himself confronting the issue of whether he would be justified in killing Hitler in his infancy in the light of subsequent history, thereby sparing millions of lives in the future. Or would the murder be immoral in that the child is an innocent being and the monster Hitler later became may have been shaped by a variety of factors? There is also the matter of whether or not the time traveler wants to commit murder, which in fact he does not, and especially the murder of a child. The example of Abraham's sacrifice of the innocent Isaac in the Old Testament is also weighed and measured.

A diametrically different stance toward Serb-Croat and Serb-Muslim relations was taken by the prominent Bosnian Serb writer and political figure Vuk Drašković (b. 1946). He is best known for his novel *Nož* (*The Knife* (1983), a grim recounting of the massacre of an entire Serb family by their Muslim neighbors on Christmas Day 1942 in a Bosnian village inside the Ustasha-controlled Croatian fascist state. Only a boy is spared the slaughter, but he is raised as a Muslim with a hatred of Christian Serbs. When he later falls in love with a Serbian girl, he gradually comes to understand the need for tolerance between Bosnian Serbs and Bosnian Muslims, who share essentially the same language and ethnic origin and who have been divided only by religion. The title of the novel refers to the Bosnian Muslim and Croatian Ustasha ritual of kissing a knife as the preferred instrument of death for Serbs.

Drašković was widely criticized for publishing his novel on the grounds that at a time when the official emphasis was on the need to create an all-encompassing Yugoslav identity, depicting Croatian and, especially, Muslim atrocities against the Serbs during World War II was inflammatory and divisive. Responding to this criticism, Drašković issued a rebuttal in 1989 under the title *Odgovori* (Rejoinders). Moreover, the same year in which Rejoinders appeared in print he published the novel *Ruski konzul* (The Russian Consul), in which he demonstrated a similar Serbian nationalism and ethnic intolerance. The focus in this instance is on the yet greater differences separating Serbs and Albanians in Kosovo. Drašković even carried over his main character, Alija Osmanović (alias

Ilja Jugović before his conversion to Islam), from *The Knife,* who appears with his original Serbian name and has been reconverted to the Serbian Orthodox Church. The Russian Consul portrays the Kosovo Albanians as fiercely anti-Serb and intent on achieving their goal of driving the Serbs from Kosovo by any and all means.

In the light of the views conveyed by such novels as *The Knife* and The Russian Consul, it may be hard to imagine that Drašković was once the leader of an opposition party in the Serbian parliament known as Srpski Pokret Obnove (SPO; Serbian Movement of Renewal) and that he was quite visible in antigovernment demonstrations in Belgrade in March 1992. However, he eventually joined the government and became an outspoken supporter of Slobodan Milošević during the Kosovo campaign of spring 1999. Besides his fiction, Drašković also published a book on the political situation in Yugoslavia from 1980 to 1992 and another on Serbian-Albanian relations in Kosovo.

The Persistence of Serbian Nationalism

Notwithstanding the court of world opinion and the ongoing trials of former Serbian politicians and military personnel involved in atrocities in Bosnia and elsewhere, it would appear that a significant percentage of the Serbian population still supports its discredited leaders and their policies. A case in point are the novels (if they can be called that) published in 2005 by such notorious figures as Milorad Ulemek (b. 1965) and Dr. Radovan Karadžić (b. 1945).

Ulemek—perhaps known best by his nom de guerre, "Legija," a reference to his service in the French Foreign Legion—was Serbia's most infamous paramilitary soldier and has been accused of some of the worst atrocities of the Yugoslav wars. He is also a former commander of the Red Berets, the military branch of the Serbian secret police. In 2004 Ulemek surrendered to Serbian police in Belgrade, where he was put on trial not for crimes related to the Balkan wars but for the assassination of Prime Minister Zoran Djindjić, who was gunned down outside his office in March 2003. After he was taken into custody, his common-law wife turned over to the Serbian publisher Mihailo Vojnović the manuscript of his novel *Gvozdeni rov* (Iron Trench). Written while Ulemek was on the run, the novel has proven a huge success in Serbia, with sales of over 70,000 copies, a record for that country. Essentially about a Serbian soldier reflecting on his experiences while lying critically wounded in a trench, the novel surprisingly—in view of its authorship—raises questions about the sacrifices made during the war in Bosnia. It is for that reason that some have characterized the book as philosophical in nature and have compared it to Albert Camus's *The Plague.* But if Ulemek adopts a philosophical stance in Iron Trench, the hostile anti-Muslim tone of the work leaves no doubt as to its author's true sympathies.

Widely regarded as the chief architect of the policy of ethnic cleansing in Bosnia, Dr. Radovan Karadžić, the chief spokesman of the Bosnian Serbs and a professional psychiatrist, went into hiding in 1996 to avoid arrest and prosecution. He has still managed to elude the authorities. While underground, Karadžić published three literary works: a children's book, a selection of his poetry, and a play. But his most enthusiastically greeted work to date is the novel *Čudesna hronika noći* (The Miraculous Chronicle of the Night), which was launched at the Belgrade Book Fair in October 2004. The book is mostly autobiographical. In roughly the first half, Karadžić describes his life in Sarajevo until the beginning of the 1980s. The second half is devoted to the eleven months he spent in prison as a kind of revenge by the Serbian secret police because of his refusal to serve as an informant for them. In the opinion of the well-known Serbian writer and visual artist Momo Kapor (b. 1937), a nationalist like Karadžić and a member of the Committee to Protect the Truth of Radovan Karadžić, "It is equal to the best pages in Serbian literature" (*The New York Times*, Friday, January 21, 2005). Kapor further compares the novel to James Joyce's *Dubliners*.

A native of Sarajevo himself, Kapor lamented the destruction of the city during the Bosnian War and vividly recalled its past in his generally well received "Sarajevo trilogy": *Poslednji let za Sarajevo* (The Last Flight for Sarajevo, 1995), a picaresque tale of sorts built around the adventures of a Yugoslav Airlines steward named Slobodan ("Bob") Despot; *Hronika izgubljenog grada* (Chronicle of a Lost City, 1997), a personal reminiscence of life and culture in Sarajevo before its destruction; and *Čuvar adrese* (The Address Guard, 2000). The war theme is also paramount in Kapor's collection of stories *Smrt ne boli: Priče iz poslednjeg rata* (Death Doesn't Hurt: Stories from the Last War, 1997) and in his *Lep dan za umiranje* (A Lovely Day to Die, 1999), which deals specifically with the seventy-eight-day NATO bombing of Belgrade.

Before its implosion, the Socialist Federal Republic of Yugoslavia was a state of considerable geopolitical importance. It was also widely respected as a model of a communist government that was both economically and politically liberal. But it took only a decade after Tito's death to reveal the extreme fragility of Yugoslav federalism and the multiethnic and multireligious harmony portrayed in the microcosm of pre–Balkan War Sarajevo in the tales of Isak Samokovlija (1889–1955). The old South Slavic tribalism that was thought to be a thing of the past burst to the surface with appalling ferocity and before long engulfed Yugoslavia in some of the worst fighting and atrocities of the blood-soaked twentieth century. The guns are silent now; the diplomats and politicians have taken over. Ethnic and religious separation has become the means of conflict resolution. But the end to the sad story of Yugoslavia has not yet been written. Six small, and weak, independent states—Bosnia-Herzegovina, Croatia, Macedonia, Montenegro, Serbia, and Slovenia—have taken the place of the former Socialist Federal Republic of Yugoslavia. But the festering issue of the status of Kosovo still remains to be resolved. In part now a plaything of international politics, the region faces a future that is anything but clear, and the potential for more tribal conflict cannot be ruled out.

10

Glimpses of the Other World

America Through Eastern European Eyes

Once the drumbeat of vilification of the West, and the United States in particular, began with the Cold War in the early 1950s, trips to the West became exceptionally difficult for Eastern Europeans. Because of their status in society, artists and intellectuals, who were expected to fall in step with the official party line, faced even higher hurdles. As the dust settled from such tumultuous events as the passing of Stalin in 1953, the revolution in Hungary in 1956, and the Warsaw Pact invasion of Czechoslovakia in 1968, domestic policies ameliorated in Eastern Europe. Travel to the West became easier, and there was no shortage of writers anxious to take advantage of the opportunity to finally glimpse the other side of world. They traveled beyond the Berlin Wall for a variety of reasons: to participate in conferences; to give readings; to attend international PEN meetings; to accept invitations to lecture at universities, and so on.

Probably the most important vehicle by which Eastern European writers were able to come to the United States was the International Writing Program initiated by the University of Iowa. This impressive cultural initiative was officially launched in 1967 and by now has brought well more than a thousand foreign writers to Iowa, including a number of Eastern Europeans.

Romanians

Where this chapter begins is fairly unimportant; most of the literatures of Eastern Europe are represented to one extent or another. But if there could be an ideal point of departure, it might well be the poem "Occidentul" (The West," 1990) by Mircea Cărtărescu, the leading figure of Romanian postmodernism and one of the freshest voices in Romanian literature since the end of World War II. The impact on Cărtărescu of the West, and of the United States in particular, was huge—greater than what he expected it to be—and what he writes about it in his typically long narrative poem (which has been slightly shortened here) could be extrapolated to any number of other Eastern European writers as well:

The West stuffed my mouth full.
I saw New York and Paris, San Francisco and Frankfurt,
I was places I never even dreamt of going.
I returned with a heap of photos
and with death in my chest.
I believed that I meant something and that my life meant
something. . . .
Oh, my world no longer exists!
my world no longer exists!
my wretched world, in which I counted for something. . . .
I now see how limited my horizons
and the horizons of literature
since I saw the Sears Tower
and from the Sears Tower, way up, I saw Chicago,
bathed in mist . . .
What would I be there? A delighted man, happy
to the point of madness
but one whose life is ending
with his definitely screwed up life like the worm in the kirsch bottle . . .
I saw men for whom the law on abortions
is more important than the breakup of the Soviet Union . . .
I saw San Francisco, the blue gulf with ships
and farther out the ocean with forested islands
in the Pacific, if you can imagine that! . . .
I can't find my place in life, I'm no longer from here
and can't be from there
But poetry? I feel like the last Mohican
laughable like Denver the Dinosaur
The best poetry is the poetry that's bearable
only bearable, otherwise nothing.
For ten long years we created good poetry
without realizing how bad the poetry really was. . . .
The West opened my eyes . . .
I leave other things behind that until today were my life,
Along with other beliefs, in which I believed,
together with other loves that I loved.
I can no more,
I can no more, I can no more. . . .[1]

Other Romanian literary visitors to the United States preceded and followed
Cărtărescu, and some wrote of their impressions, though none quite as compel-
lingly. The novelist Alexandru Ivasiuc (1933–1977), together with his wife,
the journalist Tita Chiuper-Ivasiuc, participated in the University of Iowa's
International Writing Program in 1968 on a grant from the Ford Foundation.

While in the United States, Ivasiuc gave lectures on Romanian literature at Columbia University and at the University of California at Berkeley. On his way back to Romania, he stopped in Great Britain, where he lectured at Oxford University. The novelist Ştefan Bănulescu (b. 1926) came to the Iowa program in 1971, remaining for one year. He was followed there a year later by the poet Ana Blandiana and her husband, Romulus Rusan. They stayed in Iowa from December 1973 to May 1974, then went on an extended bus tour of the United States.

Of subsequent Romanian writers who visited the United States, two in particular, Liliana Ursu and Daniela Crăsnaru, both well-known poets, were moved enough by their experiences to find inspiration in them for some of their poetry. Ursu has a more than passing familiarity with the United States and American culture. She has held two Fulbright grants to teach Romanian language and literature at Pennsylvania State University, and has also taught creative writing at the University of Louisville, Kentucky. In 2003 she was named Poet-in-Residence at the Stadler Center for Poetry at Bucknell University. Her six books of translations include many poems by American and English poets. Demonstrating her knowledge of American poetry, she alludes on several occasions to Randall Jarrell, John Berryman, and Sylvia Plath, and has also written a memoriam to Ezra Pound. In order to contribute to a better appreciation of Romanian literature in the English-speaking world, Ursu has translated several Romanian writers into English for her anthology *Fifteen Young Romanian Poets: An Anthology of Verse* (1982). She has also collaborated with the American poet Tess Gallagher on translations of some of her own poems from Romanian into English.

Although she has not dedicated any single collection of poetry to Americana as such, Ursu has included several poems drawn from her American experiences in her nearly one dozen volumes of published poetry. In several of these the emphasis falls heavily on the unsettling sense of immense distance separating her from her homeland and on the peculiar loss of identity she seems to experience in a new land so far from home. She has also written on the emotional baggage of a writer coming from Eastern Europe to the New World, as in the poem "Am aura tristă a celor care vin din Europa de Est" ("I Have the Sad Aura of People from Eastern Europe"), from the post-Ceauşescu *Angel Riding a Beast:* "I have the sad aura of people from Eastern Europe / as if from some kind of Inferno. / I don't know / how much of me has survived. . . . / Our nights were stolen, / standing in queues for meat, / or for butter or milk, / or cooking until dawn / because when morning arrived, / as if by bad magic, / the fire in the stove had turned to stone. / During the day we walk like schizophrenics / through this world that seems / more and more like a mental hospital / because we thought one thing, / but said another. . . . / From home / all the letters I get / have the same stamp: / the crucifixion of our Lord Jesus Christ."[2] Another poem, "Spălarea inimii sau Europa de vănzare" ("Washing Out the Heart; or, Europe for Sale"), was inspired by her experiences as a teacher of Romanian to

American students, some of them of Romanian origin: "The dice were thrown, but I couldn't see how they turned up. / NOROC [Good Luck] was the first word I wrote on the board for my students / who study Romanian with me, / these kids who remake the voyage of Columbus in reverse order / sailing toward their ancestors, traveling on the ark of a Latin language / they journey, without knowing, toward my Transylvania, / a California of the old world" (25).

The literary fruit of Daniela Crăsnaru's sojourn at the University of Iowa's International Writing Program was a small collection of seven poems on American themes, written originally in English in 1993 and grouped under the heading "Seven Illusory Contours of America." As evidenced in texts by other Eastern European writers who spent time in the United States, her experience of America brought forth memories of the past. In the case of "A Fairy Tale" this meant the recollection of the deportation to the desolate Bărăgan Plain of her grandparents, who were considered "rich exploiters" because they owned two cows and a ewe. Remembering how her grandmother would often repeat the hopeful phrase "The Americans will come to rescue us someday," heard often throughout Eastern Europe in the darkest days of communism, Crăsnaru closes the poem with the somber words "The Americans did not come," which she likens to the bursting of the classic fairy tale of "Little Red Riding Hood."[3]

Another poem, "Retirement Building; or, Vanilla Death," recalls the time in Iowa when Crăsnaru and other participants in the writing program were temporarily housed in the Walden Place retirement community because of the floods that swept Iowa City in 1993. The pastel colors all around in the building, and the large figures of cats and dogs in the lobby, only served to distract the inhabitants of the home from the inevitability of death. The poem "Grammar" strikes a political note, as Crăsnaru takes as her point of departure the American flag, which seems to flutter everywhere, and connects it to the war in Vietnam and the fighting in Somalia and Kuwait. The lure of American democracy is expressed in "The Streets of Philadelphia" and "Western People, Eastern Creatures." Crăsnaru tries to come to grips with it, to understand it, but the embrace is not immediate, as she acknowledges in "The Streets of Philadelphia": "And I, striving to translate into Romanian, / without success, / that cardinal point from the most democratic / declaration of principles in the world. / Trying to understand what it is to pursue happiness / simply because one must" (109). "Maybe here life is worth living," she muses in "Western People, Eastern Creatures," which may explain the myriad of health phobias in the United States—"That's why they want to be immortal." But as she is about to lick the stamp on a postcard with a panoramic view of Chicago, she hesitates ("There could be a lot of bacteria"), and then asks: "This new feeling: a shortcut to madness / or a small step toward democracy?" (110). Sad feelings of homelessness, of otherness, even of rejection form the subject of Crăsnaru's last two American poems, "New York, NY" and "Homeless."

Daniela Crăsnaru kept no book of memoirs of her stay in the United States, no diary or journal; she did not make America the subject of a major work of fiction. But her seven poems touchingly capture the complex feelings of an Eastern European trying to fathom the appealing and yet disturbing reality of America.

South Slavs: Slovenes, Serbs, Bulgarians, Macedonians

Although coming from a country much smaller than Romania, Slovenian writers have been especially well represented among the Eastern Europeans who visited the United States for one reason or another. Certainly one of the best known—based on the large body of his poetry available in English translation, his broad range of contacts with American poets, and his extensive readings at American college campuses and elsewhere through the years—is Tomaž Šalamun (b. 1941). Besides his participation in the University of Iowa's International Writing Program in the early 1970s, when he came for two years, he has also held residencies at the writing colonies of Yaddo and McDowell and was the recipient of a Fulbright Fellowship to Columbia University. Šalamun was eventually tapped for government service and in 1996 was named Slovenian cultural attaché in New York. Among his many collections of poems, perhaps the most engaging from the point of view of Šalamun's perceptions of America is the volume *Praznik* (Holiday, 1976), which includes several poems about Yaddo and one on New York ("Prvič, ko sem prišel v New York City," "The First Time I Came to New York").

The novel *Posmehljivo poželenje* (*Mocking Desire*, 1993) by Drago Jančar is a young Slovene's account of the time he spent in New Orleans as the assistant in a creative writing course to a professor at an unspecified university (Tulane?). Arriving in the New World as a dispassionate but sharp-eyed observer of the American scene, the narrator (Gregor Gradnik) soon becomes as if hypnotically drawn into the sensuous and sleazy subculture of New Orleans. Attentive to his duties as the assistant to Professor Fred Baumann, who is hard at work on a study of melancholy, Gregor still has ample time for the hard-drinking and pot-smoking characters he befriends in local bars. Even as he describes, and analyzes, them and their mores against the background of the daily routine of the French Quarter, Gregor finds himself lured by similar temptations. His relationship with a sweetheart back home in Slovenia slowly but surely becomes relegated to a back burner as Gregor's life becomes filled with the sights and sounds of his present reality. Casual sex is as much a part of the scene as drugs and drink, and Gregor is no paragon of virtue. Yet as he becomes enmeshed in the coils of New Orleans bohemia, he remains ever alert to the ironies he observes all around him and the cultural differences between the tiny Slovenia he has temporarily left behind, and periodically misses, and the gigantic United States. The considerable appeal of Jančar's book lies in the author's narrative skill, his shrewdness of observation and character portrayals, and his humor.

The poet Boris A. Novak (b. 1953), a Belgrade native who studied literature and philosophy in Ljubljana, was president of the Slovenian PEN Club from

1991 to 1996 and, after January 1994, worked with the Peace Committee of the International PEN, organizing assistance for exiles from the former Yugoslavia as well as for writers from besieged Sarajevo. During the summer of 1991 he was a visiting lecturer on poetry at the University of Tennessee (Chattanooga) for one semester. He published over three dozen books from 1977 to 1999, among them ten collections of poetry for adult readers, including a volume of translations and adaptations of Provençal sonnets and ballads. One of the best known of his books is the bilingual Slovene-English edition, *Vrtnar tišine / Gardener of Silence* (1990).

Andrej Blatnik (b. 1963), an impressive contemporary Slovenian writer, is another "alumnus" of the University of Iowa's International Writing Program. Known primarily for his 1990 novel *Menjave kož* (*Skinswaps*), he is also the author of a second novel, *Tao ljubezni* (The Tao of Love, 1996), and a book of essays about everyday culture, *Gledanje cez ramo* (Looking Over the Shoulder, 1996). In 2000 Blatnik published a collection of sixteen mostly first-person short narratives based on his stay in the United States. The collection is titled *Zakon želje* (The Law of Desire) and deals primarily with a subject dear to Blatnik's heart, male-female relations. Before coming to the United States in 1993 as the recipient of a Fulbright Fellowship that enabled him to participate in the Iowa program, Blatnik also visited Japan in 1987 on a Japanese government grant. His impressions and observations from that trip are also reflected in his writings, but are less substantive than those related to America. In 2001 Blatnik published the book *Papirnati labirinti* (Imaginary Labyrinths), subtitled *Vodič za autostopere po američkoj metafikciji i njezinoj okolici* (A Guide to Autostops Through American Metafiction and Its Neighborhood); it had originally appeared in 1994 under a slightly different title. Essentially a study of American prose from Mark Twain to Nicholson Baker's *Vox* (1992), the publication also includes brief summaries of the novels discussed in the main body of the text.

Other writers from the former Yugoslavia able to spend time in and write about the United States include the Serbs David Albahari, Nina Živančević (b. 1957), and Vladimir Pištalo (b. 1960). A worthy representative of Yugoslav postmodernism, Albahari has long had a serious interest in Anglo-American literature, as attested by his translations from English. A well-traveled writer who has spent time in the United States, Albahari resettled in Canada in 1994 in the wake of the Yugoslav wars. His novel *Mamac* (*Bait,* 1996) has a western Canadian setting and reflects his own experiences as a recent immigrant.

Albahari's novel *Cink* (Tsink) was published in English translation (by Albahari himself) under the title *Tsing*. This fairly small work of just under a hundred pages, dealing in part with Albahari's impressions of America based on an earlier trip, had originally been published in 1988. But *Tsing* is anything but a linear narrative of an American sojourn. Deeply interested for much of his career in matters of language and narrative, Albahari has brought several layers of narration together in *Tsing*. One consists of italicized sections of a novel-within-a-novel about a father-daughter relationship that constitutes the fictive part of *Tsing* as whole. This imagined father-child tale dovetails with the principal narrative thrust of the novel, which is a personal reflection of his own relationship with his beloved father very near the end of his life. In a sense, *Tsing* is an homage to Albahari's father. Much of this is recollection undertaken by Albahari during a stay at the University of Iowa's International Writing Program and in other locations during his travel in the United States, especially the Southwest.

When not engaged in such recollection, Albahari ponders the impact on himself of the immensity of America. He was, he recalls, lonely in America, at times unbearably so. But contradiction, like paradox, is no stranger to Albahari. Later in *Tsing* he speaks of his fondness for big cities, recalling that someone once noted that metropolises are necropolises, "for they offer the safety and certainty of disappearance: you become nobody, you don't exist, you're not there." The imagined/reality dichotomy also shapes his attitude toward America:

> I realized then why I could never establish a true relationship with America: I recognized in everything the repetition of movie scenes. The waitress looked like a waitress from a movie with Jack Nicholson, the town I lived in for several months was the town I had already seen in dozens of motion pictures. I walked, as it were, through movie sets . . . , and there was not a single moment that was really and truly mine, I was a copy of a copy; in the best of circumstances, a reflection in the mirror, unreality in the sea of imagined reality.[4]

But Albahari was no consistently somber traveler in time and space. He makes clear that he is strongly attracted to women, and he recalls his six-day fling with a Navajo woman named Alice in a hotel high above the Grand Canyon. Throughout *Tsing,* images of Albahari's father intrude on other thoughts, whether erotic or grotesque, as, for example, in his recollection of an experience in Arizona:

> I heeded the advice of a student tourist guidebook and in Tuba City, at a restaurant called "The Truck Stop," I had "the best taco in the world," the traditional dish of the Navajo Indians and Mexicans. While I was eating, a drunk Indian vomited in the toilet. He reminded me of my father. He threw up the same way, with loud moans, as if the vomit was tearing his esophagus, or as if something was being taken away from him that he wanted to keep and had long thought of as his. Despite everything, the taco was excellent. (30)

Whatever else it may be, *Tsing* is in essence a literary parting with a father, a celebration of his life and death.

Nina Živančević came to the United States in 1974 and lived in the country for several years before eventually moving to France. While in the United States she learned English well enough to write original poetry in it, as in the volume *More or Less Urgent* (1988). A decade later, a volume of prose written originally by Živančević in English was brought out under the title *Living on Air Fiction* (1998). Her previous prose work, *Inside and Out of Byzantium* (1994), is in fact a collection of personal reminiscences set in different American and European locales and translated by Živančević herself and others. In 2000 Živančević returned to her native Serbian to write *Prodavci snova* (The Dream Merchants), an account of her trip from New York to Paris before she knew French; the colorful characters she met in Europe, mostly in the arts; and her ill-fated, drug-filled trans-Atlantic romance with her French lover.

Vladimir Pištalo, a native of Sarajevo, came to the United States in 1993 at the invitation of the McDowell writers' colony in New Hampshire. Rather than return to war-torn Bosnia, he remained in America for the purpose of pursuing postgraduate university studies. He subsequently received his M.A. and Ph.D. degrees in European and American history at the University of New Hampshire. On 4 July 2002 he became an American citizen. Best known as a short-story writer, he is the author of such collections as *Slikovnica* (Picture Book, 1981), *Kraj veka* (The End of the World, 1990), *Vitraž u sećanju* (Stained-Glass Memories, 1994) , and *Priče iz celog sveta* (Tales from the Whole World, 1997), as well as the 1987 novella *Korto Malteze* (Corto Maltese).

America as a literary theme crops up first in his collection Stained-Glass Memories. The book is divided into three parts, one of which is titled simply "Amerika" ("America"); it is further subdivided into "Pismo o Tesli, kralju patuljaka" ("Letter About Tesla, the King of Midgets"), "Ljuto" ("Spicy"), "Vidjeni sa Meseca" ("Seen from the Moon"), "Loptanje sa suncem" ("Playing Soccer with the Sun"), "Čovek bez lica" ("The Man Without a Face"), and "Uskrs u Novom svetu" ("Easter in the New World"). These are short pieces of just a few pages, and one of them, "Playing Soccer with the Sun," in fact relates a story about Iceland told to Pištalo by someone else. The others are fairly inconsequential, each encompassing a single episode. One may be worth mentioning: "Letter About Tesla, the King of Midgets" is in the form of a letter to a friend named Mara (probably Mara Miloš, a friend from his days at the Yaddo literary colony). In it he recounts the oddities he finds in the American press as represented by a newspaper with the name *Weekly World News*. Apart from a spate of stories about Bill and Hillary Clinton, he learns that thousands of people send letters every day to God addressed, "Lord God, Jerusalem, Israel," and signed, for example, "Your Friend, Jimmy." He also finds an item about the Yugoslav scientist Nikola Tesla (1856–1943), who taught for a number of years at Columbia University. Tesla is described as "the man who invented the twentieth century." The newspaper, of course, had his name spelled wrong. Recalling Isabel Allende's remark that North American magical realism finds its expression in tabloids just like *Weekly World News,* Pištalo notes that according to the paper the newest research shows that ninety out of a hundred extraterrestrials are dwarfs. No doubt as a form of flattery, the paper situates Tesla among such dwarfs and creatures from another planet. Others, however, will suggest that Tesla is a figure of American magical realism and will place him alongside other mythological beings. The appearance of his short biography among the miracles of this world is no different than the news that God receives letters sent to Jerusalem.[5]

Pištalo's 1997 book, Stories from the Entire World, is a collection of seventeen stories ostensibly dealing with the experiences of émigrés from various countries whom Pištalo apparently met in the United States. Somewhat longer than those in Stained-Glass Memories, the stories are not especially informative about life in America as seen through the immigrant prism, despite their occasional American university settings. For the most part they seem invented primarily for the sake of humor, for which Pištalo has an undeniable talent. In "Vesela nauka" ("Happy Scholarship"), for example, a Brazilian postgraduate student in history at the University of Maine addresses a letter to his adviser, a Professor Viliam Falkoner, asking his support for a grant to enable him to attend an academic conference in Atlanta, Georgia. Apart from the amusing, sometimes bizarre rationale he offers for wanting to attend the Atlanta conference, he also lists among the items for which he needs funding "the icon of political correctness, 'Lifestyles' brand condoms." The rest of the stories—even the longest and the best, "Smrt u Las Vegasu" ("Death in Las Vegas"), with its cast of oddball Yugoslav characters—are much along the same lines.

Bozhidar Bozhilov (b. 1923) and Lilyana Stefanova are among the best-known Bulgarian writers who visited America and wrote about it. A poet, novelist, and playwright, Bozhilov in 1979 published a lighthearted account of his stay in the United States as a participant in the University of Iowa's International Writing Program, under the title *Putnitsite ot "Sivata Hrutka"* (Traveling with Greyhound, 1979).[6] His visit began on 2 September 1975. After describing his initial disorientation at finding himself in so different and in some ways bewildering an environment as the United States, the otherwise well-traveled Bozhilov then proceeds to describe his subsequent American experiences in a series of both short and long individually titled narratives. His style throughout is casual, with a fair amount of reconstructed dialogue, and his intent is clearly not to provide either a diary or a linear account. Instead, his focus is on the offbeat and entertaining. Thus in one section he delves into the linguistic origins of the title of the newspaper *The Des Moines Register;* in another he notes his reactions to a large outdoor exhibition of student sculpture mounted in the center of Iowa City and called "The Naked Drum." But the bulk of Traveling with Greyhound is, in fact, devoted to his travels through such states as California and Florida via Greyhound.

Stefanova, a globe-trotting poet and the author of several books about her experiences in the former Soviet Union, Japan, and Mexico, also wrote a book about America, *Edna esen v Amerike* (One Fall in America, 1964; it was republished in 1979 in a single volume together with her Mexican travel book *Vulkanite na Meksiko dimyat* [The Volcanoes of Mexico Are Smoking]). In 1980 she returned to the United States in order to participate in the University of Iowa's International Writing Program. One Fall in America is a casual account, like most such books, of her travels through the United States as a member of the Kutev (or Koutev) Bulgarian National Ensemble, a song and dance folklore troupe. The company started its tour in New York and then set forth in two buses to perform in a number of other American cities. She mentions her meetings in New York with, for example, a youngish-looking Professor Bill Harkins of the Columbia University Department of Slavic Languages, with whom she enjoyed talking about Slavic folklore and Soviet literature. Once on the road, Stefanova occasionally provides her readers with descriptions of the cities she visits as well as some historical information about them—for example, about Springfield, Illinois, and Abraham Lincoln.

Performances of the Bulgarian National Ensemble seem to have been eminently successful and Stefanova dutifully notes the warm reception they received. This was to be expected. But what clearly emerges from One Fall in America is Stefanova's keen interest in describing meetings with old and newer Bulgarian residents of the United States whom she encounters at practically every performance of the troupe. There are people who have been in the United States for many years, have forgotten how to speak Bulgarian, but harbor nostalgia for the old country. And there are newer immigrants who ask about relatives they had to leave behind and their chances of being able to return to communist Bulgaria to visit them. A few confide in her the political nature of their departure and offer excuses for it. In many cases, particularly with older immigrants, Stefanova feels compelled to note the considerable economic and social progress Bulgaria has made since the end of World War II.

If she does not come across as a political hack by dwelling on negative aspects of life in America, she also does not stray far from the official line. As one might perhaps expect, given the time frame of her first American journey, she draws attention, for example, to the plight of the blacks in the United States in the sections of her book dealing with Kansas City and especially New Orleans. Here is how she describes her initial impressions on entering the black section of Kansas City:

> Old dingy single-story houses with narrow windows and gloomy entryways. Filthy yards, where a yellowing tuft of grass peers out here and there between rusty tin cans and rags. Children, just black kids, in stiff cowboy pants and cheap shirts. Frail negresses stretching out colored laundry. The movements of black-skinned people expressing depression and humiliation, sorrow and servitude.[7]

The full reality of racism and segregation hit her the hardest, however, during her stay in New Orleans, her account of which takes on an indignant, accusatory tone as she recites the many striking contrasts between the living conditions of blacks and whites. But as she recalls the heroism of the three young men who went to Mississippi to register black voters and were murdered by the Ku Klux Klan, and the immense following inspired by Martin Luther King Jr., she expresses belief in the inevitability of change.

Another prominent feature of Stefanova's One Fall in America is her strong Bulgarian national pride. Rarely does she miss an opportunity to extol the virtues of the "new" Bulgaria. She is especially hard on Bulgarians who have made money in the United States or Canada and have turned their backs in shame on their motherland. Here and there Stefanova also genuflects in the direction of Engels, doubtless regarding this as perhaps less obvious political pandering than citations from the writings of Lenin. Finding herself in Chicago on May Day, together with a fellow Bulgarian, "an old Chicago worker," she recalls the first May Day in 1886 and declares: "The streets of Chicago speak with the angry voice of tens of thousands of workers. Mills, factories, workshops, offices—are silent. It is awesome when the working class expresses its mind! Then the skyscrapers of New York will tremble; the industrial giants of Philadelphia, Detroit, Baltimore, St. Louis, Milwaukee will shudder . . . This universal, overwhelming strike, that battle for the eight-hour work day, that May First assault Engels calls 'one of the most remarkable events of the year 1886'" (113).

Stefanova's pride in Bulgaria was reaffirmed in other ways as well. In one of the more surprising sections of her book, she recalls an encounter with several middle-aged American "progressives"—teachers in a local college—who approached her after the Bulgarians' concert. Apart from their obvious contempt for racism and segregation, she was especially struck by the words of the eldest of the group: "I have known and loved you for some time. I have read books by Georgi Dimitrov. And his speech in Leipzig. A great Bulgarian. A great communist. Missus, comrade, you have no idea how fortunate you are. You just don't know!" (229). Politeness would surely have brought forth expressions of esteem for the Bulgarian people and their folk arts. For Stefanova, this comment translates into "deep respect for socialist Bulgaria," as if admiration for the political system in Bulgaria had indeed been intended. Although it may seem dubious that the Bulgarian Communist Party boss Georgi Dimitrov would have his American admirers, it is not out of the question, in view of his stunning defense at the Leipzig trial of those implicated in the Reichstag fire in Berlin in 1933. The speech, which won Dimitrov his freedom, was hailed around the world.

The propagandistic dimension of One Fall in America becomes more pronounced in the sections after Stefanova returns to New York, some of which are devoted to a visit to the editorial office of the Communist Party newspaper *The Worker,* where she meets the editor in chief, James Jackson, and a followup rendezvous with Jackson at which they discuss the situation of the blacks in America, the American "progressive" movement, American literature, Cuba, and the Korean and Vietnam wars. On the way to their next stop, Montreal, the Bulgarians learn about the assassination of President John F. Kennedy and the subsequent arrest of Lee Harvey Oswald. When more information comes their way about Oswald's background—his Russian wife, his stays in the Soviet Union and Cuba—they fear a severe anticommunist reaction that could possibly bring a halt to their tour. But after the American Department of State announces that there are no links between Oswald and any foreign powers, they are reassured that their performances will continue as scheduled. As they prepare to return to Bulgaria after their final Canadian appearance, they bid their final goodbyes to their American tour conductors and new Canadian friends and are told how truly successful the entire tour by the Bulgarian National Ensemble had been.

Two major Macedonian writers who published accounts of their travels in the United States, Meto Jovanovski (b. 1928) and Bogomil Gjuzel (b. 1939), were both affiliated with the University of Iowa's International Writing Program. Gjuzel's visit was the earlier of the two. An important post–World War II poet, Gjuzel was a writer-in-residence at the University of Iowa in the academic year 1972/1973. He came to Iowa with a good knowledge of English; he had majored in English language and literature at the university in Skopje from which he graduated in 1963, and he had also spent the academic year 1964/1965 at Edinburgh University on a British Council stipend. Known primarily for poems and tales with Macedonian themes and others inspired by ancient Macedonian myths and legends, he was also the author of the travel book *Kuća cel svet* (Home Is the Whole World, 1974) as well as one poem inspired by the flood he witnessed in Iowa, "Flood at the International Writers' Workshop." Jovanovski came to Iowa for the academic year 1979/1980 as an Honorary Fellow in Writing and later published an informal and rather entertaining account of his travels in the United States (as well as in Europe and Israel) under the title *Kluchevite na Manhatan: Zapisi od zapadnite predeli* (The Keys to Manhattan: Notes from Western Lands, 1983).

Gjuzel's Home Is the Whole World, as published in book form in 1974, also incorporates a previously serialized account of his trip to Ireland in the mid-1960s, *Moeto pateshestvie vo Irska* (My Journey to Ireland). It is considerably shorter than the part of the book devoted to the United States, which consists mainly of an account of his travels across the country by Greyhound bus, a means of transportation that both was cheap and offered more scenic possibilities. Having finished five and a half months in Iowa City, Gjuzel was off on his trip. After boarding the bus in Des Moines, he headed west to Salt Lake City and then California. With good reason, Gjuzel titled the California section of his travel book "Poets, Friends, and Acquaintances." Witty and urbane, he made friends easily and already had contacts in America he was anxious to renew—American poets he had met at the annual Struga (Macedonia) Poetry Festivals. San Francisco (which he refers to usually as "Frisco") was an obvious destination. He lost no time in getting together with the city's literary luminaries, but was disappointed at not being able to meet the Beat poet Lawrence Ferlinghetti at his famous City Lights bookshop. From San Francisco he went to nearby Berkeley, the West Coast's intellectual Mecca at the time, where he was soon in the company of the winner of the 1984 Pulitzer Prize for Poetry, Caroline Kizer (b. 1925), and her outspoken and quirky daughter Ashley, with whom he spent many hours in conversation. It was also on this leg of his trip that Gjuzel met the American "cult" poet of the esoteric and occult, Robey Edward Duncan (1919–1988), as well as the politically radical poet Denise Levertov (1923–1997), then a teacher at Stanford University, who was well known for her outspoken exploration of female spirituality and sexuality.

From California, Gjuzel visited Las Vegas, Flagstaff (Arizona), and the Grand Canyon, then went on to Albuquerque (oddly missing Santa Fe and Taos). His next ports of call were Dallas—where he paused to ruminate on the assassination of President John F. Kennedy—New Orleans, Miami Beach, Atlanta, Chapel Hill (North Carolina), and Washington, D.C., where he met Milne Holton, a professor of literature at the University of Maryland and a translator of Macedonian literature. From the Washington, D.C., area, he headed north to Boston, Buffalo, and Toronto. After that it was back to Iowa, where he pursued his friendship with Paul Engel, the head of the International Writing Program at the university, and his Taiwanese wife. In New York, near the end of his stay in America, Gjuzel also made the acquaintance of the highly regarded poet Louis Simpson (b. 1923), the winner of the Pulitzer Prize for Poetry in 1964, who was affiliated at the time with the State University of New York at Stony Brook, Long Island. He also became friends with that prodigious translator of Yugoslav literature, the poet Charles Simić, who later wrote the introduction to P. H. Liotta's translation of Gjuzel's poetic cycle *Wolf at the Door.*

Jovanovski's The Keys to Manhattan, in the edition published in 1983, comprises three separate multipart sections, whose chronology suggests that the original account of his trip to America under the sponsorship of the University of Iowa ("The Keys to Manhattan") was written in early 1977. This is the kernel of Jovanovski's book and the source of the title of the 1983 edition. The other sections were added in 1980 and 1982. Those from 1980 comprise an account of his travels from Western Europe back to Skopje, and cover such things as an international PEN conference in Stockholm; travels in the American Southwest accompanied by American friends; relations with his black girlfriend, Fatima, who sees him through a period of illness and then departs, forever, to New York; encounters with fellow passengers on airplanes, and his lecture on Macedonian literature before students in his friend Sam's class at the University of Oregon in Portland. The episodes from 1982 are devoted to his Iowa friend Polly's thoughts on revolution and the turbulent 1960s; conversations with American friends centered mostly on music; and Jovanovski's experiences in Israel on a trip to the Middle East. Thus, although the point of departure was Jovanovski's invitation to the University of Iowa, the Iowa experiences form only a small part of The Keys to Manhattan, as they do also in Gjuzel's Home Is the Whole World. Jovanovski's book is primarily a collection of disparate episodes from his extensive travels, narrated in a breezy style and with a heavy emphasis on dialogue. His sense of humor is especially evident in those places where he recalls conversations with naive Americans about Yugoslavia and Macedonia—as for example on a flight from Denver to Portland, Oregon, when his neighbor has trouble understanding how Jovanovski could be from two states at the same time, never mind his owning up to being a communist.

One can only be impressed with how well-connected Jovanovski was socially, even more so perhaps than Gjuzel. It seems that wherever he traveled, friends were there waiting for him, many of them Americans. If lacking in any real cultural or intellectual content, Jovanovski's The Keys to Manhattan makes for lively reading, very much the kind of work one might expect from a world traveler who knows his way around, makes friends easily, and excels as a raconteur. Since The Keys to Manhattan is unavailable in English, acquaintance with Jovanovski would have to rest on such works of his available in translation as the novel *Budaletinki* (Simpletons, 1973; translated as *Cousins*) and *Faceless Men, and Other Macedonian Stories* (1992). Jovanovski can also be seen as a film actor in the ambitious Macedonian film *The Great Water* (1994), directed by Ivo Trajkov.

Poles and Czechs

Polish writers have been among the most prolific on the subject of America. One of the earliest to come to the United States in the postwar period and to write about it was Lenta Główczewska. But Główczewska is actually not representative of those Eastern European writers who came to America for one or various reasons, traveled in the country, were perhaps affiliated with an international literary program, and subsequently returned home and wrote about their experiences.

Lenta Główczewska was an art historian who moved to the United States in 1962. She studied English at the University of North Carolina in Raleigh and subsequently moved to New York. From 1983 to 2002 she published a regular series of reportage about Manhattan for the Polish journal *Zeszyty Literackie*. Dealing with aspects of life in the metropolis, especially its vibrant artistic and cultural scene, the articles are on average about six pages long. The last, dated "Winter 2002," is titled "Po 11 września 2001" ("After 9/11, 2001"). Główczewska's highly readable contributions to *Zeszyty Literackie*, the first of which—dated 1983–1984, and dealing with the reopening of the newly renovated Museum of Modern Art—were published in book form in 2004 under the title *Nowy Jork: Kartki z metropolii 1983–2002* (New York: Postcards from the Metropolis, 1983–2002), with a preface by the Polish poet Julia Hartwig.

More typical, and among the earliest of the postwar Polish writers who wrote about America based on their own experiences, was the very talented but ill-fated Halina Poświatowska. She remained in America for close to three years, from August 1958 to July 1961. Suffering from a serious heart ailment, Poświatowska came for an operation, following which she underwent a long convalescence in the Deborah Heart Foundation sanatorium. As her recovery progressed, Poświatowska took advantage of the free time on her hands to study English, to become more familiar with the new world she had now become a part of, and, finally, to earn a college degree. While staying with relatives in New Jersey, and as her health improved, she began exploring New York City and became fascinated with the area around Columbia University. She enrolled for a course in English there in the summer of 1959. By the time the summer was over, Poświatowska had received affirmative answers from three of the several colleges and universities she had applied to seeking admission with financial aid. One of these was Smith College, in Northampton, Massachusetts. Enthusiastic about the all-women's college on the advice of friends and relatives, she began her studies there on 24 September 1959. When she returned to Poland nearly three years later, she held a degree from an American college.

Although life at Smith started out pleasantly enough, before long Poświatowska came to regard her residence there as oppressive, a period of confinement she compared to life in a sanatorium. She was one of thirty foreign students at Smith at the time who felt themselves a breed apart and were often lonely. Nevertheless, Poświatowska did make friends, and describes warmly her relations with a Japanese girl and a trip to Florida by car with fellow Smith students. Poświatowska's competence in English also troubled her. She worked intensely at the language, but never reached the level of fluency she sought. Whenever she could, she fled to New York, where she felt more at home and in the vicinity of which she had relatives she could fall back on for support.

Poświatowska's sojourn in the United States in general was a mixed blessing. She satisfied her curiosity about American life and about New York City, which had long fascinated her. But despite a few, ultimately unsatisfying, romantic liaisons—including one with a married visiting professor of philosophy one summer while studying at Columbia—she was never quite at ease in America. Her academic experiences were only fitfully gratifying, and her social life was not wholly a success. She seemed to be able to relate easily to people, but at times felt awkward trying to deal with the demographic complexities of American life. Once back in her own country, she completed her studies in Kraków in 1963 and the following year became an assistant in the Department of the Philosophy of Natural Sciences at the Jagiellonian University. But her heart condition worsened and in 1967 she passed away.

Before her death, the sensitive and gifted young woman had managed to write several poems on American subjects as well as a two-hundred-page prose narrative based on her nearly three years in the United States. The autobiographical work, *Opowieść dla przyjaciela* (Tale for a Friend), was originally published in 1998 in the third volume of Poświatowska's collected works, and in 2000 as a separate book. The male addressee of Tale for a Friend remains a mystery and may be no more than a literary device to engage the reader directly. There are references to her husband, Adolf Poświatowski, a student at the Łódź Institute of Theater and Film who died years before the book appeared in print, and to another male admirer (unfortunately a married man with a family) with whom she fell in love in yet another sanatorium. Whoever the addressee, Tale for a Friend is compelling reading. Written simply, in confessional style, Poświatowska pours out her innermost feelings and thoughts as she recalls the history of her heart problems, her many hospital visits, her stays in various sanatoria, the support of her immediate family, her decision to travel to the Philadelphia area for heart surgery, her convalescence afterward in the Deborah sanatorium in New Jersey, her struggle to learn English, and the postoperative events in her life.

She is candid but not self-pitying throughout the work, as in her account of the foredoomed relationship with her husband, who was also suffering from a serious heart condition when the two met in the fall of 1953 in the sanatorium in Kudów, Poland. Despite the strenuous objections of her family and doctors, Halina accepted Poświatowski's proposal of marriage. As their conditions steadily worsened, the couple contemplated suicide together. But fate decreed otherwise. Adolf died of a heart attack in a hotel room in the spring of 1956, less than three years after they were married. Halina outlived her husband by eleven years.

After Poświatowska's works with American settings, a decade or more was to elapse before the appearance of the diaries spanning the years 1978–1985 by Kazimierz Brandys. Bearing the common title *Miesiące* (Months), the diaries were published in four volumes by the Instytut Literacki in Paris. Collectively, they represent, as we have seen, a highly valuable resource for anyone interested in Polish and Polish émigré politics and culture in the period of the late 1970s through the late 1980s. Although he had visited the United States on a previous occasion, his main stay in the country occurred in 1982/1983, when he was invited by Columbia University as writer-in-residence for that academic year. Brandys was to teach a lecture course on Polish literature, in Polish, something he had specified. He arrived in September 1982 and left after the spring semester in 1983.

On the whole, the account of his affiliation with Columbia in the third book of Months is not very expansive. He seems to have enjoyed his contact with students, of whom he had a good opinion, but he says little else about life at the university—limited undoubtedly by his less-than-fluent English—apart from his comfortable residence in Butler Hall. He looked up Polish friends in the New York area, and managed to take in some of the city's vibrant cultural life. Like other visitors to New York, he could not help but record his impressions of Harlem, which he stumbled upon by mistake. But his remarks reflect the abysmal fear of the black man not uncommon among Europeans and especially among Eastern Europeans, whose encounters with blacks were historically rarer. As he recalls at one point:

> I got onto the wrong bus and rode into the very center of Harlem. Black men in hats were sitting on benches in front of houses, while here and there groups of black youths were shuffling about. The bus was taking me ever farther away from home. I get up and approach the driver. I mention my address and ask him where I have to get off. . . . Don't get off now; I'll show you a stop where you can transfer. *A long way* . . . I withdraw, sit down in my former seat as we pass empty, littered squares. Wasn't it here that Professor Freidman, who had decided to visit Harlem, was stabbed? I feel out of place. The bus is quiet. The blacks don't look at me, but I know they sense my unease. Although they appear to be looking straight ahead, I'm certain that out of the corner of their eyes they see and avert their gaze from this white spot, the only one in the entire bus. I am

alone among their bronze, desert faces, like a chicken in a lions' cage. . . . The black driver calls me over and points out something with a finger. I see a subway station. The bus stops. I get out, and run. I run with my cane, fall into a crowded tunnel, and suddenly—again a lion's cage. No, an iron box, brown, a shout, a crush of people, just black faces with gleaming teeth and the whites of their eyes, and me in the midst of them, pressed in from all sides. . . . A strange feeling. For the first time in my life I experienced the fear of a white man for the future of the white race.[8]

After Poświatowska, the most prominent Polish women poets to write about America were Julia Hartwig, Ewa Lipska, Anna Czekanowicz, and Marzena Broda. Hartwig published two books of poems inspired by her stays in the United States from 1971 to 1974 and again from 1979 to 1982. They are both titled *Americana*. The poems in both volumes tend to consist of fleeting poetic impressions, mostly of observed landscapes, and are permeated with a sense of melancholy. Some of the poems focus on a single human figure enveloped in the aura of Americana like a Norman Rockwell painting. Hence Mr. Robert Knox, who preferred to close his Alabama restaurant rather than yield to the new law of desegregation and became so popular that he went on to become governor of the state. He has since opened a new, desegregated restaurant, where he regularly entertains his customers by whistling the melody "Alabama Jubilee" through a megaphone to the accompaniment of an old pianola ("Pianola pana Knoxa," "Mr. Knox's Pianola"); and the Norwegian-born Mr. Petersen, who never married, never attended church although he read the Bible and was religious, and who after his death left thirty thousand dollars to an old-age home in his native town of Gol, the annual interest from which was to be used for the purchase of wine for the residents of the home, "despite the fact that he himself drank only rhubarb wine / and from time to time a can of beer" ("Wino pana Petersena," "Mr. Petersen's Wine"). In the short concluding poem to her second *Americana* volume, Hartwig simply but eloquently expresses the dream/reality dichotomy of her American experiences: "I used to see these cities in dreams / San Francisco and New Orleans / Later on, I saw them with my own eyes / However, in my dreams the same landscapes as before return / mocking what I experienced as well as my four senses."[9]

Hartwig has also published travel diaries, including, for example, *Dziennik amerykański* (American Diary, 1980) and *Zawsze powroty: Dzienniki podróży* (Always Returns: Travel Diaries, 2001). Unlike her earlier American Diary, Hartwig's Always Returns deals mostly with her stays in Paris from 2 January 1986 to 7 November 1986, from 4 October 1987 to 4 November 1987, and from 6 November 1988 to 27 September 1992. After her first stay in Paris, Hartwig flew to the United States, where she remained for less than a month, returning to Europe on 28 November 1986. Although she and her husband, the writer and critic Artur Międzyrzecki, visited their daughter Daniela and son-in-law Keith, who had been living in New York for several years, the principal reason for the trip to the United States at this time was to spend a few weeks in Iowa City.

This was not Hartwig's first visit to Iowa. In 1970 she had been a participant in the University of Iowa's International Writing Program. In her preface to her *Always Returns*, Hartwig mentions other Polish writers who had preceded or followed her into the Iowa program, among them Julian Stryjkowski, Jan Józef Szczepański, Zbigniew Bieńkowski, Andrzej Kijowski, Marek Nowakowski, Marek Skwarnicki, Janusz Głowacki, and Adrianna Szymańska. Kijowski, Skwarnicki, Szczepański, and Szymańska also contributed to the impressive Iowa-based writings of the Polish literary visitors. Hartwig's remarks on her fairly short stay in the United States in November 1986 appear on pages 203–226 of *Always Returns*. But she was busier in Iowa than she expected, mainly because of a lecture on Apollinaire that she was asked to give (she says that it cost her two weeks' time), while husband Artur also gave a lecture on contemporary European poetry. The Iowa notes mostly recall new and old friends she met with in Iowa City. She also mentions a moving talk by a visiting Chinese writer who spoke about the Cultural Revolution and his forced labor for several years on a farm. In New York she stayed with Daniela and Keith in their apartment in a shabby neighborhood on Second Avenue and 84th Street. Hartwig also mentions at one point the modest lifestyle of the former Polish actress Elżbieta Czyżewska, who had left Poland a few years earlier after marrying the American writer David Halberstam and where she had lived in grand style. On 12 November, Hartwig was in Cambridge, Massachusetts, for a couple of days. While at Harvard, she gave a poetry reading that was attended by some forty people, including a prominent professor of Polish, Wiktor Weintraub, and his wife and of which a video was made.

Ewa Lipska was granted the Kościelski Fund Award (Geneva) in 1973, and the following year received an invitation from the International Writing Program of the University of Iowa that enabled her to spend the fall semester of academic year 1975/1976 in the United States. Her "American" poems date from this period and appeared in print for the first time in the collections *Piąty zbiór wierszy* (Fifth Collection of Verse, 1978) and *Nie o śmierć tutaj chodzi lecz o biały kordonek* (It's Not About Death Here, But a White Chenille, 1982). In 1979 she was given the Robert Graves PEN Club award. "Nowy Jork miasto porwane" ("New York, the Hijacked City," 1982), the longest, and best, of Lipska's "American" poems and one of the best by an Eastern European poet in general, negates the poet's own express intention not to write a poem about New York. Nevertheless, she writes a striking one in which the great metropolis "moves slowly like a freight train / infected with the epidemic of time."[10] She can see her reflection in the "dark-ringed eyes / of that eternally insomniac city. / On white paper sheets / I note down sleep." Her comments on New York landmarks are Lipska at her best, the banal rejected. Hence: "From the fifty-ninth floor / of the Pan Am Building / I observe / the hopeless flight of light / from the General Motors ad. / . . . / In the bar of the Piccadilly Hotel / on 227 W 45th Street / I sit / between epochs / like a bookmark."

But wherever she goes, she is haunted by the plight of those she left behind, by feelings of guilt at having left them: "But even here they look at me / from beyond frozen window panes / from beyond the dead side / and they cry out: treason treason. / How come you're here / How come we're there. / We sleep on the dead side / and you on the living. You're against us." But, as she declares, she can find no words for them, no gifts to leave them. In Pennsylvania Station she sends a letter to her "Departed Friend"—who figures as well in her poem "Dwa listy" ("Two Letters")—admonishing her now-deceased friend, who had hoped to dissuade her from leaving ("*You're leaving for San Francisco / and I'm dying*"), "not to be posthumous / take a real interest in something / don't abuse death. / Grab hold of victory over the grave."

In the end she speaks of New York lying on her like "an oversized coat. / You mustn't wear this city over you—a waiter says to me. / I leave him a tip / for the service of thought." As she departs the Piccadilly Hotel after packing New York into her suitcases and flies away over the city, in her mind's eye she sees "the last subway car / with no station / falling onto an empty plain. . . . The blue-gray air / meticulously wrapping / the abandoned hotel / at the torn-off collar of the street." The final image is that of the city's "yellowing scarf" hanging out of her suitcase.

A somewhat similar if more simply expressed sense of dislocation informs the poem "Iowa Iowa Iowa" by Anna Czekanowicz (b. 1952), a leading poet of the Gdańsk literary community. A native of Sopot on the Baltic, she studied at Gdańsk University and made her literary debut in 1976 with a small collection of poems entitled *Ktoś kogo nie ma* (Someone Who Isn't There). Subsequent volumes of poems by Czekanowicz include *Więzienie jest tylko we mnie* (Prison Is Merely Within Myself, 1978), *Pełni róż obłędu* (A Full House of the Roses of Madness, 1980), *Najszczersze kłamstwo* (The Sincerest Lie, 1984), and *Śmierć w powietrzu* (Death in the Air, 1991). This last collection of poems, Death in the Air, contains texts inspired by her stay at the University of Iowa's International Writing Program. "Iowa Iowa Iowa," the best of them, is largely a modest description of sights along Iowa Avenue in Iowa City (hence the title of the poem). Czekanowicz's favorite shop is a cheap bookstore where she likes to read the books. Noting her interest, a salesman is surprised that she never buys any. Czekanowicz offers the explanation that she has no home in Iowa and is just walking around without really knowing where she's going. This is typical of her attitude toward travel, which she views as a suspension of life, as in the poem "wiersz podróżny" ("travel poem"): "It's a waste of time to look for life in travel / there are only suitcases / packed and unpacked / carried in and carried out / airplanes trains taxis / palms stretched out for tips."[11] Unexpectedly perhaps, toward the end of "Iowa Iowa Iowa" she makes the apparently critical but wry observation that there are no mice or ants on the lawns around the little white houses, only cockroaches. She then declares, "I'm getting to like them more and more / because day by day / I'm aiming my shoe better / even at these most humble examples / of the American standard of living" (10). And as her thoughts lead back to Gdańsk, and home, a subtle note of regret colors her concluding remark: "I'll no doubt be wasting this talent / in Gdańsk."

Marzena Broda's volume *Cudzoziemszczyzna* (Foreignness, 1995) contains a number of poems from 1989 to 1995 that were composed in various places along the Atlantic seaboard: New York City, New Jersey, Bar Harbor, Swan Island, and South Beach. Few of the poems deal with the locales as such. Deeply sensitive to nature, Broda writes mainly of her reactions to the sights and sounds of nature associated with the locales, as in the poems "Sztorm nad Swan Island" ("Storm Over Swan Island") and "Po wizycie: patrząc z South Mountain w stronę Bath Beach" ("After the Visit: Looking from South Mountain Toward Bath Beach"). These reactions are often tinged with melancholy, even sadness. In one of her best texts in Foreignness, "Dom iguany" ("House of the Iguana"), written in long prosaic lines in New Jersey in December 1994, her thoughts about nature's wondrous power of renewal are inspired by the sight of an iguana in a cage. She speaks of entering "this strange house": "I feel at home, on an island that is not in a *Geography of the World*."

The only poems characterized by specificity of space are those written in Bar Harbor, Maine, in 1993: "Tren dla Marguerite Yourcenar" ("A Lament for Marguerite Yourcenar") and "Mount Desert Island." Broda deeply admired Yourcenar (as she did the Russian poets Marina Tsvetaeva and Sofia Parnok) and traveled to Maine to visit the house on Mount Desert Island, Petite Plaisance, where Yourcenar and Grace Frick, her partner, secretary, and translator, had once lived together. Writing after Yourcenar's death, Broda asks: "Do you know already where her land is, or must I conclude / that I have approached the summit standing on the threshold of Petite Plaisance? / Believe me, I truly wept when I saw these doors." "Mount Desert Island" is dedicated to the memory of Grace Frick and operates as a poetic characterization of the now-deserted house and its once illustrious inhabitants. Yourcenar and Frick built the house on an island so as to find peace as far away from people as possible. But it did not work out that way, and in the end "one old woman was caring for another." Although they had lived together on their island for fifty years, it was "hardly a moment" to Broda. For the poet, Petite Plaisance becomes a metaphor for life's ephemerality. Although her visit there was brief, Broda declares that "that night gave me forever the closeness that I desired."[12]

The much-honored Solidarity-affiliated poet Tomasz Jastrun, whom we met previously as the author of Notes from a Vicious Circle (1983), an account of political prisoners during the crackdown on the Solidarity movement, was also the author of an engaging book about America published in Berlin in 1989 under the title *W złotej klatce: Notatnik amerykański* (In the Gilded Cage: An American Notebook). Writing in a casual, laconic manner, occasionally omitting verbs, Jastrun is anything but an uncritical admirer of the American scene. The New York subway system, for example, is portrayed in this way: "The metro is a hundred years old and more or less looks it. Dirt, alternating waves of cold and heat, deafening noise. The metro saves the city from suffocation, but is at the same time its nightmare. Fat rats scurry between the rails. In the tangle of corridors criminals feel best, the solitary and weak the worst. The stations are poorly indicated, which is why beginning users are doomed to confusion. Some of the cars are air-conditioned, but you never know what you're liable to encounter. When you exit the oxygenated aquarium, a wave of odor strikes you all the stronger. Nevertheless, the passengers, although condemned to sweating, don't smell badly. A dictate of cleanliness and frequent change of clothing in the course of the day rules here. A trip to outlying districts of the city often lasts for hours, the cars decorated with graffiti shake mercilessly. Flocks of insistent beggars flit through them."[13]

While in New York, Jastrun looked up Polish acquaintances Janusz Głowacki and Andrzej Czeczot, among others. Janusz Głowacki—who made a success as an émigré writer in New York, especially with his play *Hunting Cockroaches*—takes him to a peep show, where he feels uncomfortable because all the women in it are naked and he's dressed. Jastrun comments on nearly everything: American television programs, a Pułaski Day parade in Manhattan, AIDS, beggars, a rodeo, Mormons, and so on. His travels are extensive, ranging by bus and car across the Midwest to the West Coast, through the cowboy and Indian country of the Southwest, into the Old South, back to Chicago, and finally into New England and New York. People he meets are glad to hear that he is from Poland but know next to nothing about the country except for Solidarity, Lech Wałęsa, and Pope John Paul II. In Chicago he meets the Polish émigré writer Tymoteusz Karpowicz, but finds him crabby and complaining. While in Berkeley, California, he visits the street Czesław Miłosz lives on but notes caustically that unlike the pope, for example, Miłosz does not embrace the unfortunate, referring to other less fortunate Polish émigrés, writers included. Moreover, Miłosz doesn't want to meet with everyone, which, to Jastrun, is "much to be regretted" (78). Although he makes no mention of even trying to meet Miłosz, it seems likely that though Jastrun might have liked such a meeting he was rebuffed.

In by all means the most interesting aspect of his small book, Jastrun devotes much attention to the outlook of Solidarity-era émigrés in the United States, their attitude toward Poland, and their relations with older Polish émigrés. He reports conversations with Polish émigrés he meets who express views extremely critical of other émigrés for, among other things, their prejudices brought from Poland, and also toward Polish-Americans. He quotes Leszek Waliszewski, for example, as complaining that "most people in America understand that the best medicine is tolerance and patience. Our countrymen rarely accept this proposition. In Poland we became crippled. We have so much envy and intolerance" (115). Other relatively recent émigrés share with Jastrun their thoughts on the situation in Poland as they perceive it, on Solidarity, Martial Law, and how many of the political émigrés still feel emotionally bound up with the Solidarity cause. Before returning to New York, Jastrun met with Stanisław Barańczak on a visit to Harvard and stayed with him and his family for a week. He also met with the well-known Polish-Jewish writer Henryk Grynberg and recalls his meetings with other Polish Jews expelled from Poland after the 1968 "anti-Zionist" campaign; they remain, he notes, more faithful to Poland than their native land was to them. A readable, and interesting, account of his travels in America, Jastrun's In the Gilded Cage makes the greatest impression on the reader for his effort to come to grips with the dilemma of the Polish political émigrés caught between the promise of America and a sometimes guilt-ridden nostalgia for the troubled land they left behind and to which few intend to return.

Adam Zagajewski, the most celebrated of contemporary Polish writers, has enjoyed intimate ties with the United States. He has taught in the University of Houston's Creative Writing Program and once gave a well-publicized poetry reading and lecture at the Guggenheim Museum, introduced by the late Susan Sontag. Unlike Jastrun, however, he has never published any diary of his visits to the United States or any other book based on his experiences in America.

It was quite different with his slightly younger colleague, Grzegorz Musiał (b. 1952). Musiał lived in the United States from 1989 to 1990; while there he worked on the translations contained in his anthology of fifty-five contemporary American poets, *America, America!* Apart from five poems on America included in his small collection *Smak popiołu* (*Taste of Ash,* 1992),[14] Musiał's most substantive writing on America is to be found in his diary, *Dziennik z Iowa* (Iowa Journal, 2000). Casual, candid, sardonic, insightful, at times even self-mocking, the book is clearly the work of a writer who is receptive to a host of new impressions but never abandons his critical stance toward them. Bemused at the very idea of thirty or more foreign writers being herded together in the middle of Middle America by the hosts of the University of Iowa's International Writing Program, Musiał never completely abandons his sense of the ridiculousness of the whole business. Although his stay in Iowa, then Canada, then back again in Iowa spans such momentous international political events as the destruction of the Berlin Wall and the collapse of the Eastern European communist regimes, Musiał comments on them briefly, indeed never dwelling on them. He prefers instead to keep his focus on what is more immediately at hand.

His collaboration with Daniel Weissbort, the well-known translator from Russian and other languages, was fruitful, and Weissbort ran interference for him on numerous occasions. Among the literary stars Musiał met in the United States, the Russian poet Josip Brodsky and the American "Beat" poet Allen Ginsberg are the most memorably etched in Iowa Diary. Sensing a certain emotional fragility, combined with an undeniable made-for-America posturing, about Brodsky, Musiał engages in a degree of psychoanalysis in what he writes about him:

> He is afraid of something, he feels in himself something like the pressure of someone else's death. He defends himself with a poorly suited irony taken from Auden that fits him like an Oxford dinner jacket fits an Orthodox church deacon.
>
> How to dream of power with an ironic smirk of the West stuck on neurotically vibrating lips? How to be a tragic clown out of Shakespeare on an American college campus?[15]

Although he admired Ginsberg as a poet, translated him, and wrote a poem about him, Musiał wasn't easily taken in by him. He soon discovered that Ginsberg was cheap, and a hypochondriac. At one point, much to his surprise, Ginsberg phoned Musiał to invite him to dinner. "I'll be the first person in the world to whom Ginsberg proposed dinner. And I had such a nasty thought for the reason that the Great Poet is universally known for his reluctance to deprive himself of the legal tender of the Federal Reserve Bank." But when the time came for Musiał to make his way over to Ginsberg's place in New York City's East Village, he had a certain foreboding and decided to call ahead first. In a sickly voice, Ginsberg informed him that they weren't going out to dinner after all as he was sick abed. But, Ginsberg suggested:

Come on over anyway, but I don't have anything to eat. On First Avenue, between Twelfth and Thirteenth streets, there's a little Polish restaurant, "Christina." Get me some chicken soup and bring it along.

Musiał thought:

Oho. A rich American was supposed to treat a poor Pole to dinner, and now the rich Pole is going to be feeding a poor American. (143)

Interrupting an altercation between a waitress and the proprietress at the restaurant, Musiał has an interesting suggestion for the waitress on how she can hang on to her job. Showing her the copy of Ginsberg's *Collected Poems* that he had with him, with a photograph of Ginsberg on the back of the glossy red jacket, Musiał tells her:

A great American poet often eats here.—I tap on the photograph with a finger.—He's the greatest, the whole world knows him and everyone's mad about him. He lives just around the corner from here, so all you have to do is advertise that "the greatest American poet eats in our bar."
    Zocha looks dissatisfied, and says:
    Eee, I know him, the bald guy, never leaves a tip. I was just telling Basia that if he comes again, you wait on him, he's never left me even a cent. (123)

And when he finally called on Ginsberg, the poet, knowing of Musiał's medical training, asked him to check him over! Musiał's diagnosis, to himself, was *hipochondria poetica*.
    No less entertaining is a conversation between Daniel Weissbrot and Musiał, quoted on pages 145 and 146 in Iowa Diary, about the expense of having different writers—Eastern European and American—in for lectures, and the appalling ignorance of most American students about the Eastern Europeans. Musiał's

wit can at times be quite caustic, as in his characterizations of American students and his sense of something mildly absurd about the Iowa program that brought him to the United States in the first place. But his anthology of translations from contemporary American poetry, *Ameryka, Ameryka! Antologia wierszy amerykańskich po 1940 roku* (America, America! An Anthology of American Poetry After 1940, 1994), as well as his individual translations of Allen Ginsberg and others, amply attests his love for America and its culture.

Of the Czech literary visitors to New York who subsequently wrote about their experiences, none was more expansive than Miroslav Holub (1924–1998). One of the major Czech writers of the twentieth century, Holub was a man of science as well as letters and the author of many books. Although known primarily for his voluminous poetry, he was also a prolific prose writer who had a first-hand knowledge of the United States as the result of several visits to the country between 1951 and 1980. His appointment in 1956/1957 as a visiting investigator in the Department of Immunology of the Public Health Research Institute of the City of New York was of particular value in solidifying his relationship with a city of which he grew immensely fond. Holub drew on his New York experiences as well as his travels from one coast of America to the other in three short books; *Anděl na kolečkách: Poloreportaž z USA* (Angel on Wheels: Polo Reportage from the USA), which was published in 1964; *Žit v New Yorku* (Living in New York, 1969); and *beton: verše z new yorku a z prahy* (concrete: poems from new york and prague, 1970). Peppered with quotes from and allusions to several American writers, among them Gertrude Stein, Henry Miller, and such poets as Laurence Ferlinghetti, Allen Ginsberg, Robinson Jeffers, Kenneth Patchen, and Karl Shapiro, Angel on Wheels is a collection of short prose vignettes ranging in length from a small paragraph to at most a page or page and a half. Casual in style, they have the character often of impressionistic, "on the run" observations of a wide variety of American phenomena drawn from Holub's travels.

But if Holub's reputation as a writer and scientist made possible his travels in America, the political realities of contemporary Czechoslovakia imposed an unstated demand for political correctness, communist style. Hence Holub's emphasis, wherever appropriate, on the contrasts, incongruities, and inequalities of American life. As an example of both his style and outlook, here is a small piece entitled "Město pod městem" ("City Beneath a City"), in which the subject is the notorious Emile Griffith–Benny Paret boxing match of 1962 that resulted in Paret's death:

> On Eighth Avenue there's a queue for tickets to the fights in Madison Square Garden. . . .
> But beneath this city there's another city, an underground city, dark and indefinable, where it's already been decided that tonight in Madison Square Garden,

Griffith will demolish Benny Paret. . . . The doctors have been bought off, a worn-down Paret will keep on boxing, he won't be counted out on time, because of the need for a sensation caught by the cameras.

That evening, Griffith slaughtered Banny Paret in the ring. Paret died after ten days of agony and ten days of sensational reports in the press. . . .

A city beneath a city, governed by love, lust, death, and dollars. To a certain extent, it's everywhere the same.[16]

Such ideologically motivated jabs notwithstanding, Holub covers a lot of ground in Angel on Wheels and offers his Czech readers many interesting and curious glimpses of what life in the United States was like at the time. He writes about popular culture, high culture, the achievements of American science and technology, sports, the press, and literature. With respect to the latter, he paints a rather grim picture of the harm done by the narrow-mindedness and political conservatism of "official" American criticism and censorship. Thus, the San Francisco Beat poets (Ferlinghetti, Ginsberg, Corso) have been marginalized as "lightweight." "Left-oriented" poets (like those affiliated with the review *Masses and Mainstream*) are "understandably" similarly relegated to the margins. So, too, were such poets as Robinson Jeffers, Kenneth Patchen, and Karl Shapiro, who edited what Holub characterizes as the only "mainstream" literary review, *Poetry.* In Shapiro's case, the problem, according to Holub, was his anarchistic views and engaged poetry. So, too, Eli Siegel and his "little group" in New York. Henry Miller, the "dean of American literature," who gave the only thorough interpretation of contemporary American life ("according to Shapiro"), has not only been marginalized but also partly exiled because the censors judged his *Tropics* to be immoral. Holub adds that this does not surprise him, "although I understandably disagree." In Holub's view, the writers of "strong voice" in the tradition of Walt Whitman and, in contemporary America, Henry Miller, "have been sentenced to a life that is so distant from their ideal of American society" (79–80).

Except for the fact that Living in New York, unlike Angel on Wheels, deals exclusively with New York and incorporates slightly longer pieces, this 1969 book by Holub is cast in much the same spirit. New York is the "most inconvenient" of American cities, and the most contaminated. "It's possible to love New York," he writes at one point, "when you see it from New Jersey, or from an airplane. Or from Europe." Holub then proceeds to casual observations on different aspects of life in New York, including the layout of its streets, its architecture, its different neighborhoods, the other boroughs, its black and white ethnic issues, its hotels and restaurants, museums, television programs, and so on. Each mini-essay in the book is preceded, or prefaced, by a quote from (usually) an American source (a few from the *New York Times,* for example), in Czech translation, of course—including ads that Holub felt set the "tone" for the following piece. On the whole, Holub does a fair job of maintaining the integrity of his breezy book of New York vignettes, with its very broad coverage and well-informed outlook. Although he cannot refrain from aligning himself with what the communists liked to call "progressive thought" on such hot issues as the war in Vietnam and American nuclear policy, Living in New York is anything but blatantly ideological and does what Holub obviously intended it to do: give his average Czech reader a glimpse into and feel for the life of one of the greatest cities in the world.

Holub's much smaller book of poems, concrete: poems from new york and prague, was, again, inspired mainly by New York. Most of the poems reflect Holub's fascination with the city and its surroundings. There are poems on such New York landmarks as the Van Wyck Expressway, the New York subway system, a Brooklyn cemetery, Jersey City, Park Avenue, East River Drive, Rockefeller Center, a weekend in Long Beach, Harlem, and the Bowery. A few of the poems were inspired by articles in the *New York Times,* such as this one from June 1967, which Holub titles "Nalezená poezie: Debata o Středním Východě, New York" ("Discovered Poetry: Debate About the Middle East, New York"):

> The police placed
> anti-Soviet demonstrators
> on the south side of 47th Street
> and on the north side, pro-Soviet demonstrators.
> However,
> the police didn't know what to do
> with Josef Mlot-Mroz from Salem, Mass.,
> who was standing in the rain
> on First Avenue,
> with an American flag made of make-believe stones
> in his left fist.
> He held a poster with the inscription:
> The Jews are murderers,
> Communism is Jewish.
> From the beginning to the End.
> Wipe out communism.
> Polish Fighters for Freedom, Inc.
> The police captain,
> Francis R. Kelly,
> Had first led Mr. Mlot-Mroz
> to the southern side.
> But after a short conversation,
> the policeman went away,
> shaking his head and mumbling,
> I just don't know where
> to put him.[17]

An East German Visitor

One of the most notable East German writers to spend time in the United States and subsequently write about his experiences was the multifaceted and hugely prolific Günter Kunert (b. 1929). As the son of a Jewish mother, Kunert was denied admission to any institution of higher learning under the Nazis. It was only after World War II that he was able to enroll in the College of Applied Art in Berlin. Although literature soon became his true passion, Kunert's graphic skills were later put to good use in his illustrations for several of his own books. By the late 1940s he was making his way as a professional writer in East Berlin. A gifted poet as well as prose writer, widely respected for his reportage, Kunert was especially admired for his parodies and grotesque satires. In 1962 he was honored with the Heinrich Mann Prize and within a few years had already earned international recognition. From September 1972 to January 1973, on invitation of the University of Texas at Austin, he gave a series of guest lectures on the literature of the German Democratic Republic.

His American experiences and impressions provided the material for his engaging travel book *Der andere Planet: Ansichten von Amerika* (The Other Planet: Postcards from America, 1975). It was one of the very few times a book about America appeared on the East German market free of the usual ideological trappings. Austin was Kunert's first port of call after arriving in New York City, and his account of his stay in the Texas capital sets the tone for The Other Planet as a whole. Cultural and political observations are not his primary concern; his preference lies instead with descriptions of places, occasionally augmented by brief historical notes, and observations on what (to him) appear to be oddities of American life (including western garb and the extreme informality of student dress) compared to what he was used to in Europe. In contrast to other Eastern European accounts of travel in America, Kunert's is remarkably free of individuals. Although he mentions an Austin apartment house neighbor who speaks what he calls the best Berlin dialect of the 1920s and supplies him with "real" coffee ("You certainly can't drink American coffee; it's quite undrinkable"[18]) and copies of the New York Jewish German-language newspaper *Der Aufbau,* about the only individuals singled out for (mere) mention are the chairman of the Foreign Language Department at the University of Iowa and a professor of German at the University of Northern Iowa whom he meets during stopovers in Iowa City and Cedar Falls. After visits to Chicago and New Orleans (with particular attention to its cemeteries and the Conti wax museum), Kunert left no stone unturned on travel through the Southwest, visiting San Antonio, El Paso, Santa Fe, the Ancoma Indian reservation, and White Sands National Monument, before heading on to Washington, D.C., and New York City. His remarks on Yorkville, the predominantly German neighborhood of New York, in the section "East 86th Street," and the presence there during World War II of the pro-Nazi German-American Bund under Fritz Kuhn, make for interesting reading. Taking due note at one point in his coverage of New York City of the American porn scene, Kunert can't refrain from quoting this ad from a magazine, which he views as revealing of the American psyche: "Are you spending many uninteresting hours in your automobile? You can arouse yourself sexually with AUTO SUCK. Vigorous suction accompanies you everywhere. Plug AUTO SUCK into the cigarette lighter. Its soft feminine rubber opening will stroke and suck you with erotic suction energy. Feel how the juices of orgasm are drawn from your body. Lifelike inner rubber vaginal lips surround the penis and dispense hours of pleasure both while driving and parking. 35 dollars" (181).

After his obviously satisfying American sojourn, Kunert became Writer-in-Residence at the University of Warwick in England. His experiences there were also reflected in his writings, most notably in his book of lyrics *Englische Gedichte* (English Poems, 1975) and in *Ein englisches Tagebuch* (An English Diary, 1978). When the popular East German poet and entertainer Wolf Biermann was stripped of his GDR citizenship in 1976 while on a tour of West Germany, Kunert was one of a number of German writers and intellectuals who protested the action. Two years later, he and his wife left East Germany for the West, settling in Schleswig-Holstein. More publications and exhibitions of his graphic work and painting further enhanced his reputation. In 1983 he received an honorary doctorate from Allegheny College in Pennsylvania, and in 1985 delivered the prestigious Frankfurt Poetics Lectures.

I I

The Postcolonial Literary Scene in Eastern Europe Since 1991

Although the end of communist domination of Eastern Europe and the Soviet Union in the period 1989 to 1991 initially brought exhilaration, this was soon followed by a more sober realization that the transition from communism to a postcommunist era was not going to be an easy one.

The legacy of political stagnation, economic mismanagement, and bureaucratic inefficiency was not easily overcome. Before serious progress toward implementation of a free market economy could be made, many manifestations of the old system had to be cleared away, and the task appeared daunting. The closing of anachronistic and wasteful factories, the withdrawal of state support for many industries, and the raising of prices in order to bolster currencies and cope with inflation came down particularly hard on some segments of the population, especially pensioners and the elderly. Many jobs were lost, and before long social problems had begun to manifest themselves.

An entrepreneurial class able to acquire controlling shares in industries and to buy property eventually produced a bumper crop of domestic millionaires and even multimillionaires. Imported automobiles and other pricey foreign commodities soon became commonplace, notwithstanding the inability of many to afford them. As life suddenly started to become increasingly more expensive, the gulf between haves and have-nots grew wider. Chronic maladies of capitalist states now became the afflictions of the newly postcommunist states of Eastern Europe and the former Soviet Union. Crime—including the surfacing of home-grown mafias—prostitution, drug use, and sexually transmitted diseases supplanted alcoholism as weightier social problems.

Although their populations were more homogeneous by and large than those of Western societies beset with massive immigration from former colonies, Africa, and the Balkans, minorities were still sufficiently represented to provoke prejudice. The remnants of the German and Hungarian populations of Romania, above all in Transylvania, became targets of discrimination and repression. So too did the Gypsies of the Czech and Slovak republics. Although the Holocaust had considerably reduced the numbers of Jews still living in

Eastern Europe, signs of residual anti-Jewish sentiment have appeared from time to time. The irony here is inescapable. With Jews now a greatly diminished presence throughout Eastern Europe, the growing nostalgia for the past has given rise as well to a new curiosity, even interest, about the Jewish communities of old, once so numerous in most of the countries of Eastern Europe. This is especially true of younger people who grew up in the postwar era with little or no direct knowledge of anything Jewish. The renovation of some structures associated with the Jewish past, the opening of small museums and libraries devoted to Jewish history and culture, annual festivals of Jewish culture, and significant publication about the former Jewish communities—while obviously positive developments—have still not eradicated traces of ill will toward Jews.

Nationalism, that old Eastern European bugaboo, has also reared its ugly head. The relatively slow economic recovery, relative to Western Europe, notable in such countries as Albania and Romania, coupled with considerable pressure to meet the requirements for entry into the European Union, have also tended to stoke the smoldering embers of nationalism. This is especially true of those countries caught up in the Balkan wars of the 1990s, principally Croatia and Serbia. In a throwback to the old days of the communist era, antidemocratic authoritarian rule, as in post-Soviet Belarus (and Russia itself), has reappeared as what might be called postcommunist neocommunism.

The picture that emerges thus from an overview of more than fifteen years of postcommunist Eastern Europe is anything but one-sided: progress and reversals in both the political and economic spheres (as exemplified, for example, in the collapse of "pyramid" financial schemes in Albania in December 1996 and early 1997 and riots over economic mismanagement in Hungary in October 2006), enthusiasm and malaise, hope and frustration, with much still remaining to be accomplished. In order to get a sense of the impact on literary culture of the great transformation underway in Eastern Europe since 1989, I propose to approach the matter by means of certain discrete thematic groupings. The first to be addressed will be new writing from two of the more important cultures to emerge from the breakup of the Soviet Union, Lithuania and Ukraine.

Manifestations of a New Post-Soviet Sensibility in Lithuania

The sundering of the Lithuanian literary community in 1940 as a result of the incorporation of Lithuania into the Soviet Union was at last rectified when the country came free of Soviet power in 1991 and became an independent state. This is not to suggest by any means that the large émigré Lithuanian community immediately reestablished itself in the homeland. But the split between Soviet Lithuanian writers, necessarily subservient to the norms of Soviet literary culture, and their kith and kin in the free world was effectively at an end. Indeed a number of exile writers who were able to do so returned to Lithuania and joined in the enterprise of reestablishing a unitary Lithuanian literature.[1] The achievements of this new postcommunist Lithuanian literature have been impressive for the fairly short period of its independence. Among relatively younger poets who were born in the 1950s and later, and most of whose works appeared after the collapse of Soviet rule in Lithuania, the most prominent are Kornelijus Platelis (b. 1951), Nijolė Miliauskaitė (1951–2002), Antanas A. Jonynas (b. 1953), Donaldas Kajokas (b. 1953), Aidas Marčėnas (b. 1960), Eugenijus Ališanka (b. 1960)—perhaps the brightest star of the new Lithuanian poetry—and Gintaras Grajauskas (b. 1966). In prose, Jurgis Kunčinas (1947–2002), Ričardas Gavelis (1950–2002), Jurga Ivanauskaitė (1961–2007), Renata Šerelytė (b. 1970), Herkus Kunčius (b. 1965), and Marius Ivaškevičius (b. 1973) have dominated the literary scene.

Kornelijus Platelis, Lithuanian Vice-Minister of Culture and Education from 1991 to 1993 and a former president of the Lithuanian PEN Club, is a prominent poet and one of the country's more important intellectuals. He is the author of six volumes of poetry, the most recent being *Luoto kevalas* (The Hull, 1990), *Prakalbos upei* (Speeches to a River, 1995), *Atoslūgio juosta* (Tidal Wave, 2000), and, in English, *Snare for the Wind*. Nijolė Miliauskaitė, a highly regarded poet who won the 1996 Lithuanian Writers' Union Prize, published *Uršulės S. portretas* (Portrait of Uršula S., 1985), *Uždraustas jeiti kambarys* (The Forbidden Room, 1995), and *Sielos labirintas* (Labyrinth of the Soul, 1999). Composed in a style of simplicity and clarity, rarely more than several lines in length, many of her poems intertwine recollections of girlhood dreams and fears with understated allusions to World War II, the Holocaust, and occupation as well as to the harsh realities of the present. In her strolls about a landscape of urban nightmare, Miliauskaitė is often accompanied by her frequent companion, "Franz K." The bleak solitude of a number of her poems is relieved by the poet's fondness for flowers and gardens and other warming signs of spring and summer. Miliauskaitė's poetry is a melancholic yet enchanting world of fading photographs and the tenderness of grandmotherly memories.

Antanas A. Jonynas, a 1978 recipient of the Gėlė Prize for the best debut by a lyric poet for *Metai kaip strazdas* (Year Like a Blackbird), subsequently won the Lithuanian Writers' Union Prize for best book of the year for *Nakties traukinys* (Night Train, 1991) and was also nominated for the State Prize of the Republic of Lithuania that same year. He has since published *Toks pasaulis* (Such a World, 1995) and two bilingual collections, *Mohnasche / Aguonų pelenai* (Moonash, 2002; German-Lithuanian) and *In Time / Laiko inkliuzai* (2002; English-Lithuanian). Donaldas Kajokas, an experimental poet known most for miniatures of seven lines each, has published in the post-Soviet period such volumes of poetry as *Žuvusi avis* (A Dying Sleep, 1991), *Drabužėliais baltais* (White Clothing, 1994), *Meditacijos* (Meditations, 1997), and *Mirti reikia rudenį* (One Must Die in Autumn, 2000). All of Gintaras Grajauskas's poetry has appeared since 1991 and includes the collections *Tatuiruotė* (The Tattoo, 1993), *Atsiskyrėlio atostogos* (A Hermit's Holiday, 1996), *Katalogas* (The Catalogue, 1997), and *Kaulinė dūdelė* (The Bone Flute, 1999). Aidas Marčėnas began his career as a poet with the collection *Šulinys* (The Well) in 1988. All subsequent books of poems by him were published in the 1990s and 2000; these include *Angelas* (The Angel, 1991); *Dulkės* (Dust, 1993); *Metai be žiogo* (The Year Without Locusts, 1994); *Vargšas Jorikas* (Poor Yorick, 1998); *50 eilėraščių* (50 Poems, 1999); and *Dėvėti* (Threadbare, 2001). Known primarily for his preference for the sonnet, Marčėnas writes mostly about everyday life in Vilnius or of his recollections of childhood in the nearby village of Antakalnis.

Eugenijus Ališanka's first volume of poetry, *Lygiadienis* (Equinox, 1992), signaled the arrival of an important new voice in Lithuanian poetry. It won the Zigmas Gėlė Prize awarded annually to the best debut book of Lithuanian poetry. *Peleno miestas* (*City of Ash,* 1995), his next volume, is his only book of poetry to be translated thus far into English. It is also one of his finest. A poet primarily of autumnal, wintry, and nocturnal landscapes, of snow, short days, hard-frozen earth, and of solitudes, Ališanka is also a poet who, like any dweller of the north, welcomes summer and sun. Attracted as well to myth and ancient lore, hints of which appear in his poetry, he is acutely aware of the material out of which language is constructed—vowels, consonants, syllables—and frequently makes this the subject of his verse.

When Ričardas Gavelis's *Vilniaus pokeris* (Vilnius Poker, 1989) first appeared, critics hailed it as a "literary bomb." Its scandalous reputation—from the perspective especially of conservative nationalists and moralists—was based not only on its graphic and brutal sex scenes, but also on Gavelis's debunking of some Lithuanian national myths and patterns of thinking that had become dear to many of his countrymen. A novel in part about the Lithuanian passion for basketball and in part a mystery novel involving the macabre murder of a beautiful young woman, Vilnius Poker encompasses a broad range of Lithuanian attitudes toward the Russians during the Soviet period. Paranoia, sport as an outlet for pent-up feelings of nationalism, and the strategies by which Lithuanians sought to adapt to and resist Soviet rule are all woven into the fabric of the novel. The totalitarian force alluded to only by the pronoun "They" in Vilnius Poker, but understood as the Soviet KGB, comes even more vividly to life in Gavelis's next novel, *Jauno žmogaus memuarai* (Memoirs of a Young Man, 1991). Through his central character, the "young man" of the title, Gavelis demonstrates that because of the circumstances prevailing at the time (meaning, of course, Soviet domination), a free, active, and responsible life was not possible. Caught in the claws of the totalitarian monster first portrayed in Vilnius Poker, Gavelis's antihero is transformed by ideological terror into a "sexless metaphysical worm." This kind of unsparing analysis of the totalitarian regime, for which Gavelis became well known, grew even sharper in such later novels as *Vilniaus džiasas* (Vilnius Jazz, 1993), *Prarastų godų kvartetas* (Quartet of Lost Desires, 1997), and *Septyni savižudybės būdai* (Seven Ways of Committing Suicide, 1999), which are all thematically linked to his previous works.

Gavelis was very much an urban writer, and Vilnius—for Lithuanians synonymous with "city"—operates almost as an independent actor, as a metaphysical condition, in any case always more than mere background, locale, or setting. Vilnius in Gavelis's works is at once a phantasmagoria, a labyrinth, an ethnic and national melting pot, and a mythical beast, as in his short-story collection *Taikos balandis: Septyni Vilniaus apsakymai* (Pigeon Freedom: Seven Vilnius Stories, 1995). But the most telling image of Vilnius is the one evoked by Gavelis in Vilnius Poker:

> There's no escaping the fact that the only real thing there is the ancient castle in the new city: a lonely tower emerging out of the overgrown slope of the hill—Vilnius's phallic symbol. It reveals all secrets. The symbolic phallus of Vilnius: short, blunt, and impotent. For ages it has been unable to use its pseudo-mighty organ. A red three-story tower, a phallic NOTHING, shamelessly on display to one and all, a symbol of Vilnius's helplessness. A castrated city, a huge symbol of castrated Lithuania, crammed onto every postcard, into every photo album, every tourist brochure. A symbol of shame. It is unseemly to hide one's impotence, not admit it, or at least to pretend that one is still capable of something. But this city lost everything a long time ago—even its self-respect. The only thing left here are lies, absurdity, and fear.[2]

Gavelis turns apocalyptical in his other major work from 1995, the novel *Paskutinioje žemes žmunių karta* (The Last Generation of Earthlings, 1995). Here Vilnius is destroyed by an explosion of the earth's surface.

Gavelis's surrealistically postmodern texts encompass as well sharp analyses of character. The same can be said for his journalistic writing, for example, his 1994 book *Nemirtingumas* (Immortality), a portrait in essence of the journalist Vitas Lingis, the thirty-three-year-old deputy editor of *Respublika* murdered in 1993 by the Lithuanian underworld, whose activities he had begun investigating.

A few years older than Gavelis, Jurgis Kunčinas (1947–2002), who was a university-trained specialist in German language and literature and a highly respected translator from German, began his literary career as a lyric poet. He published his first collection of prose, the short-story collection *Vaizdas į menulį* (View of the Moon), the same year that Gavelis broke into print. In some ways resembling Gavelis, with a similar inclination toward the grotesque, Kunčinas peoples his world with an original assortment of characters: tramps, alcoholics, con artists, and, of particular interest, artistic bohemians of the Soviet era. With a fondness for detail and atmospherics, he is one of the most interesting of contemporary Lithuanian writers for his backward glance at the now-defunct Soviet period. View of the Moon was followed by two more collections of short stories, *Laba diena, pone Enrike!* (Good Morning, Mr. Enrikas) and *Menestreliai maksi paltais* (Minstrels in Overcoats), both published in 1996, and by the novels *Glisono kilpa* (The Glison Loop, 1991), *Tūla* (Tūla, 1993)—which some regard as his best work—*Blanchisserie arba Žverinas-Užupis* (Blanchisserie; or, Žverinas-Užupis, 1997), *Kilnojamosios Rentgeno stotys* (Mobile X-Ray Stations, 1998)—the work for which he is now perhaps best known—and, published also in 1998, *Bilė ir kiti* (Bilė and Others).

Tūla, Kunčinas's second novel—which was awarded the Lithuanian Writers' Union Prize in 1993—is a bittersweet love story about a young man's (the narrator's) all-consuming but doomed passion for the eponymous heroine, told against the background of a drab, spiritless Soviet Lithuania in the 1980s. The overall squalor of the environment contrasts with the often poetic quality of the first-person narrative. Also enhancing the textural richness of the novel is Kunčinas's affectionate depiction of a colorful assortment of characters surrounding Tūla and the verisimilitude with which he evokes the shabby Vilnius neighborhood of Užupis, where the story takes place. This fondness for specific Vilnius locales is evident as well in the 1997 novel Blanchisserie; or, Žverinas-Užupis (like Užupis, Žverinas is a district of Vilnius). Kunčinas's narrator is a familiar type in his fiction, and the kind for which he had a definite affinity—a homeless vagrant who drinks a lot. Tūla, the unlikely object of his romantic fixation, is a young woman from a good home. As with Gavelis, an element of the fantastic is woven into the first-person narrative: the narrator has the ability to change into a bat whenever he wants so as never to lose sight of his beloved. At the end, after her untimely demise, the young man buries an urn with her ashes beneath the floor of her small house along the shore of the Vilenka River. It bears the cryptic inscription: "Here lies Tūla. God knows her real name."

One of Kunčinas's very best works, Mobile X-Ray Stations is a sly novel, obviously autobiographical in part, about the involvement of the narrator in the making of a film about an abandoned Soviet-era mobile X-ray station for testing possible TB cases. Beginning with a kind of preface wherein Kunčinas exposes what might be termed Lithuanian self-pity about the injustices done them by history, he then moves through a series of recollections of friends who committed suicide or were accidentally killed, inferring that the malaise and frustrations of the Soviet period bore some of the responsibility for the alcoholism that most had in common. A surprise visit to the narrator's home by a film director leads to a small excursion and the narrator's stumbling across the old abandoned X-ray bus. The director then jumps on the idea of making a movie about the mobile station and the plot is launched.

Among younger contemporary Lithuanian writers, two of the most noteworthy are the postmodernists Herkus Kunčius (b. 1965) and Marius Ivaškevičius (b. 1970). Often characterized as a playful nihilist with a fondness for Louis-Ferdinand Céline, Vladimir Sorokin, and Henry Miller, Kunčius delights in provoking and shocking. He began his career with the publication of his novel *Ir dugnas visada priglaus* (Even a Precipice Always Offers Shelter, 1986) in the journal *Metai*. Several of his subsequent novels also first saw light in the same journal: *Matka Pika* (Mother Pika, 1998), *Sparnu vaška urna* (The Winged Wax Urn, 1999), and *Barbarei šventykloje* (Barbarians in the Temple, 2002). Apart from plays that have been staged, he also published a volume of essays and other short prose under the title *Pilnaties linksmybes* (The Fullness of Life and Its Pleasures, 1999).

Kunčius's postmodernist nihilism, absurdism, and fondness for pure literary fantasy, although evidenced earlier, come to the fore vividly in the novel

Būtasis dažninis laikas (The Imperfect Tense, 1998), which, like the earlier Even a Precipice Always Offers Shelter, draws on Kunčius's long stay in Paris. His lead character is a booze-loving, cynical intellectual living in the French capital who has an utter disdain for French culture, which he reviles at every opportunity. Much the same outlook pervades his novels *Ekskursija: Casa Matta* (An Excursion: Casa Matta, 1998) and *Mano kova bambino* (My Struggle, Bambino, 1999). Both works are essentially fragmentary in design. Excursion: Casa Matta deals ostensibly with the adventures of a Polish cavalry regiment between the wars in what is obviously Wilno (the Polish name for Vilnius), and the funeral, amid much pomp and ceremony, of the beloved horse Kasztanka (Chestnut) of Marshal Józef Piłsudski, the head of the Polish state through much of the interwar period. A sexton opines at one point that the mare's death, most likely from reactive tuberculosis, could have been caused only by saboteurs who travel the length and breadth of the country spreading the disease to man and beast alike. But little seems to have anything to do with anything else in this absurdist novel built around the technique of the collage, and many scenes are written in dialogue, as if Kunčius was calling attention to his affinities with the theater of the absurd. My Struggle, Bambino is made up of utterances of all kinds, witty and otherwise, the basic sense of the work summed up in the author's disclaimer that he has no message, never wanted to have anything to say, and still doesn't.

Similarly absurdist in nature is Kunčius's 1996 short novel *Pelenai asilo kanopoje* (Ashes on the Donkey's Hoof), about a young man in a topsy-turvy world in which his newly won job as city executioner is held in high esteem, despite the personal restrictions it imposes. Because of the need to devote himself completely to his new responsibilities, he must, for example, abandon any thought of marriage and he is forewarned that lonely, trying days lie ahead of him. But he is willing to do whatever it takes because of the prestige attached to the executioner's position:

> I am the city executioner. I am the hangman and proud of my responsibilities. It strokes my self-esteem when people notice me and appreciate me. That's a big thing because others wouldn't even dare dream of a similar offer even if they waited until a ripe old age. But it's me they took notice of. Me they took notice of and chose from hundreds, thousands, and millions. . . .
>
> I can't assert that the beginning was easy. Everything happened. Successes, joys, and disappointments. I'll also never forget my first execution. I was all worked up before the debut, and was sweating. I remember—I couldn't sleep all night. Please let everything just go well, just go well. . . .
>
> It went well. This time it went very well. To tell the truth, I was still far from being a master, still far from perfection. Nevertheless, I did all right. I detached the head from the body with a single blow. It rolled, unconcerned, into the wicker basket, and then the mayor approached me, embraced me, kissed me, and was delighted that he had chosen me. I felt like I had grown wings. My state of mind was indescribable.[3]

That the novel is set, probably in France, sometime during the eighteenth century is apparent from this excerpt, in which the young executioner speaks of his desire to keep up with things in the world in view of the importance of his position:

> I follow literature, subscribe to journals, exchange correspondence with Voltaire, Diderot, Montesquieu, and Jean-Jacques Rousseau, who sends me juicy plums every fall. (10–11)

But then, in Kunčius's absurd world, chronology doesn't mean much, as we realize when he mentions, virtually in the same breath, that "in free moments, when I stretch out a little and read the existentialists, I often think about existence. It's interesting to me" (10). He then goes on to mention that he realizes that "life is boundless joy. 'It's worth being loved,' my friend Camus used to stress. Albert is his first name" (11).

Marius Ivaškevičius, the youngest of the writers being discussed here, began his career as a correspondent with the Vilnius daily *Respublika* after graduating from Vilnius University with a degree in Lithuanian studies. He published his first work of fiction, the short-story collection *Kam vaiku* (To Whom the Children), in 1996. It made enough of an impression for several of the stories to be translated into other European languages, including French and German. Two years later, Ivaškevičius published the novel *Istorija nuo debesies* (History from a Cloud), which quickly came to be regarded as one of the most important Lithuanian literary works of the decade. Although not a novel to be read with any more than a certain curiosity by the foreign reader, it is an interesting text for its imaginative blend of myth and national history. Writing partly under the spell of a grandmother's story-telling and partly under the influence of the lore and legends of his native region, Ivaškevičius devised a unique way of viewing the thousand-year-old history of the Lithuanian state.

Women writers have also made their presence in Lithuanian literature strongly felt since the country regained its independence. The two best known are Jurga Ivanauskaitė and Renata Šerelytė.

Jurga Ivanauskaitė's reputation rests on the novels *Menulio vaikai* (Children of the Moon, 1988), *Pragaro sodai* (Gardens of Hell) and *Ragana ir lietus* (The Witch and the Rain), both published in 1993, *Agnijos magija* (Agnija's Magic, 1995), and *Sapnų noblokšti* (Dream Borne, 2000). She has been much admired as a pioneer of a new feminine-oriented literature that defends a woman's right to emotion in a highly technologized civilization and against the taboos of a society twisted by Catholic values. In search of final truths at an important juncture in her life, Ivanauskaitė traveled to India to learn from the Dalai Lama. The heroes of her prose fiction are typical children of an era influenced by nihilism and pragmatism.

Arguably her most successful novel to date, The Witch and the Rain brings together most of the signature elements of Ivanauskaitė's fiction. It is the story of a young woman named Vika who consults a female psychiatrist (Norma) about her burning need to forget her lover. He is none other than a charismatic priest, an old friend of her invalidic father, who has decided to enter a monastery and before doing so ends the relationship with Vika. As she describes her passionate romance with the priest, Paulius, the narrative shifts back and forth between Vika's account and that of Mary Magdalene about her all-consuming love for Jesus. Desperate to forget Paulius, Vika plunges into casual, mostly sexual relationships (hence the parallel with Mary Magdalene) that are described in graphic detail. This is clearly all part of Ivanauskaitė's feminist agenda. The men with whom Vika takes up are loathsome, with little but sex on their minds and a degrading attitude toward women. This feminist antipathy toward men carries over as well into the biblical scenes. The apostle Peter wants to drive Mary Magdalene away from Jesus because she is a woman and as such has no value. But Jesus does not repel the fallen woman, the sinner who according to the Old Testament was to be condemned to stoning. Instead he washes her feet and makes a place for her at his side. It is as if Ivanauskaitė were arguing the equal right of women to God's mercy.

Another commonplace in Ivanauskaitė's fiction is her knowledge of and admiration for the Tibetan people and their culture, the result of her travels there and contacts with the Dalai Lama. Although there is little of this in The Witch and the Rain, it is the major thrust of her essayistic writing, as contained in *Ištremtas Tibetas* (Forbidden Tibet, 1996), *Kelionė į Šambala* (A Journey to Shambala, 1997), and *Prarasta pažadetoji žemė* (The Lost Promised Land, 1999).

A graduate in Lithuanian studies of Vilnius University, Renata Šerelytė made her literary debut in 1995 with the short-story collection *Žuvies darinejimas* (Preparing Fish). This was followed by two more collections in 1997, *Balandų ratas* (The Circle of the Deaf) and *O ji tepasake miau* (And She Just Said Meow). Richly atmospheric and drenched in self-irony, the stories depict the emptiness and despair mostly of provincial Lithuania under the Soviets. Šerelytė inclines toward an expressionistic style rich in striking character portraits that are often grotesque in their caricature-like qualities. Her first novel, *Ledynmečio žvaigždės* (Stars of the Ice Age, 1999), won the Žemaitė Prize. Leaving behind a provincial town, with its characteristic drunks, parasites, and cranks, and a grotesque home environment, a young woman settles in Vilnius, now a haven of the arts in newly independent Lithuania. After completion of her studies, she begins working as an editor while harboring the ambition to become a writer. Although she wanders the labyrinthine paths and byways of the city and experiences a variety of sexual adventures along the way, the existential transformation she had hoped for fails to materialize. Šerelytė was also the author (under the name Skomantas) of the historical tale *Prakeiktas kardas* (The Accursed Sword), about the last years of the reign of the Lithuanian king Mindaugas, and in 1997 made her debut as a dramatist with *Stoglangis* (The

Window in the Roof), with which she won the Open Society's competition for children's and youth theater.

Ukrainian Literature Fields a Major Writer

Undoubtedly the brightest star of contemporary post-Soviet Ukrainian literature is the poet and prose-fiction writer Oksana Zabuzhko (b. 1960). Her major prose works are the intriguingly titled *Pol'ovi doslidzhennia z ukrains'koho seksu* (*Field Studies on Ukrainian Sex*), which was written in 1994 and published for the first time in 1996, and the longish story *Divchatka* (Girls, 1998). Both texts were completed on trips abroad, the first during the fall of 1994 when Zabuzhko held a Fulbright Fellowship in the United States (at Harvard University and the University of Pittsburgh), and the second at the Rockefeller research retreat, the Villa Serboni, in Bellagio, Italy, in 1998.

Field Studies on Ukrainian Sex, Zabuzhko's best work to date, would seem to have a solidly autobiographical base despite her disclaimers to the contrary. The parallels with Zabuzhko's own life in Ukraine as she was growing up as well as her experiences in the United States as a Fulbright Fellow are simply too striking to dismiss out of hand. Not far from the end of the novel she undertakes a long excursion into the subject of the fear bred into many of her generation by the political conditions in Ukraine under the Soviets. Like so many other Ukrainians, her father was arrested with little or no provocation when armed men simply showed up at the door and dragged him off. Zabuzhko recalls her mother as a product of the famine of the 1930s and the repression that followed. Much of Zabuzhko's loathing of the Soviet system is vented in her remarks about the persistent campaign of the Soviets against the Ukrainian language and Ukrainian creativity. Her resentment over Ukrainians' submissiveness to the Soviets analogizes with her resentment over a woman's submissiveness to men, beginning with her relationship with her own father. *Field Studies on Ukrainian Sex* has anything but a tight structure and easily accommodates pontifications by Zabuzhko about man and art in the contemporary world (her outlook is generally bleak). The prose narrative is also interspersed with lines of verse and snippets from her own poetry.

Zabuzhko's unequivocal feminist perspective on the male (dominant)–female (submissive) relationship—which, as we've seen, also has a political dimension vis-à-vis the long Soviet overlordship of Ukraine—comes through vividly as well in one of her best poems, "Klitemnestra" ("Clytemnestra"), from her collection *Avtostop* (Hitchhike) of 1994. In this instance, the loathing of men is couched in even stronger terms than in *Field Studies on Ukrainian Sex*:

> Agamemnon's coming—
> he's mounting the stairs, and the sun
> shines at his back,
> and he's clanging with brass,

like an idol stuffed with war, and the leather
thongs of his armor are squeaking . . .
Take it off, I don't want it!
I don't desire the animal smell of his mouth,
or his hands with their black-stained nails—
those hands
rip the clothes
from me, as from a corpse on the battlefield,
and under the nails the coils and scruff
from the clothes and hair of the fallen
are probably still rotting.
Perhaps I'm really not a woman—
I don't want to scream and twist from mortal pleasure,
impaled by his gleaming blade,
amid spills of stinking sweat,
beneath a burden more unbearable than imperial power—under his body,
sprinkling me with the sticky juices of death: I hate
the delicate bitch's whines that will involuntarily
escape from my throat at that moment,
I hate the wave of languor that will embrace me . . .[4]

In 2001 Zabuzhko published a small collection of short pieces under the title *Reportazh iz 2000-go roku* (Reportage from the Year 2000). The essays deal almost entirely with Ukrainian themes, including several about her native city of Kiev, of which she professes herself to be an ardent admirer. This follows hard on the heels of her first published collection of essays, *Khroniki vid Fortinbras: Vibrana eseïstika 90-kh* (The Chronicles of Fortinbras: Selected Essays from the '90s, 1999). (The use of Fortinbras in the title echoes her previous collection of poetry first published in English, *Enter Fortinbras: A Kingdom of Fallen Statues: Poems and Essays by Oksana Zabuzhko* [Toronto: Wellspring, 1996].) The volume contains her well-known essay "Apologiya poeziï v kintsi 20-go stolittya" ("An Apology for Poetry at the End of the Twentieth Century") as well as other essays on literature and politics, again oriented mostly toward circumstances in postcommunist Ukraine. One of the most interesting deals with the woman writer in colonial culture, "Zhinka-avtor u kolonial'niy kul'turi, abo znadobi do ukraïn'skoï gendernoï mifologiï" ("The Woman Author in a Colonial Culture; or, Studies in Ukrainian Gender Mythology").

With respect to the culture of present-day Ukrainian society, Zabuzhko sees it as post-totalitarian, postcommunist, postcolonial, and, at the same time, "post-tragic," the idea being that it has lost its capacity to experience reality as tragedy. Zabuzhko's essays in general establish her as a writer of high intelligence, broad learning, and a sophisticated ability to tie together culture and politics. *Sestro, sestro* (Sister, Sister), which was originally published in 1999 and reprinted in 2003, is a collection of novellas and short stories containing the well-known "Divchatka" ("Girls") and "Inoplanetyanka" ("The Woman from Another Planet").

Crime, Punishment, Sex, and More Sex: The Postcommunist Urban Landscape

The path in Eastern Europe from state socialism and communist ideology to democracy and the free market has been rocky. Unemployment is widespread, and with it much grumbling. Outmoded state-subsidized industrial plants have had to be abandoned, giving rise to sometimes harsh economic as well as social dislocations. Progress has certainly not been negligible in the years since the collapse of communism in the late 1980s and early '90s, and there are significant differences from country to country. But the rate of progress, both politically and economically, has been uneven.

To a casual observer, life seems to be good. Luxury goods, including the latest model automobiles, are much in evidence; food is plentiful; new restaurants from the modest to the luxurious dot the urban landscape; the newest representatives of international hotel chains are everywhere; commercial and residential renovation and construction proceed at an impressive pace; a sharp increase in tourism has significantly added to the economy; and European Union and NATO membership—those highly visible rewards of good behavior—have already been achieved or are soon slated to be.

But freedom obviously has its price. Unemployment and the hunger for wealth have spawned crime of every conceivable sort. The Eastern European equivalent of Mafia gangs has sprung up throughout the region. Prostitution is rampant and in many cases organized as a "white slave" trade, as the talented Albanian writer Elvira Dones demonstrates graphically in her searing novel *Yjet nuk vishen kështu* (Stars Don't Dress Like That, 2000). Drugs are easy to come by and are widely used, giving rise to the health problems associated with substance abuse in the more prosperous West. Venereal disease, above all AIDS, is now a fact of life in Eastern Europe. Intolerance, in the form primarily of prejudice against local minorities, such as Gypsies in the Czech Republic and Slovakia, have become well known. And the problems legacied by the Bosnian War and the fighting in Kosovo have yet to be resolved definitively. Young people, often rootless, flock to cities in search of excitement and succumb to familiar lures. Increasingly expensive housing has put a severe strain on marriage, with divorce and infidelity greater problems now than they were under the communists.

The reappearance of former communists in positions of authority has bred considerable resentment and has given rise to de facto vendettas. Although most of the governments in Eastern Europe are pro-Western in orientation, in a few, such as Belarus and Ukraine, voters are torn between democratically inclined politicians and those favoring a new, closer relationship with Russia. Attempts to influence elections in these states by the Russians, such as the transparent intervention of the Russian president Vladimir Putin in the Ukrainian presidential election of 2004, are all too obvious.

The atmosphere of this postcommunist era has become a popular issue among contemporary Eastern European writers. Consider, for example, some Czech and Slovak examples. In his well-received novel of 1996, *Poslední stupeň důvernosti* (The Last Stage of Intimacy; translated as *The Ultimate Intimacy*), the prolific Czech writer Ivan Klíma (b. 1931) has touched on many of the ills of contemporary Eastern European society in a work set in Prague that deals primarily with fidelity and infidelity in marriage, and the dichotomy between faith and faithlessness in spiritual and moral life. The passionate affair between an otherwise upstanding Protestant minister and a woman who comes to him from a troubled second marriage serves as the context in which Klíma examines ideas of faith, spirituality, and God in society. Through a polyphonic narrative structure involving an omniscient author, the intimate diaries of the minister, and letters by several characters both major and minor, Klíma weaves a tale of complex marital and romantic relationships within the framework of the new postcommunist society. The minister's daughter by his first wife becomes pregnant by a young ex-con befriended by the minister, who believes that in order to raise the funds he needs to do good in the world he has to resort to trafficking in drugs. The ramifications of the drug problem in the new Czech Republic are fully explored by Klíma in the novel.

When not addressing the ills besetting society in the postcommunist period, Klíma makes it clear that crimes of the communist past will not be forgotten by himself and his contemporaries any more than they are forgotten by his characters. These include the terrible toll on the rural population brought about by agricultural collectivization; the frequent arrests and interrogations of citizens on the flimsiest of charges; the doings of the dreaded state security police; the communist persecution of the churches; groundless political imprisonment; the ruination of people with views regarded as opposed to the official positions of the regime; and so on.

The novels of the younger writer Michal Viewegh (b. 1962) brim with the realia of contemporary big-city life in Prague. His first novel, the fairly short *Názory na vraždu* (Thoughts on Murder), appeared in 1990. Narrated in the first person (like almost all of Viewegh's fiction), it is about the strange circumstances surrounding the death of a young schoolteacher. Viewegh's typical characters are mostly young people, often living on the fringes of society, young rebels without a cause, and out-of-the-ordinary types such as the few Vietnamese in Thoughts on Murder. Viewegh's second novel, *Báječná léta pod psa* (The Fabulous Awful Years, 1993; translated as *The Lousy Years of Blissful Living*)—which is set still in the communist period—was an immediate success and was widely translated. It was followed in 1994 by his next big success, *Výchová dívek v Čechách* (Bringing Up Girls in Bohemia), in which he returns to contemporary Prague. Narrated in a lighter vein, the novel chronicles the seriocomic results of the campaign by a Prague crime boss to hire a writer who will help his very independent daughter satisfy her own literary ambitions.

In his major work, the novel *Balada o sestupu* (*Ballad of Descent*, 1992), Martin Vopěnka (b. 1963), a Prague native who was trained as a nuclear physicist but gave up science for literature, seems to look back at the communist period and ahead to the postcommunist Eastern European era. Although *Ballad of Descent* was published in 1992, it was written between 1988 and 1990, thus while the communists were still clinging to power in Czechoslovakia, but at a time when the winds of change could already be felt. The novel has the quality of a dystopian allegory and could as well have been considered under the rubric of "allegory" in chapter 5.

With no indication as to the year, two young friends, Martin and Tomáš, the narrator, board a train in Prague and set out on a journey to the "Other Country" ("Ta země"). Which country is a question that remains unanswered, although there are ample hints along the way that Romania is intended. When the narrator speaks with dismay of mass demolition in the center of the town and "the heart of the town being stolen," it seems obvious that he has Bucharest in mind and the mind-boggling project by the Romanian dictator Nicolae Ceaşescu, who razed a huge part of the city in order to erect on the site his mammoth House of the People. Moreover, the people the Czechs meet soon after they arrive have Romanian names and the local speech is identifiable as Romanian. When Martin and Tomáš reach the Other Country, it appears to be an armed camp, in fact in a State of Emergency. Tomáš expresses disillusionment, because, as he says, "the State of Emergency that has been declared here, showing the ruling group's complete loss of touch with the interests of the citizens, immediately threatens my own corrupted country. There too the rights of the individual are no more than grains of sand under the feet of the powerful."[5] Remarks of this nature help establish the time frame of the novel.

While in the Other Country, where civil unrest is spreading, workers are in revolt, and armed troops are everywhere, the focus soon shifts away from the urban setting to a dense winter landscape of woods and mountains. The journey of the Czechs, especially the narrator Martin, into this landscape becomes a journey into the self, a journey of discovery, lyrical rather than epic in design. An aura of mystery and strangeness pervades much of Vopěnka's book, no more so than in the mountain episodes. Reality and imagination intertwine and a dreamlike quality infuses everything. Martin has come to know love in the Other Country in the form of the girl Livie, the daughter of a teacher and his family who befriended the Czechs soon after their arrival and with whom he has a brief but passionate love affair. However, Martin comes to realize that she cannot leave with him, that he has failed to save her from the chaos of her own country. When, at the end of the novel, Martin appears to awaken as if from a long dream, Livie's answer to his earlier question, "What do you really want from Life?"—"I want it to have value" (86)—and its implications for his own quest for identity in a totalitarian society may be the greatest gift he takes with him on his journey home.

Vopěnka's own Jewishness may also shed light on the underlying meaning of his novel. "Liberated" of a sense of ethnic identity and pride by the ideology of communist Czechoslovakia, Martin's journey may also be seen as a quest for his Jewish roots. In a revealing scene in the novel, he converses with a candlestick in Livie's home that he fears may fall and hurt him:

> "You frighten me," I whispered timidly. "I'd rather you tell me something ancient and beautiful."
>
> "It wouldn't be so ancient or beautiful. It's the story of a human quest that led back to where it started. And of yet another quest.". . .
>
> "I'd be a liar if I said I understood you," I replied. "My mother is of Jewish origin, father's not. I've always been trying to discover what I have Jewish in me. I've met it at every step of the way, but have been unable to catch it. It's like a puppy chasing its own tail."
>
> "If you were a Jew at heart, the tail would plug your mouth. But let's rather talk about me. I'm nothing now but a family memento. A reminder of roots. That's really my problem." (60)

And somewhat later in the same chapter the subject of the candlestick and its link with Jewishness comes up again, this time between Martin and Livie:

> "This teapot you were asking about," she started laboriously, as if she felt some debt, "it belonged to Momma's parents. Momma comes from a Jewish family. The candlestick in the room belonged to them too.". . . The candlestick recalled Jewishness, hers and mine. "Yes," I realized, "I am Jewish as well. Why did I forget to tell her?" (88)

Not to be outdone by their Czech cousins, especially since the peaceful division in 1993 of Czechoslovakia into the Czech Republic and the Republic of Slovakia, Slovak writers have turned their own capital city of Bratislava into a similar albeit smaller locus of iniquity, postcommunist style. When it appeared in 1991, the first volume of Peter Pišt'anek's (b. 1960) raw and violent novelistic trilogy, *Rivers of Babylon*—its English title derived from a Boney M song— caused a sensation. There simply had never been anything like it in Slovak. Its uniqueness was confirmed by the great enthusiasm for the 1998 film based on it that was directed by Vladimir Balco. Drawing heavily on the techniques of pop fiction, the cartoon strip (the style of the illustrations throughout the novel), pornography, and the thriller, the novel recounts the meteoric rise to power of a lowly boilerman named Rácz who works in the fashionable hotel Ambassador, "somewhere in Central Europe" (a thinly veiled Bratislava). In order to impress his future father-in-law with his enterprise, Rácz hits on the idea of using his ability to control the heat throughout the hotel in order to make people do his bidding. He is soon able to extort money as well as sexual favors (for which he has an insatiable appetite) from the hotel guests and staff. Before long, his growing financial assets and ruthlessness enable him to assemble a coterie of flunkies who stand ready to do his every bidding. He eventually takes over the hotel and then begins acquiring other properties, until his tentacles reach throughout Slovakia and beyond.

Pišťanek's obscenely violent view of the world gives the huge novel its punch and comments in its own way on postcommunist Slovak society. That some choose to view the work as a political allegory seems evident from its film history. Although plans were afoot to convert the first novel into a film not long after its publication in 1991, it was not until 1998 that the film was released. The Slovak Ministry of Culture had originally promised a state subsidy to enable production to move forward, but it reneged on its promise when the former Slovak prime minister within the Czechoslovak Republic, Vladimír Mečiar, became newly independent Slovakia's first prime minister. The figure of the rapacious Rácz had apparently struck too close to home for the former boxer, who was known for a tough autocratic style with little patience for democratic procedures. When the film was finally ready, there were those who took issue with certain changes that had been made to heighten the moral element in the novel, as represented by the characters Fredy Špáršvajn and Video Urban, a cheap pimp and black-marketeer. The filmmakers also made the tempting political reading more obvious, subsequently describing the cinematic version of *Rivers of Babylon* as Slovakia's first underground film. It became the Slovak Republic's official submission for an Oscar in the foreign film category.

The second novel in the trilogy, subtitled *Alebo drevená dedina* (The Wooden Village), appeared in 1994. Five years later, the third and last part came out, this time subtitled *Fredyho koniec* (The End of Fredy). These subsequent parts of *Rivers of Babylon* demonstrate Pišťanek's imagination at its wildest. The action moves at an ever-faster pace. Plots and counterplots for and against Rácz and his empire run rampant; the previously moralistically inclined Fredy (now referred to as the second Larry Flint) and Video Urban become the wealthy operators of a successful pornographic film company called Fredy Vision. In the third novel Slovakia has become so successful because of Rácz's enterprises that it stirs the enmity of a faraway Chechnya-like archipelago of vague Tartar-Turkish-Mongol character named Džundža (the name possibly inspired by Mikuláš Džurinda, Vladimír Mečiar's successor as Slovak prime minister). Oddly enough, in the novel Džundža has a substantial Slovak minority population that it oppresses and tries to turn away from everything Slovak; as one character describes the situation:

> But to be a Slovak isn't just a matter of blood. Above all it's a matter of will and feeling. There are many Slovaks, especially in the cities, who have borrowed Džundžian models, and in fact have become white Džundžians. They have accepted Džundžian nationality and have obtained Džundžian citizenship. And some have even submitted to plastic surgery on their eyes and lips in order not to look like Slovaks.[6]

When combat breaks out between Džundža and its Slovak insurgents, Fredy undergoes another transformation and becomes the "coolest" reporter covering the fighting, later joined also by Urban. By the end of the trilogy, the Džundžian Slovaks are victorious, thanks to the Czech cousins who have come to their aid, and the way is now open to build a new multiethnic state to be known as the Republic of the Slovak Archipelago. The republic, however, soon becomes an empire. Rácz, now a happily married man, appears at the end after a long hiatus in order to share the victory of the Džundžian Slovaks and to help in the reconstruction of the country.

With its large cast of pulp magazine characters and numerous allusions to Czech-Slovak relations before and after the peaceful separation of the two republics, contemporary politics in postcommunist Slovakia, current events in the Middle East and Central Asia, the deposed and executed Romanian dictator Nicolae Ceauşescu, and the Romanian Securitate, Pišťanek's *Rivers of Babylon* was bound to intrigue readers. And when the film based on the first novel—the best of the three—was finally released, it renewed interest in the trilogy as a whole.

If a political subtext could possibly be read into *Rivers of Babylon,* there is no mistaking the subversive element in Pišťanek's 1995 book *Skazki o Vladovi* (Tales of Vlado). This is a collection of stories about a certain Prince Vlado, an autocratic ruler who is adored by his subjects. But although they worship every word that tumbles from his lips, they understand none of it.

Slovenia, a small nation with an attractive but small capital, would seem to be no less insulated from the ills of contemporary urban civilization than the rest of Eastern Europe—or at least judging from contemporary Slovenian literature. Consider, for example, the older writer Peter Božič, whose fiction since the late 1980s has dealt primarily with the Ljubljana drug and crime scene in communist and postcommunist times. A successful journalist and dramatist, Božič also became well known for short stories and novels hailed by critics as the first modernist prose in Slovenia. Although his earlier murder mystery I Killed Anita (1972), and his World War II novel *Očeta Vincenca smrt* (The Death of Father Vincenc, 1979) were well received, his popularity reached new heights with the appearance in 1987 of his gritty short novel *Chubby Was Here* (its original title in English echoing the American "Kilroy Was Here" graffiti of World War II fame). Subtitled Notes from Memory, the work is presented as a recollection of the Ljubljana subculture of drugs, prostitution, and homeless youths in the 1960s and '70s, with allusions to the political unrest of 1964, 1968, and 1970. The novel pivots on the mysterious disappearance of Chubby, a reputed dope dealer and murderer who has assumed near-mythic proportions. More in line with *Chubby Was Here* than with his earlier work, Božič's relatively more recent writing from the 1990s, such as the novels Man and Shadow and Behold the New Authority, deal similarly with the dark undercurrent of contemporary urban life with its rampant casual and professional sex and drug trafficking. With army deserters, jailbirds, exotic characters such as the dancer Cica Oriental, and allusions to the Albanian mafia, Behold the New Authority lays fair claim to a more cosmopolitan character than Božić's previous works.

Other contemporary but younger Slovenian writers—for example, Brane Mozetič (b. 1958), Andrej Morovič (b. 1960), Mart Lenardič (b. 1963), Aleš Čar (b. 1971), and Polona Glavan (b. 1974)—follow similar paths in their exploration of contemporary Slovenian society. A certain sense of alienation, the absence of clear goals, and the willingness to yield to the thrill of the moment pervade their work. Language is street-tough, jarring, often monosyllabic. As in Božić, but with much less of his exoticism, drink, drugs, casual, graphically described sex, love as animalistic conquest, the supercharged atmosphere of the disco, physical aggression, and insensitivity are the staples of a seemingly aimless everyday existence. The model, as we have seen, is the new fad of pulp fiction, as represented, for example, by the Sin City stories of the American writer Frank Miller and such immensely popular films as *Pulp Fiction, Kill Bill,* and *Sin City.*

A widely respected poet, Brane Mozetič (b. 1958) is a leading figure in Ljubljana's gay literary community, editor of the gay journal *Revolver,* and currently director of the Center for Slovenian Literature. He is the author of several books of poems, one of which, *Metulji* (*Butterflies,* 2000), was translated into English in 2004. He has also published two collections of short fiction, *Pasijon* (*Passion,* 1993), which was translated into English in 2005, and *Zgubljena zgodba* (Lost Harmony, 2001), as well as an anthology of homoerotic love under the title *Modra svetloba: Homoerotična ljubezen v slovenski literaturi* (Blue Light: Homoerotic Love in Slovenian Literature, 1990). Mozetič is an aggressively homosexual writer, and one of the roughest of the species. His prose works, narrated for the most part in the first person, almost as stream of consciousness, describe the attraction to certain males, the games of gay contact and conquest, the rough coupling, the gratuitous violence, drug use, the association of sex and death, and the frequent sense of disgust at being unable to realize an ideal, to find another person capable of true feeling.

After graduating high school in his native Ljubljana, Andrej Morovič traveled abroad, where he sought out the subculture in such cities as Berlin and New York while keeping himself alive by working as a day laborer. After he returned to Slovenia in the 1990s, he became a champion of so-called alternative culture. In more recent years he has gained a certain prominence also as a social activist and speaker at international forums. After *Bomba la petrolia* (Bomba la petrolia) in 1989, he published two other novels, *Tekavec* (The Courier, 1991) and *Vladarka* (The Ruler, 1997), and four collections of short stories. In most of his works, beginning with *Bomba la petrolia,* the pace is torrid, as characters race from country to country and from city to city in search of drink- and drug-drenched adventure; the settings—European, American, Asian, Australasian—are urban, and tough; the focus is on the young, and multinational; the sex (straight, gay, transvestite)—always very near the center of a Morovič novel or short story—is frequent, unromantic, and graphic. And—in accordance with what has become virtually normative for this type of fiction in Eastern Europe—allusions to American pop culture abound. The works of William Burroughs are required reading. Often narrated in the first person, Morovič's style is brisk, unadorned, straight to the point; slang permeates his speech. That Morovič has remained consistent in his writing since *Bomba la petrolia*, albeit with more deft touches of light humor and irony, is evident from The Ruler, a first-person narrative by an itinerant female expert in sadomasochism.

In Mart Lenardič's story "Program Plus," from the collection *Še večji Gatsby* (The Greater Gatsby, 1994), a young man's obsession with a TV beauty he encounters in a disco is inadvertently thwarted by the reappearance of the girl-friend he came with but hoped he could palm off on friends. Frustrated, he finally rids himself of the girlfriend but fails to make contact with the beauty. Desperate, he falls into a kind of mad state for several days, until he sees the beauty on TV and, as if trying to drag her out of the appliance, destroys it and then hurls it out a window. When he comes to, he reaches for the phone, but only to call the friend he tried so hard to get rid of. Flush with victory and full of himself, the young boxer in Lenardič's story "Fajter" ("The Fighter"), also from The Greater Gatsby, comes home to his woman and wants to make love to her. After all, in the shower after his winning bout, he had "cleaned his dick" with "special lovingness" in anticipation of the big night ahead. But the object of his desire rebuffs him because she has to be up very early the next morning. When a similar failure recurs on successive nights, she finally confesses that she has fallen in love with a concert violinist. The boxer seeks out his rival, bangs him around, then reconciles with his girlfriend through a virtual rape. The violence and sex in these stories by Lenardič reflect more than anything else the hold on the new postcommunist generation of Eastern European writers of the dynamics of the Western pulp fiction genre as represented by both Pišt'anek and Božić.

The ubiquity of such garish and sensationalist writing in small countries like Slovakia and Slovenia (and not only these two) may suggest that for younger writers especially popularity and even international status are achievable with this style. Otherwise, one is hard pressed to explain what we find in this by no means unusual excerpt from the title story of the collection *V okvari* (Out of Order, 2003) by Aleš Čar, the author of such novels as *Igra angelov in netopir-jev* (The Game of Bats and Angels, 1997) and *Pseći tango* (Dog Tango, 1999):

> The woman wanted to continue with her efforts to animate me down below but I stopped her, and with the tips of my fingers closed her eyelids: she grew calm though I could see that she was confused. I leaned in toward her face, let out a stream of spit, aiming at the ring of mascara around her eye. The spittle fell slowly so I adjusted and it hit her left eye. She opened her right eye, looked at me bewildered and then pressed the lid down again. The second time I missed and the saliva fell on the edge of her lips. The third time, I hit right below the right eye and smeared her lashes so it looked like she'd been crying and, in that instant, I was ready: I turned her around, leaned her over the toilet, braced my

hands against the tiles above the seat and plunged into her. We tried to control
our breathing. The woman untied the scarf around her neck, though it probably
wasn't necessary. Because on the other side of the thin partition they had started
to fuck like crazy.[7]

In Čar's first novel, The Game of Angels and Bats—a success in Slovenia and
winner of a literary prize for a first novel—he espoused essentially the same
outlook on life as in his subsequent writing. The central figure is Father Faus,
the new parish priest in a small mining town, who at the very beginning of his
church service meets the woman who proves his undoing, the morally loose,
troubled Nasja. Strongly attracted to her, Faus loses no time in taking up her
company. Making matters worse, he succumbs not only to the femme fatale,
but also to alcohol and drugs. When Nasja gets married, the priest is unable
to free himself from bad company despite his awareness that he is sinking into
a hell of his own making. He traffics with prostitutes and contracts a case of
gonorrhea that lands him in a mental hospital, where he also finally meets up
again with Nasja. Faus is typical of Čar's main characters—hedonistic, nihil-
istic, inhabitants of a small world with all its weaknesses from which they are
unable to extricate themselves.

Čar's next novel, *Pseći tango* (The Dog Tango, 1999), is built around the figure of the young Ljubljana writer Viktor Viskas. When we meet him in August
1999, he is alone on a road, by himself, without funds, girlfriends, or ideas
about the future. No matter what he grabs hold of to try to improve his lot, he
meets with failure. But his greatest friends and supporters are dogs, who seem
to adore him. Full of ironic observations about the contemporary political scene
in Slovenia, the novel uses the character of Viskas to encapsulate a generation
in transition from socialism to the new postsocialist era. Čar's style is brisk
and cinematic as it follows Viskas along at a hectic pace through the Slovenian
capital.

Polona Glavan, a comparative literature and English major at Ljubljana
University who had already begun making a name for herself in the short-story
genre, published her first novel, *Noč v Evropi* (A Night in Europe), in 2001.
The action of the novel takes place within a ten-hour time frame, mostly on the
night express train from Paris to Amsterdam. Characters originating from the
four corners of the globe converge on the train at the Gare du Nord, and their
interaction forms the substance of the five-chapter novel. However, the baggage
they carry with them is already familiar from the works of such other younger
Slovenian writers as Čar and Morovič: an absence of clearly defined goals in
life, the desire thus to live for the moment with little or no thought to the future,
free and easy sex and shifting romantic loyalties, drugs, smoking and drinking,
and the seemingly never-ending quest for new experiences.

Andrej Blatnik (b. 1963), a leading light of contemporary Slovenian literature, first attracted favorable attention with his novel *Šopki za Adama venijo*
(The Bouquet for Adam Is Withering, 1983), regarded in Slovenia as the first

independent book of the generation of the 1980s. He has cemented his reputation with his later novels *Plamenice in solze* (Torches and Tears, 1987), *Tao ljubezni* (Tao of Love, 1996), and *Biografije brezimenih* (Biographies of the Nameless, 1989), an important text in the maturation of Slovenian literary postmodernism. In the English-speaking world, Blatnik is best known for his short-story collection *Menjave kož* (*Skin Swaps*), a significant part of which was written in the Ledig House International Writers' Colony in northern New York (see chapter 10) and which appeared at the beginning of the 1990s. *Skin Swaps* was followed by a second collection of short stories, *Zakon želje* (The Law of Desire, 2000). The work may be regarded as a sequel to *Skin Swaps*. The number of stories in both collections is exactly the same, sixteen, although no special importance need be attached to the number. They are all dated between 1991 and 2000 and, as in *Skin Swaps,* are ten to thirty pages long.

The terrain with which Blatnik is most comfortable is that of the relations between the sexes, which he treats with sophistication, good humor, and irony. Chance encounters, fleeting relationships, resigned farewells, misunderstandings, and reconciliations are the stuff of many of his stories. In view of his travels, especially in the United States, the human landscape is frequently cosmopolitan. His style is direct and laconic, in both prose narration and dialogue, as, for example, in the opening lines of "O čem govoriva" ("What We Were Talking About"), the first story in The Law of Desire: "I met her in the American Center. I had to return Carver's book *What We Talk About When We Talk About Love,* which I had read as much of as I could. I walked in uneasily, involuntarily, because I saw that the librarian was waiting for me with a stern look and shaking his head since today was the deadline for the book's return."[8] The reference to the highly regarded "minimalist" American short-story writer Raymond Carver (1930–1988) discloses a shaping influence on Blatnik's writing. So too does the epigraph to the story "Uradna verzija" ("Official Version'), a quotation from the songwriter David Byrne's lyrics in *Women vs. Men:* "So remember be careful / should one cross your path / One innocent movement / and it could be your last / No one knows how it started / and God knows how it'll end / The fighting continues / Women versus Men."

An outsider from early on who spent a year and a half in prison for deserting the army during the Martial Law period, the Pole Andrzej Stasiuk has a keen understanding of the outsider mentality and drew on it on more than one occasion in his writing. Leaving the urban environment of Warsaw, where he was born, he settled in an abandoned house in an out-of-the-way mountain village near the Ukrainian border. A poet, playwright, and literary critic, Stasiuk got his breakthrough with his novel *Biały kruk* (*White Raven,* 1995). A group of Warsaw friends, all men in their early thirties, wisecracking and cynical, decide to leave behind the drabness of their everyday lives and plunge into a wilderness adventure in winter in the remote mountain region Stasiuk himself had come to know so well. The lighthearted camaraderie of the men is soon challenged, however, when one of them senselessly kills a Polish border guard who has stopped them to check their IDs and backpacks. The rest of the novel details their attempt to outrace the pursuers they imagine will soon be upon them. The weather progressively worsens and the men's trek turns harrowing. By the end of the novel some of their number are dead from natural causes and the remainder are trudging on into a snowstorm that is sure to consume them. Description of the awesome landscape the men traverse on their odyssey is punctuated by stops in villages, where they meet a variety of local people. This breaks up the tedium of the near-constant challenge of nature and provides some occasional if rough humor as well as additional danger. The murder of the border guard occurs early in the novel, thereby allowing Stasiuk to trace the disintegration of the solidarity of the men in the wake of the crime. The deeper they plunge into the wilderness, staying off main roads to elude pursuers, the harder the going gets and the more the fabric of their relationship tears.

There is another dimension to the novel. The first-person narrative moves not only through space but through time as the narrator returns to different stages of the men's past lives up to the initiation of the ill-fated trip. The purpose of this is twofold: to sketch their backgrounds and relations with one another and, more important, to paint a depressing picture of the drabness and dreariness of life under communism, a life of seeming purposelessness filled with alcohol and the smoke of cheap cigarettes. Recalling the excesses of their youth, one of the group asks, rhetorically:

> How on earth did we manage to pull it off? How did we manage not to die from alcohol, cigarettes, sleepless nights when, having finished all our shitty schools, we struck camp in those rooms for weeks, months on end? Our bodies were taking it in and cried for more. . . . Sometimes someone tried to make contact with reality, yielded to motherly despair and started looking for a job, found it and left it.[9]

When one of the group asks another, "Tell me, what were you doing in 1980?," this dialogue, typical of many in the work, ensues: "The usual stuff. Nothing." "And '81?" "Same shit.'" "'82?" "Likewise" (200).

In a broad sense an allegory of postcommunist life in Poland, *White Raven* attracted much attention on its publication, which was then augmented by the popularity of the film based on it. The novel was awarded three of Poland's prestigious literary awards, those of the review *Kultura* (1994), the Koscielski Foundation (1995), and S. B. Linde (2002). Stasiuk has also added to his reputation with The Walls of Hebron, about his time in prison, and *Opowieści galicyjskie* (*Galician Tales*), a stunning portrait in the form of prose ballads about a mythical village—much like the remote border community he has lived in—trying to make sense of and adjust to the new economic realities of the 1990s. With his newest novel, *Dziewięć* (Nine, 2004), Stasiuk has again returned to the genre of crime fiction. Set in Warsaw in the early 1990s, and crammed with realia of the Polish capital, the novel deals with the growing criminal entanglements of a small-time entrepreneur who is unable to repay a loan. On its surface a crime novel, the book serves as a vehicle for Stasiuk to paint a depressing picture of contemporary Eastern European money lust and rapidly declining values.

These declining values are very much at the center of the popular first novel—*Lampa i Iskra Boża* (The Lamp and the Divine Spark, 2002; translated into English as *Snow White and Russian Red*)—by the young Polish writer Dorota Masłowska (b. 1983). Drenched in the drug, sex, and violence culture of post-communist Eastern European fiction, The Lamp and the Divine Spark also comes illustrated in the original edition with comic book–style drawings reminiscent of those gracing the pages of Pišt'anek's *Rivers of Babylon;* it also easily brings to mind the Czech Jachým Topol's *City Sister Silver.* The Lamp and the Divine Spark consists of one long obscenity-ridden free-associative, at times hallucinatory, first-person narrative by the principal character, the young man Andrzej Robakoski, nicknamed Nails. His contempt for women, politics, the communist past, the postcolonial economic exploitation of Poland by the Russian mafia—as he sees it—the violation of the rights of animals, and society at large colors virtually every page of the novel. The women Andrzej takes up with after his girlfriend Magda leaves him seem to live on drugs and suffer, disgustingly, from their aftereffects. Masłowska, anything but a prude, leaves little to the imagination.

Similarly depressing views of postcommunist capitalism, albeit through the prism of more imaginative texts, have been expressed by the Hungarian writer Ágotá Bozai (b. 1965) and the Bulgarian Alek Popov (b. 1966). A freelance writer, with one previously published novel, Bozai has done well internationally with her best work to date, *Tranzít glória* (1998; translated into English as *To Err Is Divine*). At the center of Bozai's narrative is the high-principled school-teacher Anna Lévay. Overweight and prone to sweating, she suddenly becomes aware of a halo above her head one evening while taking a bath. Although she regards herself as an atheist, Anna now believes that sainthood—and the miracles associated with it, such as the gift of healing—has been conferred on her. Before long she falls prey to an opportunistic neurologist at a local hospital, who makes a fortune exploiting Anna's saintly powers. The town she lives in becomes inundated with people suffering from a variety of maladies, all looking for cures they have been led to believe Anna possesses. Honest and upright, she finds consolation from the drabness and sorrow of her life—her husband was killed in the 1956 revolution and her only son emigrated permanently to the West—in learning (mastering the Basque language, for example). The sheer drudgery of Anna's life, compounded by her reluctance to recognize her new-found powers, contrasts sharply with the greed and entrepreneurial spirit of the neurologist.

The author of several popular collections of short stories, among them *Drugata smurt* (The Other Death, 1992), *Mrusni sunishta: Raskazi na uzhasa i absurda* (Dirty Dreams: Stories of Horror and the Absurd, 1994), *Zeleviyat tsikul* (Cabbage Cycle, 1997), *Putiyat kum Sirakuza* (The Road to Syracuse, 1998), and *Nivo za naprednali* (Advanced Level, 2002), Popov published his first novel, *Mission: London,* in 2001. Like Bozai's *To Err Is Divine,* it quickly became a success both nationally and internationally. A recognized writer as well of radio plays and film scripts, Popov has won several literary awards and also served as cultural attaché of the Bulgarian embassy in London from 1997 to 1998. At present he is director of the (Bulgarian) Center for Books for Children and Young Adults, editor in chief of the literary review *Rodna rech,* and press secretary for the Bulgarian PEN Center.

If Popov's short stories spin lurid tales of sex and crime, often with an international flare, *Mission: London* is a satirical-absurdist work about ludicrous events involving the Bulgarian embassy in London, a setting Popov obviously knew well from his own service there. Narrated by an omniscient author, *Mission: London* focuses on the antics of members of the embassy staff and others on its periphery. In the most bizarre scheme, a young domestic servant at the embassy, who does double duty as a nightclub stripper to make ends meet, is hired to dress up as Princess Diana for the gratification of the fantasies of well-heeled private clients. All the while, the clueless newly appointed Bulgarian ambassador is in the throes of planning a gala charity dinner to which Queen Elizabeth herself will be invited. Interest also centers on a planned exhibition on "Hygiene in the Bulgarian Lands," at which the Bulgarians hope to present what they claim as a Bulgarian invention, the world's first toilet. But since the British have a well-documented claim to this distinction, Bulgarian officials are loath to do anything that might hamper their efforts to smooth Bulgaria's integration into Europe.

Beneath the lightheartedness of Popov's tale is the indeed serious matter of Bulgaria's ambition to be welcomed into the European Union and the view of Western nations that Bulgaria has a way to go—socially, economically, environmentally, politically—before this can happen. The conflicting views of East and West toward each other in the postcommunist era—and these not limited just to Bulgaria—lie at the core of Popov's novel. Against the background of the events described in *Mission: London,* the picture painted of conditions back in Bulgaria is anything but flattering, and the worst nightmare of any of the embassy personnel is the thought that at a certain time they will have to leave London and return home. Popov's *Mission: London* is certainly no significant literary breakthrough, but Popov is a good, racy storyteller, and the novel is entertaining even as it broaches a serious subject. However, in the long run Popov's many short stories may prove more rewarding reading.

Other contemporary Bulgarian writers deal with similar themes. Nikolai Valchinov (b. 1950), an actor and film director as well as a writer, describes in *Sezonat na kanarchetata* (The Season of Canaries, 1993)—which was eventually made into a movie—the humiliations and sacrifices suffered by the individual under the communist regime. Somber and pessimistic, the novel concerns the tormented relationship between a mother and her son. No sooner is he released from prison than the son learns from his mother that he was born out of rape and that because of circumstance she was unable to raise him. In a flashback, the mother reveals how she was forced to marry her rapist in totalitarian Bulgaria, the son of an important party official who had no other interest in her whatsoever. In order to isolate her from family and child, her mother-in-law arranged to have her committed to an asylum, where she was forced to work at hard labor and to submit to sex with the authorities. After many years she finally managed to escape. In the final blow, when she at last unburdens herself to her son, he can only look at her with hatred and disgust.

Similarly devoted to unmasking the evils of communist totalitarianism, but more imaginative, are the thirteen stories and novellas in Evgeni Kuzmanov's (b. 1941) collection *Foto "Lazur"* (Photo-Azur, 1990). By means of allegory or fantastic absurdity, Kuzmanov depicts the means by which the totalitarian system robs the individual of his freedom and values. The universal character of his work is underscored by the fact that all his heroes are named Petrov (the Bulgarian Everyman). However, unlike Valchinov, Kuzmanov avoids simplistic black-and-white portrayals of the underdog. Although theirs is a losing battle, his characters manage to voice their own individuality and thus preserve a fair measure of integrity. Understandably, his book could not be published in Bulgaria until after the collapse of communism.

The falling away of taboos, particularly in the areas of sex and substance abuse, is, as we have seen, a dominant characteristic of works by younger Eastern European writers, notably women. But writers whose careers were launched before the end of communism have also joined in the whittling away of taboos related to that dismal era. This is especially true, for example, of the Hungarian woman writers Érszebet Gálgoczi (1930–1989) and the much younger Ágata Gordon (b. 1963). Gálgoczi came into the limelight when her 1980 novel *Törvényen belül* (Within the Law; translated as *Another Day*) was made into a popular film by Károlyi Makk and released under the title *Egymásra nézve* (Regarding One Another). The novel concerns two female journalists, Éva and Livia, who are in love with each other. Éva is killed in mysterious circumstances while trying to cross the border, and the novel then moves to recount her affair with Livia through flashbacks. Outspoken politically, Éva cannot bring herself to confess her lesbian attraction for Livia. Only when she is interrogated by a detective after Livia's husband shoots her does she become explicit about their relationship. Gálgoczi's novel is built on the parallels between political dissent and sexual dissent. Éva is thus a rebel on both counts, as indeed Gálgoczi herself was.

Ágata Gordon's *Kecskéruzs* (Goat Rouge, 1999) is her first novel. Although patently about lesbian love, the novel is neither openly erotic nor in any way prurient. It is rather an intensely introspective and lyrical self-examination by the heroine, the young girl Leona who begins to notice in adolescence that she is attracted to members of the same sex. Constructed as a series of lyrical pictures and divided into forty small, unpunctuated chapters marked off by lines of poetry on separate pages in different print styles, the novel retraces Leona's childhood romances until her great love, Isolda, enters her life. Together with another couple, Gerle and Paloma, Leona and Isolda retreat to a hideaway in the woods, where they are free to love as they wish away from public scrutiny. But Isolda betrays Leona with Paloma and Leona is eventually left alone in their once-idyllic retreat. She is taken to a hospital by friends and there comes under the care of the heterosexual Dr. Orsolya Hostell. A "light" novel in terms of a certain playfulness and undeniable superficiality, Goat Rouge attracts attention more for its subject than its literary merits.

Lesbianism also forms the subject of the 2000 novel *Rok perel* (The Year of Pearls) by the Czech writer Zuzana Brabcová, whom we have met previously as the author of the novel Far from the Tree. As she traces the love affair between a forty-year-old wife, mother, and successful professional editor and a twenty-four-year-old woman, Brabcová's narrative skill soon becomes evident. The novel's emotional intensity comes from the transformation of the older woman's life. Previously stable and calm—at least on the surface—it becomes dramatically altered by her inability at a certain point to control her erotic attraction for another woman. As she struggles with her own desires, the relationship with the younger woman becomes progressively obsessive and masochistic.

Another yet graver social taboo, incest, crops up in the first novel by the talented Hungarian poet Zsuzsa Rakovszky. Published in 2002, *A kigyó ámyéka* (The Snake's Shadow) is a historical novel set in the year 1666 in Löcse (now Levoca, in Slovakia) and Sopron among Hungary's ethnic German population. Although most of Hungary was then under Turkish occupation, these two towns remained outside the orbit of Turkish power. But that did not spare them destruction in the near-constant warring between Catholic and Protestant factions and the ravages of plague. The novel's central character, and its narrator, is Orsolya Lehmann, who at a young age loses her mother to plague. Her father remarries, but the baby that his new wife (also named Orsolya) bears is stillborn. The plot then becomes more intricate, as Orsolya's father devises a plan to save the honor of his daughter, who has been seduced by a young aristocrat and becomes pregnant. His plan, by which Orsolya pretends to be his wife, and his second wife (the other Orsolya) his daughter, also serves the far darker purpose of satisfying his incestuous feelings toward his own daughter. With Orsolya's illegitimate child born secretly, the family settles in Sopron. When the second wife, Orsolya, dies unexpectedly, father and daughter find themselves trapped in the forbidden relationship from which neither is able to break free. The strength of the narrative, the quality of the writing, particularly in the descriptions of nature, the nuanced psychological insights, and the intriguing historical background lift Rakovszky's novel far above the ordinary and explain the splendid reception that it enjoyed among critics and public alike.

A young girl also stands at the center of Rakovszky's second novel, *A hullócsillag éve* (The Year of the Falling Stars, 2005). Again set mostly in Sopron, near the Austrian border, the novel is also historical except that this time the history is considerably more recent, the first half of the 1950s. The central figure of the novel is again a young girl, Piroska. After the death of her father in 1952, she grows up in a cramped apartment with her widowed mother and an elderly domestic servant. Because of the family's bourgeois origins, life is anything but easy for them in this bleak period of early postwar Hungarian communism when social tensions were deliberately exacerbated by the regime. Rakovszky handles this important dimension of the novel with impressive understanding, particularly in her depiction of what Piroska is forced to experience in nursery school. Rakovszky is no less skilled at depicting the unfolding of a young girl's consciousness as she gradually becomes aware of the situation around her, both privately and in the larger social context of the times. Another dimension of the novel involves the mother's romantic attachments. Strongly attracted to the theater critic Bartha, who cannot free himself of the domination of his lover, a secret police agent, and who escapes to Vienna during the Hungarian Revolution of 1956, she finally settles for the less colorful but steady Pista, who has returned from a Soviet labor camp, where he was interned as a prisoner of war.

The Year of the Falling Stars remains in the end a sensitively written tale of thwarted hopes and dreams (the "falling stars" of 1956 alluding metaphorically not simply to the red stars [of communism] tumbling from buildings during the revolution). Although narrated in the third person, the novel is constructed mainly of Piroska's thoughts, impressions, and recollections. These are interspersed with fragments of letters and diaries that seem to have at best only a tenuous connection to the main concerns of the novel and recall Rakovszky's use of similar material in The Snake's Shadow. And, as in her first novel, Rakovszky the poet makes ample use of passages of lyrical power to capture the fearful and fragile world of the child.

Eastern European Narratives of Recollection

The end of the communist era unleashed a flood of literary works united by the common thread of recollection. As if free of the demons of the recent past, writers sought to review and reassess the events they lived through in the post–World War II period. For the first time they were able to talk openly about the ordeals they had to endure in order to get books published, the long delays at times in their efforts to meet the demand for changes on the part of censors, and the problems with unsympathetic critics. Some insisted on viewing their personal situation from the broader perspective of what it meant to be a creative artist in a totalitarian society.

But revisiting the past for other writers, especially younger ones, meant above all an attempt to recreate through remembrance their earlier years, when childhood was a time of traditional values, before the full impact on these values of a communist social and political order could be felt. The experience of dislocation was in some instances the engine that drove such recollection. Apart from the dislocation brought on by the departure from a native town or village, there was the more wrenching dislocation of physical resettlement within new borders drawn in the aftermath of the war and the consequent shifting of populations. There was hardly a people in Eastern Europe that remained unaffected by such dislocation. Germans were expelled from areas ceded to Poland, while

Poles were resettled in cities like Danzig/Gdańsk and Breslau/Wrocław that were at first alien to them; Polish Wilno and Lwów became, respectively, the Lithuanian Vilnius (now the capital of Lithuania) and the Ukrainian Lviv; and Hungarians and Germans who had been in Romania for generations and longer were discomforted into leaving during the Ceauşescu era. The accommodation to the new, and the sense of discovery that was a dimension of it, was often accompanied by a nostalgic yearning for the old.

Nostalgia looms large in much of this literature, prompted in part by the desire to recapture a time of innocence associated with childhood and in part by the need to find anchors in the uncertainties of postcommunist society. These tendencies are much in evidence, for example, in contemporary Polish and Slovak literatures.

Typical of the nostalgic writing inspired by memories of family and childhood are the prose and poetry of the Pole Aleksander Jurewicz (b. 1952). A native of the village of Lida, which is located in what used to be Soviet Belorussia and is now the independent state of Belarus, Jurewicz began turning his attention to the past in his novella *W środku nocy* (In The Middle of the Night), which dates from 1980 and is where the Lida theme first appears in any significant way. The growing compulsion to revive the past led to his second novella, *Lida* (1990; 2d ed. 1994), for which Jurewicz won the Czesław Miłosz Prize and that of the Maria and Jerzy Kuncewicz Foundation. A mixture of prose and some poetry, with excerpts of letters from his grandmother from 1989, the novella recreates in a splendidly evocative way—including the local dialect—the circumstances of his departure from Lida and arrival in Poland at the age of five. Since much of the text consists of dialogue, the work may be considered bilingual.

The extraordinary detail in the descriptions of landscape, movement, and attitudes (including resentment and even anger on the part of Poles with respect to the large influx of newcomers from the east) suggests that *Lida* is more creation in fact than recreation. This hardly diminishes its stature. Moreover, the feeling for the passage of time is effectively conveyed through the shift of perspective from that of the five-year-old to that of the thirty-five-year-old looking back on his own distant past. The warmth of *Lida*'s nostalgia is also enhanced by the mythic element woven into the narrative. The novella closes with a series of poems grouped under the title "Kronika Lidzka 1986" ("Lida Chronicle, 1986") that view the landscape of Lida in the present and in which the narrator addresses the five-year-old boy of the past in the second person. Seen from the present, the past assumes the contours of a dream.

Still unable to let go of his Lida past, Jurewicz returned to it yet again in his next work, *Pan Bóg nie słyszy głuchych* (The Lord Does Not Hear the Deaf, 1995). A short text of under a hundred pages, The Lord Does Not Hear the Deaf is a first-person narrative in which Jurewicz recalls his growing up in rural Belorussia (Belarus) and his very close relationship with his grandfather, who stands at the center of this warm remembrance of a time past. The author notes his grandfather's habit of sleeping with a small packet of Belorussian soil beneath his pillow that he would withdraw from time to time and hold in his hands like a prayer book as he recited his evening prayers. The memoir indeed begins with the figure of the grandfather in the forefront of the narrative. At the end, the narrator departs on a train that will carry him into the new phase of his life, far from the grandfather who is integrally bound up with the dearest memories of the past. The uprootedness Jurewicz experienced in his own life when he was wrenched from Lida in his youth remains the overarching concern of his writing.

The incorporation of the Baltic port of Danzig/Gdańsk into post–World War II Poland and the exodus of Germans from the city has given rise to a curious phenomenon in postcommunist Polish literature. Younger Polish writers born there after the war have developed over time an intense interest in the city's Germanic past and its dual cultural heritage. This somewhat parallels the broader interest in Poland's Jewish heritage since the annihilation of most of the country's Jewish population and the destruction of many of the most important monuments associated with the Jewish past. Two writers whose names are most often linked with the "Danzig/Gdańsk phenomenon" in recent Polish literature are Stefan Chwin (b. 1949) and Paweł Huelle (b. 1957).

Although he began his career several years earlier, Chwin rose to a celebrity he had not previously enjoyed with the publication of his novel *Hanemann* (1995; translated as *Death in Danzig*). Critically situated in the contemporary current of "mythographic" prose—also sometimes referred to as the literature of "small fatherlands"—Hanemann, however, is not easily typecast within the boundaries of this genre. Obviously reflective of Chwin's obsessive fascination with a specific locale, in this case German and Polish Gdańsk, as well as with objects as signs of historical continuity, Hanemann operates within what at the outset appears to be a criminal plot. Hanemann himself is a doctor on the staff of an anatomical institute. When he first appears he is confronted with the corpse of a woman he obviously knows well who lost her life in a ferryboat accident and on whom he is now expected to perform an autopsy. However, he cannot bring himself to do it, and leaves the institute amid a swirl of gossip. Before long the scene abruptly shifts to the evacuation of townspeople from Gdańsk before the arrival of Russian troops in World War II. With few exceptions, Hanemann's characters are all German, as is Hanemann himself. Chwin's technique of weighting his text with enumerations of families quitting the city, the minutiae of their activities at the time, and the objects they are taking with them or abandoning makes for slow, at times even ponderous reading. Nevertheless, this serves as an effective means of conveying the cumulative impact of the dislocations of war.

Chwin's novel *Esther* appeared in 1999. Unlike Hanemann, Esther is set primarily in Warsaw in the early twentieth century; it assumes a cosmopolitan air through its characters who travel between Heidelberg and Vienna and its strong Russian dimension, in view of the fact that Warsaw at the time was a part of the Russian Empire. Although Esther deals less directly and prominently with the Danzig/ Gdańsk setting of Hanemann, Chwin's characteristic concern with the matter of Polish ethnic diversity and attention to the details of an urban setting are very much in evidence. Instead of being divided into chapters, the novel is broken up into a number of smaller units, each separately titled, thereby creating the impression of a series of looser episodes. The novel closes with two discrete structural components, an epilogic section in which the author kaleidoscopically reviews the subsequent fate of characters and objects from the Russian Revolution through World War II, and an italicized section titled "Sandals in Hand" that links up with the italicized quasi-preface to the book.

Both sections appearing in italics are set in the present. The prefatory one, "Ulica Nowogródzka 44" ("44 Nowogródzka Street"), is related by the narrator, a son of the Ciekliński family, which stands at the center of the novel as a whole. Long-standing residents of Warsaw, the Cieklińskis were finally uprooted by the Warsaw Uprising of 1944 during World War II and resettled in the Gdańsk region, where their two sons, Andrzej and Aleksander, were born. Filled with the memories of their years in Warsaw of his parents and grandparents, the narrator, whom we may presume from the context to be the younger brother, Andrzej, finally makes his way to the apartment house on Nowogródzka, which has somehow miraculously survived all the great upheavals of the twentieth century. During his first time in Warsaw, on a trip clearly intended as a recovery of the past, with old photographs as well as family memories as his guides, the narrator begins the process of recall, establishing the temporal setting of the novel proper as either 1898 or 1900. Contemporary reality reappears in the second italicized section, at the end of the book, where the first-person narrative yields to that of an omniscient author who shares with the reader Andrzej's thoughts as he is about to leave Warsaw.

The penultimate narrative voice, to which the novel belongs, is that of the elder Ciekliński son, Aleksander. Although crowded with events and Chwin's familiar concentration on locales and objects as defining place, in a kind of loving reconstitution of early-twentieth-century Warsaw, the novel has a specific focus, that of the young woman, Esther, after whom the novel is named. Esther is a French and German tutor from Danzig by way of Vienna whom the Cieklińskis hire for their two sons. The novel begins in fact with news of the arrival in Warsaw of Esther Simmel and from that moment on barely loses sight of the character. Esther soon becomes an integral part of the family and beloved by all. But before long she falls ill, apparently with malaria. The family consults several physicians, but with little success. In desperation, they turn to a Russian healer who is clearly modeled on the figure of Rasputin. The healer, however, abandons his "cure" when he cannot suppress the demon (or demons) unleashed from within Esther in a scene reminiscent of the once-popular American movie *The Exorcist*. This is hardly the only strange circumstance in the novel. As if woven together of a series of digressive elements, which take on a life of their own, other strange events create an atmosphere of melodrama, tension, and at times unreality.

The other Polish writer prominently identified with the thematics of Danzig/ Gdańsk, Paweł Huelle, became an instant celebrity with the publication of his first novel, *Weiser Dawidek* (David Weiser; translated as *Who Was David*

Weiser?, 1987). His subsequent two collections of stories, *Opowiadania na czas przeprowadzki* (Stories for a Time of Moving, 1991; translated as *Moving House*) and *Pierwsza miłość i inne opowiadania* (First Love, and Other Stories, 1996), fared less well critically. Following the publication of a new collection based on his two previous books of stories, *Byłem samotny i szczęśliwy* (I Was Lonely and Happy, 2002), Huelle returned to his Gdańsk past in his newest novel, *mercedes-benz; z listów do Hrabala* (Mercedes-Benz; From Letters to Hrabal, 2002).

Who Was David Weiser? is Huelle's most celebrated work to date. It has been regarded as the most important Polish literary debut of the 1980s and has been widely translated; it was also made into a film by Wojciech Marczewski. Set in Gdańsk and its environs in the summer of 1957, thus twelve years after the end of World War II, *Who Was David Weiser?* presents a narrator who carries the reader with him into the world of his childhood past. The tale is set in motion with the schoolhouse interrogation of three twelve-year-olds concerning the strange disappearance of their playmate, David Weiser. The first-person narration is also focused on discovering the elusive truth about the extraordinary Weiser, a quest complicated by the reluctance of anyone who ever knew him to talk about him. Previously an object of derision, mostly because of his Jewish origin, Weiser gradually grows into a figure of magical stature. He is credited with all sorts of powers and knowledge (in particular, the whereabouts of a cache of World War II weapons). Truth be known (it is not to his schoolmates), Weiser in a sense was almost literally hoist with his own petard: a pyromaniac who also liked playing with explosives, he died in a blast inside a tunnel.

Mercedes-Benz, which came out in 2002, is another, this time more light-hearted, work of nostalgia. The narrator (easily identified with Huelle himself) recalls the mortification he felt the first time he sat behind the wheel of a small Fiat with a female driving instructor at his side. In order to put off the final day of reckoning as long as possible, he coaxes from his imagination a tale centered on the fine automobiles owned by his two grandfathers: one a Citroën crushed by an express train from Wilno, the other a Mercedes requisitioned by the Soviets in the Lwów area during their invasion of Poland in 1939. A family history as well as an excursion into the troubled Eastern European history of the past and present, especially during the interwar period, the novel is also an exercise in intertextuality. The work begins in fact with a line in Czech addressed to the Czech novelist Bohumil Hrabal: "Milý pane Bohušku, a zase život udělal mimofiádnou smyčku" ("My dear Mr. Bohušek, life has once again rolled an uncanny loop"). Huelle is alluding to Hrabal's own earlier attempts at learning how to ride a motorcycle, which he made the subject of a humorous story. Focusing on the parallels between his own novice driving experiences and those of Hrabal, Huelle weaves a running monologue with the Czech author into his own narrative.

While hardly the only prominent Slovak writer to explore the past of his own youth, Milo Urban (1904–1982) fashioned an entire tetralogy out of the material. As a representative of an older generation of Slovak writers who began their careers before World War II, Urban had summoned up his past as early as 1970 when his book *Zelená krv: Spomienky hájnikovho syna* (Green Blood: Remembrances of a Gamekeeper's Son) was first published. In its 323 pages, Urban carries his readers on a nostalgic, leisurely, and remarkably detailed journey back to the very beginning of his life and thence through childhood to the completion of secondary school and his first attempt at writing a novel. Green Blood was eventually followed by what is regarded as the second part of his memoiristic tetralogy, *Kade-tade po Halinde: Neveselé spomienky na veselé roky* (Here and There Across Halinda: Unhappy Memories for Happy Years), which first appeared in 1992. If indeed Urban thought of Green Blood as the first in a series of volumes of a retrospective nature, political circumstances in Czechoslovakia intervened to delay publication of the second volume until considerably later.

Here and There Across Halinda covers primarily the period of the 1920s, when Czechoslovakia emerged as an independent state following the breakup of the Austro-Hungarian Empire in the aftermath of World War I. The book covers such topics as relations between the major ethnic communities in the new state—Czechs, Slovaks, Jews, and Hungarians—as well as Urban's school years, his apprenticeship with the journal *Slovenský národ,* and bohemian life in contemporary Bratislava. *Slovenský národ* folded in 1926, and Urban had been associated with it since its inception. In general, Here and There Across Halinda is engagingly written, casual, light, full of informative tidbits about people and places. Urban's favorite haunt, the Astória coffeehouse in Bratislava, is lovingly recalled, and the reception of his first novel—and one of his best books—*Živý bič* (The Living Whip, 1927) is described in detail, including the Czechoslovak president Tomáš Garrigue Masaryk's enthusiastic comment, "Dobrá práca" ("A good piece of work"), before he even knew who the author was.[10] Although not primarily concerned with political issues, Urban far from ignores them. But arguably the strongest appeal of the book is the picture it evokes of interwar Slovak journalism. Although he had cooperated also with the journal *Slovanské pohľady,* Urban's loyalties were with *Slovenský národ;* when it closed, he says there were few opportunities for him to work as a journalist except for Communist Party–affiliated newspapers.

The rest of Urban's tetralogy consists of *Na brehu krvavej rieky: Spomienky novinára* (On the Shore of a River of Blood: A Journalist's Memoirs, 1994) and *Sloboda nie je špás: Spomienky dôhodcu* (Freedom Is No Joke: A Pensioner's Memoirs), which he had completed in 1977 but which remained unpublished until 1995. This last volume may in some ways be the most interesting of Urban's memoirs, as it covers the turbulent period from 1948, when the communists took power in Czechoslovakia, to the late 1970s. Noteworthy in the book, as we previously observed, is Urban's candor concerning the Slovak treatment of Jews during World War II. Urban's minimal attention to the situation of the Jews in postwar Slovakia is more than adequately compensated for by the writer Miloš Žiak's *Jewropean* (1997). Although not a work of fiction, it sheds much light on the fate of the Slovak Jews in the post–World War II period, the reasons behind their support of the new communist regime, and their status in a postcommunist independent Slovak state.

For the prominent, and highly idiosyncratic, Slovak writer Dušan Mitana memories of the past were bound up with his hometown cemetery. Indeed, his principal book of recollections is entitled *Môj rodný cintorín* (My Native Cemetery, 2000). It is a warm, often amusing, and eccentric account of his small-town family life and the role played in the community by its cemetery. The cemetery has a twofold meaning for Mitana: it is the repository of living memories, and it is the actual town cemetery, the repository of the physically deceased.

Religion obviously had an important place in the community, but as one might expect from Mitana, it was anything but straightforward, traditionalist Catholicism. This becomes evident on the first page of the work when he describes the grandfather's benediction at mealtime:

> Grandfather began dinner with the words: "Peace unto you," and we, his disciples, responded: "And to your spirit too." And he answered: "Thanks be to God, that He has granted us this Jell-o, may you enjoy it. Amen." We hurried up since we wanted to finish eating before the arrival of the [Lutheran] minister. We knew that they'd be here at four. Two or three times a month they stopped off at our place. For a discussion.[11]

Religious discussions, among Catholics, atheists, and Protestants, took place fairly often and were quite lively—as, for example, the one described in chapter 5 among a minister, a priest, Mitana's grandfather, and other members of the family, where serious, comic, and folkish elements combine. A Jewish motif is introduced when, at the end of several chapters, Mitana interpolates passages from the Kabala, in Hebrew, as supportive of certain "prophecies." Also interwoven into his narrative are excerpts from a bibliographic oddity—Fr. Ján Maliarik's *Celo-Zemský Universalný Štát* (The All-World Universal State), which was written, as Mitana describes it, in "Slovak-Czech-Polish-Hindi-Hebrew" and was the inspiration for his own study of foreign languages.

The role of superstition in the town, and Mitana's ability to extract humor from almost anything, is demonstrated in the reaction that he describes to the supposition at one point that a late snowfall forebodes the end of the world. When that should come to pass, the question is asked what will people live on, how will they be able to continue making slivovica, that "foul psychostimulant of organic origin used and abused since ancient times even in the northeastern region of western Slovakia." There then follows a short disquisition on the origin of slivovica:

> Slivovica is worse than alcohol, that medicinal, intoxicating drink whose name derives from the word AL—unequivocal proof of its Arabic origin. . . . The first producer of ALcohol was evidently ALlah. He gave it to the Arabs as a gift of God.

But the moment they began to abuse it, he instituted—through his intermediary Mohammed—the uncompromising law of abstinence and permitted them to drink either on the sly or in foreign lands. And in place of alcohol, he bestowed crude oil on them, by which he definitively liquidated them. (160–161)

In her own family memoir, *Víc než jeden život* (More Than One Life, 1994), Miloslava Holubová (b. 1913), a senior member of the Czech literary community, drew a compelling family portrait that grows progressively darker over the course of the story. Although it is disarmingly casual and offbeat at the outset, little by little there accumulate details that shed light on a dysfunctional family tyrannized by a father who seems incapable of communicating with his children and a wife incapable of communicating with her husband. After twenty-six years of marriage, he asked his wife for a divorce the night before she left for a sanatorium with a serious illness, romanced a girl thirty years his junior, made a mess of everything, including the family business, and even failed at a suicide attempt, which further strained relations with his children. After the father's death, his children discover boxes and boxes of personally revealing journals, which they decide to burn after reading some of them. A few poignant excerpts from these journals are incorporated, in italics, into the text of the memoir. With both their parents eventually gone, the children engage in seemingly endless discussions about the personalities of both and what made them so incompatible. At the end of the account, the author describes the pilgrimage she and her siblings make to their father's favorite mountain in order to at last scatter the ashes they had kept in an unmarked urn for ten years.

The popular Czech entertainment figure Halina Pawlowska (b. 1955)—a talk show hostess, editor of an illustrated entertainment magazine, and author of a series of popular "women's novels" devoted in the main to the tragicomic aspects of relations between the sexes—published in 1994 her semiautobiographical novel *Díky za každe nové ráno* (Thanks for Each New Morning). A year later it was made into an award-winning film of the same name for which Pawlowska herself wrote the screenplay. What distinguishes Pawlowska's book from similar narratives of adolescence and life in general in the period of so-called normalization is the fact that her perspective is not only that of a woman, but that of a member of the Ukrainian minority living in Prague. The protagonist's father (like Pawlowska's own) is a Ukrainian poet from Transcarpathian Ruthenia, and much of the book's poignancy and humor derive from the family's cross-cultural eccentricity. Thanks for Each New Morning is a warm, stylistically uncomplicated narrative about Pawlowska's family background, her father (in particular), their neighbors in Prague, and Ukrainian "parties" held in Prague just before Christmas at which she was expected to perform her father's poems.

With *Smeh za lešeno pregrado* (Laughter Behind the Wooden Fence, 2000), the prominent Slovene writer Jani Virk (b. 1962) published an engaging, richly detailed, in some ways poignant first-person narrative about the small town in

Slovenia in which he grew up, his family background, the local public school, the accidental drowning of his only real friend, which he witnessed, and the impact on the townspeople of the last years of World War II, the liberation, and the beginning of collectivization under Tito. The time frame of the novel is the decade from 1951/52, when the narrator was seven years old and about to enter school, to the spring of 1961. A running dialogue with his lively, earthy alter ego (printed in italics), who is preoccupied with the female body, adds another voice, as it were, to the narrative and functions as the prism through which the past is often viewed or commented on. Although politics is not the main focus, Laughter Behind the Wooden Fence spans some of the harshest years of Yugoslav communism and manages to fold in reflections of the reality of the times without calling undue attention to them. When, at the end of the novel, Pavel, the narrator, yearns to duplicate the space feat of the Soviet Union's first astronaut, Yuri Gagarin, by hurtling across national frontiers, the meaning is clear.

An acknowledged masterpiece of contemporary Bulgarian literature, and fairly well represented in translation (although not into English), Ivaïlo Petrov's Before I Was Born and Afterward (1973) combines autobiography, Bulgarian history in the early decades of the twentieth century, a knowledgeable picture of pre–World War II Bulgarian village life, and social criticism into a compelling whole. Born in 1923, Petrov began his literary career with the publication in 1953 of a collection of stories entitled *Krushtenie* (Baptism). Like his later short novel *Na chizhda zemia* (On Foreign Soil, 1982), the collection focuses on the fortunes of the ordinary soldier in World War II, which Petrov himself had participated in toward the end of the war. His breakthrough as a writer came with the novel Nonka's Love (1956), which deals with the impact on a young peasant woman of the transformation of Bulgarian rural society brought on by communist agricultural collectivization and industrialization. As we have seen earlier, this was one of the great issues of post–World War II Bulgarian, and Eastern European, literature.

In the light of the devastation brought to Croatia and Bosnia-Herzegovina by the wars of the Yugoslav succession of the 1990s, one can easily appreciate the temptation on the part of writers from these regions to revive a happier past. The Croatian Josep Cvenić (b. 1952) is a case in point. His native town of Osijek was one of those villages most devastated during the fighting. Cvenić paid tribute to it by reviving memories of his youth there in his 1997 novel, *Kajinev pečat* (The Mark of Cain). Cvenić's newer novel, *Kraljica noći* (The Queen of the Night, 2000), is also set in Osijek, and may have an autobiographical substratum. Originally composed as a scenario for a television film, and only subsequently developed into a novel, it tells the story of a fifteen-year-old rower named Marko who is in training for a race to be held on the Drava River, which runs through Osijek. The importance of the event is underscored by the fact that it will be attended by none other than "Comrade Tito"—an almost abstract figure in the work—who will personally fire the start pistol.

Although the novel has a political dimension to it—the race becomes the means by which Marko secures his father's release from jail, where he had been held as a dissident—it is primarily about the sexual maturation of a young man. In a curious twist, Marko, the favorite of the race, suffers from a potentially serious condition known as cryptorchismus, or an undescended testicle. During hospitalization, his affair with a nurse named Jagoda reverses his medical condition. Marko and his team go on to win the race, which he dedicates to Jagoda, and his father is subsequently freed. The "queen of the night" of the title refers to a type of cactus that is distinguished by the beauty of its flower, which opens only at night. The rather insubstantial yet undoubtedly autobiographical story of Marko, Jagoda, and Marko's salvation from probable infertility serves primarily to point up the artistically generative power of Cvenić's memories of his badly battered but beloved city of Osijek.

Mythologizing the Past: Some Polish Examples

Recreating the past in the spirit of myth is a noteworthy trend in several novels by the prominent contemporary Polish writers Piotr Szewc (b. 1961) and Olga Tokarczuk (b. 1962).

A native of the southeastern city of Zamość, Szewc attracted considerable attention with his first novel, *Zagłada* (*Annihilation*, 1987), which has been translated into English, French, German, and Italian. *Annihilation* is a small novel that sets out to recreate the atmosphere of the Jewish quarter of Zamość on a July day in the year 1934. Recovering the Jewish past has indeed become one of the hallmarks of postcommunist Polish literature. And where Jews have become scarce to the point of near invisibility, the imagination has come into play, as in the works of Stefan Chwin and Paweł Huelle. But where the Danzig/Gdańsk writers make individual Jews the focus of such novels as *Esther* and *Who Was David Weiser?*, Szewc's *Annihilation* has as its goal the recreation of an entire community that is frozen, as it were, in time—indeed on a specific day in time—and thus able to be immortalized before such communities were erased from the map and from the memory of most people. In a quiet, almost lyrical act of evocation, Szewc admirably succeeds in bringing to life a single day in the life of the Zamość Jewish population, with nary a hint at the terrible future just a few years away.

Szewc repeated his first literary success in his next novel, *Zmierzchy i poranki* (*Sunsets and Sunrises*, 1999). The setting is again southeastern Poland, although no specific mention is made of the city of Zamość. And again, the novel assumes the form of a recreation of a single day in the life of the community—its evocation rendered all the more vivid by the absence of chapter division. But unlike *Annihilation*, Sunsets and Sunrises does not focus primarily on Jews, although the small community is the dominant part of the town's landscape. Instead Szewc's emphasis is on various aspects of womanhood as represented by several dominant female characters, above all the shopkeeper Salomea Goldman, the paramour of Dr. Henryk Tarnowski, and the bakery proprietress Fajga Katz, and as seen through the eyes of the young boy Piotruś. No less realistic than *Annihilation* in its extraordinary detail, Szewc's second novel seeks to capture the harmony of everything in the community—people, nature, animals, and things (as, for example, the mechanical dolls in the watch-maker Chaim Brondwein's shop)—as they move from the dark of night to the light of day. The town in which Sunsets and Sunrises is set is thus a living organism in which plants, animals, and objects are anthropomorphized and move to similar rhythms. To cite a single example: as night sets in, the windows of Samuel Kahan's mill, "seen from Krasnobrodzka Street . . . recalled sunken eyeholes. The mill fell asleep. It still grumbled, as if scattered handmills were going around inside it now of their own volition; it gasped, shook, and breathed deeply, albeit more freely."[12]

Olga Tokarczuk, another outstanding member of the contemporary Polish literary community, and a trained psychologist, is known for her metaphysical and psychological interests. Both are much in evidence in her first two novels, *Podróż ludzi Księgi* (The Journey of the People of the Book, 1993) and *E.E.* (1995), which is set in early-twentieth-century Wrocław when it was part of Prussia and known by the name Breslau. In large measure a family novel, the "E.E." of the title is Erna Eltzner, a frail, sickly, fifteen-year-old girl who suddenly acquires parapsychological powers, who is then utilized in séances, and for whose treatment the family doctor advises an exorcist. At the end of the tale she is running a sewing shop and appears to have no recollection of the strange doings of her earlier life. Tokarczuk's two subsequent novels, *Prawiek i inne czasy* (Prawiek and Other Times, 1996) and *Dom dzienny, dom nocny* (House of Day, House of Night, 1998), brought her well-deserved international celebrity. *Prawiek* was published in French translation in 1998 under the title *Dieu, les temps, les hommes, et les anges,* and an English translation of *House of Day, House of Night* came out in 2002, the same year in which the novel won the Berlin Brücke prize.

With Prawiek Tokarczuk has gone deeper into the meaning and relevance of the past as time and space. Prawiek is the name of a small Polish town that figures as the setting of the work. The word in Polish actually means "distant or remote time"; it can also be taken to mean the universal past. In delineating the small-town relationships out of which the story is woven, Tokarczuk underscores their ultimate meaninglessness by suggesting that everything that happens is an instrument of time yet ultimately unnecessary to time, which moves on regardless. The novel in a sense makes time its most important element through its division of each chapter into small units, each of which is called *czas,* "time." The "freezing" of a past moment in time, as in Szewc's *Annihilation,* may serve purposes of nostalgia, but to Tokarczuk nothing in the past can be "frozen" because of the relentless process of time. Yet the novel also seems to propose—and this becomes more evident in her subsequent novel—that no matter how small, how trivial something may in fact be, it has meaning as a part of something larger. It is a part of a bigger picture, in other words, and it is the meaning of that greater entity that the characters in the novel struggle to grasp.

House of Day, House of Night operates within a known geographical space. It is set in the small Polish Silesian town of Nowa Ruda on the Czech border, the town where Tokarczuk herself lived when she wrote the novel. This part of Silesia belonged to Germany before World War II but was ceded to Poland by the Yalta and Potsdam treaties. In a by-now familiar shift of populations, Poles who had been displaced in the east from territory annexed by the Soviet Union were resettled in the "regained" territories of the west in a situation analogous to that of the demographic changes in Danzig/Gdańsk after the war.

Divided into a number of small units and beginning with a dream recounted by the narrator, *House of Day, House of Night* conveys a deep sense of alienation and displacement. Once the narrator and her husband are settled in Nowa Ruda, she begins to collect bits of information about the town's residents. It is these fragments, if you will, only tenuously linked by geography and history, that create the novel's random structure within the framework of the narrator's diary. The focus is much of the time on the town's oddities, like the drunk Marek Marek, who believes he had shared his body with a bird and finally succeeds in hanging himself after a few failed attempts. Or Franz Frost, who receives nightmares transmitted by a newly discovered planet. To protect himself he carves a helmet of ash wood but refuses to substitute a real helmet for it when war erupts and he thus is killed. The death of her son and others from eating poisonous mushrooms provides the pretext for the narrator's sharing a recipe based on them. Other similarly bizarre recipes also appear in the book. One of the strangest episodes recounts the martyrdom of Saint Kummernis. When she mysteriously grows a beard, she rejects her father's demands that she shave it off because she thinks it makes her look like Christ. Her father then kills her in disgust and anger.

In a deceptively straightforward prose style, Tokarczuk weaves an intricate and oddly compelling tale—simultaneously humorous, bizarre, and depressing—assembled from separate narrative sequences and much indebted to the obvious inspiration of magical realism. Boundaries between dream and day, the real and the imagined, dissolve, life appears a dream, and dream life, hence the title, the "house of day" connoting day, the "house of night" dream, both sides of the coin of human existence intimately bound up with the other. A serious student of philosophy, Tokarczuk holds Jung in great esteem, and the influence of his thought lies just below the surface of her novel.

Political Reckoning in Albania, Slovakia, and Germany

Albania makes an interesting case study of postcommunist political reckoning in the light of the harshness of the Enver Hoxha regime and the tremendous sense of relief experienced by most Albanians after its downfall. Among the earliest, and most important, responses to the new political climate came from the respected writer Fatos Kongoli.

A native of Elbasan, in central Albania, and a mathematician by training, Kongoli is the author of a novel tetralogy published between 1992 and 2001: *I humburi* (The Lost, 1992); *Kufoma* (The Cadaver, 1994); *Dragoi i fildishtë* (The Ivory Dragon, 1999); and *Endrra e Damokleut* (The Dream of Damocles, 2001). In The Lost, Kongoli follows the career of a young man, Thesar Lumi, who in March 1991 changes his mind at the last moment and decides against joining the many Albanians then attempting to flee to Italy by boat. The episode of the March 1991 exodus also reappears briefly in The Dream of Damocles. Relying on his wiles, Lumi eventually gains entry into the university and from there into the small circle of the powerful then ruling Albania. Kongoli is often at his best when depicting the small tight world of the politically powerful but pathologically paranoid. Although this dimension of communist-era Albania is in evidence in The Lost, the novel's main focus is on the corruption and degradation of Albanian daily life in the 1960s and 1970s, the period of Kongoli's own youth. Blending interior monologue, dialogue, and narration, The Lost remains one of the most resonant novels to come out of Albania in the early 1990s.

In The Cadaver, which followed The Lost by two years, Kongoli again uses a single character, the somewhat ludicrous, self-abnegating, and self-deprecating Festim Gurabardhi, an employee of a publishing house, to expose the inner rot of the last years of Albanian communism. Even more so than in The Lost, Kongoli seems to positively delight in exposing the political and sexual intrigues of the Albanian establishment. Capable of withering satire, Kongoli also cannot resist the temptation to lay into the pomposities and absurdities of big-city publishing, Albanian style. It was a milieu he himself knew well from his employment with the major Tirana publishing house Naim Frashëri.

Kongoli's third novel, The Ivory Dragon, by all means his most cosmopolitan work in terms of its international cast of characters, is also the most obviously autobiographical part of the tetralogy. As a young man Kongoli had the opportunity to visit China while a student. This was during the period of the Albanian-Chinese alliance of the 1960s and '70s, when for the Albanians China represented a counterbalance to the weight of the Soviet Union, with which it had broken off relations. Chinese state paranoia and the intrusion of politics into the everyday lives of foreign students, including their romantic relationships, motivate much of the intrigue of The Ivory Dragon.

While The Ivory Dragon is perhaps Kongoli's most interesting novel, The Dream of Damocles is surely his darkest. A young man commits suicide in the apartment of his friend, the narrator, in the autumn of 1997. Searching his apartment for any sign of a suicide note, the narrator stumbles across a notebook written by the deceased in which he recounts in vivid detail his tragic romance with a young woman whose family belonged to the political elite under the Hoxha regime. Pain over the forbidden relationship, which culminates in the girl's death, had plunged the young man, Ergys, into the depths of despair and a no man's land between sanity and insanity before his suicide.

The year before Kongoli published the first part of his tetralogy, another major Albanian writer, Neshat Tozaj, the author of the controversial novel The Knives (1989), began writing his memoirs. This was the time when Albania was moving toward its first pluralistic elections. The memoirs appeared in 1993 under the title Why I Speak: Retrospectives; the volume constitutes one of the most revealing looks at Albania in the crucial period of transition from dictatorship to democracy. An expert on forensic identification who worked first in the Department of the Interior in Peshkopi and then in its central offices in Tirana, Tozaj had a firsthand knowledge of the workings of the Sigurimi, the Albanian state security apparatus. Apart from revealing some of its methods in his recollections, he also uses this postcommunist publication to make amends for any inadvertent professional help he may have provided the Sigurimi in their harassment and persecution of political opponents.

Tozaj's memoirs were followed in 1998 by an interesting collection of largely political and literary essays from 1997–1998 by the versatile and cosmopolitan writer Teodor Laço (b. 1936). The political pieces in *Kohë për të kujtuar / Kohë për të harruar* (A Time to Remember / A Time to Forget), as Laço's collection is titled, cover Albanian and non-Albanian events and personalities, for example, the Romanian dictator Nicolae Ceauşescu, whose fall is seen from an Albanian perspective, and the former Albanian president and later prime minister Dr. Sali Berisha, whose repressive crackdown of political opponents and mismanagement of the calamitous "pyramid" investment schemes of the 1990s caused widespread dismay with his once-democratic government.

Anton Baláž, whom we met previously as the author of The Camp of Fallen Women (1993), is one of several Slovak writers who have settled their own score with Stalinism. In Baláž's case, it was in the form of the short satirical novel *Hijó, kone stalinove* (Heigh Ho, Stalin Horses) published in 1992. A journalist by training, Baláž became actively involved in politics from 1991 to 1993, first with the Peasant Social Union and then from 1993 to 1996 as an employee in the office of the president of the new Slovak Republic. Since 1999 he has been affiliated with the National Center of Media Communications in Bratislava.

Not all writers who suffered at the hands of the communist regime in Slovakia were willing to wait until the collapse of the system to express their views on what they had endured. Consider the case of Dominik Tatarka, a pillar of contemporary Slovak literature who was an ardent believer in communism and a supporter of the communist regime in the early post–World War II years. But when his faith soured, he turned with a vengeance on the system he had once admired. His absurd and grotesque antitotalitarian novella *Démon súhlasu* (The Demon of Consent, 1956), and his later denunciation of the Soviet invasion of Czechoslovakia in 1968, only aggravated the antagonism of the regime toward him. He became a literary nonperson and was denied permission to publish after 1969. His response to the ban appeared only much later, and beyond the borders of the Czechoslovak state, in the form of his most provocative literary work, *Písačky* (Jottings, 1984; published in Cologne, Germany). Regarded as a singular event in communist-era Slovak prose, Jottings is a celebration of love and an exuberant hymn to freedom in the form of an autobiographical novel of an uninhibited sexual nature. Inspired by his experiences in Paris, where Tatarka studied for a year before World War II, and his subsequent visit to the city, it is built around his relationship with the well-born Russian Orthodox woman he addresses variously throughout the book as "Dear Lutécia, Parízia, Letícia, Lutica, Čiča , the Most . . . You, my bony, hungry, eternally fasting, and absolutely familiar little body."[13] Consisting entirely of monologues and real or imagined intimate conversations between Tatarka and his lady love, Jottings surges with eroticism and sexual dynamics from beginning to end. Jottings was followed by the related but less explosive *Navrávačky* (Tapings, 1986; also published in Cologne, Germany). As evidence of Tatarka's official status as a nonperson even as late as 1987 his name was excluded from the multivolume *Dejiny slovenskej literatúry 4: Slovenská literatúra po roku 1945* (History of Slovak Literature 4: Slovak Literature After 1945), published by the Slovak Pedagogical Publishing House in Bratislava.

Since the fall of the Berlin Wall and the reunification of Germany there has been a flood of literature by former East German writers seeking—in many cases for the first time freely—to take stock of the reality of the now-defunct German Democratic Republic. Some of the best examples of this type of literature were written by Ernst Loest, the author of the previously discussed It Takes Its Course; or, Trouble on Our Level. Loest was also the author of several works capturing the complex attitudes of many East German citizens toward their own wartime past and their postwar life in the GDR. A former American prisoner of war, Loest could easily relate to their experiences.

The fairly short Today We Have a Visitor from the West consists of monologues by two former citizens of the GDR, who cast a rueful look back on their life under the communist regime. The second monologue is the more interesting of the two. It is spoken by a newly retired schoolteacher who had belonged to the Hitler Youth before the war and had taken a HY training course in shooting in the spring of 1943 in Silesia. After forty-four years educating children, he regards himself as a failure for not getting rid of Margot Honecker, the wife of the East German head of state who was GDR Minister for Education for a time, and for the fact that he and his fellow teachers were a cowardly bunch of conformists. Nevertheless, he expresses disappointment at the failure of socialism to triumph in East Germany and feels that he had no cause for complaint when he was dismissed from his job as a school principal in 1980 because his son had fled to the West via Yugoslavia. It was, however, his son's action that cost the schoolteacher his job and ruptured the relationship between father and son. Reflecting on his war years with little trace of repentance, he recalls how he had been a member of the Waffen SS and had participated in action against the Americans at Remagen. After the war, however—like so many others in East Germany—he had his SS tattoo removed, less out of shame than out of fear of the consequences.

Since the collapse of the GDR, access to State Security archives has led to a spate of revelations about the inner workings of the once-dreaded Stasi and the complicity of a number of writers (Sascha Anderson and Hermann Kant, among others) in their intelligence-gathering operations. In order to set the record straight by showing the extent to which he was an object of interest to the Stasi, Loest published in 1991 the book The Stasi Were My Eckermann; or, My Life with the Bedbug, which consists almost entirely of authentic state and secret police files about his case. In 1997 and 2003, respectively, he published another two books of nonfiction about parting company with the GDR and, again, about his problems with the censors over his novel It Takes Its Course; or, Trouble on Our Level. The first, When We Came West: Thoughts of a Literary Border-Crosser, is a collection of fifty short pieces on a wide variety of subjects, many of interest to historians of the GDR. The second, The Fourth Censor: The Novel *Es geht seinen Gang* and the Shady Characters, is a compelling insider's view of the workings of the East German literary establishment, especially the pressures on writers to cooperate or suffer the consequences, the weakness of those who both conformed and informed for the Stasi, and the petty intrigues fostered by the regime.

Émigré Experience

The number of Eastern Europeans dislodged by political events and economic conditions in the region since the end of World War II is staggering. And in this instance I am speaking not about literary exiles of the celebrity of Czesław Miłosz, Milan Kundera, or Ismail Kadare, but rather of the many thousands of ordinary people, from every walk of life, who, though not dislocated by wars from World War II to the Yugoslav campaigns of the 1990s, felt that conditions in their own countries made further residence there out of the question. Such events as the Hungarian Revolution of 1956, the anti-Semitic campaign in Poland in 1968, the Warsaw Pact invasion of Czechoslovakia that same year, the suppression of the Solidarity movement in the 1980s before its rebirth, the disintegration of Yugoslavia in the fires of the wars of the 1990s, and the collapse of the "pyramid" money schemes in Albania in 1997 have been catalysts for migration. In some cases, people returned home and picked up the threads of the lives they had left behind. In a far larger number of cases, once in emigration they chose to remain there and create new lives for themselves. How such people have fared, and are faring, has emerged as a current in contemporary postcolonial and postcommunist Eastern European literature. There is, to be sure, no balance sheet to be weighed and measured. If we give credence to works of literature, many created by artists who themselves have known life in emigration, then the picture is overwhelmingly bleak.

Some of the bleakest pictures are to be met in Albanian and Czech literatures, but in truth no Eastern European literature has a monopoly on bleakness in this respect. The Albanian writer Elvira Dones (b. 1960), who has lived in Switzerland since 1988, published her first novel, *Dashuri e huaj* (A Foreign Love), in 1997. It deals with the moral dilemma of an Albanian woman who must decide between remaining abroad with a foreigner she falls in love with on her first trip out of Albania or returning home for the sake of her family obligations there. A Foreign Love was translated into Italian in 1998 and attracted some attention because of its glimpse into the still little-known world of post-Hoxha Albanian society. Of greater resonance was her novel Stars Don't Dress Like That. This violent and sordid work exposes the terrible plight of Albanian girls who are seduced from provincial towns and villages into the "white slave" trade in prostitution operated by the thriving and vicious Albanian Mafia in such countries as Italy and Greece. The novel is built around the fate of the principal narrator, Leila, who is taken to Italy by her fiancé on the promise of a better life—only to be severely beaten by him, gang-raped by his Mafia cohorts, and then sold into slavery to ply her new trade on the streets of Milan. At novel's end, she finally returns to her Albanian homeland, in a coffin, with her father who hasn't seen her in three years nervously waiting to claim her remains. But Leila's story is but one of many, as Dones amply demonstrates in the cases of Elena, Laura, Teuta, Entela, Mynyre, and other teenage Albanian girls whose maltreatment and degradation at the hands of thugs and bullies ultimately serves as an indictment of an entire nation.

Sordid, insensitive, and lacking any moral compass is the world of the rootless portrayed in the "émigré" novel cycle of the Czech writer Iva Pekárková, which we have touched on in a previous chapter. Although she eventually reaches America, Pekárková's devil-may-care, amoral heroine has to first pass nearly a year in a brutal and degrading detention center for Eastern European refugees in Traiskirchen, Austria. This is the subject of *The World Is Round,* in which the sexual element in *Truck Stop Rainbows* is amplified and becomes even more graphic. Communal sex and brutal gang rapes are everyday occurrences, as Pekárková recalls one gruesome episode in particular:

And it smelled everywhere, smelled here in such a way that wouldn't let you forget what happened to that Polish girl in the coat red as a flower and all pissed up in the back. How could you not know about it, with all of Trais buzzing about it, the Albanians (or was it the Romanians?) got her—no, no, no, it was the Albanians, I know all about it. They dragged her off to their room, and not to rape her in a normal, humane way, so to speak, one, two, three, and that's that—sure, that happens—but not that crew, they stripped her completely from the waist down and screwed her with her legs spread on the lower bunk, and then so as not to have to trouble themselves with her too much, they tied her feet to the top bunk with belts . . . And they took turns on her, at least thirty of them, then they brought their buddies over to have a go too, and they were too lazy to go to the can for water, so they washed her underneath with beer . . . Well, you can just imagine how it stank, the whole mattress soaked with Kronenbier.[14]

In *Gimme the Money*, the last novel in her "émigré" cycle, Pekárková follows her expatriate heroine (now named Jindřiška) to New York, where she marries an African Muslim fellow immigrant named Talibe. Talibe's principal appeal, initially anyway, lay in his ability to help secure her a green card for purposes of employment. But difficulties in the marriage soon appear:

> Conversation between Talibe and his wife had been notoriously frozen for months. Perhaps it never existed at all, but they hadn't noticed it before. Jindřiška . . . was obliged to sit at home, not go anywhere (but nevertheless bring in as much money as possible—how, it wasn't entirely clear), change the sheets every day for the benefit of some tribal spirit who refused to live in soiled beds, clean, cook, look after Talibe's well-being, open her legs whenever he was in the mood, and keep her mouth shut just in case she was unhappy about anything.[15]

The relationship is further complicated by Talibe's stubborn clinging to African ways and his insistence that she wed his "cousin" Ouagadougou so that he too might obtain a green card. When she tries to explain that bigamy is against the law, Talibe replies that since her first marriage was in Manhattan and the second one will take place in the Bronx, everything should be just fine. Willing or not, Jindřiška goes through with the wedding and the oddities of attendant West African customs, among them the groom's inspection of the bride's uncircumcised genitalia. This focus on the tenacity of tribal customs among African immigrants in Harlem is one of the novel's most interesting aspects. *Gimme the Money* is cynical, sordid, and unsentimental, as all of Pekárková's writing to date; the title itself refers to the ever-present danger of holdups, and murder, faced by New York cabbies—the fate, in fact, that befalls Talibe. But *Gimme the Money* does manage a happy ending. After a harrowing, drawn out attempt on her life by a white passenger who appears to be the murderer of Talibe, Jindřiška stabs him to death in self-defense. She subsequently finds love, walks out on Ouagadougou, and heads west with her new lover in a "borrowed" taxi.

The award-winning Polish dramatist Janusz Głowacki (b. 1938), who had the opportunity to observe the Polish (and Russian) émigré scene in New York in the late 1970s and 1980s, made it the subject of two of his best plays, *Polowanie na karaluchy* (*Hunting Cockroaches*, 1986) and *Antygona w Nowym Yorku* (*Antigone in New York*, 1992). *Hunting Cockroaches* is an absurdist glimpse into the wretched lives of a couple of Polish émigré artists in New York in the post-Solidarity period. The play has had phenomenal success on the foreign stage. Its world premiere took place at the Manhattan Theater Club in New

York in 1987, and it was subsequently staged in more than fifty American theaters as well as in a number of other countries. *Antigone in New York,* a great success in its own right, is set in that favorite haunt of the homeless in New York City, Tompkins Square Park. It features a group of three homeless people—a Polish émigré, a Russian-Jewish émigré artist, and a young Puerto Rican girl of the streets—who become involved in a bizarre plot to retrieve her dead boyfriend's body from Potter's Field, where the anonymous dead are buried, for a "decent" burial in Tompkins Square Park. This play, too, has been widely staged throughout the world, beginning with the Arena Stage production in Washington, D.C., in 1993.

One of the bright stars of contemporary Polish writing about Poles abroad is Manuela Gretkowsa (b. 1964). In late 1988 she resettled temporarily in Paris, where as a writer she sought her material primarily among Polish and other émigrés, Slavic and non-Slavic. A prolific author, she has published six books to date: *Tarot paryski* (Parisian Tarot, 1993); *Kabaret metafizyczny* (The Meta-physical Cabaret, 1994); *My zdies' emigranty* (We're Emigrants Here, 1995; title in Russian in the original); *Podręcznik do ludzi* (A Manual on People, 1996); *Światowidz* (1998; the title refers to an old Slavic deity with four faces); and *Namiętnik* (The Man of Passion, 1998).

Gretkowska's first three books deal mostly with life as an outsider in France. With a keen power of observation and a delicious sense of humor she writes about cultural oddities she comes across in Paris as well as about emigrants she encounters during her stay abroad. Her writing is casual, witty, and highly entertaining. In The Metaphysical Cabaret (1994), a slight book of a little over a hundred pages, her focus is on a Parisian cabaret on the Rue Chabanais, its star performer a stripper named Beba Mazeppo, the proud possessor of two clitorises whose fond desire is to marry a man with two penises. Before long, however, Gretkowska sets off on excursions into medieval European art and above all Greek and Jewish history and thought, of which her knowledge is undeniably impressive. As if somehow to underline the marginality of her sub-ject, Gretkowska arranges the sections of her book as extended footnotes, each marked off by an asterisk and situated beneath a line dividing the text proper (here nonexistent) and the footnote. Asterisks in the body of most footnotes lead to explanations in subsequent footnotes and so on.

We're Emigrants Here (1995), wherein émigré experience is more directly addressed, takes the form of an informal diary beginning in the fall of 1988. The entries are either by season or by month until Gretkowska gets to October 1989, when they become daily, albeit not in regular sequence. Days are skipped and before long we are in July, where the book ends with a final entry for the 22nd of the month. When not sharing her observations on the mores of emi-grants and native Parisians or playing with identity (at times pretending to be a Russian in order to elicit the differing reactions of foreigners toward Poles and Russians), Gretkowska's lively intellectual curiosity leads her to various cultural and academic venues and eventually results in a scholarly work on the parallels between the Greek goddess Artemis and Mary Magdalene. In the course of her research she also furthers her study of Hebrew, the Kabala, and Hasidism, to which a number of pages are devoted in The Metaphysical Cabaret and which was reflected earlier in Parisian Tarot.

Raising the issue of the phenomenon of the émigré's frequent self-loathing as an émigré and his or her repudiation of his native land and culture, she recounts the words of one young Pole she came across in the French capital:

> I've simply stopped feeling a Pole and that's that. If I still had a Polish passport, I'd toss it into the Seine. I've always suspected that between Poland and me there's something that's not quite right.[16]

He then recalls what happened when he met some Poles who had come to Paris to earn money as handymen (a frequent motif in contemporary Polish literature). In a bar one night, after much drinking, the other Poles stand up at the stroke of midnight and sing the Polish national anthem. When they finish, they ask him why he doesn't join in. His answer: "And what kind of an anthem is it that begins in desperation with the words 'Has Poland not yet perished?' It's perishing, it's perishing, and it can't stop perishing. We have to change the hymn, or we'll end badly." His attempts to convince the others that the medieval *Bogurodzica Dziewica* (The Virgin Mother of God) would be a more fitting hymn, and would link Poland with the whole of knightly Europe and the Christian West, fall on deaf ears. But he continues nevertheless: "Poles have been singing *Jeszcze Polska* . . . (Poland has still not . . .) since pre-school and what good have they had from it? From that Poland that still hasn't perished journalists, councillors of state, and engineers have been coming here to earn their bread as manual laborers." At this, his fellow Poles denounce him for being a Pole no longer and then toss him out the door.

Most of the émigrés from Eastern Europe left for both political and economic reasons. In many cases they left in search of freedom; in many other cases they left to escape want. But there were instances where they left because they belonged to an ethnic minority that had begun to experience discrimination. Apart from Albanians and Serbs driven out of their traditional places of habitation in Kosovo during the Balkan wars, the most notorious example of ethnically motivated emigration in Eastern Europe involves the Germans of Romania.

A very old community going back centuries, the Romanian Germans, usually known as Saxons, lived primarily in the Banat region of the country or in Transylvania. There may be no better introduction to the way of life of these Romanian Germans—apart from sociological studies—than the poet Ioana Ieronim's book *Triumful paparudei* (Fool's Triumph, 1992). Herself of Romanian-German origin, Ieronim (b. 1947) was moved to write *Fool's Triumph* by the imminent destruction after the communist takeover of Romania of the Saxon Transylvanian community where she had spent her childhood. In essence a series of prose poems by a poet of impressive sensitivity and nuance, *Fool's Triumph* paints a warm picture of a village life ruled by rituals of tradition doomed to extinction, both by secret police arrests and expropriation.

Another Romanian-German writer, Herta Müller (b. 1953), who was forced to leave Romania in 1987 because she refused to cooperate with the Securitate, has written about the plight of Romanian Germans who have left Romania and resettled in Germany, as she herself did. Unlike Ioana Ieronim, however, Müller writes in German. Her first novel, the slender *Der Mensch ist ein grossser Fasan auf der Welt* (Man Is a Big Pheasant in the World, 1986; translated as *The Passport*), consists of a series of short, loosely related prose pieces built around the figure of the village miller Windisch, whom circumstances are forcing to migrate from Romania. He has applied for his passport and is waiting for the rest of the family to receive theirs. The mainspring of Müller's writing is obviously her desire to convey the sense of despair about their future in Romania on the part of the German ethnic minority.

Like Ieronim, her canvas of German village life is meticulously detailed, and sometimes no less poetic. Townspeople and small everyday events come vividly to life. But in one respect Müller differs from Ieronim, and that is in her propensity for images of cruelty, especially toward animals. The skinner who finds his vocation early in life by skinning a goat live in the village square is a good example. Husband-wife relations are more often than not coarse, sometimes brutal. It is as if the dire circumstances of the community impose a near-constant state of nervousness, fear, and hostility. Amidst requisitioning and expropriation, the urge to emigrate grows desperate and it soon becomes known that the fast track to the precious baptismal certificates and passports runs through the private quarters of the local parish priest and militiaman:

> The night watchman has told Windisch that the priest has an iron bed in the sacristy. In this bed he looks for baptismal certificates, with the women. "If things go well," said the nightwatchman, "he looks for the baptismal certificates five times. If he's doing the job thoroughly, he looks ten times. With some families he loses and mislays the applications and the revenue stamps seven times. He looks for them on the mattress in the post office storeroom with the women who want to emigrate."[17]

And so it is with Windisch's daughter Amalie, who he once vowed would not fall into the same trap as the other women. But near the end of the novel she gives herself to the priest and the militiaman at the same time. The baptismal certificates and passports thus obtained, the Windisches pack their possessions into suitcases and prepare to leave Romania for Germany and an uncertain future.

Müller followed *The Passport* with three other novels, all available in English translation: *Reisende auf einem Bein* (*Traveling on One Leg*, 1989); *Herz-Tier* (Heart-Beast, 1993; translated as *The Land of Green Plums*); and *Heute wär ich mir lieber nicht begegnet* (Today I'd Prefer Not to Meet Anyone, 1997; translated as *The Appointment*). The first deals with the experiences of a German woman emigrant from Romania, Irene, who now resides in Germany. It is Müller's best-known and perhaps most highly regarded novel. Consisting in the main of short declarative sentences and dialogue written in a matter-of-fact style yet full of poetic images, the novel depicts the essentially lonely life of its heroine, a loneliness, however, that she is able to control. Feeling little or no remorse over leaving dictatorial Romania—always referred to as "the other country" ("das andere Land")—Irene also finds that adjusting to her new life in Germany is less than satisfying. The officials she runs across at the immigration office are much like the officials she remembers from Romania. Even their dress is similar. Politically regarded, and treated as an alien, her life gravitates among three men she meets along the way: Franz, a fellow emigrant from Romania who seems incapable of returning her love; Stefan, a friend of Franz's toward whom she is ambivalent; and Thomas, a bookseller and homosexual.

Toward the end of the novel Irene receives two letters, one from the German Senate for the Interior informing her that in a week she has to report to be invested with German citizenship, about which she is anything but jubilant; and the other from a friend still in Romania. When she opens the letter from Romania, she is plunged back into the atmosphere of doom and death she had left behind:

> She opened Dana's letter. The drummer had hanged himself, Dana wrote. The back of the chair pressed against her back. The drummer was exactly Irene's age. . . . Irene knew a time would come when the living and the dead would be equally divided. But later, this time would come later, she thought earlier. This time would come only then when a person himself didn't have much longer to live. There were some friends that were as old as Irene and dead. Since they died, they had begun to look alike. A resemblance on the edge. But it was the same edge.[18]

In *The Land of Green Plums* the focus is not on the problematic adjustment to life in the West of emigrant Romanian Germans, but rather on the frequent harassment and interrogations to which young village people—Romanian Germans who are now university students—are subjected on the mere suspicion that they are contemplating emigration. Of the students whose fates Müller traces in this bleak and disturbing novel, the most poignant case is that of Lola, who wants to study Russian for four years; she joins the Communist Party, commits suicide in her last year of school by hanging herself by a belt in a closet, and is posthumously denounced for this in public by the party. The most overtly political of Müller's novels, *The Land of Green Plums* introduces the figure of the sinister Captain Pjele of the Romanian secret police, a kind of Grand Inquisitor whose job is to ferret out the students who scheme to flee the country and in some cases to continue to harass them even in emigration. Anyone considered still an enemy of the regime, for whatever reason, could enjoy no feeling of security in another country. One day, one of the narrator's friends, Edgar, receives a telegram. The message is simple, and chilling: "Early in the morning, six weeks after emigrating, Georg lay on the pavement in Frankfurt outside the transit hostel. Six floors up was an open window. The telegram said: Death was instantaneous."[19] One by one most of the circle of friends dies, by their own hand or otherwise.

Müller's newest novel, *The Appointment,* is much like *The Land of Green Plums,* although in this instance the representative of the Securitate is Captain Albu. Also narrated in the first person, the novel recounts the drab life of the narrator and her second husband, Paul, in between visits to Captain Albu, as if these visits were defining that life. As suggested by Müller, most Romanian Germans seem to live in dread of being summoned to Captain Albu's office for interrogation about their desire to emigrate, or about plans for emigration that have already been formulated. The mood of the interrogation is a strain on both parties, as the narrator describes her own experiences:

> During the interrogation I sit at the small table, twisting the button in my fingers, and answer calmly, even though every one of my nerves is jangling. Albu paces to and fro; having to formulate the right questions wears at his calm. As long as I keep my composure there's the chance he'll get something wrong—maybe everything. . . .[20]

Years now after the fall of the Ceauşescu dictatorship, Müller's accounts of the dread of being caught in the crosshairs of the Securitate are still chilling, the more so for being the experience of so many ordinary citizens throughout Eastern Europe in the communist period.

Minority Issues

Slovak Hungarians Have a Voice

Although it is more usual to think of the Slovak minority in Hungary (going back to Austro-Hungarian imperial times), in fact since the creation of the Czechoslovak state after World War I and the peaceful separation of Czechs and Slovaks in 1993 Hungarians have represented the largest ethnic minority in Slovakia. They are fortunate in having their own literary representative in the form of the popular, and prolific, writer Lajos Grendel (b. 1948), who won the coveted Hungarian Kossuth Prize in 1999.

Educated at Comenius University in Bratislava and now head of the Kalligram publishing company, which is located in the Slovak capital, Grendel writes often of the Hungarian minority in Slovakia, and often from an ironic and critical point of view that sets him apart from other Hungarian-Slovak writers. Typical of Grendel's style and outlook is the novel *Éleslövészet* (*Live Fire*), which was originally published in 1986 together with *Galeri* (Gang of Hoodlums) and *Áttételek* (Metastases). Divided into three sections—"First Settling of Accounts: Historical," "Second Settling of Accounts: Literary," and "Third Settling of Accounts: Final"—*Live Fire* begins promisingly as an account of the early history of the Slovak capital Bratislava that is based on scrolls found in the "Olsavszky house." But before long, it develops into a self-titillating exercise in by-now banal postmodernist jibing at narratology. The insistent effort to be clever, and entertaining, is signaled by the first lines of the novel, which should be taken as a harbinger of things to come:

> We shall talk secretively of the events collected herein, so as to derive a bit of (malicious) pleasure for ourselves, and not only because they aren't sunny in the least. . . . The narrator's task is none too easy, for he can round out the passages only with the instinctive control of his experiences and with the bitter grimace of a historical fiasco. Nothing encourages him toward further work. Not even the author's message (if indeed there is one), although the ambiguity of the presumed message (to be nastier: its ambiguous unintelligibility) happens to incite our sensitivity today—here and now. Nor is the tangle of vague allusions a call for further narrative thinking, or for that matter even for cautious commentaries.[21]

Once the novel parts company with the first, "historical," section, it becomes a meandering teaser about the narrator and his work in some editorial office, relations between Hungarians and Slovaks, occasional scraps of history, and events that take place on a certain July 32.

Also in 1999 Grendel published one of his best works, the short novel *Tömegsír* (Mass Grave). A satire on the absurdities to which provincialism often gives rise, the novel is narrated in the first person by a middle-aged historian at Bratislava University. As a result of the postcommunist policy of returning once-confiscated family property to its rightful owners, he has come into possession of a parcel of land in a village populated by Hungarians. While in the process of digging a well the villagers unearth a mass grave but have no clue as to the identity of the bones or of the circumstances of death. Perplexed by the discovery, the village authorities are torn between keeping the discovery secret or of finding a way to put it to their advantage. Enter a respected local pharmacist named Dömötör, who believes that the bones are those of innocent people who were brought there and slaughtered during World War II by the Germans. The authorities seize on the idea and erect a plaque honoring those who died there. But before long, the discovery of the mass grave, and the underlying story behind it, are lost in a detailed account of our historian's life in Bratislava, including and especially his relations with women, sexual and otherwise. The point of all this may be Grendel's desire to portray the historian as cynical and opportunistic. He couldn't seem to care less about the mass grave, but when the villagers keep pressing him on the matter, about the only way he can get them off his back is by going to live in the village and, in a sense, becoming one of them. Perhaps the high point of the novel is the splendidly satirical party at a hunting lodge, where the village officials, and the pharmacist Dömötör, try to win over the historian, plying him with food, drink, and girls. The pharmacist is upset, and offended, by the historian's lack of willingness to cooperate with them, at least at this stage. If the Bratislava historian is portrayed as cynical even toward history, the pharmacist is an entertaining caricature of a provincial figure who thoroughly enjoys the esteem in which he is held by the villagers and their adulation of him.

Grendel's fondness for the absurd and grotesque, usually in the context of Hungarian-Slovak relations, shows up in other works, for example, his short-story collections *Einstein harangjai* (Einstein's Bells, 1998), subtitled *Abszurdisztáni történet* (Tales from Absurdistan), *Esmeralda szivárványai* (*Esmeralda's Rainbows*, 1999), and *Szép históriák* (Nice Stories, 2001) and his volume of essays and articles *Hazam, Abszurdisztán* (My Native Land, Absurdistan, 1998). Although he may seem at times to overdo postmodernist literary play, Grendel nevertheless has a robust sense of humor, a feeling for the absurdities around him, an impressive narrative skill, a flair for the erotic, and a keen knowledge of his own people as a minority in the Slovak lands.

Slovaks in Hungary Also Have a Voice

One of the most successful Hungarian novels of the late 1990s was *Jadviga párnája* (Jadviga's Pillow, 1997), by Pál Závada (b. 1952), himself a member of the small Slovak community located mainly in the Békés region in the southeastern part of Hungary. Relying heavily on the diary form as the structural spine of the novel, he tells the story of a prosperous Slovak peasant named András Osztatni whose wife, Jadviga, long refused to reciprocate his love, both emotionally and physically. This is revealed primarily in his diary for the years 1915 to 1922, when his marriage finally collapses upon his discovery that his wife has had a lover even from before their marriage and that he is not the father of their second son. The diary details not only his troubled relationship with his strange and complex wife but also the routine of his life as a farmer and the situation of the Slovak minority in Hungary. After his death, in the 1930s, Jadviga discovers András's diary and proceeds to make her own entries in it. These serve a twofold purpose: to put her own interpretation on András's account of their marriage and to record events since his death. The diary, begun by András and added to by Jadviga, is continued by their youngest (and illegitimate) son, Misu, who documents the family's eventual collapse, including his own moral failure when he becomes a police informer during the communist era. The diary ends with the year 1987. The great strength of Závada's novel, apart from its linguistic range—from András's refined peasant speech to Jadwiga's more urbane intellectual style to Misu's coarse, proletarianized speech—lies in the wholly credible way he has brought home to his readers a minority ethnic community with its own culture and customs.

Závada wrote two more novels set in the Hungarian-Slovak milieu. The first, *Milota* (2002), is interesting mostly for the history it incorporates of the Slovak community of the great Hungarian *púszta*, or plain. More successful is Závada's third novel, the unmistakably autobiographical *A fényképész utókora* (The Photographer's Legacy, 2004), which is again set among the Slovaks of Hungary with several minor characters from the previous two novels reappearing in it. In his newest work, Závada intertwines three different stories. The first begins with a team of sociographers (Závada himself is a trained sociologist) who are photographed by a Jewish photographer, Miklós Buchbinder, as they talk with local people. This part of the novel chronicles the fates of the people in Buchbinder's photographs through 1957. It serves, in a sense, as a minihistory of Hungary's vicissitudes as a nation from the interwar period through World War II and down to the Revolution of 1956 and its aftermath. The second story follows the lives of the children and grandchildren of the people photographed in the first story from the spring of 1968 to the Soviet invasion of Czechoslovakia. Adam Korén, one of these grandchildren, is the central figure of the third part of the story. The lives of the descendants of those in one way or another connected with Buchbinder's original photographs are brought together through Korén's life and associations in the present. Although The Photographer's Legacy comes close to dissipating its energy through a certain fragmentariness, Závada's use of an unidentified first-person plural narrator introduces a cohesive element.

Although written in Hungarian rather than Slovak, Závada's works provide a vivid collective portrait of the Slovak community in Hungary that has been part of the fabric of Hungarian society and culture for hundreds of years.

Vibrant, disturbing, compelling, the literature of Eastern Europe since the collapse of communism clearly demonstrates the tenacious hold on the creative imagination of over half a century of totalitarian rule. In attempting to wrestle with this odious legacy, and to navigate the currents and crosscurrents of societies moving into a future of their own making, the gifted writers in this chapter, and indeed throughout this book as a whole, remind us once again that however unfamiliar the Eastern European cultures may seem, cultural alienation must not supplant political truncation if a true union of the European nations is to exist.

Notes

1. "World War II in the Literatures of Eastern Europe"

1. Imre Kertész, *Sorstalanság* (Budapest: Magvető, 1975), 333.

2. Ferenc Karinthy, *Budapesti tavasz* (Budapest: Karinthy, 1997), 223.

3. Jozef Leikert, *Testament svedomia* (Bratislava: Astra, 1996), 33.

4. Milo Urban, *Sloboda nie je špás* (Bratislava: Slovenský spisovateľ, 1995), 102–103.

5. Anton Baláž, *Tábor padlých žien* (Bratislava: Slovenský spisovateľ, 1993), 17.

2. "Postwar Colonialism, Communist Style"

1. Czesław Miłosz, *Zdobycie władzy* (Kraków: Znak, 1999), 194.

2. Slobodan Selenić, *Memoari Pere Bogalja* (Belgrade: Prosveta, 1968), 93.

3. Milan Kundera, new preface to Penguin edition of *Life Is Elsewhere,* trans. Peter Kussi (New York: Penguin, 1986), v.

4. Milan Kundera, *Život je jinde* (Toronto: Sixty-Eight Publishers, 1979), 291.

5. Milan Kundera, *Kniha smíchu a zapomnění* (Toronto: Sixty-Eight Publishers, 1981), 9.

6. See Ismail Kadare, *Dialogue avec Alain Bosquet,* trans. Jusuf Vrioni (Paris: Fayard, 1995), 38.

7. The text of Kadare's verses on the U-2 spy plane incident and his interpretation of the event can be found in his poem "Shënime për brezin tim" in Ismail Kadare, *Vjersha dhe poema të zgjedhura* (Tirana: Naim Frashëri, 1966), 68–69.

8. Dritero Agolli, *Vepra letrare 1* (Tirana: Naim Frashëri, 1980), 269.

9. Agolli, *Vepra letrare 2,* 135.

10. Arshi Pipa, *Albanian Stalinism: Ideo-Political Aspects* (Boulder, Colo.: East European Monographs, 1990), 263–264 n. 3.

11. D. R. Popescu, *Vînătoarea regală* (Bucharest: Eminescu, 1976), 224–225.

12. Alexandr Kliment, *Nuda v Čechách* (Prague: Československý spisovatel, [1990]; 2001), 44.

3. "In the Aftermath of the Great Dictator's Death"

1. Alexander Kliment, *Nuda v Čechách* (Prague: Československý spisovatel, [1990]; 2001), 86–87.
2. Sławomir Mrożek, *Vatzlav; Ambasador* (Paris: Instytut Literacki, 1982), 50.
3. Václav Havel, *Hry: Spisy 2* (Prague: Torst, 1999), 97.
4. Václav Havel, *Pokoušení* (Munich: Obrys/Kontur–PmD, 1986), 108.
5. For the best collection of these in English, see Ludvík Vaculík, *A Cup of Coffee with My Interrogator: The Prague Chronicles of Ludvík Vaculík*, trans. George Theiner (London: Readers International, 1987).
6. Zuzana Brabcová, *Daleko od stromu* (Frankfurt: Index, 1987), 9.
7. Dritëro Agolli, *Shkëlqimi dhe rënia e shokut Zylo* (Tirana: Dritëro, 1999), 319–320.
8. Quoted on the back cover of Ismail Kadare, *The Palace of Dreams* (New York: Arcade, 1993).
9. Erich Loest, *Es geht seinen Gang oder Mühen in unserer Ebene* (Stuttgart: Deutsche Verlags-Anstalt, 1978), 18.

4. "Fleeing the System: Literature and Emigration"

1. The best book on Pipa is the Albanian study by Uran Kalakulla, *Arshi Pipa: Njeriu dhe vepra* (Tirana: Toena, 1999). It contains a fairly lengthy discussion of the animosity between Pipa and Kadare.
2. Ismail Kadare, *Albanian Spring: The Anatomy of Tyranny*, trans. from the French by Emile Capouya (London: Saqi, 1995), 187 n. 1.
3. Kadare, *Albanian Spring*, 58–59.
4. Bujor Nedelcovici, *Aici și acum* (Bucharest: Allfa, 1998), 123.
5. Bujor Nedelcovici, *Jurnal infidel: Pagini din exil, 1987–1993* (Bucharest: Eminescu, 1998), 36.
6. Pavel Kohout, *Bílá kniha: O kauze Adam Juráček* (Toronto: Sixty-Eight Publishers, 1978), 43.
7. Milan Kundera, *Kniha smíchu a zapomnění* (Toronto: Sixty-Eight Publishers, 1981), 169.

5. "Internal Exile and the Literature of Escape"

1. Ludvík Vaculík, *A Cup of Coffee with My Interrogator: The Prague Chronicles of Ludvík Vaculík*, trans. George Theiner (London: Readers International, 1987), ii.
2. Ismail Kadare, *Piramida* (Paris: Çabej MÇM, 1995), 16–17.
3. Tibor Déry, *G. A. úr X.-ben* (Budapest: Szépirodalmi Könyvkiadó, 1964), 364. The quotes in this paragraph are all from the same page.

6. "Writers Behind Bars: Eastern European Prison Literature, 1945–1990"

1. The Romanian poet Ruxandra Cesereanu has undertaken an impressive project dealing with political prisons and torture in communist Romania. To date, she has published *Călătorie spre centrul infernului: Gulagul în conştiinţa românească* (1998); *Panopticum: Tortura politică în secolul XX, studiu de mentalitate* (2001); and *Memorialistica şi literatura închisorilor şi lagărelor comuniste: Eseu de mentalitate* (2005).

2. Nicolae Steinhardt, *Jurnalul fericirii,* 7th ed. (Cluj-Napoca: Dacia, 2000), 83–85.

3. Arshi Pipa, *Autobiography: 1988* (Tirana: 2000), 28–29.

4. Visar Zhiti, *Kujtesa e ajrit* (Tirana: Shtëpia Botuese e Lidhjes Shkrimtarëve, 1993), 57.

5. Vizar Zhiti, *Hedh një kafkë te kembit tuaja: Poezitë e burgut, 1979–1987* (Tirana: Naim Frashëri, 1994), 107.

6. Venko Markovski, *Goli Otok: The Island of Death. A Diary in Letters* (Boulder, Colo.: Social Science Monographs, 1984), 30–31.

7. An English translation of the work, by Stephen M. Dickey and Bogdan Rakić, was published by Northwestern University Press in 2005 under the title *How to Quiet a Vampire.*

8. Slavko Goldstein, *Moj slučaj* (Ljubljana: Cankarjeva Založba, 1989), ix.

9. Jiří Mucha, *Living and Partly Living,* trans. Ewald Hosers (London: Hogarth, 1967), 18.

10. Jiří Hejda, *Žil jsem zbytečně: Román mého života* (Prague: Melantrich, 1991); see esp. 281–385.

11. Jiří Hejda, *Sonety zpívané šeptem ve stínu šibenice: Ruzyně–Pankrác–Mirov–Leopoldov–Valdice, 1950–1962* (Prague: Anthropos, 1993), 15.

12. Lenka Reinerová, *Alle Farben der Sonne und der Nacht* (Berlin: Aufbau, 2003), 18–19.

13. Ludvík Vaculík, *A Cup of Coffee with My Interrogator: The Prague Chronicles of Ludvík Vaculík,* trans. George Theiner (London: Readers International, 1987), 47–48.

14. Karel Pecka, *Motáky nezvěstnému* (Toronto: Sixty-Eight Publishers, 1980), 88–89.

15. Eva Kantůrková, *Přítelkyně z domu smutku* (Cologne: Index, 1984), 10.

16. *Homecoming, and Other Stories,* trans. Katharina M. and Christopher C. Wilson; foreword trans. George Szirtes, 2d printing (Budapest: Corvina, 1995), 9–10.

17. Ádám Bodor, *A börtön szaga* (Budapest: Magvető, 2001), 90–91.

18. For English translations of these works, see *Volcano and Miracle: A Selection from* The Journal Written at Night, trans. Ronald Strom (New York: Viking, 1996), and *A World Apart,* trans. Joseph Marek (London: Heinemann, 1951; trans. Andrzej Ciokosz [Joseph Marek], New York: Arbor House, 1986).

19. Andrzej Stasiuk, *Mury Hebronu* (Warsaw: Wyd. Głodnych Duchów, 1992), 33.

7. "The Reform Imperative in Eastern Europe: From Solidarity to Postmodernism"

1. Julian Kornhauser and Adam Zagajewski, *Świat nie przedstawiony* (Kraków: Wydawnictwo Literackie, 1974), 126.

2. Janusz Anderman, *Brak tchu* (London: PULS, 1983), 49.

3. Nicolae Manolescu, quoted in Mircea Horia Simionescu, *Dicţionar onomastic: Text integral* (Bucharest: ALLFA, 2000), 661.

4. Mircea Cărtărescu, *Levantul* (Bucharest: Humanitas, 1998), 146.

5. Svetislav Basara, *Kinesko pismo* (Belgrade: Dereta, 1997), 5.

6. Svetislav Basara, *Ukleta zemlja* (Belgrade: Vreme knjige, 1995), 37.

7. See Ana Lucic's interview with Vedrana Rudan posted on the Dalkey Archive Press Web site: http://dalkeyarchive.com/context/1650/interview-with-vedrana-rudan.

8. Georgi Gospodinov, *Estestven roman* (Sofia: Korporatsiya Razvitie KDA, 1999), 31.

9. Jiří Kratochvil, *Medvědi román* (Brno: Atlantis, 1990), 264.

10. Jiří Kratochvil, *Uprostřed nocí zpěv* (Brno: Atlantis, 1992), 193.

11. Kratochvil, *Medvědi román*, 110.

12. Jiří Kratochvil, *Avion* (Brno: Atlantis, 1995), 168–169.

13. Daniela Hodrová, *Théta* (Prague: Československý spisovatel, 1992), 19.

14. Michal Ajvaz, *Druhé město* (Prague: Mladá fronta, 1993), 29.

15. Pavel Vilikovský, *Večne je zelený . . .* (Bratislava: Slovenský spisovatel', 1989), 60.

16. Dušan Mitana, *Návrat Krista* (Levice: Kalaman Kertész Bagala, 1999), 343.

17. Jana Bodnárová, *Tiene papradia* (Bratislava: Slovenský spisovatel', 2002), 111.

18. Michal Hvorecký, *Lovci & zberači* (Bratislava: techno.sk, 2002), 68–69.

19. Michal Hvorecký, *Posledný hit* (Bratislava: Ikar, 2003), 21.

8. "Eastern European Women Poets of the 1980s and 1990s"

1. Wisława Szymborska, *Wiersze wybrane: Wybór i układ Autorki* (Kraków: a5, 2000), 199.

2. Anna Świrszczyńska, *Mówię do swego ciała / Talking to My Body*, trans. Czesław Miłosz (Kraków: Colonel Press, 2002), 83, 85, 87.

3. Julia Hartwig, *nim opatrzy się zieleń: wybór wierszy* (Kraków: Znak, 1995), 199.

4. Halina Poświatowska, *Wiersze wybrane* (Kraków: Wydawnictwo Literackie, 2003), 73.

5. Taken from Ewa Lipska, *Wakacje mizantropa* (Kraków: Wydawnictwo Literackie, 1993), 296.

6. Marzena Broda, *Cudzoziemszczyzna* (Poznań: a5, 1995), 55.

7. Sylva Fischerová, *Velká zrcadla* (Prague: Československý spisovatel, 1990), 27.

8. Jana Bodnárová, *Še-po-ty* (Bratislava: Slovenský spisovatel', 1995), 29.

9. Saša Vegri, *Naplavljeni plen* (Ljubljana: Državna založba Slovenije, 1961), 47.

10. Saša Vegri, *Tebi v tišino* (Ljubljana: Nova revija, 2001), 23.

11. Elizaveta Bagryana, *Izbrani stihotvoreniya* (Sofia: Bulgarski pisatel, 1968), 51.

12. Blaga Dimitrova, *Otvud lyubovta* (Sofia: Narodna mladezh, 1987), 158.

13. Nevena Stefanova, *Otkroveniya* (Sofia: Bulgarski pisatel, 1973), 73–74.

14. Vanya Petkova, *Greshnitsa* (Sofia: Bulgarski pisatel, 1968), 66–67.

15. Vanya Petkova, *Tsiganski romans* (Sofia: Narodna mladezh, 1984), 13.

16. Katica Kulavkova, *Medjusvet* (Skopje: Nebesna, 2000), 14–15.

17. Katica Kulavkova, *Nova pot* (Skopje: Misla, 1984), 55–56.

18. Nina Cassian, *De îndurare* (Bucharest: Eminescu, 1981), 13, 89.

19. Ileana Mălăncioiu, *Linea vieţii* (Bucharest: Cartea Românească, 1982), 160.

20. Ileana Mălăncioiu, *Poezii* (Bucharest: Vitruviu, 1996), 12.

21. Ana Blandiana, *Poeme/Poems,* English trans. Dan Duţescu (Bucharest: Eminescu, 1982), 212.

22. Ana Blandiana, *100 de poeme* (Bucharest: Tinerama, 1991), 13.

23. Grete Tartler, *Cuneiforme* (Timişoara: Helicon, 1997), 42, 48.

24. Liliana Ursu, *Piaţa aurarilor* (Bucharest: Cartea Românească, 1980), 22.

25. Doina Uricariu, *Vindecările* (Bucharest: EE, 1998), 242, 151.

26. Denisa Comănescu, *Barca pe valuri* (Bucharest: Cartea Românească, 1987), 12.

27. Mariana Marin, *Atelierele, 1980–1984* (Bucharest: Cartea Românească, 1990), 27.

28. Carmen Firan, *Locuri de trăit singur* (Bucharest: Cartea Românească, 1997), 17.

29. Ruxandra Cesereanu, *Antologia poeziei româneşti de la origini până azi,* ed. Dumitru Chioaru and Ioan Radu Văcărescu (Piteşti: Paralela 45, 1998), vol. 2, 581–582.

30. Ruxandra Cesereanu, ed., *Deliruri şi delire: O antologie a poeziei onirice româneşti* (Piteşti: Paralela 45, 2000), 46.

31. Simona Popescu, *O mie şi una de poezii româneşti,* ed. Laurenţiu Ulici (Bucharest: Du Style, 1997), vol. 10, 170–172.

32. Mimoza Ahmeti, *Delirium* (Tirana: Marin Barleti, 2001), 29.

33. Mimoza Ahmeti, *Pjalmimi i luleve* (Tirana: ORA, 2002), 20–23.

34. Luljeta Lleshanaku, *Palca e verdhë* (Prishtina: Gjon Buzuku, 2000), 106.

35. Luljeta Lleshanaku, *Gjysmëkubizëm* (Tirana: Eurorilindja, 1996), 54.

36. Elke Erb, *Der Faden der Geduld* (Berlin: Aufbau, 1978), 39.

9. "The House of Cards Collapses: The Literary Fallout of the Yugoslav Crises of the 1990s"

1. Danilo Kiš, *Čas anatomije* (Belgrade: Nolit, 1978), 31.

2. Drago Jančar, *Konec tisočletja, račun stoletja* (Ljubljana: Mladinska knjiga, 1999), 84–85.

3. Semezdin Mehmedinović, *Sarajevo Blues,* trans. Ammiel Alcalay (San Francisco: City Lights Books, 1998), 18.

4. Bisera Alikadić, *Grad hrabost/City of Courage* (Sarajevo: Medjunarodni centar za mir, 1995), 12–13.

5. Ferida Duraković, *Serce tame: Sarajevo, 1973–1993* (Sarajevo: Bosanska knjiga, 1994), 109–110.

6. Nenad Veličković, *Konačari,* 4th ed. (Sarajevo: Omnibus, 2003), 93.

7. Zlatko Dizdarević, *Sarajevo: A War Journal,* trans. Anselm Hollo, ed. Ammiel Alcalay (New York: Fromm International, 1993), 71.

8. Svetislav Basara, *De bello civile* (Belgrade: Vreme, 1995), 69–71, 72.

9. Stjepan Čuić, *Abeceda licemjerja* (Zagreb: Prova, 1992), 47.

10. Miljenko Jergović, *Sarajevski Marlboro* (Zagreb: Durieux, 1994; 4th ed., 1996), 56.

10. "Glimpses of the Other World: America Through Eastern European Eyes"

1. The poem has never been published in Romanian. Quoted and translated here by me with the kind permission of Mircea Cărtărescu.

2. Liliana Ursu, *Înger călare pe fiară* (Bucharest: Cartea Românească, 1996), 27–28.

3. Daniela Crăsnaru, *Sea-Level Zero* (Rochester, N.Y.: BOA Editions, 1999), 105.

4. David Albahari, *Cink* (Belgrade: Dereta, 1995), 19–20.

5. Vladimir Pištalo, *Vitraž u sećanju* (Belgrade: Vreme knjige, 1994), 114.

6. Selections from the book in English translation by Cornelia Bozhilova were published by Ohio University Press (Athens) in 1980 under the title *American Pages.*

7. Lilyana Stefanova, *Edna esen v Amerika. Vulkanite na Meksiko dimyat* (Sofia: Narodna mladezh, 1979), 156.

8. Kazimierz Brandys, *Miesiące: 1982–1984* (Paris: Instytut Literacki, 1984), 74–75.

9. Julia Hartwig, *nim opatrzy się zieleń: wybór wierszy* (Kraków: Znak, 1995), 55, 57, 67.

10. All citations from Lipska's "Nowy York, porwane miasto" here are from Ewa Lipska, "Nowy Jork miasto porwane," *Nie o śmierć tutaj chodzi lecz o biały kordonek* (Kraków: Wydawnictwo Literackie, 1982), 115–119.

11. Anna Czekanowicz, *Śmierć w powietrzu* (Gdańsk: Graf, 1991), 7.

12. Marzena Broda, *Cudzoziemszczyzna* (Poznań: a5, 1991), 35.

13. Tomasz Jastrun, *W złotej klatce: Notatnik amerykański* (Berlin: Veto, 1989), 9.

14. For English translations of these poems—"All Souls' Day on the Bay," "Dusk at San Diego Beach," "Looking at Photographs," "Poem for Allen," and "I'm Sick / America of the Dark Sycamores Along the Street . . ."—see: *Poems of Grzegorz Musiał: "Berliner Tagebuch" and "Taste of Ash,"* trans. Lia Purpura (Madison, N.J.: Fairleigh Dickinson University Press, 1998).

15. Grzegorz Musiał, *Dziennik z Iowa* (Warsaw: Open, 2000), 85.

16. Miroslav Holub, *Anděl na kolečkách: Poloreportaž z USA* (Prague: Československý spisovatel, 1964), 30–31.

17. Miroslav Holub, *Beton: verše z new yorku a z prahy* (Prague: Mladá Fronta, 1970), 24–25.

18. Günter Kunert, *Der andere Planet: Ansichten von Amerika* (Munich: Hanser, 1975), 53.

11. "The Postcolonial Literary Scene in Eastern Europe Since 1991"

1. For a good overview of Lithuanian literature in English, including the period of Soviet occupation and postcolonialist developments, see the collective *Lithuanian Literature* (Vilnius: Vaga, 1997), a publication of the Institute of Lithuanian Literature and Folklore.

2. Ričardas Gavelis, *Vilniaus pokeris,* 2d ed. (Vilnius: Vaga, 1990), 58.

3. Herkus Kunčius, *Pelenai asilo kanopoje. Smegenu padažas. Eksursija: Casa Matta* (Vilnius: Lietuvos rašytoju sajungos leidykla, 2001), 6–7.

4. Oksana Zabuzhko, "Klitemnestra," *Avtostop* (Kiev: Ukraïns'kyï pys'mennyk, 1994), 67.

5. Martin Vopěnka, *Balada o sestupu* (Prague: Rozmluvy, 1992), 21.

6. Peter Pišt'anek, *Rivers of Babylon: Fredyho koniec* (Bratislava: Fénix, 1999), 199.

7. Aleš Čar, *V okvari* (Ljubljana: Študentska založba, 2003), 47–48.

8. Andrei Blatnik, *Zakon želje* (Ljubljana: Študentska založba, 2000), 11.

9. Andrzej Stasiuk, *Biały kruk* (Poznań: Obserwator, 1995), 192.

10. Milo Urban, *Kade-tade po Halinde: Neveselé spomienky na veselé roky* (Bratislava: Slovenský spisovatel', 1992), 248.

11. Dušan Mitana, *Môj rodný cintorín* (Levice: Koloman Kertész Bagala, 2000), 5.

12. Piotr Szewc, *Zmierzchy i poranki* (Kraków: Wydawnictwo Literackie, 1999), 142.

13. Dominik Tatarka, *Písačky* (Cologne: Index, 1984), 7.

14. Iva Pekárková, *Kulatý svět* (Prague: Společnost Josefa Škvoreckého, 1993), 69–70.

15. Iva Pékarková, *Dej mi ty prachy* (Prague: NLN, 1996), 19.

16. All quotes from Gretkowska are from Manuela Gretkowska, *My zdies' emigranty,* 3d corrected ed. (Warsaw: W. A. B., 2001), 142.

17. Herta Müller, *Der Mensch ist ein grosser Fasan auf der Welt* (Berlin: Rotbuch, 1986), 43.

18. Herta Müller, *Reisende auf einem Bein* (Berlin: Rotbuch, 1989), 158.

19. Herta Müller, *Herz-Tier* (Reinbek bei Hamburg: Rowohlt, 1993), 224.

20. Herta Müller, *Heute wär ich mir lieber nicht begegnet* (Reinbek bei Hamburg: Rowohlt, 1997), 20.

21. Lajos Grendel, *Éleslövészet. Galeri. Áttételek* (Bratislava: Madách, 1986), 9–10. A later edition of *Éleslövészet* was published in 1999 with the new subtitle *Nem (zetiségi) antiregény* (Nationality Antinovel). There is a play of words here: "nem" means "no, not," and "nemzet" means "nation." So "nem (zetiségi)" suggests a nationality that is and is not one.

Further Reading

Agee, Chris, ed. *Scar on the Stone: Contemporary Poetry from Bosnia.* Newcastle upon Tyne: Bloodaxe, 1998.

Barańczak, Stanisław, and Clare Cavanaugh, eds. and trans. *Polish Poetry of the Last Two Decades of Communist Rule: Spoiling Cannibals' Fun.* Evanston, Ill.: Northwestern University Press, 1991.

Born in Utopia: An Anthology of Modern and Contemporary Romanian Poetry. Jersey City: Talisman, 2006.

Bradbrook, Bohuslava. *A Handbook of Czech Prose Writings: 1945–2005.* Portland, Ore.: Sussex Academic Press, 2007.

Büchler, Alexandra, ed. *Allskin, and Other Tales by Contemprary Czech Women.* Seattle: Women in Translation, 1998.

———, ed. *This Side of Reality: Modern Czech Writing.* London: Serpent's Tail, 1996.

Castro, Michael, and Gabor C. Gyukics, eds. and trans. *Swimming in the Ground: Contemporary Hungarian Poetry.* St. Louis: Neshui, 2003.

Čašule, Ilija, and Thomas Shapcott, eds. and trans. *An Island on Land: Anthology of Contemporary Macedonian Poetry.* North Ryde, N.S.W.: Macquarie University, 1999.

Catalano, Alessandro. *Sole rosso su Praga: La letteratura ceca tra socialismo e underground, 1945–1995: Un'interpretazione.* Rome: Bulzoni, 2004.

Chitnis, Rajendra A. *Literature in Post-Communist Russia and Eastern Europe: The Russian, Czech, and Slovak Fiction of the Changes, 1988–1998.* New York: RoutledgeCurzon, 2005.

Cooper, Henry R., Jr., ed. *A Bilingual Anthology of Slovene Literature.* Bloomington, Ind.: Slavica, 2003.

Cornis-Pope, Marcel. *The Unfinished Battles: Romanian Postmodernism Before and After 1989.* Iaşi: Polirom, 1996.

Czerwiński, E. J. *Contemporary Polish Theater and Drama (1956–1984).* New York: Greenwood, 1988.

Debeljak, Aleš, ed. *The Imagination of Terra Incognita: Slovenian Writing, 1945–1995.* Fredonia, N.Y.: White Pine, 1997.

Deletant, Andrea, and Brenda Walker, trans. *An Anthology of Contemporary Romanian Poetry.* London: Forest, 1984.

———. *Silent Voices: An Anthology of Contemporary Romanian Women Poets.* London: Forest, 1986.

Elsie, Robert. *History of Albanian Literature.* 2 vols. Boulder, Colo.: East European Monographs, 1995.

Fairleigh, John, ed. *When the Tunnels Meet: Contemporary Romanian Poetry.* Newcastle upon Tyne: Bloodaxe, 1996.

Farnoaga, Georgiana, and Sharon King, eds. and trans. *The Phantom Church, and Other Stories from Romania.* Pittsburgh: University of Pittsburgh Press, 1996.

Firuţa, Corina, trans. *Questions at the Turn of the Millennium: Contemporary Romanian Poetry: A Sampler / Întrebări la sfîrşit de mileniu: Din poezia română contemporană.* Bucharest: Eminescu, 1984.

French, Alfred. *Czech Writers and Politics, 1945–1969.* Boulder, Colo.: East European Monographs, 1982.

Goetz-Stankiewicz, Marketa, and Phyllis Carey, eds. *Critical Essays on Václav Havel.* New York: G. K. Hall/Twayne, 1999.

———. *The Silenced Theatre: Czech Playwrights Without a Stage.* Toronto: University of Toronto Press, 1979.

Gömöri, George, and George Szirtes, eds. *The Colonnade of Teeth: Modern Hungarian Poetry.* Newcastle upon Tyne: Bloodaxe, 1996.

Gorup, Radmila J., and Nadežda Obradović, eds. *The Prince of Fire: An Anthology of Contemporary Serbian Short Stories.* Pittsburgh: University of Pittsburgh Press, 1998.

Hawkesworth, Celia, ed. *A History of Central European Women's Writing.* New York: Palgrave, in assoc. with School of Slavonic and East European Studies, University College, London, 2000.

———. *Voices in the Shadows: Women and Verbal Art in Serbia and Bosnia.* Budapest: Central European University Press, 2000.

Hogan, Ed, Askold Melnyczuk, et al., eds. *From Three Worlds: New Ukrainian Writing.* Moscow: Glas, 1996.

Jackson, Richard, and Rachel Morgan, eds. *The Fire Under the Moon: Contemporary Slovene Poetry.* 2d rev. ed. Chattanooga, Tenn., and Elgin, Ill.: Poetry Miscellany/Black Dirt, 1999.

Kadare, Ismail. *Dialogue avec Alain Bosquet.* Trans. Jusuf Vrioni. Paris: Fayard, 1995.

———. *Entretiens avec Eric Faye.* Paris: J. Corti, 1991.

Kelertas, Violeta, ed. *Baltic Postcolonialism.* Amsterdam: Rodopi, 2006.

Konrád, George. *The Melancholy of Rebirth: Essays from Post-Communist Central Europe, 1989–1994.* Trans. Michael Henry Heim. San Diego: Harcourt Brace Jovanovich, 1995.

Kopač, Radim, ed. *Czech Literature at the Turn of the Millenium / Neue tschechische Literatur an der Jahrtausendwende.* Prague: Ministry of Culture of the Czech Republic, 2003.

Kraszewski, Charles S. *The Romantic Hero and Contemporary Anti-Hero in Polish and Czech Literature: Great Souls and Grey Men.* Lewiston, N.Y.: Edwin Mellen Press, 1998.

Lahusen, Thomas, and Evgeny Dobrenko, eds. *Socialist Realism Without Shores.* Durham, N.C.: Duke University Press, 1997.

Lappin, Elena, ed. *Daylight in Nightclub Inferno: Czech Fiction from the Post-Kundera Generation.* North Haven, Conn.: Catbird, 1997.

Leeder, Karen J. *Breaking Boundaries: A New Generation of Poets in the GDR, 1979–1990.* Oxford: Clarendon, 1996.

Liehm, Antonin, and Peter Kussi, eds. *The Writing on the Wall: An Anthology of Contemporary Czech Literature.* Princeton: Karz-Cohl, 1983.

Kubilius, Vytautas, ed. *Lithuanian Literature.* Trans. Rita Dapkutė and Diana Bartkutė. Vilnius: Vaga, 1997.

Lukić, Sveta. *Contemporary Yugoslav Literature: A Sociopolitical Approach.* Ed. Gertrude Joch Robinson; trans. Pola Triandis. Urbana: University of Illinois Press, 1972.

March, Michael, ed. *Child of Europe: A New Anthology of East European Poetry.* New York: Viking Penguin, 1990.

———, ed. *Description of a Struggle: The Picador Book of Contemporary East European Prose.* London: Picador, 1994.

Mihailovich, Vasa, ed. *South Slavic Writers Since World War II.* Detroit: Gale, 1997.

Mihailovich, Vasa D., and Steven Serafin, eds. *South Slavic and Eastern European Writers.* Detroit: Gale, 2000.

O'Doherty, Paul. *The Portrayal of Jews in GDR Prose Fiction.* Amsterdam: Rodopi, 1997.

Owen, Ruth J. *The Poet's Role: Lyric Responses to German Unification by Poets from the GDR.* Amsterdam: Rodopi, 2001.

Pipa, Arshi. *Albanian Literature: Social Perspectives.* Munich: R. Trofenik, 1978.

———. *Albanian Stalinism: Ideo-Political Aspects.* Boulder, Colo.: East European Monographs, 1990.

———. *Contemporary Albanian Literature.* Boulder, Colo.: East European Monographs, 1991.

Porter, Robert. *An Introduction to Twentieth-Century Czech Fiction: Comedies of Defiance.* Brighton: Sussex Academic Press, 2001.

Predan, Alja, ed. *Contemporary Slovenian Drama.* Ljubljana: Slovene Writers' Association, 1997.

Pynsent, Robert B. *Modern Slovak Prose: Fiction Since 1954.* London: Macmillan, 1990.

Radaković, Borivoj, Matt Thorne, and Tony White, eds. *Croatian Nights: A Festival of Alternative Literature.* Trans. Celia Hawkesworth. London: Serpent's Tail, 2005.

Raifi, Mensur, ed. *The Roads Lead Only One Way: A Survey of Modern Poetry from Kosova.* Trans. John Hodgson and Fiona Cullen. Priština: Kosova Association of Literary Translators, 1988.

Richter, Milan, and Daniela Humajová, eds. *Album of Slovak Writers: Authors and Texts.* Bratislava: Slovak Literature Information Centre, 2001.

Segel, Harold B. *The Columbia Guide to the Literatures of Eastern Europe Since 1945.* New York: Columbia University Press, 2003.

Serafin, Steven, ed. *Twentieth-Century Eastern European Writers.* First series. Detroit: Gale, 1999.

———, ed. *Twentieth-Century Eastern European Writers.* Second series. Detroit: Gale, 2000.

————, ed. *Twentieth-Century Eastern European Writers*. Third series. Detroit: Gale, 2001.

Short, David. *Essays in Czech and Slovak Language and Literature*. London: School of Slavonic and East European Studies, University of London, 1996.

Simic, Charles, ed. and trans. *The Horse Has Six Legs: An Anthology of Serbian Poetry*. St. Paul, Minn.: Graywolf, 1992.

Slavov, Atanas. *The "Thaw" in Bulgarian Literature*. Boulder, Colo.: East European Monographs, 1981.

Sorkin, Adam J., and Kurt Treptow, eds. *An Anthology of Romanian Women Poets*. Boulder, Colo.: East European Monographs, 1994.

Sorkin, Adam J., Bogdan Stefănescu, Radu Andriescu, et al., eds. and trans. *Speaking the Silence: Prose Poets of Contemporary Romania*. Piteşti: Paralela 45, 2001.

Sruoginis, Laima, ed. and trans. *The Earth Remains: An Anthology of Contemporary Lithuanian Prose*. Boulder, Colo.: East European Monographs, 2003.

————, ed. *Lithuania in Her Own Words: An Anthology of Contemporary Lithuanian Writing*. Vilnius: Tyto alba, 1997.

Steiner, Peter. *The Deserts of Bohemia: Czech Fiction and Its Social Context*. Ithaca, N.Y.: Cornell University Press, 2000.

Šutić, Miloslav, ed. *An Anthology of Modern Serbian Lyrical Poetry (1920–1995)*. Belgrade: Serbian Literary Magazine, 1999.

Szakolczay, Lajos, ed. *Give or Take a Day: Contemporary Hungarian Short Stories*. Budapest: Corvina, 1997.

Tate, Dennis. *The East German Novel: Identity, Community, Continuity*. Bath: Bath University Press, 1984.

Tempest, Peter, trans. *Anthology of Bulgarian Poetry*. Sofia: Sofia Press, 1980.

Tighe, Carl. *The Politics of Literature: Poland, 1945–1989*. Cardiff: University of Wales Press, 1999.

Topčić, Zlatko, ed. *Forgotten Country: A Selection of Bosnian-Herzegonian Stories*. Sarajevo: Association of Writers of Bosnia-Herzegovina, 1997.

————, ed. *Forgotten Country: War Prose in Bosnia-Herzegovina (1992–1995)*. Sarajevo: Assoc. of Writers of Bosnia-Herzegovina, 1997.

Tötösy de Zepetnek, Steven, ed. *Comparative Central European Culture*. West Lafayette, Ind.: Purdue University Press, 2002.

Tradition and Innovation in Contemporary Literature. P.E.N. Club. Hungarian Centre. Budapest: Corvina, 1964.

Trensky, Paul. *Czech Drama Since World War II*. White Plains, N.Y.: M. E. Sharpe, 1978.

Turczi, István, ed. *At the End of the Broken Bridge: Twenty-Five Hungarian Poems, 1978–2002*. Manchester [England]: Carcanet; Edinburgh: Scottish Poetry Library, 2005.

Wachtel, Andrew Baruch. *Making a Nation, Breaking a Nation: Literature and Cultural Politics in Yugoslavia*. Stanford, Calif.: Stanford University Press, 1998.

————. *Remaining Relevant After Communism: The Role of the Writer in Eastern Europe*. Chicago: University of Chicago Press, 2006.

Walker, Brenda, and Michaela Celea-Leach, trans. *Young Poets of a New Romania: An Anthology*. London: Forest, 1991.

Zawacki, Andrew, ed. *Afterwards: Slovenian Writing, 1945–1995*. Buffalo, N.Y.: White Pine, 2000.

Index

Abdihoxha, Ali: *Kronika e një nate,* 18; *Një vjeshtë me stuhi,* 18; *Tri ngjyra të kohës,* 18

Academica Civica Foundation, 250

Academy of Arts and Sciences of Bosnia and Herzegovina, 118

Adcock, Fleur, 252

Aeschylus, 96

Agee, Chris, 267

Agolli, Dritëro, 159; "Baballarët," 50, 83; *Shkëlqimi dhe renia e shokut Zylo,* 83–84

Agopian, Ştefan: *Manualul întâmplărilor,* 199; *Sara,* 199; *Tache de catifea,* 199, 200; *Tobit,* 199

Ahmeti, Mimoza: *Bëhu I bukur,* 258; *Delirium,* 258–259; *Pjalmimi i luleve,* 258; *Sidomos nesër,* 258

Ajvaz, Michal, 210; "Bílí mravenci," 216; *Druhé město,* 215–216

Albahari, David, 272–273; *Cink,* 295–296; *Mamac,* 273, 295; *Opis smrti,* 273

Albania, vii, 14, 114; China and, 86–88, 151; communists and nationalists, 17–20; Gheg and Tosk dialects, 153; Gjirokastër, 19, 95; Italian campaign, 17–18, 151; Kosovo campaign and, 273–288; prison camps, 151–160; Purge of Liberals, 20; Sigurimi (secret police), 84, 97, 151, 357; Soviet Union and, 86, 87, 95; Ushtria Çlirimtare Kombëtare, 14; World War II, 17–20

Albanian Union of Writers and Artists, 17

Albanian writers: absurd and grotesque, literature of, 84–86, 160; postcommunist writings, 355–357; women poets, 258–260

Albin Michel publishing house (Paris), 101, 102–103

Alexandrova, Rada, 244

Alia, Ramiz, 97

Alianţa Civică (Civil Alliance), 197

Alibali, Jusuf, 84

Alikadić, Bisera: *Grad hrabrost,* 268–269

Ališanka, Eugenijus, 320; *Lygiadienis,* 321; *Peleno miestas,* 321

allegory, 125–133

Almanul literar (journal), 101

American League of Writers, 175

American Military Mission (Albania), 52

American motifs, 335–336

American Vocational School, 52

Amfiteatru (journal), 199

Anderman, Janusz, 191, 195–196; *Brak tchu,* 195; *Fotografie,* 192, 196; *Kraj świata,* 195

Anders, Władysław, 2, 188
Anderson, Sascha, 261
Andreev, Leonid, 127
Andrić, Ivo, 167–168; *Gospodjica,*
    117, 118; *Na Drini ćuprija,*
    117–118; *Prokleta avlija,* 168;
    Travnička hronika, 117, 128
Andrzejewski, Jerzy, 4; *Popiół i*
    diament, 5, 40; *Wielki Tydzień,* 5, 6
anticommunism, 14–15, 40–41
anti-Semitism, x, 1, 170; Romania,
    27–28, 148
Antisthius. *See* Steinhardt, Nicolae
Antonescu, Ion, viii–ix, 28, 29
Apitz, Bruno, 36–37
Apostrof (journal), 253
Aralica, Ivan: *Četverored,* 27, 120
Arbanas, Nevenka, 243
Argeş (journal), 249
Arp, Hans (Jean), 261
Arrow Cross (Nyilaskereszt), ix, 20, 23
Arsenijević, Vladimir: *Andjela,* 282;
    Mexico: Ratni dnevnik, 282; *U*
    potpalublju, 281–282
Association of Hungarian Journalists in
    Romania, 253
Auschwitz, 8, 10, 21–22, 24
Axis, allies of, vii, 13, 20–29

Babeţi, Adriana, 200
Bagryana, Elisaveta, 233, 244
Baláž, Anton, 33–35; *Hijó, kone*
    stalinove, 357; *Krajina zabudnutia,*
    34; *Tábor padlých žien,* 34–35, 357
Bălcescu, Nicolae, 124
Balk, Theodor, 175
Balkans, 264; women poets, 241–260;
    World War II, 17–20. *See also*
    Albania; Bosnia-Herzegovina;
    Bulgaria; Croatia; Kosovo; Macedo-
    nia; Montenegro; Romania; Serbia;
    Slovenia; Yugoslavia
Balkan wars, x, 114, 166
Balla, Zsófia, 185
Balli Kombëtar (National Front)
    (Albania), 14
Baltag, Cezar, 60
Baltic states, 39

Bănulescu, Ştefan, 60, 292
Banuş, Maria, 233
Barańczak, Stanisław, 191, 310; *Ironia*
    i harmonia: Szkice o najnowszej
    literaturze polskiej, 194–195
Barandov film studios, 170
Barbarian group (Kraków), 238
Barbu, Eugen: *Caietele princepelui,*124;
    *Groapa,*124; *Încognito: Cine-*
    *roman,*124; *Miresele,*124;
    *Princepele,*124
Basara, Svetislav, 277; *De bello civili,*
    206, 278; *Looney Tunes: Manično-*
    paranoična istorija srpske
    književnosti u periodu 1979–1990,
    206; *Sveta mast: Manično-*
    paranoična istorija srpske
    književnosti, 206, 278–279; *Ukleta*
    zemlja, 206–207
Beckett, Samuel, 181
Bednár, Alfonz, 34; *Hodiny a minúty,*
    36; *Sklený vrch,* 35–36
Behrürhung ist nur eine Randerschei-
    nung: Neue Literatur aus der DDR
    (Kirsch and Anderson), 261
Belgrade Circle, 279
Beneš, Eduard, 71
Benka, Urszula, 236–237; *Chronomea,*
    238; *Dziwna rozkosz,* 238; *Nic,*
    238; *Perwersyjne dziewczynki,* 238;
    Ta mała tabu, 238
Berliner Ensemble theater, 63
Berling, Zygmunt, 2
Berlin Wall, fall of, ix, 89, 190, 264
Berlin workers' strikes (June 1953), ix,
    66
Bernstein, Ingrid. *See* Kirsch, Sara
Bessarabia, 145; deportation/slaughter
    of Jews, viii, 20, 27, 28
Best Book of the Year (Romania), 150
Beyer, Frank, 125
Białoszewski, Miron, 6, 238
Biblioteka "Kultura," 3
Bibliotheque Polonaise, 98
Bienek, Hans, 190
Bieńkowski, Zbigniew, 307
Biermann, Wolf, 262, 317
Blandiana, Ana, 247, 249–250, 292;

Ochiul de greier, 250; *Octombrie, noiembre; decembrie,* 249

Blatnik, Andrej, 204; *Papirnati labirinti,* 295; *Menjave kož,* 204, 295, 338; *Šopki za Adama venijo,* 337–338; *Zakon želje,* 295

Bleiburg, Austria, massacre, 27

Bodiu, Andrei, 203

Bodnárová, Jana, 218, 239; *Aféra rozumu,* 221, 222; *bleskosvetlo/bleskotma,* 221, 240; *2 cesty,* 221, 222; "Ľahký dych stúpa k nebu," 221, 240; *Neviditeľná sfinga,* 221, 240; *Še-po-ty,* 221, 240; *Terra nova,* 221, 240; *Tiene papradia,* 221–222, 223, 240; video-poviedky, 222–223; *Závojovaná žena,* 221, 240; *Z denníkov Ida V.,* 221, 222, 240

Bodor, Ádám: *Az érsek látogatása,* 185, 230–231; *Az Eufratesz Babilonnál,* 230; *A börtön szaga,* 185–186; *Sinistra körzet,* 185, 230

Bogdan, Ivo, 112

Bogomil heresy, 116, 119

Bogusławski, Wojciech, 81

Bojetu, Berta: *Besede iz hiše,* 209; *Filio ni doma,* 209–210; *Pticja hiša,* 209; *Žabon,* 209

Borovský, Karel Havlíček: *Král Lávra,* 125–126

Borowski, Tadeusz, 21, 40; *Gdziekolwiek ziemia,* 7–8; *Kamienny świat,* 8; *Pożegnania z Marią,* 8

Boškovski, Jovan: *Rastrel,* 116; *Solunski atentatori,* 116

Bosnia, 117, 119; Young Bosnia movement, 117, 168

Bosnia-Herzegovina, viii, 12–13

Bosnian Muslims, 119, 163, 266–273

Bota e re (journal), 152

Botta, Emil, 252

Bourne, Daniel, 196

Bozai, Ágotá: *Tranzít glória,* 340

Bozhilov, Bozhidar: *Putnitsite ot "Sivata Hrutka,"* 298

Božič, Peter: *Chubby Was Here,* 140, 334; *Človek in senca,* 140; *Jaz sem ubil Anito,* 140; *Očeta Vincenca smrt,* 140, 334; *Zdaj, ko je nova oblast,* 140, 334–335

Brabcová, Zuzana, 68; *Daleko od stromu,* 77–79; *Rok perel,* 343

Brandys, Kazimierz: *Antygona,* 46–47; *Człowiek nie umiera,* 46; *Matka Królów,* 46, 47; *Miasto niepokonane,* 46; *Między wojnami,* 46–47; *Miesiące, 1978–1979,* 191, 305; *Miesiące, 1980–1981,* 191, 305; *Obrona Grenady,* 46, 47; *Obywatele,* 47; *Samson,* 46–47; *Troja miasto otwarte,* 46; *A Warsaw Diary, 1978–1981,* 191

Bratić, Radoslav, 164

Brecht, Bertolt, 63, 89, 190

Broda, Marzena, 237; *Cudzoziemszczyzna,* 238–239, 309; *Światło przestrzeni,* 238

Brodsky, Josip, 311

bruLion (quarterly), 238

Bucharest Writer's Association, 101

Buchenwald, 10, 36

Buczkowski, Leopold: *Czarny potok,* 2–3; *Wertepy,* 2

Bukovina, 100; deportation/slaughter of Jews, viii, 20, 27, 28

Bulatović, Miodrag, 279; *Heroj na magarcu,* 15–16; *Rat je bio bolji,* 15–16

Bulgaria, 12–13, 39, 208; as ally of Axis, vii, viii, 13, 20–27

Bulgarian writers: escapist literature, 133–137; historical writing, 116–117; women poets, 244–246

Bulić, Vanja: *Tunel: Lepa sela, lepo gore,* 272

Cádra, Fedor: *Jediný deň života,* 33

Călinescu, Matei, 60

Calvino, Italo: *Le città invisibili,* 227

Canon of Lek Dukagjini, 49, 96

Carcer Magni Principatus Transilvaniae, 145

Čar, Aleš, 335; *Igra angelov in netopirjev,* 337; *Pséci tango,* 336, 337; *V okvari,* 336–337

Cârneci, Magda (Magdalena Ghica), 247, 253–254; *Chaosmos*, 253; *Hipermateria*, 253

Cărtărescu, Mircea, 200; *Jurnal*, 203; *Jurnal II: 1997–2003*, 203; *Levantul*, 201–203; "Occidentul," 290–291; *Orbitor*, 201; *Postmodernismul românesc*, 201; *Travesti*, 201; *Visul*, 201–202

Cartea Românească publishing house, 199

Carver, Raymond, 338

Cassian, Nina (Renée Annie Cassian), 248; *Cronofagie*, 248; "Gimnastica de dimineața," 248; *La scara 1/1*, 248; *Loto-poeme*, 248; *Numărătoarea inversă*, 248; *Spectacol în aer liber*, 248

Catholic mysticism, 172

Ceaușescu, Elena, ix

Ceaușescu, Nicolae, ix, 97, 100–101, 129, 197; prison camps under, 144, 146, 148–150

Cesereanu, Ruxandra, 247; *Deliruri și delire*, 256; *Oceanul Schizoidian*, 255–256

Charter 77 movement, 75, 106, 107, 177

Chesterton, G.K., 138

chetnik *(četnik)*, 13–14, 42

China, Albania and, 86–88, 151

Chiuper-Ivasiuc, Tita, 291–292

Church of Mary (Kraków), 123

Church of St Jacob (Levoča), 123

Chwin, Stefan: *Esther*, 346–347, 353; *Hannemann*, 346

Cinci (Marin, Bucur, Lefter, Ghiu, Mușina), 254

Ciomoș, Virgil, 150

Codreanu, Corneliu Zelea, 28, 29, 148

collectivization, forced, 55–65

Comănescu, Denisa, 247; *Barca pe valuri*, 252–253

Committee on National Liberation (Poland), 41

Committee to Protect the Truth of Radovan Karadžić, 289

Communist League of Yugoslavia, 165

Confederation of Political Prisoners (Slovak), 181–182

Constantinescu, Emil, 199, 200

Ćosić, Dobrica, 276; *Srpsko pitanje—demokratsko pitanje*, 274–275; *Vreme smrti*, 114, 274

Crăsnaru, Daniela, 247, 251–252, 292, 293–294; *Letters from Darkness*, 251–252

Creangă, Ion, 55

crime novels, 38, 136, 137–142

Croatia, vii, x, 27, 280–283; Ustasha *(Ustaša)*, viii, ix, 13, 20, 118, 287

Croatian Democratic Union, 165

Croatian Mass Movement *(Masovni pokret, Maspok)*, 165

Croatian Social-Liberal Party, 165

Croatian writers: historical, 120; postmodernism, 207; prison literature, 164–166; women poets, 242–244

Cseres, Tibor: *Foksányi-szoros*, 26; *Hideg napok*, 24–25; *Őseink kertje: Erdély*, 26; *Vérbosszú Bácskában*, 24–26; *Vízaknai csaták*, 26

Csurka, István, 68, 79; *Túrógombóc*, 80

Čuić, Stjepan: *Abeceda licemjerja*, 282–283; *Staljinova slika i drugi priče*, 135; *Tridesetogodišnje priče*, 135

Cuvîntul (review), 199

Cvenić, Josep: *Kajinev pečat*, 352; *Kraljica noći*, 352–353

Cyril, St., 122

Czapski, Józef: *Na nieludzkiej ziemi*, 4; *Wspomnienia starobielskie*, 4

Czarne publishing house, 188

Czech Brethren, 123

Czech Index series, 179

Czech Literary Fund, 217

Czechoslovakia, x, 30; elections (1946), 71–72; émigré writers, 104–111; National Front Government, 72; occupied, 9–12; Prague Spring (1968), 46, 66, 105, 106, 107, 109, 169, 178; resistance, 11–12; Velvet Revolution (1989),

170; Warsaw Pact invasion of, 66, 70, 86, 106

Czech writers: absurd and grotesque, literature of, 68, 71–79, 107–108, 126–128; émigrés, 104–111; historical writing, 126–128; poetry, 172–175; postmodernism, 210–218; prison literature, 169–182; urban landscapes, 330–332; women poets, 239–241

Czeczot, Andrzej, 310

Czekanowicz, Anna: "Iowa Iowa Iowa," 308; *Ktoś kogo nie ma*, 308–309; *Śmierć w powietrzu*, 308–309

Czyżewska, Elżbieta, 307

Dachau, 8

Dacia publishing house (Cluj), 150

Dalmatia, 120

Davičo, Oskar: *Medju Markosovim partizanima*, 14; *Pesma*, 14

Dayton Agreement, 266, 272

Dejiny slovensky literatury 4: Slovenská literatúra po roku 1945, 358

De Rada, Girolamo, 153

Déry, Tibor: *A befejezetlen mondat*, 130; *Börtönnapok hordaléka: Önélejtrazi jegyzetek*, 130, 183; *Felelet*, 130, 182; *Három asszony*, 183; *Itélet nincs*, 183; *Liebe Mamuskam*, 183; *G.A. úr X.-ben*, 130–131, 182; *Niky, egy kutya története*, 130

Déry Archive, 183

Despot, Slobodan, 274

Detection Club (England), 138

Dežulović, Boris: *Christkind*, 287; *Greatest Shits*, 286; *Jebo sad hiljadu dinara*, 286–287

Dimitrov, Georgi, 300

Dimitrova, Blaga: "Dokosvaniya," 244

Dinescu, Mircea, 103

Divadlo na Vinohradech (Theater in the Vineyards), 106, 127

Dizdar, Mak (Mehmed Alija): *Kameni spavač*, 119; *Stari bosanski epitafi*, 119; *Stari bosanski tekstovi*, 119

Dizdarević, Zlatko: *Sarajevo: A War Journal*, 272

Djilas, Milovan, 167; *Land Without Justice*, 169; *Memoir of a Revolutionary*, 169; *The New Class (Nova klasa)*, 168, 169; *Razgovori sa Stalinom*, 168–169; *Rise and Fall*, 169; *Tamnica i idea*, 169; *Tito: The Story from Inside*, 169; *Wartime*, 169

Djindjić, Zoran, 288

Dobiáš, Rudolf, 181–182; "Koniec šalieného storočia, 182; *Svedecto troch križov*, 182; *Tajni ľudia*, 182; *Temná zeleň*, 182; *Zvony a hroby/Príbehy z prítmia*, 182

Dobrescu, Caius, 203

Dobršek, Albina. *See* Vegri, Saša

Dobrudja region, 62

Dones, Elvira: *Dashuri e huaj*, 360; *Yjet nuk vishen kështu*, 329, 360

Dragojević Srdjan, 272

Drakulić, Slavenka, 282–284

Drašković, Vuk: *Nož*, 287; *Ruski konzul*, 287–288

Dubček, Alexander, 75, 211

Dumitru, Petru: *Au Dieu inconnu*, 55; *Cronică de familie*, 54; *Drum fără pulbere*, 54; *Dușmănie*, 54; *Incognito*, 54–55; *Les Initiés*, 55; *L'Extrème Occident*, 55; *L'Homme aux yeux gris*, 55; *Nopțile de iunie*, 54; *O sută de kilometri*, 54; *Rendez-vous au Jugement dernier*, 54–55; *Le Sourire sarde*, 55

Duraković, Ferida, 269–270; *Serce tame: Sarajevo, 1973–1993*, 268–269

Dva tisíce slov (Two Thousand Words) manifesto (Vaculík), 75

Džurinda, Mikuláš, 333

East German Writers' Union, 37, 190

East Germany. *See* German Democratic Republic

Edice Petlice (Padlock Editions), 75

Egymásra nézve (film, Gálgoczi), 342

Eliade, Mircea: fantastic, literature of, 133–134; *Domnișoara Christina*, 100, 134; *India*, 100; *Isabel și apele*

Eliade, Mircea (*continued*)
    diavolului, 100; *Maitreyi,* 99, 134;
    "Nouăsprezece trandafiri," 100;
    "Pelerina," 100; *Şantier,* 99–100;
    Şarpele, 100, 134; scholarly works,
    99; *Secretul Doctorului Honig-*
    berger, 100, 134; "Tinereţe fără de
    tinereţe," 100, 134–135
émigrés, literature about, 359–366
émigré writers, xii, 89, 310–311;
    Czech, 104–111; in France, 98–104;
    Kadare and Miłosz, 92–97; Roma-
    nian, 99–104; Romanians, in
    France, 99–104; Yugoslav, 111–112
Eminescu Publishing House (Romania),
    252
Endeavor (anthology), 159
Engel, Paul, 302
Enver Hoxha Museum, 129
Epicenter theater, 286
Erb, Elke, 260–261
Erb, Ewald, 260
escapist literature: allegory, 125–133;
    Albanian writers, 128–129; Bulgar-
    ian writers, 120–121, 136–137;
    Croatian writers, 135–136; Czech
    writers, 125–128, 137–140; East
    German writers, 140–142; Hungar-
    ian writers, 130–133; past, recollec-
    tion of, 115–125; Polish writers,
    121–125, 129–130, 137; Romanian
    writers, 133–135; science fiction,
    spy novels, fantastic literature,
    133–137; Slovenian writers, 140;
    World War I and interwar period,
    114–115
Esprit (review), 102
Esterházy, Péter: *Bevezetés*
    szépirodalomba, 48; *Harmonia*
    caelestis, 47–48; *A szív segédigéi,*
    228; *Kis magyar pornográfia,*
    227–228; *Termelési-regény,* 48, 227
Estonia, x, 39
ethnic cleansing, x, 266, 274

Fal'tan, Samo: *O Slovanskom národ-*
    nom povstaní, 31; *Partizánska vojna*
    na Slovensku, 31; *Slovaci v*
    partizánskych bojoch v Sovietskom
    sväze, 31; *Víťazné stretnutie,* 31
fantastic, literature of, 133–136
Federal People's Assembly (Yugosla-
    via), 168
Federal Republic of Germany (Bundes-
    republik), 36
Femeia în roşu (Mihăieş, Nedelciu, and
    Babeţi), 200
Feral Tribunea (weekly), 27, 286
Ferko, Milan: *Krádež svätoštefanskiej*
    koruny, 122; *Medzi ženou a Rímom,*
    122; *Prvá láska nastorako,* 123;
    Šestdesiat jeden krokov k slovenskej
    identite: Zvrchované Slovensko,
    123; *Slováci a maď'ari: Subor študii,*
    123; *Stary narod, mladý štát,* 123;
    Sto slávnych Slovákov, 123; *Svä-*
    topluk, 122; *Svätopluk a Metod:*
    Oheň života, oheň skazy, 122;
    Svätoplukovo dedičstvo, 122;
    Velkomoravské záhady, 123
Filipović, Zoran: *Sarajevo,* 268
Firan, Carmen, 247, 254–255; "Natură
    moartă cu scaune libere," 255
Fischerová, Sylva: *Chvění závodních*
    koní, 239; *Šance,* 239; *Velká zrcadla,*
    239; *V podsvětním městě,* 239
France, as home for émigrés, 98–104
Frank, Anne, 254
Franz-Ferdinand, Archduke, 117
Frick, Grace, 309
Friedrich II, 125
Friedrich Wilhelm I, 125
Fuchs, Bohuslav, 213
Füssli, Caspar, 123
Fühmann, Franz: *Böhmen am Meer,*
    37; *Fahrt nach Stalingrad,* 37; *Das*
    Gottesgericht, 37; *Das Judenauto:*
    Vierzehn Tage aus zwei Jahrzehnten,
    37; *Kamaraden,* 37; *Kapitulation,*
    37; *Die Nelke Nikos Gedichte,* 37
Fultz, Harry, 52

Gałczyński, Konstanty Ildefons, 40
Gálgoczi, Érszebet: *Törvényen belül*
Gallimard publishing house (France),
    93, 146

Gavelis, Ričardas, 320, 321–322;
Jauno žmogaus memuarai, 321;
Nemirtingumas, 322; *Paskutinioje
žemes žmunių karta*, 322; *Taikos
balandis: Septyni Vilniaus apsaky-
mai*, 322; *Vilniaus pokeris*, 321
Gazeta literară (journal), 60
Gazeta Wyborcza (journal), 196
Gdańsk shipyard strike, 130, 197
German Communist Youth Organiza-
tion, 37
German Democratic Republic (GDR),
ix, 36–38, 63–65, 66
German Democratic Republic writers:
crime fiction, 140–141; East
German Writers' Union, 37, 190;
prison literature, 189–190; Sixth
Writer's Congress, 262; United
States, view of, 316–317; women
poets, 260–263
Gheorghiu-Dej, Gheorghe, 144
Gherla prison (Romania), 145, 147,
149, 185–186
Ghetto Uprising (1943), 5, 6, 38
Gierek, Edward, 130
Ginsberg, Allen, 311–312
Gjata, Fatmir, 17; *Këneta*, 18, 52;
Kënga e partizanit Benko, 18;
Përmbysja, 18; *Pika gjaku*, 18;
Tana, 52; *Ujët fle, hasmi s'fle*, 18
Gjuzel, Bogomil: *Kuća cel svet*,
301–302; *Wolf at the Door*, 302
Glavan, Polona, 335; *Noč v Evropi*,
337
Globus (weekly), 286
Głowacki, Janusz, 307; *Antygona w
Nowym Yorku*, 361; *Połowanie na
karaluchy*, 310, 361
Główczewska, Lenta: *Nowy Jork:
Kartki z metropolii 1983–2002*, 303
Goethe, Johann Wolfgang von, 69, 152
Gogol, Nikolai, 84–85, 195
Goli otok (Barren Island), 42, 161–163
Gołubiew, Antoni: *Bolesław Chrobry*,
121
Goma, Paul, 99, 145; *Camera de
alături*, 145; *Chassée-croisé*, 146;
*Les chiens de la mort, ou, La passion
selon Pitești*, 146; *Dans le cercle*,
146; *Din Calidor: o copilărie
basarabeană*, 146; *Garde inverse*,
146; *Gherla*, 146, 147; *Ostinato*,
145, 146–147; *Le tremblement des
homme: Peut-on vivre en Roumanie
aujourd'hui*, 146; *Ușa (Elles étaient
quatre)*, 145
Gombrowicz, Witold, 68
Gomułka, Władysław, 130
Göncz, Árpád, 68, 183–184; *Haza-
érkezes*, 184; *Magyar Médeia*, 79;
Mérleg: Hét drámaja, 184; *Perse-
phone*, 79; *Rácsok*, 79–80, 184;
Sarusok, 79
Gordon, Ágatá: *Kecskéruzs*, 342–343
Gorky Institute of World Literature
(Moscow), 18, 51, 95
Gorky, Maksim *Mat'*, 51
Gospodinov, Georgi: *Cheresata na edin
narod*, 207; *Estestven roman*, 207;
Lapidarium, 207
Gotovac, Vlado, 164–166; *Moj slučaj*,
166; *Okovana Bosna: Razgovor*,
164; *Pisma protiv tiranije*, 166; *U
svakodnevnom*, 164
Gottwald, Klement, 72, 170, 173
Grajauskas, Gintaras: *Tatuiruotė*, 320
Grassy, József, 25
Great Dictator. *See* Stalin, Josef
Great Water, The (film), 303
Grendel, Lajos: *Éleslövészet*, 366–367;
Tömegsír, 367–368
Gretkowska, Manuela: *Kabaret
metafizyczny*, 362; *My zdies' emi-
granty*, 362–363; *Tarot paryski*, 362
Grigorescu, Lucian, 254
Grynberg, Henryk, 310
gulags (prison camps, Soviet Union), 4,
143
Guliashki, Andrei: *Otdelenie za reani-
matsiia*, 136; *Poslednoto prikliuche-
nie na Avakum Zahov*, 136; *Prikli-
ucheniiata na Avakum Zahov*, 136;
Ubiistvoto na ulitsa "Chekhova,"
136; *Zhivotut i prikliucheniiata na
Avakum Zahov*, 136
Gypsies, viii, x, 2, 17, 20, 318, 329

Habsburg empire, viii, 109, 117, 122, 124, 126

Halberstam, David, 307

Hartwig, Julia, 235–236, 303, 307; *Americana*, 306; *Chwila postoju*, 236; *Czułość*, 236; "Mówiąc nie tylko do siebie," 236; *Obcowanie*, 236; *Przemija postać świata*, 236; *Zawsze od nowa: 100 wierszy*, 236; *Zawsze powroty: Dzienniki podróży*, 306–307

Havel, Václav, 68, 75, 104, 106; imprisonment of, 180–181; *Chyba*, 181; *Largo Desolato*, 73–74; *Pokoušení*, 74; *Vyrozumění*, 72–73; *Zahradní slavnost*, 72, 73, 126; *Ztížená možnost soustředění*, 73

Hejda, Jiří: "Na smrt Luisy," 174–175; *Sonety zpívané šeptem ve stínu šibenice: Ruzyně–Pankrác–Mirov–Leopoldov–Valdice, 1950–1962*, 173–174; *Útěk*, 173; *Žil jsem zbytečně:Román mého života*, 173

Helsinki Watch Commission, 282–283

Herbert, Zbigniew, 193–194

Herling-Grudziński, Gustaw: *Don Ildebrando: Opowiadania*, 187; *Dziennik pisany nocą*, 187–188; *Gorący oddech pustyni*, 187; *Inny świat*, 187–188, 189; *Opowiadania zebrane*, 187; *Portret wenecki: Trzy opowiadania*, 187; *Skrzydła ołtarza*, 187; *Wieża i inne opowiadania*, 187

Hermlin, Stephan (Rudolf Leder), 37–38; *Abendlicht*, 38; *Die Zeit der Gemeinsamkeit*, 38

Herz, Juraj, 139

Heydrich, Reinhard, 54

Heym, Stephen: *Fünf Tage im Juni: Der Tag X*, 66

Hilbig, Wolfgang: *Der Brief*, 141; *Eine Übertragung*, 141, 142; *Ich*, 141, 142; *Die Weiber*, 141, 142

Hirt, Josef, 17

historical writing, 114–115; Albania, 128–129; Bulgaria, 116–117; Croatia, 120; Czechoslovakia, 126–128; Hungary, 130–131; Macedonia, 116; Poland, 121–125, 129–130; Romania, 124–125; Slovakia, 122–124

Hodrová, Daniela, 210, 227; *Komedie*, 214; *Kukly*, 214, 215; *Perunův den*, 214; *Théta*, 214–215; *Trýznivé město*, 214

Hoffmanová, Věra. *See* Legátová, Květa

Holan, Vladimir, 79

Hollo, Anselm, 272

Holmes, Sherlock, 138

Holocaust, 1, 21, 69, 318–319

Holub, Miroslav: *Anděl na kolečkách: Poloreportaž USA*, 313–314; *beton: verše z new yorku a z prahy*, 313, 315; *Žit v New Yorku*, 313, 314–315

Holubová, Miloslava: *Víc než jeden život*, 351

Honecker, Erich, 89

Horák, Jozef: *Hory mlčia*, 31, 32

Horáková, Milada, 173

Horáková & Co., 173

Hoxha, Enver, 14, 19, 49, 83, 87, 94, 120, 129; prison camps, 151; *The Titoites: Historical Notes*, 158

Hrabal, Bohumil, 68, 78, 348

Hronský, Jozef Ciger, 32–33; *Chlieb*, 32; *Jozef Mak*, 32; *Svet na trasovisku*, 33

Huelle, Paweł, 346; *mercedes-benz; z listów do Hrabala*, 348; *Weiser Dawidek*, 347–348, 353

Hungarian Communist Party, 186

Hungarian community in Romania, x, 253, 318

Hungarian Republic of Soviets, 186

Hungarian Revolution (1956), ix, 66, 67, 82, 130, 145, 182

Hungarians, Slovak, 366–369

Hungarian writers: absurd and grotesque, literature of, 79–83; postmodernism, 227–232; prison literature, 182–187; urban landscapes, 340, 342–344

Hungary: as ally of Axis, 20–27; Arrow Cross (Nyilaskereszt), ix, 20, 23; compliance with Nazi Germany, vii–viii, 13. *See also* Transylvania

Husák, Gustáv, 109, 211

Hussites, 214

Hvorecký, Michal, 218; *Lovci & zberači*, 224; *Posledný hit*, 225–226; "Prvé vít' azstvo supermarketov," 224–225; *Silný pocit čistoty*, 224

Ieronim, Ioana (Ioana Brânduş), 247, 250; *Triumful paparudei*, 363–364

IKESZ (Illegális Kommunistaellenes Szervezet), 185

Iliad (Homer), 128

Ilinden Uprising (Macedonia), 115–116

Index publishing house (Cologne), 78

Instytut Literacki (Insitut Litteraire), 6, 40, 93, 98, 191, 195

international appeals for amnesty, 165, 173, 279

International Center of Culture (Tirana), 229

International Writing Program (University of Iowa), xii, 10, 199, 245, 248, 260, 291–292, 294–295, 301–302, 307, 316

Iron Guard (Garda de fier), 28, 29, 148, 185

Isaeva, Lyudmila, 244

Isaković, Antonije: *Tren 2*, 162

Isanos, Magda, 233

Istrati, Panait: *Cantonul părăsit*, 59; *Dincolo de nisipuri*, 59; *Somnul de la amiază*, 59

Italy, 13, 17–18, 151

Ivanauskaitė, Jurga, 320; *Ragana ir lietus*, 325, 326

Ivanova, Mirela, 244

Ivasiuc, Alexandru, 291–292

Ivaškevičius, Marius, 320; *Istorija nuo debesies*, 325; *Kam vaiku*, 325

Jančar, Drago, 265–266; *Posmehljivo poželenje*, 294, "Spomini na Jugoslavijo," 265

Janevski, Slavko: *Čudotvorci*, 115; *Devet Kerubinovi vekovi*, 115; Kukulino octology, 115; *Selo zad sedumte jaseni*, 115

Jarry, Alfred, 126

Jaruzelski, Wojciech, 130, 191

Jasenovac (concentration camp, Croatia), viii, 161

Jašík, Rudolf: *Mrtví niespievaja'*, 31, 32; *Námestie svätej Alžbety*, 33

Jastrun, Tomasz, 191; *Bez usprawiedli- wienia*, 196; *Kropla, kropla*, 196; *Obok siebie*, 196; *Tylko czułość idzie do nieba*, 196; *W złotej klatce: Notatnik amerykański*, 309–311; *Zapis z Błędnego Koła*, 197, 309; *Życie Anny Walentynowicz*, 197

Jebeleanu, Eugen: *Ceea ce nu se uită*, 54; *Elegie pentru floarea secerată*, 54; *Lidice, Cîntece împotriva morţii*, 54; *Poeme de pace şi de luptă*, 54; *Surîsul Hiroşimei*, 54

Jergović, Miljenko: "Brada," 285–286; "Kondor," 286; *Sarajevski Marl- boro*, 285–286

Jews, x, 1, 7; in Albania, World War II, 24, 84; in Czechoslovakia, 10, 175; deportation of, viii, 6–7, 20, 27–28; in former Yugoslavia, 161, 273; in Poland, 1, 4–8; Romanian, viii–ix; Slovak, 30, 33

Johanides, Ján: *Slony v Mauthausene*, 33; *Súkromie*, 33

J(ohannes) R. Becher Literary Institute, 64, 89

Jonynas, Antanas A.: *Metai kaip strazdas*, 320; *Nakties traukinys*, 320

Joseph II, 145

Jovanovski, Meto: *Kluchevite na Manhatan: Zapisi od zapadnite predeli*, 301, 302–303

Jurewicz, Aleksander: *Lida*, 345; *Pan Bóg nie słyszy głuchych*, 345–346; *W środku nocy*, 345

Kadare, Elena, 258

Kadare, Ismail, 84–85, 153, 258; as émigré writer, 94–97; *Autobiografia*

Kadare, Ismail (*continued*)
  e popullit në vargje, 85, 96; *Dasma*,
    48–49, 95; *Dialogue avec Alain
    Bosquet*, 49; *Dimri i madh*, 87, 95;
    Dimri i vetmisë së madhe, 87, 95;
    Dosja H., 85–86, 96; *Eskili, ky
    humbës i madh*, 96; *Ftesë në studio*,
    48, 96, 97; *Gjenerali i ustrishë së
    vdekur*, 4, 19, 49, 95; *Koncert në
    fund të dimrit*, 87–88; *Kronikë në
    gur*, 19, 95, 97; *Nëntori i një
    kryeqyteti*, 19–20, 95; *Nëpunësi i
    pallatit të ëndrrave*, 85, 87; *Nga një
    dhjetor në tjetrin: Kronikë, këmbim
    letrash, persiatje*, 96–97; *Pallati i
    ëndrrave*, 85, 87; *Përbindëshi*, 4, 19,
    49, 95, 128; *Printemps Albanis*, 48;
    Tri këngë zie për Kosovën, 276–277;
    Ura me tri harqe, 95–96, 275–276
Kafka, Franz, 69, 84
Kajokas, Donaldas: *Žuvusi avis*, 320
Kalist, Zdeněk, 172
Kantůrková, Eva: *Dvanáct rozhovorů*,
    179; *Přítelkyně z domu smutku*,
    179, 180; *Sešly jsme se v této knize*,
    179–180
Kapor, Momo, 289
Kapuściński, Ryszard: *Cesarz*, 129,
    130; *Imperium*, 130; *Jeszcze dzień
    życia*, 129; *Szachinszach*, 129, 130;
    Wojna futbolowa, 130
Karadžić, Radovan, 267, 271,
    288–289; *Čudesna hronika noći*,
    289
Karahasan, Dževad: *Dnevnik selidbe*,
    119, 266–267; *Istočni divan*, 119,
    267
Karinthy, Ferenc: *Aranyidő*, 23–24;
    Budapesti ösz, 24; *Budapesti tavasz*,
    23; *Epepe*, 24, 132–133
Karinthy, Frigyes, 23
Karpowicz, Tymoteusz, 238, 310
Katyń murders, 3, 4
Kertész, Imre, 20–23; *Felszámolás*,
    21–22; *Kaddis a meg nem szlületett
    gyermekért*, 21; *A kudarc*, 21–22;
    Sorstalanság, 20–23
Khotin, Battle of, 119

Khrushchev, Nikita, 87
Kielce massacre, 5
Kijowski, Andzrej, 307
Kingdom of Serbs, Croats, and Slo-
    venes, 24–25, 168
Kirsch, Rainer, 261, 262
Kirsch, Sara (Ingrid Bernstein), 260,
    261–263
Kiš, Danilo, 264–265, 272, 278, 279;
    Cas anatomije, 265; *Grobnica za
    Borisa Davidovića*, 265
Klíma, Ivan, 78: *Posledni stupeň
    důvernosti*, 330
Kliment, Alexandr: *Marie*, 105; *Nuda v
    Čechách*, 60–61, 67, 104–105, 106
Kne, Maja, 241; *Ko bo s čudovito
    gladkim gibom ukazala finale*, 242;
    Popisovanje in rondo, 242
Knobelsdorf, G. W. von, 125
Knox, Ronald Arbuthnot: *The Body in
    the Silo*, 138; *Footsteps at the Lock*,
    138; *The Viaduct Murder*, 138
Kocbek, Edvard: *Listina: Dnevniški
    zapiski od 3 maja do 2 decembra
    1943*, 16; *Pred viharjem*, 16;
    *Slovensko poslanstvo: Dnevniški s
    poti v Jajce*, 16; *Strah in pogum*, 16;
    *Tovarišija: Dnevniški zapiski od 17
    maja 1942 do i maja 1943*, 16
Kohout, Pavel, 104, 106–107; *August,
    August, August*, 127–128; *Bílá
    kniha: O kauze Adam Juráček*,
    107–108; *Hvězdná hodina vrahů*,
    139–140; *Z deníku kontrarevolu-
    cionáře*, 107
Kongoli, Fatos: *Dragoi i fildishtë*, 88,
    356–357; *Endrra e Damokleut*, 356;
    I humburi, 88, 356; *Kufoma*, 88,
    356
Konrád, György, 68; *A cinkos*, 82;
    essays, 82–83; *Kerti mulatság*, 82;
    A látogáto, 81–82; *A városalapító*,
    61, 82
Konwicki, Tadeusz, 2; *Sennik
    współczesny*, 8–9
KOR (Committee for the Defense of
    Workers), 194
Kornhauser, Julian, 98, 194

Kosovo, ix, 13, 155, 161, 264; ethnic cleansing, x, 266, 274; resettlement of Serbs, 275

Kosovo campaign, literature about, 273–288

Kostunica, Vojislav, 266

Kovač, Mirko: *Životopis Malvine Trifkovića*, 277–278

Krall, Hanna, 196

Krasnahorkai, László: *Az ellenállás melankóliája*, 228; *Az urgai fogoly*, 229; *Háború és háború*, 229–230; *Kegyelmi viszonyok: Halálnovellák*, 228; *Rombolás és bánat az Ég alatt*, 229; *Sátántangó*, 228

Kratochvil, Jiří, 227; *Avion*, 213–214; *Lehnie, bestie!*, 214; "Ma lásko, Postmoderno," 210; *Medvědi román*, 210–212, 213; *Noční tango*, 214; *Upostřed nocí zpěv*, 212–213; *Urmedvědi*, 211

Kritika letrare (review), 151

Kulavkova, Katica, 246–247

Kultura (review), 98

Kun, Béla, 186

Kunčinas, Jurgis, 320; *Glisono kilpa*, 322; *Kilnojamosios Rentgeno stotys*, 322, 323; *Tūla*, 323; *Vaizdas į menulį*, 322

Kunčius, Herkus, 320; *Būtasis dažninis laikas*, 323–324; *Ekskursija: Casa Matta*, 324; *Ir dugnas visada priglaus*, 323; *Mano kova bambino*, 324; *Pelenai asilo kanopoje*, 324–325

Kundera, Milan, 68; as émigré writer, 92, 104, 108–110; *Identity*, 109; *Ignorance*, 109–110; *Immortality*, 109; *Kniha smíchu a zapomnění*, 45–46, 108–109; *Nesnesitelná lehkost bytí*, 108, 109–110; *Slowness*, 109; *Směšné lásky*, 108; *Valčík na rozloučenou*, 108; *Žert*, 43, 44–45, 108; *Život je jinde*, 43–44, 108

Kunert, Günter: *Der andere Planet: Ansichten von Amerika*, 316–317

Kunsági, Erzsébet (Böbe), 183

Kupecký, Jan, 123–124

Kuśniewicz, Andrzej, 121; *Eroica*, 122; *Król obojga Sycylii*, 122; *Lekcja martwego języka*, 122; *Nawrócenie*, 122; *Stan nieważkości*, 122; *W drodze do Koryntu*, 122

Kutev/Koutev (Bulgarian National Ensemble), 299–301

Kuzmanov, Evgeni: *Foto "Lazur,"* 342

Kuźnica literary group (Łódź), 7

Laço, Teodor: *Kohë për të kujtuar/Kohë për të harruar*, 357

Lalić, Mihailo: *Lelejska gora*, 14

Landovský, Pavel, 75

landowning nobility *(szlachta)*, 55

land redistribution policy, 64–65

language, under communism, 132–133

Lasker-Schuler, Else, 263

Latvia, 39

League of Albanian Writers, 152

Lederer, J., 178

Legátová, Květa (Věra Hoffmanová), 11–12; *Jozova Hanule*, 12; *Želary*, 12

Lehenová, Tat'jana, 239; *Cigánský tábor*, 241; "Malá nočná mora," 240; *Pre vybranú spoločnosť*, 240–241

Leikert, Jozef: *Testament svedomia*, 29–30

Leipziger Volkszeitung (newspaper), 89

Lem, Stanisław: *The Cyberiad*, 133; *The Futurological Congress*, 133; *More Tales of Pirx the Pilot*, 133; *Pokój na ziemi*, 133; *Solaris*, 133; *The Star Diaries*, 133; *Tales of Pirx the Pilot*, 133

Lenardič, Mart, 335; *Še večji Gatsby*, 336

Lendíc, Ivo, 112

Lengyel, József, 185; *Elejétöl végig*, 185–186

Lenin Shipyard (Gdańsk), 197

Lidice (Czechoslovakia), 54

Lingis, Vitas, 322

Lipska, Ewa, 236; *Białe truskawki/
White Strawberries*, 237; *Dom
spokojnej młodości*, 237; *Gdzie
indziej*, 237; *Godziny poza godzinami*, 237; *Ludzie dla
początkujących*, 237; *Nie o śmierć
tutaj chodzi, lecz o biały kordonek*,
237, 307; "Nowy Jork miasto
porwane," 307–308; *Pet Shops, and
Other Poems*, 237; *Piąty zbiór
wierszy*, 237; *Przechowalnia
ciemności*, 237; *Sklepy zoologiczne*,
237; *Strefa ograniczonego postoju*,
237–238; *Wiersze*, 237; *Żywa
śmierć*, 237

Lipski, Leo (Lipschuetz, Lep), 187;
Dzień i noc, 188

Literární listy (journal), 75

Literární noviný (journal), 211

literary subterfuge, xii, 67–68, 113,
251–252

Literatur (journal, Munich), 243

Lithuania, xii, 39, 94, 319–327

Ljubljana subculture, 140

Lleshanaku, Luljeta, 258, 259–260;
Gjysmëkubizëm, 260; *Palca e
verdhë*, 260

Loest, Erich, 189–190; pseudonyms,
141, 189, 190; *Als wir in den
Westen kamen: Gedanken eines
literarischen Grenzgangers*, 190;
Durch die Erde ein Riss, 89; *Ein
Sacshe in Osnabrück*, 141; *Es geht
seinen Gang oder Mühen in unserer
Ebene*, 88–91, 141, 190, 358, 359;
Froschkonzert, 141; *Heute kommt
Westbesuch*, 190, 358–359; *Jungen,
die übrig bleiben*, 88–89; *Nacht
über dem See*, 88–89; *Pistole mit
sechzehn*, 141; *Die Stasi war mein
Eckermann, oder: Mein Leben mit
der Wanze*, 190, 359; *Der vierte
Censor: Vom Enstehen und Sterben
eines Romans in der DDR*, 190,
359; *Der Zorn des Schaffes: Aus
meinem Tagewerk*, 190

Lourie, Richard, 191

Lubonja, Fatos T., 159

Lubonja, Todi, 159

Luceafărul (review), 145, 198

Lustig, Arnošt, 9–11; *Dita Saxová*, 11;
*Modlitba pro Kateřinu Horovitzo-
vou*, 10; *Nemilovaná: Z deníku
sedmnáctileté Perly Sch.*, 10–11;
Neslušné sny, 10; *Noc a naděje*, 10;
Tma nemá stín, 10; *Ulice ztracených
bratří*, 10

Macedonia, viii, 20, 161, 264; Ilinden
Uprising, 115–116; women poets,
246–247

Mackiewicz, Józef: *Droga do nikąd*, 4;
Nie trzeba głosno mówić, 4

Makarovič, Svetlana, 241–242; *Kaj
lepega povej*, 242; *Križantema na
klavirju: Šansonska besedila S. M.*,
242; *Pesmi o Sloveniji: Za tuje in
domače goste*, 242

Makk, Károlyi, 342

Mălăncioiu, Ileana, 247, 248–249;
Linia vieţii, 249; *Pasărea tăiată*, 249

Maliarik, Ján: *Celo-Zemský Universalný Štát*, 350

Maliq land reclamation (Albania),
52–53

Manea, Norman, 99, 101, 124; *Ani de
ucenicie ai lui August Prostul*, 100,
101; *Atrium*, 100; *Captivi*, 100;
Cartea fiului, 100; "Composite
Biography," 100–101; *Despre
clovni: Dictator şi artistul*, 100, 101,
124; *Octombre oră opt*, 100; "The
Trenchcoat," 100; "A Window on
the Working Class," 100; *Zilele şi
jocul*, 100

Manolescu, Nicolae, 101, 198

Mantov, Dimitur: *Albigoiska legenda*,
117; *Han Krum*, 117; *Ivan Asen II:
Tsar i samodurets*, 117; *Tsar
Petrovo vreme*, 117; *Tsar Simeon*,
117; *Zubato sluntse*, 116–117

Mao Zedong, 86, 88

Marčėnas, Aidas, 320–321; *Šulinys*,
320

Marcus Aurelius, 122

Máriássy, Félix, 23

Marin, Mariana, 247; *Aripa secretă*, 254; *Atelierele, 1980–1984*, 254; *Cinci*, 254; "Elegie, XII," 254; *Mutilaria artistului la tinereţe*, 254; *Un război de o sută de ani*, 254

Marko, Petro: *Nata e Ustikës* (Ustica Night), 17–18; *Qyteti i fundit*, 17–18

Markovski, Venko: *Goli Otok: The Island of Death. A Diary in Letters*, 161–162; "Suvremenni paradoksi," 161

Márton, Áron, 185

Masaryk, Jan, 72

Masaryk, Thomas, 72

Masłowska, Dorota: *Lampa i Iskra Boża*, 340

Matica Hrvatska publishing house (Croatia), 165

Mečiar, Vladimir, 333

Mehmed II, 116

Mehmedinović, Semezdin: *Sarajevo Blues*, 267

Meine Träume fallen in die Welt: Ein Else Lasker-Schuler Almanach, 263

Menschen im Krieg: Erzählungen über den 2. Weltkrieg von Autoren aus der Deutschen Demokratischen Republik und der Sowjetunion, 37

Merth, František Daniel: *Den Madian*, 172–173; *Na jihu království*, 173; *Orančína píseň*, 173; *Refrigerium*, 172; *Sedm písní*, 173

Metai (journal), 323

Methodius, St., Apostle to the Slavs, 122

Michnik, Adam, 196

Mickiewicz, Adam: *Dziady*, 69

Międzyrzecki, Artur, 306, 307

Mihailović, Dragoslav: *Frede, laku noć*, 162–163; *Goli otok*, 162, 163, 164; *Kad su cvetale tikve*, 162; *Lov na stenice*, 162; "Od jedan put su ubili dvadesetak ljudi," 163; *Petrijin venac*, 163

Mihailović, Draža, 13–14, 42

Mihăieş, Mircea, 200

Miliauskaitė, Nijolė: *Uršules S. portretas*, 320

Milošević, Slobodan, x, 161, 266, 276, 279, 281, 288

Miłosz, Czesław: as émigré witer, 92–94, 98, 310; Jan Syruć as pseudonym, 93; awarded National Order of Merit, 200; "Biedny chrześcianin patrzy na ghetto," 6; "Campo di fiori," 6; *Dolina Issy*, 94; *Obrachunki*, 200; *Pieśń niepodległa*, 93; *Rodzinna Europa*, 94; *Trzy zimy*, 93; *Wiersze*, 93; *Zdobycie władzy*, 41–42, 93–94; *Zniewolony umysł*, 40–41, 42, 93–94, 96

Mináč, Vladimir: *Dlhý čas čakania*, 31; *Generácia*, 31; *Živi a mŕtvi*, 31

Mitana, Dušan Krist, 218; *Hľadanie strateného autora*, 140, 220; *Koniec hry*, 140; *Krst ohnom*, 221; *Môj rodný cintorín*, 350–351; *Návrat Krista*, 220–221; *Nočné správy*, 140, 220

Mňačko, Ladislav: *Smrt' sa volá Engelchen*, 31, 32

Moldavia, 124

Molotov-Ribbentrop pact, 3

Montale, Eugenio, 151

Montenegro, 13, 114, 161, 264; resettlement of Serbs, 275; writers, 14–15

Moravia, 74, 122

Moric, Rudo, 124

Morovič, Andrej: *Bomba la petrolia*, 335–336; *Vladarka*, 335

Mozetič, Brane: *Metulji*, 335; *Modra svetloba: Homoerotična ljubezen v slovenski literaturi*, 335; *Pasijon*, 335; *Zgubljena zgodba*, 335

Mrożek, Sławomir, 68, 69–70, 98, 191; "Donosy," 192; *Karol*, 70; *Męczeństwo Piotra Oheya*, 70; *Opowiadania i donosy: 1980–1989*, 70; *Policja*, 70; *Striptease*, 70; *Tango*, 71; *Vatzlav*, 70–71

Mucha, Alfons, 170

Mucha, Jiří, 169–172; *Living and Partly Living*, 170–172; *Oheň proti ohni*, 169

Müller, Heiner: *Die Umsiedlerin; oder Das Leben auf dem Lande*, 64

Müller, Herta: *Der Mensch ist ein grosser Fasan auf der Welt,* 364; *Herz-Tier,* 364–366; *Heute wär ich mir lieber nicht begegnet,* 364–365, 366; *Reisende auf einem Bein,* 364–365
Müller, Inge, 64
murder mysteries, 136
Murrer, Ewald: *Mlha za zdí,* 217; *Sny na konci noci,* 217–218; *Zápisnik pana Pinkého,* 217–218
Musaraj, Shevqet: *Epopeja e Ballit Kombëtar,* 17; "*Isha unë Çobo Rrapushi,*" 17, 51; *Shtek më shtek me partizanët,* 17
Musiał, Grzegorz: *Ameryka, Ameryka!,* 311, 313; *Dziennik z Iowa,* 311–312; *Smak popiołu:* 311
Muslim-Croat republic, 266
Muslims, Bosnian, 119, 163, 266–273
Mustafaj, Besnik, 151; *Boshi,* 159, 160; *Daullja prej letre,* 159; *Fletorja rezervat: Shënime jashtë valixhes diplomatikë,* 159; *Midis krimeve dhe mirazheve: Ese,* 159; *Një saga e vogël,* 159–160; *Vapa,* 159
Mutafchiev, Petur, 116
Mutafchieva, Vera: *Letopis na smutnoto vreme,* 116; *Poslednite Shishmanovtsi,* 116; *Ritsariat,* 116; *Suedinenieto pravi silata,* 116

Nabokov, Vladimir, 102–103
Nádas, Péter: *Az égí és a földi szerelemről,* 232; *Emlékiratok könyve,* 231; *Év könyv: Ezerkilencszáznyolcvanhét-ezerkilencszáznyolcvannyolc,* 232; *A fotografia szép története,* 231–232
Nágy, Imre, 24
Naim Frashëri publishing house (Albania), 155, 356
Napoleon, 118, 120
Nass, Waldemar. *See* Loest, Erich
nationalism, 251, 265, 288–289, 319
National Theater (Czechoslovakia), 177

Natzweiler-Struthof concentration camp, 17
Naum, Gellu, 203
Nazi Germany, vii; eastern European allies, vii–viii, 13–14, 29–36
Neagu, Fănuş: *Ningea în Bărăgan,* 59
Nedelciu, Mircea, 200
Nedelcovici, Bujor, 99; *Aici şi acum,* 101, 102; *Al doilea mesager,* 101, 103; *Jurnul infidel: Pagini din exil, 1987–1993,* 102, 103; *Le matin d'un miracle / Dimineaţa unui miracol,* 102; *Somnul insulei,* 101
Nëntori (journal), 18, 95, 128
Neumann, Emmanuel, 148
Nezavisna Država Hrvatska (Independent State of Croatia) (NDH), 12–13
Njavro, Juraj: *Glava dolje ruke na ledja,* 166
Nobel Prize in Literature, 20, 92, 94, 117, 118, 234
Noica, Constantin, 148, 149, 251
North Atlantic Treaty Organization (NATO), x, 266, 282
Novak, Boris A., 294–295
Novi sad massacre, 25–26
Novotný, President, 178
Nowakowski, Marek, 307; *Chłopak z gołębiem na głowie,* 193; *Gdzie jest droga na Walnę,* 193; "*Grisza, ja tiebie skażu,*" 193; *Homo Polonicus,* 193; *Notatki z codzienności: Grudzień 1982–Lipiec 1983,* 191, 193; *Osiem dni w ojczyźnie,* 193; *Portret artysty z okresu dojrzałości,* 193; *Powidoki 2,* 193; *Powidoki: Chłopcy z tamtych lat,* 193; *Powidoki 3: Warszawiak pilnie poszukiwany,* 193; *Raport o stanie wojennyn,* 191, 192, 193; *Strzały w motelu George,* 193; *Życiorys Tadeusza Nawalanego, czyli Solidarość ma głos,* 193
Nyilaskereszt (Arrow Cross), ix, 20, 23

occult, tales of, 135
Odojewski, Włodzimierz, 3–4; *Wyspa ocalenia,* 3; *Zasypie wszystko, zawieje . . . ,* 3; *Zmierzch świata,* 3

Odrodzenie (journal), 40, 235–236
oneiric poetry, 255–256
Oprea, Marius, 203
Orizont (weekly), 200
Örkény, István, 68; *Egyperces novellák*, 79; *Pisti a vérzivatarban*, 79
Orthodox Christianity, 116
Osers, Ewald, 170
Oslobodjenje (newspaper), 272
Ostrovskii, Nikolai: *Kak zakalyalas' stal'*, 53
Osvobodilna fronta (journal), 16
Ottoman rule, 115–117, 119–120

Paçrami, Fadil, 84
Pahlavi, Mohammed Reza, 129
Pahor, Poris: *Nekropola*, 16–17; *Parnik trobi nji*, 16; *V labirintu*, 16
Palace of the People (Bucharest), 129
Paleologu, Alexandru, 149, 199
Paris Peace Treaty of 1921, 24
Parnicki, Teodor: *I u możnych dziwny*, 121; *Koła na piasku*, 121; *Nowa baśń*, 121; *Słowo i ciało*, 121; *Srebrne orły*, 121
Parnok, Sofia, 239, 309
Paruit, Alain, 102
Paul, Master (artist), 123
Pauză de respirație (Popescu, Bodiu, Dobrescu, and Oprea), 203
Pavelić, Ante, viii, ix, 13
Pavić, Milorad: *Hazarski rečnik: Roman-leksikon u 100,000 reči*, 204, 205; *Predeo slikan čajem*, 204–205; *Stakleni puž: Priče sa interneta*, 205; *Unutršnaja strana vetra ili roman o Kheri Leandru*, 204–205
Pawlikowska-Jasnorzewska, Maria: *Pocalunki*, 233; *Surowy jedwab*, 233
Pawlowska, Halina: *Díky za každe nové ráno*, 351
peasant literature, 120–121; Bulgaria, 61–62; Hungary, 61, 62–63; Romania, 55–61
Pecka, Karel: *Motáky nezvěstnému*, 177–178; *Na co umírají muži*, 177; *Pasáž*, 139

Pekárková, Iva, 110–111; *Dej mi ty prachy*, 111, 361; *Kulatý svět*, 111, 360; *Péra a perutě*, 111, 360–361
Pekić, Boris: *Godine koje su pojeli skakavci: Uspomene iz zatvora ili antropopeja, 1948–1954*, 164; *Hodočašće Arsenija Njegovana*, 163; *Odmor od istorije*, 164; *Sentimentalna povest Britanskog carstva*, 163–164; *Skinuto sa trake: Dnevničke zabaleške i razmišljanja, 1954–1983*, 164; *Vreme cuda*, 163
Perišić, Miodrag, 275
Përpjekja (journal), 159
Petkova, Vanya, 244; *Greshnitsa*, 245–246
Petlevski, Sibila: "Hrvatska koreografia," 243–244; *Koreografia patnje*, 243–244; *Spin Off: Antologija novijeg američkog pjesništva*, 243; *Skok s mjesta*, 243; *Sto aleksandrijskih epigrama*, 243
Pětofi Circle, 24
Petrescu, Camil, 148; *Bălcescu*, 124; *Un om între oameni*, 124
Petrescu, Radu, 198
Petreu, Marta (Rodică Marta Crişan, 247, 253
Petrov, Ivailo (Prodan Petrov Kiuchukov): *Haika za vultsi*, 61, 62; *Krushtenie*, 352; *Na chizhda zemia*, 352; *Nonkinata liubov*, 61; *Predi da se rodia i sled tova*, 61
Pfeiffer, Hans: *Kochrezepte für Kriminalgerechte, oder, Wie man einen Kriminalroman schreibt*, 141; *Mord ohne Motiv*, 141; *Die Mummie im Glassarg: Bemerkungen zur Kriminalliteratur*, 141; *Sieben Tote brauchen einen Mörder*, 141
Phanariotes (Romania), 124
Phantasma, the Center for Imagination Studies, 255
Pilinszky, János: *Harmadnapon*, 26; "KZ-oratórium," 26; *Nagyvárosi ikonok: Összegyűjtött versek*, 26–27; *Trapéz és korlát*, 26
Piłsudski, Józef, 324

Pipa, Arshi, 52, 53–54, 96–97, 151–152; as émigré, 152–153; *Albanian Folk Verse: Structure and Genre*, 153; *Albanian Literature: Social Perspectives*, 153; *Albanian Stalinism*, 153, 158; *Autobiography: 1988*, 153–155; *Contemporary Albanian Literature*, 153; *Hieronymus De Rada*, 153; *Libri i burgut*, 151; *Montale and Dante*, 151; "Neli," 153–154; *The Politics of Language in Socialist Albania*, 153; *Studies on Kosova*, 155; "Trilogia Albanica," 153; *Zhvillimi politik i shtetit shqiptar, 1912–1962*, 154–155

Pištalo, Vladimir, 295; *Priče iz celog sveta*, 297; *Vitraž u sećanju*, 297

Pišt'anek, Peter: *Fredyho koniec*, 333–334; *Rivers of Babylon*, 332–333, 334, 340; *Skazki o Vladovi*, 334

Platelis, Kornelijus: *Luoto kevalas*, 320

Poland, vii; fall of, 1–9; Great Emigration, 98; Jews in, 1, 4–8; Katyń murders, 3, 4; landowning nobility *(szlachta)*, 55; Martial Law, 191, 192, 193; Molotov-Ribbentrop pact, 3; Piast kings, 121; postcommunist social change, 193; Poznań riots, ix, 66; Slovakia and, 30; Solidarity, xii, 7, 70, 130

Polish Government-in-Exile, 2, 39, 71, 187

Polish Home Army, 40, 42, 68, 71

Polish People's Army, 38

Polish Workers' Party, 8

Polish writers: absurd and grotesque, literature of, 68–71; émigré, in France, 98–99; historical writing, 121–125, 129–130; postmodernism, 226–227; prison literature, 187–189; science fiction, 133; United States, views of, 303–313; urban landscapes, 338–340; women poets, 234–239, 303

Popescu, Dumitru Radu: *Fuga*, 58–59; *Vînătoarea regală*, 57–58

Popescu, Simona, 247, 256–258; *Exuvii*, 203, 204; *Noapte sau zi*, 203, 257–258; *Salvarea speciei: Despre suprarealism și Gellu Naum*, 203; *Xilofonul și altre poeme*, 256; *Pauză de respirație*, 256; *Juventus*, 256

Popov, Alek: *Mission: London*, 340–341

Popova, Nadya, 244

Popović, Danko, 276; *The Bloodblossoms of Kosovo*, 275

Popovici, Titus: *Setea*, 28, 59; *Străinul*, 28–29, 59

positive heroes, 48, 120

Poświatowska, Halina, 236, 303–305; *Dzień dzisiejszy*, 237; *Hymn bałwochwalczy*, 237; *Jeszcze jedne wspomnienie*, 237; "Lustro," 237; *Oda do rąk*, 237; *Opowieść dla przyjaciela*, 304

Poświatowski, Adolf, 304–305

Potrč, Ivan: *Andante patetico*, 166; *Menuet za kitaro*, 166–167; *Na kmetih*, 166, 167

Poznań riots (Poland), ix, 66

Prague Spring (1968), 46, 66, 105, 106, 107, 109, 169, 178

Preda, Marin: *Cel mai iubit dintre pămînteni*, 56; *Delirul*, 56; *Desfășurarea*, 56; *Ferestre întunecate*, 56; *Marele singuratic*, 56, 57; *Moromeții*, 56–57

prison camps: 143–144; Burrel prison (Albania), 152, 159; Bytízu Příbrami (Czechoslovakia), 177; "Devil's Yard" (Istanbul), 168; Gherla prison (Transylvania), 145, 147, 149, 185–186; Heřmanice (Moravia), 180; Jilava (Romania), 148; Leopoldov (Slovakia), 173; Pankrác (Czechoslovakia), 181; Pitești (Romania), 146; Qafë-Bari (Albania), 155; Ruzyně (Czechoslovakia), 176, 180; Soviet *gulags*, 4, 143; Spaç copper mine (Albania), 159; Starobielsk (Poland), 4; Vorkuta (Siberia), 190. *See also* concentration camps

prison literature: Albania, 151–160;

Croatia, 164–166; Czechoslovakia, 169–182; German Democratic Republic, 189–190; Hungary, 182–187; Poland, 187–189; Romania, 144–150, 185–186; Slovenia, 166–167; Yugoslavia, 160–169

Prize of the Romanian Writer's Union, 101, 102, 198, 199

propaganda, 19–20, 54

psycho-gram texts, 240

PULS Publications, 195

Puls (quarterly), 196

Putrament, Jerzy, 40

Radinska, Valentina, 244

Rákocsi, Mátyás, 79

Rakovszky, Zsuzsa: *A hullocsillag éve,* 343–344; *A kigyó ámyéka,* 343

Rebreanu, Liviu: *Ion,* 55; *Răcoala,* 55; *Răfuiala,* 55

recollection, narratives of, 344–353; Polish writers, 353–355

Red Army, 32, 71, 106

Red Berets (Serbian secret police), 288–289

Reinerová, Lenka, 175–177; *Alle Farben der Sonne und der Nacht,* 175–176

resistance, ix; Albania, 14; Czechoslovakia, 11–12, 173; Poland, 1, 4, 6; Slovakia, ix, 32–33; Yugoslavia, 13, 168, 274

Respublika (journal), 322, 325

Révai, József, 130

Revista Fundaţiilor Regale, 148

Revista Scriitorilor Români (journal), 100

revues, 178–179

Rilindja Demokratike (newspaper), 128

Rilindja (Renaissance), 120

Robbe-Grillet, Alain, 104

Rohia (monastery), 150

România Literară (review), 101, 199

Romania, 12; as ally of Axis, 27–29; antifascist movement, 29; anti-Semitism, 27–28; Ceauşescu regime, ix, 97, 100–101, 129; compliance with Nazi Germany, vii–viii, 13; deportation of Jews, 28; Hungarian community in, x, 253; peasants, 55–56; Phanariot rulers, 124; Securitate, 100, 146, 148, 185; society, 28–29; Tripartite Pact, 12

Romanian Academy, 60

Romanian Cultural Center (New York City), 254

Romanian Germans (Saxons), 363

Romanian Orthodox faith, 149, 150

Romanian writers: émigré writers in France, 99–104; fantastic, literature of, 133–135; historical writing, 124–125; prison literature, 144–150; United States, views of, 290–294; women poets, 247–258

Romanian Writer's Union, 101, 149, 198, 253

Rosenberg, Ernestin, 183

Różewicz, Tadeusz: *Akt przerywany,* 69; *Będą się bili,* 68; *Białe małżeństwo,* 69; *Kartoteka,* 68–69; *Na czworakach,* 69; *Pułapka,* 69; *Śmieszny staruszek,* 69; *Stara kobieta wysiaduje,* 69

Rožanc, Marjan: *Ljubezen,* 19, 166; *Metulj,* 166; *Roman o knjigah,* 166

Rudan, Vedrana: *Ucho, grlo, nož,* 207

Rudnicki, Adolf: *Epoka pieców,* 7; *Kupiec Łódzki,* 7; *Niekochana,* 7; *Szekspir,* 7

Rumelia, 116

Rumkowski, Chaim, 7

Rusan, Romulus, 292

Russia, 329–330

Russo-Turkish war of 1769–1791, 200

Rymkiewicz, Jarosław Marek, 4; *Rozmowy polskie latem 1983,* 7; *Umschlagplatz,* 6–7

Šalamun, Tomaž: *Praznik,* 294

Salivarová, Zdena, 106, 138, 139; *Honzlová: Protestsong,* 76–77

samizdat editions, 77, 78, 113, 177

Săptămînă (weekly), 124

Sângeorzan, Adrian, 255

Sarkadi, Imre: "A kútban," 63; *A gyáva,* 62–63; *Körhinta,* 63

Saxon school of poetry, 260–261
Scar on the Stone: Contemporary Poetry from Bosnia (Agee, ed.), 267
Schreyer, Wolfgang: *Unternehmen Thunderstorm,* 38
Schulz, Bruno, 68
Schwartz, Gheorghe, 124–125; *Cei o suta: Anabasis,* 125; *Cei o suta: Ecce homo,* 125; *Mâna albă,* 125
science fiction, 133, 224, 287
Sebastian, Mihail: *Journal, 1935–1944: The Fascist Years,* 27–28
secret police, 74, 84, 89; Securitate, 100, 146, 148, 185; Serbian, 288–289; Sigurimi, 84, 97, 151, 357; Stasi, 89, 142, 190, 359
Selenić, Slobodan: *Memoari Pere Bogalja,* 43; *Ocevi i oci,* 14–15
Selim III, 116
Selimović, Meša: *Derviš i smrt,* 118; *Tišine,* 118–119; *Trvava,* 119
Selimović, Šefkija, 118
Semilian, Julian, 255
Serb-Bulgarian war of 1885, 116
Serb-Croat War of 1991, 279
Serbia, viii, x, 20, 26–27, 114, 161, 264, 288–289; Kosovo campaign and, 273–288
Serbia-Montenegro, x, 114, 161
Serbian Academy of Arts and Sciences, 118
Šerelytė, Renata, 320; *Ledynmečio žvaigždės,* 326; *Prakeiktas kardas,* 326; *Stoglangis,* 326–327; *Žuvies darinejimas,* 326
Shapllo, Dalan, 17; *Kohë lufte,* 18; *Vepra dhe probleme të realizmit socialist,* 18
Shehu, Bashkim, 151, 157–158, 282; *L'automne de la peur,* 158; *Gostia,* 158; *Një kohë tjetër: Novelë e tregime,* 157; *Rrugëtimi i mbramë i Ago Ymerit,* 158
Shehu, Mehmet, 84, 151; murder of, 157–158
Sidran, Abdulah: *Slijepac pjeva svome gradu,* 268

Síla, Jiří, 179
Sima, Horia, 148
Šimecká, Martin, 68; *Žabí rok,* 77
Simić, Charles, 302
Simonescu, Mircea Horia: *Asediul locului comun,* 198; *Brevariul (Historia calamitatum),* 198; *Dicţionar onomastic,* 198–199; *Dupa 1900, pe la amiază,* 198; *Febră,* 198; *Învăţaturi pentru Delfin,* 198; *Ingeniosul bine temperat,* 198; *Jumatate plus unu,* 198; *Licitaţia,* 198; *Nesfârşitele primejdii,* 198; *Paltonul de vară,* 198; *Rapirea lui Ganymede,* 198; *Redingota,* 198; *Toxicologia sau Dincolo de bine şi dincoace de rau,* 198
Sixty-Eight Publishers (Toronto), 105, 106, 107, 111, 139, 177
Skenderberg, 95–96
Skomantas: *see* Šerelytė, Renata
Škutina, Vladimir: *Presidentův vězeň,* 178; revue literature, 178–179
Škvorecký, Josef, 45, 76, 104, 105, 137–139; *Hříchy pro pátera Knoxe,* 138; *Konec nylonového věku,* 106; *Konec poručíka Borůvky,* 138; Lieutenant Borůvka detective novels, 106, 137–138; *Návrat poručíka Borůvky,* 138; *Smutek poručíka Borůvky,* 106, 137–138; *Tankový prapor,* 106; *Zbabělci,* 105–106
Skwarnicki, Marek, 307
Slanský, Rudolf, 72, 170
Slanský affair, 175, 176–177
Slavici, Ioan: *Mara,* 55
Slavs, South, 114, 120; fantastic, literature of, 135–136; postmodernism, 204–210; United States, view of, 294–303. *See also* Bosnia-Herzegovina; Bulgaria; Croatia; Macedonia; Serbia; Slovenia
Slovakdom, 122–123
Slovaks, Hungarian, 368–369
Slovakia, vii–x, 29–36; Catholics, 32–33; compliance with Nazi

Germany, vii, 13; deportation of Jews, 30; language, 122–123

Slovak National Uprising (SNP), ix, 29–36

Slovak-Russian relations, 31–32

Slovak writers: crime fiction, 140; historical writing, 122–124; postmodernism, 218–226; on Slovak National Uprising, ix, 29–36; urban landscapes, 332–334; women poets, 239–241

Slovenian writers, 16–17, 19; postmodernism, 209–210; prison literature, 166–167; United States, view of, 294–295; urban landscapes, 335–338; women poets, 241–242

Slovenian Writer's Association, 242

Slovenský národ (journal), 349

Slovenský denník (newspaper), 181

Socialist Unity Party (East Germany), 37, 89

Solacolu, Ion, 146

Solidarity, xii, 7, 70, 130; literature of, 191–197. *See also* Poland

Solzhenitsyn, Aleksandr: *Arkhipelag Gulag*, 143; *Odin den' v zhizni Ivana Denisovicha*, 143, 187

Sophocles: *Antigone*, 126–127

Sorkin, Adam, 253

Soviet Union, 4, 10; collapse of, ix, 143

Spasse, Sterio: *Afërdita*, 50; *Afërdita përsëri në fshat*, 50–51; *Ata nuk ishen vetëm*, 50, 120–121; *Kryengritësit*, 120; *Nga jeta në jetë: Pse?*, 50, 120; *Rilindasit*, 120

Spiró, György, 68, 79, 80–81; *Az ikszék*, 81; *Az Imposztor*, 81; *Csirkefej*, 81

Spring of Nations (1848), 124

Srpski Pokret Obnove (SPO; Serbian Movement of Renewal), 288

Stade, Martin: *Der himmelblaue Zeppelin*, 64; *Junge Bach*, 125; *Der König und sein Narr*, 125; *Meister von Sanssouci*, 125; *Der närrische Krieg*, 125; *Der Präsentkorb*, 64; *Der Windsucher*, 64; *Zwischen Schlehdorn und Paradies: Der Junge Bach*, 125

Stalin, Josef, 66–67, 86, 171

Stambolinski, Aleksandur, 115

Stancu, Zaharia: *Carul cu foc*, 56; *Clopote și struguri*, 56; *Descult*, 56; *Jocul cu moartea*, 56, 114; *Printre stele*, 56; *Uruma*, 56

Stănescu, Nichita, 60, 252

Stanev, Emiliian: *Ivan Kondarev*, 115; *Legenda za Sibin, preslavskiia kniaz*, 116

Stasiuk, Andrzej: *Biały kruk*, 188, 338–339; *Dukla*, 189; *Dziewięc*, 189, 339–340; *Jadąc do Babadag*, 189; *Mury Hebronu*, 188, 189; *Opowieści galicyjskie*, 189, 339; *Przez rzekę*, 189

State Jewish Museum (Prague), 11

Stefanova, Lilyana, 244; *Edna esen v Amerike*, 298–301; *Kogato sme na dvadeset godini*, 245

Stefanova, Nevena, 244; *Pomruknali siyaniya*, 245

Ștefoi, Elena, 247, 253

Steinhardt, Nicolae (Nicu-Aurelian), 145; *Essai sur une conception catholique du judaisme*, 148; *Illusions et réalités juives*, 148; *Încertitudini literare*, 150; *În genul lui Cioran, Noica, Eliade . . .*, 148; *Între viață și cărți*, 150; *Jurnalul fericirii*, 147, 149–150

Stevanović, Vidosav, 277; *Hristos i psi*, 280; *Ista stvar*, 280–281; *La niege et les chiens*, 280; *Milošević: Jedan epitaf*, 281; *Ostrvo Balkan*, 280; *Sneg u Atini*, 280; *Testament; Roman u 52 bdenja*, 279–280

Stojanović, Radosav, 275

Strittmater, Erwin: *Katzgraben: Szenen aus der Bauernleben*, 63; *Ochsenkutscher*, 63; *Ole Bienkopp*, 63–64

Stryjkowski, Julian, 307

Štúr, L'udovít, 123

Stwosz, Wit (artist), 123
Sudetenland, 1
surrealism, 197, 239, 248
Svätopluk, duke of Moravia, 122
Świat nie przedstawiony (Zagajewski and Kornhauser), 98
Swir, Anna (Anna Świrszczyńska), 6; *Budowałam barykadę*, 6, 235; *Jestem baba*, 6, 234; "Kobieta rozmawia ze swoim udem," 235; *Szczęśliwa jak psi ogon*, 234; *Wiatr*, 234
Szabasów (Poland), 2
Szálasi, Ferenc, ix, 20, 23
Szczepański, Jan Józef, 307
Szczypiorski, Andrzej, 4, 191; *Grzechy, cnoty, pragnienia*, 192; *Początek*, 5–6, 192
Szép, Ernő, 20; *Az ötödik pecsét*, 23; *Emberszag*, 23
Szewc, Piotr: *Zagłada*, 353; *Zmierchy i poranki*, 353–354
Szymańska, Adrianna, 307
Szymborska, Wisława: *Dlageto żyjemy*, 234; "Jawa," 234; *Koniec i początek*, 234; "Pod jedną gwiadzką," 234; *Widok z garnkiem piasku*, 234; *Wielka liczba*, 234; *Wszelki wypadek*, 234

Tagliche Rundschau (newspaper), 89
Tarr, Béla, 228
Tartler, Grete: *Achene zburătoare*, 250; *Apa vie*, 250; *Astronomia ierbii*, 250; *Europa naţiunilor, Europa raţiunilor*, 251; *Hore*, 250; *Scrisori de acreditare*, 250; "Teatru de umbre," 250–251
Tatarka, Dominik: *Démon súhaslu*, 357–358; *Navrávačky*, 358; *Písačky*, 358; *Prvý a druhý úder*, 32
Ťažký, Ladislav, 29–32; *Ámenmária, samí dobrí vojaci*, 31–32; *Dunajské hroby*, 32; *Evangelium čatára Matúša*, 32; *Pochovol som ho nahého*, 32; *Vojenský zbeh*, 32
Teksty drugie (periodical), 194
Ţepeneag, Dumitru, 99, 102; *Aşteptare*, 104; *Călătorie neizbutită*, 104; *La défense Alékhine*, 104; *Român la Paris: Pagini de journal, 1970–1972*, 104; *Zadarnică e arta fugii*, 104
Tesla, Nikola, 297–298
Theresienstadt, 10
Third Five-Year Plan (Albania), 86
Thirty-Year War, 123
Tirana, 128–129
Tirana House of Culture, 152
Tiso, Monsignor Jozef, viii, 30, 32, 34
Tito, Jozif Broz, ix, x, 13–14, 168; break with Stalin, 151, 160, 161; Croatia and, 165; partisans, 13, 16, 42, 168
Titoist Atrocities in Vojvodina, 1944–1945: Serbian Vendetta in Bácska, 26
Tokarczuk, Olga, 227, 228; *Dom dzienny, dom nocny*, 354, 355; *E.E.*, 354; *Podróż ludzi Księgi*, 354; *Prawiek i inne czasy*, 354–355
Tomaš, Stefan, 119
tombs *(stećci)*, 119
Topol, Jáchym, 210; *Sestra*, 216–217, 340; *Výlet k nadražní hale*, 217
Topol, Josef, 216
Toruńczyk, Barbara, 98
Totozani, Shemsi, 152
Tozaj, Neshat: *Bisede për një shok*, 84; *Në emër të popullit*, 84; *Në gjurmë të të tretit*, 84; *Pse flas: Retrospektivë*, 84, 357; *Rrëmbimi i arkivit*, 84; *Shalom*, 84; *Thikat*, 49, 84, 357
Trajkov, Ivo, 303
Transnistria, viii–ix, 20, 27, 28
Transylvania, viii, 26, 29, 114, 145, 185, 230. *See also* Hungary
Tribuna (review), 249
Tribuson, Goran: *Bijesne lisice*, 136; *Gorka čokolada*, 136; *Noćna smjena*, 136; *Praška smrt*, 135; *Siva zona*, 136; *Zavirivanje*, 136
Tripartite Pact, 12
Trojan, Ondřej, 12
Tsankov, Aleksandur, 115
Tsvetaeva, Marina, 239, 243, 309
Tudjman, Franjo, 27, 164, 165
Tudor, Corneliu Vadim, 103

Tulli, Magdalena: *Skaza*, 226; *Sny i kamienie*, 226, 227; *Tryby*, 226, 227; *W czerwieni*, 226, 227

Ţutulescu, Ion, 254

Twisted Spoon Press (Prague), 217

Tyrmand, Leopold: *Zły*, 137, 140

Ugrešić, Dubravka: *Ministarstvo boli*, 284; *Muzej bezuslovne predaje*, 284

Uhde, Milan: *Děvka z města Théby*, 126–127; *Král Vávra*, 125–126

Ukraine, x, xii, 3

Ukrainian writers, 327–329

Ulemek, Milorad: *Gvozdeni rov*, 288

Union of (Romanian) Exile Writers, 102

United States: Czech views of, 313–315; East German views of, 316–317; Polish views of, 303–313; Romanian views of, 290–294; South Slavs, views of, 294–303

University of Aurel Vlaicu, 125

University of Iowa International Writing Program. *See* International Writing Program

Urban, Milo, 348–349; *Kade-tade po Halinde: Neveselé spomienky na veselé roky*, 349; *Na brehu krvavej rieky: Spomienky novinara*, 349; *Sloboda nie je špás: Spomienky dôhodcu*, 349; *Zelená krv: Spomienky hájnikovho syna*, 349; *Živý bič*, 349

Uricariu, Doina, 247, 252; *Vindecările*, 252

Ursu, Gheorghe, 248

Ursu, Liliana, 247; *Corali*, 251; *Înger călare pe fiară*, 251; *Ordinea clipilor*, 251; *Piaţa aurarilor*, 251; *Viaţa deasupra oraşului*, 251; *Zona de protecţie*, 251

Ushtria Çlirimtare Kombëtare (National Liberation Movement) (Albania), 14

Ustasha *(Ustaša)*, viii, ix, 13, 20, 118, 287

Vaculík, Ludvík, 68, 74–75; *Dva tisíce slov* manifesto, 75; *Morčata*, 75–76; *Sekyra*, 74, 75

Valchinov, Nikolai: *Sezonat na kanarchetata*, 341–342

Večerní Divadlo theater (Brno), 126

Vegri, Saša (Dobršek, Albina): *Konstelacje*, 241; *Mesečni konj*, 241; *Naplavljeni plen*, 241; *Ofelia in trojni aksel*, 241; *Tebi v tišino*, 241

Velea, Nicolae, 59–60; *Cutia cu greieri*, 60; *Dumitraş şi cele două zile*, 60; *În razboi un pogon cu flori*, 60; *Poarta*, 60; *Zbor jos*, 60

Veličković, Nenad: *Konačari*, 270–271

Vezhinov, Pavel, 136–137; *Az sum atomna*, 137; *Daleche ot bregovite*, 137; *Nauchnofantastichni noveli*, 137; *Siniiat zalez*, 136; *Vtora rata*, 136–137

Viaţa Românească (review), 60, 249

Vida, Viktor, 111–112; *Obrana hrvatske cjelokupnosti i javnih radnika*, 112; *Sabrane pjesme*, 112; *Sužanj vremena*, 112; *Svemir osobe*, 112

videopoviedky ("video tales"), 222–223

Vidmar, Maja, 241; *Liebhaftige Gedichte*, 242; *Način vezave*, 242; *Ob vznožju*, 242; *Prisotnost*, 242; *Razdalje telesa*, 242

Viewegh, Michal: *Báječná léta pod psa*, 330; *Názory na vraždu*, 330; *Výchová dívek v Čechách*, 330

Vígszínház (Comedy Theater) (Budapest), 80

Vilikovský, Pavel: *Kôň na poschodí, slepec vo Vrabl'och*, 218–219; *Slovenský Casanova*, 219; *Večne je zelený . . .*, 218, 219–220

Viorel, Titus. *See* Popovici, Titus

Virk, Jani: *Smeh za lešeno pregrado*, 351–352

Vis and Ramin (Georgian romance), 261

Voiculescu, Vasile, 197; *Povestri*, 135

Vojnović, Mihailo, 288

Vojvodina (Yugoslavia), 24–25

Volanská, Hela: *Stretnutia v lasoch,*
30–31
Vopěnka, Martin: *Balada o sestupu,*
331–332
Voskovec, Jiří, 126
Vrioni, Jusup, 98
Vrkljan, Irena: *Doba prijatelstva,* 243;
Marina, ili, o, biografii, 243; *Svila,*
škare, 242–243; *U koži moje sestre:*
Berlinske pjesme, 243
Vukovar (Croatia), 166

Walentynowicz, Anna, 197
Wałesa, Lech, 130, 197, 310
Waliszewski, Leszek, 310
Wallace, Edgar, 185
Wallachia, 124
Walldorf, Hans. *See* Loest, Erich
Wańkowicz, Melchoir: *Bitwa o Monte*
Cassino, 2
Warsaw Ghetto, 6–7
Warsaw Independent Poets and Artists
Publishing House, 237
Warsaw Uprising (1944), 8, 38, 41,
235; Ghetto *Uprising* (1943), 5, 6,
38
Ważyk, Adam: *Poemat dla dorosłych,*
47
Weil, Jiří: *Na střeše je Mendelssohn,*
11; *Život s hvědou,* 11
Weimar Republic, 63
Weintraub, Wiktor, 307
Weissbort, Daniel, 311, 312
Werich, Jan, 79, 126
Witkiewicz, Stanisław Ignacy, 68
women poets, xii, 233–234; Albania,
258–260; Balkans, 241–260;
Bosnia, 268–270; Bulgaria,
244–246; Croatia, 242–244; Czechs
and Slovaks, 239–241; German
Democratic Republic, 260–263;
Macedonia, 246–247; Poland,
234–239, 303; Romania, 247–258;
Slovenia, 241–242
World War I, 114–115, 168
World War II, vii, 1–9, 36–38
Writer's Union (GDR), 63, 64, 89

Wyspiański, Stanisław, 81
Wyszyński, Stefan Cardinal, 69

Xhuvani, Dhimitër: *Përsëri në këmbë,*
53–54; *Tuneli,* 53
Xoxa, Jakov: *Juga e bardhë,* 52; *Lumi i*
vdekur, 51–52

Yalta Treaty, 39, 121
Young Bosnia organization, 117, 168
Yourcenar, Marguerite, 309
"Yugonostalgia," 284
Yugoslav Army of National Liberation,
118
Yugoslav Communist Party, 168
Yugoslavia, vii, 84, 114; Albania and,
151; break with Stalin, 151, 160,
161; communism, 13–14; émigré
writers, 111–112; fall of, 264–265;
Jews, deportation of, 161; postmod-
ernism, 204; prison literature,
160–169; resistance, 13; western
attitude toward, 159–160; World
War II, 12–17. *See also* Balkan
wars; Bosnia-Herzegovina; Croatia;
Serbia-Montenegro; Kosovo;
Macedonia; Slovenia
Yugoslavia, Federal Republic of, 42,
274, 289
Yugoslav Writers' Union, 265

Zábrana, Jan, 106
Zabuzhko, Oksana: "Apologiya poeziï
v kintsi 20-go stolittya," 328;
Avtostop, 327–328; *Khroniki vid*
Fortinbras, 328; "Klitemnestra,"
327–328; *Pol'ovi doslidzhennia z*
ukrains'koho seksu, 327; *Reportazh*
iz 2000-go roku, 328; *Sestro, sestro,*
328–329
Zadar, 120
Zagajewski, Adam, 191, 193–194;
Drugi oddech, 194; *Dwa miasta,*
194; *Solidarność i samotność,*
98–99, 194; *W cudzym pięknie,* 194
Zahradníček, Jan: *Čtyří léta,* 172; *Dům*
strach, 172

Zapis (journal), 193, 194

Závada, Pál: *A fényképész utókora*, 369; *Jadviga párnája*, 368; *Milota*, 369

Zeszyty Literackie (journal), 98, 193, 194, 303

Zhiti, Visar, 151; "Çastet ikin," 155; *Ferri i çarë (Roman i vërtetë)*, 157; *Hedh një kafkë te këmbit tuaja: Poezitë e burgut*, 155, 156–157; *Kujtesa e ajrit*, 155–156, 157; *Rruget e ferrit*, 157; *Si shkohet në Kosovë*, 157; *Valixhja e shqyer e përrallave*, 157

Zhou Enlai, 86, 88

Žiak, Miloš: *Jewropean*, 349

Živančević, Nina, 295; *Inside and Out of Byzantium*, 297; *Living on Air Fiction*, 297; *More or Less Urgent*, 296–297; *Prodavci snova*, 297

Živković, Zoran: *Nemogući priče*, 136

Zog, King, 51, 160

Zúbek, L'udo: *Doktor Jesenius*, 123; *Jar Adely Ostrolúckej*, 123; *Oltar majstera Pavla*, 123

Zupan, Vitomil: *Levitan*, 166, 167; *Igra s hudičevim repom*, 167